Two week loan

Please return on or before the last
date stamped below.
Charges are made for late return.

VRML

Clearly Explained

Second Edition

John Vacca

AP PROFESSIONAL

AP PROFESSIONAL is a division of Academic Press

Boston   San Diego   New York
London   Sydney   Tokyo   Toronto

 AP PROFESSIONAL
An imprint of ACADEMIC PRESS
A division of HARCOURT BRACE & COMPANY

Find us on the Web! http://www.apnet.com

This book is printed on acid-free paper. ∞

Academic Press
525 B Street, Suite 1900, San Diego, CA 92101-4495
1300 Boylston Street, Chestnut Hill, MA 02167

United Kingdom Edition published by
ACADEMIC PRESS LIMITED
24-28 Oval Road, London NW1 7DX

Library of Congress Cataloging-in-Publication Data
Vacca, John R.
      VRML clearly explained / John Vacca. -- 2nd ed.
         p.   cm.
      Includes index.
      ISBN 0-12-710008-3 (alk. paper). -- ISBN 0-12-710009-1 (CD-ROM)
        1. Computer graphics. 2. Three-dimensional display systems.
  3. Virtual Reality. 4. VRML (Computer program language)
  5. Internet (Computer network) I. Title.
  T385.V3223   1997
  006--dc21   97-42710
                                        CIP

Printed in the United States of America
97 98 99 00 CP 9 8 7 6 5 4 3 2 1

This book is dedicated to my stepson, Leo Ornelas, a soldier

and a veteran of Desert Storm. He serves his country well and I am proud of him.

Contents

Acknowledgments

There are many people whose efforts on this book have contributed to its successful completion. I owe each a debt of gratitude and want to take this opportunity to offer my sincere thanks.

A very special thanks to my editor Tom Stone, whose initial interest and support made this book possible. I also thank editorial assistant Karen Wachs, who provided staunch support and encouragement when it was most needed. Thanks to my production editor, Julie Champagne, whose fine editorial work has been invaluable, and Andrew Williams of Benchmark Productions, Inc. Thanks also to my marketing manager Kira Glass, whose efforts on this book have been greatly appreciated.

Thanks to my technical editor, Pat Dalberg, whose expertise in Internet and intranet technology were indispensable. In addition to his work as technical editor, Pat contributed technical support and time toward the creation of the CD-ROM, without which this book would have been less than complete.

Thanks to my wife, Bee Vacca, for her love, her help, and her understanding of my long work hours.

I wish to thank the organizations and individuals who granted me permission to use the research material and information necessary for the completion of this book (cited in the CD-ROM), and the software and demonstrations in the CD-ROM.

As always, thanks to my agent, Margot Malley, for guidance and encouragement over and above the business of being an agent.

Introduction

No one really knows how many people actually are on the Internet. Recent estimates have put the number at 60 million Netizens in America. One forecast even predicted a worldwide Internet population of 400 million by the year 2008. A new study, however, took much of the hype out of cyberspace. An industry survey put the number of people in the United States with direct access to the Internet at 13.8 million. In addition, 10 million use commercial online services exclusively. While not as explosive as some had predicted, growth has continued to remain robust. The industry survey envisions 14 million new users by the end of 1998. Nevertheless, much in the survey is not surprising. Internet users, for instance, prove to be 4-to-3 male versus female—mostly young and relatively well-to-do. Still, demographic measurements will be critical to commercial users who fuel the Internet's undeniable but hard to quantify surge.

Web Sites for Virtualnauts

More Web statistics than you can handle? After all, the World Wide Web (WWW) is jazzy but confusing, but not so confusing that the good life can't be had by all.

For example, imagine a wine shop (www.telematix.ie/mccabes/index.html) where the salesperson is a chatty virtual reality (VR) interactive expert who delivers strong opinions but always amiably and without a trace of condescension. Or, virtual snippets from the latest alternative rock tracks. Expert advice on gardening, bicycling, and movie reviews from a self-proclaimed typical teenager. That's the WWW today.

The WWW teems with information, opinions, and advice on just about every topic you can think of—and most of it is free to anyone who pays $27 or so a month for an Internet account. Think of it now as a VR multinational library and coffee house all rolled into one. A novice virtualnaut can drown in the sheer volume of VR stuff out there on the Web—the inner sanctum of the Internet that graduates from plain text to 3-D graphics, virtual reality, and photos (and is careening into sound and video).

The Flatness of the Internet

Today's WWW promises to be realized with a new technology called *Virtual Reality Modeling Language* (VRML). VRML is literally the glue that allows a range of technologies, including multimedia-equipped personal computers, high-speed communications, and others, to bring networked virtual reality to the end user. The key to VRML's potential success lies, however, in the explosive growth of the Internet—that phenomenon of cyberspace has an almost palpable reality for users. Many people talk of going to an Internet site, or a particular Internet address, and say: "I've been there." This is a testament to the power of human imagination. The Internet today is largely a text-based, or at best a two-dimensional graphical (the Web) environment. VRML promises to take this strongly imaginative experience of cyberspace and enhance it significantly through multimedia technology.

The Origin of VRML

The abbreviation VRML sounds somewhat like the abbreviation for another Internet standard: HTML, or *Hyper-Text Markup Language*. HTML is a standard that allows the creation of hypertext documents on the World Wide Web that contain links to other documents, either on the same computer or across the globe.

While VRML utilizes Web technology, it really has no relation directly to HTML. It is not 3-D HTML as its name might suggest. In fact, VRML was developed by technologists in the field of graphics and 3-D rendering who foresaw the potential benefit of bringing three-dimensionality to the World Wide Web.

In particular, engineers at Silicon Graphics—the same company that developed the technology that allowed the stunning morph effects in the film *Terminator 2: Judgment Day*—had a major part in its initial specification. Their Open Inventor 3-D technology was chosen by an independent standards group as the underpinning for VRML. A portion of this technology with enhancements to support networking form the basis for VRML as we know it today.

How VRML Works

VRML is in fact not a programming language in the strictest sense. At least, it is not what programmers refer to as a *compiled language*. This is where a software program can issue instructions directly to the computer without the need for an intermediary program called an *interpreter*.

VRML code consists of descriptions of 3-D scenes, and the expected behavior of those scenes based on actions of the user. The code is (like HTML) actually written in plain text or ASCII format. It commonly consists of hundreds or even thousands of polygons (the basic building block of a three-dimensional scene on a computer).

When the user encounters a VRML-based site, the VRML viewer or browser receives instructions from the server on the other end. The server ends VRML code, commonly called a *homespace* or *world* to the viewer, which then interprets the instructions and displays the initial scene elements.

Each world is a self-contained environment that is loaded locally for navigation. The files range in size from 100 kilobytes to several megabytes, so bandwidth directly affects download/access time. Once the world is loaded, the user's experience is dictated by CPU performance. Higher-performance processors handle more MIPS, allowing faster and smoother navigation through the world.

Given the relatively low performance and limited bandwidth of today's installed base of personal computers, developers will begin to build VRML sites so as to minimize the back-and-forth communication between the viewer and the server-based VRML programming code. One way to do this is to utilize the power and storage capacity of the PC itself to store certain VRML elements such as commonly used texture maps and audio files in a local reference file.

As the user moves through the environment, the client viewer and the server are in intermittent contact—exchanging requests and instructions as the user clicks on links to other worlds, audio displays, streaming video, and complex behaviors. VRML worlds will become true multimedia experiences on the World Wide Web.

Who Should Read This Book?

This book is primarily for programmers and nonprogrammers alike who are interested in learning how to use VRML to create virtual reality environments and 3-D graphics on the Internet. This will include graphics designers and programmers, marketing professionals, advertising professionals, publishers, software developers, and game developers.

What's So Special About This Book?

This book thoroughly explains how to use VRML for creating 3-D graphics and virtual reality applications for the Internet. No previous experience with VRML is required and all of the latest standards are covered.

The key features of this book include, but are not limited to, the following:

♦ Contains extensive coverage of OpenGL Graphics Standards, fundamentals, and libraries
♦ Provides numerous VRML applications as examples as well as VRML browsers
♦ Includes a tutorial on graphic techniques from polygon edges to rasterization
♦ Contains the latest VRML standards developed by the VRML Consortium
♦ Provides instructions for installing and configuring specific 3-D viewers or browsers that are required to view VRML files
♦ Includes the latest VRML applications in the areas of architecture, art, astronomy, telemedicine, biomedical sciences, chemistry, sports, animation, military science, space, commercial uses, computer science, and engineering
♦ Features a CD-ROM that includes links to over 40 VRML browsers and the applications that they support (authoring tools, modeling, viewers, etc.) and examples that show how to create your own applications

Organization of This Book

This book presents instant Internet gratification for those would-be 3-D graphics Web cruisers who are tantalized by all the hoopla of VRML, but haven't got a clue about how to view any of the interactive virtual reality environments. You'll begin by exploring the future of the last great multimedia virtual information mall to come to the WWW—VR 3-D graphics. You'll continue your exploration of VRML by learning to implement the language in order to create any type of 3-D applications, advertisements, or Web pages that are needed by corporate decision makers, business owners, and technical professionals.

Many people feel daunted by the prospect of cruising the Net, in part because of all the techie terms in cyberspace. This book will put you at ease in using the 3-D viewers and browsers to view the VRML applications. The final part of this book concludes by linking you—the interactive virtualnaut—to resources around the world with effective and easy-to-use VRML browsers that allow the display of text, video, graphics, and sound on a local computer screen. In other words, the book concludes with a description of what the future of Virtual Reality on the Net holds for you.

Part I: Identifying the Future

In this part of the book, a discussion is presented about why VRML is literally the glue that allows a range of technologies—including multimedia-equipped personal computers, high-speed communications, and others—to bring networked virtual reality to the end user. You will be able to identify the key standard to VRML 2.0/VRML97's potential success in the explosive phenomenon known as the Internet.

Next, you discover why VRMLScript is the required scripting language for VRML 2.0. You also will examine OpenGL: the high-performance tool for 3-D graphics applications.

Next, you examine why Silicon Graphics' Open Inventor object-oriented 3-D toolkit is proposed as the basis for VRML. In addition, you are given a brief overview of an interactive tool for exploring VR applications over the Internet via Netscape and other browsers.

Finally, Part I reaches its climax with a discussion of real virtual reality on the Internet. It also describes the development of the architecture of the MOO-based HTML collaborative hypermedia system and its support for the emerging VRML 2.0/97 standard.

Part II: Implementing the Future

Part II begins by outlining a direction for the implementation of these virtual reality environments as users create their own VRML

Web sites. Part II of the book, which includes Chapters 8 to 13, explores the theme introduced in Chapter 8, *The VRML Consortium*, by thoroughly explaining how users can create and implement virtual reality applications on the Internet via the VRML 2.0/97 standard.

Next, it presents a brief overview of Living Worlds—another Working Group of the VRML Consortium whose charter is to define a conceptual framework and specify a set of interfaces to support the creation and evolution of multiuser (and multideveloper!) applications in VRML 2.0. It also discusses how some of the folk connected to the Universal Avatars (UA) initiative working together with the Mitsubishi Electronic Research Lab (MERL), proposed an Open Community (OC) architecture based on the SPLINE system.

Additionally, Part II discusses the development and implementation of Open Inventor as an object-oriented 3-D toolkit offering a comprehensive solution to interactive graphics programming problems. Part II also takes a thorough look at the VRML specifications themselves. It concludes with a description of the Open GL graphics system: what it is, how it acts, and what is required to implement it.

Part III: Distributed Virtual Environments

Part III presents visions of what the Web community wants to be able to do with VRML. It also takes a look at Distributed Virtual Environments (DVEs)—the sharing of virtual worlds and the new Internet technologies that promise even richer forms of interpersonal interactions. Next, Part III describes how virtual worlds present programmers with unprecedented problems. It also discusses how vendors will need a common platform customized for social interaction in order to develop a true mass market.

Part III also shows how the careful filtering of objects on a moment-by-moment basis, with networking schemes to match, can prevent virtual worlds from being swamped by their own data. In addition, Part III discusses how some soldiers are driven by guts, and others by computers. It shows how military trainees can fight virtual battles against software foes without knowing who's real and who isn't.

Finally, Part III concludes with a discussion of how users need information about the locations of objects in a virtual environment if it is to function well. Their ears, not only their eyes, must have it.

Part IV: Results and Future Directions

Part IV begins the visionary quest of visiting the numerous proposed VRML research projects and systems. It describes the preliminary ideas for extending the World Wide Web to incorporate virtual reality (VR)—the primary focus of this book. Next, you learn how various considerations have governed the selection and presentation of graphical operators in OpenGL. The theme contains a detailed discussion of OpenGL's procedural interface that allows a graphics programmer to describe rendering tasks— whether simple or complex—easily and efficiently. You even learn about VRML behavior engine technology that allows simulations as well as documentation through which a reader accesses and links them with an embedded component distributed on the Net.

In addition, Part IV also looks at the numerous VRML applications that have been developed for viewing and interacting on the Internet. As you near conclusion, you are guided through the development of ongoing realistic VR projects within the commercial, military, academic and medical communities, and amusement that will eventually be imported to the Internet as possible VRML applications. Finally, how far can high-performance VRML go? In what directions will it develop? How fast will it evolve? These questions and more are discussed in this part of the book by examining the various pieces of the puzzle and looking at application trends and future possibilities.

What's on the CD-ROM?

The CD-ROM in this book should be thought of as links to a treasure trove of tools and software that you can use to build your 3-D graphics and virtual reality applications for the Internet. Here's a quick-and-dirty overview of what is contained in the CD-ROM:

- **Neat VRML Sites.** Links to dozens of sites that have lists of sites and accompanying URLs.
- **The VRML Repository.** A resource for information relating to VRML and accompanying URLs.
- **The OpenGL Graphics System Utility Library.** A set of routines designed to complement the OpenGL graphics system is included by providing support for mipmapping, matrix manipulation, polygon tessellation, quodrics, NURBS, and error handling.
- **OpenGL Graphics with the X Window System.** A description of GLX and the OpenGL extension to the X Window System.
- **GLX Extension for OpenGL Protocol Specification.** A description of the network protocol for GLX as it is encapsulated within the X protocol bytestream.
- **Newsgroups and Mailing Lists.** Links to dozens of discussion groups, newsgroups, and mailing lists are provided for your enjoyment.
- **Software/Browsers.** Links to dozens of browsers for viewing VRML files.
- **VRML Applications.** Links to dozens of VRML applications that have been developed for viewing and interacting on the Internet, as well as various VR applications that are in the process of being designed for implementation on the Net.
- **Tools/Software.** Last but not least, the CD-ROM also includes links to a comprehensive interactive array of shareware and demo versions of some of the most popular 3-D and VRML Web Browsers, Authoring Tools, Viewers, 3-D modeling tools, and other VRML products.

A Word from the Author

Most information on the WWW is already free, as is much software. Experienced virtualnauts, not used to paying for things they download, may be reluctant to pay as they go. As spectacular as Web technology is, it still has a considerable way to go to become attractive to the millions of consumers who are used to the amenities of mall and catalog culture.

In time, though, everything from home appliances to automobiles could be linked to a virtual reality environment on the Web. As it so grows, so will VR applications such as telemedicine, in which rural doctors will share virtual diagnostic tools like MRIs with specialists around the world. Or a car might plug into a holographic VR intranet in which engineers at a manufacturing plant could comment on the car's condition in a holodeck-type setting. Perhaps home refrigerators will report their inventory to grocery store computers that they are running low in food staples and require home delivery—billed to the customer's account. The customer could then select new items by viewing them in a virtual grocery store. Nevertheless, all of this VR commerce will begin in earnest on the Web only when the computer becomes as easy to use as a telephone or a microwave oven.

If you're looking to use the Web in this way now, it would be worth your while to phone a help-line consultant to learn how to use the 3-D software and seek help often to figure out how to negotiate virtual space. The computer is evolving into an information appliance. But that day won't truly arrive until computers get easier to use and conveyors—telephone and cable companies—hook up homes with high-speed data lines that end those annoying delays when virtualnauts try to download their favorite VRML application from a Web site.

Remember, the Web is out there! Have fun!

John R. Vacca
34679 TR 382
Pomeroy, Ohio 45769
(614) 985-3667 (voice)
(614) 985-3668 (fax)
jvacca@hti.net (Internet)

Part One

Identifying the Future

1

Bringing 3-D Environments to the Web: The VRML Connection

I am a raven. Sshh, don't tell anyone, I'm really an author doing an undercover investigation of distributed virtual reality environments, and I'm posing as a raven.

As I flap about this virtual place, which appears to be some kind of starship, I see I have plenty of company. A small terrestrial fish named Terminator. A Zombie named Red Eye. And a big penguin—or at least the gigantic head of a penguin—named Alpha.

We're all roaming the corridors of this starship, looking each other over but not saying much of anything, like a bunch of sideshow freaks auditioning for a fourth remake of "The Night of the Living Dead."

I start to float toward a doorway and it slides open for me. I'm in a room lined with windows through which the stars and galaxies shine.

Another raven, named Cassandra, approaches.

"Great minds think alike," she says in what I take to be a fraternal gesture from a fellow bird.

"I suppose," I reply.

Neither of us says anything more and Cassandra continues on her way. I begin to wonder why such great minds couldn't think of anything else to talk about.

A futuristic surrealistic dream? Not quite. As it turns out, Cassandra was actually a colleague of mine from her home in Turin, Italy.

Suddenly, more 3-D environments like this chat room scenario just described are popping up all over the Web and in internal corporate Internets or intranets. The reason is *Virtual Reality Modeling Language* (VRML), a programming language for describing multi-user interactive simulations—virtual environments networked via the Internet and hyperlinked over the Web.

We're also seeing more workstation vendors, animation vendors, and *virtual reality* (VR) software vendors than ever before coming to market—with all kinds of new 3-D Web browsers, Builders, and authoring tools. At the VRML97 Technical Symposium '95, VRML and related products were all the rage. The consensus at the Symposium was that 1997 would be the year for VRML, or a bust. So, what's going on? What does it all mean?

Why All the Excitement about VRML?

VRML is the natural successor to *Hypertext Markup Language* (HTML) which is widely used today in the creation of Web content and Web browsers. While HTML displays data in static, 2-D representations, VRML enables organizations to create environments that initiate the real 3-D world we live in. In other words, VRML is to 3-D what HTML is to 2-D. VRML is the whole point. Without a standard 3-D graphics interchange format, the whole 3-D World Wide Web (WWW) is pointless.

Furthermore, whereas HTML specifies how two-dimensional documents are represented, VRML is a format that describes how three-dimensional environments can be explored and created on the World Wide Web (WWW). Since 2-D is really just a subset of 3-D, any two-dimensional object can be easily represented in a three-dimensional environment. In Mark Pesce's book, *VRML: Browsing and Building in Cyberspace*, Tim Berners-Lee, the father of the Web, reasons that VRML is the future of the Web because it is more natural for us to be immersed in a three-dimensional space than to click our way through hyperlinked pages.

Demand for VRML is being driven by its potential for commercial applications. Major corporations such as Visa International, Inc. are attracted to the notion of building 3-D worlds for their customers to visit, perhaps creating a truly memorable experience that causes them to return.

One of the limitations of HTML Web sites is that regardless of how beautiful or intriguing the 2-D graphics are, the customer still experiences a flat, text-oriented world that pales next to TV or the real world. Therefore, a new medium must do one of two things to last: It must either lead the user to an economic transaction, in which case the value of the medium is as an advertising vehicle, or it must provide the user with an experience he or she is willing to pay for. VRML is unique in that it can do both.

The construction industry already uses VRML to explore exact representations of architectural drawings and models before starting to build. The real estate industry is already capitalizing on VRML by showing houses on the Internet to long-distance clients. The games industry is already a huge VRML user. Chemists use VRML to visualize molecules before they are chemically synthesized.

VRML and the Internet are also helping Visa to create virtual branch offices rather than invest in the construction of physical offices. Visa is finding out that investing in bricks and mortar is no longer the way to reach new customers. This new interface will give financial institutions the opportunity to use cyberbricks and cybermortar to build environments in which they can offer services to consumers— at only a fraction of the investment of the traditional branch.

Using VRML, Visa is developing virtual banking and retailing applications delivered via the Internet called the Electronic Courtyard. These services will combine the power of multiuser virtual reality and partially secure transaction processing. Visa warns though, that there is currently no readily available, secure way to prevent fraud or theft when giving out a Visa card number or other sensitive information over an open network like the Internet. For this reason, Visa strongly encourages consumers, merchants, and financial institutions to avoid using Visa card accounts over open networks until there is a secure transaction system in place.

The Electronic Courtyard includes an interactive bank branch where consumers can pay bills, check account balances, transfer funds, and apply for loans. It also includes virtual online malls and catalogs. For example, Visa's Market Square (as shown in Figure 1.1) is a virtual mall that offers a wide array of goods and services from computer software, electronics, clothing, medical products, personal protection products, home-business services (mainly Internet-related), jewelry, sports cards, art, and much more. Depending on the product and company, online, phone, and mail ordering options are available.[1]

The Electronic Courtyard also represents a radical departure from traditional text and icon-based applications. Rendered in rich 3-D graphics, the virtual environment lets users explore their surroundings from a first-person perspective using their mouse or keyboard. Within virtual rooms, users can interact with other individuals, like bank tellers, loan officers, financial advisers, and salespeople, who can help them conduct business on line or purchase merchandise electronically.

A whole new breed of Web browsers and programming tools is being developed to accommodate this medium. Corporate devel-

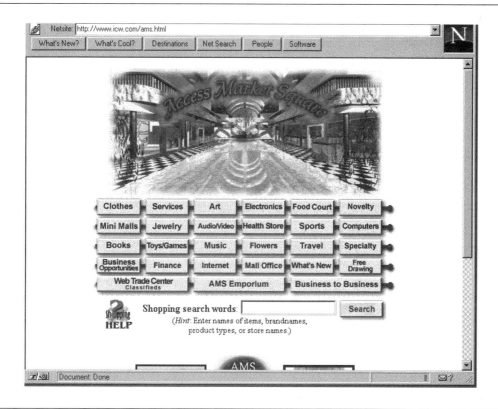

Figure 1.1 Visa's virtual mall—Market Square.

opers have their choice of three major types of products: VRML viewers, related products that provide VRML extensions to existing HTML browsers, and VRML authoring tools.

VRML viewers, like HTML browsers, are standalone applications written for PCs running Microsoft Windows, the Apple Macintosh, or other PCs or workstations. They allow the PC user to visit and navigate VRML worlds. Viewers typically feature controls for moving forward and backward, remembering or recording "camera positions" (3-D bookmarks that allow the user to return to a particular location later on), and handling essential functions like preventing the user from accidentally "walking" into or through a wall.

Many firms are continuing to develop extensions to HTML browsers that provide VRML capabilities as enhancements or plug-ins to existing Web browsers, for example, Netscape Navigator or Microsoft Internet Explorer. These products enable users to access VRML worlds with their current browser technologies. Many of these same companies developing VRML viewers are also developing homespace development tools which let developers design and build 3-D worlds in VRML format and incorporate Internet-standard audio files, video files, and behavior engines.

VRML, therefore, presents an opportunity to move away from proprietary tool-centered formats toward a more neutral geometry format. Technologically, VRML's primary advantage today is its independence and its flexibility.

Commercial acceptance of VRML depends on many factors. Certainly a commitment on the part of software companies to build tools and viewers is critical, and this has been demonstrated with the flood of products in recent months.

One problem that VRML users encounter today is incompatibility between their browser software and the many 3-D worlds they visit. Some browsers can view worlds built only with the creator's tools. Others view an array of worlds but are limited in the number of advanced features, behaviors, or site enhancements they can interpret. Advancement of the VRML standard itself, and adherence to that standard by software companies, is essential if VRML technology is to become widely deployed.

The VRML Standard: A Strategic Platform in the Making

VRML is also very exciting to the 3-D entertainment community because it represents a platform-independent multimedia file format for delivering interactive 3-D animation content to low-bandwidth devices. With the advent of games such as Quake and Duke Nukem 3-D, end-user expectations for entertainment titles have increased dramatically.

Three-dimensional oriented game play has helped create new and addicting entertainment experiences for end users. However, the technology (authoring tools and 3-D rendering engines) used to create these games is typically proprietary, and is expensive to create and maintain. Because of its proprietary nature, this technology is not available to the general game development community and does not support industry standards. In fact, many developers have been forced to delay or abandon the development of innovative new 3-D games due to a lack of commercially available authoring tools and standards-based playback technology.

By agreeing on a standard specification for sharing 3-D graphics or virtual worlds over the WWW, 3-D graphics can move outside of niche application areas and into everyday use. The new VRML 2.0 specification has changed the playing field for 3-D software development and deployment. The VRML 2.0 specification was finalized at SIGGRAPH in August 1996. This new 3-D graphics standard represents a platform-independent multimedia file format for delivering interactive 3-D animation content to low-bandwidth devices. The VRML 2.0 format is a significant improvement over VRML 1.0, adding interactivity programming, animation, programmable events, multimedia elements, scripting, and a prototyping node that will allow developers to extend the language without the need for proprietary extensions. For example, these new additions to the VRML specification will allow game developers to quickly create compelling 3-D-based games for distribution on both the World Wide Web and CD-ROM. See Chapter 12, *Virtual Reality Modeling Language (VRML) Specifications*, for an in-depth discussion of the new VRML 2.0 and beyond specification.

The latest draft of this 3-D graphics specification, VRML97 (the name of the ISO/VRML standard), replaces the 1996 version (VRML 2.0) and has been submitted to the *International Standards Organization* (ISO) as a *Draft International Standard* (DIS). It is almost identical to VRML 2.0 but with numerous improvements to the specification document and some functional differences. (See Appendix I, *List of Summary Changes to the Spec* in the companion CD-ROM, and Chapter 2, *The Emerging VRML Standard*, for a thorough discussion of this evolving standard.) All of this is exciting because there are compelling reasons to believe that 3-D graphics can be built and deployed to enable better ways to entertain, communicate, learn, and conduct business.

What's going on here is that one good idea leads to another. Very few people saw the Web coming. Even fewer saw 3-D on the Web looming over the horizon. Now that 3-D and the Web are irrevocably wed, people are raving about the brave new world. SIG-GRAPH, the premier show for interactive media technologies and solutions, has never been truer to its image. What better environment than the free-spirited SIGGRAPH to help disseminate the notion of the Web as a carrier of interactive media technologies? And of course serious businesses have become interested in making some extra money with the concept!

What all this means is that everybody is exploring new possibilities. It is still too early for a sure voice to be heard over the Web's cacophony. The experiments of today will pave the future for real applications of 3-D environments on the Web. By 1998, with the large percentage of personal computers (the client of choice for Web exploration) equipped with on-board 3-D acceleration and increased line bandwidth, 3-D will be the natural choice for navigating the Web and visualizing distributed information. The inherent topology of the Web, with all of its interconnections, is certainly not two-dimensional, and better visualization tools are required. By providing an extra dimension, 3-D seems to fill the gap.

Current 3-D Environments on the Web

An increasing number of 3-D environments are available on the Web frontier. Each environment is different. There are sites displaying objects of all kinds: online chat sessions; real-estate agents putting 3-D houses on line for potential customers to wander through; ticket sellers constructing virtual stadiums so spectators can preview their seats and the angle from which they will view the game; and product displays.

Companies like Paragraph, Black Sun International, and others have already built or are already working to build virtual worlds in VRML because of an industry-wide agreement on a common standard. They represent only the beginning of a trend that has the potential to transform the Web into a 3-D, interactive experience. The game players and entertainment companies know it's already out there.

For example, Newfire, Inc. (as shown in Figure 1.2) and other leading companies developing VRML-based content creation software will provide game developers with a wealth of resources, including:

- Pervasive, freely available 3-D rendering engines, embedded in VRML-enabled Internet browsers and standalone applications.
- Commercial-quality authoring tools to create immersive 3-D content, such as game levels, characters, and interactive game play.
- A fast-growing community of VRML experts and a wide variety of books, training materials, and public domain utilities.[2]

Further examples like Dimension X's Liquid Reality shown in Figures 1.3 through 1.8 provide an interactive 3-D experience— you can interact with objects in the environment in real time.[3] Figure 1.3 (Helix) shows off Liquid Reality's motion and sound capabilities (see the accompanying CD-ROM for Helix's sound capabilities). The trusses woosh as they go by in full stereo splendor and the helix makes strange alien noises.

Intervista Software's VRML browser, WorldView, allows you to view the VRML models and Web sites shown in Figures 1.9 through 1.11.[4] TGS and SGI have WebSpace Navigator and Cosmo Player (see Figure 1.12). These three all act as external helper applications to a regular Web browser, although they've all gone In Plane with Netscape Navigator to be viewed from within the regular browser window.[5] They also provide *static* 3-D spaces; you can wander through the spaces but can't interact with anything in the spaces.

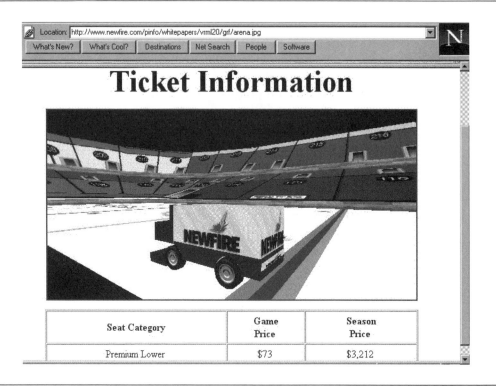

Figure 1.2 Using Newfire's Torch 3-D player as an Internet browser plug-in, developers are creating cool multimedia 3-D web pages like this online commerce example.

What is currently available are not 3-D worlds but more like 3-D islands—some with links to other islands. Most of the 3-D environments available are simply 3-D models translated to VRML. They are really just preliminary demo environments put out by R&D organizations. Very few models exist that take advantage of key VRML features like level of detail, the ability to include other nodes from across the Web, and so on.

The Good, the Bad, and the Ugly

The current crop of 3-D environments on the Web covers the entire gamut—the good, the bad, and the ugly. The same sins committed

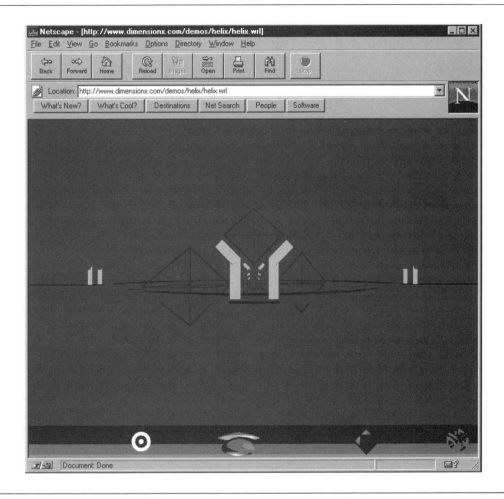

Figure 1.3 Dimension X's Liquid Reality Helix demo.

when creating traditional Web pages continue to be well represented in 3-D. The key aspects of the Web are *content* and *form*. The very nature of the Web makes it impossible to separate both. The ideal 3-D environment offers a well-thought structure, easy navigation, and above all, useful content. Today's 3-D environments are still largely exploratory in nature and more a vehicle for learning the new medium than a carrier of content—although that appears to be changing in the area of content creation.

Figure 1.4 Dimension X's Liquid Reality Kenwood 3-D Room demo.

Efficiently Creating Cross-Platform Titles

Though it seems that 3-D environments are somewhat of a weak carrier of "content," the efficient creation of cross-platform titles is the "holy grail" for content creators (see Figure 1.13).[6] Because VRML 2.0 is an interpreted language, VRML content can be played on any computing device with a client-based VRML player. VRML games will play back on any standard PC operating system,

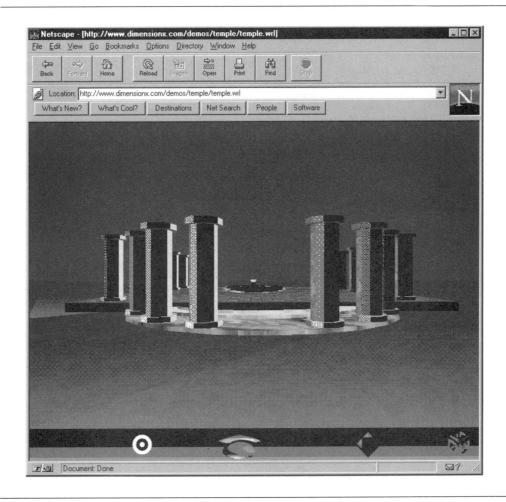

Figure 1.5 Dimension X's Liquid Reality Temple demo.

including Windows, Mac OS, and Unix. For further information on content creation see Appendix J, *Content Creation and Delivery on the Web*, in the companion CD-ROM.

Multiplayer Online Gaming

Within a few years, online gaming will be the dominant form of computer "recreation." The inherently small file sizes and compression

Figure 1.6 Dimension X's Liquid Reality Hammer demo.

ratios of VRML-based content are well suited for online game distribution. File sizes for comparable JPEG and GIF files can be two to three times larger and the files are not interactive. Because VRML is an interpreted file format, much like HTML, today's online game networks and their associated client/server protocols will easily handle VRML traffic.

One of the most frequently asked questions about VRML 2.0 is, "how can I add multiplayer capabilities?" While the VRML 2.0 specification doesn't provide a specific protocol for handling mul-

Figure 1.7 Dimension X's Liquid Reality in the System demo.

tiple players, a number of companies, including Silicon Graphics, IBM, Sony, and Black Sun Interactive, have joined together to propose a Living Worlds' API that will allow developers to author games independent of the specific underlying multiplayer technology. This will allow a VRML game developer to create his or her content without worrying about what type of multiuser technology is implemented in the users' players. See Chapter 9, *Living Worlds*, for an in-depth discussion on the "Living Worlds" API.

Online Component Development with CD-ROM Games

Developers with significant investments in CD-ROM titles can also use VRML to deliver enhancements and upgrades—new levels, characters, accessories, and behaviors—over networks. This hybrid approach to title deployment will provide developers with an efficient delivery mechanism and maximized incremental income that would have otherwise necessitated production of additional CD-ROM SKUs. See Chapter 23, *Other VR Research*, for an in-depth discussion about advanced interactive CD-ROM games like the "Virtual Titanic" (from CyberFlix) that makes users feel like they have joined the doomed passengers, and the "Virtual Einstein" (from Carnegie Mellon University) that allows users to hold a conversation with the physicist who died in 1955. A digitized video short demonstrating "Virtual Einstein" is also contained in the companion CD-ROM.

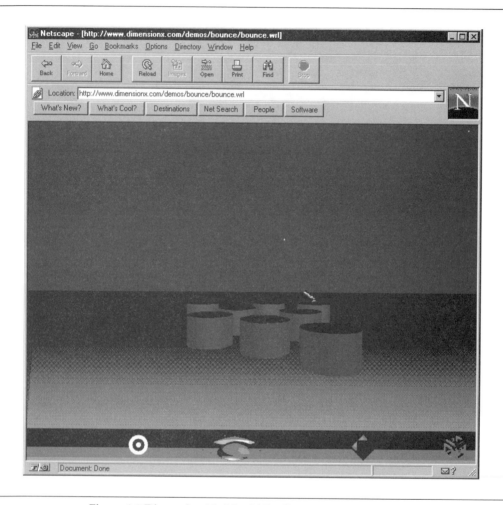

Figure 1.8 Dimension X's Liquid Reality Bounce demo.

Speed Is Not Enough with VRML 2.0 Technology

The 3-D environments this author has viewed so far have not been very interesting. This is a result of several factors: First, the viewers are pretty slow, even on something as high-end as an SGI Indigo Extreme; second, the ones viewed so far have not been com-

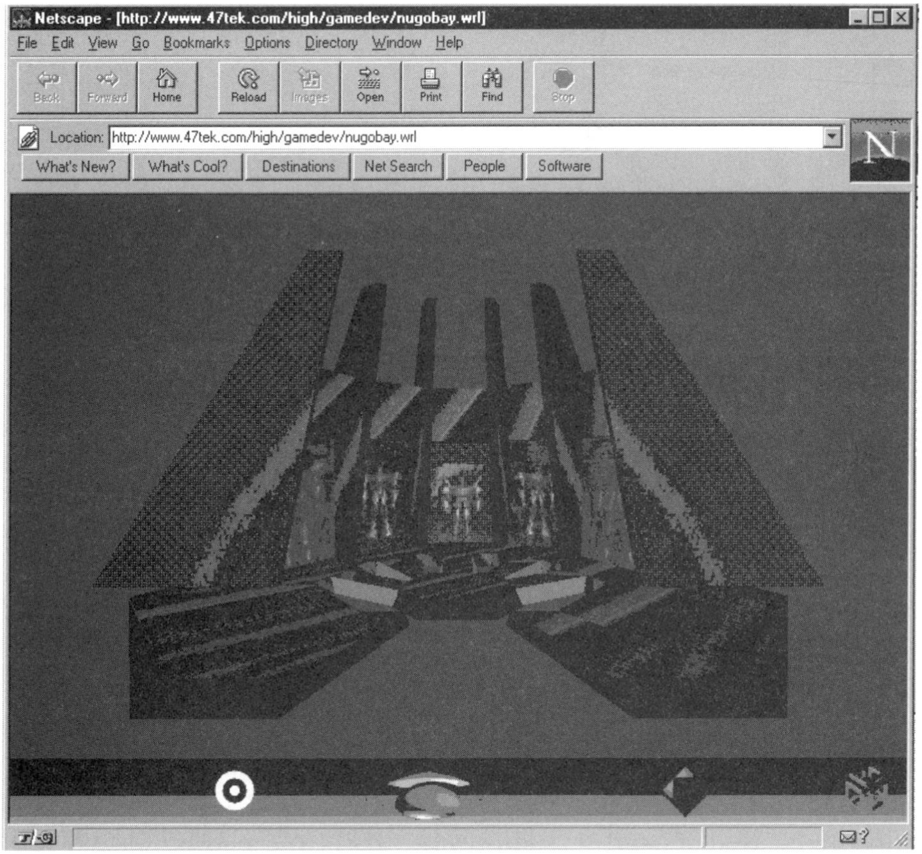

Figure 1.9 GoMan Launch Bay.

pressed and have to run on several megabytes (MB), which is a long download time even on a fast connection; and finally, VRML 2.0/VRML97 as a language is still in its infancy and static scenes with a few hyperlinks cannot be all that interesting. Therefore, it appears that the single most important element in creating an interesting 3-D environment experience is rendering speed.

Rendering Speed

In order to invest in a new commercial technology, entertainment title developers require high-performance playback and a

Figure 1.10 Virtual Parts.

well-designed architecture that allows for customization. *High-performance playback* and *customization* are the key words here in the creation of a satisfying 3-D experience with rendering speed. Slow rendering (in other words, a low frame-update rate) forces a user to navigate in a series of jerky, nonfluid movements that ultimately degrade or destroy the experience. Many of the first-generation VRML players incorporated slow z-buffer-based rendering engines (great for photorealistic rendering) that did little to improve on the navigation experience. Game-based engines typically employ some sort of *Binary Space Partitioning* (BSP) based rendering solution (for real-time playback), which helps to speed the rendering of static environments. With videogame platforms like the Sony Playstation and Nintendo 64 offering better rendering speeds, and Quake and Duke Nukem 3-D establishing new levels of expectations for PC-based games, VRML-based rendering technology must be as fast or faster than other options, as shown in Figure 1.14.[7] See Chapter 20, *VRML Concepts*, for an in-depth discussion on 3-D modeling for speed.

Nevertheless, people are still learning how to take full advantage of VRML. Simply converting existing 3-D models into VRML via file translators does not usually yield good results. VRML is designed for use on low-end machines over low-bandwidth networks. Polygon count and file sizes are important concerns. Two

Figure 1.11 Space Station.

unique features of VRML that help manage these concerns are the *Level of Detail* (LOD) *node* and the *Inline node,* as shown in Figures 1.15 and 1.16, respectively.[8]

LOD Node

The LOD node allows the author to specify multiple representations of objects at varying complexities. The version of the object

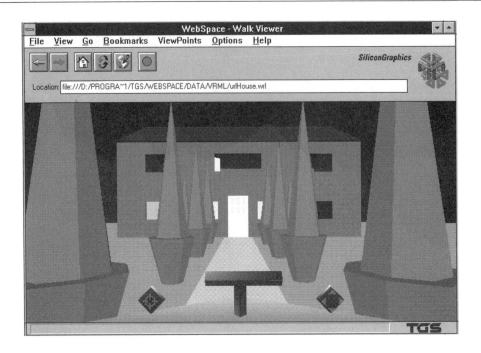

Figure 1.12 WebSpace Navigator.

that is displayed is chosen automatically, based on the distance between the object and the user's eyepoint. This is a time-honored trick used for years in real-time visual simulation applications. Effective use of the LOD node greatly improves graphics performance by helping to limit the total number of polygons displayed at any one time.

In other words, the LOD node specifies various levels of detail or complexity for a given object, and provides hints for browsers to automatically choose the appropriate version of the object based on the distance from the user. The level field contains a list of nodes that represent the same object or objects at varying levels of detail, from the highest to the lowest level of detail, and the range field specifies the ideal distances at which to switch between the levels. For example:

Figure 1.13 Newfire's Torch provides game developers with an interactive 3-D player for deploying entertainment WebSpace Navigator titles on the Web.

```
LOD {
  exposedField MFNode   level    []
  field        SFVec3f  center   0 0 0
  field        MFFloat  range    []
}
```

The center field is a translation offset in the local coordinate system that specifies the center of the LOD object for distance calculations. In order to calculate which level to display, first the distance is calculated from the viewpoint, transformed into the local coordinate

Figure 1.14 Newfire's Torch's rendering performance allows the creation of large-scale, photorealistic, fully texture-mapped worlds without downsampling textures. Model generated using Lightscape Visualization System software with full radiosity-based textures.

space of the LOD node (including any scaling transformations), to the center point of the LOD. If the distance is less than the first value in the range field, then the first level of the LOD is drawn. If the distance is between the first and second values in the range field, the second level is drawn, and so on.

If there are N values in the range field, the LOD will have N+1 nodes in its level field. Specifying too few levels will result in the last level being used repeatedly for the lowest levels of detail; if more levels than ranges are specified, the extra levels will be

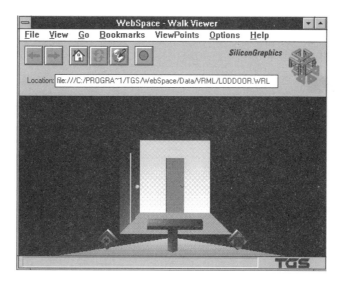

Figure 1.15 LOD (Level of Detail) node.

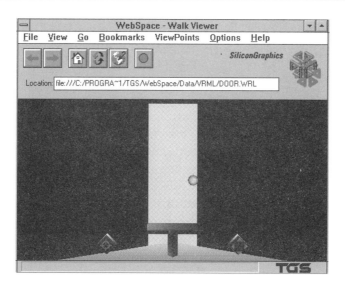

Figure 1.16 Inline node.

ignored. The exception to this rule is to leave the range field empty, which is a hint to the browser that it should choose a level automatically to maintain a constant display rate. Each value in the range field should be greater than the previous value; otherwise, results are undefined.

Authors should set LOD ranges so that the transitions are smooth from one level of detail to the next. Browsers may adjust which level of detail is displayed to maintain interactive frame rates, to display an already fetched level of detail while a higher level of detail (contained in an Inline node) is fetched, or may disregard the author-specified ranges for any other implementation-dependent reason. For best results, specify ranges only where necessary and nest LOD nodes with and without ranges. Browsers should try to honor the hints given by authors, and authors should try to give browsers as much freedom as they can to choose levels of detail based on performance.

LOD nodes are evaluated top-down in the scene graph. Only the descendants of the currently selected level are rendered. Note that all nodes under an LOD node continue to receive and send events (routes) regardless of which LOD level is active. For example, if an active TimeSensor is contained within an inactive level of an LOD, the TimeSensor sends events regardless of the LOD's state.

Inline Node

The Inline node points to other VRML files and can be used to break up large VRML files into smaller pieces. As a VRML file is being read into the user's machine, the browser interprets the file and builds the appropriate geometry. When the browser encounters an Inline node in the VRML file, it begins fetching this new piece. In the meantime, the user can begin navigating through the scene even while it is being constructed. This is especially useful if the user has a low-bandwidth network connection.

In other words, the Inline node is a grouping node that reads its children data from a location in the World Wide Web. Exactly when its children are read and displayed is not defined; reading the children may be delayed until the Inline is actually visible to the viewer. The URL field specifies the URL containing the children. An Inline with an empty URL does nothing. For example:

```
Inline {
    exposedField MFString  url           []
    field        SFVec3f   bboxCenter  0 0 0
    field        SFVec3f   bboxSize    -1 -1 -1
}
```

An Inline's URLs will refer to a valid VRML file that contains a list of children nodes at the top level. The results are undefined if the URL refers to a file that is not VRML or if the file contains non-children nodes at the top level. If multiple URLs are specified, the browser may display a URL of a lower preference file while it is obtaining, or if it is unable to obtain the higher preference file.

The *bboxCenter* and *bboxSize* fields specify a bounding box that encloses the Inline's children. This is a hint that may be used for optimization purposes. If the specified bounding box is smaller than the actual bounding box of the children at any time, then the results are undefined. A default bboxSize value, (-1 -1 -1), implies that the bounding box is not specified and if needed must be calculated by the browser.

When Inlines are wrapped inside LODs, a double advantage occurs. If the user happens to navigate away from the location of an Inlined part of the scene and never activates the LOD that contains this Inline, the browser will not even attempt to load that part of the scene across the network. This is especially efficient since it reduces both network traffic and polygon count.

Until recently, it's been difficult for VRML authors to take advantage of these features of VRML because to do so would require carefully editing the VRML text files to add these nodes at the appropriate place in the scene. This requires intimate knowledge of the VRML file format. However, interactive VRML authoring applications are now appearing that greatly simplify this task. With the use of these tools, we will begin to see more and better-performing VRML sites than are currently available.

Build It and They Will Come

Builders of 3-D environments range from universities to businesses to individuals just passing through who are interested in exploring the new medium. Recently there has been a proliferation of sites of architectural nature, where buildings and, sometimes, the main components of a town are represented. Another trend is to offer conference attendees a glimpse of an exhibition floor plan, complete with booth and vendor information. The ability to walk through a conference before even getting there is the perfect planning tool to optimize one's time.

It's still early for VRML, but more and more 3-D sites are going up every day. Just as the number of HTML Web pages grew exponentially over the last four years, so will the number of VRML sites increase.

Most of the VRML work being done right now is coming from the entertainment and commercial arenas versus the academic and research institutions of just a couple of years ago. These include architecture, art, astronomy, avatars, biomedical, chemistry, commerce/data visualization, company presence, communication, educational, entertainment, geography, mathematics, personal presence, product demonstration, simulated physical experience, site navigation, and sports.

Ease of Build

Most tools for building 3-D environments on the Web are existing applications modified to save files in the VRML format. As such, the difficulty in building these environments has little to do with the Web itself. Perhaps the main challenge is not of a graphical nature but rather how to attach Web-specific information (URLs) to existing or newly created 3-D models. A limitation of today's 3-D environments on the Web is their artificial nature. Some models lack floors or ceilings; some even lack walls—certainly not what Web warriors might expect.

There are two basic steps to building 3-D environments for use on the Web: building the geometry and adding links. Building 3-D models is not rocket science but it can be tedious. Good modeling tools are widely available as far as file translators to convert geometry to the VRML format. Structuring the geometry into Inlines and LODs as described earlier can be difficult or easy, depending on your access to interactive VRML authoring tools. The same is true for enriching VRML sites by adding links to other Web-based content.

Nevertheless, every day it is becoming easier to build 3-D Web sites because the industry is embracing the VRML 2.0 and VRML97 standards. All of the 3-D modeling packages are now exporting VRML files. All of the vendors of 3-D models are now offering VRML versions of their wares. Soon 3-D objects will become a commodity product. This is inevitable. With VRML products becoming more and more accessible, it makes it that much easier for you or me to create a 3-D Web site. Nonetheless, the authoring software still has a long way to go before it is trivial to build a 3-D Web site.

Ease of Build on the Web

The following are some very specific applications for 3-D on the Web (both Internet and intranet), where 3-D will not only add value but will actually drive growth of the Web. These are only the first steps to a more immersive Web experience.

Entertainment

Online games where users can become totally immersed in the environment have been the first to really take advantage of 3-D technology. However, the future of entertainment on line is even more intriguing than the 3-D games of today. Someday, with additional input technology, sports games will be recorded in 3-D. Imagine being able to rerun a specific play from a football game. You could move around on the field and see it from the eyes of the quarterback, any one of the players, or from above. 3-D could let you watch a performance from anywhere on the stage, zooming in and out from the characters and sounds that you find most intriguing. 3-D will add more interaction and fun to many aspects of entertainment well beyond games, as shown in Figures 1.17 through 1.21.[9]

Product Demonstration

Catalog sales is a multibillion-dollar business—the buyer purchases an item based on seeing a small photograph. Imagine how much more powerful catalog sales would be if you could actually demonstrate the product for the buyer. Take something simple like buying a bookcase. It would be so much more interesting to actually see the bookcase with the different finishes. It would be more compelling to be able to put a large binder or dictionary on the shelf to see if it fits. You could also type in your room dimensions so you could see if the desired bookcase will fit between the door and the window. Maybe upon moving it around, you decide a larger bookcase would look better. That is just one example of the number of products that would benefit by being demonstrated in 3-D on the Web. Here are just a few more:

- ◆ Appliances, large and small
- ◆ Automobiles
- ◆ Items where you need configuration information such as parts and accessories:
  - ◆ Ski racks
  - ◆ Luggage
  - ◆ Computers
- ◆ Toys
- ◆ Furniture
- ◆ Boats

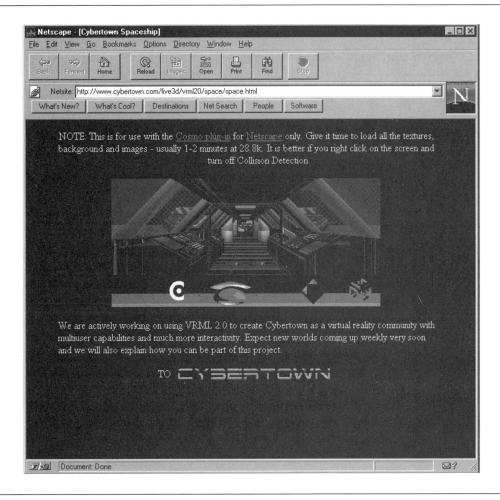

Figure 1.17 Cybertown Spaceship.

3-D product demonstrations will soon be one of the driving factors for companies wanting to use the Web to market their products. See Figures 1.22 through 1.25 for a glimpse of the future of 3-D product demos on the Internet and intranets.[10]

Communication Space

This technology does not always have to mirror real physical objects or spaces. Internet chat spaces have been among the first to

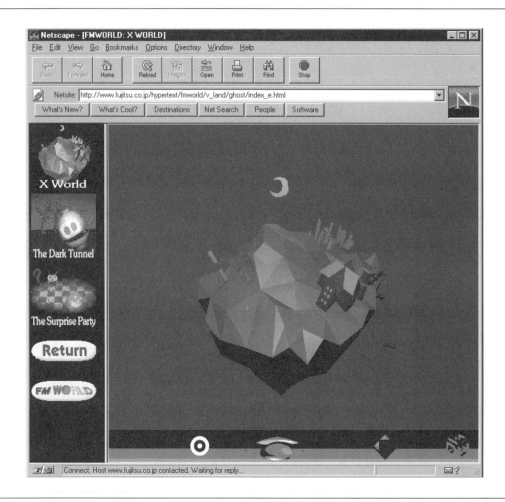

Figure 1.18 X World from Fujitsu Limited's FM World.

widely adopt 3-D on the Web. Getting people together in one location without them physically being there is certainly one of the
most compelling innovations of the Web. One of the compelling
reasons for Web chat is the anonymity it provides. With *avatars*
(figures to represent individuals), people preserve their anonymity and yet can see a physical presence in the room. Just being able
to visualize the number of people in a chat room adds a new
dynamic to chat rooms (see Figure 1.26).[11]

Figure 1.19 Netscape's Virtual Drive-In.

The next step for 3-D communications space is the corporate meeting. Take the example of a company that has engineering in the United States and manufacturing in Asia. A 3-D prototype of a product can be manipulated on the display without engineering and manufacturing having to physically be in the same space. Engineering can provide a complete walkthrough of assembly of a new product without ever leaving the office. Companies will

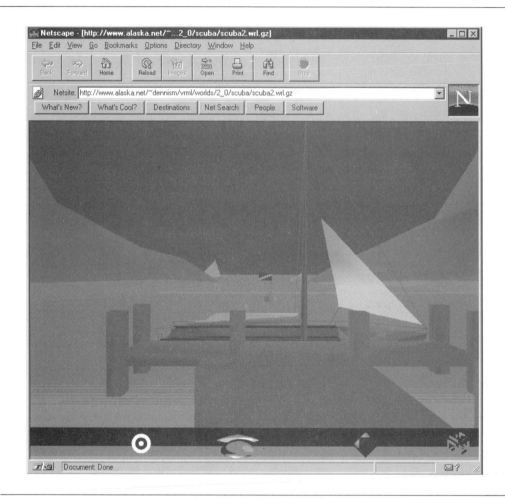

Figure 1.20 VR Group's South Seas Paradise which can be explored above and below the water surface.

save a great deal of time and money when communication becomes this easy.

Another benefit of this type of interaction is the record and replay capability. If the hand off from engineering to manufacturing is recorded in this medium, manufacturing engineers who were

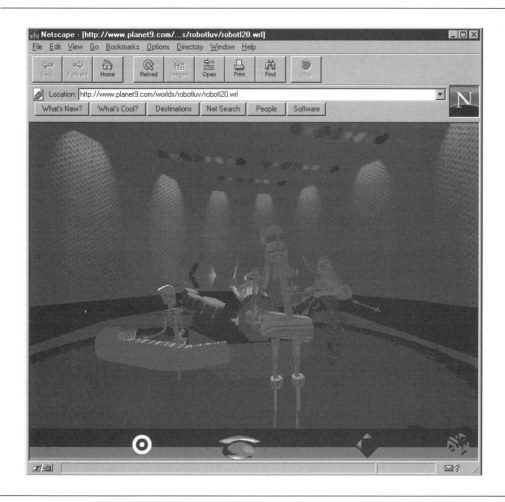

Figure 1.21 Planet9 Studio's Robot Luv.

unable to attend the online meeting can have all the benefits of the engineering hand off at their fingertips.

The final benefit of meetings in cyberspace is use of alternative media. Data visualization in 3-D can be a more powerful way to present statistics (see the "Data Visualization" section later in this chapter). With VRML you can integrate video, graphics, audio,

Figure 1.22 Bob Crispen's '57 Chevy.

and text presentations right into a single virtual meeting room. For all of these reasons, 3-D will make communication easier and more powerful.

Product Support/Documentation

Training videos are becoming an important part of corporate Web sites, but in many manufacturing facilities a training video is not

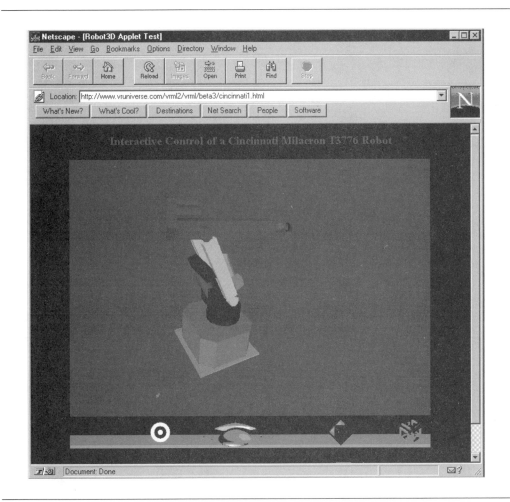

Figure 1.23 Markus Roskothen's Interactive Control Robot Arms: Cincinnati Milacron T3776 Robot.

enough. Assembly of complex parts is better communicated through 3-D interaction with the part as shown in Figure 1.27.[12] How many times have you picked up assembly instructions and tried to find the parts that match the diagram? Two dimensions do not supply an accurate view of an object. With 3-D the viewer selects the angle of the presentation and can interact with objects at his or her own pace.

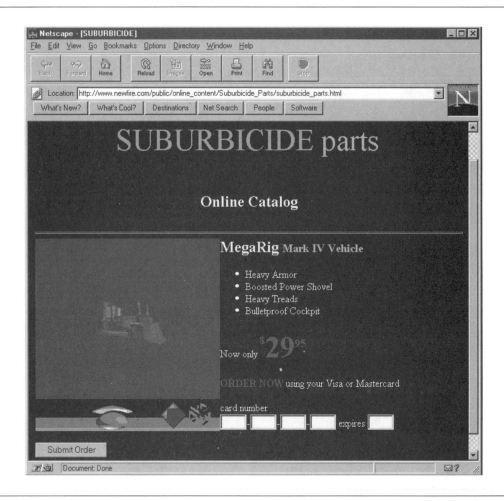

Figure 1.24 Newfire Inc.'s Suburbicide parts.

It is not just manufacturing facilities that can benefit from showing assembly in 3-D. A 3-D depiction of how to add memory or a disk drive to your computer would be extremely helpful.

The interactive nature of VRML 2.0 also allows the content author to highlight areas of interest. In the example shown in Figure 1.27 there could be a circle around the screws that you

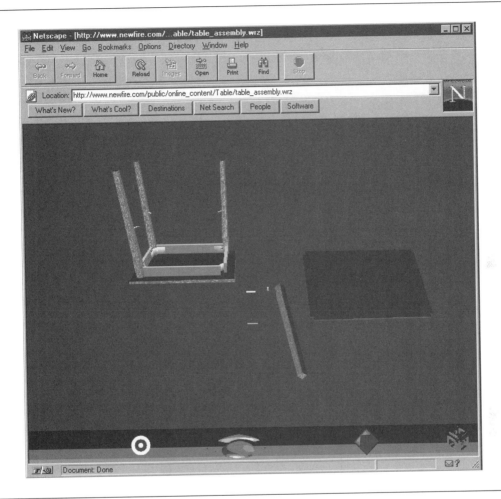

Figure 1.25 Newfire Inc.'s Table Assembly demo.

have to remove first to get the cover off your PC, then arrows can be used to point to the right slots. In the future you may get children's toys with assembly instructions in 3-D on a CD or Web site. The cost of producing these instructions with VRML will be much less expensive than a similar cost to do an instructional video production. For any type of assembly instruction, VRML is a much more effective medium than simple 2-D line drawings

Figure 1.26 Black Sun Interactive's Avatar Rooms.

and less expensive than other alternatives. See Chapter 23, *Other VR Research*, for an in-depth discussion on using VRML to access manufacturing parts data.

Architecture

The one application for 3-D that I hear mentioned all the time is "real estate walkthroughs." Most of you at one time or another have

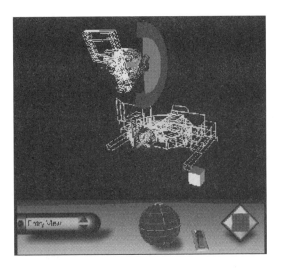

Figure 1.27 Single part rendered solid in context of wireframe saw.

tried to search for a house to buy. You've seen rental Web sites that have apartment layouts. That is a great start, but wouldn't you really like to walk through a door and see how the apartment looks and feels as shown in Figure 1.28? [13] How high is the ceiling? What is the first thing you notice when you walk in?

Real estate for sale or rent is just the beginning, however; the medium is much more powerful than that. You could wander through Frank Lloyd Wright's Marin Civic Center or take a trip to the Louvre without ever leaving your home. If you were moving into a new office your architect could show you how your new office building is going to look to customers who first walk through your door. Another application is for architects and designers to show home remodels on line. Different treatments to a room can easily be added or removed such as finishes on cabinets or draperies. Allowing people to get a feel for physical spaces is certainly one of the most powerful implementations of the technology.

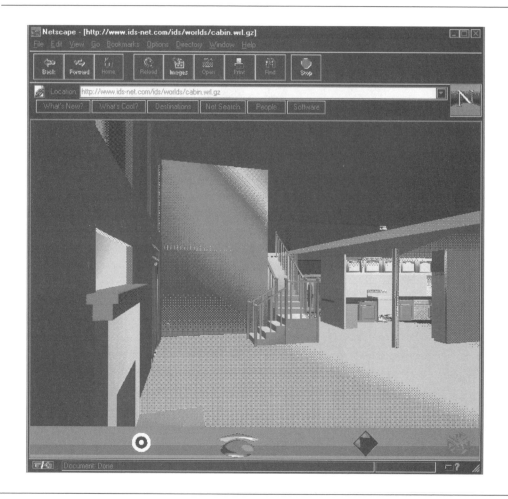

Figure 1.28 Virtual Cabin/Apartment by Integrated Data Systems.

Simulated Physical Experience

To take the architecture example one step further, imagine checking out a vacation destination ahead of time. You could walk through the hotel, step out on the balcony, see the view, and wander through a resort—all without leaving your living room. Figure 1.29 shows an architectural view of a simulated physical experience.[14]

Figure 1.29 American Gothic: a creepy house created by the folks at Construct.

3-D can be used to provide a simulated physical experience that you may not be able to otherwise achieve without being there. How many times have you looked up something in the Yellow Pages and seen an address that should be familiar? But you really don't have any idea where it is in relation to familiar landmarks. A map in 3-D would be extremely useful when taking a ride on top

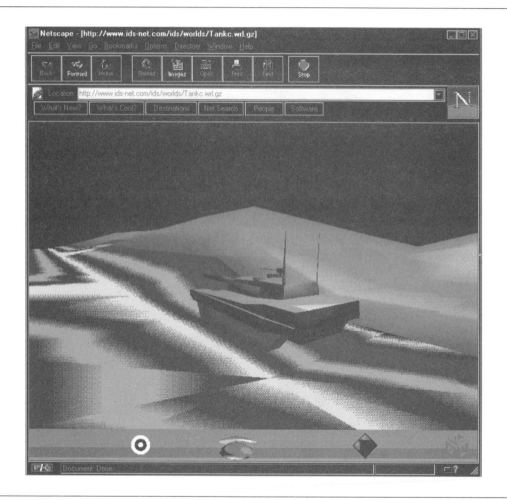

Figure 1.30 VRML tank.

of a VRML 2.0 tank as shown in Figure 1.30.[15] Have you ever noticed that tourist maps are often in 3-D? Locations are much more recognizable when you can see familiar landmarks.

Another example is trade shows. Tens of thousands of people swarm to COMDEX each year. What if you went and couldn't make it to the west hall? Wouldn't it be nice to go back to your

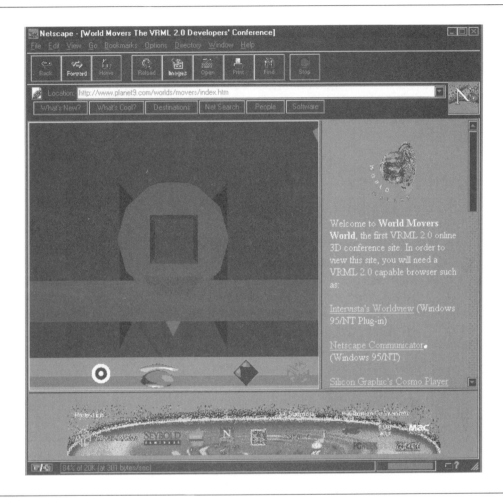

Figure 1.31 WORLD Movers World VRML 2.0 Developers' Conference by Planet9 Studios.

office and stroll through the west hall? You could see all the exciting new announcements and never have to talk to a sales rep! In fact, you could spend the week in Hawaii browsing the Web in the evenings and come back with a complete report on all COMDEX announcements! It's not COMDEX, but Figure 1.31 shows the WORLD Movers World VRML 2.0 Developers' Conference.[16]

One last area of enhanced user experience is the online tour guide. Have you ever been lost in a site trying to find specific information? What if you had a guided tour of a site? With 3-D an avatar can lead you through a site, quickly pointing you in the right direction. This is just one more way that VRML technology can provide a more interactive experience. Now, let's see how easy it is to access and interact with these VRML/3-D applications.

Ease of Access

Interacting with 3-D information on the Web can be a frustrating experience. On the one hand, the inherent limitations in bandwidth and computing power on the client side restrict the complexity and richness of 3-D environments to mere sketchy models. On the other hand, the very fact that humans are used to living in a 3-D environment makes the Web a sterile place. All interaction cues we all depend on to live in our 3-D world merely disappear when surfing the Web. Current research has concentrated almost exclusively on file formats and rendering performance at the expense of better user interaction models. Lack of proper user interaction support is the second-biggest impediment to making 3-D on the Web reach widespread use; lack of interacting and compelling content is the first. Let's be honest: Going through walls and flying upside down can be appealing to certain types of users but the novelty wears off pretty quickly. The next generation of 3-D environments will offer easily affordable immersive VR on the Web with better display and input devices, provide intelligent content and intelligent access, take care of detecting collisions, and direct users to interesting places.

Nevertheless, viewing 3-D environments on the Web today requires a VRML-compatible browser or viewing application. Currently quite a few are available on various platforms (see www.sdsc.edu/vrml/browsers.html#Live3D or www.sdsc.edu/vrml/browsers.html), as shown in the example in Figure 1.32. How good the experience of browsing 3-D sites is depends on a

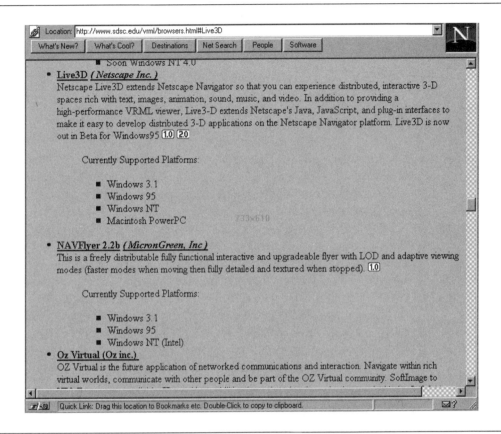

Figure 1.32 San Diego Super Computing Center.

number of factors. Obviously the more graphics horsepower you have in your computer and the faster connection you have to the Internet, the smoother the experience will be. But other factors come into play as well.

A good VRML authoring package, as shown in Figure 1.33, helps an author take full advantage of the power of VRML to perform well in low-end situations.[17] Making extensive use of LODs and Inlines will help tremendously. Structuring the geometric data as efficiently as possible and compressing the VRML files using standard compression routines, such as gzip, will also help. Adding a

Figure 1.33 VRML authoring package.

list of camera views to the scene will also do much to help the user navigate by providing a guided tour to preferred viewpoints.

Browsers are getting pretty stable now but are by no means perfect yet. It's best to have a standalone browser. Of course, the best navigation paradigms are those that leverage what people already know. Games like DOOM have been used as inspiration.

The Practical Value of 3-D Environments on the Web

Seen as the next interaction metaphor—whether on the desktop or in distributed fashion—3-D promises to expand our ability to interact with the surrounding digital world. The very nature of the World Wide Web, where information acquires a multidimensional character, fosters the use of 3-D graphics as a natural interface. Existing HTML-based pages cannot adequately convey the Web's topology-cyberspace that knows no boundaries.

Today, three major areas of practical uses for 3-D environments on the Web exist: navigation, data visualization, and network mapping. Previous examples in this chapter have shown how 3-D is useful for examining objects and spaces on the Web but it will also find substantial uses about for offline software applications. The following are some of the first areas where we will see practical uses for 3-D environments in other software applications.

Navigation

The 2-D display is fairly limiting in the amount of information that can be presented. Considerably more information can be represented in 3-D space. Intervista has come up with some powerful prototypes of Web site navigation in 3-D space that show how much easier it is to find your way around when the site is represented in 3-D space. For example, the Crispen Café shown in Figure 1.34 allows you to browse the Crispen Family WWW site via VRML 2.0.[18] This 3-D navigation will also allow Webmasters to put more information in a space without increasing the complexity.

Data Visualization

Visualizing data refers to the many scientific and technical uses of VRML, which are among the most popular applications today. Several examples of this are in the fields of chemistry, biology, mathematics, astronomy, and environmental sciences. Other practical

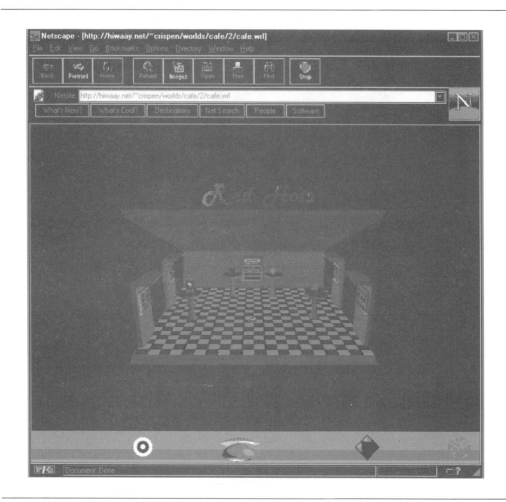

Figure 1.34 The Crispen Café.

examples of this type of 3-D interactive environment include electronic merchandising (virtual mall for shopping), cyberbanking (virtual teller), and virtual government (a government that has staffing on line to interact with citizens 24 hours a day).

In other words, data visualization has long been one of the primary uses of 3-D technology. Analysts and scientists have been using expensive workstations to show them statistics in three dimensions for 20 years because there is a far greater quantity and quality of statistical information that can be presented in 3-D. But with the recent advances in technology mentioned throughout this chapter, everyone will soon have this capability.

Although current applications like Microsoft Excel offer 3-D graphs, they are static in nature. With VRML the charts can change dynamically and the user will be able to change their viewpoints of the data as shown in Figure 1.35.[19]

Network Mapping

Most companies have a complex network of computer systems that are often represented on a network management system in flat 2-D space. The amount of information that can be displayed in such a way is very limited. With VRML technology the information can be displayed in 3-D, dynamically updated, and behaviors can be displayed for areas in the network where there are problems—making it much easier for a network administrator to recognize and correct problems.

A similar example of this technology is file system representation. With hard disks becoming larger and people using networks of systems, finding information becomes more difficult. A 3-D representation of file systems can present more information in a simpler format.

These, examples (navigation, data visualization, and network mapping) show just a few areas where 3-D will make the computing experience more powerful and interesting than ever before. Yet these are only the beginning—with 3-D and cyberspace the imagination is the only limitation for where we will go next.

Available Tools for Browsing and Building VRML Worlds

Most tools today fall in one of the following categories: VRML browsers, VRML authoring packages, or 3-D creation tools. Since

Figure 1.35 Visible Decisions Inc. (VDI) has done a considerable amount of data visualization with VRML. In this example, Market Conditions shows the state of different indexes around the world and also a historical performance of a stock exchange.

the whole market is still very young, the tools vary not only by features but also by navigation paradigms and object manipulation methods. In addition, the tools differ considerably in terms of ease of learning, ease of use, reliability, price, and system requirements.

Although VRML is still new, 3-D creation tools have been around for a long time. Whereas many CAD packages allow for 3-D design, the preferred tools for game designers and multimedia producers have been modeling and animation packages like the ones listed in the VRML Repository (www.sdsc.edu/vrml/repository.html). Although VRML does now support animation, it is still a good idea to purchase a 3-D creation tool from a vendor that will be able to add functionality as VRML continues to evolve into a language for describing interactive multiparticipant environments.

Although some 3-D creation tools already allow models to be saved in VRML, others require you to purchase or download separate translation utilities that convert from the vendor's internal format to VRML. Direct VRML output is preferable to converters, since something always gets lost during a translation. It is a good idea to make sure that the tool you are considering not only writes VRML files but also can import them. In addition, you should be aware of what elements get lost when you save a scene in VRML rather than in the vendor's format; otherwise, you'll find yourself with completely washed-out scenes because your tool supports light attenuation but VRML doesn't. Since there are various levels of VRML support, you should also check to what extent VRML is supported. For example, most modeling packages cannot write out VRML primitives.

Although most 3-D creation tools are developed by established vendors, many VRML 2.0 browsers are written by companies that were started after the first VRML spec was drafted in late 1994. Most of these companies have a networking rather than a 3-D graphics background but they were able to beat larger competitors to the market because they recognized the importance of VRML early on. See Tables 1.1, 1.2, and the "VRML 2.0 Browser Comparison Features" sidebar for a comparison of the latest version of these VRML 2.0 browsers and their accompanying advanced features, as well as those listed in the VRML Repository (www.sdsc.edu/vrml/repository.html).[20]

Table 1.1 VRML 2.0 Browser Implementation Comparison General Information

Browser	Platform	Current Version	Script node language(s)[1]	Rendering Library	ImageTexture formats	Texture size[2]
CASUS Presenter	SGI, Solaris	1.0a9	Java (no security)	Kahlua/Inventor	GIF, JPEG, XBM	$x,y = 2^n$; HW max
Community-Place	PC	2.0PR D16/R16	Java	Renderware or Direct3D	BMP, GIF, JPEG, RAS	128x128(?)
CosmoPlayer for SGI	SGI	1.0.2	VRMLscript	OpenGL	GIF, JPEG, PNG, RGB	$x, y = 2^n$; HW max
CosmoPlayer for PC	PC	1.0	VRML-/JavaScript	Renderware	GIF, JPEG, PNG, BMP, RGB	256x256
GLView / OGL	PC	3.03	VRMLscript	OpenGL	BMP, GIF, JPEG, PPM, RGB, TGA	no restrictions(?)
GLView / D3D	PC	3.03	VRMLscript	Direct3D	BMP, GIF, JPEG, PPM, RGB, TGA	?
LiquidReality	PC, SGI, Solaris, Linux	1.0b17	Java	ICE (proprietary) and D3D on PC	GIF, JPEG, XBM, PNG	no restrictions
OpenWorlds	SGI	0.2	Java C++, C, Lisp[3]	Performer or OpenGL	?	?

Table 1-1 Continued.

Browser	Platform	Current Version	Script node language(s)[1]	Rendering Library	ImageTexture formats	Texture size[2]
OzVirtual	PC	2.0b3	Java	Renderware	BMP, GIF, JPEG, PNG (Portable Network Graphics)	256x256
RealSpace Viewer	Mac/PC	2.0 beta	VRMLscript and rst:*	Proprietary	BMP, GIF, JPEG, PICT	No restrictions(?)
Torch	PC	1.0a3	Java	Polyman (proprietary)	GIF, JPEG	No restrictions
VRwave	SGI, DEC Solaris, Linux, Alpha IIPUX, (others?)	.8	will be Java	OpenGL/Mesa	GIF, JPEG, XBM	$x,y = 2^n$ IIW/Mem max
WorldView	PC	2.0	Java and JavaScript	Direct3D	BMP, GIF, JPEG, PPM, RAS, PNG	?

Table 1-2: VRML 2.0 Browser Implementation Comparison Advanced Features

	1	2	3	4	5	6	7	8	9	10	11	12	13	14	15	16	17	18
CASUS	No	Yes	Yes	Yes	Yes	No	No	No	No	Yes	Yes	Yes	No	No	Yes	No	Yes	Yes
Sony CP	Yes	Yes	Yes	Yes	No	No	No	No	Yes	Yes	Yes	Yes	Yes	No	Yes	Yes	Yes	?
CP/SGI	Yes	Yes	Yes	Yes	Yes	Yes	Yes	Yes	Yes	Yes	Yes	Yes	IRIX 6.X only	6.20 6.4 only	Yes	Yes	Yes	Yes
CP/PC	Yes	Yes	Yes	Yes	?	?	?	Yes	Yes	Yes	Yes	unlit IFS not ILS	Yes	one per scene	Yes	Yes	Yes	courds not repeat
GLV/ OGL	Yes	Yes	Yes	Yes	Yes	Yes	Yes	Yes	No	Yes	No	Yes	No	No	Yes	Yes	Yes	Yes
GLV/ D3D	Yes	Yes	Yes	Yes	Yes	Yes	Yes	Yes	No	No	No	unlit only	No	No	Yes	Yes	Yes	Yes
LR	Yes	No	Yes	Yes	No	No	Yes	Yes	Yes	Wire frame	Yes	Yes	PC only	No	Yes	Yes	Yes	?
OW	No	No	No	No	No	No	No	Yes	Yes	No	?	Yes	Yes	?	No	No	OGL only	Yes
Oz	No	Yes	Yes	Yes	No	No	No	Yes	Yes	No	Yes	No	Yes	Yes	Yes	Yes	Yes	Yes
RSV	Most- ly	Yes	Yes	Yes	Yes	Yes	Yes	Yes	Yes	Yes	Yes	No	Yes	Yes	Yes	Yes	Yes	No
Torch	No	Yes	Yes	Yes	Yes	Yes	Yes	Yes	No	No	?	Yes	Yes	Yes	Yes	Yes	Yes	?
VRW	No	?	?	?	?	?	?	No	No	No	No	?	No	No	No	No	+	No
WV	Yes	Bro- ken	Yes	Bro- ken	Yes	No	No	Yes	Yes	Yes	Yes	Mini- mally	Yes	No	Most- ly	No	?	No

56

VRML 2.0 Browser Comparison Features

The following features are considered and cross-referenced to Table 1.2:
1. Extrusion node
2. PROTOs (some support, more than just parsing)
3. PROTOs with Script nodes in them
4. PROTOs with Script nodes in them with IS
   As an example (for #4), the following gives problems in some browsers:

```
PROTO Something [ field SFFloat random 0.0 ] {
        ...
        Script
{#this line is the problem
            field SFFloat someField IS random
            url []
        }
}
```

5. PROTOs using other PROTOs in them
6. EXTERNPROTOs (single PROTO in a file)
7. EXTERNPROTOs (single PROTO referred to in a file of many)
8. PlaneSensors
9. Collision
10. Text node
11. MFVec3f events—see test world in Figure 1.36
12. colorPerVertex as shown in Figure 1.37
13. uncompressed PCM WAVE support
14. MIDI support
15. TouchSensors—test world (same as MFVec3f in Figure 1.36)
16. Cylinder-/SphereSensors
17. Inlines
18. Correct texture mapping (default, as shown in Figure 1.38) and repeatS/-T

NOTE: The current version of this information can always be found at: http://zing.ncsl.nist.gov/~gseidman/vrml/comparison

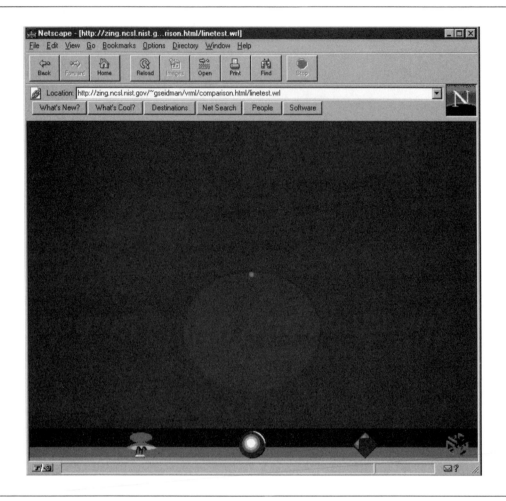

Figure 1.36 MFVec3f events test world.

What Are the 3-D Tools For?

The current crop of 3-D Web tools are still mostly of experimental nature or adaptations of existing applications. The trend for content creation is to take existing 3-D applications and change them to save as models in the VRML format. For 3-D browsing, the easiest approach is to rely on a traditional Web browser (Netscape

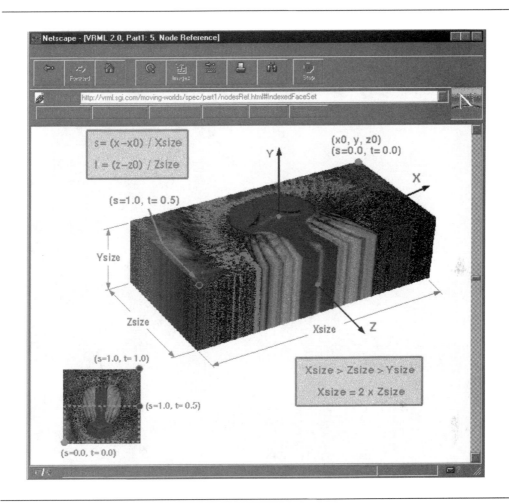

Figure 1.37 colorPerVertex.

being the all-time favorite) as a front end and to develop a compatible helper application.

The 3-D Web browsers let any Web user experience a 3-D Web site. The 3-D Web builders let any Web site creator add 3-D functionality to a Web site. World builders, such as the ones listed in the VRML Repository (www.sdsc.edu/vrml/repository.html), enable users to build 3-D environments, and 3-D browsers enable people to view 3-D sites on the Web.

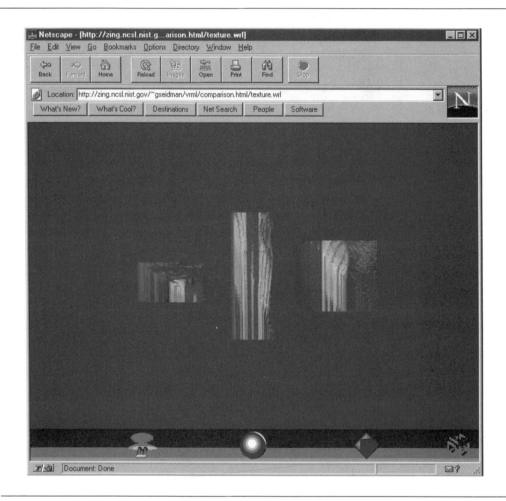

Figure 1.38 Correct texture mapping (default).

What a Difference a 3-D Web Tool Makes

Since products differ so widely, you need to evaluate which features are essential and which ones would be merely nice to have.
For example, if you already have certain 3-D models in house that
you want to use, you need to make sure that your VRML authoring tool can import those objects. In particular, you should make

sure that your tool imports VRML objects, or else you will not be able to take advantage of all the objects that you can grab off of various VRML sites on the Web.

Even if you rely heavily on prebuilt models, chances are that you will want to create a few objects of your own or merely modify some of the ones that you found on the Web. If you already have a modeling tool and your artist knows how to use it, you probably don't need to purchase another. However, you should keep in mind that many traditional 3-D modelers were built with photorealistic output in mind and may be overly complicated or lack features essential for interactive 3-D graphics.

Although most modelers still force you to work in wireframe mode, the latest breed of tools allows you to manipulate texture-mapped objects in real time. Before spending a lot of money on a high-end tool, you should evaluate whether traditional modeling features, such as lathing and extrusions, are sufficient or whether you will need advanced functions, like organic deformations and 3-D Booleans. Deformations can add sizzle to your environment but they also bump up file size and place a heavy burden on your visitors' computers that need to render your environments in real time.

Although it is always a good idea to keep the average configuration of your target audience in mind, you also need to check which authoring tools run on your platform and how much memory they require. If you have an SGI you have access to some of the best modeling tools in the industry. However, you will pay a high price for your software and the selection of VRML authoring tools will be much more limited than on the PC. Pricing for Macintoshes is more in line with those for the PC but software selection is much more limited.

Your best selection of tools will be on the PC, and the stiff competition will continue to keep prices both for software and hardware lower than on any other platform. However, some tools may require you to purchase more RAM, or you may have to deal with incompatibilities and crashes. Since most of your users will explore your VRML worlds with Windows browsers, you should have a very good reason if you choose *not* to use the PC as your primary development platform.

Rather than settling on one VRML tool you may consider purchasing several and using each of them for the tasks for which they are best suited. In this case you need to make sure that the best tools interoperate well and that there are no unexpected surprises when transferring scenes from one tool to the next.

If you have existing 2-D assets you should make sure that your VRML tool can leverage these assets. If you want to use 2-D illustrations, you should make sure that you can import at least PostScript files. You can convert most imagemaps to JPEG format but it is a good idea to check out what bitmap formats are supported by both your VRML authoring and browsing tools. Compatibility problems are minimized, of course, if you choose an integrated tool that can do it all. However, unless you want to optimize your VRML site for a particular browser you still need to check on how your scenes look in the most common browsers.

Since VRML is still hot, you will encounter many packages that claim to do VRML authoring. Please keep in mind that VRML is an ASCII format and that any text editor can technically claim to be a VRML authoring tool. However, unless you enjoy working directly with a straight ASCII file you should make sure that you can create levels of detail and inline objects without having to do any editing by hand. If modeling is not your strongest suit, you should select a tool that includes polygon reduction, so that you don't have to model levels of detail separately.

Although you need strong 3-D creation tools to generate the objects and spaces you want, the material-editing capabilities will determine how those objects and spaces will look. To keep maximum flexibility you should look for tools that let you assign material attributes not only for entire objects but also on a per-face basis. For example, you might want to use one texture map for someone's pants and another for his belt. Since texture maps increase the amount of data that has to be transferred, you should look for advanced paint tools, for example, vertex painting. Vertex painting allows you to create multicolor gradients across surfaces and often eliminates the need for texture maps.

When evaluating VRML tools, you should pay close attention to options for reducing file size. By stripping out normals, ASCII formatting, and default values, a good VRML tool can reduce file sizes by as much as 60 percent. Files can be reduced even further by collapsing hierarchies, reducing precision, using VRML primitives, and saving only one instance of an object that appears in various places. If you use gzip after having trimmed the VRML file to the bone, you may end up with files that are only 4 percent of their original sizes. This will dramatically speed up loading times for your users and it will allow you to serve more users without adding disk space or bandwidth.

However, if you don't recommend a specific VRML tool for browsing you will have to be careful about what tricks you employ to reduce file size. For example, many browsers do not accept zipped VRML files. If you do not have a tool that includes VRML browsing you need to be prepared for a lot of testing and switching between your browser and your authoring application to make sure the links work. The navigation is more comfortable and all the objects look right. You may also have to switch to a separate browser to see whether Inlines load as intended and whether objects that contain levels of detail are displayed properly.

When recommending browsers to visitors of your site, you should check how each of them performs on a similar system. The differences in speed can be quite dramatic. Some browsers are already set up to take advantage of a new breed of 3-D acceleration chips. Other factors to consider are ease of use and stability. Many of the newer browsers have not been tested adequately so it is safer to recommend a browser that has been thoroughly debugged. Ease of use is to a certain extent a matter of taste. Some people prefer to use extensive navigation controls whereas others feel more at home just using the mouse and keyboard shortcuts. A good browser gives you lots of choices for navigating around.

If you do decide to recommend a VRML tool for browsing, you should check with the developer of the tool to see whether you can make it available for downloading from your site. Many developers will be honored that you chose their tool and will allow you to distribute it free of charge. If the tool you distribute also includes authoring capabilities, you may find that your visitors will want to add to your VRML site or make improvements. In this case you should let them know ahead of time what your policy is regarding VRML scenes uploaded to your server.

The Future Promise for 3-D Environments on the Web

This technology is truly going to change our way of life. Imagine logging on in Houston and playing basketball in 3-D on the Web with your friend in Moscow. Imagine flying through a virtual store, trying out virtual products, and purchasing those you want to buy. Imagine accessing a database in 3-D whereby you can actually grab a 3-D data entity in front of you and inspect it. Imagine traveling to Antarctica on the Web. All of these things will ultimately be possible when 3-D starts coming in at the chip level for personal computers.

When the Chips Are Down

A number of 3-D graphics microprocessors from companies like Rendition, 3Dlabs, and others are already on the market, either incorporated in computers or as part of accelerator cards that can be added to PCs for $200 or less. Some industry analysts estimate that by the end of 1997 about 28 million home computers will have 3-D acceleration; that number could jump to 104 million by the end of 1998.

The good news for computer makers is that both VRML and PC-based 3-D programs run best on machines with lots of microprocessing horsepower. Apple is hoping its RISC chips (designed in conjunction with Motorola and IBM) will make the company's line of PowerPCs the machines of choice for 3-D graphics. Intel is also working on a 3-D strategy with a division of Lockheed-Martin that makes flight simulators for the military. And Microsoft is working on a microchip project, code-named Talisman.

It all amounts to a vast, unexplored cyberspace that has the potential to change the entire computing paradigm from that of a graphical desktop to a three-dimensional desk that looks and behaves like its real-world counterpart. In other words, the coming of 3-D is about dramatically simplifying the interface so users don't have to think when they walk up to a computer. It's a practical modeling of the real world in such a way that people can intuitively understand what the computer's trying to tell them. The irony, of course, is that the person leading the way into this brave new 3-D world is likely to be a small, fat man in red overalls named Mario.

The World Is Not Flat—It's 3-D!

In any event, 3-D on the Web today reminds me of Christopher Columbus. When Columbus was sailing west in his quest for a round earth he reached a point where he was hopelessly lost. Legend has it that he gathered all the sailors and exclaimed: "We've arrived at uncharted waters much sooner than I had anticipated. Rejoice!" This is the current situation with 3-D on the Web. Several explorers are experimenting with different paradigms, looking for brand new opportunities. Whether it be in education or entertainment, the future promise for 3-D environments on the Web relies on bringing users a level of experience otherwise impossible.

From Here

VRML is literally the glue that allows a range of technologies— including multimedia-equipped personal computers, high-speed communications, and others—to bring networked virtual reality to the end user. The next chapter identifies the key standard to VRML 2.0/VRML97's potential success in the explosive phenomenon known as the Internet.

Endnotes

1   Access Market Square, Inc., Visa International Inc., Foster City, CA, 1997.

2   Newfire, Inc., 12901 Saratoga Ave., Suite 4, Saratoga, CA 95070, 1997.

3   Dimension X, 181 Fremont St., Suite 120, San Francisco, CA 94105.

4   Intervista Software, Inc., 181 Fremont St., Suite 200, San Francisco, CA 94105.

5   Template Graphics Software, Inc. (TGS), 9920 Pacific Heights Blvd., Suite 200, San Diego, CA 92121, 1997.

6   Newfire, Inc., 1997.

7   Ibid.

8   Template Graphics Software, Inc. (TGS), 1997.

9   Intervista Software, Inc., 1997.

10 Ibid.

11 Ibid.

12 Ressler, Sandy. "Using VRML to Access Manufacturing Data," National Institute of Standards and Technology (NIST), 1997.

13 Intervista Software, Inc., 1997.

14 Ibid.

15 Ibid.

16 Ibid.

17 VREAM, Inc., 223 West Erie St., Suite 600, Chicago, IL 60610, 1997.

18 Intervista Software, Inc., 1997.

19 Visible Decisions Inc., 100 Wall St., Suite 605, New York, NY 10005, 1997.

20 "Gregory Seidman's Browser Implementation Comparison (VRML 2.0 Only)," National Institute of Standards and Technology (NIST), 1997.

2

The Emerging VRML Standard

In his ground-breaking 1985 science fiction novel *Neuromancer*, author William Gibson defined what he called *cyberspace*, a future world in which humans would interface directly with computers and intranets in a digital reality that seemed as real, or perhaps *more* real, than our physical world.

Gibson's vision was more fiction than science. But he did foresee that advances in computer and communications technology would, perhaps sooner than anyone thought at the time, yield a rich, highly interactive, intranet environment that for all intents and purposes is Gibson's cyberspace.

Today that environment promises to be realized in part with *Virtual Reality Modeling Language*, or *VRML*. As discussed in Chapter 1, VRML is a next-generation programming standard that allows personal computer users to visit and move through three-dimensional environments over the Internet, with much of the graphical sophistication of interactive videogames or CD-ROM software. In VRML, you can manipulate objects in 3-D space—rotate them, zoom in on detail, fly around them. For example, instead of just looking at a blueprint of a building an architect has finished, he or she could take you inside to look around. Or, instead of clicking on text and pictures to take you to different places on the Net, you could walk through doors, up stairways, or fly through windows.

A whole new breed of Web browsers has been developed to accommodate this new medium. We're seeing lots of workstation vendors, animation vendors, and VR software vendors coming to market—with all kinds of VRML Web browsers, builders, and authoring tools.

The VRML Standard

The official organization developing VRML technology is, first, the whole community. The official organizations tasked with leading the latest version of the standard are the VRML Consortium (VC), VRML Review Board (formerly the VRML Architecture Group (VAG)), Living Worlds (LW), and Open Community. With the creation of the VRML Consortium, what was originally the VRML Architecture Group handed off its responsibilities to the VRML Review Board (VRB) and associated working groups at its final meeting in December, 1996. The VRML Architecture Group initially consisted of eight technical experts who endeavored to focus and articulate the sentiments of the VRML community in order to foster the development of a scaleable, fully interactive standard for cyberspace. The VAG, working with the VRML community, created the process for what became VRML 2.0. They recommended that the VRML Review Board have primary responsibility for VRML technology, and that its principal tasks be recognizing, guiding, and accepting or rejecting the recommendations of working groups. They also recommended that the VRB consist of seven technical members, to be elected by the VRML Consortium membership. The VRML Consortium, Inc., is a nonprofit corporation with the mission of fostering and evangelizing VRML as the open standard for 3-D multimedia and shared virtual worlds on the Internet. The VRML Consortium's goals are to:

♦ Foster the ongoing development of the VRML specifications and standards.
♦ Promote rapid industry adoption of, and adherence to, the VRML specification.
♦ Offer opportunities for the VRML development community to meet and cooperate in the evolution of VRML.
♦ Educate the business and consumer communities on the value, benefits, and applications of VRML.
♦ Support the creation of conformance tests to ensure VRML interoperability.
♦ Liaison with educational institutions, government research institutes, technology consortia, and other organizations that support and contribute to the development of specifications and standards for VRML.[1]

In other words, the VRML Consortium was formed to provide a forum for the creation of open standards for VRML specifications, and to accelerate the worldwide demand for products based on these standards through the sponsorship of market and user education programs. VRML applications have been actively pursued by many organizations for quite some time. This community has spearheaded the development of the VRML 1.0 and 2.0 specifications, which provide the basis for the development of associated applications. The organizations involved in this effort felt that the creation of an open consortium focused exclusively on VRML would provide the structure necessary to stabilize, standardize, and nurture VRML for the entire community.

The VRML Consortium as shown in Figure 2.1 (see http:// vag.vrml.org/consort/Specs.html) also controls the VRML97 specification documents (VRML/ISO Draft for International Standard (DISISO/IEC DIS 14772-1)). [2] This document has been submitted to ISO for a vote; however, as of this writing, the docu-

ment still has not been voted on. The results of the vote are expected to be known before the end of 1997. See Chapter 8, *VRML
Consortium,* for an in-depth discussion on the VRML Consortium
and VRML Review Board.

Living Worlds (http://www.livingworlds.com/draft_1/lw_title
.htm#Top), on the other hand, is an initiative to define a conceptual framework and specify a set of interfaces to support the creation
and evolution of multiuser (and multideveloper!) applications in
VRML 2.0. The charter of the Living Worlds group is to distill its
experience with avatar-based interaction in VRML 1.0 into a pro-

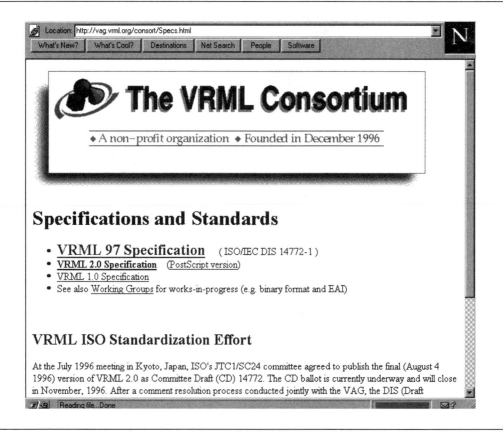

Figure 2.1 The VRML Consortium specifications and standards.

posed standard for distributed object interaction in VRML 2.0. The LW effort aims at a single, narrow, well-defined goal: to define a set of VRML 2.0 conventions that support applications that are both interpersonal and interoperable.[3] See Chapter 9, *Living Worlds*, for a thorough discussion on Living Worlds.

Finally, Open Community (formerly known as Universal Worlds) is a proposed open standard for multiuser virtual worlds. It consists of extensions to Java and VRML 2.0, and is designed to integrate with the Universal Avatars and Living Worlds specifications. The proposal is a combined effort of MERL (Mitsubishi Electric Research Lab) and members of the Universal Avatars development team. It is based on the SPLINE (Scaleable Platform for Large Interactive Networked Environments) software architecture developed by MERL.

Open Community (http://www.merl.com/opencom/) enables the simultaneous interaction of thousands of geographically distant users in real time, with interactive behaviors, voice chat, 3-D graphics, and positional audio.[4] Applications that are compliant with Open Community will be able to make real-time modifications and extensions to the environment while it is running, so that the content of an environment can grow and expand dynamically in proportion to the talent of the user community. All of this is possible through an open Java interface at both the intranet and application programmer levels. For more information, see Chapter 10, *Open Community*, for a thorough discussion on Open Community.

Implications of the VRML Standard

VRML enables the communication and sharing of 3-D objects and worlds. That alone is very powerful—allowing chemists, for example, to publish 3-D models that they can use to communicate some aspect of molecular structure that they're studying.

The VRML97 standard is continuing to evolve to include more complex notions, such as objects that change over time. This will allow even more compelling applications to be created.

VRML Browser Standards

Browsers should implement every VRML feature, but some don't. Since VRML 2.0/97 is a little more open, the browsers implement different effects (lighting models). Some browsers extend the standard. Among VRML browsers are the following:

- ◆ CASUS Presenter from the Fraunhofer Institute for Computer Graphics in Darmstadt, Germany (as part of the DZ-SIMPROLOG project), provides a platform for doing animation in VRML (see Figure 2.2). (SGI and Solaris browser based on Open Inventor.)[5]
- ◆ CosmoPlayer for PC from SGI (see Figure 2.3). (PC browser not based on Open Inventor.)[6]
- ◆ Community-Place from Sony Corporation (see Figure 2.4). (PC browser not based on Open Inventor.)[7]

For more information on VRML 2.0/97 browser standards see Tables 1.1 and 1.2 in Chapter 1, *Bringing 3-D Environments to the Web: The VRML Connection*. Now let's take a look at VRML development technology.

VRML Development Stage

The VRML technology is still immature, and current implementations are crude at best. An emerging standard for emerging technology, VRML currently does little more than whet the appetite for the inevitable evolution of this still crude discipline. Specifically, VRML V2.0 defines objects; textures; lights; sound; extrusion nodes; PROTOs with some support more than just parsing; PROTOs with Script nodes in them; PROTOs with Script nodes in them with IS; PROTOs using other PROTOs in them; EXTERNPROTOs (single PROTO in a file); EXTERNPROTOs (single PROTO referred to in a file of many); PlaneSensors; collision; text nodes; MFVec3f events; colorPerVertex; uncompressed PCM WAVE support; MIDI support; TouchSensors; Cylinder-/SphereSensors; Inlines; correct texture mapping; and cameras. However, VRML 2.0/97 still lacks some important features of interactive 3-D, such as object behaviors and cause-and-effect relationships.

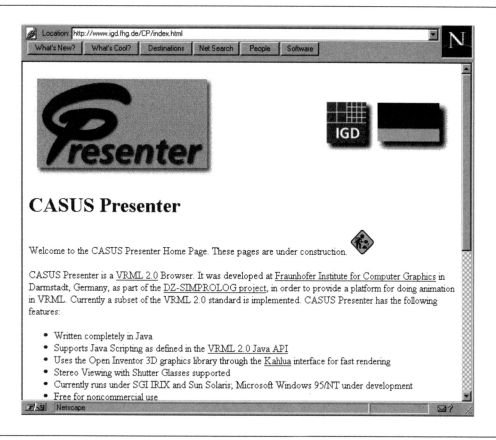

Figure 2.2 CASUS Presenter.

Many factors will push the evolution of this technology along. Intel and Motorola, for example, love compute-intensive technologies because applications based on those technologies help pull the new, more powerful computers into the market. Another group is backing the concept of cable modems, which allow you to experience the Internet through your cable line. Cable modem vendors are going to back VRML applications because Internet applications that are sexy and need a lot of bandwidth are what ultimately create their market. Microsoft is pushing 3-D in a big way. Thus, there are a lot of companies with substantial power that will push this technology into the market. At the same time, the amazing things

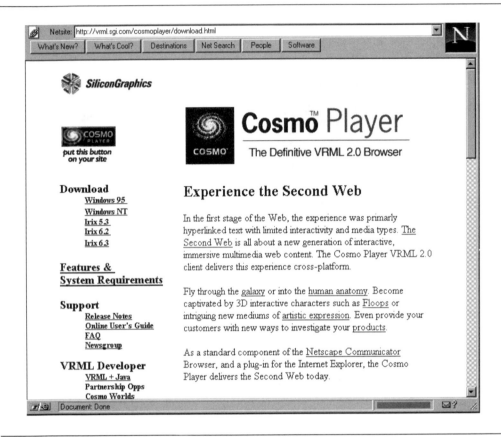

Figure 2.3 Cosmo Player.

that you will be able to do with this technology will cause consumers to pull it into the market.

VRML is, for the time being, still an evolving organism. The VRML Consortium has submitted the VRML/ISO Draft for International Standard (DIS) to the ISO for a vote. This document, ISO/IEC DIS 14772, is the official and complete specification of the Virtual Reality Modeling Language. The challenges the VRML Consortium faces are several. On the one hand, it is clear that the current specification is still somewhat of a compromise, and that

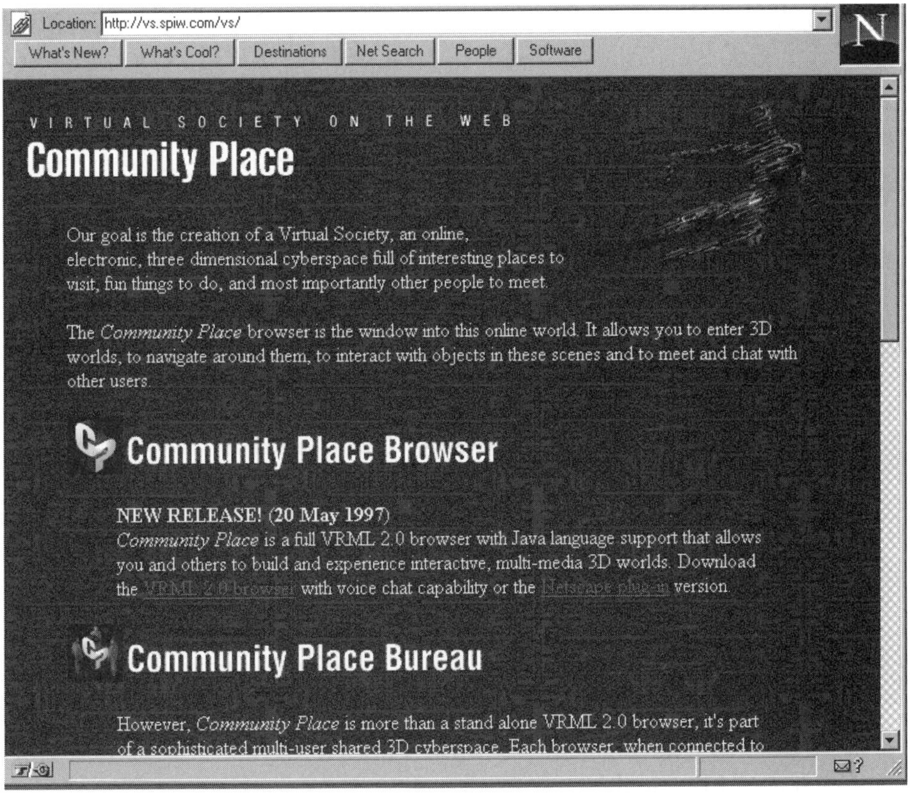

Figure 2.4 Community-Place.

changes are inevitable. On the other hand, there is strong pressure for managing changes in a way that minimizes the impact on existing commercial ventures. This latter point is very important, since widespread adoption of VRML as a standard for 3-D graphics on the Web will not happen until developers can stop chasing what is still a moving target.

Existing and potential VRML developers face another type of challenge: the parser itself. The VRML syntax and the required integration with 3-D graphics libraries alien to VRML create problems of their own. Most current browsers rely on a publicly available parser (QVlib) that, although a good starting point, does have its shortcomings. The fact that VRML is a subset of SGI's Open Inventor file format, and that QVlib itself had its roots in Open Inventor leads to files that cannot be rendered correctly. A VRML validation suite, or perhaps a reference implementation, are sorely missed.

The VRML community, during SIGGRAPH '96, braced itself for the unavoidable schism that VRML V2.0 brought. VRML V2.0 specified support for behaviors, a topic for which multiple and often conflicting solutions exist. Someone once said that instead of standing on each other's shoulders and moving forward, 3-D graphics professionals always stand on other people's toes. Perhaps the best contribution the VRML Architecture Group made on August 4, 1996, was the release of the official VRML 2.0 Specification at SIGGRAPH '96 in New Orleans. At the fifth VAG meeting in New Orleans, the VAG finalized the formal announcement of the VRML 2.0 Specification, agreed to issue RFPs for a compressible binary format and an external authoring interface to the VRML 2.0 specification, and initiated the formation of the VRML Consortium.

Apples QuickDraw 3-D API

The notion of extensibility through plug-ins has been implemented by Apple Computer as part of its 3-D graphics program, QuickDraw 3-D API. Apple's 3-D graphics API (application program interface) empowers developers and end users, allowing them to extend that product's core behavior in a well-defined manner, as shown in Figure 2.5.[8] This means that as time goes by, with the natural evolution of 3-D and related technologies, the API (a specific library where an executable application program can be created) can be kept current and fulfill the needs of an ever-growing number of users.

QuickDraw 3-D API is, naturally, the preferred way to render 3-D scenes on Power Macintosh systems. It provides real-time, interactive rendering for simple 3-D models. It is now available for the Mac OS, Windows 95, and Windows NT.

QuickDraw 3-D RAVE (Rendering Acceleration Virtual Engine) is currently available for the Mac OS, Windows 95, and Windows NT platforms. It is the foundation technology used in QuickDraw 3-D, and provides ultra-fast, real-time, workstation-quality 3-D graphics on both Power Macintosh computers and PCs.

An integral part of QuickDraw 3-D is its 3-DMF file format. Not unlike VRML, 3-DMF also has support for Web attributes, and an integral custom attribute architecture that supports plug-ins at the operating system level. Some see 3-DMF and VRML as competitors. That might be true at a very low level, but let's not miss the

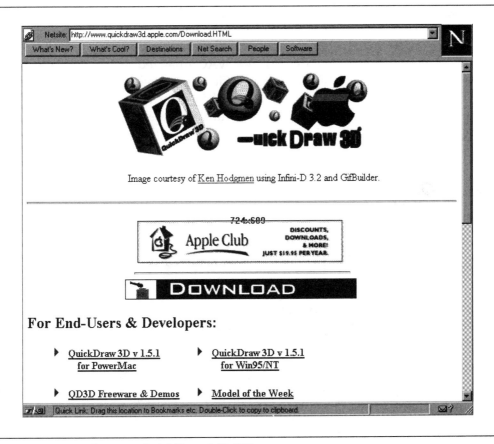

Figure 2.5 QuickDraw 3-D API.

forest for the trees. In the big scheme of things, users want the freedom to pick and choose whatever format serves their needs. The market is big enough to support multiple formats, and users will dictate their segmentation. For example, VRML, as a committee-driven effort, is a compromise (and a very good one indeed); it addresses most customers' needs, but not all. Enter 3-DMF. Its close integration at the operating system level offers users the ability to take 3-D information well beyond the Web domain and into the existing corporate infrastructure.

VRML 2.0/97 is currently in common use by most VRML browsers. It basically defines the geometry, textures, sound, and basic lights. Although it's not fully interactive, it does include some interactivity provided by the introduction of Java-based behaviors. You can load a world and fly through it, but the objects themselves do not always or fully respond to user input. Dimension X (recently acquired by Microsoft) in San Francisco (www.dimensionx.com) has created some great examples of VRML worlds with Java-charged behaviors attached to models. VRML 2.0/97 (in its spec) also includes a good deal of what Dimension X has done with its Liquid Reality software development kit (SDK). Other companies, such as MultiGen, Sense8, and Superscape, have many years of experience in building behaviors into real-time models. Their contributions are sure to be valued as well.

Availability in the Commercial World

Let's try to distinguish between commercially *available* and commercially *viable*. This is a central issue for any Web-based business today. Right now, we're creating a multibillion-dollar industry by spending billions creating it. The people really making a profit today, however, are companies selling modems (until Intel puts 10 MBps cable modem access on the mother board), companies selling Internet access (until AT&T and the Baby Bells launch their services defensively), people creating Web pages on a fee-for-service basis (not really scaleable), and magazines and books telling us all about it (always a good bet).

As with many technologies, the market for VRML is being driven largely by its potential for commercial applications. Major corporations are attracted to the idea of building 3-D worlds for their customers to visit, perhaps creating a truly memorable experience that causes them to return over and over again. One of the limits of today's HTML-based Web sites is that, regardless of how beautiful their 2-D graphics are, the customer still experiences a flat, text-oriented world that can seem disappointing when compared with television or, for that matter, the real world. As a result, the customer may not be compelled to pay a return visit to learn more about the company or its products. Corporate developers currently have their choice of three major types of products: VRML viewers, related products that provide VRML extensions to existing HTML browsers, and VRML authoring tools.

VRML Viewers

Similar to HTML browsers, VRML viewers are standalone software packages, written for PCs running Microsoft Windows 97 or higher, the Macintosh, or other PCs or workstations that allow the PC user to visit and navigate VRML worlds. They typically feature controls for moving forward and backward, the ability to remember or record camera positions (3-D bookmarks that allow the user to return to a particular location later on), and handle such essential things as preventing the user from walking into or through a wall.

Extensions to HTML Browsers

Many firms are developing products that provide these capabilities as enhancements or plug-ins to existing Web browsers, such as Netscape Navigator or Microsoft Explorer. These products allow users to access VRML worlds with their current browser technologies.

VRML Authoring Tools

Many of the same firms developing VRML viewers are also developing homespace development tools. These tools allow developers to design and build the 3-D worlds in VRML format, and to incorporate Internet-standard audio files, video files, and behavior engines that allow user interaction with, and animation of, 3-D objects in a world.

Thus, many firms are bringing viewers and development tools to market, and many of the products have already shipped. As with any new technology, however, corporate developers and end users are taking a cautious approach. They know from experience that the second, or even third, version of a standard or product is often the one that contains the most satisfying combination of functionality, performance, and an attractive price.

A new medium must do one of two things to last. It must either lead the user to an economic transaction (in which case, the value of the medium is as an advertising vehicle), or provide the user with an experience he or she is willing to pay for. VRML is unique in that it can do both. We're speaking of *interactive advertising*. Many such applications have already been deployed by advertisers. As the VRML spec continues to improve, and Internet/Web and 3-D accelerator penetration into the home increases, we'll see a rapid increase in the demand for better, more compelling interactive advertisements delivered over the Web, using VRML. Look for critical mass in 1998.

VRML's Planned Use by Vertical Industries

Vertical industries, such as the construction industry, are already using VRML to explore exact representations of architectural drawings and models prior to beginning actual construction. The real estate industry is capitalizing on VRML worlds, showing houses on the Internet to potential long-distance clientele. The museum industry is quite far along in offering 3-D worlds of various well-known pieces of art. The games industry is already a huge VRML market, and online 3-D chat worlds are becoming more popular.

Chemists are using VRML to visualize molecules before they're chemically synthesized. Travel companies are using VRML as a navigational aid in advertisements. Game publishers are using VRML to promote their 3-D games on the Web (Sega's Vectorman). Manufacturers are using VRML as an aid in training workers about production processes. Designers and architects are using VRML to help clients visualize their buildings before they're built. Advertisers are using VRML to sell real estate, cars, electronics, games, and even groceries.

Planned Applications for VRML's Use

The very fact that VRML can use existing technology is one of its major attractions to Internet technologists. This means that, in the very near future, a large number of PC users will be able to visit sites already in existence today.

Potential applications of VRML, if the market continues to grow as expected, are both varied and remarkable. The following represent a few examples of VRML applications that might be built, given the state of the today's technology.

Engineering Applications

Engineering is a field that is largely dependent on graphical tools for visualizing and even building models for various products, as shown in Figure 2.6.[9] The ability for engineers to use VRML to work on such 3-D models—across an intranet in a collaborative way—holds strong appeal for companies trying to increase productivity and cut costs.

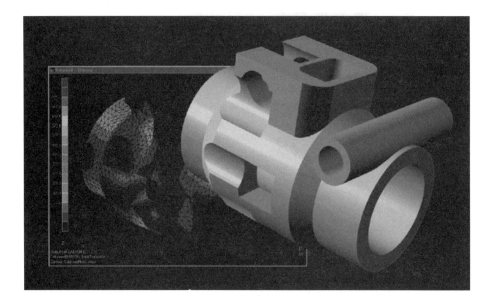

Figure 2.6 COSMOS/M: Finite element analysis (FEA) application for engineers working with design, analysis, and optimization.

Research, Including Medical Research

Medical researchers might use VRML to share across vast distances not only their ideas, in text or chart form, but also their 3-D models of molecules or genes; or even a surgical simulation prototype of the brain, as shown in Figure 2.7.[10] This could not only speed up research but also spur ideas for *new* research.

VRML is considered by the medical community to be the future of medicine and medical research. Not only will it play a key role in medical education, but it is likely that it will be used to a limited extent in patient care. As far as training is concerned, many physicians agree that virtual reality surgery will become a very useful tool. Computer imaging of human anatomy already gives students an excellent understanding of physiology. As a supplement to a Gross Anatomy class, a computer becomes a very practical study

Figure 2.7 VRML simulated surgical prototype of the brain.

aid. It is easy to review class material by using software that depicts a human body and allows you to remove layers of tissue as you would in class. The idea of virtual surgery takes this one step further. Three-dimensional graphics can depict a surgical setting in which a virtual human body can be dissected by a student. If the student was going to study the procedure for a bypass operation, the computer could clog arteries of the heart. The student would then have the opportunity to virtually perform the surgery. This has two major benefits. The first is that 3-D will give students (and professionals) a chance to prepare for uncommon surgeries. (In the past, the only way you could learn to do a procedure is by actually operating on a real person.) The second major benefit is that students can learn without putting real people at risk.

In the distant future, it is quite possible that VRML will be used in clinical medicine. Many medical centers are already experimenting with *telemedicine*—a concept based on the idea that patients can be treated by physicians in other parts of the world. NASA has already done a great deal of pioneering work in the field of telemedicine, and this field has grown to encompass many new technologies which have the possibility of improving health care and cutting costs. Telemedicine encompasses a wide variety of technologies and applications including, but not limited to, medical informatics, virtual reality medical tools, and remote consultation. In other words, patients would go to clinics where nurses or physicians' assistants would hook them up to various monitors so that a physician, who is in another place, could examine them. Clearly, this is not the ideal medium for a doctor-patient relationship, but in areas having a shortage of physicians, this may be a vital alternative. Initially, it is expected that this technology will only be used in cases that require an expert's opinion. A world-renowned physician would be able to give second opinions without ever actually meeting the patient. There is speculation that many, many years down the line, doctors will perform "remote" surgery on patients living in other parts of the world. Surgeons would have to wear head-mounted devices that showed them an image of the actual patient. They would also have to wear gloves that would precisely monitor their every motion, so that a computer stationed with the patient could receive these movements, and make accurate incisions. At this point in time, this idea seems more like science fiction than an actual possibility, but today's science fiction is tomorrow's science fact!

Commercial Applications and Marketing

The World Wide Web holds great appeal to firms wishing to establish direct links to customers; in particular, via electronic advertising on their homepages. VRML holds the potential to enhance the customer/product experience dramatically. For example, customers could visit virtual malls and virtual shops, and pick up and look at the products they are thinking about purchasing (see Figure 2.8).[11] Or, vacationers could visit a resort in advance and walk through the hotel's facilities, including the guest rooms, while checking out amenities, reviewing a schedule of local events, and pondering the streaming video view out the window.

Virtual Museums and Art Galleries

It would be possible to build a virtual museum in which users could browse around and look at works of art from various angles, as

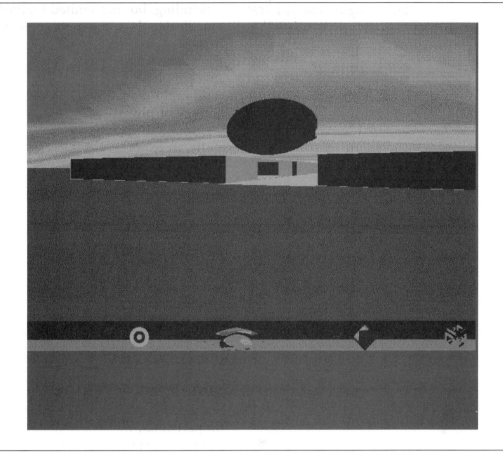

Figure 2.8 VRML Mall.

shown in Figure 2.9.[12] Although this certainly could not match the richness of a live experience, the ability to combine 3-D images of art with text and explanatory information could make VRML-based museums a significant source of art education and enrichment.

Art has always had, and will continue to have, the problem of inaccessibility. If students wanted to experience Michaelangelo's David, they couldn't just catch the next plane to Florence. Rather, they would have to settle for the picture in their art textbook.

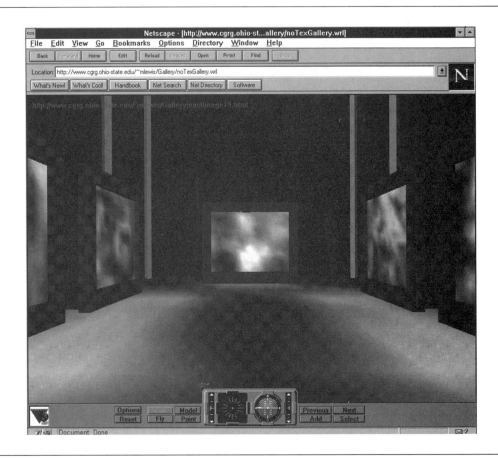

Figure 2.9 VRML art gallery: Abulafia Gallery (ACCAD, Ohio State University).

Countless times, art history professors stress the importance of seeing the actual image, rather than just a slide or picture. Andy Warhol's rendition of the Mona Lisa, in which he presents 30 photocopies of Leonardo's original, tells us that there is something to be said for the actual work that comes from the hands of an artistic genius and is not degraded by mechanical reproduction. Three-dimensional technology will never be able to bring people the real thing, and will only be able to render virtual images. However, considering that most people will not have the luxury of traveling around Europe to go museum-hopping, virtual art galleries are not such a bad thing. VRML technology would give people with access to the World Wide Web the opportunity to take virtual tours through some of the best, and most famous, museums in the world. Of course, both paintings and sculptures would be represented on a 2-D screen, but at least VRML would allow the spectator to rotate sculptures and virtually walk around them. Reconstruction of ancient ruins would also be effective, for a 3-D image is easily navigated by a VRML browser. Again, computer-generated images are no substitute for the real thing, but they have the capabilities of being better substitutes than we have now.

Implications of VRML in the Client-Server Environment

In the client-server environment, VRML allows the development of a 3-D standard for the exchange of 3-D information over the Internet and among various systems. This creates a very powerful medium for interchange of information.

VRML brings interactive 3-D to client-server environments. If you can think of ways in which having interactive 3-D objects or 3-D environments be components of your particular client-server application and can add value, you probably should start to study up on virtual reality as a technology. The biggest impact may be in the area of graphical user interfaces, in that an intuitive 3-D interface can make a lot of sense for many companies.

Corporations worldwide are discovering the strategic advantages of using internal Web sites for disseminating information company-wide. Not only do the thorny issues of groupware computing get alleviated, but internal Web sites open the door to finally tracking the Holy Grail: concurrent engineering. In the context of concurrent engineering, the need to unambiguously share product information across divisions makes 3-D a definite win. First of all, the added dimension of 3-D graphics increases the level of understanding among those accessing information. Then, the existence of a common database, composed of a well-defined format to represent 3-D information, makes it possible to move information from the conceptual-design phase down to manufacturing, without losses. Transferring data from one application to another is akin to moving sand from one place to another: When you move sand, you always drop some sand and pick up some dirt.

VRML as it exists today still lacks the richness necessary to represent the different data types and, even more important, the relationship among all data components. Until that happens, VRML will be confined to representing the graphics portion of a product's data. Perhaps that is not a bad idea, since graphics and VRML go hand in hand. Ideally, VRML is versatile enough to play along with other richer file formats. In that scenario, VRML would be the carrier of graphical information whereas, perhaps, the intelligence behind a model would be carried by another file format.

Implications of VRML in Client-Server Applications Development Environments

VRML has no special implications for client-server applications development environments. You may use the server to download a VRML environment, but after that the role of the server (and even the Internet) is minimal. You can view the VRML environment off line without losing anything. However, the server has become more important as VRML environments have become more functional. Right now, many companies rely on servers in their non-VRML environments to enable multiuser communication, to convey positioning, to update environments, and to show changes to them (either since your last visit or while you are there). The server also plays this role in VRML+ spaces. Nevertheless, we are already starting to see VRML (specifically) and virtual reality (in general) integrated into client-server development software. This allows the physical and logical components of the intranet—software and data—to be accessible and maintainable through intuitive, interactive 3-D interfaces.

Business and Technology Advantages of VRML

Despite its rapid evolution to date, the computer is still deficient in one very important area. Specifically, we as humans live in a 3-D world, yet the computer represents us with 2-D text and images. What the concept of VRML brings to the worlds of business and technology is, both literally and figuratively, a new dimension. Not only does it finally bring 3-D to the computer, but it also delivers interactive 3-D to us. VRML delivers 3-D to us quickly and efficiently across a wire, whether it be a local area network or the World Wide Web. Exactly what this technology gives us is difficult to say, just as it was difficult to predict useful applications of the computer when it was first conceptualized and commercialized. Suffice it to say that, over time, more and more people will come to understand the power of interactive virtual reality. Its applications will become more and more prevalent, materializing in ways we probably cannot predict at this time.

VRML allows us to go places that we currently cannot go, and to see things that we currently cannot see; either because of physical, logistical, or financial constraints, or because the places and things do not exist in our physical world. You cannot go inside of your computer because you are too big. You cannot visit the Playboy Mansion because access is restricted. You cannot test drive a new car design because building a prototype is too expensive. You cannot walk through a database and examine data connections because no such place exists. You cannot travel to the moon or perhaps even to the Bahamas because it is too expensive. You cannot pick up hazardous materials because it is not safe. Virtual reality lets us do all the things that we currently cannot do. The applications are limited only by the imagination.

VRML allows information to be represented in a 3-D format, which is better matched to the delivery of certain types of information and allows the user to interact with the information presented. This has dramatic technological implications. VRML allows technology currently available only to users of high-powered workstations (with expensive software) to be available to consumers and individuals in corporations with common PCs via the Internet. The business implications are that corporations can use VRML software to allow engineering designs to be reviewed by a larger number of individuals in various locations. This has resulted in improved marketing and product review. Additionally, consumers are now able to better review products and to receive better service information.

For the industry as a whole, VRML as an emerging standard presents an opportunity to move away from proprietary tool-centered formats toward a more neutral geometry format. This presents new business challenges. VRML is, in a unique way, a new medium. Throughout the history of communication, economic value, in any medium, is shared among the content author or copyright holder and the publisher/distributor. We must continue to build into the VRML specification ways to identify the original author and copyright holder of the model, and perhaps the path that model took to get to the ultimate viewer.

Technologically, VRML's primary advantages today are its independence and its flexibility. Since VRML is not sponsored by any single authoring tool or platform, the specification is independent and able to improve as quickly as the architecting parties can agree. Of course, it's a rare case (VRML being the exception) in this industry that a committee-created specification ever reaches the status of *de facto* standard. This is usually because the committee members (with the exception of the old VAG and the present VRML Consortium), with their built-in biases, can rarely agree on a neutral and advanced standard quickly enough to make it relevant to the market. It's like herding cats. However, in this case, there is significant leadership from neutral parties (Pesce, Parisi, Bell and others) who have shown an ability to help bring closure to issues quickly, and then promote the result with religious fervor.

However, VRML's polygonal format comes with the same challenge of any polygonal format—its resolution is relatively fixed. Today's user is able to dial in the desired resolution (based on bandwidth, and local processor and 3-D accelerator capability). This has required some nontrivial extensions to today's VRML specification.

Another challenge today is that many of the early viewers were optimized to ship sooner and render later. About half have taken the opportunity to take advantage of some of the powerful and quick real-time rendering tools available. This has already changed, and Moore's Law (and 36 new PC 3-D accelerator cards already on the market) has blessed us with the ever-increasing desktop 3-D power.

Requirements for Business Benefits of VRML

One wonderful aspect of VRML is that it surpasses language barriers. Content that is not culturally biased makes a site more attractive to a general audience. When we use spaces to communicate, we appeal to fairly fundamental cause-and-effect relationships. For example, other cultures may not understand American humor or moral debates; however, visitors from China may enter a Notre Dame world and instinctively know that this is a sacred space, and behave accordingly. Without having to read the literature, visitors leave with a sense of what Notre Dame is all about. In this way, businesses can apply international symbols and signs to conduct business over the Internet.

Commercial acceptance of VRML depends on a large number of factors. Certainly a commitment on the part of software companies to continue to build tools and viewers is critical, and this has already been demonstrated with the flood of products in the last year. There are perhaps three critical success factors for VRML and VRML-based products: standardization, content development, and the installed base of PCs and modems.

Standardization

One problem that VRML users encounter today is incompatibility between their browser software and the many 3-D worlds they visit. Some browsers view only worlds built using that company's tools. Others view a broad number of worlds but are limited in the number of advanced features, behaviors, or site enhancements they can interpret or process. Advancement of the VRML standard itself to the ISO (which has been done), and adherence to that standard by software companies, is essential if VRML technology is to continue to become widely deployed and used.

VRML standardization to increase compatibility among worlds and browser technologies is essential to improving user experiences and encouraging them to continue their exploration of the 3-D Web. As is the case with the current Netscape extensions (the site optimized for Netscape Navigator), many firms have marketed VRML viewers that are optimized for sites developed using their tools, or sell tools that build sites that look best when accessed with their viewer. These added features are among the differentiating factors in initial product choice, and ultimately help guide future standard specifications.

Development of Content

Another market driver is the widespread development of worlds and homespaces with meaningful content. It won't do anyone a lot of good to pour hundreds of thousands of VRML viewers into the market if there is nowhere for users to go or nowhere that they *want* to go. Developers need to start building more worlds now, and get familiar enough with VRML that they can imagine capabilities that go beyond the current technology, thus providing valuable feedback to the industry. However, developers also need to pay attention to such issues as polygon count, file size, network bandwidth, and others so that end users don't have to wait forever to download a world or wait even more than half a second for a movement they have initiated to display on the screen.

The Installed Base

Finally, and perhaps most critical, is the current state of the Internet and the installed base of personal computers. As it stands today, VRML works with many of the existing PCs, which in the home market are largely 486 machines with some multimedia capabilities, connecting to the Internet with 28.8 KBps modems.

Critically, the vast majority of PCs being sold today are more powerful and have higher-speed modems. This, combined with improvements in the Internet itself, means that just about the time that VRML is ready for prime time (that is, a large number of worlds are built), the installed base of technology should have changed, allowing for the making and using of VRML to be quite satisfying for the end user.

The Future

Clearly, VRML has great promise as a technology to help carry the Internet into the future. The ability to use 3-D virtual-reality types of interfaces in an intranet environment holds the potential for developing new applications that allow multiple users to experience rich environments (in some cases, simultaneously) connected over vast distances.

In order for this technology to become a reality, highly functional standards-based tools need to be on the market, together with a large number of VRML-based sites developed that recognize the reality of today's Internet and PC technology. Within the next year, it may become obvious whether the market is meeting its critical success factors and VRML really is destined to become the wave of the future.

From Here

Whether VRML is destined to become the wave of the future is really in the eye of the visionaries. The next chapter describes VRMLScript, the required scripting language for VRML 2.0. It also defines a "plug-in" API for the moving-worlds VRML 2.0 spec's Script node, thus allowing any language to easily be added to execute the scripts. Finally, the next chapter also addresses Dimension X's standard VRML scripting interface for Java bindings of the VRML API.

Endnotes

1 Deepak Kamlani. VRML Consortium, Inc., San Ramon, CA, 1997.

2 Ibid.

3 Yasuaki Honda, Sony Corp.; Mitra, ParaGraph International; Bob Rockwell, Black Sun Interactive; and Bernie Roehl, University of Waterloo, 1997.

4 MERL—A Mitsubishi Electric Research Lab, Mitsubishi Electric Corporation of Japan, Cambridge, MA, 1997.

5 Fraunhofer Institute for Computer Graphics, Darmstadt, Germany, 1996/97.

6 Silicon Graphics, Inc., 2011 North Shoreline Blvd., Mountain View, CA 94039.

7 Sony Corporation, 550 Madison Ave., New York, NY 10022.

8 Apple Computer, Inc., 1 Infinite Loop, Cupertino, CA 95014.

9 Structural Research & Analysis Corporation, 12121 Wilshire Blvd., Suite 700, Los Angeles, CA 90025.

10 Hiroshi Oyama, M.D., Head of MedVR project, National Cancer Center Hospital, 5-1-1, Tsukiji, Chuo-ku, Tokyo 104, Japan.

11 Ocnus' Rope Company, Inc. (ORC), webmaster@ocnus.com, 1997.

12 Advanced Computing Center for the Arts and Design (ACCAD), Ohio State University, 1224 Kinnear Road, Columbus, OH 43212-1154 .

3

VRMLScript

VRMLScript grew out of the need for a lightweight script language in VRML. It is a subset of the JavaScript language, with VRML data types supported as JavaScript built-in objects.

This chapter describes VRMLScript, the required scripting language for VRML 2.0/97. The language is intended to be very lightweight to allow simple scripts to be used in the construction of behaviors for worlds. It provides functions called when events come into the Script, access to fields within the script, logic to operate on the fields, and the ability to send events out from the script.

Script Structure and Syntax

The script syntax is based on JavaScript. No BNF (Backus-Naur Form) for JavaScript is currently available, so the BNF (formal method of specifying context-free grammars) for the language is presented here. The differences include:

- A semicolon is required at the end of expressions (it is optional in JavaScript). This was done to allow parsing by the YACC (Yet Another Compiler Compiler) parser generator.
- The optional *var* keyword is not allowed.
- The object referencing syntax is not allowed (neither the "[", "]" notation nor the "." notation).
- The break and continue syntax is not supported.

Protocol Supported in the Script Node

The url field of the Script node contains a URL to a file containing the VRMLScript text. The *vrmlscript:* protocol allows the script to be placed inline as follows:

```
Script {
    url "vrmlscript:
        function foo() { ... }"
}[1]
```

In other words, the *vrmlscript:* protocol is specific to VRML. It can be used only in the url field of the Script node. It allows inlining of VRMLScript functions. All UTF8 characters are allowed as well as the newline character, facilitating multiline scripts. Unlike other URLs no character need be escaped except the double quote, which is done with (/").

The Script node is also used to program behavior in a VRML scene. Script nodes typically receive events that signify a change or user action, contain a program module that performs some computation, and effect changes somewhere else in the world. Each Script node has associated programming language code that is executed to carry out the Script node's function. The url field can also contain a URL to a file containing the VRMLScript.

Handling EventIn

Events to the Script node are passed to the corresponding VRMLScript function in the script. For example:

```
Script {
    eventIn SFBool start
        url "... function start() { ... perform some operation ... }"
}²
```

In the example just shown, when the start eventIn is sent, the start() function is executed.

Passing Parameters

Each eventIn is passed a corresponding data value. In the example this would be an SFBool type. Also, the time each eventIn was received is available as an SFTime value. These are passed as parameters to the VRMLScript function:

```
url "vrmlscript:function start(value, timestamp) { ... }"
```

The parameters can have any name. The function can have no parameters, just the value or the value and timestamp. If the function has more than two parameters the extra parameters are not filled in. To VRMLScript the value is numeric with 0 being false and 1 being true. The timestamp is a floating-point value containing the number of seconds since midnight, January 1, 1980.

Processing of Incoming Events

Some implementations of the Script node may choose to defer processing of incoming events until a later time. This could be done as an optimization to skip executing scripts that do not affect visible parts of the scene, or because rendering has taken enough time to allow several events to be delivered before execution can be done. In this case, the events are processed sequentially, in timestamp order. After the last eventIn is processed, the eventsProcessed function is called. This allows lengthy operations to be performed or status checks to be made once rather than in each eventIn function. Any eventOut generated during the execution of this function has the timestamp of the last eventIn processed.

Accessible Fields

The fields, eventIns, and eventOuts of a Script node are accessible from its VRMLScript functions. As in all other nodes the fields are accessible only within the Script. The Script's eventIns can be routed *to* and its eventOuts can be routed *from*. Another Script node with a pointer to this node can access its eventIns and eventOuts just like any other node.

VRML Datatypes

All VRML datatypes have an equivalent object in VRMLScript. All MFFields can be dereferenced into their corresponding SFField using the VRMLScript indexing mechanism. If "a" is an MFVec3f and you perform the operation "b = a[3]," then "b" contains an SFVec3f which is the third element of a. The scalar quantities (SFInt32, SFBool, SFFloat, ...) become numeric values, SFString becomes a VRMLScript String object, and the vector quantities (SFRotation, SFVec3f, ...) allow access to their individual scalar components using the VRMLScript indexing mechanism. In the preceding example, after the operation "c = b[1]," c would contain element 1 (the Y component) of b.

Availability of EventOuts and Fields of the Script Node

Fields defined in the Script node are available to the script by using its name. Its value can be read or written. This value is persistent across function calls. EventOuts defined in the script node can also be read. The value is the last value sent. Assigning to an eventOut sends that event at the end of event execution. This implies that assigning to the eventOut multiple times during one execution of the function still only sends one event, and that event is the last value assigned.

Availability of EventOuts and Fields of Other Script Nodes

The script can access any exposedField, eventIn, or eventOut of any node to which it has a pointer. For example:

```
DEF SomeNode Transform { }
Script {
        field SFNode node USE SomeNode
    eventIn SFVec3f pos
            url "...
      function pos(value) {
          node.set_translation = value;
      }"
}3
```

This sends a set_translation eventIn to the Transform node. An eventIn on a passed node can appear only on the *left* side of the assignment. An eventOut in the passed node can appear only on the *right* side, which reads the last value sent out. Fields in the passed node cannot be accessed, but exposedFields can either send an event to the "set_..." eventIn or read the current value of the "..._changed" eventOut. This follows the routing model of the rest of VRML.

Block Scoped Statements

VRMLScript statements are block scoped the same as other C-like languages. A statement can appear alone in the body of an *if* or *for* statement. A body with multiple statements, or compound statements, must be placed between "{" and "}" characters. This constitutes a new block and all variables defined in this block go out of scope at the end of the block. Statements of a compound statement must be separated by the ";" character. For example:

```
if (a < b)
    c = d;          // simple statement

else {              // compound statement
    e = f;          // e is local to this block
    c = h + 1;
}                   // e is no longer defined here[4]
```

Statements with Conditions

The *if* statement evaluates an expression and selects one of two statements for execution. A simple *if* statement executes the statement following the condition if the result of the expression evaluation is not 0. The *if...else* statement additionally executes the statement following the *else* clause if the result of the expression evaluation is 0. For example:

```
if (a < 0)   // simple if statement
    <statement>

if (b > 5)   // if...else statement
    <statement>
else
    <statement>[5]
```

Looping Behavior Statements

The *for* statement contains three expressions that control the looping behavior, followed by a statement to which the loop is applied. It executes its first expression once before loop execution. It then evaluates its second expression before each loop and, if the expression evaluates to 0, exits the loop. It then executes the statement, followed by evaluation of the third expression. The loop then repeats, until looping is terminated, either by the second or third expression evaluating to 0. In typical use, the first expression initialized a loop counter, the second evaluates it, and the third increments it. For example:

```
for (i = 0; i < 10; ++i)
    <statement>
```

Valid Expression Statements

Any valid expression in VRMLScript can be a statement. The two most common expressions are the *function call* and the *assignment* expression. Both of these statements are thoroughly discussed later in this chapter.

Immediate Return Statement

The *return* statement does an immediate return from the function regardless of its nesting level in the block structure. If given, its expression is evaluated and the result returned to the calling function. For example:

```
if (a == 0) {
    d = 1;
    return 5 + d;
}6
```

Expressions

Expressions are the basic instructions of each function. Each expression requires one or two values. Resultant values can be used in further expressions building up compound expressions. Precedence rules are used to order evaluation. The default rules can be overridden with the use of the "(" and ")" characters to bracket higher precedence operations.

Assigning Expressions

An expression of the form *expression = expression* assigns the result of the right-hand expression to the expression on the left-hand side. The left-hand expression must result in a variable into which a value may be stored. This includes simple identifiers, subscripting operators, and the return value of a function call. For example:

```
a = 5;              // simple assignment
a[3] = 4;           // subscripted assignment
foo()[2] = 3;       // function returning an array7
```

Logical Expressions

Logical expressions include *logical and* ("&&"), *logical or* ("| |"), *logical not* ("!"), and the comparison operators ("<", "<=", "==", "!=", ">=", ">"). *Logical not* is unary, the rest are binary. Each evaluates to either 0 (false) or 1 (true). The constants true and false can also be used. For example:

```
a < 5
b > 0 && c > 1
!((a > 4) || (b < 6))
```

Arithmetic Expressions

Arithmetic expressions include *and* ("&"), *or* ("|"), *exclusive or* ("^"), *not* ("~"), *negation* ("-"), and the operators ("+", "-", "*", "/", "%"). *Not* and *negation* are unary, the rest are binary. For example:

```
5 + b
(c + 5) * 7
(-b / 4) % 6
(c & 0xFF) | 2568
```

Built-In Objects

Not all of the built-in objects from JavaScript are supported. In particular, none of the Window objects are supported, but the String, Date, and Math objects are. Additionally, VRMLScript has a Browser object which contains several VRML-specific methods.

Browser Object

The *Browser* object gives access to several aspects of the VRML browser. Since VRMLScript directly supports all VRML field types, the parameters passed and the values returned are as described there. The methods on the Browser object are shown in Table 3.1:

Table 3.1 Browser Object Methods[9]

getName()	Get a string with the name of the VRML browser.
getVersion()	Get a string containing the version of the VRML browser.
getCurrentSpeed()	Get the floating-point current rate at which the user is traveling in the scene.
getCurrentFrameRate()	Get the floating-point current instantaneous frame rate of the scene rendering, in frames per second.
getWorldURL()	Get a string containing the URL of the currently loaded world.
loadWorld(url)	Load the passed URL as the new world. This may not return.
replaceWorld(nodes)	Replace the current world with the passed list of nodes.
createVRMLFromURL(url, node, event)	Parse the passed URL into a VRML scene. When complete, send the passed event to the passed node. The event is a string with the name of an MFNode eventIn in the passed node.
createVRMLFromString(str)	Parse the passed string into a VRML scene and return the list of root nodes from the resulting scene.
addRoute(fromNode, fromEventOut, toNode, toEventIn)	Add a route from the passed eventOut to the passed eventIn.
deleteRoute(fromNode, fromEventOut, toNode, toEventIn)	Remove the route between the passed eventOut and passed eventIn, if one exists.

Math Object

The *math* object is taken from JavaScript. It consists of the keyword *math* dereferenced with the functions supported by the package. For example:

```
a = math.sin(0.78);
dist = math.sqrt(a*a + b*b);
```

Date Object

The *date* object is also taken from JavaScript. It consists of the keyword *date* dereferenced with the functions supported by the package.

Now that we've covered the main introductory highlights of VRMLScript, let's look at the specifics of the VRMLScript node authoring interface.

VRMLScript for Script Nodes

This part of the chapter takes a very close look at VRMLScript as a scripting language for VRML 2.0/97 Script nodes. Because of this, it has many advantages over other script languages (such as Java). For example:

- ♦ Scripts can be included in source form, inline rather than in a separate URL.
- ♦ All VRML 2.0 data types are supported directly. Some, like the vector types, have built-in methods (such as cross-product and normalize) to simplify working with them.
- ♦ Receiving eventIns is handled with separate functions to ease development and to speed processing.
- ♦ Sending eventOuts is done with simple assignment.
- ♦ Scalar data (SFTime, SFInt32, SFFloat, SFBool) can be used directly in expressions. The JavaScript number

object converts directly to any of the four scalar datatypes. For instance, you can add three seconds to an SFTime value with a = time + 3.

♦ Constructors are available for most datatypes to ease creation and conversion of data.

♦ A full set of JavaScript-compatible math, date, and string objects is available.

♦ The full set of JavaScript string methods and properties are available. Scalar values automatically convert to strings when concatenated. This makes construction of URLs and VRML strings (for use in createVRMLFromString) easy.

VRMLScript Language

The script syntax has similarities to JavaScript as well as several other scripting languages. VRMLScript was designed to be parsed by YACC and is therefore an LALR(1) grammar.

LALR(1) ("Look Ahead Left-to-right Rightmost" derivation) is defined as the class of context-free grammars that Bison (like most other parser generators) can handle; a subset of LR(1) (Left-to-right Rightmost). In other words, LALR is a compiler-compiler system, used for parser generation. The LALR translator construction system includes an LALR parser algorithm.

Bison, on the other hand, is a general-purpose parser generator that converts a grammar description for an LALR(1) context-free grammar into a C program to parse that grammar. Once you are proficient with Bison, you may use it to develop a wide range of language parsers, from those used in simple desk calculators to complex programming languages.

Bison is upward compatible with YACC: All properly written YACC grammars ought to work with Bison with no change. Anyone familiar with YACC should be able to use Bison with little trouble. You need to be fluent in C programming in order to use Bison or to understand the source code in this chapter.

There are conflicts with all though. Sometimes reduce/reduce conflicts can occur that don't look warranted. Here is an example:

```
%token ID
%%
def:        param_spec return_spec ','
            ;
param_spec:
                type
            |   name_list ':' type
            ;
return_spec:
                type
            |   name ':' type
            ;
type:           ID
            ;
name:           ID
            ;
name_list:
                name
            |   name ',' name_list
            ; 10
```

It would seem that this grammar can be parsed with only a single token of look-ahead: When a param_spec is being read, an ID is a *name* if a comma or colon follows, or a *type* if another ID follows. In other words, this grammar is LR(1).

However, Bison, like most parser generators, cannot actually handle all LR(1) grammars. In this grammar, two contexts, *that* after an ID at the beginning of a param_spec and *likewise* at the beginning of a return_spec, are similar enough that Bison assumes they are the same. They appear similar because the same set of rules would be active—the rule for reducing to a *name* and that for reducing to a *type*. Bison is unable to determine at that stage of processing that the rules would require different look-ahead tokens in the two contexts, so it makes a single parser state for them both. Combining the two contexts causes a conflict later. In parser terminology, this occurrence means that the grammar is not LALR(1).

In general, it is better to fix deficiencies than to document them, but this particular deficiency is intrinsically hard to fix; parser generators that can handle LR(1) grammars are hard to write and tend to produce parsers that are very large. In practice, Bison is more useful as it is now.

When the problem arises, you can often fix it by identifying the two parser states that are being confused and adding something to make them look distinct. In the previous example, adding one rule to return_spec as follows makes the problem go away:

```
%token BOGUS
...
%%
...
return_spec:
            type
        |   name ':' type
        /* This rule is never used.  */
        |   ID BOGUS
        ;11
```

This corrects the problem because it introduces the possibility of an additional active rule in the context after the ID at the beginning of return_spec. This rule is *not* active in the corresponding context in a param_spec so the two contexts receive distinct parser states. As long as the token BOGUS is never generated by yylex, the added rule cannot alter the way actual input is parsed.

In other words, to be properly recognized, the %{ and %} should each be situated at the beginning of a line. The specified Java code in <code> will then be copied into the lexical analyzer class created by Java-Lex. For example:

```
class Yylex {
... <code> ...
}
```

This permits the declaration of variables and functions internal to the generated lexical analyzer class. Variable names beginning with yy should be avoided, as these are reserved for use by the generated lexical analyzer class.

In this particular example, there is another way to solve the problem: Rewrite the rule for return_spec to use ID directly instead of via *name*. This also causes the two confusing contexts to have different sets of active rules, because the one for return_spec activates the altered rule for return_spec rather than the one for *name*. For example:

```
param_spec:
          type
     |    name_list ':' type
     ;
return_spec:
          type
     |    ID ':' type
     ;12
```

Variables and Object Types

Data in VRMLScript is represented as objects. The object types correspond to the VRML field types. A variable contains an instance of an object, and can be predefined (appearing in the Script node) or defined locally.

In other words, each sphere node, for example, might have a different radius, and different spotlights have different intensities, colors, and locations. These parameters are called *fields*. A node can have 0 or more fields. Each node specification defines the type, name, and default value for each of its fields. The default value for the field is used if a value for the field is not specified in the VRML file. The order in which the fields of a node are read does not matter. For example, "Cone { bottomRadius 1 height 6 }" and "Cone { height 6 bottomRadius 1}" are equivalent. There are two kinds of fields: *field* and *exposedField*. Fields define the initial values for the node's state but cannot be changed and are considered private. ExposedFields also define the initial value for the node's state but are public and may be modified by other nodes.

Literals, Names, and Values

A VRMLScript variable holds an instance of an object. If a name is defined as a field or eventOut of the Script node containing the script, there is a variable with that same name available globally to the script. The type of this variable is always the type of the field or eventOut. Assignment to this variable converts the expression to its type or generates a run-time error if a conversion is not possible. (See a thorough discussion on Data Conversion later in the chapter.)

The names specified in the declaration of a function (the data value and the timestamp) are local to the function in which they are declared. It is a run-time error to assign to the names of these variables.

Local variables can be created simply by assigning to a name that does not yet exist. Assigning to such a variable causes it to take the type of the expression, so these local variables always have the type of the last assignment. Local variables are scoped by the block in which they were first introduced. Once that block is exited, the variable ceases to exist. Variables corresponding to eventOuts or fields of the Script node are global in scope.

Variable names must start with a lowercase character ("a" through "z"), an uppercase character ("A" through "Z"), or an underscore ("_"). Subsequent characters can be any of these or a digit ("0" through "9"). Variable names are case sensitive.

Numeric, Boolean, and string literals are allowed. Numeric literals can be integers in decimal (417), hex (0x5C), or octal (0177) notation. They can also be floating-point numbers in fixed (1.76) or exponential (2.7e-12) notation. All numeric literals are of the number type. Boolean literals can be "true" or "false" and have the Boolean type. String literals can be any sequence of UTF8 characters enclosed in single quotes (""), and have the type String. Special (nonprintable) characters can be included in a string using the following escape sequences as shown in Table 3.2.

Here are some examples:

```
Script {
    field          SFFloat aField  0
    field          SFVec3f aVector 0 0 0
    eventOut   SFInt32 anEventOut
    eventIn    SFBool  event

  url "vrmlscript:
    function event(value, timestamp) {
        if (aField == 1.5) {
            a = true;    // 'a' contains a boolean
        }

        if (a) {          // this is NOT the same 'a' as above!
            value = 5;   // ERROR,
                         //    can't assign to function parameter!
```

Table 3.2 Escape Sequences[13]

Sequence	Meaning
\b	backspace
\f	form feed
\n	new line
\r	carriage return
\t	tab
\'	single quote (apostrophe)
\"	double quote
\\	backslash

```
        }

    aField = anEventOut;    // SFInt32 converted to SFFloat
    b = aField;             // 'b' contains a number
    b = anEventOut;         // 'b' now contains a different
                            // number
    aField = aVector;       //   ERROR,
                            //      can't assign SFVec3f to
                            // SFFloat!
    s =   'Two\nLines';     //   's' contains a String

    } "
} 14
```

Fields and Objects

For each field and eventOut in the Script node containing the script there is a corresponding global variable with the same name. Field variables are persistent; they keep their last stored value across function calls. Local variables, on the other hand, are destroyed on exit from the block in which they were defined. Local variables defined in the outermost block of a function are destroyed when the function exits so they do not persist across function calls.

EventOut variables are very similar to field variables in that their values persist across function calls. But when an assignment is made to an eventOut variable an event is generated.

Every object has a set of *properties* and *methods*. *Properties* are names on the object that can be selected (using the "." operator), then used in an expression or as the target of an expression. (See a discussion on Object and Function Definitions later in the chapter.)

Methods are names on the object that can be called (using the function call operator) to perform some operation on the object. For example:

```
function someFunction() {
    a = new SFColor(0.5,  0.5,  0.5);
```

```
    b = a.r;                    // 'b' contains 0.5
    a.setHSV(0.1, 0.1, 0.1);   // 'a' now contains new properties
}15
```

The value *a.r* selects the property which corresponds to the red component of the color. The value *a.setHSV()* selects the method which sets the color in HSV space.

Construction of Objects

For each object type there is a corresponding *constructor* (see "Object and Function Definitions" later in the chapter). Constructors typically take a flexible set of parameters to allow construction of objects with any initial value.

MF objects are essentially arrays so they always take 0 or more parameters of the corresponding SF object type. A value of a given datatype is created using the new keyword with the datatype name. For instance:

```
a = new SFVec3f(0, 1, 0);   // 'a' has an SFVec3f containing 0,
                            // 1, 0
b = new MFFloat(1, 2, 3, 4) // 'b' has an MFFloat containing 4
                            // floats
```

Implicit Type Conversion of Data

Combining objects of different types in a single expression or assignment statement will often perform *implicit type* conversion. Rules for this conversion are described in Table 3.3:

Table 3.3 Implicit Type Conversion[16]

Type	Rules
String	Combining a String with any number or Boolean type produces a String.
	Use parseInt() or parseFloat to convert a String to a number.

Table 3.3 Continued.

Type	Rules
Number and Boolean types	Assigning a number or Boolean expression to a fixed variable (field or eventOut) of scalar type (SFBool, SFInt32, SFFloat, SFTime) converts to the type of the fixed variable.
Vector types	Only combine with like types.
SFVec2f SFVec3f SFRotation SFColor	Dereference (foo[1]) produces a value of number type.
SFImage	Assignment ("=") and selection (".") are the only allowed operations.
	Can only assign SFImage type.
SFNode	Assignment ("=") and selection (".") are the only allowed operations.
	Can only assign SFNode type.
MF types	Only combine with like types.
MFString MFInt32 MFFloat MFVec2f MFVec3f MFRotation MFColor MFNode	Dereference (myArray[3]) produces the corresponding SF type. Dereferenced SF types follow same rules as normal SF types.

Array of Objects

Most *SF* objects in VRMLScript have a corresponding *MF* object. An *MFObject* is essentially an array of objects, with each element of the array having the type of the corresponding SF object. All MF objects have a length property which returns or sets the number of elements in the MF object. Array indexes start at 0. If vecArray is an MFVec3f object then vecArray[0] is the first SFVec3f object in the array.

Dereferencing an MF object creates a new object of the corresponding SF object type with the contents of the dereferenced element. Assigning an SF object to a dereferenced MF object (which must be of the corresponding type) copies the contents of the SF object into the dereferenced element.

VRMLScript Statements

VRMLScript statements are block scoped the same as other C-like languages. A statement can appear alone in the body of an *if* or *for* statement. A body with multiple simple statements, or compound statements, must be placed between "{" and "}" characters. This constitutes a new block and all variables defined in this block go out of scope at the end of the block. All simple statements must end with the ";" character. For example:

```
if (a < b)
    c = d;   // simple statement, c is local to the if statement

else {       // compound statement, c is no longer defined here
    e = f;   // e is local to the else block
    c = h + 1;
}            // e is no longer defined here[17]
```

Statements with Conditions

The *if* statement evaluates an expression, and selects one of two statements for execution. A simple *if* statement executes the statement following the condition if the result of the expression evaluation is not 0. The *if...else* statement additionally executes the statement following the *else* clause if the result of the expression evaluation is 0. For nested *if...else* statements, the *else* clause matches the nearest *if* statement. Braces can be used to override this. For example:

```
if (a < 0)   // simple if statement
    <statement>

if (a == 0)
    if (b > 5)  // if...else statement
```

```
    <statement>
else            // this else clause matches the 'if (b > 5)'
                // statement
    <statement>

if (a == 0) {
    if (b > 5)
        <statement>
}
else                // this else clause matches the 'if (a == 0)'
                    // statement
    <statement>18
```

Statements with Looping Behaviors

The *for* statement contains three expressions that control the loop-ing behavior, followed by a statement to which the loop is applied. It executes its first expression once before loop execution. It then evaluates its second expression before each loop and, if the expression evaluates to 0, exits the loop. It then executes the statement, followed by evaluation of the third expression. The loop then repeats, until looping is terminated, either by the second expression evaluating to 0 or until a break statement is encountered. In typical use, the first expression initializes a loop counter, the second evaluates it, and the third increments it. For example:

```
for (i = 0; i < 10; ++i)
    <statement>
```

The *while* statement contains a single expression that controls the looping behavior, followed by a statement to which the loop is applied. Before each loop it evaluates the expression and, if the expression evaluates to 0, exits the loop. Otherwise, it executes the statement and tests the expression again. The loop continues until terminated by the expression evaluating to 0 or until a break state-ment is encountered. For example:

```
while (i < 10)
    <statement>
```

Valid Expression Statements

Any valid expression in VRMLScript can be a statement. The two most common expressions are the *function call* and the *assignment*. A further clarification of these expressions will be made later in the chapter.

Immediate Return Statement

The *return* statement does an immediate return from the function regardless of its nesting level in the block structure. If specified, its expression is evaluated and the result is returned to the calling function. For example:

```
if (a == 0) {
    d = 1;
    return 5 + d;
}
```

Exiting Break Statement

The *break* statement exits the deepest enclosing looping statement. Execution continues at the statement following the looping statement. For example:

```
while (i < 0) {
    if (q == 5)
        break;
    <other statements>
}

// execution commences here upon break.19
```

Jumping Continue Statement

The *continue* statement jumps to the end of the deepest enclosing looping statement. Execution continues at the end of the loop. In the case of the *for* statement, the third expression is evaluated and then the second expression is tested to see if the loop should be continued. In the case of the *for...in* statement, the next element is assigned to the variable and the loop is continued. In the case of the *while* statement, the expression is tested to see if the loop should be continued. For example:

```
for a in colorArray {
    if (a[0] > 0.5)
        continue;
    <other statements>

    // loop commences here upon continue.
}20
```

Combining Expressions with Operators

Expressions combine variables, objects, constants, and the results of other expressions with *operators*. The result of an expression evaluation is always another expression. In this way compound expressions can be built out of simpler ones. Operators combine one (unary), two (binary), or three (tertiary) values. *Unary* operators are placed before (prefix) or after (postfix) the value to be operated on. *Binary* operators are placed between the values to be operated on. *Tertiary* operators always consist of two symbols, with one symbol placed between each pair of values to be operated on. For example:

```
a = -b;          // unary prefix operator
a = b++;         // unary postfix operator
a = b + c;       // binary operator
a = b ? c : d;   // tertiary operator
a = b * c + d;   // compound expression
                 // the product of b * c produces a value which
                 // is added to d21
```

Assignment Operator Results

An expression of the form *expression = expression* assigns the result of the right-hand expression to the expression on the left-hand side. The left-hand expression must result in a variable into which a value may be stored. This includes simple identifiers, subscripting operators, members of objects, and the return value of a function call. For example:

```
a = 5;              // simple assignment
a[3] = 4;           // subscripted assignment
foo()[2] = 3;       // function returning an MFField
```

In addition, a set of shorthand operators exist for doing a binary operation using the left-hand expression and the right-hand expression, then assigning the result to the left-hand expression. These operators are *plus-equal* ("+="), *minus-equal* ("−="), *times-equal* ("*=") *divide-equal* ("/="), *mod-equal* ("%="), *and-equal* ("&="), *or-equal* ("|="), *xor-equal* ("^="), *shift-left-equal* ("<<="), *shift-right-equal* (">>="), *shift-right-fill-zero-equal* (">>>="). For example:

```
a += 5;             // adds 5 to the value of a and assigns it to a
a[3] &= 0x0000FFFF; // performs bitwise-and of a[3] and 0x0000FFFF
// assigning result to a[3]
```

Arithmetic Operators

Arithmetic operators include *negation* ("-"), *ones-complement* ("~"), *increment* ("++"), *decrement* ("—") and the operators ("+", "-", "*", "/", "%"). *Negation* and *ones-complement* are prefix unary. *Increment* and *decrement* are prefix or postfix unary. The rest are binary. For example:

```
5 + b
(c + 5) * 7
(-b / 4) % 6
(c & 0xFF) | 256
```

The *increment* and *decrement* operators behave differently depending on whether they are used as *prefix* or *postfix* operators. In either case, if the expression to which the operator is applied is a variable, the value of that variable is incremented or decremented. A value is also returned from the expression. When used as a *prefix* operator the value returned is that of the expression after the increment or decrement. When used as a *postfix* operator the value returned is that of the expression before the increment or decrement. For example:

```
a = 5;          // Value of 'a' is 5
b = a++;        // Value of 'b' is 5, value of 'a' is 6
c = ++b;        // Value of 'c' is 6, value of 'b' is 6
```

Bitwise Binary Operators

Bitwise operators include *and* ("&"), *or* ("|"), *exclusive or* ("^"), *left shift* ("<<"), *right shift* (">>"), and *right shift, zero fill* (">>>"). These are all binary operators and are valid on any scalar type. When they are applied the scalar value is converted to an SFInt32 before the operation, and back to the original expression type after. Therefore, roundoff errors can occur when applying them to SFFloat or SFTime values. The shift operators shift the operand on the *left* side the number of bits specified by the operator on the *right* side. The difference between *right shift* and *right shift, zero fill* is that the former preserves the sign of the left operator and the latter always puts a zero in the most significant bits. For example:

```
a & 0x0FF       // clears upper 24 bits of 'a'
a >> 5          // shift 'a' 5 bits to the right, sign extend
```

Logical Expressions and Comparison Operators

Logical expressions include *logical and* ("&&"), *logical or* ("||"), *logical not* ("!"), and the comparison operators ("<", "<=", "==", "!=", ">=", ">"). *Logical not* is prefix unary, the rest are binary. Each evaluates to either 0 (false) or 1 (true). The constants true, false, TRUE, and FALSE can also be used. For example:

```
a < 5
b > 0 && c > 1
!((a > 4) || (b < 6))
```

Comparing String Operators

All the comparison operators can be used to compare strings for lexicographic order. Additionally, the operators "+" and "+=" can be used to concatenate two strings. Any expression involving a string and any scalar type will first convert the scalar to a string and then perform the concatenation. Conversion of a string to a scalar type can be done with the functions *parseInt()* and *parseFloat()*. For example:

```
'A one and ' + 'a two'        // result is "A one and a two"
'The magic number is ' + 7    // result is 'The magic number is 7'
a = 5;                        // 'a' contains an SFTime
a += 'is correct';            // 'a' is now the String '5 is correct'
```

Operator Precedence Rules

Precedence rules are used to order evaluation. In the preceding compound expression example *multiplication* ("*") is evaluated before *addition* ("+"). For operations of equal precedence evaluation, order is shown in Table 3.4. The default rules can be overridden with the use of the "(" and ")" characters to bracket operations to be performed first. For example:

```
a = b + c * d;   // c * d is evaluated first
a = (b + c) * d; // b + c is evaluated first
a = b * c / d;   // b * c is evaluated first
                 // ('*' and '/' have equal precedence, evaluation
                 // order is left-to-right)
```

Order of precedence is (unless otherwise stated) left to right.

Table 3.4 Order for Operations of Equal Precedence Evaluation[22]

Operator	Type Operator	Comments
comma	,	
assignment	= += -= *= /= %=	
<<= >>= >>>= &= ^= |=	right-to-left	
conditional	?:	tertiary operator
logical-or	||	

Table 3.4 Continued.

Operator	Type Operator	Comments
logical-and	&&	
bitwise-or	|	
bitwise-xor	^	
bitwise-and	&	
equality	== !=	
relational	< <= > >=	
bitwise shift	<< >> >>>	
add/subtract	+ -	
multiply/divide	* / %	
negate/increment	! ~ - ++ —	unary operators
call, member	() [] .	

Script Node's URL Field Protocol Support

The *url* field of the Script node may contain a URL that references VRMLScript code. For example:

```
Script {  url "http://foo.com/myScript.vs"  }
```

In addition, the *vrmlscript: protocol* allows the script to be placed inline as follows:

```
Script {  url "vrmlscript: function foo() { ... }"  }
```

Also, the url field may contain multiple URLs and thus reference a remote file or inline code as shown in the following example:

```
Script {
    url [ "http://foo.com/myScript.vs",
          "vrmlscript: function foo() { ... }" ]
}
```

Finally, the file extension for VRMLScript source code is .vs; and, the MIME type for VRMLScript source code is defined as follows: application/x-vrmlscript

EventIn Handling in the Script Node

Events sent to the Script node are passed to the corresponding VRMLScript function in the script. It is necessary to specify the script in the url field of the Script node. The function's name is the same as the eventIn and is passed two arguments: the event value and its timestamp (as discussed next). Also, if there isn't a corresponding VRMLScript function in the script, the browser's behavior is undefined. For example, the following Script node has one eventIn field whose name is start:

```
Script {
    eventIn SFBool start
    url "vrmlscript: function start(value, timestamp) { ... }"
}
```

In the preceding example, when the start eventIn is sent, the start() function is executed.

The EventIn Function and Parameter Passing

When a Script node receives an eventIn, a corresponding method in the file specified in the url field of the Script node is called, which has two arguments. The value of the eventIn is passed as the first argument and the timestamp of the eventIn is passed as the second argument. The type of the value is the same as the type of the eventIn, and the type of the timestamp is SFTime.

eventsProcessed() Events Received Method

Authors may define a function named *eventsProcessed* which will be called after some set of events has been received. Some implementations will call this function after the return from each eventIn function, while others will call it only after processing a number of eventIn functions. In the latter case an author can improve performance by placing lengthy processing algorithms which do not need to be executed for every event received into the eventsProcessed function.

For example, let's say the author needs to compute a complex inverse kinematics operation at each timestep of an animation sequence. The sequence is single-stepped using a TouchSensor and button geometry. Normally the author would have an eventIn function execute whenever the button is pressed. This function would increment the timestep and then run the inverse kinematics algorithm. But this would execute the complex algorithm at every button press and the user could easily get ahead of the algorithm by clicking on the button rapidly. To solve this, the eventIn function can be changed to simply increment the timestep and the IK algorithm can be moved to an eventsProcessed function. In an efficient implementation the clicks would be queued. When the user clicks quickly the timestep would be incremented once for each button click but the complex algorithm will be executed only once. This way, the animation sequence will keep up with the user.

The eventsProcessed function takes no parameters. Events generated from it are given the timestamp of the last event processed.

initialize() Method Function for Processing Preparation

Authors may define a function named *initialize* which is called when the corresponding Script node has been loaded and before any events are processed. This can be used to prepare for processing before events are received, such as constructing geometry or initializing external mechanisms.

The *initialize* function takes no parameters. Events generated from it are given the timestamp of when the Script node was loaded.

shutdown() Method Function

Authors may define a function named *shutdown* which is called when the corresponding Script node is deleted or the world containing the Script node is unloaded or replaced by another world.

This can be used to send events informing external mechanisms that the Script node is being deleted so they can clean up files, etc.

The *shutdown* function takes no parameters. Events generated from it are given the timestamp of when the Script node was deleted.

Accessing Fields from the VRMLScript Functions

The fields, eventIns, and eventOuts of a Script node are accessible from its VRMLScript functions. As in all other nodes the fields are accessible only within the Script. The Script's eventIns can be routed *to* and its eventOuts can be routed *from*. Another Script node with a pointer to this node can access its eventIns and eventOuts just like any other node.

Accessing eventOuts and Fields of the Script Node

Fields defined in the Script node are available to the script by using its name. Its value can be read or written. This value is persistent across function calls. EventOuts defined in the script node can also be read. The value is the last value sent.

Accessing EventOuts and Fields of Other Nodes Which Have a Pointer

The script can access any exposedField, eventIn, or eventOut of any node to which it has a pointer. For example:

```
DEF SomeNode Transform { }
Script {
    field SFNode node USE SomeNode
    eventIn SFVec3f pos
    directOutput TRUE
    url "...
        function pos(value) {
            node.set_translation = value;
        }"
}23
```

This sends a set_translation eventIn to the Transform node. An eventIn on a passed node can appear only on the *left* side of the assignment. An eventOut in the passed node can appear only on the *right* side, which reads the last value sent out. Fields in the passed node cannot be accessed, but exposedFields can either send an event to the "set_..." eventIn, or read the current value of the "..._changed" eventOut. This follows the routing model of the rest of VRML.

Sending Assigned eventOuts

Assigning to an eventOut sends that event at the completion of the currently executing function. This implies that assigning to the eventOut multiple times during one execution of the function still only sends one event, and that event is the last value assigned.

Function and Object Definitions

There are a fixed set of objects in VRMLScript, each of which have a fixed set of properties (values) and methods (functions). For all object types except Math, there are functions to create an instance of the object. The supported set of objects are:

- ◆ parseInt and parseFloat functions
- ◆ Browser
- ◆ Math
- ◆ SFColor
- ◆ SFImage
- ◆ SFNode
- ◆ SFRotation
- ◆ String
- ◆ SFVec2f
- ◆ SFVec3f
- ◆ MFColor
- ◆ MFFloat
- ◆ MFInt32
- ◆ MFNode
- ◆ MFRotation
- ◆ MFString
- ◆ MFVec2f
- ◆ MFVec3f
- ◆ VRMLMatrix

parseFloat and parseInt Functions

The *parseFloat* and *parseInt* functions are provided to convert a String value to an SFInt32 or SFFloat value. For example, the parseInt(s, [radix]) converts the passed String, "s", to an integer valued number, using the optional passed numeric "radix" as the base. If the radix is omitted, base 10 is assumed. Numbers can be in decimal (123), hexadecimal (0x5C), or octal (0177) notation and may be preceded by a minus sign ("–"). Conversion stops at the first unrecognized character. If the string begins with an unrecognized character, 0 is returned.

On the other hand, parseFloat(s) converts the passed String, "s" to a floating-point valued number. Numbers can be in fixed (1.23) or exponential (12E3) notation, and both the mantissa and exponent may be preceded by a minus sign ("–"). Conversion stops at the first unrecognized character. If the string begins with an unrecognized character, 0 is returned.

Browser Object

This part of the chapter discusses the methods available in the browser object, which allows scripts to get and set browser information. The browser interface provides a mechanism for scripts contained by Script nodes to get and set browser state, such as the URL of the current world. This part of the chapter also describes the semantics and functions/methods that the browser interface supports. A C-like syntax is used to define the type of parameters and returned values, but is hypothetical. In this hypothetical syntax, types are given as VRML field types. Mapping of these types into those of the underlying language (as well as any type conversion needed) is described in the appropriate language reference.

In addition, decision logic and state management is often needed to decide what effect an event should have on the scene—"if the vault is currently closed AND the correct combination is entered, then open the vault." These kinds of decisions are expressed as Script nodes that receive events from other nodes, process them, and send events to other nodes. A Script node can also keep track of information between execution (managing internal state over time). This part of the chapter also describes the general mechanisms and semantics that all scripting languages must support.

Event processing is done by a program or script contained in (or referenced by) the Script node's url field. This program or script can be written in any programming language that the browser supports. Browsers are not required to implement any specific scripting languages in VRML 2.0.

Finally, a Script node is activated when it receives an event. At that point the browser executes the program in the Script node's url field (passing the program to an external interpreter if necessary). The program can perform a wide variety of actions: sending out events (and thereby changing the scene), performing calculations, communicating with servers elsewhere on the Internet, and so on.

Unique Math Object

The *Math* object is unique in VRMLScript in that there is exactly one globally available instance of the object, named *Math*. Properties can be accessed using the syntax Math.<property-name>. Methods can be invoked using the syntax Math.<function-name> (<argument-list>).

Corresponding SFColor Object

The *SFColor* object corresponds to a VRML 2.0 SFColor field. All properties are accessed using the syntax sfColorObjectName.<property>, where sfColorObjectName is an instance of a SFColor object. All methods are invoked using the syntax sfColorObjectName.method(<argument-list>), where sfColorObject-Name is an instance of a SFColor object.

Corresponding SFImage Object

The *SFImage* object corresponds to a VRML 2.0 SFImage field, where .sfImage1ObjectName = new SFImage(x, y, comp, array). Here x is the x-dimension of the image and y is the y-dimension of the image. *Comp* is the number of components of the image (1 for grayscale, 2 for grayscale+alpha, 3 for rgb, 4 for rgb+alpha). All these values are scalar. Array is an MFInt32 field containing the x*y values for the pixels of the image. The format of each pixel is the same as the PixelTexture file format.

Corresponding SFNode Object

The *SFNode* object corresponds to a VRML 2.0 SFNode field, where sfNodeObjectName = new SFNode (vrmlstring). Here vrmlstring is an ASCII string containing the definition of a VRML 2.0 node. Each node may assign values to its eventIns and obtain the last output values of its eventOuts using the sfNodeObjectName .eventName syntax.

Corresponding SFRotation Object

The *SFRotation* object corresponds to a VRML 2.0 SFRotation field, where sfRotationObjectName = new SFRotation(x, y, z, angle). Here x, y, and z are the axis of the rotation and angle is the angle of the rotation (in radians). All values are scalar.

Also, sfRotationObjectName = new SFRotation(axis, angle), where axis is an SFVec3f object whose value is the axis of rotation and angle is the scalar angle of the rotation (in radians). In addition, sfRotationObjectName = new SFRotation (fromVector, toVector) fromVector and toVector are SFVec3f valued objects. These vectors are normalized and the rotation value that would rotate from the fromVector to the toVector is stored in the object.

Corresponding String Object

The *String* object corresponds to a VRML 2.0 SFString field, where stringObjectName = new String(number), and number is any scalar expression. Also, stringObjectName = new String(string)— where string is any UTF-8 string expression.

Corresponding SFVec2f Object

The *SFVec2f* object corresponds to a VRML 2.0 SFVec2f field. Each component of the vector can be accessed using the x and y properties or using C-style array dereferencing (sfVec2fObjectName[0] or sfVec2fObjectName[1]).

Corresponding SFVec3f Object

The *SFVec3f* object corresponds to a VRML 2.0 SFVec3f field. Each component of the vector can be accessed using the x, y, and z properties or using C-style array dereferencing (sfVec3fObjectName[0], sfVec3fObjectName[1] or sfVec3fObjectName[2]).

Corresponding MFColor Object

The *MFColor* object corresponds to a VRML 2.0 MFColor field. It is used to store a one-dimensional array of SFColor objects. Individual elements of the array can be referenced using the standard C-style dereferencing operator (mfColorObjectName[index], where index is an integer-valued expression with 0<=index<length and length is the number of elements in the array). Assigning to an element with index > length results in the array being dynamically expanded to contain length elements. All elements not explicitly initialized are set to SFColor(0, 0, 0).

Corresponding MFFloat Object

The *MFFloat* object corresponds to a VRML 2.0 MFFloat field. It is used to store a one-dimensional array of SFFloat objects. Individual elements of the array can be referenced using the standard C-style dereferencing operator (mfFloatObjectName[index], where index is an integer-valued expression with 0<=index<length and length is the number of elements in the array). Assigning to an element with index > length results in the array being dynamically expanded to contain length elements. All elements not explicitly initialized are set to 0.0.

Corresponding MFInt32 Object

The *MFInt32* object corresponds to a VRML 2.0 MFInt32 field. It is used to store a one-dimensional array of SFInt32 objects. Individual elements of the array can be referenced using the standard C-style dereferencing operator (mfInt32ObjectName[index], where index is an integer-valued expression with 0<=index<length and length is the number of elements in the array). Assigning to an element with index > length results in the array being dynamically expanded to contain length elements. All elements not explicitly initialized are set to 0.

Corresponding MFNode Object

The *MFNode* object corresponds to a VRML 2.0 MFNode field. It is used to store a one-dimensional array of SFNode objects. Individual elements of the array can be referenced using the standard C-style dereferencing operator (mfNodeObjectName[index], where index is an integer-valued expression with 0<=index<length and length is the number of elements in the array). Assigning to an element with index > length results in the array being dynamically expanded to contain length elements. All elements not explicitly initialized are set to NULL.

Corresponding MFRotation Object

The *MFRotation* object corresponds to a VRML 2.0 MFRotation field. It is used to store a one-dimensional array of SFRotation objects. Individual elements of the array can be referenced using the standard C-style dereferencing operator (mfRotationObjectName[index], where index is an integer-valued expression with 0<=index<length and length is the number of elements in the array). Assigning to an element with index > length results in the array being dynamically expanded to contain length elements. All elements not explicitly initialized are set to SFRotation(0, 0, 1, 0).

Corresponding MFString Object

The *MFString* object corresponds to a VRML 2.0 MFString field. It is used to store a 1-dimensional array of String objects. Individual elements of the array can be referenced using the standard C-style dereferencing operator (mfStringObjectName[index], where index is an integer-valued expression with 0<=index<length and length is the number of elements in the array). Assigning to an element with index > length results in the array being dynamically expanded to contain length elements. All elements not explicitly initialized are set to the empty string.

Corresponding MFVec2f Object

The *MFVec2f* object corresponds to a VRML 2.0 MFVec2f field. It is used to store a 1-dimensional array of SFVec2f objects. Individual elements of the array can be referenced using the standard C-style dereferencing operator (mfVec2fObjectName[index], where index is an integer-valued expression with 0<=index<length and length is the number of elements in the array). Assigning to an element with index > length results in the array being dynamically expanded to contain length elements. All elements not explicitly initialized are set to SFVec2f(0, 0).

Corresponding MFVec3f Object

The *MFVec3f* object corresponds to a VRML 2.0 MFVec3f field. It is used to store a one-dimensional array of SFVec3f objects. Individual elements of the array can be referenced using the standard C-style dereferencing operator (mfVec3fObjectName[index], where index is an integer-valued expression with 0<=index<length and length is the number of elements in the array). Assigning to an element with index > length results in the array being dynamically expanded to contain length elements. All elements not explicitly initialized are set to SFVec3f(0, 0, 0).

The Manipulating VrmlMatrix Object

The *VrmlMatrix* object provides many useful methods for performing manipulations on 4x4 matrices. Each element of the matrix can be accessed using C-style array dereferencing (vrmlMatrixObjectName[0][1] is the element in row 0, column 1). The results of dereferencing a VrmlMatrix object using a single index (vrmlMatrixObjectName[0]) are undefined.

Source Code Reference Implementation of VRMLScript

Source code for a reference implementation of VRMLScript is available in the archive vrmlscript.zip. This source is freely available for use in adding VRMLScript to your browser. Please read the readme.txt file contained in that package. It lists the restrictions for use, which are:

- ◆ You must credit Silicon Graphics for the code.
- ◆ You cannot sell the source.
- ◆ If you redistribute this package, you must do so intact, including the readme.txt file.

♦ You may not use the code for purposes other than implementing a VRMLScript compiler and interpreter.

The package contains everything you need to parse and interpret VRMLScript. Also included are classes to implement the datatypes, including vector and quaternion math, a general MF array class, string functions and time functions. Currently it is packaged for use on a PC with Windows 95 and 97 and Microsoft Developer Studio.

Defining a Plug-In API for the VRML 2.0 Spec's Script Node

This part of the chapter represents an attempt at defining a plug-in API for the VRML 2.0 spec's Script node; thus allowing any language to easily be added to execute the scripts. Some advantages of using a plug-in architecture are:

♦ The burden on the browser writers is lighter—they only have to implement a simple interface, not one (or even two) language binding(s) and/or interpreter(s).

♦ The burden on the content creators is lighter—they don't need to learn yet another language. As long as a plug-in is available for their favorite language, they can write VRML worlds in it.

♦ Compatibility is ensured—all VRML browsers will use the same plug-in, making sure that a script in any given language will execute identically across different browsers.

♦ People equipped to write language interpreters/run-time environments get to do what they are best at. People writing VRML browsers get to do what they are best at.

♦ And best of all: No work is wasted. Been working long nights inventing a new language called VRMLScript? Made a nice Java link lately? Convert it to a plug-in and everyone will benefit from it.[24]

Content Creators

Will the content creators need to care? The answer is *not necessarily*. Behold the following illustration as shown in Figure 3.1.[25]

The content creators write or export VRML files and write scripts in their favorite language. So from a content creator's point of view, you only need to know that "this is great," and stop reading here!

Seriously, none of what is written in this part of the chapter is of immediate interest to a content creator—this is aimed at browser writers and spec writers! See the following example (ATLAST language plug-in) in which the content creator only writes the .wrl and .atl files. This is a sample plug-in using John Walker's wonderful FORTH-like threaded language ATLAST as discussed in the sidebar, "A T L A S T: Autodesk Threaded Language Application System Toolkit:"

The Script Node

The following is what the content creator will need to write! For example:

```
DEF OpenVault Script {
    # Declarations of what's in this Script node:
    eventIn SFTime openVault
```

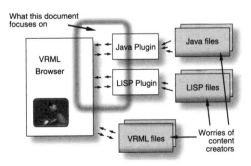

Figure 3.1 Content creator worries.

```
eventIn SFBool combinationEntered
eventOut SFTime vaultUnlocked
field SFBool unlocked FALSE

# Implementation of the logic:
url "vault.atl"
}26
```

The VAULT.ATL File

The following is what the content creator will need to write! For example:

```
variable vaultUnlocked

    variable locked

    : init ( )
        "vaultUnlocked" getStringNumeral vaultUnlocked !
        1 locked !
    ;

    : openVault ( SFTime -- )
        locked 0= if
            vaultUnlocked @ sendEvent \ SFTime is already on the
                                      \ stack
        then
    ;

    : combinationEntered ( SFBool -- )
        drop                \ Drop the SFBool, don't need it
        1 locked !          \ Set the variable
    ; 27
```

The ATLAST Plug-In Source

The ATLAST plug-in source needs to use a rewritten atlast which keeps all state-variables in a struct pointed to by atl_instance_ptr, to be able to have several instances of the interpreter. For example:

```c
#include "atlast.h"

    struct browserCallback *browser = NULL;

    int sendEvent();

    static struct primfcn prims[] = {
        {"0SENDEVENT", sendEvent,
        {NULL,         (codeptr) 0}
    };


    int VPCanHandle(char *languageId)
    {
        /* If it's ATLAST, say we can handle it! */

        if (strcmp(languageId, "language/atlast") == 0 ||
            stricmp(languageId, ".atl") == 0) return TRUE;

        return FALSE; /* Dunno what it is! */
    }

    void *VPInitInstance(char *URL, struct browserCallback *cbks)
    {
        dictword *dw;

        browser = cbks;

        atl_init(); /* Initialize ATLAST */

        atl_primdef(&prims); /* Let ATLAST know about "sendEvent" */

        dw = atl_lookup("init"); /* Find function named "init" */

        if (NULL != dw) atl_exec(dw); /* Call it, if present */

        return atl_instance_ptr; /* Dirty, just return atlasts
                                 /* instance pointer */
    }
```

```
    void *VPFunctionHandle(void *instance, char *name)
    {
        atl_instance_ptr = instance; /* Set the right instance */

        return atl_lookup(name); /* Lookup the dictionary word */
    }


    void VPEventIn(void *instance, void *functionHandle, int
dataType, void *data)
    {
        atl_instance_ptr = instance; /* Set the right instance */

        /* Put datatypes on the ATLAST stack. Never mind the wierd
syntax to push
          the items onto the stack, OK?! Blame John Walker... :-) */

        switch (dataType)
        {
          case SFBool:
              Push = *(int *)data;   /* Pushes bool onto stack */
              break;
          case SFTime:
              Push = 0; /* Make room for a float */
              Push = 0; /* Make room for a float */
              SREAL0(*(double *)data);
              break;
              .

              .

              .

        }

        atl_exec(functionHandle);  /* Calls that ATLAST function */
    }

    /* Called from the ATLAST code */
    void sendEvent()
    {
        int numeral;
```

```
    numeral = D0; /* Get the numeral (top of stack) */
    Pop; /* Pop item off stack */

/* TBD: Get data of stack. Does datatype need to be passed?  */

    browser->sendEvent(numeral, data);
}28
```

A T L A S T: Autodesk Threaded Language Application System Toolkit

ATLAST is an attempt to make software component technology and open architecture applications commonplace in the mainstream software market. It is both a software component which can be readily integrated into existing applications, providing them with a ready-made macro language and facilities for user extension and customization, and a foundation upon which new applications can be built in an open, component-oriented manner.

ATLAST was developed at Autodesk, Inc. Autodesk returned the rights to John Walker in 1991 and he subsequently placed the program in the public domain.

ATLAST is based on the FORTH-83 language but has been extended in many ways and modified to better serve its mission as an embedded toolkit for open, programmable applications. ATLAST is implemented in a single file, written in portable C; it has been ported to many different machines and operating systems, including MS-DOS, OS/2, the Macintosh, and a wide variety of Unix machines. ATLAST includes native support for floating-point C-like strings, Unix-compatible file access, and a wide variety of facilities for embedding within applications. Integers are 32 bits and identifiers can be up to 127 characters; extensive stack and heap pointer checking is available to aid in debugging. ATLAST may be configured at compilation time to include only the facilities needed by a given application, thus saving memory and increasing execution speed (when error checking is disabled).

Virtually every industry analyst agrees that open architecture is essential to the success of applications. And yet, even today, we write program after program that are closed—that the users cannot program—that admit of no extensions without our adding to the source code. If we believe intellectually, from a sound understanding of the economic incentives in the marketplace, that open systems are better, and have seen this belief confirmed repeatedly in the marketplace, then the only question that remains is, why? Why not make every program an open program?

Well, because it's HARD! Writing a closed program has traditionally been much less work at every stage of the development cycle: easier to design, less code to write, simpler documentation, and far fewer considerations in the test phase. In addition, closed products are believed to be less demanding of support, although I'll argue later that this assumption may be incorrect.

The Painful Path to Programmability

Most programs start out as nonprogrammable, closed applications and then painfully claw their way to programmability through the introduction of a limited script or macro facility, succeeded by an increasingly comprehensive interpretive macro language which grows like topsy and without a coherent design as user demands upon it grow. Finally, perhaps, the program is outfitted with bindings to existing languages like C.

An alternative to this is adopting a standard language as the macro language for a product. This approach has many attractions. First, choosing a standard language allows users to avail themselves of existing books and training resources to learn its basics. The developer of a dedicated macro language must create all this material from scratch. Second, an interpretive language, where all programs are represented in ASCII code, is inherently portable across computers and operating systems. Once the interpreter is gotten to work on a new system, all the programs it supports are pretty much guaranteed to work.

Third, most existing languages have evolved to the point that most of the rough edges have been taken off their design. Extending an existing language along the lines laid down by its designers is much less likely to result in an incomprehensible disaster than growing an ad-hoc macro language feature by neat-o feature.

Unfortunately, interpreters are slow, slow, slow. A simple calculation of the number of instructions of overhead per instruction that furthers the execution of the program quickly demonstrates that no interpreter is suitable for serious computation. As long as the interpreter is deployed in the role of a macro language, this may not be a substantial consideration. However, as soon as applications try to do substantial computation, the overhead of an interpreter becomes a crushing burden, verging on intolerable. The obvious alternative is to provide a compiled language. But that, too, has its problems.

Introducing ATLAST

ATLAST is a toolkit that makes applications programmable. Deliberately designed to be easy to integrate both into existing programs and newly developed ones, ATLAST provides any program that incorporates it most of the benefits of programmability with very little explicit effort on the part of the developer. Indeed, once you begin to "think ATLAST" as part of the design cycle, you'll probably find that the way you design and build programs changes substantially. I'm coming to think of ATLAST as the "monster that feeds on programs," because including it in a program tends to shrink the amount of special-purpose code that would otherwise have to be written, while resulting in finished applications that are open, extensible, and more easily adapted to other operating environments such as the event-driven paradigm.

The idea of a portable toolkit, integrated into a wide variety of products, all of which thereby share a common programming language, seems obvious once you consider its advantages. It's surprising that such packages aren't commonplace in the industry. In fact, the only true antecedent to ATLAST that John Walker says he's encountered in his whole twisted path through this industry was the universal macro package developed in the mid-1970s by Kern Sibbald and Ben Cranston at the University of Maryland. That package, implemented on Univac mainframes, provided a common macro language shared by a wide variety of University of Maryland utilities, including a text editor, debugger, file dumper, and typesetting language. While ATLAST is entirely different in structure and operation from the Maryland package, which was an interpretive string language, the concept of a cross-product macro language and appreciation of the benefits to be had from such a package are directly traceable to those roots.

Summary and Conclusions

Everything should be programmable. Everything! John Walker has come to the conclusion that to write almost any program in a closed manner is a mistake that invites the expenditure of uncounted hours "enhancing" it over its life cycle. Further tweaks, "features," and "fixes" often result in a product so massive and incomprehensible that it becomes unlearnable, unmaintainable, and eventually unusable.

Far better to invest the effort up front to create a product flexible enough to be adapted at will to users' immediate needs. If the product is programmable in a portable, open form, user extensions can be exchanged, compared, reviewed by the product developer, and eventually incorporated into the mainstream of the product.

It is far, far better to have thousands of creative users expanding the scope of one's product in ways the original developers didn't anticipate. In fact, working for the vendor without pay is better than having thousands of frustrated users writing up wish list requests that the vendor can comply with only by hiring people and paying them to try to accommodate the perceived needs of the users. Open architecture and programmability not only benefit the user and make a product better in the technical and marketing sense, but confers a direct economic advantage upon the vendor of such a product—one mirrored in a commensurate disadvantage to the vendor of a closed product.

The chief argument against programmability has been the extra investment needed to create open products. ATLAST provides a way of building open products in the same, or less, time than it takes to construct closed ones. Just as no C programmer in his or her right mind would sit down and write his or her own buffered file I/O package (when a perfectly fine one was sitting in the library), why reinvent a macro language or other parameterization and programming facility (when there's one just sitting there that's as fast as native C code) for all but the most absurd misapplications? After all, it only takes less than 51K. Also, with every gew-gaw and optional feature at its command enabled all at once, it is portable to any machine that supports C by simply recompiling a single file. It can also be integrated into a typical application at a basic level in less than 15 minutes.

Is John Walker proposing that every application suddenly look like FORTH? Of course not; no more than output from PostScript printers looks like PostScript, or applications that run on 80386 processors resemble 80386 assembly language. ATLAST is an intermediate language, seen only by those engaged in implementing and extending the product. Even then, ATLAST is a chameleon which, with properly defined words, can look like almost anything you like, even at the primitive level of the interpreter.

Again and again, Walker states that he has been faced with design situations where he knew that he really needed programmability but didn't have the time, the memory, or the fortitude to face the problem squarely and solve it the right way. Instead, according to Walker, he feels he ended up creating a kludge that continued to burden him through time. This is just a higher-level manifestation of the nightmares perpetrated by old-time programmers who didn't have access to a proper dynamic memory allocator or linked list package. Just because programmability is the magic smoke of computing doesn't mean we should be spooked by the ghost in the machine or hesitant to confer its power upon our customers.

Don't think of ATLAST as FORTH. Don't think of it as a language at all. The best way to think of ATLAST is as a library routine that gives you "programmability," in the same sense other libraries provide file access, window management, or graphics facilities. The whole concept of "programmability in a can" is odd—according to Walker, it took him two years from the time he first thought about it until he really got his end effector around it and crushed it into submission.

Open is better. ATLAST lets you build open programs in less time than you used to spend writing closed ones. Programs that inherit their open architecture from ATLAST will share, across the entire product line and among all hardware platforms that support it, a common, clean, and efficient means of user extensibility. The potential benefits of this are immense.[29]

Again, this part of the chapter is only intended as an example of how such an interface (VRML scripting language plug-in architecture) could be done. Only specific examples are provided for the Windows platform. Don't confuse these VRML Language plug-ins with NETSCAPE plug-ins!! The functionality is very similar but these plug-ins are plugged directly into the VRML browser, regardless of whether the browser itself is running as a NETSCAPE plug-in or not!

The Appearance of a Script Node

The following example is the appearance of a Script node:

```
Script {
        exposedField MFString url                [ ]
        field         SFBool    directOutputs FALSE
        field         SFBool    mustEvaluate  FALSE
        # And any number of:
        eventIn       eventTypeName eventName
        field         fieldTypeName fieldName initialValue
        eventOut      eventTypeName eventName
}[30]
```

The node consists of a set of fields, eventIns, eventOuts and a url for the script to be executed. For our purposes we concentrate on the events and the url.

Finding the Interpreter/Run-Time Environment: Scripts languageId

When the VRML browser encounters a script node, it looks at the URL and tries to extract information from it. First of all, if the protocol supports MIME-types (such as http:// transfers), the mimetype is used. Second, if the protocol doesn't support MIME-types but is a file-access protocol (such as file:// at local hard disk access, or other MIME-less file transports such as FTP), the extension is used. Finally, if the protocol isn't a file transport protocol, the protocol name itself is used (to support inline protocols such as SGI's proposed vrmlscript:// protocol or the data:// protocol).

Language Plug-In Directory

The directory from which to load the language plug-ins must be established. The following search method is used: First, if a VRMLPLUG-INS environment variable or .INI-file setting exists, the plug-ins are loaded from the directory or directories specified in that variable. Second, if the variable is missing or the plug-in is not found, search the PLUG-IN subdirectory under the VRML browser itself.

Finding the Path

The path(s) found in the previous step is searched for files named *.vrp. (Virtual Reality Plug-in). For example: Under Windows, these are 32-bit DLL files with a .vrp extension.

Each .vrp file is loaded (if not already loaded and known, of course!) and the first function in the file is called:

```
int VPCanHandle( char *languageId ); // Ordinal #0
```

For example, under Windows this is accomplished by calling the function with a fixed ordinal.

The function is then passed one parameter, the languageId as found in the earlier step. For example, if it was a MIME-type, the type is passed as a string("language/javabc"). Second, if it was an extension, the extension including period is passed (".lsp"). Finally, if it was a protocol, the protocol including colon is passed ("javascript:"). In other words, by including the period or the colon the module can determine what is being passed.

The function being called simply returns 0 (can't handle this language) or 1 (can handle it). If it passes 1, the search ends. If no appropriate plug-in is found, an error message is displayed, and the user is, if possible, routed to an appropriate resource to download the correct plug-in.

Running Scripts: Initializing the Plug-In

When the plug-in has been loaded and it's time to execute the script, the function VPInitInstance is called by the VRML Browser:

```
void *VPInitInstance(char *URL, struct browserCallback *cbks);
// Ordinal #1
```

Two parameters are given by the VRML Browser to the plug-in. The first parameter URL is a pointer to the (full) URL as seen in the url field in the Script node. This way, an inline protocol (such as "javascript:" or similar) can choose to make a local copy of the string, compile it into an internal bytecode, or whatever. If it's a file-URL of some kind, it's time to go fetch that file now (or set up another thread to fetch it, or whatever).

The second parameter is a pointer to a struct browserCallback which is a struct containing function pointers for calling back into the VRML browser from the plug-in. This struct is described next.

The VPInitInstance function must also set up one "context" for this process to run in. Remember, the same language plug-in can be called from many Script nodes in one file. Each of these instances need to keep their data separate.

The handle or pointer to this "local data" is then returned by VPinitInstance. If there is an error, VPInitInstance returns NULL, and the browser must take appropriate action. This pointer is kept by the VRML browser and passed in all subsequent calls from the VRML Browser to the language plug-in.

Language Plug-In Functions

The browser callback struct contains the functions the language plug-in is allowed to call back into the browser. For example:

```
struct browserCallback {
        int    (*getStringNumeral)(char *string);
// Get a string numeral
        int    (*sendEvent)(int numeral, void *arguments);
// Send an event
        void *(*callFunction)(int numeral, void *arguments);
// Call a browser function
        .
        . ?? more ??
        .
    };31
```

The available functions are:

```
int getStringNumeral (char *string)
```

The preceding function enumerates all string expressions that would otherwise need to be passed over the interface into an integer representation. This can be used in many ways, depending on what kind of language is being implemented:

♦ A "load time" (semi) compiling language can enumerate strings directly into its bytecode representation.
♦ A compiled language (C, Java) can explicitly use this function in its code.
♦ An interpreted language can keep a hash table of strings mapped to numerals.

Numerals are used for node names, field names, function names for browser callbacks, etc. Numerals are *not* used for actual string processing operations. For example:

```
int sendEvent (int numeral, void *data)
```

The preceding function sends an event (specified in the eventOut of the Script node). The name of the event is given as a numeral, "data" is a pointer to the data in the appropriate format (as declared in the Script node). For example:

```
void *callFunction (int numeral, void *data)
```

The preceding function calls a browser function.

Enumeration

Enumeration may, for efficiency's sake, need to go both ways. The browser calls this function:

```
void *VPFunctionHandle(void *instance, char *name) // Ordinal #2
```

The first time the VRML browser is about to call a script it will need to know the handles of the functions and event-handlers in that script as provided by the plug-in. Furthermore, a handle can be anything (represented here as a void pointer), simply something that uniquely identifies a given event/function name and that your plug-in can understand and know how to call the correct piece of the script.

You may want to have direct function pointers, you may want to have an index into an array of functions, or you might simply want to remember the string (strdup() it into the handle!). The VPFunctionHandle, on the other hand will be called once for each name the browser needs to resolve in that instance (Script node). The actual calls will be used using that handle, not the string. If the event doesn't exist in the script, NULL is returned, and the Browser must report an error.

Called from the Script Node

The only way to be called from the Script node is when an event arrives, thus the name of the function. For example:

```
void VPEventIn(void *instance, void *functionHandle, int
dataType, void *data) // Ordinal #3
```

The event handler is called with the instance identifier; the functionHandle as established earlier (which exact meaning is defined by your VRML plug-in); and, the data member points to the event data. The type declared in the Script node is passed in "type."

Standard Java Bindings of the VRML Scripting API

This part of the chapter looks at Dimension X's proposal for the standard Java bindings of the VRML API. In order to get a different perspective on the VRML 2.0/97 specifications, their proposal addresses some of the most serious shortcomings of the bindings described in the Java Reference appendix of the specification discussed in Chapter 12, *Virtual Reality Modeling Language (VRML) Specifications*. The most serious of these shortcomings concerns the interface—which is impossible to implement for a VRML browser written completely in Java.

The Java VRML API bindings that Dimension X is proposing as a standard are based on the Java and External API appendices. The

Moving Worlds spec is located at http://vrml.sgi.com/moving-worlds/, with the Java section of the spec at http://vrml.sgi.com/moving-worlds/spec/part1/java.html.

The changes Dimension X is suggesting are designed to make the Java VRML API fulfill some essential requirements:

♦ Implementation in any language should not be precluded.
♦ It must be memory efficient.
♦ It must be well-defined and syntactically correct.
♦ It should be sufficiently general to support advanced implementations of VRML. [32]

Summary of Changes

The following is a summary of the changes Dimension X is proposing. Reasons for the changes are also included.

Scheme for Handling eventIns in Scripts

The current Java VRML API proposal specifies the scheme for handling eventIns in Script nodes. According to this scheme, a different method of a Script subclass is called for every eventIn defined for a script, and the name of this method is based on the name of the eventIn. However, in Java, there is no means to construct a method name at run time and call it. This event-handling technique for scripts only works if you are calling into the Java VM from C or some other low-level language, and is unable to be implemented by a completely Java-based VRML browser.

In Dimension X's proposal, when a Script node receives an eventIn, its handleEvent method is called. The specific eventIn is passed as a parameter.

The Browser Class Is Non-Static

It's conceivable that multiple VRML browsers will be running in the same Java VM, or that multiple independent scenes will be simultaneously displayed within a browser. To support this, Dimension X renamed the Browser class to Scene (since it really represents a particular scene and not a browser) and made the methods non-static. A script node can call getScene() to determine which scene and browser "own" it.

Class Hierarchy Changes

Node and eventIn have been changed from an interface to a class. The eventIns are now logically represented using eventIn objects, rather than overloading the Field class. Formerly, eventIns were representing using Fields, but the value of such fields was undefined. Similarly, eventOuts are represented using the new eventOut class.

The package vrml.node has been removed and Node and Script are both in the package vrml. Field and ConstField have similarly been moved from the vrml.field package into the vrml package (although the various field subclasses are still in vrml.field). Dimension X feels that related basic functionality should be grouped together in the same class. Script now inherits from Node, since a Script is a kind of Node.

All of the multiple-valued field types (MFString) have new common superclasses MField or ConstMField. These in turn inherit from Field and ConstField, respectively.

The Exceptions

None of the field accessor methods declare that they throw an ArrayIndexOutOfBounds-Exception, since it is a RuntimeException. Also, there are no methods in the Script class which throw java.lang.Exception, and there is no need in Java to make such a declaration.

All of the exceptions in the vrml package except for VRMLSyntax-Exception have been changed to extend RuntimeException (or more specifically, IllegalArgumentException) instead of Exception since they can only be thrown as a result of a programmer error.

Subclassing them from Exception requires that all uses of the methods have try/catch clauses around them, which is inconvenient and unnecessary.

InvalidVRMLException is renamed to VRMLSyntaxException to distinguish it from the other exceptions, which are RuntimeExceptions. Also, a new exception InvalidFieldChangeException exists. This may be thrown as a result of all sorts of illegal field changes, for example:

- Adding a node from one Scene as the child of a node in another Scene.
- Creating a circularity in a scene graph.
- Setting an invalid string on enumerated fields, such as the fogType field of the Fog node.

It is not guaranteed that such exceptions will be thrown but a browser should do the best job it can. In addition, new Runtime-Exceptions, InvalidNodeTypeExceptions, and InvalidNavigation-TypeExceptions are declared.

Field Class Methods

The *getValue* and *setValue* methods for the field classes are designed to require as little memory allocation as possible. In particular, the getValue methods are passed arrays and write into the arrays, rather than returning arrays as in the existing spec. When returning arrays, if the arrays are freshly allocated each time, memory inefficiency results; if not, a security problem is introduced because the script could modify the arrays and thus interfere with other scripts or even damage the internals of the browser.

The *insertValue, addValue, deleteValue*, and *size* methods are present in all of the multivalued field classes. Currently, most of the multivalued fields have only a *setValue* method for the entire set of values. Also, for the convenience of the programmer, all *set/get* methods on fields are overloaded and take many different kinds of parameters, minimizing the need to manually convert between different parameter representations.

Other Various Changes

A *create* method is added onto Script nodes. The various methods on Script such as *getEventIn*, *getEventOut*, *getField*, *getExposedField*, and *getInternalField* are not guaranteed to return correct values before the call to create (in the constructor). Script nodes should put initialization code here rather than in the constructor; this allows browsers to properly initialize the objects. For a browser written in Java, it is very inconvenient to do all initialization in the constructor because no parameters can be passed in.

The New Execution Model

When a new Script object is constructed, its *create* method is invoked. The getEventIn, getEventOut, getField, getExposedField, and getInternalField are not guaranteed to return correct values before the call to create—*create()* is called exactly once during the life of a script object. The Script node should do any initialization in the create() method rather than in its constructor. In general, it should not even define its own constructor, and instead let the default no-argument constructor apply.

When a script receives an event, its handleEvent() method is called. The method is called with one parameter, an Event object. The event object has three values associated with it, which can be retrieved using methods on the Event: an eventIn (representing which eventIn was triggered), a ConstField (representing the value that was sent), and a double (the timestamp). The script can determine which eventIn was triggered by comparing the eventIn of the Event to eventIn objects previously retrieved using the Node method getEventIn(String), or simply by calling getName() on the eventIn to determine its name.

A script can also define an eventsProcessed() method, which is called with a count and an array of queued events. The default implementation of eventsProcessed() calls handleEvent() with each array entry. The browser may or may not call eventsProcessed() instead of calling handleEvent() directly. In particular, it will never do so if the Script node sets the mustEvaluate field to true, but may do so otherwise. The purpose of this method is to allow Scripts that are not particularly concerned with the exact timing of the events received to generate fewer outgoing events by processing many events at once.

Note that the arguments to handleEvent() and eventsProcessed() (in particular, the Event objects, the ConstField object returned from the getValue() method on the Event class, and the array of Events passed to eventsProcessed()) may be reused after the call to handleEvent() returns. Thus, any Script that wants to hang on to any of these objects after the call to handleEvent() or eventsProcessed() returns must make a copy using the provided clone() methods on Event and ConstField. This is done to avoid having to newly allocate memory each time an event is received or sent.

If the directOutput field of a Script node is false, a browser may throw an exception if the Script attempts to do some illegal operation such as establishing a new route. However, such behavior is not guaranteed. For example:

```
Script {
    url "Example.class"
    eventIn    SFBool start
    eventOut   SFBool on
    field      SFBool state TRUE
}

// Java implementation
import vrml.*;
import vrml.field.*;

public class Example extends Script
{
    private SFBool state;
    private EventIn start;
    private EventOut on;
```

```
    public void create()
    {
        state = (SFBool) getInternalField("state");
        start = getEventIn("start");
        on = getEventOut("on");
    }

    public void handleEvent(Event e)
    {
        if (e.getEventIn() == start)
        {
            postEvent(on, e.getValue());
            state.setValue((ConstSFBool) e.getValue());
        }
    }
}33
```

Another example:

```
DEF ImANode Transform {}
Script {
    field SFNode node USE ImANode
    eventIn SFVec3f pos
    url "Example2.class"
}

import vrml.*;
import vrml.field.*;

public class Example2 extends Script
{
    private SFNode node;
    private EventIn pos;

    public void create()
    {
        pos = getEventIn("pos");
```

```
        node = (SFNode) getInternalField("node");
    }

    public void handleEvent(Event e)
    {
        if (e.getEventIn() == pos)
        {
            SFVec3f translation =
                (SFVec3f) node.getValue().getExposedField("transla-
tion");
            translation.setValue((ConstSFVec3f) e.getValue());
        }
    }
}34
```

Class Hierarchy Division

The classes are divided into two packages: *vrml* and *vrml.field*. *vrml.field* contains the implementations of fields and constant fields. All the other classes are in *vrml*. Note that the base classes of the fields are in *vrml* not *vrml.field*. For example:

```
java.lang.Object
        vrml.Node
                vrml.Script
        vrml.Event
        vrml.EventIn
        vrml.EventOut
        vrml.Browser
        vrml.Field
                vrml.field.SFBool
                vrml.field.SFColor
                vrml.field.SFFloat
                vrml.field.SFImage
                vrml.field.SFInt32
                vrml.field.SFNode
                vrml.field.SFRotation
                vrml.field.SFString
```

```
                        vrml.field.SFTime
                        vrml.field.SFVec2f
                        vrml.field.SFVec2f
                        vrml.MField
                                vrml.field.MFColor
                                vrml.field.MFFloat
                                vrml.field.MFInt32
                                vrml.field.MFNode
                                vrml.field.MFRotation
                                vrml.field.MFString
                                vrml.field.MFTime
                                vrml.field.MFVec2f
                                vrml.field.MFVec2f
                        vrml.ConstField
                                vrml.field.ConstSFBool
                                vrml.field.ConstSFColor
                                vrml.field.ConstSFFloat
                                vrml.field.ConstSFImage
                                vrml.field.ConstSFInt32
                                vrml.field.ConstSFNode
                                vrml.field.ConstSFRotation
                                vrml.field.ConstSFString
                                vrml.field.ConstSFTime
                                vrml.field.ConstSFVec2f
                                vrml.field.ConstSFVec2f
                                vrml.ConstMField
                                        vrml.field.ConstMFColor
                                        vrml.field.ConstMFFloat
                                        vrml.field.ConstMFInt32
                                        vrml.field.ConstMFNode
                                        vrml.field.ConstMFRotation
                                        vrml.field.ConstMFString
                                        vrml.field.ConstMFTime
                                        vrml.field.ConstMFVec2f
                                        vrml.field.ConstMFVec2f
java.lang.Exception
        java.lang.RuntimeException
                vrml.InvalidRouteException
                vrml.InvalidFieldException
```

```
vrml.InvalidEventInException
vrml.InvalidEventOutException
vrml.InvalidExposedFieldException
vrml.InvalidNavigationTypeException
vrml.InvalidNodeTypeException
vrml.InvalidFieldChangeException
vrml.VRMLSyntaxException
```
[35]

Pros and Cons of VRMLScript

Finally, this part of the chapter looks at the pros and cons of VRMLScript. It attempts to dispel a few misconceptions, clarify a few concepts, and make a few lists of advantages and disadvantages.

Misconceptions

The use of Java for scripting in VRML would mean including Java source or bytecode within script nodes: FALSE. Java source would never reach the client computer, and bytecode would be referred to by URL, just like a texture or inline.

On the other hand, this could be TRUE, with some efforts. Including Java source means the browser needs to compile it. Suppose a browser is distributed with Sun's JDK, the browser can folk the compiler of Java. Including bytecode is far more easy. Although it is not text, you can encode using uuencode (for instance). [36]

For reasons that have been discussed before, there's a belief in the VRML community that the inclusion of Java source code is highly inadvisable. Most go along with it anyway—especially with respect to binary files with one addition: insert "necessarily" between "would" and "mean." There are two circumstances when the inclusion of Java bytecode in the VRML file makes excellent sense:

The first is in a file inclusion, perhaps along the lines of the data:
URL. This should also be encoded, so technically speaking, the file
is still text.

The second is in the binary form of the VRML file. Here, there
doesn't seem to be any objection whatsoever to including the bytecode directly. And, there are a great many good things about doing
that: chiefly speed and, as a weak second, verifiability (one
assumes that undetected errors in the encoded binaries are infre-
quent). [37]

The source code for the JavaVM would be required to write a
browser which supports scripting in Java: FALSE. There is talk of
a JavaVM DLL coming from Sun, there is talk (and even some
action) to include Java binary support within most OS platforms
(OS/2, MacOS, Win95/NT, Unix), but Sony came up with the simplest solution in their CyberPassage; the browser is mostly native
code, but it is native code called from a Java class and the whole
thing runs under the JavaVM that is freely available and distributed with the Java Development Kit.

There was never a clearly defined or required external or internal
API as a part of Moving Worlds: TRUE. There were two sample
(read: plausible) external APIs (for C and Java) included as appendices but they were only reference material, not part of the proposal.

However, that is not entirely accurate. The appendices describe
internal scripting language bindings to be used by the Script node
(not "external APIs"). It is now obvious that the spec is not clear
enough on this topic since so many people have made a similar
interpretation. Now let's look at the concepts.

Concepts

People have been using the term "External API" to mean a number of things, but they can all be classified as *explicit* or *implicit*
interprocess communication. The ideas are: a network socket or

sockets a browser listens to and to which scripts can send commands to change the scene; an object code library (C/C++/Fortran/Tcl/whatever can link to it) that takes care of the nitty-gritty of IPC for the programmer; and a Java class library (package) of classes which take care of the nitty-gritty of IPC for the programmer.

Not to say that these are in any sense mutually exclusive. One could, for example, have sockets within the object code library or class library. The most significant part of preparing a VRML browser for a given platform is the implemention of this API. And (further quibble) the scene need not change as a result of the operation of the External API, but the state of a node within the scene or related to the scene may change.[38]

People have been using the term "Internal API" to mean a number of things, but they can all be classified as a set of "function calls" that can be used in Java or JavaScript or VRMLScript or whatever the browser may support internally, interpreting these "calls" as commands to modify the scene. In fact, this has been referred to as the "Browser Interface" in both the old Moving Worlds' spec and the new. Call it what you like.[39]

The VRMLScript that Gavin Bell (of SGI) is proposing has begun as a strict subset of JavaScript in the sense of reverse-engineering. The language has been created to follow the syntax and semantics as closely as can be gleaned from JavaScript documentation and behavior. It is to be an interpreted language included in plain text (not a URL) in Script nodes calling an Internal API to modify the scene. There is debate over whether a BNF, a YACC specification, or even a full-fledged parser will be provided by the proponents. Now let's look at the pros and cons.

Pros and Cons

The three viable scripting concepts are: first, communication with arbitrary scripts, on the client system or otherwise, through network sockets using something like a binary command language to alter the scene and receive events. In other words, the thrust of proposal (1) is the "binary command language," not the network sockets. Of course, a key benefit of standardizing such a "command language" is that we can then turn around and pump this byte-stream across a variety of universal communication mechanisms, such as (a) network sockets, (b) C streams or pipes, (c) memory buffers. Depending on how "binary" we go, the overhead of version (c) might be no more than a few memcpys.[40]

Java bytecode support can be either internal to the browser, or running in a separate browser process, or even running in the same VM as the browser itself (CyberPassage), where scripts can subclass a standard class or classes to alter the scene and receive events by having methods called with events. Java-/VRMLScript support, on the other hand, is where the browser interprets scripts which can alter the scene through an internal API of "function calls" and receive events by being called.

So what about the more generic idea of standardizing a "foreign function interface"? In other words, a generic C API for language interpreters that would allow "function calls" to be made across language barriers. An example is Netscape's JRI (Java Runtime Interface—but it's not as Java-specific as the name would imply).[41]

There are advantages and disadvantages to each of these. Table 3.5 clearly shows the pros and cons of all of these scripting concepts. In the end, the decision is really yours.

Table 3.5 Advantages and Disadvantages of Scripting Concepts[42]

	Advantages	Disadvantages
Network Sockets	Requires no language support (with the exception of the command API). Allows distributed computing. Includes/provides networking (e.g., for	May have nasty overhead for socket communication from a machine to itself. Provides no platform independence for client-side script execution. Provides no execution

Continued

Table 3.5 Continued.

	Advantages	Disadvantages
	multiuser environments). Scripts are likely to be native (compiled code), thus run quickly. Gives the programmer access to all resources on the machine running the script (e.g., network, threads, databases, etc.). Code can be written in language with network any support, so nearly everyone should be able to use it.	security for client-side script execution. Poorly defined, as yet, exactly how the communication will take place and how or whether scripts will be fetched or told to execute. Network latency may be a problem. Requires use of low-level socket interface (steep learning curve).
		Requires packet sniffing, binary translation, and/or stack tracing to debug.
Java Bytecode	Threads and networking are built in, including URL fetching. Easily reusable code. Platform-independent client-side execution with security. Strong typing, decent debugger, and object-oriented paradigm make debugging as easy as possible. Executes faster than an interpreted (ASCII) language. Large base of programmers, class libraries, and development environments. Freely available VM implementations (DLL and OS support soon, JDK JavaVM available now).	Slower than native code. Requires overhead of the JavaVM for even tiny scripts. Steep learning curve for those not familiar with programming, specifically OOP. It may be difficult to extend the API later. Bytecode must be shipped over the network. Bytecode must be maintained and compiled separately from the VRML.

Table 3.5 Continued.

	Advantages	Disadvantages
	Has a reference implementation (CyberPassage). Source could possibly be generated by VRML editors to perform simple scripting tasks. Bytecode can be compiled from languages other than Java (Ada, etc.). Gives the programmer access to windowing and dialog services for further user interaction.	
VRMLScript	Simple, easy to learn. Small scripts can be executed quickly. Minimally difficult to implement, and a free parser may be provided. Similar to JavaScript, which has an installed base of programmers. Executes within the browser process (no extra processes or overhead). Code is encapsulated in the VRML file.	No network or thread support (no multiuser). Is interpreted, thus scripts must be fairly simple. May be too simple to script interesting behaviors or to execute quickly enough. Typeless and lacks its own process or stack, thus difficult to debug. No local variables. If VRMLScript is defined to be a subset of JavaScript, then VRMLScript should follow any changes made to JavaScript, otherwise they can easily be separate languages. If you allow them to be separate languages then, contrary to what Gavin said to Rodger, we try to define a new language.

From Here

This chapter has thoroughly described the ins and outs of VRMLScript, the required scripting language for VRML 2.0. The next chapter briefly examines OpenGL: the high-performance tool for the 3-D graphics applications.

Endnotes

1 *The Moving Worlds VRML 2.0 Specification: VRMLScript Reference*, Silicon Graphics, Inc., 2011 North Shoreline Blvd., Mountain View, CA 94039.

2 Ibid.

3 Ibid.

4 Ibid.

5 Ibid.

6 Ibid.

7 Ibid.

8 Ibid.

9 Ibid.

10 Chris Marrin and Jim Kent, "Proposal for a VRML Script Node Authoring Interface: VRMLScript Reference," Silicon Graphics, Inc., 2011 North Shoreline Blvd., Mountain View, CA 94039.

11 Ibid.

12 Ibid.

13 Ibid.

14 Ibid.

15 Ibid.

16 Ibid.

17 Ibid.

18 Ibid.

19 Ibid.

20 Ibid.

21 Ibid.

22 Ibid.

23 Ibid.

24 Håkan "Zap" Andersson, "VRML Scripting Language Plug-in Proposal," St Almby, Hagby, S-635 05 Eskilstuna, Sweden, 1997.

25 Ibid.

26 Ibid.

27 Ibid.

28 Ibid.

29 John Walker, "Autodesk Threaded Language Application System Toolkit," kelvin @ fourmilab . ch, 1997.

30 Håkan "Zap" Andersson, "VRML Scripting Language Plug-in Proposal," St Almby, Hagby, S-635 05 Eskilstuna, Sweden, 1997.

31 Ibid.

32 Chris Laurel and Ben Wing, "VRML Scripting Interface for Java," Dimension X, 181 Fremont St., Suite 120, San Francisco, CA 94105.

33 Ibid.

34 Ibid.

35 Ibid.

36 Yasuaki Honda, "Scripting Concepts: Pros and Cons," Sony, 1997.

37 Bob Crispen, "Scripting Concepts: Pros and Cons," Boeing, 1997.

38 Ibid.

39 Ibid.

40 Paul Burchard, "Scripting Concepts: Pros and Cons," Princeton University, 1997.

41 Ibid.

42 National Institute of Standards and Technology (NIST), 1997.

4

The OpenGL Graphics System

The concept of bringing 3-D environments to the Web is not new; however, before these environments can be brought over by VRML 2.0 or VRML97 they have to be developed. This is where OpenGL comes into play.

OpenGL, the high-performance tool from Silicon Graphics Computer Systems, is the premier environment for developing 3-D graphics applications. The OpenGL application programming interface (API) is a vendor-neutral, multiplatform industry standard. Licensees of OpenGL support the API on a range of computers: from PCs to workstations to all types of computers. Porting OpenGL applications among conforming OpenGL implementations is simple and easy.

Leading PC, workstation, and supercomputer vendors (including 3-Dlabs, AccelGraphics, AT&T, Cirrus Logic, Cray Research,

Daikin, Digital Equipment, Evans & Sutherland, Harris Computer, Hitachi, IBM, Intel, Intergraph, Japan Radio Company, MediaVision, Microsoft, NEC, NeTpowerm, Samsung, Sony, and Silicon Graphics) are committed to OpenGL as a strategic open standard for high-performance 3-D graphics. Third-party solutions for Apple, Hewlett-Packard, and Sun products are available from several companies, including Portable Graphics and Template Graphics Software.

OpenGL is the direct descendant of IRIS Graphics Library invented in 1982. More than 3000 applications are currently written with IRIS GL. OpenGL inherits that legacy of experience in applications development. It preserves all critical rendering functionality from IRIS GL. The OpenGL applications are, and will be, ported from IRIS GL, and new applications will be written directly with OpenGL.

Features/Application Portability

OpenGL provides a wide range of graphics abilities, from rendering a simple geometric point, line, or filled polygon to the most sophisticated lighted and texture-mapped NURBS curved surface, as shown in Figure 4.1. The more than 250 routines of OpenGL give software developers access to the following capabilities:

- ◆ geometric and raster primitives
- ◆ RGBA or color index mode
- ◆ display list or immediate mode
- ◆ viewing and modeling transformations
- ◆ lighting and shading
- ◆ hidden surface removal (depth buffer)
- ◆ alpha blending (translucency)
- ◆ anti-aliasing
- ◆ texture mapping
- ◆ atmospheric effects (fog, smoke, haze)
- ◆ feedback and selection
- ◆ stencil planes
- ◆ accumulation buffer[1]

Figure 4.1 Texture maps and shadows.

These functions are provided on every conforming OpenGL implementation to make applications (written with OpenGL) easily portable among platforms. All licensed OpenGL implementations are required to pass conformance tests and come from a single specification and language-binding document.

Architecture

The OpenGL state machine is a good model for representing graphics problems. Figure 4.2[2] provides a high-level block diagram of how OpenGL processes data. Command enter from the left and proceed through what can be thought of as a processing pipeline. Some commands specify geometric objects to be drawn, and others control how the objects are handled. All elements of the OpenGL state, even the contents of the texture memory and the frame buffer, can be obtained by an OpenGL application.

If you want to draw a 3-D model consisting of lighted, smooth shaded polygons, for example, turn on the lighting state and set your values for the material properties. Turn on the smooth shading. Set your viewing transformation. For each polygon, declare a current surface normal to define its orientation. Now that you've established the current state, issue the vertices that comprise each polygon. The OpenGL state machine will process and render those polygons into the frame buffer.

In subsequent renderings you can further enhance your model. Turn on the depth buffer and remove hidden surfaces, or even add fog or apply a texture map to your model.

Integration

The model for interpreting OpenGL commands is the client-server process, as shown in Figure 4.3.[3] A client application issues com-

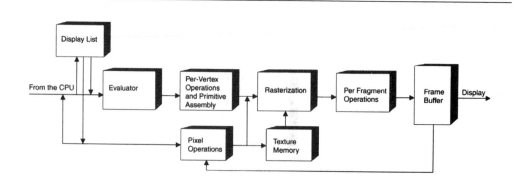

Figure 4.2 OpenGL diagram.

mands, which are interpreted and processed by an OpenGL server. The server and client may operate on different machines; thus OpenGL is network transparent. If it is not going over a network, the client-server communication can be replaced by local rendering, which may be faster.

OpenGL is hardware, window, and operating system independent, as shown in Figure 4.4.[4] On one implementation OpenGL may run with the X Window System and Unix. On another implementation OpenGL may run with Microsoft Windows, MS DOS, Microsoft Windows NT, Solaris, HP-UX, and IBM. OpenGL is compatible with other APIs, such as Xlib, OSF/Motif, IRIS Open Inventor, Image Vision, and IRIS Performer. OpenGL is callable from C, C++, FORTRAN, and Ada.

OpenGL News

Updated information about OpenGL is readily available on line. You can get source code examples, documentation, and news about product availability. Just browse the OpenGL homepage on the World Wide Web (http://www.sgi.com/Technology/openGL/opengl.html).

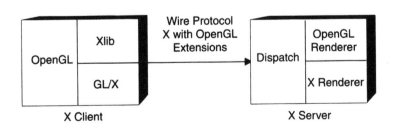

Figure 4.3 Integration.

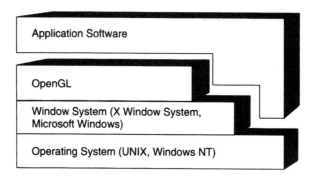

Figure 4.4 Extensibility of OpenGL.

From Here

Chapter 5 continues this theme of OpenGL with a brief but detailed overview of Open Inventor, the object-oriented 3-D graphics programming tool—a virtual must in the VRML 2.0 or VRML97 environment. A further discussion of Open Inventor can be found in Chapter 11.

Endnotes

1 Silicon Graphics Computer Systems, Corporate Office, 2011 N. Shoreline Boulevard, Mountain View, CA 94043.

2 Ibid.

3 Ibid.

4 Ibid.

5

Open Inventor Object-Oriented 3-D Toolkit and VRML

Open Inventor has taken many programmers years to design and implement and is a fairly large, very general system. VRML 2.0 or VRML97 must be much smaller to become a success; otherwise, implementations will either be incompatible or will take too long to produce. Therefore only the most commonly used subset of Open Inventor is proposed here as the basis for VRML.

The Open Inventor group at Silicon Graphics is committed to separating the ASCII file-reading code from the rest of the Open Inventor library, repackaging it, and putting it in the public domain as the start of a VRML toolkit to make implementing VRML easier. The file reader will be C++ code that produces a hierarchical structure of C++ classes. A VRML implementor would need to define appropriate render methods for these classes to implement rendering—a pick method to implement picking, etc.—or, alternatively, traverse these classes and create a completely different internal representation for the scene.

Object-Oriented File Format

At the highest level of abstraction, the Open Inventor file format is just a way for objects to read and write themselves. Theoretically the objects can contain anything—3-D geometry, MIDI data, JPEG images, anything. Open Inventor defines a set of objects useful for doing 3-D graphics. These objects are called *nodes*.

Scene Graphs

Nodes are arranged in hierarchical structures called *scene graphs*, as shown in Figure 5.1. Scene graphs are more than just a collection of nodes; a scene graph defines an ordering for the nodes. The Open Inventor scene graph has a notion of state: Nodes earlier in the scene can affect nodes that appear later in the scene. For example, a Rotation or Material node will affect the nodes after it in the scene. A mechanism is defined to limit the effects of properties (Separator nodes), allowing parts of a scene graph to be functionally isolated from other parts.

This notion of order in the scene graph may be the most controversial feature of Open Inventor. Most other systems attempt to attach properties to objects, with the properties affecting only that one object. In fact, an early prototype of Open Inventor was written that way. However, treating properties differently from geometry resulted in several problems. First, if a shape has several properties associated with it, you must still define an order in which the properties are applied. Second, some objects, such as lights and cameras, act as both shapes (things that have a position in the world) and properties (things that affect the way other

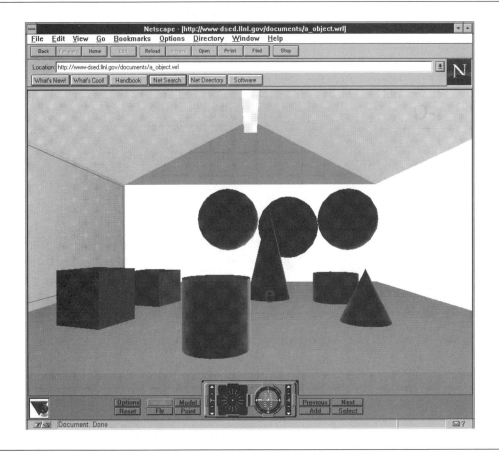

Figure 5.1 Scene graphs.

things look). Getting rid of the distinction between shapes and properties simplified both the implementation and the use of the library.

Node Contents

A node can be characterized by what kind of object it is. A node might be a cube, a sphere, a texture map, a transformation, etc.

Further, parameters distinguish this node from other nodes of the same type. For example, each Sphere node might have a different radius, and different texture map nodes will certainly contain different images to use as the texture maps, as shown in Figure 5.2. These parameters are called fields. A node can have zero or more fields.

Being able to name nodes and to refer to them elsewhere is very powerful. It allows a scene's author to give hints to applications using the scene about what is in the scene and creates possibilities

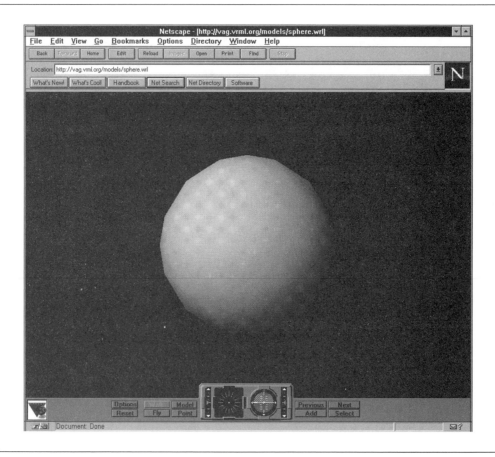

Figure 5.2 Sphere node.

for very powerful scripting extensions. Nodes do not have to be named, but if they are named, they have only one name.

Object hierarchy is implemented by allowing nodes to contain other nodes. Parent nodes traverse their children in order during rendering. Nodes that may have children are referred to as *group nodes*. Group nodes can have zero or more children.

The syntax chosen to represent these pieces of information is straightforward:

```
DEF objectname objecttype { fields children }
```

Only the objecttype and braces are required. Nodes may or may not have a name, fields, and children. The following sections describe the types of objects that should be the basis of VRML and describe details of this basic syntax.

IndexedFaceSet

Open Inventor has eight ways of specifying a polygonal shape or surface (FaceSet, IndexedFaceSet, QuadMesh, TriangleStripSet, IndexedTriangleStripSet, NurbsSurface, IndexedNurbsSurface, and Text3). To ease the implementation burden, it is proposed that only IndexedFaceSet be part of VRML, as shown in Figure 5.3. IndexedFaceSets can be used to represent any of the other polygonal shape types, are fairly space efficient, and are the most common type of geometry. IndexedFaceSet supports overall, per face, and per vertex materials and normals. IndexedFaceSet will automatically generate normals if the user doesn't specify them. Faces with fewer than three vertices will be ignored. Here is a simple example of two Open Inventor V2.0 ASCII IndexedFaceSets, showing some of its more advanced features (per vertex coloring, for example), as shown in Figures 5.4 and 5.5.

Each of the faces of an IndexedFaceSet is assumed to be convex by default. A ShapeHints node (see following) can be used to change this assumption to allow concave faces. However, all faces must be simple (they must not self-intersect).

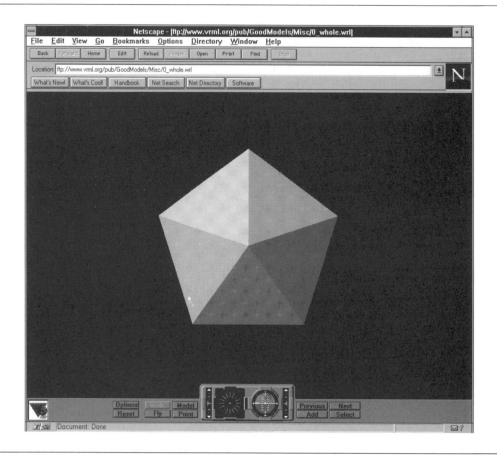

Figure 5.3 IndexedFaceSets.

If not enough normals are specified to satisfy the current normal binding, normals will be automatically generated, based on the IndexedFaceSet's geometry. If explicit texture coordinates are not specified using a TextureCoordinate2 node, default texture coordinates will be automatically generated. A simple planar projection along one of the primary axes is used, mapping the width of the texture image onto the longest dimension of the IndexedFaceSet's bounding box, with the height of the texture image going in the direction of the next-longest dimension of its bounding box.

```
#Inventor V2.0 ascii
# Two IndexedFaceSets each describing a cube.
# Normals are per polygon. The first has OVERALL material binding, and
# appears all one color.
# The second has colors indexed per vertex. This allows the colors
# to be defined in any order and then randomly accessed for each vertex.

Separator {
  Coordinate3 {
    point [      -1  1  1,   -1  -1  1,   1  -1  1,   1  1  1,
                 -1  1 -1,   -1  -1 -1,   1  -1 -1,   1  1 -1  ]
  }
  Material { diffuseColor [ 1 0 0,   0 1 0,   0 0 1,   1 1 0 ]  }# indices 0,1,2,3
  Normal {
    vector [      0.0  0.0  1.0,   1.0  0.0  0.0,      # front and right faces
                  0.0  0.0 -1.0,  -1.0  0.0  0.0,      # back and left faces
                  0.0  1.0  0.0,   0.0 -1.0  0.0  ]    # top and bottom faces
  }
  NormalBinding   { value PER_FACE_INDEXED }
  MaterialBinding { value OVERALL }
  IndexedFaceSet {
    coordIndex [ 0,  1,  2,  3, -1,   3,  2,  6,  7, -1,    # front and right faces
                 7,  6,  5,  4, -1,   4,  5,  1,  0, -1,    # back and left faces
                 0,  3,  7,  4, -1,   1,  5,  6,  2, -1 ]   # top and bottom faces
    normalIndex [ 0,  1,  2,  3,  4,   5, ]       # Apply normals to faces, in order
}
```

Figure 5.4 IndexedFaceSet describing a cube; normals are per polygon. This one has OVERALL material binding and appears all one color.

ShapeHints

The ShapeHints node gives extra information about the shapes in the scene that a renderer can use to optimize rendering, as shown in Figure 5.6. It has a faceType field that can be either CONVEX (meaning that all of the polygons in all shapes to follow are convex) or UNKNOWN_FACE_TYPE (meaning that the polygons may be either concave or convex). Its vertexOrdering field lets a renderer know whether faces are defined CLOCKWISE, COUNTERCLOCKWISE, or have an UNKNOWN_ORDERING. Its shapeType field defines whether the shape is SOLID (the faces completely enclose a volume of space) or an UNKNOWN_

```
Translation  {  translation 3  0  0  )
  MaterialBinding  { value PER_VERTEX_INDEXED  }
  IndexedFaceSet  {
    coordIndex  [ 0,   1,   2,   3,  -1,    3,  2,  6,  7, -1,   # front and right faces
                  7,   6,   5,   4,  -1,    4,  5,  1,  0, -1,   # back and left faces
                  0,   3,   7,   4,  -1,    1,  5,  6,  2, -1 ]  # top and bottom faces
    materialIndex  [ 0,   0,   1,   1,  -1,        # red/green front
                     2,   2,   3,   3,  -1,        # blue/yellow right
                     0,   0,   1,   1,  -1,        # red/green back
                     2,   2,   3,   3,  -1,        # blue/yellow left
                     0,   0,   0,   0,  -1,        # red top
                     2,   2,   2,   2,  -1 ]       # blue bottom
  }
}
```

Figure 5.5 Here colors are indexed per vertex. This allows the colors to be
defined in any order and then randomly accessed for each vertex.

SHAPE_TYPE. Open Inventor uses these hints to turn off or on
backface removal, two-sided lighting, and the tesselation of concave polygons.

ShapeHints also has a creaseAngle field used during normal generation. It is a hint to the normal generator about where sharp
creases between polygons should be created. If two faces sharing
an edge have a dihedral angle less than the creaseAngle, the normals will be smoothed across the edge; otherwise, the edge will
appear as a sharp crease.

Coordinates and Normals

Coordinate3 and Normal nodes are considered properties, like
materials or textures, as shown in Figure 5.7. Specifying coordinates and normals separately from the shape makes it much easier to extend the format to support other representations for
coordinates and normals.

If a binary format for VRML is developed, it will be worthwhile to
specify low-bandwidth alternatives to the standard Open Inventor

```
VERTEX ORDERING ENUMS
      UNKNOWN_ORDERING              Ordering of vertices is unknown
      CLOCKWISE                     Face vertices are ordered clockwise
                                       (from the outside)
      COUNTERCLOCKWISE              Face vertices are ordered counterclockwise
                                       (from the outside)

SHAPE TYPE ENUMS
      UNKNOWN_SHAPE_TYPE            Nothing is known about the shape
      SOLID                        The shape encloses a volume

FACE TYPE ENUMS
      UNKNOWN_FACE_TYPE            Nothing is known about faces
      CONVEX                       All faces are convex

FILE FORMAT/DEFAULTS
    ShapeHints   {
          vertexOrdering            UNKNOWN_ORDERING
          shapeType                 UNKNOWN_SHAPE_TYPE
          faceType                  CONVEX
          creaseAngle               0.5
    }
```

Figure 5.6 ShapeHints.

Coordinate3 and Normal nodes, which store each coordinate or normal as three floating-point numbers. Lighting is usually good enough even with byte-sized normals. A ByteNormal with normal XYZ vectors with components from (127 to 127 would save a significant amount of network bandwidth. Similarly, a ShortCoordinate3 that specified vertices in the range of (32767 to 32767 (the model would need an appropriate scale to make it reasonably sized, of course) could also save significant network bandwidth. Note that in the ASCII file format, new nodes aren't necessary; you can just limit the precision of the ASCII numbers in your scene to a few digits of accuracy. For example, instead of specifying a normal as [.7071067811865 .7071067811865 0], specify it as [.707 .707 0] to save bandwidth.

```
Coordinate3 {
    point  [ -1  1  1,    -1 -1  1,     1 -1  1,    1  1  1,
             -1  1 -1,    -1 -1 -1,     1 -1 -1,    1  1 -1  ]
  }
  Material { diffuseColor [ 1 0 0,    0 1 0,    0 0 1,    1 1 0 ]  }# indices 0,1,2,3
  Normal {
    vector  [ 0.0  0.0  1.0,    1.0  0.0  0.0,        # front and right faces
              0.0  0.0 -1.0,   -1.0  0.0  0.0,        # back and left faces
              0.0  1.0  0.0,    0.0 -1.0  0.0  ]      # top and bottom faces
  }
  NormalBinding  { value PER_FACE_INDEX }
  MaterialBinding { value OVERALL }
  IndexedFaceSet {
    coordIndex [  0,   1,   2,   3, -1,   3,   2,   6,   7, -1,    # front and right faces
                  7,   6,   5,   4, -1,   4,   5,   1,   0, -1,    # back and left faces
                  0,   3,   7,   4, -1,   1,   5,   6,   2, -1 ]   # top and bottom faces
    normalIndex [ 0,   1,   2,   3,   4,   5, ]       # Apply normals to faces, in order
  }
}
```

Figure 5.7 Coordinated and normal ModesIndexedFaceSets.

Bindings

Binding nodes (MaterialBinding and NormalBinding) specify how to apply properties to primitives. Open Inventor has eight ways of binding materials or normals to primitives. The _INDEXED bindings use the index fields in IndexedFaceSet (coordIndex, normalIndex) to index into the list of current materials or normals, as shown in the sidebar.

Specifying how materials or normals are applied to shapes allows the same set of materials (or, much less common, normals) to be used for several different shapes. For example, a program may use only a limited palette of materials that it applies to either the vertices or the faces of IndexedFaceSets. The same Material {} node may be used by all of the IndexedFaceSets, with MaterialBinding nodes switching between PER_VERTEX_INDEXED and PER_FACE_INDEXED materials.

Open Inventor has a TextureCoordinateBinding node with DEFAULT, PER_VERTEX, and PER_VERTEX_INDEXED values.

Bindings

- DEFAULT—Each shape chooses a reasonable binding. The primitive shapes and IndexedFaceSet all choose OVERALL as their default material binding; the DEFAULT normal binding for IndexedFaceSet is PER_VERTEX_INDEXED (the primitive shapes generate their own normals and ignore the normal binding).
- OVERALL—One material or normal used for the entire object.
- PER_PART, PER_PART_INDEXED—One material or normal for each part of the shape. For IndexedFaceSet, these are the same as PER_FACE and PER_FACE_INDEXED. Primitive shapes treat PER_PART_INDEXED the same as PER_PART.
- PER_FACE, PER_FACE_INDEXED—One material or normal for each face of the shape. Since primitive shapes do not have faces, they interpret these bindings the same as OVERALL.
- PER_VERTEX, PER_VERTEX_INDEXED—One material or normal for each vertex of the shape. Since primitive shapes do not have explicit vertices, they interpret these bindings the same as OVERALL.[1]

Because binding texture coordinates PER_VERTEX is very rare (PER_VERTEX_INDEXED is infinitely more common), the node should not be part of VRML.

IndexedLineSet

IndexedLineSet is just like IndexedFaceSet, only open line segments are drawn instead of polygons. For example, Figure 5.8 shows this as two line segments: The first is a closed triangle (note that the first index is repeated to close the loop), and the second is a zig-zag of four connected line segments.

```
FILE FORMAT/DEFAULTS
    IndexedLineSet   {
        coordIndex                    0
        materialIndex                -1
        normalIndex                  -1
        textureCoordIndex            -1
    }
```

Figure 5.8 IndexedLineSet.

Unlike IndexedFaceSet, an IndexedLineSet will be drawn with lighting turned off if normals are not specified. Lines with fewer than two vertices are ignored.

PointSet

Points are drawn using the PointSet primitive, as shown in Figure 5.9. Its startIndex and numPoints fields are used to specify which points from the current coordinate node should be drawn. By default, startIndex is zero and numPoints is (1, meaning draw all of them. PointSet uses the current coordinates in order, starting at the index specified by the startIndex field. The number of points in the set is specified by the numPoints field. A value of (1 for this field indicates that all remaining values in the current coordinates are to be used as points.

Like IndexedLineSet, if normals are not specified, the points will be drawn unlighted. *Note:* An IndexedPointSet primitive isn't terribly useful, because coordinates used for a PointSet aren't typical-

```
FILE FORMAT/DEFAULTS
    PointSet   {
        startIndex           0
        numPoints           -1
    }
```

Figure 5.9 PointSet.

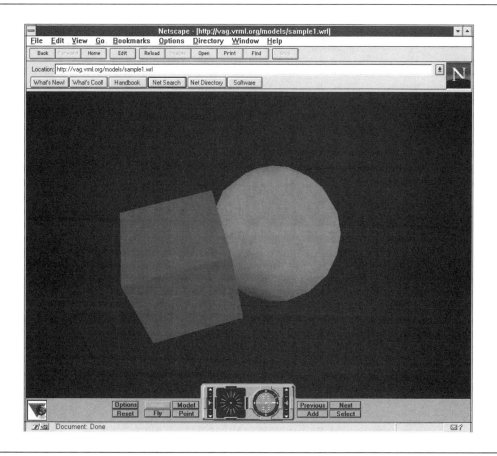

Figure 5.10 Primitive shapes.

ly shared (unlike polygons and lines, where several polygons or line segments may meet at a vertex).

Primitive Shapes

The Open Inventor Cube, Sphere, Cylinder, and Nit: yes, cubes aren't really cubes if they have different widths, heights, and depths, as shown in Figure 5.10. But a nonuniform scale can also make a sphere not a sphere.

Open Inventor has a Complexity node with a 0.0 to 1.0 value that can be used to control the quality of these shapes. The complexity control should be left to the browser, which could control the complexity to get good interactive performance.

Groups

Group nodes (Separator, Group, TransformSeparator, Switch, and LevelOfDetail) are used to create the scene hierarchy, as shown in Figure 5.11. Separator is most commonly used; it separates the effects of its children (material changes, translates/rotates/scales, etc.) from the rest of the scene.

Open Inventor's Separator node has several fields to control its caching (whether it should build a display list when rendering) and culling (whether it should draw its children, based on whether or not it is in the view volume) behavior. It is proposed that VRML require only the renderCulling field, since the caching fields is specific to APIs like GL, which have a notion of display lists (and the default, Open Inventor's AUTO caching, works very well).

Another group that is very useful is TransformSeparator, which separates the effects of transformations inside it from the rest of the scene but allows other properties to leak out. This node wasn't implemented to improve performance over Separator. On a well-implemented system, Separator should do a lazy push/pop of attributes—saving/restoring only attributes that matter. Nevertheless, the node was implemented to allow transformations to transform lights and cameras without affecting the objects that the camera is viewing or the lights are illuminating.

```
FILE FORMAT/DEFAULTS
      Group  {
      }
```

Figure 5.11 Groups.

The Switch node traverses none, one, or all of its children, based on its whichChild field. It is most useful in programs (for example, a scene may contain two representations of a world, with a named Switch used to switch between them), but it can be very useful for commenting out part of the scene.

LevelOfDetail

LevelOfDetail is a special group that traverses one of its children, based on approximately how much screen area its children occupy. It approximates the screen area by taking the 3-D bounding box of its children, projecting it onto the 2-D screen, and then taking the area of the 2-D bounding box that contains that projected 3-D bounding box. The different levels of detail are stored as the LevelOfDetail node's children. The first child should be the most detailed version of the object, with subsequent children being less detailed versions of the object. For example, here is a very simple LevelOfDetail node that displays a sphere as the most detailed object. When its bounding box is larger than 10,000 pixels (about 100 by 100), a cube as the middle level of detail (when the object is between 10,000 and 100 pixels big) displays nothing (an Info node) when it is smaller than 100 pixels:

```
LevelOfDetail {
     screenArea [ 10000, 100 ]
     Sphere { } # Highest level of detail
     Cube { }    # Next level of detail
     Info { }    # Lowest level of detail
}2
```

Will implementing this be too difficult? It wouldn't be too bad if it were a much simpler node that just chose a child based on how far away it is from the eye (called DistanceSwitch, perhaps). DistanceSwitch could switch, based on the distance of the center of its children's bounding box from the eye (but then that forces implementors to be able to figure out bounding boxes for objects); or it could just switch, based on the distance of point (0,0,0) in object space from the eye (this assumes that objects are modeled around (0,0,0) and translated into position).

Thus the Open Inventor LevelOfDetail node (Open Inventor's primitive shapes—*Cube/Sphere/Cone/Cylinder) pay attention to the current complexity value, stored in the Complexity node (a lower complexity value causes LevelOfDetail to choose simpler levels of detail). Therefore it is okay for VRML to leave complexity as a global value controlled by the browser.

Materials

Open Inventor's Material node supports a simple model for how light reflects off the surface of an object. Materials are intended to be easily implementable, not to capture a truly accurate physical description of the surface. The parameters are ambient, diffuse, specular and emissive colors, a shininess parameter (specular exponent for the geeks reading this), and how transparent or opaque the material is. The ambient, diffuse, specular, and emissive colors are specified as RGB triples in the range 0.0 to 1.0.

Open Inventor has two other material nodes: BaseColor is equivalent to a Material except that it sets only the diffuseColor for subsequent shapes. PackedColor is a compact form of BaseColor, with diffuse colors and transparency specified as 32-bit unsigned long values. The red, green, blue, and alpha components are specified with eight bits of precision. Thus BaseColor doesn't add enough functionality to justify its inclusion in VRML. However, PackedColor does use significantly less bandwidth than Material and should be included.

Textures

The Texture2 node specifies a 2-D array of colors (possibly with transparency) to be mapped onto 3-D objects, as shown in Figure 5.12. It allows the image either to be specified in an external file or to be stored in an SFImage field directly in the Open Inventor file. It also specifies how the colors should interact with the material of the object (whether they should combine with or replace the object's material) and whether the texture should repeat (see Texture Coordinates, following).

Open Inventor's Texture2 node has a model field that controls how the texture image and the object's lighted color are combined. BLEND is used with grayscale and grayscale+alpha images. It uses the intensity of the texture image to control how much of the object's color is used and how much of a constant blending color. Specified in the Texture2 Issue: for VRML, the filename field should take a URL. The same image formats as HTML should be supported. The SFImage field is an uncompressed, eight bits per component format.

Texture Coordinates

Open Inventor's primitive shapes define how the texture image is mapped onto their geometry. A TextureCoordinate2 node is used to specify how the texture is mapped onto the IndexedFaceSet primitive. The texture image is mapped into the (0,0) to (1,1) space of texture coordinates. TextureCoordinate2 allows each vertex of the IndexedFaceSet to be given a different texture coordinate, allowing arbitrary mappings. Texture coordinates outside the range (0,0) to (1,1) will either cause the texture image to repeat itself or will be clamped, causing the border pixel in the texture image to be reused, depending on the fields of the Texture2 node.

```
WRAP ENUM
    REPEAT          Repeats texture outside 0-1 texture coordinate range
    CLAMP           Clamps texture coordinates to lie within 0-1 range
    }

FILE FORMAT/DEFAULTS
    Texture2   {
        filename              " "
        image                 0   0   0
        wrapS                 REPEAT
        wrapT                 REPEAT
    }
```

Figure 5.12 Texture2 node.

The Texture2Transform node can be used to modify a shape's texture coordinates. A Texture2Transform is a 2-D version of the Transform node that transforms texture coordinates instead of vertex coordinates. It has fields that specify a 2-D translation, 2-D rotation, 2-D scale, and a 2-D center about which the transformations will be applied. Texture coordinates are either specified explicitly in a TextureCoordinate2 node or are implicitly generated by shapes. The cumulative texture transformation is applied to the texture coordinates, and the transformed texture coordinates are used to find the appropriate texel in the texture image. Note that like regular transformations, Texture2Transform nodes have a cumulative effect.

Texture2Transforms allow the default mapping of textures onto primitive shapes to be changed, as shown in Figure 5.13. For example, you might build a house out of Cube primitives (if you didn't really care about performance!) and change the Texture2Transform so that a wallpaper texture was repeated across the walls instead of the default mapping of the texture being repeated once across the faces of the cube.

Transformations

Open Inventor defines 12 transformation nodes. The following should be part of VRML. Translation has a single field that specifies an XYZ translation for subsequent objects. Note that all transformations are relative.

```
FILE FORMAT/DEFAULTS
        Texture2Transform    {
                translation   0   0
                rotation      0
                scaleFactor   1   1
                center        0   0
        }
```

Figure 5.13 Texture2Transforms.

For example:

```
Translation  {   translation  1  0  0  }
Translation  {   translation  3  5  2  1  }
Cube  {          }
```

will result in the cube's having a total translation of (4.5,2,1).[3]

Scale has a single field that specifies a relative scale. The scale will be nonuniform in the X, Y, or Z directions if all of the components of scaleFactor are not the same.

Rotation has a single field that specifies an axis to rotate about and an angle (in radians) specifying how much right-hand rotation about that axis to apply. It would have been more convenient if the angle were specified in degrees instead of radians.

MatrixTransform has a single field containing an arbitrary 4-by-4 rotation matrix. It is to be combined with previous transformations and applied to subsequent objects.

The Transform node combines several common transformation tasks into one convenient node. It has fields specifying a translation, rotation, and scaleFactor, along with scaleOrientation and center fields for specifying what coordinate axes the scale should be applied along and about which point the scale and rotation should occur.

Cameras

Open Inventor defines two types of cameras PerspectiveCamera and OrthographicCamera. PerspectiveCamera has position and orientation fields that specify the camera's location and orientation relative to world space (the space objects are in after all transformations have been applied), as shown in Figure 5.14. PerspectiveCamera also has a heightAngle that specifies how wide or narrow the field of view should be. Changing the heightAngle is like using a zoom lens to zoom in and out. The focalDistance field is a hint to browsers about where the person behind the camera is

```
FILE FORMAT/DEFAULTS
    PerspectiveCamera {
        position        0  0  1
        orientation     0  0  1  n
        focalDistance   5
        heightAngle     0.785398
    }
```

Figure 5.14 PerspectiveCamera.

looking. Browsers can use this information to do correct stereo rendering (basing the stereo eye separation on the focalDistance), to adjust how quickly the viewer should move through the scene, and to do fancy depth-of-field blur effects.

ViewportMapping, nearDistance, farDistance, or aspectRatio fields should not be part of VRML. ViewportMapping is almost always left at its default value of ADJUST_CAMERA. The near and far clipping planes distances are best calculated by the VRML browser and adjusted automatically. And we should assume that the aspectRatio will match the window. Authors who want their scenes to look squished can insert nonuniform scales.

OrthographicCamera is exactly like PerspectiveCamera. Only instead of a heightAngle field to control the field of view, it has a height field that specifies how tall the viewing volume is in world-space coordinates, as shown in Figure 5.15.

This spec doesn't define any way of specifying a recommended viewing paradigm—walk-through versus fly-through versus looking at a single object. Most common paradigms will be a single object (you just want to move around the object and look at it from all sides)—an immersive room or environment (you want to walk or fly or crawl or hop around it exploring). Smart browsers should be able to distinguish between these two cases pretty easily (using position of camera versus rest of scene, plus viewer size (focalDistance) versus rest of scene).

```
FILE FORMAT/DEFAULTS
    OrthographicCamera  {
         position           0  0  1
         orientation        0  0  1  0
         focalDistance      5
         height             2
    }
```

Figure 5.15 OrthographicCamera.

Lights

Open Inventor defines three basic kinds of lights. All lights have an intensity, color, and an on field that can be used to turn them on or off. DirectionalLight has a direction field that specifies what direction the light is traveling. A PointLight has a position in space and radiates light uniformly in all directions from that point. A SpotLight has both a location and a direction, plus fields to control the width and focus of its beam. Note that light positions and directions *are* transformed by the current transformation, allowing lights to be attached to objects.

Info

Storing arbitrary information in a file is handy for recording who created an object, copyright information, etc. The Info node contains a single field, called string, that contains an arbitrary ASCII string that can be used for this.

For example:

```
Info {
     string     "Created by Thad Beier.
Slightly ill-behaved model: has some clockwise
polygons.
Public domain.
"
}4
```

Note that newlines are allowed in string fields, allowing one Info node to contain several lines of information. Should conventions for the information inside Info nodes be established to allow browsers to interpret that information? For example, the convention for author information could be a line of the form: Author: author_name.

VRML Extensions to Open Inventor

For the first release of VRML, two new nodes were proposed: WWWInline and WWWAnchor.

WWWInline would look like this:

```
WWWInline {
     name "http://www.sgi.com/FreeStuff/
CoolScene.wrl"
     bboxCenter  0  0  4
     bboxSize   10.5  4.5  8
}
```
[5]

The name field is an SFString containing the URL for the file. A smart implementation can delay the retrieval of the file until it is rendered instead of reading it right away. Combined with LevelOfDetail, this provides an automatic mechanism for delayed loading of complicated scenes.

The bboxCenter and bboxSize fields allow an author to specify the bounding box for this WWWInline. Specifying a bounding box this way allows a browser to decide whether the WWWInline can be seen from the current camera location without reading the WWWInline's contents. If a bounding box is not specified, the contents of the WWWInline do have to be read to determine the WWWInline's bounding box.

WWWAnchor looks very much like WWWInline, except that it is a group node and can have children.

```
WWWAnchor {
      name "http://www.sgi.com/FreeStuff/
CoolScene.wrl"
      Separator  {
            Material    {      diffuseColor 0 0 .8 }
            Cube  {      }
      }
}
```

WWWAnchor is a strange node. It must somehow communicate with the browser and cause the browser to load the scene specified in its name field when a child of the WWWAnchor is picked, replacing the current scene that the WWWAnchor is part of. Specifying how that happens is up to the browser and implementor of WWWAnchor, as is implementing the picking code.

So what happens when you nest WWWAnchors (you have WWWAnchors as children of WWWAnchors)? *Suggestion:* The lowest WWWAnchor wins.

WWWAnchor also has a map field that adds the object-space point on the object the user picked to the URL in the name field. This is like the image-map feature of HTML and allows scripts to do different things, based on exactly what part of an object is picked.

For example, given this WWWAnchor:

```
WWWAnchor {
      name "http://www.foo.com/cgi-bin/pickMapper"
      map POINT
      Cube {      }
}
```

Picking on the top of the Cube might produce the URL http://www.foo.com/cgi-bin/pickMapper?.211,1.0,-.56.

Other Open Inventor Nodes

Several other Open Inventor nodes are not common enough or will be too difficult to implement to include in VRML. The following are the most interesting, along with my reasons for not including them in this chapter.

Text2, Text3, Font

Text2 is two-dimensional screen-aligned text. Adding a 2-D primitive whose size is not in 3-D object coordinates but window coordinates turns up a lot of annoying implementation issues. As 3-D text is pretty complicated to implement, implementing the full Open Inventor functionality would necessitate adding four more nodes to specify the font, coordinates for the 3-D extrusion bevel on the text, and specification whether the extrusion is a curve or a set of line segments (Font, ProfileCoordinate2, LinearProfile, and NurbsProfile). Also, allowing different fonts to be specified opens up a whole can of worms on what font names are allowed, where fonts are defined, what format fonts are in, etc.

NURBS

NURBS curves and surfaces are also complicated, especially if trimming of NURBS surfaces is supported (Open Inventor supports that). VRML can be very successful without them.

Nodekits

Open Inventor's nodekits impose a structure on the scene graph, making it easier for applications to manipulate the scene. For example, figuring out where to insert a material node to affect a picked object is not trivial for an arbitrary scene. If you use node-kits, it is trivial. Each ShapeKit has an associated AppearanceKit, and you just tell the AppearanceKit what you want the material to be. Nodekits should not be part of VRML only because they add yet another thing to be implemented, and the design must be kept as minimal as possible.

Draggers

Draggers are incredibly powerful interactive objects that respond to user interaction by moving themselves. For example, a RotateSpherical dragger will rotate itself when the mouse is clicked and dragged over it. Draggers become powerful when their fields (which change as they move) are wired to other parts of the scene, using field-to-field connections. Because behaviors, engines, and field-to-field connections should not be part of VRML, draggers should not be, either.

Array, MultipleCopy

An Array node copies its children several times, each translated differently. A MultipleCopy node is similar, except that arbitrary transformation matrices are specified. They aren't used very much (although they are useful for things like regular grids).

Blinker, Rotor, Shuttle, Pendulum

Blinker, a subclass of the Switch node, changes which child is drawn over time. Rotor is a rotation that changes over time. Shuttle is a translation that changes between two locations over time, and Pendulum changes between two rotations over time. The notion of animating objects that change over time have been fully realized with the release of VRML 2.0 and VRML97 and include full-fledged engines and behaviors.

ClipPlane

ClipPlane specifies an arbitrary clipping plane that can be used to clip out parts of the scene. Useful for specific CAD applications, ClipPlane is not very useful generally (and not typically saved as part of a scene).

DrawStyle

This functionality allows parts of the scene to be drawn as LINES or POINTS but can be left to the browser. Authors can use PointSet or IndexedLineSet if they want lines or points in their scene.

Environment

The Environment node specifies global illumination settings, such as fog and the ambient light intensity of the scene. Those are pretty advanced features that have now been implemented in VRML 2.0 and VRML97.

LightModel

Open Inventor supports either a BASE_COLOR lighting model, which is basically no lighting at all, or the default PHONG lighting model, which is a simple lighting approximation. The BASE_COLOR lighting model is useful mainly for scenes that have already had their lighting precomputed, such as a scene for which a radiosity solution has been calculated. These kinds of scenes are not common enough to justify the addition of the LightModel node to VRML.

ResetTransform, Units, AntiSquish, RotationXYZ

ResetTransform can be painful to implement correctly and is almost never specified in scene files. The same is true for AntiSquish. Also, Units shouldn't be used, because strange things happen when you nest them.

For example:

```
Separator {
    Units { units FEET }
    DEF FootCube Cube { }
    Separator {
        Units { units METERS }
        DEF MeterCube Cube { }
    }
}
```

Applications that try to be smart about rearranging the object hierarchy will have trouble figuring out exactly what effect the second Units node will have, since its effect will change if it is moved out from under the first Units node. The rules are much simpler if a simple Scale node is used instead.

RotationXYZ allows rotation about one of the primary axes. The generality of Rotation is preferred here, which allows rotation about an arbitrary axis. However, it might make sense to replace Rotation with RotationXYZ, since the general Transform node can also be used to rotate about an arbitrary axis.

TextureCoordinateEnvironment, TextureCoordinatePlane

These specify a fairly simple mapping of object geometry to texture coordinates. The TextureCoordinatePlane is now part of VRML 2.0 and VRML97. However, it does add a fair amount of complexity to a VRML implementation's code for handling texture coordinates.

Coordinate4, ProfileCoordinate2, ProfileCoordinate3

Coordinate4 specifies homogeneous coordinates (X, Y, Z, and W), which are not very common. ProfileCoordinate2 and ProfileCo-ordinate3 specify coordinates for the bevels on 3-D text and the trim curves of NURBS objects. Since 3-D text or NURBS should not be part of VRML, they aren't necessary, either.

Binary Format

To make implementation of VRML easier, a binary format should not initially be part of VRML. Experience with Open Inventor has shown that using a standard compression utility (such as com-press, pack, or gzip) to compress ASCII Open Inventor files results in files that are just as small as Open Inventor's binary format (compressing the binary format typically has very little effect). New protocols for transmitting VRML scenes are being designed. This allows servers and browsers to automatically compress and decompress ASCII VRML files to save network bandwidth. Actually, this is orthogonal to VRML. HTML files could also be stored and sent compressed to save network bandwidth. Parsing time is greatly improved with a binary format. However, for

VRML browsers the network transmission time is much greater than the ASCII parsing time.

Field Syntax

Each node has zero or more fields that store the data for the node. Each of the fields is written as the field's name, followed by the data in the field.

For example, a Sphere has a single radius field that contains a single floating-point value and is written as Sphere { radius 1.0 }. Each node defines reasonable default values for its fields, which are used if the field does not appear as part of the node's definition.

Some fields can contain multiple values. The syntax for a multiple-valued field is a superset of the syntax for single-valued fields. The values are all enclosed in brackets ([]) and are separated by commas. The final value may optionally be followed by an extra comma. If a multiple-valued field has only one value, the brackets and commas may be omitted, resulting in the same syntax as single-valued fields. A multiple-valued field may also contain zero values, in which case just a set of empty brackets appears.

Field Classes

Single-valued fields have type names that begin with SF. Multiple-valued fields have type names that begin with MF. Open Inventor defines 42 types of fields.

VRML should consist of the subset used by the nodes defined by VRML, which are:

```
*       SFFloat
*       MFVec3f
*       SFVec3f
*       MFColor
*       SFColor
```

```
*      SFRotation
*      SFMatrix
*      SFEnum
*      SFBitMask
*      MFString
*      SFString
*      SFImage
```

Some of the types for fields are tied to the C programming language (Float; Open Inventor also has Long and Short). It will be misleading on some machines. An Open Inventor SFFloat is a 32-bit floating-point number, even though floats are larger or smaller on different machines.

Naming

A node may be given a name by prepending its definition with the reserved token DEF, followed by whitespace, the name of the node, and whitespace to separate the name from the type of the node. For example, to give the name SquareHead to a Cube, use the following: DEF SquareHead Cube {}. Names must not start with a digit (0–9), and must not contain ASCII control characters, whitespace, or the following characters: +,\,',",{}.

Note: The + character is illegal for compatibility with Open Inventor programs in which the characters after the + are used to disambiguate multiple nodes with the same name. For example, a user of an Open Inventor program may give two nodes the name Joe; when written, these might appear as Joe+0 and Joe+1. The other characters are illegal, to make parsing easier and to leave room for future format extensions.

Instancing

A node may be the child of more than one group. This is called *instancing* (using the same instance of a node multiple times, or aliasing or multiple references by other systems). It is accomplished by using the USE keyword.

The DEF keyword both defines a named node and creates a single instance of it. The USE keyword indicates that the most recently defined instance should be used again. If several nodes were given the same name, the last DEF encountered during parsing wins. DEF/USE is limited to a single file. There is no mechanism for using USE on nodes which is used DEF in other files.

For example, rendering this scene will result in three spheres being drawn. Both of the spheres are named Joe; the second (smaller) sphere is drawn twice:

```
Separator {
    DEF Joe Sphere { }
    Translation { translation 2 0 0 }
    DEF Joe Sphere { radius .2 }
    Translation { translation 2 0 0 }
    USE Joe
}
```

Extensibility

Open Inventor's file format has two mechanisms to support easy extensibility: self-declaring nodes and alternative representations for nodes. Objects that are not built in write out a description of themselves first. This allows them to be read in and ignored by applications that don't understand them.

This description is written just after the opening brace for the node and consists of the keyword fields, followed by a list of the types and names of fields used by that node. To save space, fields with default values that won't be written also will not have their descriptions written.

For example, if Cube was not built into the core library, it would be written like this:

```
Cube {
    fields [ SFFloat width, SFFloat height,
SFFloat depth ]
    width 10 height 4 depth 3
}
```

By describing the types and names of the Cube's fields, a parser can correctly read the new node. Field-to-field connections and engines (which are not part of VRML 2.0 or VRML97) require that the parser know the names and types of fields in unknown nodes. It isn't good enough just to search for matching curly-braces outside of strings and store unknown node contents as an unparsed string.

The other feature that allows easy extensibility is the ability to supply an alternative representation for objects. This is done by adding a special field, named alternateRep of type SFNode, to your new nodes. For example, to implement a new kind of Material that supported indexOfRefraction, a regular Material would be needed as an alternative representation for applications that do not understand RefracMaterial.

The file format would look like:

```
RefracMaterial {
    fields [ SFNode alternateRep, MFFloat
indexOfRefraction,
        MFColor diffuseColor ]
    indexOfRefraction 0.2
    diffuseColor 0.9 0.0 0.2
    alternateRep Material { diffuseColor 0.9 0.0
0.2 }
}
```

Open Inventor uses DSOs (dynamic shared objects; DLLs, or dynamic link libraries, on the Windows NT port of Open Inventor) to support run-time loading of the code for a new node. A RefracMaterial.so is needed, with an implementation (written in C++) of the new RefracMaterial. At this point existing Open Inventor applications will then work, thus recognizing the new node, and *not* use the alternateRep. However, it is beyond the scope of VRML to try to define a method for the dynamic loading of platform-independent code across the network. That issue is completely independent of VRML.

Header

For easy identification of VRML files, every VRML file must begin with the characters:

```
#VRML  V2.0  utf8
```

Any characters after these on the same line are ignored. The line is terminated by either the ASCII newline or carriage-return characters.

It would be a little more convenient if VRML shared the same identifying header as Open Inventor (Open Inventor ASCII). However, in the long run there will be many fewer problems if it is easy to distinguish VRML files from Open Inventor files. It would be trivial to write a translator for VRML to Open Inventor and only moderately difficult to write one for Open Inventor to VRML that tesselated any primitives that were not part of VRML (NURBS) into IndexedFaceSets.

Comments

The "#" character begins a comment. All characters until the next newline or carriage return are ignored. The only exception to this is within string fields, where the # character will be part of the string.

Comments and whitespace may not be preserved. In particular, a VRML document server may strip comments and extraneous whitespace from a VRML file before transmitting it. Info nodes should be used for persistent information, such as copyrights or author information.

Whitespace

Blanks, tabs, newlines, and carriage returns are whitespace characters wherever they appear outside of string fields. One or more whitespace characters separate the syntactical entities in VRML files, where necessary.

File Contents

After the required header, a VRML file contains exactly one VRML node. That node may in turn contain any number of other nodes.

Open Inventor allows a series of root nodes to be parsed from a single file. This causes problems for filters that operate on Open Inventor files. (Instancing between the nodes in the different roots tends to get broken as each root is worked on independently.) It doesn't really add any functionality.

File Extension

The standard file extension for VRML files is .wrl for world. In the future this may change to .mdl for model, to reflect that a scene would more likely be built from component models as opposed to being assembled from a collection of worlds.

Coordinate Space Conventions

Open Inventor's default unit is the meter. Open Inventor uses a right-handed coordinate system. If you are looking at your computer monitor, the default Open Inventor coordinate axes are +X toward the right, +Y toward the top, and +Z coming out of the screen toward you.

The consensus on the mailing list was +X right, +Y into the screen, and +Z up. Is it worth having VRML be incompatible with Open Inventor? It is also easy for a translator to add a Rotation node.

Terminology and Features

- Platform independence—This is an ASCII file format that has already proved to be easily transportable to other platforms.
- True 3-D information (not prerendered texture maps a la DOOM)—All of the primitives are true 3-D objects.
- PHIGS-ish lighting and view model—Material, the lights, and PerspectiveCamera give a simple but powerful way of specifying views and lights.
- Unrecognized data types are ignored (to leave open future development)—Extensibility has been designed in.
- Hierarchical data structure—Groups create the hierarchy, with Separators providing appropriate encapsulation so subparts do not affect their parents.
- Lightweight design—You'll have to judge, but it should be kept minimal.
- Convex and concave objects allowed—IndexedFaceSets allow arbitrary geometry.
- Fill-in-the-details support (pictures in a museum)—LevelOfDetail combined with a lazy-load WWWInline node give this functionality.

- The file format is public domain—The Open Inventor file format is usable by anybody, and Silicon Graphics will be releasing a public domain parser for it to make it easier to write applications that understand the file format.
- Level of detail support—LevelOfDetail supports this directly.
- Geometric primitives—{Cube, Sphere, Cylinder} (Anybody want to argue hard for others?).
- Object-oriented—Most people would agree that Open Inventor is object-oriented, and that this is reflected in its file format.
- Texture mapping—Texture2 and TextureCoordinate2 provide a general method for doing simple texture mapping.
- Engines—This is the one feature that it would be a mistake to add to VRML V1.0. This can safely wait for a later version of VRML.

Is That Everything?

Not quite! Let's define a list of terms and features *here* in order to place the remainder of this chapter and the ones that follow in perspective.

Looking Ahead

Open Inventor's field-to-field connections, global fields, and engine objects (which should not be part of VRML 2.0 or VRML97) provide the infrastructure for creating objects with behaviors. Open Inventor is missing a good set of engines for doing simple keyframed animated behaviors of objects. It is also missing some simple interactive nodes, such as buttons (like the WWWAnchor node, only more general). The Open Inventor team at Silicon

Graphics is currently designing and implementing these kinds of nodes and engines.

From Here

If this wasn't enough, a further detailed discussion of Open Inventor will be coming up in Chapter 11. Chapter 20 will give a brief overview of an interactive tool for exploring VR applications over the Internet via Netscape and other browsers.

Endnotes

1 Gavin Bell, *Inventor and VRML*, Silicon Graphics, Inc., 1996.

2 Ibid.

3 Ibid.

4 Ibid.

5 Ibid.

6

Real Virtual Reality on the Internet

Today, the term "Virtual Reality" (VR) is used in a variety of ways, and often in a confusing and misleading manner. Originally, the term referred to *Immersive Virtual Reality*. In immersive VR, the user becomes fully immersed in an artificial, three-dimensional (3-D) world that is completely generated by a computer.

The *head-mounted display* (HMD) was the first device providing its wearer with an immersive experience. A typical HMD (shown in Figure 6.1) houses two miniature display screens and an optical system that channels the images from the screens to the eyes, thereby presenting a stereo view of a real virtual world.[1] A motion tracker continuously measures the position and orientation of the user's head and allows the image-generating computer to adjust the scene representation to the current view. As a result, the viewer can look around and walk through the surrounding virtual environment.

To overcome the often uncomfortable intrusiveness of a head-mounted display, alternative concepts (BOOM and CAVE) were developed for immersive viewing of virtual environments. The *BOOM* (Binocular Omni-Orientation Monitor) from Fakespace (shown in Figure 6.2) is a head-coupled stereoscopic display device.[2] Screens and an optical system are housed in a box that is attached to a multilink arm. The user looks into the box through two holes, sees the virtual world, and can guide the box to any position within the operational volume of the device. Head tracking is accomplished via sensors in the links of the arm that holds the box.

The *CAVE* (Cave Automatic Virtual Environment), as shown in Figure 6.3, was developed at the University of Illinois at Chicago and provides the illusion of immersion by projecting stereo images on the walls and floor of a room-sized cube.[3] Several persons wearing lightweight stereo glasses can enter and walk freely inside the

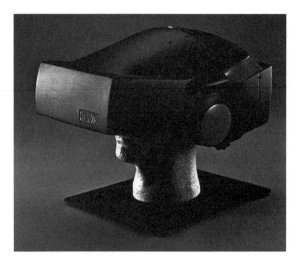

Figure 6.1 Head-mounted display (HMD).

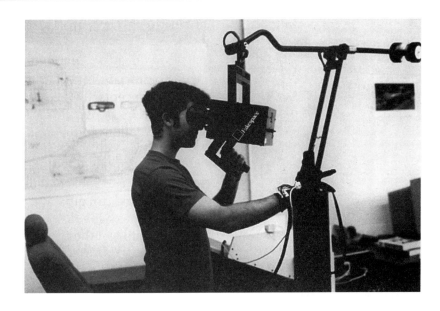

Figure 6.2 The BOOM—A head-coupled display device.

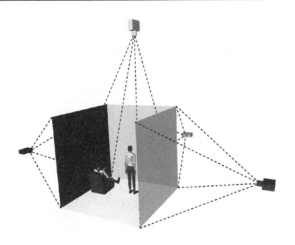

Figure 6.3 CAVE environment.

CAVE. A head-tracking system continuously adjusts the stereo projection to the current position of the leading viewer.

A variety of input devices like data gloves (see Figure 6.4), joysticks, and hand-held wands (see Figure 6.5) allow the user to navigate through a virtual environment and to interact with virtual objects.[4] Directional sound, tactile and force-feedback devices, voice recognition, and other technologies are being employed to enrich the immersive experience and to create more "sensualized" interfaces.

The unique characteristics of immersive virtual reality can be summarized as follows:

- ◆ Head-referenced viewing provides a natural interface for the navigation in 3-D space and allows for look-around, walk-around, and fly-through capabilities in virtual environments.
- ◆ Stereoscopic viewing enhances the perception of depth and the sense of space.
- ◆ The virtual world is presented in full scale and relates properly to the human size.
- ◆ Realistic interaction with virtual objects via data gloves and similar devices allows for manipulation, operation, and control of virtual worlds.
- ◆ The convincing illusion of being fully immersed in an artificial world can be enhanced by auditory, realistic (haptic), and other nonvisual technologies.

Figure 6.4 A data glove allows for interaction with the virtual world.

Figure 6.5 Moving the steering wheel.

♦ Networked applications allow for shared virtual environments. Users at different locations (anywhere in the world) can meet in the same virtual world, see each other, communicate, and interact.

Today, the term "Virtual Reality" is also used for applications that are not fully immersive. The boundaries are becoming blurred, but all variations of VR will be important in the future. This includes mouse-controlled navigation through a 3-D environment on a graphics monitor, stereo viewing from the monitor via stereo glasses, stereo projection systems, and others. Apple's QuickTime VR, for example, uses photographs for the modeling of 3-D worlds and provides pseudo look-around and walk-through capabilities on a graphics monitor.

Most exciting is the ongoing development of VRML (Virtual Reality Modeling Language) on the World Wide Web. In addition to HTML (HyperText Markup Language), which has become a standard authoring tool for the creation of homepages, VRML 2.0/97 provides 3-D worlds with integrated hyperlinks on the Web. Homepages become homespaces. The viewing of VRML models via appropriate browsers is usually done on a graphics monitor under mouse-control and, therefore, is not fully immersive. However, the data structure of VRML provides an excellent tool for the modeling and internal representation of 3-D worlds that can be transferred into fully immersive viewing systems, as shown in Figures 6.6 and 6.7.[5] The ongoing development of VRML 2.0/97 will include more interactivity, behavior, and functionality of real virtual worlds on the Internet, and shared multiuser applications.

Diganta
Saha

Figure 6.6 Escher's Penrose Staircase.

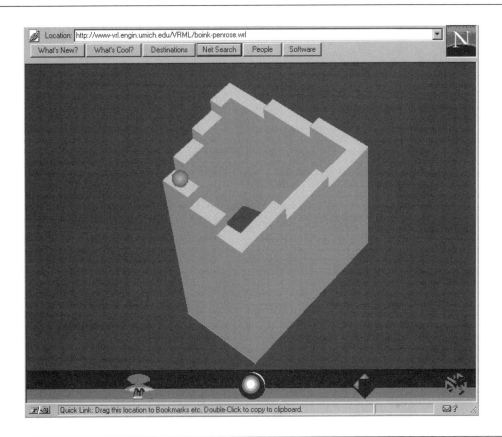

Figure 6.7 An animated 3-D VRML 2.0 model reveals the mystery of Escher's Penrose Staircase.

Other VR-related technologies combine virtual and real environments. Motion trackers are employed to monitor the movements of dancers and athletes for subsequent studies in immersive VR. The technologies of "Augmented Reality" allow for the viewing of real environments with superimposed virtual objects. *Telepresence* systems (telemedicine, telerobotics) immerse a viewer in a real world that is captured by video cameras at a distant location, and allow for the remote manipulation of real objects via robot arms and manipulators.

As the technologies of virtual reality evolve, the applications of VR become literally unlimited. It is assumed that VR will reshape the interface between people and information technology by offering new ways for the communication of information, the visualization of processes, and the creative expression of ideas.

Note that a virtual environment can represent any 3-D world that is either real or abstract, as shown in Figures 6.8 and 6.9.[6] This includes real systems like buildings, landscapes, underwater ship-wrecks, spacecraft, archaeological excavation sites, human anato-my, sculptures, crime scene reconstruction, solar systems, and so on. Of special interest is the visual and sensual representation of abstract systems like magnetic fields, turbulent flow structures, molecular models, mathematical systems, auditorium acoustics, stock market behavior, population densities, information flows, and any other conceivable system, including artistic and creative work of an abstract nature. These virtual worlds can be animated, interactive, shared, and can expose behavior and functionality.

Useful applications of real VR on the Internet include training in a variety of areas. These areas might include military, medical, equipment operation, education, design evaluation (virtual proto-typing), architectural walk-through, human factors and ergonom-ic studies, simulation of assembly sequences and maintenance tasks, assistance for the handicapped, study and treatment of pho-bias (e.g., the fear of height), entertainment, and much more.

Now let's take an in-depth look at the Virtual Reality Laboratory at the University of Michigan, and the VR research projects that are being conducted there in the areas of immersive virtual reality, augmented reality, and other variations of virtual reality.

The Virtual Reality Laboratory

The *Virtual Reality Laboratory* (VRL) at the University of Michigan (UM) is a research facility within the College of Engineering, and

Figure 6.8 Real and abstract virtual worlds—Michigan Stadium.

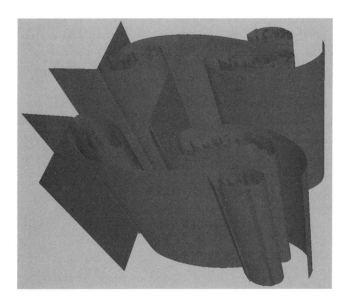

Figure 6.9 Real and abstract virtual worlds—flow structure.

is operated by the Department of Naval Architecture and Marine Engineering. Research and development at the VRL concentrate on industrial applications of immersive virtual reality, augmented reality, and other variations of virtual reality. Additional projects include architectural walk-through models, free-form shape design, accident simulations, training simulators, educational events, academic outreach activities, and more.

The VRL was created in April 1993 with initial funding from the automotive industry in Detroit. The Laboratory has expanded rapidly into a facility with state-of-the-art equipment, and is widely recognized for its pioneering research work in areas like virtual prototyping of automotive interiors and other designs, simulation of manufacturing processes, and related engineering and nonengineering applications.

The unique characteristics of immersive virtual reality provide an unrivaled instrument for the analysis of spatial arrangements found in complex mechanical systems. The VRL is developing these technologies into revolutionary concurrent engineering tools for the entire spectrum of industrial design and manufacturing processes.

A focal point of the Laboratory's research is the rapid creation of virtual prototypes from CAD/CAM databases and the modeling of behavior and functionality of these prototypes for operational simulations and engineering analysis, as well as simulation of assembly, production, and maintenance tasks. Let's look at some of these selected projects, applications, and/or areas that VRL has been dabbling in.

VR in Manufacturing Applications

This part of the chapter gives some examples of how real Virtual Reality can be used in manufacturing applications. The robot shown in Figure 6.10 is a Mitsubishi MOVEMASTER EX.[7]

Robot Animations

Many robots, like the one shown in Figure 6.11, are animated, but you have to have a Live3D plug-in, which is not available on all

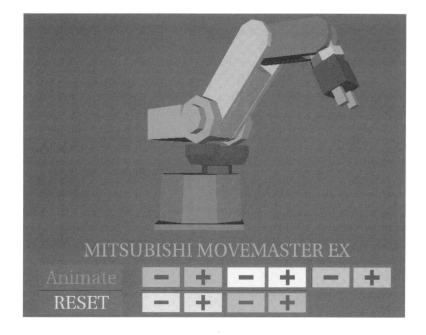

Figure 6.10 Animated robot.

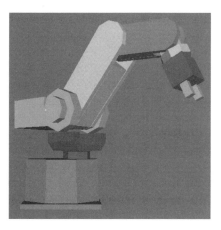

Figure 6.11 Robots in manufacturing applications.

platforms.[8] To animate the robot on all platforms, this model was ported to VRML 2.0/97 (see Figure 6.12).[9] There, it's possible to use scripts for the animation.

There are a couple of ways to interact with the robot, as shown in Figures 6.13 and 6.14.[10] If a mouse button is pushed over the bottom of the robot, it moves by itself. A second selection with the mouse stops the animation. Use the buttons on the bottom of the viewer to move the parts of the robot manually.

Next, let's look at another of these selected immersive virtual reality projects from VRL: virtual prototyping of automotive interiors.

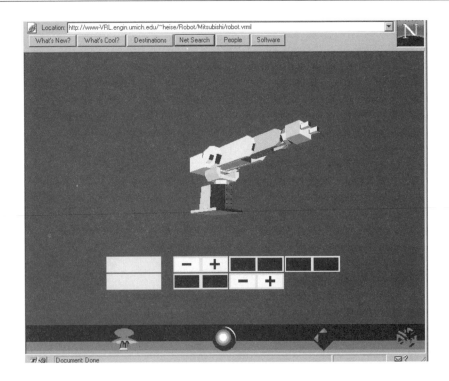

Figure 6.12 Animating the robot model on all platforms with VRML 2.0/97.

Figure 6.13 Production process.

Figure 6.14 The production process with VRML 2.0/97.

Designing Automotive Interiors with Virtual Prototyping

During the design of an automobile, detailed mockups of the interior are built to study the design and evaluate human factors and ergonomic issues. These physical prototypes are expensive, time-consuming, and difficult to modify.

Immersive virtual reality provides an effective alternative. A virtual prototype can replace a physical mockup for the analysis of design aspects; for example, layout and packaging efficiency; visibility of instruments, controls, and mirrors; reachability and accessibility; clearances and collisions; human performance; aesthetics and appeal; and more (see Figure 6.15).[11] A person, placed in a seating buck, is immersed in the virtual interior and can study the design and interact with the virtual car (see Figure 6.16).[12]

In a 1993–95 project sponsored by Chrysler Corporation, VRL researchers studied the process of *Virtual Prototyping* (the many steps required for the creation of a virtual representation from a CAD/CAM model, and for the subsequent use of the prototype in immersive VR). VRL researchers implemented a systematic

Figure 6.15 Virtual prototyping.

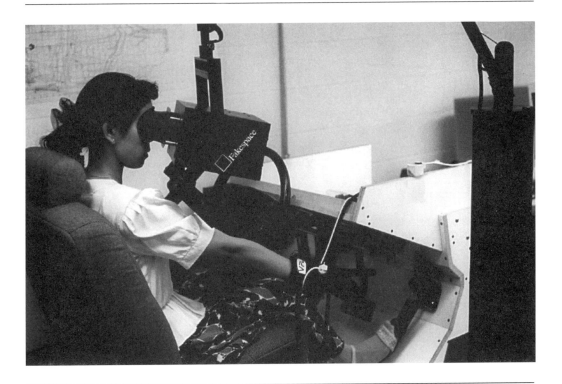

Figure 6.16 A seating buck is used for immersive viewing and interaction.

approach and developed a suite of interactive tools, automatic algorithms, and data formats that covered the entire process.

The time required for the creation of a virtual prototype was reduced from several weeks or months to a few hours. This significant step toward the goal of *Rapid Virtual Prototyping* proved that the application of VR can shorten the design cycle time, reduce costs, and allow for improved market response with products that have been optimized through the study of a larger number of "virtual" design alternatives.

The steps of the virtual prototyping process can be summarized as follows:

- ◆ Extraction of geometry from a CAD/CAM model
- ◆ Tessellation: approximation of geometry by polygons and polygon meshes
- ◆ Complexity reduction: decimation and stitching to various levels of detail
- ◆ Prototype editing: color, material properties, vertex normals, lighting, etc.
- ◆ Precise texture mapping for the representation of detailed elements
- ◆ Additional geometry: external surroundings and other elements
- ◆ Calibration of virtual display with physical elements of seating buck
- ◆ Scripting of functionality and behavior for operational tasks[13]

Some of the preceding steps are briefly explained and illustrated in the following sections of this chapter.

Decimation and Tessellation

The geometry of automotive interiors consists almost exclusively of curved surfaces. The given CAD/CAM model uses a mathematical representation for these free-form shapes (B-splines, NURBS, etc.). The virtual prototype, however, has to present the geometry via computer-graphics primitives like points, lines, or polygons.

Curved surfaces have to be approximated by polygon meshes using *tessellation* algorithms, as shown in Figure 6.17.[14] Typically, large numbers of polygons are created (several millions for an interior). *Decimation* algorithms reduce the polygon count to a level that allows for real-time rendering response at a desired rate of 20 to 30 frames per second during immersive viewing.

Stitching Algorithm

The CAD/CAM model of a surface typically consists of several trimmed surface patches that are connected along common boundaries, as shown in Figure 6.18.[15] Tessellation and decimation of

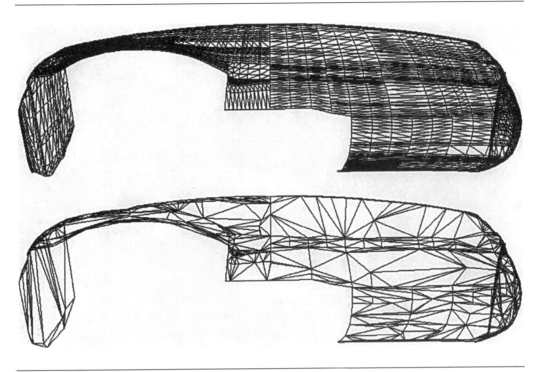

Figure 6.17 Initial tessellation of a dashboard and result of polygon decimation.

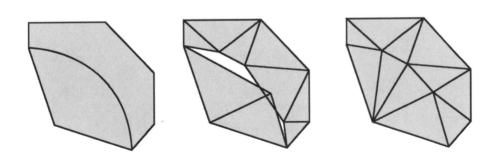

Figure 6.18 Stitching along the common boundary of two surface patches.
Left—common boundary; center—tessellation; right—stitching.

individual patches create gaps or overlaps between these patches. A *stitching* algorithm "sews" the disconnected patches together and creates a uniform polygon mesh with shared vertices at the patch boundaries.

Pasting Precise Images

The modeling of elements with complex details like instruments, radio, or air outlets requires large numbers of polygons. *Texture maps* are an excellent tool to reduce geometric complexity. Computer renderings or photographs of these elements are converted into bitmaps, and a cut-out of the image is pasted precisely at the correct location within the virtual prototype (see Figures 6.19, 6.20, and 6.21).[16]

Calibration and Physical Seating Buck

To place a person properly inside the virtual automotive interior, and to allow for realistic (haptic) interactions with essential elements, a *physical seating buck* is used in this application. The buck consists of a seat, steering wheel, foot pedals, and stick shift (see Figure 6.22).[17] The virtual interior is presented via a stereoscopic display device. A precise *calibration* of the virtual display with the

Figure 6.19 A photo is converted into a texture map.

Figure 6.20 The texture map is placed at the correct location.

Figure 6.21 Use of textures for other elements and for external surroundings.

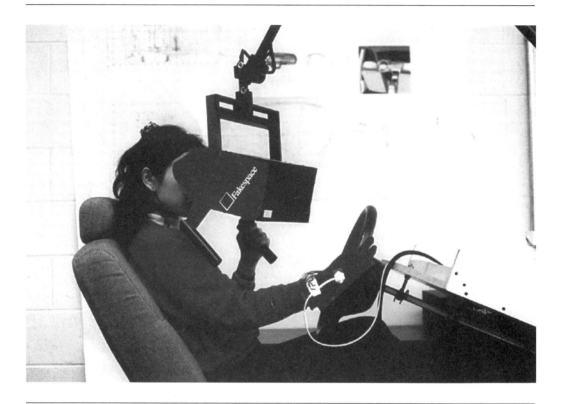

Figure 6.22 The seating buck provides the essential physical elements.

physical elements of the seating buck is instrumental for the usefulness of the virtual prototype. When the user grabs the virtual steering wheel with the data glove–controlled virtual hand (see Figure 6.23), he or she must feel the physical steering wheel at the very same location.[18]

Behavior and Functionality of the Prototype

For the final use of the virtual prototype, interaction with the interior needs to be defined by specifying the prototype's response to operations by the user. *Functionality* and *behavior* of the prototype is scripted in the form of event-action relations. For example, if the user touches a radio button with the data glove (event), sound will

Figure 6.23 An immersive display device presents the virtual interior at a calibrated location.

be generated (action). Touching another control may start or stop the windshield wiper. Virtual pop-up menus can be called up for the modification of interior colors, lighting environment, and other settings (see Figure 6.24).[19]

Immersive Virtual Reality in the Ship Production Process

In the context of Agile Manufacturing Systems, the design and production of portions of a PD 337 Navy cargo ship were studied by VRL researchers using immersive virtual reality, as shown in Figure 6.25.[20] Ships of this size are being built by combining pre-fabricated sections (building blocks) into the final assembly.

Figure 6.24 Changing the light settings via a virtual pop-up menu.

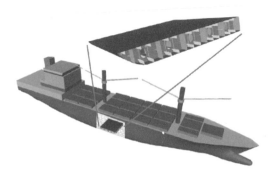

Figure 6.25 Portions of a PD 337 Navy cargo ship.

Virtual Prototyping Sections

The design of a double bottom section, a building block located at the bottom of the ship (shown in Figure 6.26), was provided as an AutoCad model and converted into a virtual prototype.[21] An immersive walk through the full-scale representation of this complex steel structure immediately revealed severe design flaws that are typically found in initial CAD/CAM models. For example, several compartments were not accessible for welding operations, and many of the longitudinal stiffeners were accidentally attached to the wrong side.

Virtual prototypes of building blocks allow for early detection of design errors, and avoid the significant costs that occur if these errors are realized later in the manufacturing process. In addition, possible assembly sequences, accessibility and reachability for welding operations, and the use and movement of equipment inside and outside the section can be studied (see Figures 6.27, 6.28, and 6.29).[22]

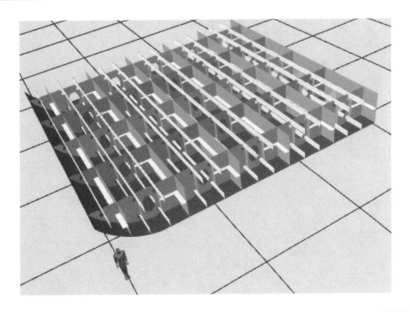

Figure 6.26 Double bottom section overview (top plate removed).

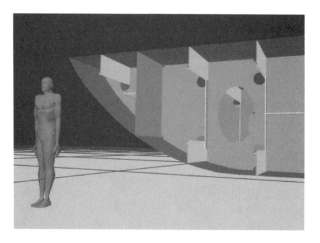

Figure 6.27 Selected view #1 from the outside.

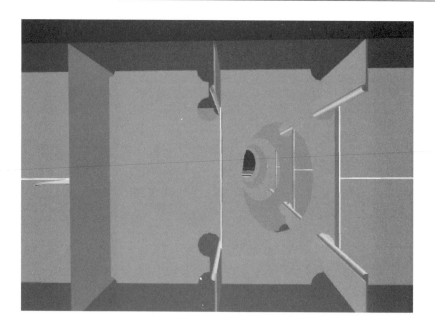

Figure 6.28 Selected view #2 from the outside.

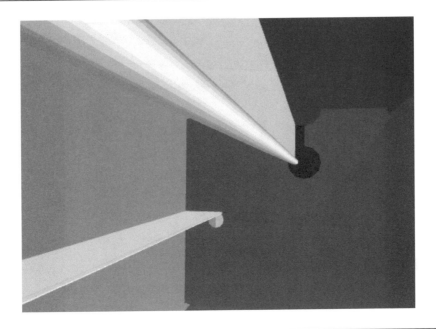

Figure 6.29 Selected view #3 from the inside.

The Second Stage: Assembly Sequence

In a second stage of this project, the *assembly sequence* of the double bottom section was simulated based on the standard practice procedures of a given shipyard, as shown in Figure 6.30.[23] An animated virtual prototype of the assembly process was created that allowed for the study of clearances and possible collisions during the process, required welding operations at the various stages (see Figures 6.31 through 6.36), necessary crane operations, and other production aspects.[24]

The Barcelona Pavilion: An Architectural Walk-Through

The *Barcelona Pavilion*, designed by Mies van der Rohe, was a German entry for the 1929 World Exposition at Barcelona. The pavilion existed for six months and disappeared during the shipping back to Germany. Although its existence is now confined to

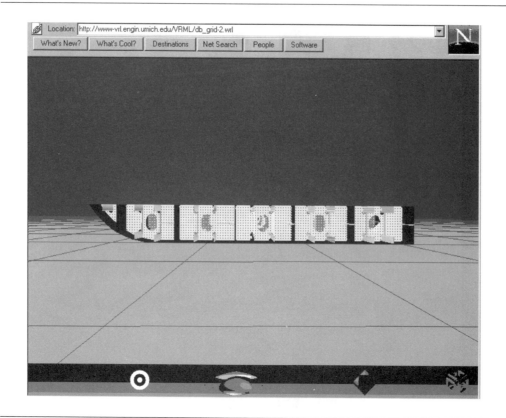

Figure 6.30 Climb through the VRML 2.0/97 model and inspect the double bottom for design flaws.

cyberspace, the Barcelona Pavilion is still considered to be the most famous masterpiece of modern architecture.

An excellent presentation of the Barcelona Pavilion (shown in Figure 6.37)—with exquisite renderings, background information, and a tour via HTML or QuickTime VR—is available on the Web from the School of Architecture Property and Planning at the University of Auckland, New Zealand. You can visit the Barcelona Pavilion at http://archpropplan.auckland.ac.nz/virtualtour/barcelona/barcelona.html.[25]

Figure 6.31 Stage 1 of the assembly sequence.

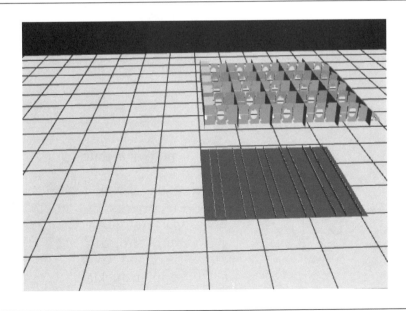

Figure 6.32 Stage 2 of the assembly sequence.

Figure 6.33 Stage 3 of the assembly sequence.

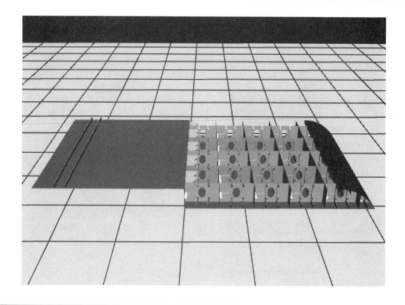

Figure 6.34 Stage 4 of the assembly sequence.

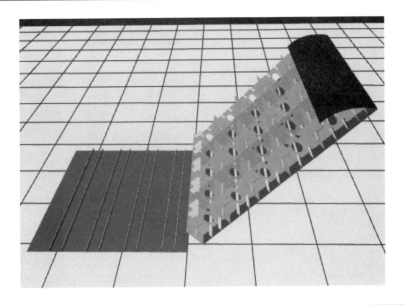

Figure 6.35 Stage 5 of the assembly sequence.

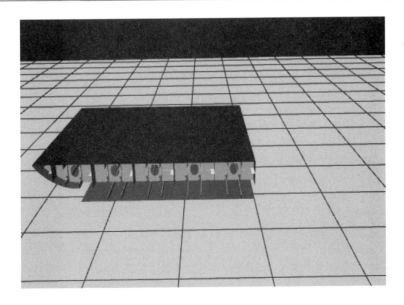

Figure 6.36 Stage 6 of the assembly sequence.

Figure 6.37 The Barcelona Pavilion.

VRL researchers developed a model of the pavilion (based on data obtained from SGI) for experiments in immersive virtual reality and for the study of the following topics:

- Geometry simplification via polygon reduction algorithms
- Real-time rendering techniques in immersive VR; frame rate optimization
- Human relation to a full-sized representation in immersive VR
- Navigation through and around the pavilion; diving into the pool
- Texture mapping on flat and curved surfaces; translucent surfaces
- Model representation in VRML, including level-of-detail nodes
- Animation via shuttle, pendulum, rotor, and blinker nodes in VRML

The test version from the VRL researchers is different from the original pavilion, and the animation placed into the model may not be appropriate regarding the intended spirit of this building. It is the hope of the VRL, however, that these sacrileges (shown in Figures 6.38 through 6.46) do not offend the many admirers of Mies van der Rohe's work.[26]

Figure 6.38 View 1 of the Barcelona Pavilion.

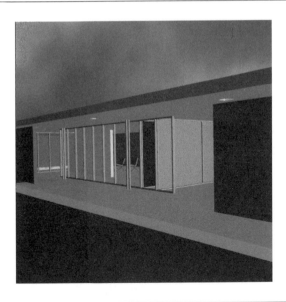

Figure 6.39 View 2 of the Barcelona Pavilion.

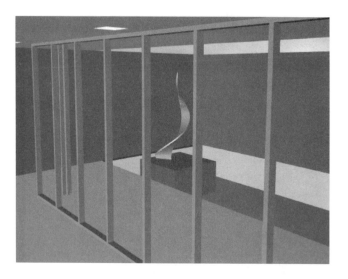

Figure 6.40 View 3 of the Barcelona Pavilion.

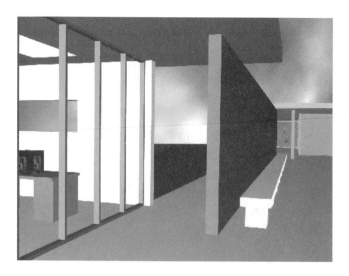

Figure 6.41 View 4 of the Barcelona Pavilion.

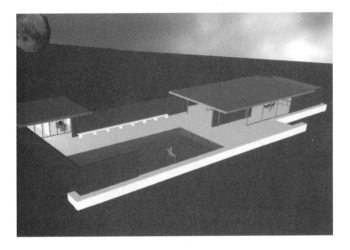

Figure 6.42 View 1—Bird's-eye view of the Barcelona Pavilion.

Figure 6.43 View 2—Bird's-eye view from a close-by moon of the Barcelona Pavilion.

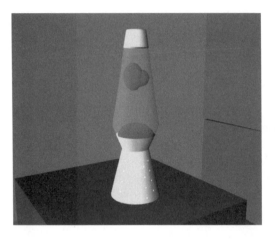

Figure 6.44 Still frame of lava-lamp animation.

Figure 6.45 Still frame of jumping-monitor animation.

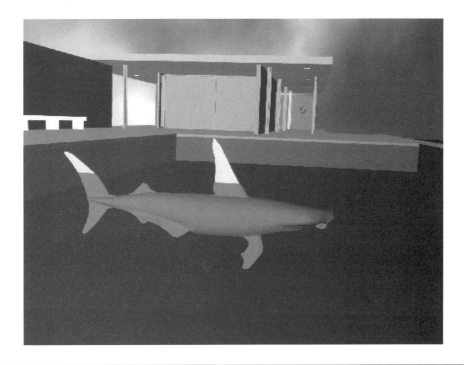

Figure 6.46 Still frame of circling-shark animation.

Simulated Accident

This project shows the virtual reconstruction of a deadly accident that was presented to the jury of a court case, and involved the replacement of a telephone pole by a work crew. The existing pole was sawed off a few feet above the ground. In a proper design, the incoming and outgoing telephone cables and the anchored workers are supposed to keep the sawed-off pole in a balanced position. In this case, however, the cables had been attached to the wrong side of the pole, and the workers were attached too low and did not properly bisect the angle between incoming and outgoing cables. As a result of the unanticipated forces, the sawed-off pole started to move, and pushed a member of the work crew against the rear wheel of a utility truck, causing severe injuries (see Figures 6.47 through 6.50).[27]

Figure 6.47 Scene overview and Stage 1 of the accident.

Figure 6.48 Scene overview and Stage 2 of the accident.

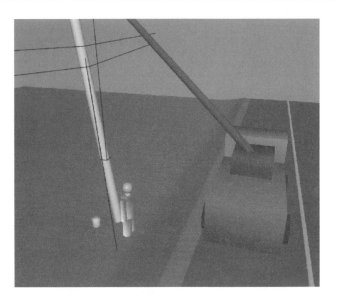

Figure 6.49 Scene overview and Stage 3 of the accident.

Figure 6.50 Scene overview and Stage 4 of the accident.

Immersive Virtual Reality Prototyping in Yacht Design

This project, sponsored by the Marine Hydrodynamics Laboratory, created a virtual sailing yacht from an AutoCad representation (see Figure 6.51) to study the difficulties, limitations, and benefits of immersive virtual reality in an application that deals with arrangement problems and narrow spaces.[28] The 3-D interior and exterior of the yacht were modeled in great detail, and with extensive use of texture mapping (shown in Figures 6.52 and 6.53).[29]

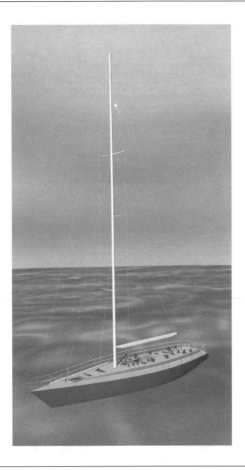

Figure 6.51 Virtual prototyping of a sailing yacht.

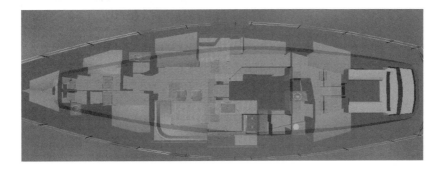

Figure 6.52 This top view (with the deck made translucent) shows the interior arrangement.

Figure 6.53 A view of the deck as seen from the helm.

The study highlights the usefulness of immersive virtual reality in yacht design and related marine applications. Layout and interior arrangement can be studied in a full-scale, 3-D virtual representation that provides the user with walk-through (see Figures 6.54 through 6.56) and fly-over capabilities (see Figures 6.57 through 6.59).[30] The user experiences a realistic impression of a complex design and can evaluate the yacht before it is built.

From Here

Now let's look at a prelude to the future development of VRML: *multiuser domains* (MUD) and *multiuser object-oriented* (MOO) systems. Chapter 7 discusses the architecture of the MOO-based HTML collaborative hypermedia system and its support for the emerging VRML 2.0/97 standard.

Figure 6.54 View 1—Interior walk-through view of saloon and galley.

Figure 6.55 View 2—Interior walk-through view of saloon and galley.

Figure 6.56 View 3—Interior walk-through view of saloon and galley.

Figure 6.57 View 1—Fly-over view of the exterior.

Figure 6.58 View 2—Fly-over view of the exterior.

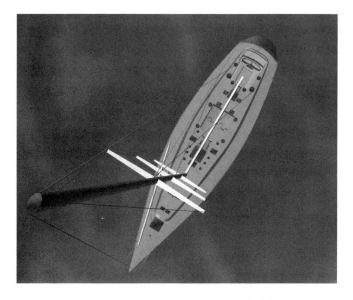

Figure 6.59 View 3—Fly-over view of the exterior.

Endnotes

1 Dr.-Ing. Klaus-Peter Beier, "Virtual Reality: A Short Introduction." Research Scientist, College of Engineering; Adjunct Associate Professor, Naval Architecture and Marine Engineering; Associate Director, Laboratory for Scientific Computation (LaSC). Virtual Reality Laboratory (VRL), University of Michigan, 2600 Draper, 225 NA&ME Bldg., Ann Arbor, MI 48109-2145, July 1996.

2 Fakespace, Inc., 241 Polaris Ave., Mountain View, CA 94043.

3 University of Illinois at Chicago, 1200 West Harrison, Chicago, IL 60607.

4 Dr.-Ing. Klaus-Peter Beier, "Virtual Reality: A Short Introduction." University of Michigan, 2600 Draper, 225 NA&ME Bldg., Ann Arbor, MI 48109-2145, July 1996.

5 Diganta Saha, University of Michigan, NAME Virtual Reality Laboratory, 1813 Willowtree Lane, Apartment # C2, Ann Arbor, MI 48105.

6 Dr.-Ing. Klaus-Peter Beier, "Virtual Reality: A Short Introduction." University of Michigan, July 1996.

7   Robot Simulations Ltd., 2892 Kew Drive, Windsor, Ontario, N8T 3C6, Canada.

8   Ibid.

9   Ibid.

10 Ibid.

11 Dr.-Ing. Klaus-Peter Beier, "Virtual Reality in Automotive Design and Manufacturing." Proceedings, Convergence '94, International Congress on Transportation Electronics, SAE (Society of Automotive Engineers), Dearborn, MI, October 1994.

12 Ibid.

13 Ibid.

14 Ibid.

15 Ibid.

16 Ibid.

17 Ibid.

18 Ibid.

19 Ibid.

20 Virtual Reality Laboratory, University of Michigan, 2600 Draper, 225 NA&ME Bldg., Ann Arbor, MI 48109-2145.

21 Ibid.

22 Ibid.

23 Ibid.

24 Ibid.

25 Ibid.

26 Ibid.

27 Ibid.

28 Marine Hydrodynamics Laboratory, University of Michigan, 126 West Engineering Building, Ann Arbor, MI 48109-1092.

29 Ibid.

30 Ibid.

7

Surrogate Travel on the Internet

This chapter describes the development of a networked collaborative hypermedia system intended to support groups of writers and scholars in writing and publishing hypertext fiction and criticism in a virtual reality environment. The current system still supports the importation of individually developed *Storyspace* hypertext documents into a MUD-based (multiuser domain) collaborative workspace for integration and expansion, and allows for the immediate publication of these dynamically generated multimedia documents with 3-D Web browsers. In addition, a forms-based writing and linking interface to the text is provided, so that writers use either the MUD-based or the forms-based authoring tools.

This chapter discusses how the *Web Object Oriented Distributed Server* (WOODS) builds on several decades of research and development in both the collaborative systems and hypermedia fields.

Many of the issues facing existing collaborative systems—the foremost being load handling—can be documented from observations of existing implementations. The next generation of collaborative hypermedia systems must address these issues with a fully scalable design solution. The MOOniverse Project at SenseMedia has implemented a scalable intranet of independent yet cohesive WOODS-based collaborative hypermedia servers known as *The Sprawl*.[1]

Since HTML is generated dynamically from an underlying database, capabilities have been added to allow for user negotiation of content and bandwidth (only small virtual reality versions of the pictures, with the audio and text in German, with movies), and to provide the bandwidth-intensive media from distributed mirror sites. This system is being used by thousands of students, writers, and theorists around the world to support such projects as hypertext writing and theory classes at Brown and Vassar; a hypermedia version of a virtual reality feature-length film; WAX, or the discovery of television among the bees; a collaborative women's hypertext fiction-writing group; the creation of an electronic journal to discuss the impact of technology on writing practices, and many more.

The World Wide Web has very quickly become one of the fundamental structures of the Internet and intranet. Although it provides a great deal of support for publishing information and navigating through it, it does not provide as much support for computer-supported collaborative work where users can collectively write, annotate, and explore hypermedia documents.

A prototype system has been developed to support a collaborative virtual reality hypermedia writing space where users may write documents, annotate each other's documents, engage in critical discussion, and have online classes or seminars. Although it was originally developed to support an undergraduate creative-writing class, it is now being used for film-based works, collaborative writing groups, and as a reviewing system for refereed journals.

Evolution of MOO-Based Collaborative Hypermedia Systems for the World Wide Web

MOO-(Multiuser Object Oriented Domain) based collaborative hypermedia systems are the result of the development and combination of both collaborative systems and hypermedia technology. Early ideas of personal information systems such as the Memex became plausible with the introduction of electronic computers. The primitive graphics of the Sketchpad system foretold of the high-resolution displays of today. The inevitable development of a universally compatible information system first described as Project Xanadu made major strides with the introduction of affordable high-performance personal computers, global interconnectivity, and new ideas in tools facilitating workgroups. Rapid advances in graphics hardware technology during the last two decades spurred the development of device-independent and object-oriented platforms such as Picosof iDrive.[2]

Text-based virtual realities were introduced with the popular Adventure exploration game, and the desire to improve and extend the original single-person game resulted in the development of multiuser, object-oriented, programmable platforms known as MOO that allow new virtual domains to be created and inhabited by many users. The World Wide Web introduced a transaction protocol and addressing standard that facilitates the exchange of different formats of media, including styled text, graphics, audio, and video. Browser software like Netscape Navigator and Microsoft Explorer provides cross-platform compatibility. *WOO* (Web Object Oriented) combines the collaborative features of MOO with the hypermedia features of the World Wide Web, creating the *CHIME* (Collaborative Hyperarchical Integrated Media Environment).[3]

Manipulation by Memex

Over 50 years ago, Vannevar Bush posed the idea for a machine that would give an individual the ability to rapidly manipulate large volumes of information. The *Memex*, as he coined it, would allow documents to be linked together with cross references that could be easily followed. Memex would provide the means to create new documents by seamlessly compositing citations from other documents at the direction of the operator. The state of the art at the time would have required the Memex to be constructed using mechanical storage and retrieval systems based on the available microfilm technology. While it addressed many of the problems of information overload and the importance of timely and flexible data retrieval, sheer mechanical complexity prevented it from ever being built.

On-Screen Manipulation by Sketchpad

The arrival of electronic computing devices using crude cathode-ray tube displays and new types of real-time input devices including keyboards, dials, and lightpens, provided an opportunity for new interactive information-processing applications. Ivan Sutherland utilized this new technology to create *Sketchpad*, a program that allowed, for example, on-screen manipulation of simple objects, the ability to describe certain properties of the objects to create, and the simulation of electric circuits. Although the graphics were primitive and the hardware bulky, Sutherland's work is clearly the precursor for the generations of interactive user interfaces that would follow.

NLS/The Internet Augmentation

The research of Douglas Engelbart began to address the issue of people working together, or collaborating, to deal with large volumes of information. The basic premise of his work deals with the issue that one individual is becoming increasingly unable to deal with the levels of complexity that are often present in many real-life problems. The goal of collaborative computing tools is to facilitate people working together to create solutions better and faster than a single individual can, if at all.

While Vannevar Bush recognized the problem of information overload, it appears he envisioned people working at their individual

Memex stations, happily sifting through large chunks of information. Englebart's work, as embodied in the Internet and his *oNLine System* (NLS), provides a real-time interactive interface that allows groups of people to communicate, cross-reference, quote, and deal with large amounts of information as a team, even remotely over long distances.

Xanadu Project

Theodore Nelson identified a new form of media, coined *Hypertext*, in the 1960s. Nelson envisioned words and ideas freed from the technological limitations of paper and ink. Nelson identified a literary issue, not a computing one, and he began to define many of the issues of hypermedia from the perspective of a literatician for the first time. Nelson described a world-spanning intranet of information repositories containing all "the information in the world" cross-referenced, linked, and "transcluded." The central tenant of his work, *Transcopyright*, provided unimpeded access to information to those quoting excerpts in a new context (transclusion) while automatically providing compensation and protection to the holder of the copyright of transcluded media.

While Nelson very accurately foretold the technical requirements of deploying his hypertext system, dubbed *Project Xanadu*, he happily left the details of actually building it to those better suited. It appears that while Nelson clearly identified many of the literary issues, and provided a means of everyone in the world having access to all the information available in the world, he addressed the issue of collaboration as people working *near* each other, not so much *with* each other.

Picosof iDrive Virtual Controller

Picosof iDrive was developed primarily as a virtual device interface and process controller. The iDrive provided a device-independent output layer in the form of an *application program interface* (API), allowing new output devices to be supported with the creation of a relatively straightforward device driver. Furthermore, iDrive provided a system-level message-passing mechanism, encouraging parallel object-oriented designs running in a preemptive multitasking operating system.

Applications built with iDrive typically comprise many instances of a few simple component objects wired together into an event-driven data flow intranet. Input is acquired through polled and interrupt-driven sensor and transducer objects, and output is rendered by various device-independent component output objects. The iDrive allows very efficient event-driven applications to be created from libraries of component objects. *System-level message passing* supports encapsulation and compatibility between components implemented, using a variety of compiled or interpreted platforms. *Device independence* allows rapid integration of new and different forms of hardware as it becomes available without requiring the modification of application software.

Excellent Adventure

The 1970s saw the installation of timeshared minicomputers at many universities around the world. For the first time, large numbers of students had access to interactive computing in the form of timeshare terminals available at on-campus computer labs. One of many "computer games" to be created in this golden age of computing is known as *Adventure*. Adventure is a text simulation of a collection of rooms or interconnected caves and outside areas that can be virtually explored and navigated by the virtual solo adventurer using simple commands like go north, pick up ax, read sign. Each player receives a certain number of points for discovering each room, and bonus points are awarded when special puzzles are solved. The original 350-point Adventure is a compelling interactive fiction that thousands of people continue to discover every year.

Adventure became the first of this new genre of computer games and soon advanced and extended. New versions of Adventure were developed sporting many new caves and puzzles. Two significant directions emerged from the early Adventure simulations: *Multiuser Domains* and *User Extensible Domains*. Multiuser

Domains allow groups of people to explore as a team or even against each other in virtual battle. User Extensible Domains allow users to extend the environment by creating new rooms and objects to their specification. These two directions recently converged along with the maturing of dynamic object-oriented programming environments, creating the object-oriented multiuser domain known as *MOO*, which is discussed in greater detail later in this chapter.

The WOO

Early in 1994, Samuel Latt Epstein's desire to incorporate the rich media features of the World Wide Web into the MOO interactive object-oriented environment led to the development of the Web MOO.[4] These are *WOO* (Web Object Oriented) enhancements that allow a MOO server to function as a collaborative hypermedia server, and a *WOO Transaction Protocol* (WTP).

WOO Transaction Protocol (WTP)

WOO Transaction Protocol (WTP) is an internet communications protocol designed to integrate two well-known Internet services: World Wide Web (WWW) and Multiuser Object Oriented (MOO) environments creating WOO. WTP provides a means for MOO servers to serve HTML documents to WWW clients like Netscape Navigator or Microsoft Explorer. WTP provides clients with the multiuser and rich programming features of MOO combined with the rich content of the entire World Wide Web.

WTP Connections: WTP provides two kinds of connections: *public connections* and *personal connections*. Public connections support WWW browsing of MOO objects by any WWW client. The WOO appears to the WWW client as an ordinary http server. HTML documents served by the WOO, however, may be created at connect time and depict current object descriptions and the descriptions of the contents of an object. Personal connections provide a means for a specific client with a registered WOO character to execute verbs as its character via *WOO URL* (WURL) requests.

WTP Public Connections (http://chiba.picosof.com/): Displays the homepage http://chiba.picodsof.com/ "object". Displays the .htext of the "object>" and the .htexts of the contents of the "object" if "object".htext==NIL. Displays the "object". description.

WTP Personal Connections (http://chiba.picosof.com/ "homemoo"/"char"/"rpassword"/"object"/"verb"/"arg"...]: Identifies the client to the WOO server as: "homemoo," the MOO a character is registered on; "char," the name of the character; "rpassword," the remote password for authentication. Upon authentication with the character's home MOO: execute "object".verb with "args" display HTML.

WOO HTML Inline Images: WOO servers providing WTP services are designed to keep mostly structural HTML in object descriptions (in db.) Large media elements including inline graphics, images, audio, video, and so forth, should be referenced via a *URL* (Universal Resource Locator) from a standard http server or by another out-db method for performance reasons.

Conclusion: WTP provides a means for WOO servers to provide the benefits of WWW and MOO by making WWW browsing a collaborative activity. Simultaneously, WTP and WOO make WWW publishing easily accessible to a whole new level of users. Anyone with a character on a WOO can publish his or her own WWW homepage to the entire world. WTP and WOO integrate the World Wide Web and distributed MOO intranets with an easy-to-create, attractive, graphical user interface.[5]

In other words, a WTP is a specification for issuing object/verb requests to a WOO server through the standard URL addressing mechanism.[6] A WOO server provides many advantages over a traditional Web or MOO server, including a collaborative, interactive, media-rich environment and a dynamic object-oriented Web server. WOO collaborative hypermedia technology was first deployed in ChibaMOO/The Sprawl, making this multiuser domain based on the fiction of William Gibson the first public-access Web server and multimedia MOO on the Internet. Rooms and objects on The Sprawl contain images and audio, as well as text descriptions. Over ten thousand people from all over the world have joined this virtual society this past year—socializing, playing games, learning, and creating objects and rooms on its several component servers. WOO technology has been adopted by Brown University (HyperText Hotel/WAXweb), the University of Nottingham (Living Documents), and many other educational and commercial organizations.

WOO was deployed initially as an object-oriented Web server in the SenseMedia Surfer.[7] The dynamic object-oriented environment is ideally suited to the creation of self-service collaborative hotlists; for example, lists of local movie theaters and points of interest, as well as online résumés, catalogs, and surveys. The object-oriented nature of the WOO server provides state-of-the-art programming features to otherwise flat traditional HTTPD World Wide Web hypermedia servers.

WOO Server Technology: The Second Generation

A second generation of ChibaMOO servers (which are discussed in greater detail later in the chapter) was deployed to provide additional capacity to the original ChibaMOO server. *WorldMOO* in Seattle, *UltiMOO* in Sydney, *HyperMOO* in Sapporo, and *MOOhalo* in Hawaii each provided full Web/MOO functionality and a level of intersite communication via remote paging and linked multi-channel facility. This second generation of WOO servers succeeded in providing additional capacity while distributing the load; however, it was still subject to the problems of an only partially scalable, hub-based design. Furthermore, while the InterMOO communication facilities functionally worked, a transparent feel was missing, preventing a feeling of cohesiveness between the different sites.

WorldMOO was the second collaborative hypermedia server to adopt the WOO server enhancements. WorldMOO provided all the same rich-content hypermedia facilities of ChibaMOO and was based on the descriptions of the real world, as rendered by people who actually lived in or visited these real-world places. WorldMOO grew beyond its available resources and, as a result of bloat of the database, WorldMOO was shut down permanently almost exactly one year after it opened.

UltiMOO, a SenseMedia/Next Online collaboration, provides a collaborative hypermedia server local to the Australian and New Zealand subnets. UltiMOO is based on a barely futuristic suburb of Sydney and provides fast local interactivity while maintaining intersite connectivity with the other ChibaMOO servers. UltiMOO is basically limited to users from Australia and New Zealand, which has limited the growth of the Australian database. This same slow growth has kept UltiMOO from fully reaching the critical mass necessary to become a thriving community on its own.

HyperMOO is primarily a research and development server dedicated to experimenting with object-oriented client technology; for example, the Intelligent Pad Development Environment developed at Hokkaido University in Japan. HyperMOO, located at the Sapporo Hypermedia Lab, was the first collaborative hypermedia server in Japan. HyperMOO has a very limited account policy and is not open to the general public.

MOOhalo is located on Oahu, Hawaii, providing collaborative hypermedia services to the residents of the Pacific Islands. MOOhalo accounts are limited to Hawaiian residents, keeping resource utilization relatively low. MOOhalo recently hosted the *Hawaiian Education Research Network* (HERN) project, bringing 250 educators together at the University of Hawaii for two weeks of intensive training on how to teach Internet collaborative and hypermedia skills to their colleagues and students.

Collaborative Hypermedia Servers for Academia

Organizations like the Language Arts Department at The University of Hawaii, the Artificial Intelligence group at The University of Nottingham, and Brown University, to name but a few, have adapted SenseMedia's WOO technology into collaborative hypermedia servers for various remote teleducation and hypermedia research projects. In these cases, growth is strictly limited by providing access to new accounts in a limited fashion, often to members of the organization and their collaborators.

Other MOOs

New collaborative environments of both the text-only and the hypermedia varieties regularly appear on the Internet. However, a majority are unable to attract users and are shut down within the first few days or weeks of operation for a variety of reasons. In a very few cases, all the ingredients necessary to launch a collaborative hypermedia server on a growth curve come together, and the more successful the work of the administrators of the environment, the sooner it overruns its resources and either must be shut down, seriously pruned, or stagnate.

Collaborative Hypermedia: The Next Generation

Next-generation collaborative hypermedia systems must address the issue of load handling and resource management. Effective load distribution appears to be the solution to the lag and bloat problems typically associated with monolithic servers. An asymmetrical multiprocessing prototype was deployed back in 1994, connecting over 1400 people using over one dozen servers in a hub-based network configuration. A symmetrical multiprocessing solution utilizing a hubless packet-routing mesh of linked servers is the heart of the next-generation, WOODS-based collaborative hypermedia environment.

Load Distribution

The requirement for scalability in the design of collaborative hypermedia systems demands new levels of flexibility in inter-server connectivity. It is crucial that mechanisms be developed that distribute the load across available resources without impeding the social nature of the collaborative hypermedia environment. Indeed, the goal is to provide a solution that allows the development of a critical mass of population necessary to create a healthy growing social system, while also providing a manageable growth path into the future.

The keys to providing effective load distribution are providing near-transparent interserver socialization and navigation. Linked user-to-user and multichannel communications features, as well as linked socialization/navigation features, allow users to communicate and socialize even between separate servers.

Rock-and-Roll Prototype

SenseMedia deployed *The Virtual Venue* on December 7, 1994, hosting the members of the band Aerosmith. Electronic Frontier Foundation and an audience of over 1400 people during a 90-minute question-and-answer session focused on individual rights and freedom of expression on and off the Internet.[8] The largest event of its kind at the time, SenseMedia's Virtual Venue consisted of a virtual auditorium with balconies connected to over a dozen servers on four continents.

The Virtual Venue utilized a hub-based network setup to connect the various servers together into a single virtual distributed server, each server supporting between 50 and 150 people in real time. This hub-based design supported nearly 1500 people and was potentially scalable to twice as many. The hub-based design, however, is very susceptible to failure of the hub, thereby disabling the entire network.

The Virtual Venue is ringed with an exhibit area featuring posters and exhibits about the participating servers and sponsors of the event. For the event, a small dedicated database consisting of the Venue and its corresponding exhibit hall were made available for installation at all the participating sites. Participants were able to wander the exhibits with their friends, and then select seats within rows of a virtual balcony for the actual event.

Installable Distributed Collaborative Hypermedia Server

The *MOOniverse Project* was launched to create a fully scalable, distributed collaborative hypermedia environment. The goal of the MOOniverse Project was a new, easy-to-install, collaborative hypermedia server/core combination known as *SprawlCore*. MOOniverse Project extends The Virtual Venue proof-of-concept prototype by replacing the hubbed intranet with a hubless, multi-point mesh. This hubless intranet, known as SunNet, provides a truly scalable, redundant, and reliable platform for the distributed collaborative hypermedia server. MOOniverse Project enhances basic MOO communication and navigation functions with hierarchical domain addressing extensions, providing seamless communication and navigation between servers.

Project MOOniverse

The MOOniverse Project consists of a WOODS-distributed server known as *SprawlCore*, and a hubless, packet-routing interserver intranet. SprawlCore-based servers achieve near-transparent socialization and navigation functionality between servers, allowing the collaborative intranet to be grown in a scalable fashion while evenly distributing increasing load. *The Sprawl* is the result of the MOOniverse Project and consists of the growing intranet of SprawlCore-based and SprawlCore-enhanced servers. Users are able to seamlessly communicate and navigate through The Sprawl, providing the advantages of both global and local communities without the resource problems typically associated with large monolithic servers.

SprawlCore Servers

The MOOniverse Project has at its heart the SprawlCore server/database combination. SprawlCore is an easy-to-install collaborative hypermedia server with a preloaded database containing all the basic Web and MOO functionality. SprawlCore is designed to closely interface with other SprawlCore servers via an efficient multipoint routing intranet, providing transparent communication and navigation between different sites.

The Intranet

The MOOniverse Project utilizes a highly reliable multipoint routing intranet known as *SunNet* in favor of a traditional hub-and-star intranet. SunNet supports both direct and indirect gateway connections using dynamic packet propagation to help maintain connectivity even around intranet outages. SunNet supports both standard and privileged remote verb execution, and is the primary intranet transport layer that InterMOO communication and navigation are based upon.

Navigation/Socialized Transparency

At the most fundamental level, the MOOniverse Project addresses the social requirements of an effective collaborative environment by encouraging a cohesive and easily navigable feel, obscuring the boundaries between physical sites.[9] Providing this level of transparency encourages users to log in to collaborative hypermedia servers geographically closest to them. Like a cellular intranet, additional servers may be deployed where there is demand for them, yet the user may participate at least at the social level anywhere within the intranet. Users benefit from fast local net, yet still have access to remote net on demand.

Primarily, SprawlCore utilizes an avatar/remote connection implementation to provide generic domain extensions to familiar MOO social and navigation commands in the form of (@dbname). This consistent and intuitive extension supports going, joining and paging, as well as InterMOO-linked channels and transparent site-linking exits.

The Sprawl

ChibaMOO is the last of the large monolithic collaborative servers. Experience shows that performance of the MOO platform degenerated geometrically. Experience with the MOOniverse Project also shows that a number of small sites working in parallel can grow to scale up to demand as necessary, and that cohesive intersite functionality encourages users to spread out the load through the intranet somewhat evenly. *The Sprawl* is the result of the MOOniverse Project and supersedes the original ChibaMOO collaborative hypermedia server with a distributed collaborative hypermedia intranet. The Sprawl now consists of a growing intranet of collaborative hypermedia servers based on SprawlCore, or including the intranet/socialization/navigation subset of SprawlCore.

The Sprawl began with the launch of Weyrmount, the first of the WOODS-based distributed servers, by more than 100 existing users who transplanted their community from the original ChibaMOO server. SnowMOO was opened to accept new users. Old Sprawl and The Caves are cleaved from the original ChibaMOO server into smaller servers for retired and current ChibaMOO users. New Chiba is being launched for new users. UltiMOO, HyperMOO, and MOOhalo are being retrofitted into the MOOniverse Project. Rupert is being launched for new users, and many other existing MOOs are being enhanced with SprawlCore functionality to smoothly plug in to The Sprawl. The Sprawl regularly supports over 100 online users who can smoothly communicate and navigate from end to end of the entire

intranet in its initial level of deployment with no appreciable server lag. WOODS-based collaborative intranets such as The Sprawl
should be able to scale into thousands of online users just by
adding servers to meet demand as necessary.

Weyrmount

Weyrmount was the first of the MOOniverse Project sites.
Weyrmount was formed by a group of Ultima Dragon enthusiasts
that had taken up residence in ChibaMOO. The Dragons numbered greater than 100 and, as a group, decided to leave
ChibaMOO for the greener pastures of a brand new MOOniverse
server. Weyrmount has succeeded farther and faster than anyone
expected, primarily because of the cohesiveness and direction of
the group of users that chose to pioneer this new collaborative
environment. Weyrmount serves as a wonderful model of how a
group of like-minded individuals create an environment and a correspondingly distinct culture, yet one that is open to visitors and
integrated and connected to other parts of the MOOniverse.

SnowMOO

SnowMOO is based on the fiction of Neal Stephanson. It was the
second of the MOOniverse Project sites.

Old Sprawl

Old Sprawl consists of recent users. The construction is from the
original ChibaMOO server retrofitted into the MOOniverse
intranet.

The Caves and New Chiba

The Caves consists of users who have been inactive since the beginning of ChibaMOO's second year, retrofitted into the MOOniverse
network. The Caves include a collaborative model of the entire
original Adventure Caves. *New Chiba*, on the other hand, is being

opened up to provide collaborative hypermedia facilities for brand new users.

UltiMoo

UltiMOO continues to serve the Australian and New Zealand communities. It has been retrofitted into the MOOniverse intranet.

HyperMOO and MOOhalo

HyperMOO has reopened as a MOOniverse-based SprawlCore server. It continues to function as a testbed for object-oriented client technology, including Intelligent Pad as well as the increasingly available Java and JavaScript systems. *MOOhalo*, on the other hand, has been reopened to the Hawaiian community as a MOOniverse SprawlCore-based server.

Rupert

Rupert, named after the last planet in Douglas Adams' *Hitchhiker's Guide Trilogy*, is a virtual cyberspace based on this fictional universe. Rupert has opened as a SprawlCore-based server.

Other Servers

Many groups are presently integrating MOOniverse distributed-server technology into their existing collaborative servers, and many new MOOniverse SprawlCore-based or derivative servers are being deployed throughout the world—taking The Sprawl to a whole new level of magnitude. The MOOniverse provides a consistent means for independent sovereign sites to link together into a cohesive intranet to benefit from the advantages of relatively small databases, as well as the cultural interchange and diverse population of an encompassing whole.

Now it's time for a little show-and-tell. Let's look at some Hypermedia Models commonly found in hypertext systems.

Hypermedia Models

The *Dexter* hypertext reference model (shown in Figure 7.1) describes a common set of abstractions found in hypertext systems in order to compare these systems and to develop interchange standards for them. Since this part of the chapter describes the interaction among three complementary hypertext systems, the Dexter model will be used to highlight differences in the approaches taken by the various systems and the techniques used to convert among them.

However, since the Dexter model does not provide for the content-ware presentation of multimedia information, the *Amsterdam hypertext model* (AHM) (shown in Figure 7.2) will also be used. This model represents multiple types of media information through the use of various channels, and also is able to specify synchronization relationships among the various parts. Although the primary multimedia mechanism (typically, Netscape) is still not able to support

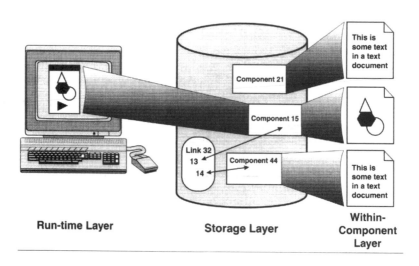

Figure 7.1 Dexter hypertext reference model.

synchronized multimedia information, and even though the World Wide Web still does not allow for the specification of temporal relationships, the information here is described in terms of an ideal virtual hypermedia implementation, not based on the limitations of any single environment.

The model used in the system consists of a central database that contains the text of each node, as well as additional information specifying the type, project information, and language of other multimedia information. This high-bandwidth multimedia information is typically stored at a number of distributed Web-site servers on a per-project basis. The centralized database contains low-bandwidth information (text and content coding) that is unlikely to change. On the other hand, the distributed multimedia servers contain high-bandwidth data (audio and video information) that will be modified much less frequently. At runtime, the central database server creates a specification of the text (based on current language and media preferences), with pointers to the

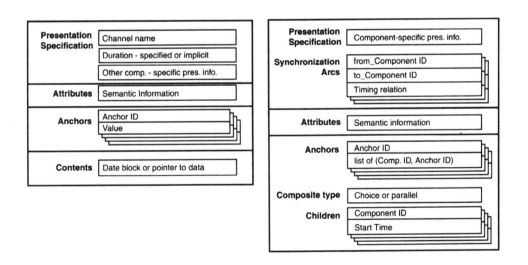

Figure 7.2 Amsterdam hypertext model.

multimedia information on the closest distributed server for that project. The model is a superset of the Dexter model, but does not provide for the synchronization and timing relationships expressed by the AHM.

Storyspace

The *Storyspace* hypertext system was developed by writers who sought to build a tool that would encourage the process of writing, and that would provide techniques useful in the creation of hypertext fiction. Storyspace uses *guard fields*, which provide for Boolean preconditions for following links. Many of the authors using Storyspace have used guard fields extensively in their writing, to provide for alternative narrative possibilities, based on what sections have previously been explored.

Storyspace has several interfaces for space (node) and link editing. These interfaces are based on the writer's preferred authoring style.

Publishing a read-only version of the text without any additional tools is easy. Several types of readers are available; they allow the user various levels of control and engagement with the text. However, they're not too overwhelming or too complex for the user.

Because of these features, and because a number of early influential hypertext fictions were written in Storyspace (Michael Joyce's *Afternoon*), this system is now used by the majority of those writing hypertext fiction in academic environments. Eastgate Systems, the publisher of Storyspace, is also the primary publisher of texts written in the system and has a catalog of a few dozen titles, distributed primarily on floppy disk.

Storyspace is a classic hypertext system, providing for one-to-many and span-to-span unidirectional links. The primary part of the Storyspace system not covered under traditional hypertext models is the guard fields, which require a significant amount of user state.

Unfortunately, Storyspace was originally intended to be a single-user and single-reader system. It provides only limited work-group and version support, and does not support simultaneous users on networked machines. The primary motivation in this work was to create a networked writing space with the narrative features of Storyspace in order to encourage the creation of collaborative fiction.

We've talked and hinted about MOO is this chapter. Now, let's get down to specifics and really discuss what it's all about!

MOO

MOO (Multiuser Object Oriented Domain) was developed by Stephen White and enhanced by Pavel Curtis, ostensibly as an advanced multiuser, user-extensible domain to the extreme, requiring that a virtual environment be constructed first before any game can be played. Indeed, the inherent open-endedness and flexibility of the MOO environment caused the focus to shift from creating multiuser domains for cave-type games to creating virtual online communities, where the focus of the thousands of participants becomes socialization as well as the growth or extension of the environment itself. While MOO has been used to implement some multiuser games, the majority of MOO environments presently on line are still virtual communities providing a place for education, socialization, and a growing number of commercial enterprises.

Building on Englebart's work, MOO provides a highly malleable and rich interactive collaboration space. It provides interactive (chat), store-and-forward (mail), posting (mailing list), and news features to its virtual denizens, many of whom have incorporated

MOO into their daily routine—staying connected to friends, colleagues, and other team members all day.

MUDs

On the other hand, *MUDs*, or multiuser domains, evolved out of multiplayer Adventure-style games in the early 1980s. These began as hack-and-slash-style games, but some of the MUDs began to evolve into more social areas somewhat reminiscent of chat lines. Although many of the earlier systems relied on hard-coded behaviors, MUD systems began to incorporate internal scripting and virtual-reality modeling languages. One particularly flexible Web-site server, MOO (MUD object-oriented), is now being widely used by the research community to support collaborative work, due to the ease of modifying the virtual-reality environment to support scholarship and sharing of information, as shown in Figure 7.3.

The MOO Web site is distributed by Xerox PARC (Palo Alto Research Center) through its study of collaborative computer systems. Although a large number of MOOs are still devoted solely to socializing, MOO systems have been established at the MIT Media Lab (collaborative environment for media researchers), the University of Virginia (postmodern theorists), CalTech (astronomers), and the Weizmann Institute of Science in Israel (biologists).

Hypertext in the MOO

It was apparent that the MOO system could be easily modified to create a hypertext fictional VR environment, since the MOO architecture of rooms connected by various passages could correspond to the hypertext architecture of nodes connected by links. It seemed that it would be especially interesting to transform Storyspace documents into MOO. This would keep the structural and narrative elements of the documents, yet provide for the possibility of additional richness by the social environment. Writers could meet their readers in their text and engage in immediate dialogues with them, or writers could arrange to meet and work on collaborative works.

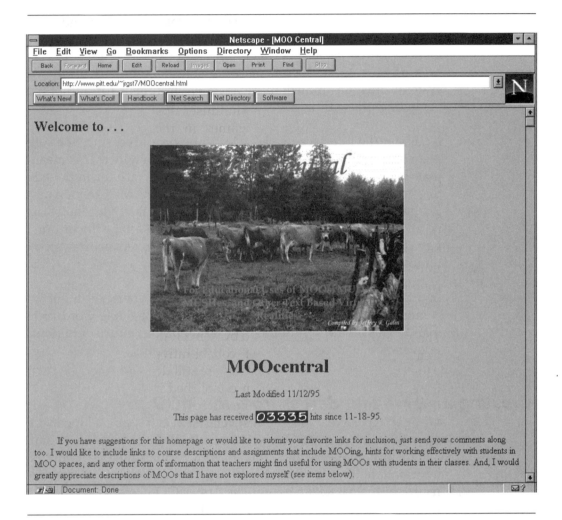

Figure 7.3 MOO.

Creation of the Hypertext MOO

The creation of hypertext authoring tools in the MOO was straight-forward, consisting of adding functionality to the generic rooms, exits, and players that already existed in the VR system. Because the MOO environment uses an interpreted object-oriented scripting language, the development of this part of the system was quite rapid.

Additionally, the importation of Storyspace documents into the MOO generally consisted of one-to-one mapping between documents and rooms, and between links and exits. A number of pre-existing Storyspace documents were able to be imported into the system; thus, an immediate rich VR environment for authors to begin to work with was created.

Note that the interface to a MOO is quite primitive, since the software was designed to work through line-mode telnet. This means that the only interface is a command-line interface (even the editors are line editors). Since many of the standard MOO commands for building VR rooms and linking them are fairly arcane (@dig north,n to Room 211), the MOO interfaces are a bit difficult for a novice to learn, since only now are computer users getting accustomed to VR interfaces.

In order to simplify the process of authoring hypertexts, all of the commonly used tools are written to consist of a one-word command. This in turn prompts the writer for as much additional information as necessary by using simple menus.

Creating a WWW Site Server from the MOO

Within the past year, people at several MOOs have developed software that allows a MOO to serve as a WWW site server, responding to http requests and dynamically formatting the requested information. This is made especially easy due to the interpretive nature of the MOO language. The first MOO-based WWW server was developed at Jay's—*HouseMOO* (JHM). This MOO was devoted to exploring networking issues (a MOO-based gopher interface was also developed). Originally, a modified version of the software was run. It ran an independent process that logs in as a character on the MOO and listens on another socket for the http requests. Recently, an integrated and modified version of the code has been developed at ChibaMOO. This code integrates the 3-D Web-site server very tightly into the MOO, without the necessity of an additional process to redirect the http requests. The VR graphical and multimedia capabilities of WWW browsers like Netscape Navigator and Microsoft Explorer provide for a much more readable publishing medium than the early 1970s look that line-mode telnet offers. However, there are many reasons to encourage the use of both interfaces. The MOO VR interface gives the user a great deal of programming control over the behavior of each node, and also allows for real-time collaboration. Until a single viewer is developed with the best qualities of the two interfaces, the MOO version and the 3-D WWW version of the database will continue to be supported.

Dynamic Delivery of HTML Texts

All of the texts are stored internally in the MOO database, which consists of objects with methods and properties defined on them. The hypertexts are stored as texts marked up with an extended version of HTML. It's described here in more detail to provide for dynamic formatting of the data. This extended version of HTML is then parsed, all dynamic links are resolved, and it is then output as pure HTML.

Extensions to HTML

Three important extensions to HTML are provided. First is the specification of a generic media type, which allows for pictures at multiple possible resolutions. This occurs with client-based specification of the preferred data bandwidth—none of which standard http supports. It also allows for the user to specify that he or she would like to receive medium-sized pictures with video, but without audio. Additionally, since the multimedia elements of the text are generally of a much higher bandwidth than the text, the specification of a number of large VR projects (WAXweb is an example of one such project) is allowed. Each of these projects has a set of mirror Web-site servers defined for it. The server determines where the incoming request is coming from, and then points all the media references to the nearest server. Unfortunately, due to the present Internet namespace, it is easy to determine the closest server only on a national level. Requests coming in from an address ending in .jp would be pointed to a mirror server in Japan, but it is difficult to distinguish between a .edu site in California and one in Maine.

Dynamic in-database virtual links are specified by using a *dyn-link* tag. This tag allows for the creation of floating links, and dynamic in-database links are specified using a dyn-link tag. This tag allows for the creation of floating virtual links and also provides for the maintenance of in-db state information passed through the URL. The state information is described later in the chapter.

Multiple-language support is provided through the <<Q lang=>> tag, which is defined as part of HTML+. The proposed definition of this tag, however, is primarily to guarantee that the language-specific layout conventions (hyphenation, text direction, etc.) are followed.

The World Wide Web

The proliferation of the Internet, combined with the adoption of a collection of transaction protocols and data formats, provided both a wealth of available information as well as an abundance of confusion when trying to locate and then access the information. Tim Berners Lee offered a consistent method of identifying both the location and the protocol used to access a particular piece of information via *a Universal Resource Locator* (URL), and a protocol for accessing information from a hypertext server (HTTP). Netscape Navigator and Microsoft Explorer use these new protocols to combine text and graphics from hypertext servers all over the world into attractive presentations on the large majority of personal computers that are now being connected to the Internet.

The World Wide Web was born of the union of these new Internet protocols; freely available hypertext client and server software by both NCSA and CERN, and the de facto adoption en masse by Internet users. The World Wide Web is a dramatic simplification of Nelson's Xanadu model, and is therefore subject to many of the limitations and problems solved by the full Xanadu architecture. However, as the first widely adopted hypertext system, the World

Wide Web is an exciting and compelling innovation that provides an incredibly effective and inexpensive means of publishing material to users all over the world.

Adding State to WWW

There's a need to pass around a great deal of state to represent the current state of the reader; however, http is specified as a stateless mechanism for transferring hypertext. One common solution to this problem is to include the state as part of the URL associated with each link. This is not an incredibly clean solution to the problem of maintaining state. Since the state of a session could become arbitrarily complex with the inclusion of guard-field information, it is currently used quite heavily in the following situations:

♦ **Authentication keys containing the current user and an encrypted password.** Once a user is authenticated, he or she is able to access the authoring tools that require special privileges, and the database is able to keep track on more internal state describing a given user's preferred authoring modes or the user's bookmarks. Additionally, this allows tracking of the ownership of virtual links and nodes.

♦ **The desired bandwidth level.** This is where the information is stored about whether to display pictures, audio, or video to the user in a VR environment.

♦ **The current state of the user interface.** A number of different interfaces may be opened or closed at any given time. The state between nodes should be maintained. These interfaces are described in greater detail later in the chapter.

♦ **The support for guard fields.** Although guard fields are not presently used, the information describing them on the individual nodes from Storyspace has been imported. This may be a feature that will be added to the state information that's stored, as documents are imported that make more extensive use of guards.

Forms-Based Authoring Tools

Most current implementations of 3-D Web viewers allow for the use of forms, which let an encapsulated user interface be included as part of the hypermedia content. Although the client deals with simple interaction (e.g., pop-up options menus), the 3-D Web-site server is responsible for handling updates from the forms. A number of expandable forms-based tools have added VR-authoring interface to the MOO. These include:

- Modifying the current media defaults, including the level of VR picture detail, the types of media, and the current language for the text and audio.
- Displaying authorship information, including the original creator of the text and a list of those who have added to it.
- Showing comments and adding one's own to the text.
- Adding and deleting bookmarks, and going to a specified bookmark.
- Adding links to the text, and creating new nodes.
- Editing the text of nodes one owns.

The first three interfaces are available to any reader of the text. Only registered users are able to add bookmarks and VR links to the text. At the moment, a user can only edit text that he or she owns, although any registered user can add VR links between texts.

Main Issues

The main issues facing the development of collaborative hypermedia servers are problems with interactivity known as lag, uncontrolled growth known as bloat, the definition of the social direction the virtual environment takes, and security.

Lag Problem

Lag is a problem that diminishes the interactive features of a collaborative hypermedia server. Lag is experienced by the user as delays in between requests or instructions issued to the server and results or responses returned by the server. Lag can be very frustrating to a user, especially when it comes intermittently in bursts or is consistently slow. Lag basically takes two forms: *server lag*, caused by the server suffering from excessive load; and *net lag*, caused by poor connectivity between user and server or server and server.

Server lag diminishes the interactive experience of collaborative hypermedia servers and is caused by the host processor bogging down under load. Excessive load is typically caused by too many users trying to simultaneously use a server, by one or more users using an inordinate share of system resources, or some combination of the two.

Net lag diminishes the interactive experience as well. It is caused by slow and/or error-ridden connections between both the user and a server, as well as between servers.

Database Bloat Concerns

Database bloat is a significant concern to collaborative hypermedia servers. The tendency for new objects and verbs to be created, along with the tendency for old objects to persist, combined with a growing daily population can lead to severe database bloat, which, in turn, leads to lag.

Social Direction of a VR Environment

The social direction of a virtual environment is determined by the users who populate the environment. Like real-life social systems, as more and more users participate in a virtual environment, the varying user demands on what direction the environment takes can cause conflict.

Security Issues

Although mechanisms for secure user authentication on the World Wide Web are constantly being developed, they currently allow for authentication for only a single document, due to the stateless nature of the protocol. Since one would rather not have the need for the reader to continually type in his or her password to be able to edit a set of pages, an authentication key has been added to the state passed around in the URL. At the moment, this consists of the user's account name (unique for the database) and an encrypted version of the password.

Consideration was given to making this encrypted password act as a token; however, it would only be valid for a limited time—possibly a day. That way, users wouldn't be able to impersonate other users for more than a short period of time. However, this would make it difficult to take advantage of the current hotlist features of Netscape Navigator and Microsoft Explorer. Since this has also been confusing to users, it hasn't been done.

Currently, the use of a public-key cryptosystem to provide for a more secure interface has been implemented. Of course, the consequences of a user impersonating another user of the system are fairly minor, limited to the ability to edit that user's texts. However, since this system is being used for more important commercial applications, security has become a critical issue.

Applications

There are presently many examples of collaborative systems existing on the Internet. The largest public-access text-based server, known as *LambdaMOO*, is regularly overwhelmed by load. *JHM* is a limited-access MOO that remains relatively inaccessible, thereby not taxing its resources. *CardiffMOO* is a small, nonpublic development MOO with restricted login hours. *ChibaMOO* is the largest public-access hypermedia server, and has addressed the load issue by moving in the direction of distributed server development. Many organizations, including schools and universities, operate text-only collaborative servers or WOO-based collaborative hypermedia servers. The main impediment to widespread use of this technology is the resource requirements of a traditional monolithic server. Next-generation distributed server technology promises to make collaborative hypermedia technology much more accessible.

LambdaMOO

LambdaMOO is the oldest and largest of the public-access, object-oriented, multiuser domains. Growing to a population of over 20,000 people over several years, LambdaMOO has become a large monolithic database consisting of a main building and its surrounding grounds as constructed by its 20,000-fold populace. LambdaMOO requires considerable resources and fortunately is sponsored by Xerox Palo Alto Research Center.

Even with very powerful servers with lots of memory, LambdaMOO often lags horribly, which prevents people from interacting smoothly. LambdaMOO often hosts more than 200 people during peak activity. The load on the server placed by more than 200 people can make the lag unbearable. LambdaMOO regularly reaps or discards users who have not logged in for several months, freeing up resources for a limited number of new users who can create new accounts. The nonscalability of the MOO server design essentially shows this to be the practical limit for a virtual environment based on MOO.

LambdaMOO has a rich social structure, providing community review of building and arbitration of issues between users. A thriving political community has evolved on LambdaMOO, providing regular new petitions and elections for positions on the various elected review boards.

LambdaMOO provides an innovative environment for collaborative educational and research activities to thousands of people. Inevitably, people that initially get involved with MOO for the social aspect get exposed to basic object-oriented programming and design principles—regardless of, though applicable to, their primary discipline.

JHM

Jay's HouseMOO was started to provide a place to discuss and develop various different projects in an environment free of the often mundane Spam or social chatter found on public MOOs. JHM is a very restricted building and programming environment; however, it provides a meeting place for many of the developers of much of the leading collaborative technologies. Since JHM is relatively small and serves a correspondingly small population, it requires very modest resources and provides very fast interactive response.

CardiffMOO

CardiffMOO is a small research site that is responsible for some of the early developments providing gateways between MOO and other MOOs, as well as between MOO and the World Wide Web. CardiffMOO is not a public MOO, and restricted operating hours keep memory and bandwidth usage to a minimum.

ChibaMOO

ChibaMOO it the world's first and largest public-access collaborative hypermedia server. ChibaMOO is a *Collaborative Hyperarchical Integrated Media Environment* (CHIME) server combining the object-oriented interactive virtual reality of MOO with the rich content hypermedia features of the World Wide Web. Denizens of this WOO (Web Object Oriented) cyberspace, based on the fiction of William Gibson, can create objects and rooms consisting of text, graphics, and sounds, as well as create dynamic WWW homepages.

Over the last year, ChibaMOO has grown to a population of over 12,000 people in a loose synchronistic anarchy or *synarchy*. Efforts to help distribute the load, including integrating WOO functionality as well as server-to-server linking facilities into parallel environments, has led to a total of slightly over 20,000 people on an intranet of 10 servers since ChibaMOO was originally opened to the public. ChibaMOO was selected as an original Netscape "What's Cool" site and, since that time, ChibaMOO has provided public-access Web services and programming facilities to people all over the world.

ChibaMOO runs on SenseMedia SGI IndigoII (or higher) servers that provide very high levels of performance. Combined with the loose intranet of parallel servers, ChibaMOO servers suffer very little lag, with a load of approximately 200 users on line of a population of several thousand. Beyond this, ChibaMOO servers begin to lag like LambdaMOO servers.

The original ChibaMOO server reached a reasonable limit after about 14 months, at which time all new account creation was terminated. SenseMedia's distributed collaborative hypermedia MOOniverse project was set in motion to solve the nonscalable architecture problem of the traditional MOO environment.

Other MOO Applications

The *HyperText Virtual Hotel* was begun by the HyperText Fiction Workshop at Brown University in 1991, using Intermedia, and ported to Storyspace in 1993. This historic collaborative document has been imported into the VR system. There it has continued to be extended and written on by writing students. The Storyspace version has also been added to. In addition, other people have written in the text and incorporated it with the other, newer areas of the VR system.

Hi-Pitched Voices (a women's collaborative hypertext fiction working group) has been the most prolific part of the HyperText MOO. This group was started to explore models of women's writing on the Net.

Another group, *RhetNet*, is also beginning to use the HyperText MOO to prepare a refereed electronic journal of technology and rhetoric. This group also held an online panel in the system, as part of the electronic version of the Computers and Writing conference.

WAXweb

WAXweb was the motivating application for the development of the 3-D Web-based viewing and authoring tools. The media composition of the film WAX depends on a paradigm that might be described as anything, in any order, at any time. The film has no dialogue, but instead, a narrator who delivers much of the story through voice-over. This fact, combined with the film's natural resemblance to hypertext and the need for audience assembly, made it a natural retrofit into a constructive hypertext.

WAXweb began as an experiment in hypermedia authoring, trying to remove the time base from the film and increasing the number of pointers. The construction of the work began by developing a base layer of 600 nodes, roughly corresponding to each spoken line in the film's monologue. In each node, accompanying the text of the monologue, is the MPEG video and the audio of that scene. Additionally, each node contains stills (about 2,000 total) representing each shot used in the video for that node. Each still has a commentary by the filmmaker. The entire text is also provided in video via English, French, German, and Japanese.

The base layer has several large-scale indexing structures:

♦ The linear path, which connects each node with the one immediately following it in the film.
♦ A tree structure, which establishes each node in its proper position in the act/scene hierarchy.
♦ Shot overview maps (like the clicking on an active still), which take you to an index of similar pictures in the film (e.g., all the other pictures of hands).
♦ Textual thematic paths, where the text of the film has embedded links between words corresponding to the overall themes of the film (e.g., the path through all the instances of the word *darkness*).
♦ A random index, which consists of a page filled with Xs, each connected to a random starting point in the film.

Through a combination of these navigational techniques, it is expected that the reader will be able to understand the ideas expressed in WAX. So far, readers who have seen WAX as a film have reacted quite positively to experiencing it as a hypertext.

In other words, WAXweb is a hypermedia version of the VR film WAX, or the discovery of television among the bees. This VR film was the first independent feature film edited using a nonlinear editing system. It was also the first film to be broadcast over the *mbone* (multimedia backbone) of the Internet. Originally, the text of the film was to be put onto the Hypertext MOO to support a collaborative VR project in which 25 writers, filmmakers, and theorists from around the world would add to the text of the movie and create a large body of associated hypertexts based on the film. Currently, this work has become the driving application for adding hypermedia functionality to the system.

Summary

As described in this chapter, the present level of implementation of MOO-based collaborative hypermedia systems for the World Wide Web demonstrates both the potential and the limits of this technology. A wide range of examples of text-only, as well as hypermedia collaborative systems, documents the issues involved with both small- and large-scale collaborative systems. The requirements of next-generation collaborative hypermedia systems demand high levels of interactivity and media-rich presentation, and must be fully scalable in order to serve the continually growing demand on resources.

SenseMedia's MOOniverse Project developed and implemented the Web Object Oriented Distributed Server (WOODS), providing a high-performance, fully scalable collaborative hypermedia server known as SprawlCore. The Sprawl consists of a collection of SprawlCore-based and SprawlCore-enhanced servers that run independently, yet are very closely, even transparently, linked at a social level. The Sprawl provides the advantages of a large encompassing population comprising smaller like-minded social groups with none of the load and resource depletion problems associated with large monolithic servers. WOODS-based collaborative hypermedia servers provide an effective means of creating really large collaborative systems from combinations of many smaller servers, making the benefits of collaborative hypermedia technology accessible to many individuals and organizations who could not previously afford the cost.

From Here

Chapter 7 has described how MOO-based collaborative hypermedia systems for the World Wide Web have evolved from the convergence of both collaborative and hypermedia systems. The next chapter provides an overview of the implementation of these environments as users create their own VRML Web sites. Part II of the book (Chapters 8 through 13) continues the theme of Chapter 8 by thoroughly explaining how users can create and implement virtual reality applications on the Internet via the VRML 2.0/97 standard.

Endnotes

1. Samuel Latt Epstein, "Woods Object Oriented Distributed Server." Director, Hypermedia Services. SenseMedia Netcasting, Division of Picosof Systems, Honolulu, HI, 1996.
2. Ibid.
3. Ibid.
4. Ibid.
5. Ibid.
6. Ibid.
7. Ibid.
8. Ibid.
9. Ibid.
10. Ibid.

Part Two

Implementing the Future

8

The VRML Consortium

The VRML Consortium, as described in Chapter 2, is the official organization tasked with extending the VRML specifications and standards into what we all want: a scalable, fully interactive cyberspace. The continued expansion of VRML specifications and standards is made possible by the *Working Group Process* of the VRML Consortium.

A *Working Group* (WG) of the VRML Consortium is a technical committee that researches and proposes solutions to specific technical problems relating to VRML. Anyone may volunteer to join a WG. Let's look at some of the research work that is being currently developed by WGs for implementation in future VRML standards and specification extensions.

Beyond VRML

This part of the chapter outlines a direction for VRML, based on the Working Group Process shown in Figure 8.1.[1] This discussion is intended as a guide to the current operating status (Formation; Research; Drafting; Proposal) or stage that each WG is in. In other words, the final result of some (not all) WGs will be to produce a *Standard* or a *Recommended Practice* (RP) of the VRML Consortium. The difference between the two tracks lies in the ultimate disposition of the proposed addition. Note that not all WGs will produce a Standard or an RP. It is entirely reasonable to decide *not* to create a new standard or RP. Each WG must follow a process and pass several milestones before a proposal is produced and considered for either of the two tracks. The focus of this chapter is to outline the priorities and purpose of the Working Groups; how to form a Working Group; how to reveal problems with VRML through the standardization process; provide technical review and guidance for the Working Groups; advise the VRML Consortium on recommended practices and standards; and, finally, make some comments about the future. The WG Process will be covered in greater detail later in the chapter.

Priorities and Purpose of WGs

Working Groups are essentially self-forming, self-regulating, and self-directed. They must meet certain criteria (see accompanying CD-ROM on the VRML Consortium) before they are recognized, but then one of the key roles of the VRML Consortium is support of the WG process. The Consortium does not support, nor does it recognize product-specific WGs. Its focus is on issues and technologies with industry-wide ramifications. This is one of the most important aspects of the WG process. Many companies and industries are already investing large amounts of time and resources to VRML technology. A WG must be able to clearly state its intentions. An ordering of priorities is paramount when trying to produce a Standard or a Recommended Practice; and, it should be one of the first orders of business when expanding VRML specifications and standards.

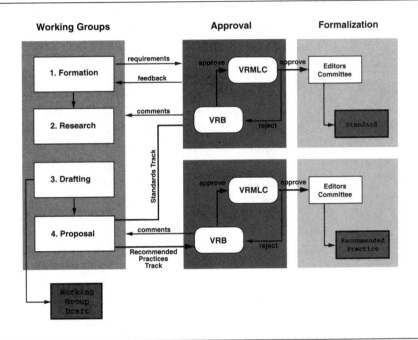

Figure 8.1 Working Group Process shows the steps needed for a proposal to be adopted by the VRML Consortium.

Additional work needs to be done in many areas. Because there are so many complicated issues, the following is a list of the currently recognized Working Groups. The WGs listed here represent only what is thought to be of importance to VRML's future. By no means is this list complete.

- ◆ **The Humanoid Animation WG**: The VRML Humanoid Animation Working Group exists for the sole purpose of creating a standard VRML representation for humanoids.
- ◆ **The Color Fidelity WG**: The purpose of the Color Fidelity Working Group is to enable world builders to create worlds with the assurance that viewers on all platforms will see them looking as good as the originals and with colors reasonably close to the originals.

- **The MetaForms WG**: The purpose of the MetaForms Working Group is to create and maintain a methodology for the specification of productions of formal grammars that may map to specific *forms* such as VRML, primarily to enable the representation of the structure and growth of *digital life-forms*.
- **The Object-Oriented Extensions WG**: The VRML OO-Extensions Working Group has been created to discuss and develop object-oriented extensions for VRML.
- **Database WG**: The goal of the VRML Database Working Group is to enable the standards-based creation of VRML business applications, where databases enable persistent, scalable, and secure delivery of VRML content.
- **External Authoring Interface WG**: The EAI Working Group is attempting to create a standard interface between a VRML world and an external environment.
- **Widgets WG**: The Widgets Working Group is an initiative to provide developers and users with a fundamental, freely available set of standard user interface widgets and a theoretical framework supporting these and all VRML widgets.
- **Compressed Binary Format WG**: The CBF Working Group has been created to discuss and develop the binary encoding of VRML files, emphasizing the reduction of file size for fast transmission, and the simplification of file structure for fast parsing.
- **Universal Media Libraries WG**: The goal of the UML Working Group is to increase the realism of VRML worlds and decrease network downloads by defining a small, cross-platform library of locally resident media elements (textures, sounds, and VRML objects) and a uniform mechanism by which VRML content creators can incorporate these media elements into their worlds.
- **Living Worlds WG**: This Working Group is involved in defining a conceptual framework and specifying a set of interfaces to support the creation and evolution of multiuser (and multideveloper!) applications in VRML

2.0. See Chapter 9, *Living Worlds*, for an in-depth discussion of this Working Group.

- **Keyboard Input WG**: The mission of the Keyboard Input Working Group is to define one or more extension nodes to allow content creators to have access to keyboard input inside their VRML worlds.
- **Conformance WG**: The goal of the Conformance Working Group is to provide a forum where conformance testing issues can be discussed. In particular, this group will identify areas where implementations are diverging, and determine appropriate courses of action.
- **Biota WG**: The mission of the Biota Working Group is to create and deploy digital tools and environments for research and learning about living systems.
- **Distributed Interactive Simulation WG**: The goal of the Distributed Interactive Simulation Working Group is to establish initial networking conventions for building multicast-capable, large-scale virtual environments (LSVEs).[2]

Now that we've looked at the current list of WGs and discussed their purposes and priorities, let's take a look at how these Working Groups are started. See the accompanying CD-ROM for more information and individual detailed descriptions of the purpose of each of these WGs.

How to Form a Working Group

A WG may be started by an individual or group. VRML Consortium membership is not required. A candidate WG must prepare a Working Group Proposal (discussed next) and submit it to the *VRML Review Board* (VRB) for recognition. The VRB provides technical review and guidance for WGs, advising the VRML Consortium on recommended practices and standards.

If the VRB accepts the proposal, the WG is added to the list of active WGs and the WG is on its way. If the VRB rejects the proposal (unusual), a detailed explanation for the rejection will be provided so that the WG can try again. Once the issues are addressed, the group may resubmit its WG proposal.

The VRB is a group elected by the VRML Consortium membership, and comprises experienced technical experts responsible for creating, directing, and coordinating the various Working Groups. See the accompanying CD-ROM for more information on the VRB.

So how does a WG submit a proposal? What are the steps involved?

Submitting a Working Group Proposal

The first step in submitting a proposal is to prepare a Web page for your WG. A template is usually provided as shown in Figure 8.2.[3] Use of this template is not required, but is recommended to make sure you include all the necessary information for the formation of your WG. You are also encouraged to add logos and structure to this template (page) to most effectively convey the information relating to your group.

The template must include:

- **Working Group title**: The official title of this WG (The Bojack Node Working Group).
- **Working Group identifier**: A short name to be used to identify your group. This will also be the name of the mailing list for this group, so it may not contain any spaces or characters that are illegal in an e-mail address. For instance, the bojack-node WG might be called *bojack-node*, and its mailing list would be called *bojack-node@someplace.com*.
- **Short description**: A one- or two-sentence description of this WG, to be placed in the current WG list.
- **Mission statement**: A short statement about the purpose of this WG.
- **Goals**: What constitutes the successful conclusion of this WG?

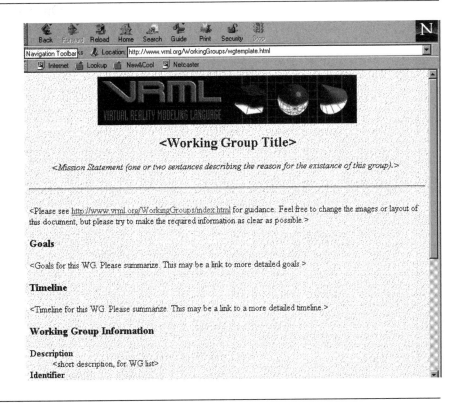

Figure 8.2 Working Group Proposal template.

- ♦ **Timeline**: What are the milestones? What is the approximate time frame of each milestone?
- ♦ **Chair and other contacts**: Identify the chairperson for the WG and important contacts who would add cohesion to the WG.
- ♦ **How to subscribe to the mailing list**: Instructions to everyone on how to subscribe to the mailing list.[4]

The second step in submitting a proposal is to create a mailing list. Before submitting your proposal, you must have your mailing list up and running, with subscription open to everyone. In the future, the VRML Consortium will provide a mailing list service for WGs.

The third step in submitting a proposal is to submit it to the VRB. Send a short message to *vrml-vrb@vrml.org*, indicating the URL for your proposal.

The fourth step in submitting a proposal is to wait for a response from the VRB. If accepted, the VRB will notify the WG chair by e-mail within one week, and will add a link to your homepage to the list of Working Groups. If rejected, an explanation will be sent to the chair, at which time the proposal can be amended and resubmitted.

Finally, the last step in submitting a proposal is to post a message to *www-vrml@vrml.org*. This message should be an open invitation to everyone to join the WG, with a pointer to the homepage. It should appear within a week of recognition.

Once your WG is started it must remain open to anyone wishing to participate. The bulk of the WG's communications should be through its mailing list. Occasional face-to-face meetings are a valuable addition to this, but minutes of such meetings should be posted to the mailing list as soon as possible. An archive of the mailing list should be kept, if possible. Archiving is a service that will be provided by the VRML Consortium server, if it is used as the mailing list server. Announcements of major milestones and other significant events may be posted to *www-vrml@vrml.org*. Key issues and updated timelines should be documented on the homepage.

Also, your homepage should be kept up to date and accessible at all times (within reason). If your server has problems keeping the Web page or mailing list accessible, they can be moved to the VRML Consortium server. This service is presently available.

Now that we've covered how a WG submits a proposal for recognition and appears on a list, let's take a closer look at the milestones of the Working Group Process or *Standardization* process that was discussed earlier (see Figure 8.1).

WG Process Milestones

As previously discussed, a WG must follow a process and pass several milestones before a proposal is considered for either of the two tracks (Standard or a Recommended Practice). Figure 8.1 showed a flowchart with the steps needed for a proposal to be adopted by the VRML Consortium. Let's take a closer look at these steps.

Formation

In this step, the WG has not yet been recognized or added to the WG list. Interested parties are sharing ideas, creating a homepage, and developing a charter for use in the WG.

Performing Research

This is the first step at which the WG is recognized and appears on the list. In this phase, the WG performs research, gathers ideas and proposals, and begins to develop consensus through open discussions, mostly on its mailing list. The group leaders should perform due diligence on addressing issues from all participants. Now is a good time for the group to solicit informal feedback from the VRB. The VRB can help make sure your group is on track for advancing to the next stages of development, and early in the cycle is a good time to get this feedback.

Working Group Draft

When the major issues have been resolved, and agreement is reached from all participants in the WG, the group begins creating a Working Group Draft. This draft documents the ideas and conclusions from the research and discussions. This document is unofficial, but it may be the final product of the group. If the group decides that its work does not need to be formalized into a standard or recommended practice, it may stop work when the WG Draft is completed. When drafting of this document commences, the group will be moved to a higher level in the WG list, upon request.

Proposal Submission

For groups that decide to submit proposals to the VRML Consortium, they will ultimately enter this phase. The decision to enter this phase must be done by consensus of the WG participants. Once consensus is reached, the group formalizes the draft into a proposal for submission. During this process, the group will be moved to a higher level in the working group list, upon request.

The proposal should try to adopt the VRML97 style if appropriate. During this phase, two independent implementations must be developed (if relevant). Once the proposal is complete, the WG submits it to the VRB to enter the Standards or Recommended Practices tracks.

Proposal Approval

Once submitted, the proposal requires approval by both the VRB and the VRML Consortium membership. If the proposal is rejected, the VRB will make comments and return it to the WG. The proposal may be resubmitted once the comments are addressed. If accepted, an Editing Committee is formed (recommended size: one to three people). At this point, the Editing Committee is responsible for editing and communications concerning the document review and ratification process.

Standards and Recommended Practices Tracks

If VRML-related products would need to adopt and conform to this document in order to be compliant, the proposal is a candidate for a Standard. Requirements for standardization are as follows:

- interoperability,
- common to wide VRML audience, and
- generally agreed upon within the community.[5]

If the proposal does not set requirements, but rather outlines common practices that will enhance the interoperability of VRML-related products, it is a candidate for a Recommended Practice.

Review and Editing

During the editing process, three drafts are produced by the Editing Committee. Initially, the proposal is reworked with minor editing and style changes. This becomes the first draft, which is submitted for public review. After the first review period, comments are incorporated and a second draft is produced and submitted for review. Upon integration of comments from this review period, the final draft is produced and ready for final vote for inclusion into the standard or recommended practices. During this editing process, no functional changes are allowed without VRB approval.

Throughout most of this chapter, the discussion has been focused on the continued expansion of VRML specifications and standards by the Working Group process of the VRML Consortium. But, is the VRML specification stable? Better yet, is it now an official *International Standards Organization* (ISO) standard? And, what part has the VRML Consortium (VRMLC) played in all of this? What is the VRMLC's relationship and/or agreement with the ISO? The next section will answer all of these questions and more.

VRMLC and ISO

The VRML specification is stable. VRML has been functionally complete since August 1996. The specification has been submitted to the ISO for ratification, where it is referred to as ISO/IEC DIS 14772-1, or (informally) as VRML97.[6] All portions of the spec are known to be implementable, and at least one company has released a browser that implements the full VRML specification. Many other browser writers have nearly completed their implementation of the specification.

VRML97

On April 4, 1997, VRML97 *Draft for International Standard* (DIS) 14772 came into being. This official document includes small technical revisions and replaces the VRML 2.0 *Committee Draft* (CD). This document was submitted to the *International Standards Organization* (ISO) to be put to a vote in the fourth quarter of 1997. If the DIS is approved, the final *International Standard* (IS) will be produced. The IS may not contain *any* functional changes from the DIS. Editorial changes are permitted. It is expected that the IS will be released in late 1997. [7]

Cooperative Agreement

The ISO is a worldwide federation of national standards bodies from some 100 countries, one group from each country. ISO is on line at *http://www.iso.ch.*

The *Joint Technical Committee 1* (JTC 1) of the International Organization for Standardization (ISO) and the *International Electrotechnical Commission* (IEC) have worked cooperatively over the past three years with the VRML community to transpose the publicly available VRML specification into an International Standard. Within JTC 1, the development work on VRML is assigned to *Subcommittee 24* (SC24) whose area of work is Computer Graphics and Image Processing. [8]

At a 1996 meeting in Kyoto, Japan, SC24 agreed to publish the final version of VRML 2.0 as *Committee Draft* (CD) 14772. The CD text was reviewed jointly by the VRML and ISO/IEC communities during a comment period that closed in late 1996. The comment resolution process lasted until early 1997 due to the extent of editorial changes that it was agreed should be made. The DIS version of the specification became available for review in both communities in the second quarter of 1997. After this review ends in the fourth quarter of 1997, there will be a final comment resolution process followed by publication of the VRML97 International Standard very late in 1997 or early 1998. The text will be published electronically as an HTML document and will mark the first time that an ISO standard has been so published.

Liaison Policy between VRMLC and ISO

The VRML Consortium has several new items of work underway that supplement the VRML specification. Both ISO/IEC JTC1/SC24 and the VRML Consortium have indicated their willingness to extend and continue the cooperative arrangement in SC24 N1599 that has led to the successful processing of the VRML97 Specification as an ISO/IEC standard.

The purpose here is to establish the detailed procedures whereby ISO/IEC JTC1 and the VRML Consortium will cooperate to continue the development of a series of ISO/IEC standards based on the work of the VRMLC, including the VRML97 Specification (DIS 14772). The following are general principles from which the details of this agreement are derived:

♦ The VRML Consortium produces *publicly available* industry specifications through an open, consensus-based process with international participation by thousands of individuals and organizations.
♦ ISO/IEC JTC1 wishes to adopt suitable industry specifications as ISO and IEC standards.
♦ Both organizations desire to harmonize their procedures so that initial technical development work is done primarily in the Consortium with provisions for ISO participation, and the final editorial and independent technical assessment work is done primarily in the ISO/IEC JTC1 with provisions for VRML Consortium participation.
♦ Both organizations desire that VRML Consortium Specifications be adopted as ISO and IEC standards as quickly as is feasible and with only minimal changes based on an agreed upon set of criteria. [9]

Final Standards Distribution

All documents developed under this agreement, including the final ISO/IEC standards, will be made available through ISO/IEC sources. They will also be made available through normal VRML Consortium sources, including the open VRML Consortium Web site.

Interchange Document

ISO/IEC documents developed under this agreement will be made available to the VRML Consortium and the VRML community by placing copies on the VRML Consortium Web site. Relevant VRML Consortium documents on the VRML Consortium Web site will be referenced in the ISO/IEC activity. No documents will be referenced that are not generally available. Notification of availability of new documents on the VRML Consortium Web site will be announced on an e-mail reflector limited to the appropriate ISO/IEC WG(s) and the VRML Consortium participants only.

Intellectual Property Rights

In accordance with VRML Consortium procedures, the text of all working documents developed under this agreement, as well as the final ISO/IEC standards, shall remain free of intellectual property right restrictions that would limit their open distribution following normal VRML Consortium practices. The name of the standards (including the words *VRML* and *Virtual Reality Modeling Language)* shall also remain free of intellectual property right restrictions. The VRML Consortium certifies to ISO/IEC that the original base document (the VRML97 specification) is free of intellectual property right restrictions and, in particular, contains no material which any organization claims is proprietary or confidential or is the subject of any patent. If and when other work beyond that based on the VRML97 specification is initiated with ISO/IEC JTC1, the VRML Consortium agrees to identify any intellectual property right restrictions to ISO/IEC in accordance with ISO/IEC policies.

Aligning Procedures

To allow coordinated review of all working documents developed under this agreement, appropriate portions of ISO and VRML Consortium procedures must be aligned. The various aspects of this alignment are described in the following sidebar, "Aspects of Aligning Procedures."

Aspects of Aligning Procedures

Liaison: The ISO/IEC JTC1 Class C Liaison mechanism will be used as a primary mechanism to enable cooperation. ISO/IEC JTC1 has appointed the VRML Consortium as a Class C liaison organization to ISO/IEC JTC1. This allows VRML Consortium members to attend ISO/IEC working meetings and to participate in the work of the ISO/IEC. The VRML Consortium accepts an ISO/IEC JTC 1 representative as a liaison representative to the VRML Review Board so that liaison in the other direction can be achieved. This representative shall have the following responsibilities:

- At the point that the VRML Review Board agrees that work should be passed to ISO/IEC JTC1 for further processing, forward documents to ISO/IEC JTC1.
- Pass formal comments from ISO/IEC JTC1 to the VRML community.
- Report on the work of the VRML Consortium at each relevant ISO/IEC JTC1 or JTC1 subcommittee meeting.
- In coordination with the VRB, provide early notification to ISO/IEC JTC1 of VRML Consortium work that is likely to eventually be submitted to ISO/IEC JTC1.

Early collaboration: Both organizations desire that any VRML Consortium specifications that are input into ISO/IEC JTC1 be as close to meeting ISO/IEC style and quality requirements as possible. To help achieve this goal, ISO/IEC JTC1 agrees to produce a *Style Guide* and provide it as an aid to VRML Consortium Working Groups for use in the original creation of their specifications.

- Participation in all VRML Consortium Working Groups is open to any individual worldwide without restriction. ISO/IEC JTC1 National Bodies are encouraged to participate in the technical work on VRML by participating in these Working Groups. Since the desire of both organizations is that technical changes shall not be made once work has been passed to ISO/IEC JTC1 for finalization, ISO/IEC JTC1 National Bodies will encourage their technical experts to participate in VRML Working Groups.

Initiation of ISO/IEC work: No work on VRML Consortium specifications shall start within ISO/IEC JTC1 until the VRB has agreed that the work will be forwarded to ISO for processing as an ISO/IEC Standard. This requirement shall not prevent individual experts who participate in the work of ISO/IEC JTC1 from simultaneously participating in the technical work of one or more VRML Consortium Working Groups. The criteria that shall be applied by the VRB with the assistance of the ISO/IEC liaison representative include:

♦ The work is of sufficient interest and importance to the VRML community to become an ISO/IEC standard.
♦ The work is complete as measured by the Style Guide described earlier.
♦ The work is technically stable.

The preferred mechanism for initiating work within ISO/IEC JTC1 is the combined NP/CD (New Work Item Proposal/ Committee Draft) ballot. One exception is work that can be processed as an additional part of an existing standard so that an NP is not required. As a general rule, submitted specifications shall have reached the status of VRML Consortium Standard by the time of their submission to ISO/IEC JTC1.

Finalization of ISO/IEC work: ISO/IEC JTC1 and the VRML Consortium agree to the following procedures for processing work once it has entered ISO/IEC JTC1:

♦ From the time of initiation of processing (normally the NP/CD ballot) through to the publication of the IS text, ISO/IEC JTC1 procedures shall be followed.
♦ The VRML Consortium can participate in this stage of the work through the Category C liaison mechanism.

> ◆   The ISO/IEC DIS text shall be published by the VRML
>   Consortium for review within the Consortium accord-
>   ing to Consortium practices simultaneously with the
>   DIS ballot within ISO/IEC.
>
> **Late-stage technical changes**: It is expected that many editor-
> ial changes may be made to a Consortium specification as it is
> processed to become an ISO/IEC standard. Technical changes to
> a specification once ISO/IEC processing has been initiated shall
> be allowed only in accordance with the following criteria:
>
> ◆   Clarification is necessary for the sake of completeness
>   or consistency.
> ◆   A serious technical flaw is found that would render the
>   specification unusable.
> ◆   Both organizations agree to the change. [10]

Joint Meetings and Rights to Publish

All formal work under this agreement will take place at appropriately scheduled ISO/IEC JTC1/SC24 meetings. VRB (or other
VRMLC-appointed technical experts) members can participate in
formal ISO through the Class C liaison mechanism. Also, both
VRML and ISO/IEC retain the rights to publish all documents
developed under this agreement according to their own practices.

Base Document and Availability of Drafts
and Other Working Documents

At the time that a VRML Consortium specification is submitted to
ISO/IEC JTC1 for processing as an ISO/IEC standard, the VRML
Consortium shall identify the base document(s) for the work. In
addition, all drafts and working documents will be freely available
to participants according to each party's normal practices.

Standards Maintenance

Both organizations agree to coordinate matters of interpretation
and defect correction in any ISO/IEC standards that result from
this agreement. When requests for interpretation or reports of

defects are submitted to ISO/IEC JTC1, they shall be forwarded to the VRML Consortium to provide solutions that shall then be processed through normal ISO/IEC JTC1 processes for defect resolution and interpretation. Thus, the ISO/IEC JTC1 agrees to establish a VRML Defects Editing Committee to work with the VRML Consortium.

From Here

The VRML Consortium, as discussed in this chapter, was formed to provide a forum for the creation of open standards for VRML specifications, and to accelerate the worldwide demand for products based on these standards through the sponsorship of market and user education programs.

The next chapter presents a brief overview of Living Worlds, another Working Group of the VRML Consortium whose charter is to define a conceptual framework and specify a set of interfaces to support the creation and evolution of multiuser (and multideveloper!) applications in VRML 2.0.

Endnotes

1 VRML Consortium, 1997.

2 Ibid.

3 Ibid.

4 Ibid.

5 Ibid.

6 Don Brutzman. "The VRML Review Board (VRB) Frequently Answered Questions (FAQ)," U.S. Navy (http://www.stl.nps.navy.mil/~brutzman/vrb_faq.html), 1997.

7 Ibid.

8 Ibid.

9 Ibid.

10 Ibid.

9

Living Worlds

Establishing standards for implementing cyberspace was the long-term goal of the infant VRML community back in 1994. It divided its goal into three sequential tasks:

- **Defining appearances**: How things in cyberspace will look.
- **Defining behavior**: How to make things move.
- **Defining distribution**: How moving worlds will be shared.[1]

Roughly speaking, these tasks defined the focus of three successive major VRML releases; however, a lot of overlap was ignored in the process. Most of the work has gone into hammering out the thousand unforeseen details involved in creating consistent compromises from multiple threads of intersecting input.

VRML 1.0 was achieved surprisingly quickly. This was accomplished by an agreement by all parties concerned to build on a preexisting ASCII file format for the descriptions of virtual object clusters. It was also based on the use of HTTP to access such files across the Internet. Thus, since there was suddenly an installed base to consider, VRML 2.0 proved harder to achieve. Therefore, two somewhat different sets of requirements needed to be reconciled by the designers of VRML 2.0:

- To refine VRML 1.0 based on the reports and recommendations of the pioneer content developers.
- To enable new kinds of content; in particular, sound and other data streams, animation, and other time-constrained interactions.[2]

VRML 2.0 was introduced at Siggraph '96. Designers are able to create an enormous range of applications through their use of VRML 2.0. It enables them to create applications for chemical or biomedical modeling to information visualization, and manufacturing design. It has now (in its turn) become the basis for a new two-pronged design process:

- *Content developers* have already begun to put the new VRML 2.0 animation and extensibility features to work, testing whether their semantics are adequate to define virtual worlds that can satisfy paying customers.
- *VRML architects* are equally busy, analyzing the requirements and articulating the design trade-offs involved in coordinating interactions among multiple human and mechanical participants in distributed virtual scenes.[3]

A number of new working groups emerged to push this dual process forward even before VRML 2.0 was formally launched. One of these, working under the name *Living Worlds* (LW), brings together a small group of developers who have already implemented proprietary systems for inserting dynamic objects (human-controlled avatars and autonomous bots) into VRML 1.0 scenes. They have also distributed the results in real time over consumer-grade Internet hook-ups. The goal of the LW group is to distill the experience gained from these systems into a proposal for a VRML97 application framework. This would enable VRML developers to populate and share their *Moving Worlds*.

This chapter describes the Living Worlds group initiative: where it comes from, the problems it addresses, the process it adopted, and the conceptual model that is its first result. This chapter also reports some initial results achieved by the LW working group. In addition, it proposes how and what has begun to be used by the LW as a foundation for a broader community effort.

Living Worlds Charter

The charter of the LW group is to distill its experience with avatar-based interaction (in VRML 1.0) into a proposed standard for distributed object interaction in VRML 2.0. The LW effort aims at a single, narrow, well-defined goal. In other words, its goal is to define a set of VRML97 conventions that support applications which are both *interpersonal* and *interoperable*.

What is meant by *interpersonal* is VRML applications that support the virtual presence of many people in a single scene at the same time. In other words, interpersonal means people who can interact both with objects in the scene and with each other.

On the other hand, *interoperable* means that such applications can be assembled from libraries of components developed independently by multiple suppliers. It also means that applications can be visited by client systems that have nothing more in common than their adherence to the VRML97 standard. What this means is that

Draft 1.0 of the LW specification, dated February 24, 1997, includes interfaces for:

- Coordinating the position and state of shared objects (including avatars).
- Information exchange between objects in a scene.
- Personal and system security in VRML applications.
- A (small) library of utilities, and some workarounds for VRML97 limitations.
- Identifying and integrating at run time interaction capabilities implemented outside of VRML and its scripts.[4]

These fundamental interfaces are both necessary and sufficient to build a first generation of shared VRML worlds. In other words, interoperability is a requirement posed by all participants in shared worlds:

- Users want to be able to take their avatars, and their favorite interactive objects, with them to different worlds.
- Component developers want to focus their efforts on building single components (avatars or portable multipurpose components such as dice or playing cards), for which there will be a larger market as more and more worlds become interoperable.
- Application developers (the authors of worlds and complete applications such as the board game) can combine best-of-breed components to yield richer results with less effort.[5]

Nevertheless, it is crucial not to overly constrain component developers by trying too early for too fine a level of interoperability. So, when developers have enough space between the standard interfaces to make things they can sell at a profit, that's when environments become conducive only to technical innovation. Thus, it is crucial to try to match component standardization with a sense of the maturity of the market.

Working Principles

Living Worlds is governed by the process that allows VRML to continue to evolve, and by a fundamental commitment to VRML itself. Thus, a number of working principles end up governing the content of the Living Worlds proposal.

Build on VRML 2.0

There is always a temptation to imagine an ideal system. In order to achieve fundamentally new results, more of a challenge is needed to apply existing capabilities. Living Worlds is not (yet) much concerned with what ought to go in VRML 2.0 or 97. It is built entirely with existing VRML 2.0 mechanisms. Anything that cannot be implemented inside the current standard is defined as *implementation specific*.

Standards

The task of a standard is to simplify the integration of independently developed components. No standard can ensure good design. Standards that overly constrain solutions stifle innovation. The focus of the LW effort is:

- ♦ To identify the minimum set of system features required to enable shared environments.
- ♦ To define the minimum set of standard interfaces required to enable application developers to combine feature sets from multiple suppliers.[6]

Architectures

As is normally the case, all of the LW initiators have their solutions based on architectures that exploit a central server. Nevertheless, enabling innovation requires that the standard not prejudge the question of how functionality is physically distributed.

Therefore, in order for the marketplace to be successful, LW must be equally as strongly committed to it. That commitment leads to further principles governing the Living Worlds process.

Running Code Requirements

The initiators of LW have all implemented interpersonal VRML environments. Many of these environments have been implemented for commercial use. The challenge here is to distill that implementation experience into a framework for interoperable components. In other words, a proposed interoperability standard can only be evaluated on the basis of multiple interoperable implementations Thus, a real-world application experience is required to development a final Proposal for VRML97.

Market Role

The goal is to give component and application developers a way to combine their best efforts, not to design the best imaginable system. The reason for this is so that more VRML worlds will get built faster. Also, the base of user experience figures into this—where LW will eventually learn what this technology is good for. Time to market is of the essence in this process as well.

Thus, the eventual technical target of LW is to produce specific enhancements to the VRML97 standard. As a way of anchoring the technical target discussion in some recognizable way, let's take a look at LW's work in shared VRML environments.

Technical Targets of the Cyberspace Infrastructure

Shared VRML environments will not be designed as single structures by LW but assembled ad hoc as they are used. They will invoke scripts as external applications in a variety of languages but not be constructed solely in VRML. They will grow ad hoc, as individuals and small groups begin to visit each other's private VRML sites and plug them together, but not be under any single operator's control.

In sum, shared VRML environments will be based on continual negotiations among independently developed software objects. Many of these objects will encounter each other for the first time at run time. Some of these will invoke input from multiple, more or less arbitrarily interacting application programs (the whiteboard, the dice, the voice-chat package). Less predictable humans will *drive* still other objects. See Chapter 14, *Sharing Distributed Virtual Worlds*, for detailed information on shared VRML environments.

With this level of complexity, individual authors of local living rooms or trade show booths cannot be expected to cope. The evolution of cyberspace, like that of any other modern human living space, depends on the establishment of a reliable infrastructure. This infrastructure could be comprised of things like facilities that provide commonly accessible solutions to the basic problems of transport and communication, traffic regulation, commercial transactions, and property protection.

Let's look at some LW scenarios for infrastructure requirements. LW identifies two basic sets of infrastructure functionality: *scene sharing* and *security*.

Sharing Scenes

The coordination of events and actions across the Net is known as scene sharing. This is what enables multiple clients to interact. In other words, these are the mechanisms for letting each other know that someone has arrived, departed, sent a message, or changed something in the scene. Let's look at some of the basic functions of this.

Run Time   How else can an avatar make its exit or entrance? Or, during a game, suddenly produce a RoboCop who takes you directly to jail? In a single-user world, this can be handled by existing VRML97 scripting mechanisms. In Living Worlds, the scene graph on every client must in principle be dynamically modifiable by any other client.

Real Time   The challenge here is to let user A see the result of whatever user B is doing (moving furniture, dodging dive-bombing birdbots), given that both network bandwidth and client processing power are always in limited supply. As soon as we get past C and begin thinking about virtual crowds, the question "Who needs to know what how often?" becomes increasingly critical to insuring overall system performance. Therefore, a subtle problem in dynamic data distribution occurs by keeping everyone as up to date as their equipment allows.

Object Driver Coordination   Coordinating local and external object drivers extends scene sharing to include not just multiple users but also multiple developers and non-VRML technologies. On the one hand, it is the basic enabling mechanism for all personal interaction (avatar motion and behavior). However, on the other hand, it is the basis for all component-based applications, from the use of electronic cash to the database access that validates your right to enter the Dragon's Lair.

Information Exchange Support Among Objects   Information exchange support among objects can be simple message strings and multimedia data arrays (a business card with your picture on it). It can also be any essential arbitrary data streams and containers (a file with your résumé in it, or your company's complete set of 1997 product maintenance manuals).

Persistent Imported Objects   Let imported objects become a permanent part of the scene. This is what makes it possible for Art's art to be updated, or Betty's birdbot to lay an egg that doesn't vanish when Betty leaves the scene. This issue is easily overlooked, but the issue is neither technically trivial nor possible to postpone. This raises the twin issues of permanent storage and access control. If you can make permanent changes to any scene you enter, then you become de facto one of its authors. All of the security issues are implied here. However, if you cannot make permanent changes to any scene you enter, or you can't make anything happen in an online world, how long are you going to find that interesting? So, if we can all potentially alter the worlds we visit together, then how and where are those changes recorded and communicated? And, under whose control? Therefore, it seems clear that implementing object persistence in shared VRML worlds will require interfaces to external database management systems. In other words, the focus will be on a separate Working Group with which close coordination will be needed.

The Living Worlds authors have all developed proprietary solutions to most of the challenges just presented. This proposal is a first attempt to devise a common VRML97 interface to support basic social interaction in multiuser virtual scenes: a public infrastructure for cyberspace. But bringing people together also means creating opportunities for conflict, both inadvertent and deliberate. To enable effective sharing, LW must simultaneously provide effective security.

Security

It takes little imagination to picture the potential for problems caused by multiuser interactions, given the possibility of such interactions in shared scenes. Faith in humanity (or in the harmlessness of pretty pets carried in by friends) is a fine thing. However, it's still a good idea to cut the cards, and to carry a big insurance policy. Functional requirements of any security system can be grouped under the basic headings *Concurrency Control*, *Conditional Access*, and *Authentication*.

Concurrency Control   Managing conflicting user actions is the most elementary issue in any shared environment. If a person tries to open a door while another person is trying to lock it, who wins? What happens if a person tries to sit in a chair that another person is trying to move?

Data and Functionality Access Control   The normal, procedural approach to access control is simply to bracket all messages between objects in security routines. In other words, what is needed is a pre-check to determine whether a message should be accepted at all, a post-check to verify that no damage has been done, and, if damage has been done, a way to identify who is to blame. Unfortunately, there is no built-in way for VRML97 to determine where a message came from. This bug must be worked around until it can be fixed (by sticking messages in an envelope with a return address). The harder problem is that VRML, being declarative rather than procedural, has no reliable definition of before and after. Thus, there is no easy way to specify conditional execution.

Users and Agents Authenticated   In principle, the Net has a solution for the problem of authenticating users and their agents. In other words, encrypted certificates should be validated by an independent authority. The problem here is to insure that certified users don't get impersonated by rogue software inside a given client system. This requires the creation of a trusted path along with a message that says it comes from component A on Art's desktop machine and therefore cannot be hacked to look as though it comes from component B on Betty's machine.

This basic infrastructure for secure scene sharing goes a long way toward enabling the creation of VRML environments that are truly interpersonal (places people can actively share). Living Worlds provides standard interfaces to support all these features. LW also provides the architectural framework that is required to implement them from a set of interoperable components. That is why the LW effort seeks to:

♦ Identify the major components that make up a multiuser system, where *component* means *any piece that may be independently supplied.*
♦ Identify the key interfaces between those components and consider how they communicate with each other
♦ Design a VRML97 application framework to support that component architecture.[7]

A major task in this effort is to get agreement on a basic conceptual framework for implementation. The previous discussion distilled a general view of some basic interaction facilities needed to support shared virtual worlds. The next section seeks to locate this list of needs in a general conceptual framework that can effectively guide LW's investigation into potentially standardizable program interfaces.

General Conceptual Framework

Figure 9.1 shows the place of the Living Worlds interface proposals in terms of a very generic Web-browser architecture. Note: The blocks do not necessarily represent code modules. The point here is to make a logical partitioning of the relevant functionality.

Legend

The shaded blocks and the interfaces 1–4 of Figure 9.1 indicate the domain of the Living Worlds proposals. Interface 5 is the External Authoring Interface proposal currently under review. Its approval

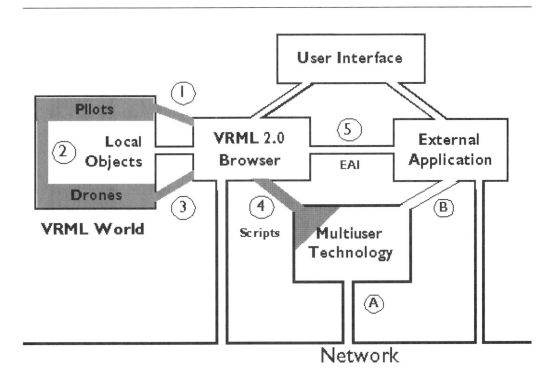

Figure 9.1 Architectural/conceptual framework.

is assumed, but it is unrelated to this proposal. Interfaces A and B are how the multiuser technology and other external applications communicate across the Net. They are essential to the implementation of shared environments; however, interfaces A and B are outside the reach of a VRML 2.0. node library.

The first thing to note about this model is that it is derived from LW's Principle (*Standards, not design*) discussed earlier. LW's goal is not a system design but an analysis that can inform a standards proposal. Thus, interfaces that support interoperation between components from independent suppliers are the only ones the model shown in Figure 9.1 identifies.

This approach leads to some definitions that may be unexpected. Let's discuss those next.

User Interface

The *user interface* (UI) accepts all user input. It also renders the virtual world in media the user can interpret. This definition bundles the mouse and video and sound drivers together with all widgets, windows, frames, menus, dialog boxes, error messages, help files, and so forth. It also includes any and all media used by the system and its human user to interact with each other. Also, no UI standards or conventions are proposed by Living Worlds.

VRML 2.0 Browser

The VRML 2.0 browser parses the content of VRML files and passes it to the UI for display to the user. Any and all changes in the actual run-time world are affected. In other words, the browser is the only component that interacts directly with the world. For instance, CosmoPlayer is a browser that uses Netscape Navigator's UI (User Interface). Also, as VRML continues to evolve, all interfaces to the browser are defined by the VRML standard. The two unlabeled browser interfaces are those that exist today as part of any VRML 2.0 system. This includes the system's access to the intranet for files (including scripts and inlines), and its link to its own UI.

VRML World

The VRML code that specifies a (set of) scene(s), plus the local code invoked by its script nodes (Java, JavaScript, TCL, etc.) is known as the *VRML World*. Since LW's purpose is to make it possible for objects to be inserted into scenes (for changes made to objects in one instance of a scene to be mirrored in other instances of that scene), it is crucial to distinguish all objects in the world as either local or shared. The latter (those whose state and/or behavior is to be distributed) communicate via the interfaces 1–3 (as shown in Figure 9.1) between *pilot* and *drone* objects. The rest of the world either behaves with local effects only or else is static.

External Application

Code that interacts with a VRML browser to realize some (set of) feature(s) not encoded in the VRML or its associated scripts is known as an *external application*. For instance, this could be a videoconferencing application that places its images on your living-room wall. The VRML standard does include an external API through which such applications can interact with the browser. Living Worlds provides a framework whereby objects in a world can negotiate their shared use of external applications. Note that external applications may well have their own independent access to the intranet. This is how most current proprietary systems for placing avatars in VRML worlds work (including those of Black Sun, Paragraph, and Sony).

Multiuser Technology

MUtech (Multi-User Technology) is a component proposed by Living Worlds to implement shared behaviors/states across the intranet. By definition, MUtechs provide all intranet communication needed for multiuser interaction beyond that provided by the browser itself. Thus, to say that future versions of VRML will include multiuser capability as part of the standard is simply to say that part of the functionality LW labels MUtech will some day become the responsibility of the browser.

The MUtech connects to the browser via standard VRML 2.0 scripts (interface 4 as shown in Figure 9.1). These semantics are a key part of the Living Worlds proposal. Interface B gives MUtechs a direct link to external applications, and through them back into the world via the browser's external API. Such interactions are likely to be extensive in real-world applications as VRML authors incorporate such things as external authentication systems or electronic cash transfers into their worlds. Nevertheless, those interfaces are outside the scope of LW's proposal.

The model shown in Figure 9.1 of the five major conceptual components, is above all a supplier's model. LW foresees both a need and a market at each of the interface thresholds in their model. Nevertheless, the fundamental difference between shared virtual environments and their predecessor platforms (that they are both multiuser and interactive) has not yet begun to be addressed by LW to any great extent. Neither has the potential that each user can interact with any other.

From Here

Living Worlds is not the only initiative aimed at accelerating the evolution of shared virtual environments. The next chapter discusses how some of the folks connected to the *Universal Avatars* (UA) initiative, working together with the *Mitsubishi Electronic Research Lab* (MERL), proposed an *Open Community* (OC) architecture based on the SPLINE system.

Endnotes

1 Living Worlds, "Concepts and Context," 1997.
2 Ibid.
3 Ibid.
4 Ibid.
5 Ibid.
6 Ibid.
7 Ibid.

10

Open Community

The creation of a seamless distributed multiuser virtual environment that connects all the 3-D worlds on the Internet is the ultimate goal of VRML and cyberspace advocates. VRML 1.0, 2.0, and 97 have brought the VR community closer to this dream but have not crossed the bridge to multiuser experiences. The open *Open Community Java/VRML 2.0 API* developed jointly by Mitsubishi Electric Research Labs, Chaco Communications, Inc., Velocity Games, and Worlds, Inc., provides a complete distributed multiuser communication infrastructure for complex virtual worlds. It provides for both *interacting* and *passive* behaviors. A passive behavior is isolated, such as an avatar waving. An interacting behavior involves two objects, such as two avatars shaking hands. A part of the architecture called *regions* allows different virtual worlds to connect to each other. Reference implementation uses peer-to-peer communication to improve speed and scalability, even though the Open Community API does not specify communication protocols. Therefore, an open networking protocol must be specified in order to create the complete cyberspace dream: A baseball player can hit a ball from one manufacturer's server into another's and smash a company's window.

Challenges

VRML and the World Wide Web promise seamless movement between 3-D worlds. This movement could stem from a virtual Saturn car dealership, where an avatar (person) can interact with a salesperson and a 3-D virtual car, to a virtual Borders bookstore where an avatar (person) can purchase a maintenance manual. VRML97 allows avatars to interact with objects in a scene. However, it provides no standard way to present those interactions to others, no standard way for individuals to sense and affect a shared state, no standard way to move from one scene to another, and no standard way to view one scene through the window of another.

How is cyberspace brought to the broadest audience? How does it help people create business, entertainment, and social environments on the Internet? Open specifications are best for problems involving numerous companies that must cooperate. The open VRML specification has brought 3-D to many people. It was embraced by both Netscape and Microsoft. This made them essentially available in every browser. Several high-quality 3-D VRML scene and object creation tools are now available. Manufacturers compete to provide the fastest, most robust, and most standard-compliant VRML viewers. The rewards go to companies that build superior technology on standards. Rewards are few and far between for those companies exploiting proprietary advantage.

Open Community

Content developers through the Open Community interface are allowed to create portable, interconnected, multiuser interactive worlds that operate on any manufacturer's Open Community server. In addition, content developers can choose servers based on added value. This would involve things such as speed, robustness, standard compliance, and additional features—especially since the Open Community API is completely open.

A content developer must build or license a proprietary multiuser API and server from a third party in order to realize a multiuser world with VRML97. Only Java allows multiuser behaviors to run portably on any machine. Thus, the developer can write the multiuser behaviors in any language.

An API-Based Approach

As previously stated, Open Community is a proposed API standard for communication within and between shared virtual worlds. It is based on the well-known SPLINE system. This system was developed at the *Mitsubishi Electronic Research Laboratories* (MERL). Living Worlds (see Chapter 9, "Living Worlds") and Open Community both ask the same questions: What aspects of the technology for shared virtual worlds should be standardized, and what should be left open for innovation?

VRML will be the language of choice for implementing multiuser virtual environments according to an assumption made by *Living Worlds* (LW). LW focuses clearly on what can be accomplished using VRML97. Anything that can't be done inside the current standard is declared by definition to be *MUtech* specific. In other words, this would be an implementation matter outside the boundary of the interface standard, much like the Living Worlds Principles (Require Running Code and Respect the role of the market).

The *Open Community* (OC) workgroup makes no assumptions about the use of VRML. OC starts with a *world model* that is a pure semantic abstraction, instead of starting with objects in a virtual space. In fact, OC worlds need not be 3-D, thus explicitly leaving open the matter of object appearance. Their goal is to insure that behaviors in different worlds (however the behaving entities may be visualized) can be coordinated among multiple participants on distributed platforms. In other words, they offer a standard set of multiuser functionality. This is made available by APIs in Java and C that can be used to implement arbitrary (in a sense, *external*) applications.

OC proposes standardizing precisely those interfaces that LW proposes to keep open. Figure 10.1 shows the two initiatives are neatly separated by the dotted line.[1] At first blush, this would seem to make their work wholly complementary—each is working on what the other has chosen to avoid. Does that mean all LW needs to do to achieve a complete standard is to integrate the two? A quick diagrammatic comparison suggests how neat the fit might be.

Figure 10.1 shows how the domain of the Open Community effort is mapped onto the LW conceptual model presented in Chapter 9 and shown in Figure 9.1. Note that the blocks do not necessarily represent code modules; the point is the logical partitioning of functionality.

This neat congruence of boundaries has not gone unnoticed. Work is already under way from both sides to bring the two efforts closer together. The OC team is looking at implementing Living Worlds' MUtech interface so that VRML developers will be able to build components that interoperate with OC environments. And the Living Worlds' MUtech providers are looking at how their work might profit from the OC APIs.

One difficulty is that of timing. When you try to standardize everything at once, there is no room left in which to experiment.

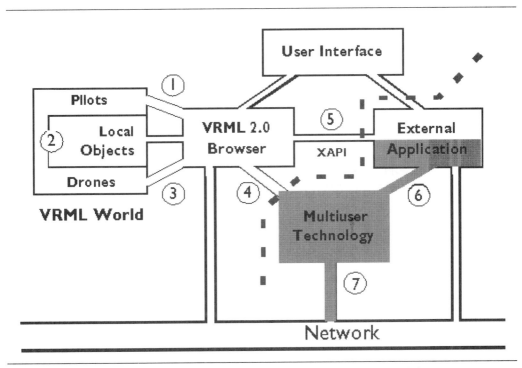

Figure 10.1 Open Community conceptual framework model.

The original strategy considered by the Living Worlds group was to propose an API standard, working solely through the newly proposed external API, and thus allow the line protocols to remain proprietary. The thinking was that any attempt to standardize the transfer protocols would pose an unreasonably high entry barrier to new suppliers and/or give one of the existing suppliers an unacceptable competitive advantage.

These same arguments, however, eventually proved to apply with almost equal strength to the idea of a wholly API-based standard. Also, the LW group was concerned that this approach did not make appropriate use of the new *ROUTEing* capability of VRML97.

The final decision was to effect all communication among objects within a scene using VRML language mechanisms, and to provide a customizable set of VRML *wrappers* through which providers could introduce proprietary features. The chosen architecture is flexible enough to allow developers to work either through the external API or directly within the browser's scripting capability.

Proposal

Open Community combines a portable, multiuser, interactive Java API with a VRML prototype layer. Using Open Community, the content developer can create a single multiuser virtual world that can operate with anyone's server. Figure 10.2 shows where Open Community fits between VRML 2.0 and multiuser content.[2] Once

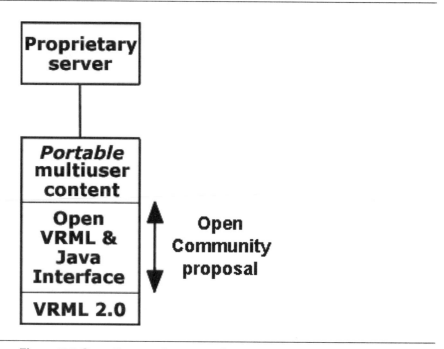

Figure 10.2 Open Community proposal.

Open Community is widely adopted, tools manufacturers can develop stable, broadly applicable authoring tools. Server manufacturers then compete on the basis of functional value.

The Open Community specification builds on Mitsubishi's SPLINE, a distributed multiuser virtual world infrastructure. Open Community includes several desirable features: It scales well through the use of regions—an important feature on the Internet. A streamed media identification system accommodates new media types easily. Peer-to-peer communication reduces latency for animation, voice, and chat communication. Strict object ownership avoids conflicts between interacting objects, allows each client to run at full speed, and lets clients sense and react to events caused by others.

Servers based on Open Community provide for truly interacting behaviors. A baseball game illustrates the difference between passive and interacting behaviors. In a world that implements only passive behaviors, a pitcher can throw a baseball and everyone else can see the ball being thrown, flying through the air, and dropping to the ground. However, the batter cannot hit the ball. In a world with interacting behaviors, the batter can obtain control of the ball, hit it, and other people can get control of the ball and catch, throw, and tag runners out.

Open Community is not totally dependent on VRML. Figure 10.3 shows a shared whiteboard running inside Netscape, under SPLINE.[3] The shared whiteboard allows any number of people to draw and view others' drawings. They can use post-it notes and audio chat to communicate with each other.

Virtual worlds' components like Chaco's multimedia server Tribe and client Pueblo will both appear as Open Community applications. Combining Open Community with Chaco's Tribe server can produce multimedia content-avatars, VRML, HTML, real-time voice, and text chat (as shown in Figure 10.4).[4]

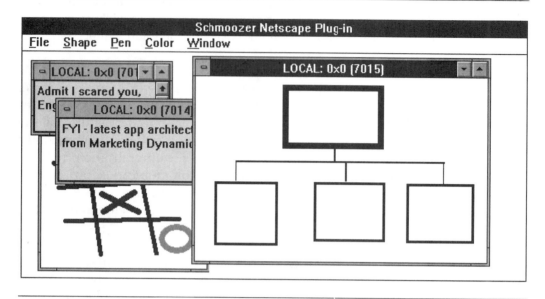

Figure 10.3 Shared whiteboard running under SPLINE.

The Universal Avatars Initiative

An associated working group called *Universal Avatars* has proposed to standardize many of the issues surrounding avatars, such as persistence, scale, and the design of better interfaces for socialization-based virtual communities. The spAvatarInfo and spAvatar classes in Open Community implement Universal Avatars' concepts. Open Community will continue to reflect the needs of the avatar community, since it is closely aligned with the Universal Avatars' initiative.

Prior Efforts

Universal Avatars builds on a wealth of prior work, including VRML97, Java, and SPLINE. Again, it is worthwhile comparing the Open Community and Living Worlds proposals.

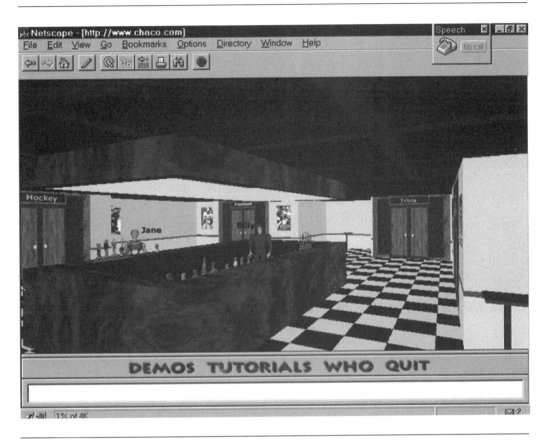

Figure 10.4 Tribe/Pueblo, VRML, HTML, and voice example.

VRML97 is a single-user, animated, 3-D virtual environment specification, which has associated automated behaviors (such as a door opening when a user clicks on the doorknob) with a 3-D object. This is sometimes referred to as *intransitive behaviors*. Through a programming API, VRML97 allows content developers to create cool, animated games and environments.

Java is an object-oriented programming language supported by all major Web browsers. It is currently used to add life to static Web pages. However, through any of a number of proposed Java interfaces for VRML97 viewers, Java can drive complex behaviors, communicate with servers, and animate avatars.

Living Worlds, shown in the middle of Figure 10.5, is a proposed specification for multiuser virtual worlds.[5] It builds on VRML 2.0 with a combination of standard and proprietary APIs. The portable VRML API of Living Worlds represents passive behaviors, and the unspecified proprietary APIs support interacting behaviors. A content developer can rely on Living Worlds to support interacting behaviors, but must build or license a proprietary multiuser API and server. Figure 10.5 shows the progression from VRML 2.0 to Living Worlds, and then to Open Community, which adds a completely portable Java API to the VRML prototype layer.

Seamless Multiuser Cyberspace on the Internet

These different APIs—from VRML 2.0, to Living Worlds, to Open Community—move us toward the ultimate goal: a seamless multiuser cyberspace on the Internet. We need the ability for individual

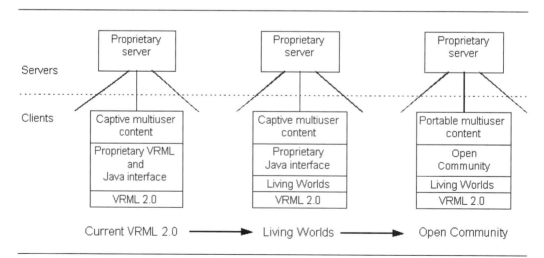

Figure 10.5 Possible scenario for integration.

worlds to refer to and include other worlds. For example, avatars should be able to look through the window of the Saturn dealership (running on a Velocity, Inc., server) and see events taking place in front of the Borders bookstore (running on a Chaco server).

To do this, a final specification for the networking protocols used between servers and clients must be created. Let's call it *Universal Cyberspace*. Once this is implemented, the batter in a virtual world can hit a baseball out of the ballpark (running on a Worlds server) and through the window of the Saturn dealership (running on a Chaco server). Figure 10.6 illustrates how that communication would take place in a Universal Cyberspace environment.[6] The reference implementation of Open Community has a good starting point for this protocol.

Summary

Open Community provides a rich Java and VRML97 API for cyberspace. This completely open specification allows content

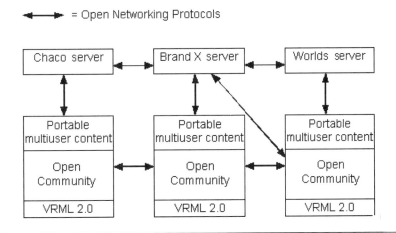

Figure 10.6 Universal Cyberspace concept.

developers to create multiuser worlds that run on any server supporting the Open Community API. This work adds value to other specifications under development, such as Universal Avatars and Living Worlds, by providing interacting behaviors between avatars, an object-ownership model, efficient communication mechanisms, and high scalability through the use of regions.

By adopting both the Open Community API and the reference implementation networking protocols, server manufacturers can create the dream of cyberspace advocates: a seamless web of 3-D spaces, where avatars can shake hands through a doorway, and where moving from store to store is a natural, uninterrupted process.

From Here

This chapter discussed Open Community as a proposed API standard for communication within and between shared virtual worlds. The next chapter presents a brief overview of Open Inventor as an object 3-D toolkit offering a comprehensive solution to interactive graphics programming problems.

Endnotes

1   MERL (Mitsubishi Electric Research Labs). "Open Community Overview," November 5, 1996.

2   Ibid.

3   Ibid.

4   Ibid.

5   Ibid.

6   Ibid.

11

Open Inventor

Open Inventor is an object-oriented 3-D toolkit offering a comprehensive solution to interactive graphics programming problems. It presents a programming model based on a 3-D scene database that dramatically simplifies graphics programming. It includes a rich set of objects, such as cubes, polygons, text, materials, cameras, lights, trackballs, handle boxes, 3-D viewers, and editors, that speed up your programming time and extend your 3-D programming capabilities. Open Inventor has the following characteristics:

- is built on top of OpenGL,
- defines a standard file format for 3-D data interchange,
- introduces a simple event model for 3-D interaction,
- provides animation objects called engines,
- provides high-performance object picking,
- is window system and platform independent,
- is a cross-platform 3-D graphics development system,

- ◆ supports PostScript printing, and
- ◆ encourages programmers to create new customized objects.
- ◆ Also, it is fun to use.[1]

IRIS Inventor Overview

IRIS Inventor was the first release of Inventor and is also known as Inventor V1.0 (Open Inventor is Inventor V2.0). IRIS Inventor is built on top of IRIS GL rather than OpenGL and has fewer features.

Inventor defines a powerful, extensible format for 3-D objects and scenes. The Inventor format is the standard for 3-D objects on Silicon Graphics machines and may become the standard for all machines.

However, Inventor is more than a 3-D object file format. It is a complete toolkit for writing interactive 3-D applications.

Inventor is for programmers writing 3-D applications and does not directly provide any way for users to create 3-D objects. Several Inventor applications have been written that create 3-D objects. Showcase V3.0, which is bundled with IRIX, is a fairly simple example. A much more sophisticated modeler called *Ez3d*, built on top of Inventor, is available from Radiance Software International.

Open Inventor contains mostly 3-D objects. There is little in the way of conventional user interface objects, such as buttons, dialogues, and menus. However, Open Inventor includes a full-fledged event model, a framework designed for 3-D user interaction, and some manipulator objects for 3-D user interface building. Note that the Open Inventor Xt Component and Utility Library includes some traditional 2-D user interface widgets.

Few GL programs achieve peak graphics performance, because most applications have natural application overhead, and many programmers lack a thorough understanding of the details and eccentricities of GL. If you are writing a simple display-only, immediate-mode GL program, it will run a bit faster using straight GL. However, if your program has scene traversal, interactivity, picking, bounding-box calculations, and other object space tasks, Open Inventor will perform better for you, because Open Inventor is specially tuned to make optimal use of GL on each SGI machine. Furthermore, Open Inventor supports render caching, which results in peak GL performance in most cases.

The VRML Consortium Architecture Group, as discussed in Chapter 11, has found that in many cases, Open Inventor programs run faster than the original GL program. Thus the programmer productivity increases easily outweigh the overhead of the toolkit.

You can use the C API and never see or use C++. However, subclassing to extend the toolkit does require C++.

Open Inventor requires SGI's C++ compiler. The GNU C++ compiler and SGI's C++ compiler produce incompatible code, and Silicon Graphics does not ship an Open Inventor library compatible with GNU C++.

An Open Inventor Sampler: Hello Cone

This part of the chapter introduces Inventor programming and some key Inventor concepts. Most of the chapter provides variations on the Hello Cone program, a simple program that displays a cone on the screen.

Hello Cone is a 20-line program that opens an XtRenderArea in a window; creates a 3-D scene consisting of a camera, a light, and a red material; adds the scene to the XtRenderArea; and then enters the Xt main event loop, which takes care of rendering the cone in response to window system events. (Bonus information you won't find in the book: Several people in the Open Inventor group at SGI believe that these examples should have been expressed in the

ASCII file format instead of being presented as programming exercises. However since Open Inventor is a programming library first and a file format second, the argument was lost. Nonetheless, the file format for the examples is being presented here. If you have an SGI machine, you can use the program "/usr/sbin/ivview" to view them.)

Here is HelloCone:

```
# Inventor V2.0 ascii
Separator {
     PerspectiveCamera
          position 0 0 4.18154
          nearDistance 2.44949
          farDistance 5.91359
          focalDistance 4.18154
     }
     DirectionalLight {}
     Material {
          diffuseColor [ 1 0 0 ]
     }
     Cone {}
}2
```

Variation 1: Using Engines to Make the Cone Spin

The first variation presented adds an engine to make the cone spin. A rotation transformation (RotationXYZ) is added to the scene, and an ElapsedTime engine is connected to the rotation's angle so that the angle of rotation in radians equals the time in seconds since the program started (the axis of rotation is set to the X-axis).

In the ASCII file format, this scene looks like:

```
#Inventor V2.0 ascii
Separator {
     PerspectiveCamera {
          position 0 0 4.18154
```

```
              nearDistance 2.44949
              farDistance    5.91359
              focalDistance 4.18154
        }
        DirectionalLight {}
        RotationXYZ {
              AXIS x
              angle = ElapsedTime{ }. timeOut
        }
        Material {
              diffuseColor [ 1 0 0 ]
        }
        Cone {}
}
```

Variation 2: Adding a Trackball Manipulator

Next, a trackball manipulator is used to allow the user to interactively manipulate the rotation of the cone. This is done by replacing the RotationXYZ node of the previous example.

This is done with a TrackballManip:

```
#Inventor V2.0 ascii
Separator {
      PerspectiveCamera {
              position 0 0 4.18154
              nearDistance 2.44949
              farDistance    5.91359
              focalDistance 4.18154
        }
        DirectionalLight {}
        TrackballManip {}
        Material {
              diffuseColor [ 1 0 0 ]
        }
Cone {}
}
```

Variation 3: Adding the Examiner Viewer

Finally, an XtExaminerViewer is used instead of a simple XtRenderArea. The XtExaminerViewer adds user interface controls to allow the user to manipulate his or her view of the scene. For example, this is like a zoom slider that controls the field of view (like a zoom lens on a camera) and thumbwheel widgets that control rotation about the screen *X* and *Y* axes, etc. The particular viewing paradigm used (ExaminerViewer, WalkViewer, FlyViewer, etc.) is not considered part of the scene and is not saved in the file format. So there is no corresponding file format example for this variant on Hello Cone.

Naming Scenes

Most Open Inventor C++ classes are prefixed with So, which stands for Scene Object (at least, that's the official explanation—insiders know that it really stands for Scenario, the internal name of the project before it had a name). All enumerated values are all uppercase, etc. The Open Inventor library also contains some useful low-level classes that are prefixed with Sb: SbLine, SbColor, and SbRotation.

Coordinate Systems

The convention for the coordinate system used by Open Inventor is a right-handed coordinate system with +z coming out of the screen. Angles are specified in radians, and objects may be defined in their own local coordinate system. The world coordinate space is the default coordinate space. An object can be transformed into world coordinates by applying all of the transformation affecting it.

Building a Scene Graph

This part of the chapter explains the concept of a scene graph and shows how to build scenes out of groups, properties, and shapes. It also describes the concepts of actions, traversal, and traversal state.

The phrase *"Open Inventor supports"* is used to indicate the features that are built into Open Inventor. Programmers can extend the toolkit to support almost anything.

Open Inventor programs store their scenes in structures called *scene graphs*. A scene graph is made up of *nodes*, which represent 3-D objects that are drawn (shapes); *properties* of the 3-D objects (properties); groups and nodes that contain other nodes are used for hierarchical grouping and others (cameras, lights, etc.).

Open Inventor defines a standard set of actions that can be applied to a scene, such as rendering, getting the world-space bounding box of the scene, or picking (finding out what objects are underneath the mouse pointer). Each node implements its own action behavior.

Nodes and Groups

Each node contains one or more pieces of information stored in fields. For example, the Sphere node contains only its radius, stored in its radius field. Each field class defines methods to get and set its values. Well-behaved nodes (all standard Open Inventor nodes are well behaved) use only the contents of their fields and their position in the scene to determine how they behave when traversed during an action.

Open Inventor supports the following shape nodes:

- Cone
- Cube
- Cylinder
- Sphere
- Text2
- Text3
- IndexedFaceSet
- IndexedLineSet
- IndexedTriangleStripSet
- FaceSet
- LineSet

- PointSet
- QuadMesh
- TriangleStripSet
- IndexedNurbsCurve
- IndexedNurbsSurface
- NurbsCurve
- NurbsSurface[3]

The way shapes are drawn is affected by property nodes in the scene. Open Inventor supports the following property nodes:

- BaseColor
- ColorIndex
- Complexity
- Coordinate3
- Coordinate4
- DrawStyle
- Environment
- Font
- LightModel
- Material
- MaterialBinding
- MaterialIndex
- Normal
- NormalBinding
- PackedColor
- PickStyle
- LinearProfile
- NurbsProfile
- ProfileCoordinate2
- ProfileCoordinate3
- ShapeHints
- Texture2
- Texture2Transform
- TextureCoordinate2
- TextureCoordinateBinding
- TextureCoordinateDefault
- TextureCoordinateEnvironment
- TextureCoordinatePlane

- ◆ AntiSquish
- ◆ MatrixTransform
- ◆ ResetTransform
- ◆ Rotation
- ◆ Pendulum
- ◆ Rotor
- ◆ RotationXYZ
- ◆ Scale
- ◆ SuffoundScale
- ◆ Transform Translation
- ◆ Shuttle
- ◆ Units[4]

The order in which the shapes are drawn is determined by group nodes, which contain other nodes known as the group's "children." Open Inventor supports the following kinds of group nodes:

Open Inventor supports the following group nodes:

- ◆ Group
- ◆ Array
- ◆ LevelOfDetail
- ◆ MultipleCopy
- ◆ PathSwitch
- ◆ Separator
- ◆ Annotation
- ◆ Selection
- ◆ Switch
- ◆ Blinker
- ◆ TransformSeparator

Open Inventor draws the scene graph in a recursive fashion, starting by drawing the first (root) node and then drawing its children (if it is a group). A property must be drawn before a shape node to affect it. The simplest kind of group node is Group, which just draws its children in order.

Separator nodes are used to isolate parts of a scene from the rest of the scene. A property node inside a Separator will not affect any nodes outside the Separator.

For example, a robot's head and body might be specified in the file format like this:

```
#Inventor V2.0 ascii
Separator {
    Separator { # Body
        Transform { translation 0 3 0
        Material { A bronze color:
            ambientColor .33 .22 .27
            diffuseColor .78 .57 .11
            specularColor .99 .94 .81
            shininess .28
        }
        Cylinder { radius 2.5 height 6 }
    }
    Separator { # Head
        Transform { translation 0 7.5 0 }
        Material { # A silver color:
            ambientColor .2 .2 .2
            diffuseColor .6 .6 .6
            specularColor .5 .5 .5
            shininess .5
        }
        Sphere { }
    }
}
```

The use of Separator nodes keeps the translation of the body from affecting the translation of the head.

The *Switch* group has a field that specifies which children should be drawn. It can be set to draw only one child, to draw no children, or to draw all of the children (in which case it acts like a Group node).

LevelOfDetail is a kind of group that draws only one of its children, based on how big the object appears on the screen. It can be used to draw a simpler version of the object, with fewer polygons when the object is far away.

Adding the same node to more than one group creates a *shared instance*. Instancing is useful for geometry that is shared. Only one copy of the geometry needs to be read in and stored in memory.

For example, we can modify the robot scene graph to add legs, like this:

```
# Inventor V2.0 ascii
Separator {
   Separator{ # Body
      Transform { translation 0 3 0 }
      Material { # A bronze color:
         ambientColor .33 .22 .27
         diffuseColor .78 .57 .11
         specularColor .99 .94 .81
         shininess .28
      }
      Cylinder { radius 2.5 height 6 }
      Separator { # Left leg
         Transform { translation 1 -4.25 0 }
         DEF +0 Group { # Shared leg geometry
            Cube { width 1.2 height 2.2 depth 1.1 }
            Transform { translation 0 -2.25 0 }
            Cube { width 1 height 2.2 depth 1 }
            Transform { translation 0 -2 .5 }
            Cube { width .8 height .8 depth 2 }
         }
      }
Separator { # Right leg
         Transform { translation -1 -     4.25 0 }
         USE +0 # Use the leg geometry again
      }
   }
   Separator { # Head
      Transform { translation 0 7.5 0 }
      Material { # A silver color:
         ambientColor .2 .2 .2
         diffuseColor .6 .6 .6
```

```
        specularColor .5 .5 .5
        shininess .5
    }
    Sphere { }
  }
}
```

The DEF/USE +0 syntax is used to refer to the same node more than once. If several nodes were multiply instanced, Open Inventor would write out each with a unique number after the plus sign {+}.

Paths

The concept of a path is important when programming Open Inventor. A *path* is a chain of nodes, from parent to child, through the scene graph. Paths are returned from picking and searching. For example, if the user clicks the mouse on the left foot of the robot, a path from the root of the scene, through the body separator, the left-leg separator, through the leg group, and finally down to the last cube in the leg group would be returned. Paths are necessary because nodes may be multiple instances. The cube representing the foot cannot be returned when the user picks on the left foot, because the same cube is used for both the left and right feet.

Fields

Each type of field has its own set of methods for getting and setting its value(s). For example, MFFloat, which is a type of field that contains zero or more floating-point values, has methods for setting one value, for deleting a range of values, and for returning the number of values currently being stored, etc.

Fields have an ignored flag that can be set and queried. Fields in nodes that are marked ignored will have no effect. The ignore flag is written to file as a "-" character after (or in place of) the field's value.

Nodes have an override flag that can be used to force temporary changes to the scene. For example, to draw everything as lines, the following program might put a line near the beginning of the scene and set its ignored flag.

```
DrawStyle { style LINES }
```

Any subsequent DrawStyle nodes in the scene will be ignored. The override flag is not written to (or read from) file.

Node Mechanisms

Nodes are managed while in memory with a reference-counting mechanism that allows a node to be created, added to a scene, and then forgotten. The node gets properly deleted when the scene is deleted, even if it is multiply instanced.

Open Inventor provides programmers with a run-time type mechanism for its node, engine, action, detail, and event classes. It allows programmers to find out whether an object is of a given type, what class an object is derived from, etc.

Nodes can be given names. Once given a name, a node can be quickly looked up by name. Names follow the rules for C++ identifiers ([a-zA-Z_] [a-zA-Z0-9_]*).

The Open Inventor group will probably relax this to be any sequence of characters not containing the characters +,',",\,{}. Open Inventor V2.0 does not check to see whether names are valid and some Open Inventor customers already have programs that give their nodes names like Object1:foo[1,14]). Names are read and written to files by using the keyword "DEF".

For example, a cube named Joe would be written as:

```
DEF Joe Cube f )
```

Note: If multiply instanced, it might be written as Joe+l 8, but its name is still just Joe.

Cameras

Cameras and Lights, the Open Inventor node classes that allow you to see the objects that you create in your graph, are relatively intuitive. Lights provide the lighting for your scene. Cameras provide the viewports to see them from.

The Camera class allows you to define a view of the scene. The two kinds of Camera nodes are *Orthographic* and *Perspective*. The Orthographic Camera class allows you to define cameras that do not preserve perspective, which can be useful for designing objects. Perspective cameras provide a more natural way of viewing scenes.

All Cameras have fields allowing you to set:

- ◆ the position of the camera in the scene;
- ◆ the orientation that the camera faces;
- ◆ the aspect ratio of the camera;
- ◆ the near and far clipping planes (so that you don't try to view things a millimeter away, or off in the extreme distance);
- ◆ a focal distance, when relevant; and
- ◆ a mapping flag, for use when the camera's proportions do not match those of the actual window that the user is looking at.[5]

When it encounters a camera during traversal of a scene graph, Open Inventor figures out the volume of space that the camera covers (based on the angles it includes and the clipping planes) and doesn't draw any objects that aren't in that space. This space is called the *view volume*. You can orient a camera toward a specific object, using the pointAt() method, or examine an entire scene, using the viewAll() method.

Perspective Cameras provide one additional field: the vertical angle that the camera covers. By contrast, Orthographic Cameras instead have a field for the height of the volume that the camera should cover. Thus Perspective Cameras have (more or less) conical view volumes, and Orthographic ones have rectangular prisms for their view volumes.

You can have multiple cameras in a scene and switch between them dynamically. However, only one camera may be active at a time, and it must come before the objects it is to view.

Lights

Like Cameras, lights should come before objects in the scene graph, and each light illuminates only the objects that come after it. There is a base class of Lights and several subclasses: Point Lights, Directional Lights, and Spotlights. All lights have several fields, indicating:

- whether the light is on,
- its intensity, and
- its color.[6]

Point Lights are balls of light at a particular point. They have one additional field, a location, and shine equally in all directions.

Directional Lights are like sunlight: They are infinitely far off and shine in one specific direction. They have one additional field, the direction of the light.

Spotlights are like real-world spotlights. They have a location in the scene and a direction of focus, as well as a falloff rate (indicating how much they are focused on one spot) and a cutoff angle beyond which no light goes. You can have an arbitrary number of lights in a scene.

Shapes, Properties, and Binding

This part of the chapter describes the basics of how you create shapes and how to apply properties to those shapes.

Shapes

All shapes are subclasses of the SoShape class. Shapes can be either simple or complex. Simple shapes include cubes, cones, spheres, and cylinders. Complex shapes allow you to describe more complex surfaces in a variety of ways—face sets, line sets, triangle strips, point sets, quad meshes, and NURBS.

Face Sets allow you to define a solid shape in terms of the polygons that make up its faces. You create an array of coordinates containing all of the vertices of all of the faces, in order. Note that this may involve duplication of vertices.

An Indexed Face Set is like a Face Set, except that the vertices are indexed. This allows you to refer to vertices in any order and to reuse them, thus often saving some space.

A Triangle Strip Set allows you to create a surface out of a collection of triangles. It works much like a Face Set but is somewhat faster to render. However, it may be more inconvenient for some shapes. A Quad Mesh is similar to a Triangle Strip Set but uses an array of quadrilaterals to define the shape instead of triangles.

Properties

You can apply a number of kinds of *properties,* each with a different node class. Whereas shape nodes tell the rendering engine to draw the shape in question, property nodes affect the *state* of the rendering, changing the way that subsequent shapes will be drawn. Thus a property must always come before the shapes it is to affect.

The following properties are available:

- ♦ Materials—affects the color and reflectivity of objects;
- ♦ Draw Style—tells the renderer how to draw shapes;
- ♦ Light Model—affects how light is treated in the scene environment, specifying ambient properties such as fog and light attenuation;
- ♦ Shape Hints—permits certain rendering optimizations;

  ◆ Complexity—allows you to specify the level of detail to be drawn; and
  ◆ Units—allows you to define your units of measurement.

A SoMaterial node affects subsequent objects in the scene. This node allows you to specify the following for each object:

  ◆ ambient color—response to ambient light,
  ◆ diffuse color—base color of the object,
  ◆ specular color—reflected color,
  ◆ emissive color—color of radiated light,
  ◆ shininess, and
  ◆ transparency.[7]

A SoDrawStyle lets you define whether shapes should be drawn as filled-in regions (the default), as outlines, as arrays of points, or left invisible. If you choose points, you can specify the size of those points. If you choose lines, you can specify the width and pattern of the lines.

A SoLightModel node allows you to specify whether to use Phong lighting (that is, use the light sources in the scene) or to just display each object in its base color. Phong lighting is the default and usually looks much more natural.

A SoEnvironment allows you to specify the *atmosphere* of the scene. Specifically you can describe:

  ◆ the intensity and color of the ambient light in the scene,
  ◆ how rapidly light attenuates away from its sources (which can be set to constant, linear, or squared attenuation),
  ◆ the kind of fog in the scene (there are several grades of fog: haze is light, fog is moderate, and smoke is quite dense),
  ◆ the color of the fog, and
  ◆ the distance at which the fog completely obscures the scene.[8]

A SoShapeHints node allows you to specify several characteristics of the subsequent shapes; doing so can speed up rendering of the scene. These hints include:

♦ the order of vertices in the faces of the shape,
♦ whether the shape is solid,
♦ whether all of the faces of the shape are convex, and
♦ the crease angle, which can help in automatically generating normals.[9]

A SoComplexity node allows you to specify how much you want the renderer to subdivide subsequent objects into polygons. If you specify less subdivision, rendering is generally faster.

You can tell it the following:

♦ to use fewer polygons for objects that are small on the screen,
♦ draw just bounding boxes,
♦ a hint about how much to subdivide (this is simply an abstract number between 0 and 1), and
♦ a hint about how carefully to texture the objects.

A SoUnits node allows you to specify the units of measurement for all subsequent shapes in the graph. Almost everything you are likely to want is available: from kilometers down to angstroms, including normal English units (feet, miles), and one or two esoteric ones (nautical miles). Meters are the default unit.

Bindings

A single Material is often insufficient for an object, particularly a complex object. Various parts or faces of the object may call for different colors or reflectivity. Thus, a SoMaterial node can actually hold an unlimited number of materials, and each field in the node can have multiple values. The way that these values are applied to objects is determined by a SoMaterialBinding node.

You can specify a number of ways to bind a list of materials onto an object:

- the default, which tries to use the best binding (usually an overall binding), uses no materials;
- an overall binding, using the first material for the entire shape;
- the use of one material for each part of the shape, where part is appropriate to the kind of object in question;
- the use of one material per part, with indexing;
- the use of one material per face, optionally with indexing; and
- the use of one material per vertex, optionally with indexing.

If you use indexing, the object in question should use a *materialIndex* field to specify which materials are bound to which parts of the shape. If you bind materials to vertices, this field interpolates between those vertices. Several color plates are provided to illustrate the way Open Inventor handles materials, lights, and bindings.

Normals

Normals can be specified explicitly or generated automatically. You can specify them explicitly in much the same way that materials are specified and bound to objects. Most complex objects can compute their normals automatically, but this process is quite compute intensive and can slow things down.

Transformations

Transformations are similar to properties in that they affect the state of the rendering engine. However, they are cumulative; a transformation adds to previous transformations, unlike properties, which replace previous properties in the state. You can specify all of the usual sorts of transformations in a SoTransform node. Specifically, you can describe:

- ◆ translation in space,
- ◆ rotation,
- ◆ scaling factor,
- ◆ scaling rotation (a rotation to apply before scaling), and
- ◆ the center point of the object for rotation and scaling.

There are also separate node classes for rotation, translation, and scaling, which are convenient if you are performing only one transformation.

Text

Both two dimensional (2-D) and three dimensional (3-D) text can be added to a scene. Two-dimensional text is always displayed facing the screen. Three dimensional text appears as an object in the scene and can be viewed from any direction. The font type and size can be changed for both types of text, and the profile of the 3-D text can be modified.

A *SoText2* node is available for creating screen-aligned text. The origin of the text is (0,0,0), and the origin is transformed by the current transformation matrix. However, the text itself always faces the screen. The text can be justified with respect to the origin, and the line spacing can be modified. The 2-D text is not affected by perspective changes. In other words, the height and width of two-dimensional text does not change as the distance from the viewer changes. Two-dimensional text is useful for labeling graphs or points in a scene.

The primary difference between *SoText3* and *SoText2* is that 3-D text has a thickness and can be displayed as solid letters. *SoText3* is not constrained to face the screen. For instance, if the camera moves above the letters, the tops of the 3-D letters are displayed on the monitor.

The shape of the text displayed with a *SoText3* node can be changed by applying a custom extrusion profile. The profile can be defined by using either a *SoLinearProfile* node or a *SoNurbsProfile* node.[10] The profile can make the text appear beveled or curved instead of blocky.

Textures

Textures can greatly increase the quality of a rendered image. Textures are used to add visual detail to a model without increasing the number of polygons in the model.

To display a textured object, you need a list of polygons comprising the object on which the texture is to be displayed and a two-dimensional bitmap or image, which is called a texture map. The mapping between the texture and the polygons is controlled by assigning texture coordinates to individual vertices.

Two-dimensional images used as texture maps can be read from file or stored in memory. Currently only SGI's RGB image format is supported on the SGIs, but there are many ways to convert image files to the SGI RGB format.

A texture map is described as being a 1×1 square. However, a texture map does not have to have the same dimension in height and in width. When a square or a rectangular bitmap is read into memory, it is assigned coordinates between 0.0 and 1.0 in both directions. These coordinates are mapped to the texture coordinates on the vertices of the polygon.

This example uses a SoTexture2 node to apply the bitmap contained in texture.rgb to a cube:

```
#Inventor V2.0 ascii
Separator {
     Texture2 {
```

```
            filename "texture.rgb-"
        }
        Cube {
        }
}11
```

The following list identifies and describes the nodes used for texture mapping:

SoTexture2   Used to specify bitmap for texturing.

SoTextureCoordinate2   Lists texture coordinates to be indexed by subsequent vertices.

SoTextureCoordinateBinding   Describes texture coordinate binding for following shape nodes.

SoTextureCoordinatePlane   To be determined.

SoTextureCoordinateEnvironment   Nodes that allow the use of spatial functions for creating texture coordinates.

SoTextureCoordinateDefault   Turns off previous texture coordinate functions.

SoTexture2Transform   Transforms a 2-D texture map.[12]

Texture maps can be used to modulate the color and the transparency of an object. Normally, when you draw shaded images, a polygon's color (or shaded color) is calculated, based on the current SoMaterial node. When a texture is used to *modulate* the color, the shaded color is combined with the texture color. When it is used as a *decal*, the texture color replaces the shaded color. With *blend* mode turned on and a one- or two-component texture map, the final color is blended between the shaded color and a constant blend color.

To map the texture onto the object, you can use the default texture mapping for the shape node, as in the previous example. However, you will often want more control over how the texture is mapped to the polygons of the object.

A SoTextureCoordinate2 node can be used to align specific texture coordinates to polygon vertices. Also, two texture coordinate functions can be applied to shapes: SoTextureCoordinatePlane and SoTextureCoordinateEnvironment.

Nodekits

Nodekits are a collection of nodes with a specified arrangement, thereby simplifying the creation of consistent, structured databases. Nodekits also support nesting hierarchies, so many levels of relative motion can occur.

The template associated with the nodekit decides which nodes can be added and where they should be placed. Therefore you don't have to create and arrange each node individually.

When a nodekit is created, particular nodes are thereby default (separator nodes and internal nodes, for example); you must explicitly request other nodes to be created. The nodes can be created in any order, because the kit will put them in the right place as specified by the nodekit catalog. You don't have direct access to "hidden children," which are the nodes you create and remove in the nodekit. The nodekit takes care of the details for you.

An example can illustrate the ease of using nodekits for application-specific objects. With a cat simulation package, there are several objects representing cats. Each cat has the same general structure in the scene graph, for example, legs and head, as well as cat-specific actions (for example, ScratchingHead()). Each cat can be dealt with in a similar way. Knowing the details of the subgraph representing ScratchingHead() isn't necessary, because the general ScratchingHead() method exists. To create these new specific objects and methods, you need to extend Open Inventor by subclassing, which is described in Inventor Toolmaker.[13]

To select parts and to set values, you use something called "set()." You can also specify part names in the nodes of the nodekits. The other two basic methods are GetPart(), which returns the requested node, and setPart(), which inserts the node given as a new part in the nodekit. There are macros for these and two methods, called SO_GET_PART() and SO_CHECK_PART(), which perform casting and, additionally, type checking.

A path can be returned from a pick or a search action. The default is SoPath, which ends the path at the nodekit. You can also choose to cast SoFullPath, which includes hidden and public children of the nodekit; or SoNodEkitPath, which contains only the nodekits (not the intermediate nodes). It is also possible to create paths to a particular nodekit part.

Each nodekit class has an associated catalog, which lists all the nodes available in the kit. The nodekit catalog describes how nodes are arranged in the subgraph (when they are selected) and lists the available parts, such as name of part, type of node, default type, whether this is the default or name of parent, and name of right sibling.

Some nodekit parts are lists of parts. These children, of type SoNodeKitListPart, are restricted to certain classes. You still use the standard group methods to operate on the parts list. The difference with these is that the group checks the type of children.

SoSeparatorKit is a class of nodekit that can be used to create motion hierarchies. Classes derived from separator nodekits inherit a childList of type SoNodeKitListPart. This aspect allows your attention to wander from each element (individual parts of each group kit) to how the parts of an object would move relative to other parts.

Again, instead of creating each node individually, specifying values for their fields, and arranging them in the proper places in a subgraph, the nodekit already knows how nodes should be arranged. All you have to do is specify which nodes you want to utilize and get and set the desired values for the nodes.

In short, nodekits are flexible, already organized (convenient), and efficient (only the nodes needed are created). You can tailor nodekits to your own groupings. An added plus is that code is readable and relatively short. Nodekits give short-cut routines for creating nodes and setting their values. Hierarchies of nodekits can be nested so that relative motion can be more easily achieved.

From Here

This chapter presented Open Inventor as an object 3-D toolkit offering a comprehensive solution to interactive graphics and as the basis for the VRML 2.0 and VRML97 standard itself. The next chapter takes a thorough look at VRML itself.

Endnotes

1 Galvin Bell, Silicon Graphics, Inc., 1994, 1995, gavin@sgi.com.

2 Ibid.

3 Ibid.

4 Ibid.

5 Mark Waks, Silicon Graphics, Inc., 1995, justin@dsd.camb.inmet.com.

6 Ibid.

7 Ibid.

8 Ibid.

9 Ibid.

10 John Barrus, Silicon Graphics, Inc., 1995, barrus@merl.com.

11 Ibid.

12 Ibid.

13 Ferguson, Silicon Graphics, Inc., 1995, snpf@ugcs.caltech.edu.

12

Virtual Reality Modeling Language (VRML) Specifications

The *Virtual Reality Modeling Language* (VRML) is a language for describing multiparticipant interactive simulations—virtual worlds networked via the global Internet and hyperlinked with the World Wide Web. VRML can be used to specify all aspects of virtual world display, interaction, and Internetworking. It is the intention of its designers that VRML become the standard language for interactive simulation within the World Wide Web.

The first version of VRML allowed for the creation of virtual worlds with limited interactive behavior. These worlds can contain objects that have hyperlinks to other worlds, HTML documents, or other valid MIME types. When a user selects an object with a hyperlink, the appropriate MIME viewer is launched. When the user selects a link to a VRML document from within a correctly configured browser, a VRML viewer is launched. Thus, VRML viewers are still the perfect companion applications to standard WWW browsers for navigating and visualizing the Web. Now VRML97 allows for richer behaviors, including animations, motion physics, and real-time multiuser interaction.

VRML Overview

The history of the development of the Internet has had three distinct phases. First was the development of the TCP/IP infrastructure, which allowed documents and data to be stored in a proximally independent way. That is, the Internet provided a layer of abstraction between datasets and the hosts that manipulated them. This abstraction was useful, but also confusing. Without any clear sense of what went where, access to the Internet was restricted to the class of sysops/Net surfers who could maintain internal cognitive maps of the data space.

Next, Tim Berners-Lee's work at CERN, where he developed the hypermedia system known as the World Wide Web, added another layer of abstraction to the existing structure. This abstraction provided an addressing scheme: a unique identifier (the Universal Resource Locator) that could tell anyone where to go and how to get any piece of data within the Web. Although useful, it lacked dimensionality. There's no *there* within the Web, and the only type of navigation permissible (other than surfing) is by direct reference. In other words, users can be directed on how to get to the VRML Forum homepage only by saying http:www.wired.com/, which is not human-centered data. So, although the World Wide Web provides a retrieval mechanism to complement the existing storage mechanism, it leaves a lot to be desired, particularly for human beings.

Finally, we move to perceptualized Internetworks, where the data has been sensualized or rendered sensually. If something is represented sensually, it is possible to make sense of it. VRML is an attempt (how successful, only time and effort will tell) to place humans at the center of the Internet, ordering its universe to our whims. In order to do that, the most important single element is a standard that defines the particularities of perception. Virtual Reality Modeling Language is that standard, designed to be a universal description language for multiparticipant simulations.

These three phases—storage, retrieval, and perceptualization—are analogous to the human process of consciousness, as expressed in terms of semantics and cognitive science. Events occur and are recorded (memory). Inferences are drawn from memory (associations), and maps of the universe are created (cognitive perception) from sets of related events. What is important to remember is that the map is not the territory, and we should avoid becoming trapped in any single representation or world view. Although we need to design to avoid disorientation, we should always push the envelope in the kinds of experiences we can bring into manifestation!

This part of the chapter discusses the success of a process that was committed to being open, flexible, and responsive to the needs of a growing Web community. Rather than reinvent the wheel, the original VRML Architecture Group (now the VRML Consortium) had adapted an existing specification (Open Inventor) as the basis from which its own work could grow, saving years of design work and perhaps many mistakes. Now the real work has begun: rendering its norspheric space.

History

VRML was conceived in the spring of 1994 at the first annual World Wide Web Conference in Geneva, Switzerland. Tim Berners-Lee and Dave Raggett organized a *Birds-of-a-Feather* (BOF) session to discuss virtual reality interfaces to the World Wide Web. Several BOF attendees described projects already under way to build three-dimensional graphical visualization tools that interoperate with the Web. Attendees agreed on the need for these tools to have a common language for specifying 3-D scene description and hyperlinks—an analog of HTML for virtual reality. The term *Virtual Reality Markup Language* (VRML) was coined, and the group resolved to begin specification work after the conference. The word *Markup* was later changed to *Modeling* to reflect the graphical nature of VRML.

Shortly after the Geneva BOF session, the www-vrml mailing list was created to discuss the development of a specification for the first version of VRML. The response to the list invitation was over-whelming: Within a week, there were more than a thousand members. After an initial settling-in period, list moderator Mark Pesce of Labyrinth Group announced his intention to have a draft version of the specification ready by the Fall 1994 conference, a mere five months away. List members generally agreed that, although this schedule was aggressive, it was achievable, provided that the requirements for the first version were not too ambitious and that VRML could be adapted from an existing solution. The list members quickly agreed on a set of requirements for the first version and began a search for technologies that could be adapted to fit the needs of VRML.

The search for existing technologies turned up several worthwhile candidates. After much deliberation, the list members came to a consensus: the Open Inventor ASCII File Format from Silicon Graphics, Inc. The Open Inventor File Format supports complete descriptions of 3-D scenes with polygonally rendered objects, lighting, materials, ambient properties, and realism effects. A sub-set of the Open Inventor File Format, with extensions to support networking, forms the basis of VRML. Gavin Bell of Silicon Graphics had initially adapted the Open Inventor File Format for VRML, with design input to the mailing list. SGI publicly stated at the time that the file format was available for use in the open market and had contributed a file format parser into the public domain to bootstrap VRML viewer development.

The second release of VRML added significantly more interactive capabilities. It was designed by the Silicon Graphics VRML team with contributions from Sony Research and Mitra. VRML 2.0 was reviewed by the VRML moderated e-mail discussion group (www-vrml@wired.com), and later adopted and endorsed by many companies and individuals. See the San Diego Supercomputer Center's VRML Repository or Silicon Graphics' VRML site in the accompanying CD-ROM for more information. The first official version of the VRML 2.0 specification was published on August 4, 1996. The latest draft of the specification, VRML97 (April 1997), replaces the August 4 version and has been submitted to ISO as a *Draft International Standard* (DIS). The following sidebar, "ISO and IEC," contains more information on these worldwide standards bodies.

ISO and IEC

ISO (the International Organization for Standardization) and IEC (the International Electrotechnical Commission) form a specialized system for worldwide standardization. National bodies that are members of ISO or IEC participate in the development of International Standards through technical committees established by the respective organization to deal with particular fields of technical activity. ISO and IEC technical committees collaborate in fields of mutual interest. Other international organizations, governmental and non-governmental, in liaison with ISO and IEC, also take part in the work. See http://www.iso.ch for information on ISO, and http://www.iec.ch for information on IEC.

    In the field of information technology, ISO and IEC have established a joint technical committee: ISO/IEC JTC 1. The Draft International Standards adopted by the joint technical committee are circulated to national bodies for voting. Publication as an International Standard requires approval by at least 75 percent of the national bodies casting a vote. See http://www.iso.ch/meme/JTC1.html for information on JTC 1.

    International Standard ISO/IEC 14772 was prepared by Joint Technical Committee ISO/IEC JTC 1, Information Technology

Subcommittee 24, Computer Graphics, and Image Processing, in collaboration with The VRML Consortium (http://www.vrm l.org) and the VRML moderated e-mail list (www-vrml@vag .vrml.org).[1]

VRML97

As previously stated in earlier in the book, VRML97 is the name of the ISO/VRML standard. It is almost identical to VRML 2.0, but with numerous improvements to the specification document and a few minor functional differences (see the summary of VRML97 features later in the chapter). VRML97 has been submitted to ISO for a vote (DIS (*Draft International Standard*)) and was finalized in July 1997 as an *International Standard* (IS).

Moving Worlds

Moving Worlds, on the other hand, is the name of the 1996 Silicon Graphics' submission to the Request-for-Proposals for VRML 2.0. It was chosen by the VRML community as the working document for VRML 2.0. In addition, it was created by Silicon Graphics, Inc. in collaboration with Sony and Mitra. Many people in the VRML community were actively involved with Moving Worlds and contributed numerous ideas, reviews, and improvements.

Requirements

As previously stated, VRML is a file format for describing interactive 3-D objects and worlds. VRML is designed to be used on the Internet, intranets, and local client systems. In addition, VRML is also intended to be a universal interchange format for integrated 3-D graphics and multimedia. VRML may also be used in a variety of application areas such as engineering and scientific visualization, multimedia presentations, entertainment and educational titles, Web pages, and shared virtual worlds.

VRML was designed to meet the following requirements:

- **Authorability**: Enable the development of computer programs capable of creating, editing, and maintaining VRML files, as well as automatic translation programs for converting other commonly used 3-D file formats into VRML files.
- **Composability**: Provide the ability to use and combine dynamic 3-D objects within a VRML world and thus allow reusability.
- **Extensibility**: Provide the ability to add new object types not explicitly defined in VRML.
- **Implementability**: Be capable of implementation on a wide range of systems.
- **Performance:** Emphasize scalable, interactive performance on a wide variety of computing platforms.
- **Scalability**: Enable arbitrarily large, dynamic, 3-D worlds.[2]

As with HTML, these are absolute requirements for an intranet language standard. They should need little explanation here.

Early on, the designers decided that VRML would not be an extension to HTML, which is designed for text, not graphics. Also, VRML requires even more finely tuned intranet optimizations than HTML. It is expected that a typical VRML scene will be composed of many more inline objects and served up by many more servers than a typical HTML document. Moreover, HTML is an accepted standard, with existing implementations. To impede the HTML design process with VRML issues and to constrain the VRML design process with HTML compatibility concerns would do both languages a disservice. As an intranet language, VRML will succeed or fail independent of HTML.

VAG also decided initially that, except for the hyperlinking feature, the first version of VRML would not support interactive behaviors. This was a practical decision intended to streamline design and implementation. Design of a language for describing interactive behaviors is a big job, especially when the language needs to express behaviors of objects communicating on an intranet. Such languages do exist. If VAG had chosen one of them, it would have risked getting into a language war. People don't get excited about the syntax of a language for describing polygonal objects; people get very excited about the syntax of real languages for writing programs. Religious wars can extend the design process by months or years. In addition, networked interobject operation requires brokering services such as those provided by CORBA or OLE. Finally, by keeping behaviors out of a version, VAG made it a much smaller task to implement a viewer. VAG acknowledged that support for arbitrary interactive behaviors is critical to the long-term success of VRML. They have been included in VRML97.

So, what's come out of the initial VAG effort, and continued on by the VRML Consortium, is that VRML is capable of representing static and animated dynamic 3-D and multimedia objects with hyperlinks to other media such as text, sounds, movies, and images. VRML browsers, as well as authoring tools for the creation of VRML files, are widely available for many different platforms.

VRML supports an extensibility model that allows new dynamic 3-D objects to be defined and a registration process that allows application communities to develop interoperable extensions to the base standard. There are mappings between VRML objects and commonly used 3-D application programmer interface (API) features.

VRML Specifications

The VRML Specification (see companion CD-ROM) is the technical document that precisely describes the VRML file format standard. It is primarily intended for implementers writing VRML browsers and authoring systems as shown in the sidebar, "High-Level Summary of the VRML Specification."

In other words, the VRML specification shown in the previous sidebar defines a file format that integrates 3-D graphics and multimedia. Conceptually, each VRML file is a 3-D, time-based space that contains graphic and aural objects that can be dynamically

High-Level Summary of the VRML Specification

VRML 1.0 provided a means of creating and viewing static 3-D worlds; VRML97 provides much more. The overarching goal of VRML97 is to provide a richer, more exciting, more interactive user experience than is possible within the static boundaries of VRML 1.0. The secondary goal is to provide a solid foundation for future VRML expansion to grow from, and to keep things as simple and as fast as possible—for everyone from browser developers to world designers to end users. VRML97 provides these extensions and enhancements to VRML 1.0:

♦ Enhanced static worlds
♦ Interaction
♦ Animation
♦ Scripting
♦ Prototyping

You can also add realism to the static geometry of your world using new features of VRML97. New nodes allow you to create ground-and-sky backdrops to scenes, add distant mountains and clouds, and dim distant objects with fog. Another new node lets you easily create irregular terrain instead of using flat planes for ground surfaces.

VRML97 provides 3-D spatial sound-generating nodes to further enhance realism—you can put crickets, breaking glass, ringing telephones, or any other sound into a scene. Also, if you're writing a browser, you'll be happy to see that optimizing and parsing files are easier than in VRML 1.0, thanks to a new simplified scene graph structure.

Interaction: No more moving like a ghost through cold, dead worlds; now you can directly interact with objects and creatures you encounter. New sensor nodes set off events when you move in certain areas of a world and when you click certain objects. They even let you drag objects or controls from one place to another. Another kind of sensor keeps track of the passage of time, providing a basis for everything from alarm clocks to repetitive animations.

And no more walking through walls. Collision detection ensures that solid objects react like solid objects; you bounce off them (or simply stop moving) when you run into them. Terrain following allows you to travel up and down steps or ramps.

Animation: VRML97 includes a variety of animation objects called *Interpolators*. This allows you to create predefined animations of many aspects of the world and then play it at some opportune time. With animation interpolators, you can create moving objects such as flying birds, automatically opening doors, walking robots, objects that change color as they move (such as the sun), and objects that morph their geometry from one shape to another. You can also create guided tours that automatically move the user along a predefined path.

Scripting: VRML97 wouldn't be able to move without the new Script nodes. Using Scripts, you can not only animate creatures and objects in a world, but give them a semblance of intelligence. Animated dogs can fetch newspapers or frisbees, clock hands can move, birds can fly, and robots can juggle.

These effects are achieved by means of events; a script takes input from sensors and generates events based on that input, which can change other nodes in the world. Events are passed around among nodes by way of special statements called *routes*.

Prototyping: Have an idea for a new kind of geometry node that you want everyone to be able to use? Got a nifty script that you want to turn into part of the next version of VRML? In VRML97, you can encapsulate a group of nodes together as a new node type, a prototype, and then make that node type available to anyone who wants to use it. You can then create instances of the new type, each with different field values. For instance, you could create a Robot prototype with a robotColor field, and then create as many individual different-colored Robot nodes as you like.[3]

modified through a variety of mechanisms. VRML defines a primary set of objects and mechanisms that encourage composition, encapsulation, and extension.

The semantics of VRML describe an abstract functional behavior of time-based, interactive, 3-D, multimedia worlds. VRML does not define physical devices or any other implementation-dependent concepts (screen resolution and input devices). In addition, VRML is intended for a wide variety of devices and applications, and provides wide latitude in interpretation and implementation of the functionality. For instance, VRML does not assume the existence of a mouse or 2-D display device. Each VRML file does however implicitly establish a world coordinate space for all objects defined in the file, as well as all objects recursively included by the file; explicitly defines and composes a set of 3-D and multimedia objects; can specify hyperlinks to other files and applications; and can define object behaviors.

An important characteristic of VRML files is the ability to compose files together through inclusion, and to relate files together through hyperlinking. For instance, consider the file earth.wrl that specifies a world that contains a sphere representing the earth. This file may also contain references to a variety of other VRML files representing cities on the earth (file paris.wrl). The enclosing file, earth.wrl, defines the coordinate system that all the cities reside in. Each city file defines the world coordinate system that the city resides in, but that becomes a local coordinate system when contained by the earth file.

Hierarchical file inclusion enables the creation of arbitrarily large, dynamic worlds. Therefore, VRML ensures that each file is completely described by the objects and files contained within it, and that the effects of each file are strictly scoped by the file and the spatial limits of the objects defined in the file. Otherwise, the accumulation of files into larger worlds would produce unscalable results (as each added world produces global effects on all other worlds). For instance, light sources have the potential of global effect since light energy theoretically does not dissipate to zero. And, if the earth file contains 200 city files, each containing 200 lights and each affecting all objects in the world, the lighting calculations would quickly become intractable. Therefore, in order to prevent global effects, light source objects are scoped by either a maximum radius or by location within the file.

Another essential characteristic of VRML is that it is intended to be used in a distributed environment such as the World Wide Web. There are various objects and mechanisms built into the language that support multiple distributed files, including inlining of other VRML files, hyperlinking to other files, using established Internet standards for other file formats, and defining a compact syntax.

Thus, VRML specifications are also intended for readers interested in learning the details about VRML. Note that many people (especially nonprogrammers) find the VRML specifications inadequate as a starting point or primer. There are a variety of excellent introductory books on VRML in bookstores—like the first edition of this book.

From Here

Now that VRML has been covered thoroughly, there also needs to be a very thorough discussion about the OpenGL Graphics System. After all, both OpenGL and Open Inventor are the bases, or foundations, on which VRML was created.

Chapter 13 describes the OpenGL graphics system: what it is, how it acts, and what is required to implement it. Programmers and experts in the computer graphics arena might also want to take a look at Appendixes C, D, and E in the companion CD-ROM for an in-depth look at the OpenGL environment.

Endnotes

1   Silicon Graphics, Inc., 2011 North Shoreline Boulevard, Mountain View, CA 94039.

2   Ibid.

3   Ibid.

13

The OpenGL Graphics System

This chapter describes the OpenGL graphics system: what it is, how it acts, and what is required to implement it. You must have at least a rudimentary understanding of computer graphics. This means that you must be familiar with the essentials of computer graphics algorithms, as well as with basic graphics hardware and associated terms.

Three Views of OpenGL

OpenGL (for Open Graphics Library) is a software interface to graphics hardware. The interface consists of a set of several hundred procedures and functions that allow a programmer to specify the objects and operations involved in producing high-quality graphical images—specifically color images of three-dimensional objects.

Most of OpenGL requires that the graphics hardware contain a frame buffer. Many OpenGL calls pertain to drawing objects, such as points, lines, polygons, and bitmaps, but the way that some of this drawing occurs (such as when antialiasing or texturing is enabled) relies on the existence of a frame buffer. Further, some of OpenGL is specifically concerned with frame buffer manipulation.

To the *programmer* OpenGL is a set of commands for the specification of geometric objects in two or three dimensions, together with commands that control how these objects are rendered into the frame buffer. For the most part OpenGL provides an immediate-mode interface, meaning that specifying an object causes it to be drawn.

A typical program that uses OpenGL begins with calls to open a window into the frame buffer into which the program will draw. Then calls are made to allocate a GL context and to associate it with the window. Once a GL context is allocated, the programmer is free to issue OpenGL commands. Some calls are used to draw simple geometric objects (points, line segments, and polygons). Others affect the rendering of these primitives, including how they are lit or colored and how they are mapped from the user's two- or three-dimensional model space to the two-dimensional screen. There are also calls to effect direct control of the frame buffer, such as reading and writing pixels.

To the *implementor* OpenGL is a set of commands for the operation of graphics hardware. If the hardware consists only of an addressable frame buffer, OpenGL must be implemented almost entirely on the host CPU. More typically the graphics hardware may comprise varying degrees of graphics acceleration—from a raster subsystem capable of rendering two-dimensional lines and polygons to sophisticated floating-point processors capable of transforming and computing on geometric data. The OpenGL implementor's task is to provide the CPU software interface while dividing the work for each OpenGL command between the CPU and the graphics hardware. This division must be tailored to the available graphics hardware to obtain optimum performance in carrying out OpenGL calls.

OpenGL maintains a considerable amount of state information. This state controls how objects are drawn into the frame buffer. Some of this state is directly available to the user: He or she can make calls to obtain its value. Some of it, however, is visible only by the effect it has on what is drawn. One of the main goals of this specification is to make OpenGL state information explicit, to elucidate how it changes, and to indicate what its effects are.

To me OpenGL is a state machine that controls a set of specific drawing operations. This model should engender a specification that satisfies the needs of both programmers and implementors. It does not, however, necessarily provide a model for implementation. An implementation must produce results conforming to those produced by the specified methods, but, there may be ways to carry out a particular computation that is more efficient than the one specified.

OpenGL Operation

OpenGL (henceforth the GL) is concerned only with rendering into a frame buffer (and reading values stored in that frame buffer). There is no support for other peripherals sometimes associated with graphics hardware, such as mice and keyboards. Programmers must rely on other mechanisms to obtain user input.

The GL draws primitives subject to a number of selectable modes. Each primitive is a point, line segment, polygon, or pixel rectangle. Each mode may be changed independently. The setting of one does not affect the settings of others (although many modes may interact to determine what eventually ends up in the frame buffer). Modes are set, primitives specified, and other GL operations described by sending commands in the form of function or procedure calls.

Primitives are defined by a group of one or more vertices. A vertex defines a point, an endpoint of an edge, or a corner of a polygon where two edges meet. Data (consisting of positional coordinates, colors, normals, and texture coordinates) are associated with a vertex. Each vertex is processed independently, in order, and in the same way. The only exception to this rule is if the group of vertices is clipped so that the indicated primitive fits within a specified region. In this case vertex data may be modified and new vertices created. The type of clipping depends on which primitive the group of vertices represents.

Commands are always processed in the order in which they are received, although there may be an indeterminate delay before the effects of a command are realized. This means, for example, that one primitive must be drawn completely before any subsequent one can affect the frame buffer. It also means that queries and pixel read operations return state consistent with complete execution of all previously invoked GL commands. In general, the effects of a GL command on either GL modes or the frame buffer must be complete before any subsequent command can have any such effects.

In the GL data binding occurs on call. This means that data passed to a command is interpreted when that command is received. Even if the command requires a pointer to data, the data is interpreted when the call is made, and any subsequent changes to the data have no effect on the GL (unless the same pointer is used in a subsequent command).

The GL provides direct control over the fundamental operations of 3-D and 2-D graphics. This includes specification of such parameters as transformation matrices, lighting equation coefficients, antialiasing methods, and pixel update operators. It does not provide a means for describing or modeling complex geometric objects. Another way to describe this situation is to say that the GL provides mechanisms to describe how complex geometric objects are to be rendered rather than mechanisms to describe the complex objects themselves.

The model for interpretation of GL commands is client-server. That is, a program (the client) issues commands, which are interpreted and processed by the GL (the server). The server may or may not operate on the same computer as the client. In this sense the GL is network transparent. A server may maintain a number of GL contexts, each of which is an encapsulation of current GL state. A client may choose to connect to any one of these contexts. Issuing GL commands when the program is not connected to a context results in undefined behavior.

The effects of GL commands on the frame buffer are ultimately controlled by the window system that allocates frame buffer resources. It is the window system that determines which portions of the frame buffer the GL may access at any given time and that communicates to the GL how those portions are structured. Therefore there are no GL commands to configure the frame buffer or to initialize the GL. Similarly display of frame buffer contents on a CRT monitor (including the transformation of individual frame buffer values by such techniques as gamma correction) is not addressed by the GL. Frame buffer configuration occurs outside of the GL in conjunction with the window system. The initialization of a GL context occurs when the window system allocates a window for GL rendering.

The GL is designed to be run on a range of graphics platforms with varying graphics capabilities and performance. To accommodate this variety, ideal behavior is specified here instead of actual behavior for certain GL operations. In cases where deviation from the ideal is allowed, the rules are also specified that an implementation must obey if it is to approximate the ideal behavior usefully. This allowed variation in GL behavior implies that two distinct GL implementations may not agree pixel for pixel when presented with the same input, even when run on identical frame-buffer configurations.

Finally, command names, constants, and types are prefixed in the GL (by gl, GL, and GL, respectively in C) to reduce name clashes with other packages. The prefixes are omitted in this chapter for clarity.

Floating-Point Computation

The GL must perform a number of floating-point operations during its operation. No specification is made here as to how floating-point numbers are to be represented or how operations on them are to be performed. Nevertheless it is required that numbers' floating-point parts contain enough bits and that their exponent fields are large enough so that individual results of floating-point operations are accurate to about 1 part in 10^5. The maximum representable magnitude of a floating-point number used to represent positional or normal coordinates must be at least 2^{32}. The maximum representable magnitude for colors or texture coordinates must be at least 2^{10}. The maximum representable magnitude for all other floating-point values must be at least 2^{32}. Most single-precision floating-point formats meet these requirements.

Any representable floating-point value is legal as input to a GL command that requires floating-point data. The result of providing a value that is not a floating-point number to such a command is unspecified, but must not lead to GL interruption or termination. In IEEE arithmetic, for example, providing a negative zero or a denormalized number to a GL command yields predictable results, whereas providing a NaN or an infinity yields unspecified results.

Some calculations require division. In such cases (including implied divisions required by vector normalizations) a division by zero produces an unspecified result but must not lead to GL interruption or termination.

GL State

The GL maintains considerable state. This chapter enumerates each state variable and describes how each variable can be changed. For purposes of discussion, state variables are categorized somewhat arbitrarily by their function. Although a description is provided of the operations that the GL performs on the frame buffer, the frame buffer is not a part of GL state.

There are two types of state distinguishers here. The first type of state, called GL server state, resides in the GL server. The majority of GL state falls into this category. The second type of state, called GL client state, resides in the GL client. Unless otherwise specified, all state referred to in this chapter is GL server state.

GL client state is specifically identified. Each instance of a GL context implies one complete set of GL server state. Each connection from a client to a server implies a set of both GL client state and GL server state.

Although an implementation of the GL may be hardware dependent, this discussion is independent of the specific hardware on which a GL is implemented. There is a concern, therefore, with the state of graphics hardware only when it corresponds precisely to GL state.

GL Command Syntax

GL commands are functions or procedures. Various groups of commands perform the same operation but differ in how arguments are supplied to them. To conveniently accommodate this variation, a notation has been adopted for describing commands and their arguments.

GL commands are formed from a name followed, depending on the particular command, by up to four characters. The first character indicates the number of values of the indicated type that must be presented to the command. The second character or character pair indicates the specific type of the arguments: 8-bit integer, 16-bit integer, 32-bit integer, single-precision floating point, or double-precision floating point. The final character, if present, is **v**, indicating that the command takes a pointer to an array (a vector) of values rather than to a series of individual arguments.

Two specific examples come from the **Vertex** command:

```
void Vertex3f ( float x, float y, float z ) ;
```

and

```
void Vertex2sv ( short v[2] ) ;[1]
```

Table 13.1 shows the correspondence of command suffix letters to GL argument types. Refer to Table 13.2 for definitions of the GL types.

Table 13.1 GL Suffix Letters and Corresponding Argument Type

Letter	Corresponding GL Type
b	byte
s	short
i	int
f	f lost
d	double
ub	ubyte
us	ushort
ui	uint

The following examples show the ANSI C declarations for these commands. In general, a command declaration has the form

$rtype$ Name { $\in$ 1234} { $\in$ b s i f d ub us ui} {$\in$ v}
([args ,] T arg1, ... , T argN [, args]) ;

Note that the declarations shown in this chapter apply to ANSI C. Languages that allow passing of argument type information, such as C++ and Ada, admit simpler declarations and fewer entry points.

Rtype is the return type of the function. The braces ({}) enclose a series of characters (or character pairs) of which one is selected; $\in$ indicates no character. The arguments enclosed in brackets ([args ,] and [, args]) may or may not be present. The N arguments *arg1* through *argN* have type T, which corresponds to one of the type letters or letter pairs as indicated in Table 13.1 (if there are no letters, the arguments' type is given explicitly). If the final character is not **v**, N is given by the digit **1**, **2**, **3**, or **4** (if there is no digit, the number of arguments is fixed). If the final character is **v**, only *arg1* is present, and it is an array of N values of the indicated type. Finally, an unsigned type is indicated by the shorthand of prepending u to the beginning of the type name (so that, for instance, unsigned char is abbreviated uchar).

For example,

```
void Normal3{fd}( T arg ) ;
```

indicates the two declarations

```
void Normal3f( float arg1, float arg2, float arg3 ) ;
void Normal3-D( double arg1, double arg2, double arg3) ;
```

However,

```
void Normal3{fd}v( T arg ) ;
```

means the two declarations

```
void Normal3fv( float arg[3] ) ;
void Normal3-Dv( double arg[S] ) ;
```

Arguments whose type is fixed (not indicated by a suffix on the command) are of one of 14 types (or pointers to one of these). These types are summarized in Table 13.2.

GL types are not C types. Thus, for example, GL type int is referred to as GLint outside this chapter and is not necessarily equivalent to the C type int. An implementation may use more bits than the number indicated in the table to represent a GL type. Correct interpretation of integer values outside the minimum range is not required, however.

Basic GL Operation

Figure 13.1 shows a schematic of the GL. Commands enter the GL on the left. Some commands specify geometric objects to be drawn, whereas others control how the objects are handled by the various stages. Most commands may be accumulated in a display list for

Table 13.2 GL Data Types

GL Type	Minimum Number of Bits	Description
boolean	1 bit	Boolean
byte	8 bits	Signed two's complement binary integer
ubyte	8 bits	Unsigned binary integer
short	16 bits	Signed two's complement binary integer
ushort	16 bits	Unsigned binary integer
int	32 bits	Signed two's complement binary integer
uint	32 bits	Unsigned binary integer
sizei	32 bits	Nonnegative binary integer size
enum	32 bits	Enumerated binary integer value
bitfield	32 bits	Bit field
float	32 bits	Floating-point value
clampf	32 bits	Floating-point value clamped to [0,11]
double	64 bits	Floating-point value
clampd	64 bits	Floating-point value clamped to [0, 1]

processing by the GL at a later time. Otherwise, commands are effectively sent through a processing pipeline.

The first stage provides an efficient means for approximating curve and surface geometry by evaluating polynomial functions of input values. The next stage operates on geometric primitives described by vertices: points, line segments, and polygons. In this stage vertices are transformed and lit, and primitives are clipped to a viewing volume in preparation for the next stage-rasterization. The rasterizer produces a series of frame buffer addresses and values, using a two-dimensional description of a point, line segment, or polygon. Each fragment so produced is fed to the next stage which performs operations on individual fragments before

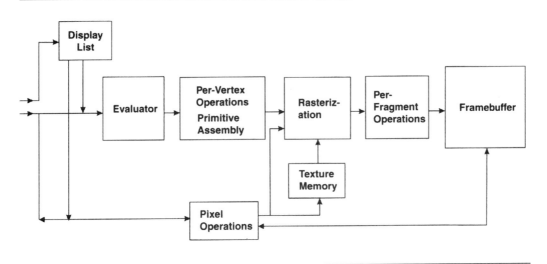

Figure 13.1 Block diagram of the GL.

they finally alter the frame buffer. These operations include conditioned updates into the frame buffer, based on incoming and previously stored depth values (to effect depth buffering); blending of incoming fragment colors with stored colors; as well as masking and other logical operations on fragment values.

Finally, there is a way to bypass the vertex-processing portion of the pipeline to send a block of fragments directly to the individual fragment operations, eventually causing a block of pixels to be written to the frame buffer. Values may also be read back from the frame buffer or copied from one portion of the frame buffer to another. These transfers may include some type of decoding or encoding.

This ordering is meant only as a tool for describing the GL, not as a strict rule of how the GL is implemented. It is presented here only as a means to organize the various operations of the GL. Objects such as curved surfaces, for instance, may be transformed before they are converted to polygons.

GL Errors

The GL detects only a subset of those conditions that could be considered errors. This is because in many cases error checking would adversely impact the performance of an error-free program.

The following command is used to obtain error information:

```
enum GetError( void ) ;
```

Each detectable error is assigned a numeric code. When an error is detected, a flag is set and the code is recorded. Further errors, if they occur, do not affect this recorded code. When **GetError** is called, the code is returned and the flag is cleared, so that a further error will again record its code. If a call to **GetError** returns **NO_ERROR**, no detectable error has occurred since the last call to **GetError** (or since the GL was initialized).

To allow for distributed implementations, there may be several flag-code pairs. In this case after a call to **GetError** returns a value other than **NO_ERROR,** each subsequent call returns the nonzero code of a distinct flag-code pair (in unspecified order), until all non–**NO_ERROR** codes have been returned. When there are no more non–**NO_ERROR** error codes, all flags are reset. This scheme requires some positive number of pairs of a flag bit and an integer. The initial state of all flags is cleared, and the initial value of all codes is **NO_ERROR**.

Table 13.3 summarizes GL errors. Currently when an error flag is set, results of GL operation are undefined only if **OUT_OF_MEM-ORY** has occurred. In other cases, the command generating the error is ignored so that it has no effect on GL state or frame buffer contents. If the generating command returns a value, it returns 0. If the generating command modifies values through a pointer argument, no change is made to these values. These error semantics apply only to GL errors, not to system errors, such as memory access errors. This behavior is the current behavior. The action of the GL in the presence of errors is subject to change.

Table 13.3 Summary of GL Errors

Error	Description	Offending Command Ignored?
INVALID_ENUM	Enum argument out of range	Yes
INVALID_VALUE	Numeric argument out of range	Yes
INVALID_OPERATION	Operation illegal in current state	Yes
STACK_OVERFLOW	Command would cause a stack overflow	Yes
STACK_UNDERFLOW	Command would cause a stack underflow	Yes
OUT-OF-MEMORY	Not enough memory left to execute command	Unknown

Two error-generation conditions are implicit in the description of every GL command. First, if a command that requires an enumerated value is passed, an enumerant that is not one of those specified as allowable for that command, the error **INVALID_ENUM** results. This is the case even if the argument is a pointer to an enumerated value if that value is not allowable for the given command. Second, if a negative number is provided where an argument of type **sizei** is specified, the error **INVALID_VALUE** results.

Begin/End Paradigm

In the GL most geometric objects are drawn by enclosing a series of coordinate sets that specify vertices and, optionally, normals, texture coordinates, and colors between Begin/End pairs. Ten geometric objects that are drawn this way: points, line segments, line segment loops, separated line segments, polygons, triangle strips, triangle fans, separated triangles, quadrilateral strips, and separated quadrilaterals.

Each vertex is specified with two, three, or four coordinates. In addition, a *current normal, current texture coordinates*, and *current color* may be used in processing each vertex. Normals are used by the GL in lighting calculations. The current normal is a three-dimensional vector that may be set by sending three coordinates that specify it. Texture coordinates determine how a texture image is mapped onto a primitive.

A color is associated with each vertex as it is specified. This *associated* color is either the current color or a color produced by lighting, depending on whether lighting is enabled. Texture coordinates are similarly associated with each vertex. Figure 13.2 summarizes the association of auxiliary data with a transformed vertex to produce a *processed vertex*.

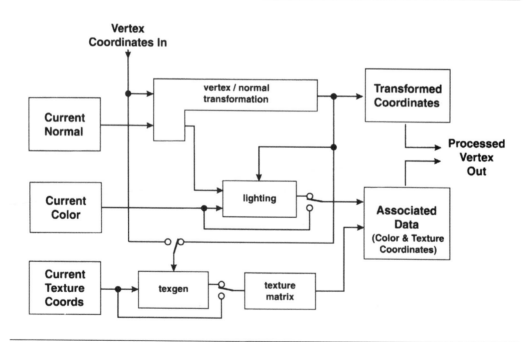

Figure 13.2 Association of current values with a vertex. The heavy lined boxes represent GL state.

The current values are part of the GL state. Vertices and normals are transformed. Colors may be affected or replaced by lighting. Texture coordinates are transformed and possibly affected by a texture coordinate-generation function. The processing indicated for each current value is applied for each vertex that is sent to the GL. The methods by which vertices, normals, texture coordinates, and colors are sent to the GL—as well as how normals are transformed and vertices are mapped to the two-dimensional screen—are discussed later.

Before a color has been assigned to a vertex, the state required by a vertex is the vertex's coordinates, the current normal, and the current texture coordinates. Once color has been assigned, however, the current normal is no longer needed. Because color assignment is done vertex by vertex, a processed vertex comprises the vertex's coordinates, its assigned color, and its texture coordinates.

Figure 13.3 shows the sequence of operations that builds a primitive (point, line segment, or polygon) from a sequence of vertices. After a primitive is formed, it is clipped to a viewing volume. This may alter the primitive by altering vertex coordinates, texture coordinates, and color. In the case of a polygon primitive, clipping may insert new vertices into the primitive. The vertices defining a primitive to be rasterized have texture coordinates and color associated with them.

Begin and End Objects

Begin and **End** require one state variable with 11 values: one value for each of the 10 possible **Begin/End** objects and one other value indicating that no **Begin/End** object is being processed. The two relevant commands are:

```
void Begin( enum mode ) ;
void End( void ) ;
```

There is no limit on the number of vertices that may be specified between a Begin and an End.[2]

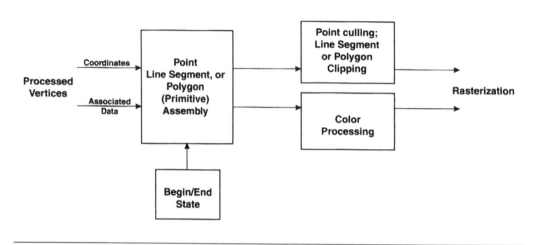

Figure 13.3 Primitive assembly and processing.

A series of individual *points* may be specified by calling Begin with an argument value of POINTS. No special state need be kept between Begin and End in this case, since each point is independent of previous and following points.

A series of one or more connected line segments, or *line strips*, is specified by enclosing a series of two or more end points within a Begin/End pair when Begin is called with LINE-STRIP. In this case the first vertex specifies the first segment's start point; the second vertex specifies the first segment's end point and the second segment's start point. In general, the ith vertex (for $i > 1$) specifies the beginning of the ith segment and the end of the i - lst. The last vertex specifies the end of the last segment. If only one vertex is specified between the Begin/End pair, no primitive is generated.

The required state consists of the processed vertex produced from the last vertex that was sent (so that a line segment can be generated from it to the current vertex) and a Boolean flag indicating whether the current vertex is the first vertex.

Line loops, specified with the LINE-LOOP argument value to Begin, are the same as line strips, except that a final segment is added from the final specified vertex to the first vertex. The additional state consists of the processed first vertex.

Individual line segments, or separate lines, each specified by a pair of vertices, are generated by surrounding vertex pairs with Begin and End, when the value of the argument to Begin is LINES. In this case the first two vertices between a Begin and End pair define the first segment, with subsequent pairs of vertices each defining one more segment. If the number of specified vertices is odd, the last one is ignored. The state required is the same as for lines but it is used differently: a vertex holding the first vertex of the current segment and a Boolean flag indicating whether the current vertex is odd or even (a segment start or end).

A *polygon* is described by specifying its boundary as a series of line segments. When Begin is called with POLYGON, the bounding line segments are specified in the same way as line loops. Depending on the current state of the GL, a polygon may be rendered in one of several ways, such as outlining its border or filling its interior. A polygon described with fewer than three vertices does not generate a primitive.

Only convex polygons are guaranteed to be drawn correctly by the GL. If a specified polygon is nonconvex (in particular, if its bounding edges, when projected onto the window, intersect anywhere other than at common end points), the rendered polygon need lie only within the convex hull of the vertices defining its boundary.

The state required to support polygons consists of at least two processed vertices (more than two are never required, although an implementation may use more). This is because a convex polygon can be rasterized as its vertices arrive, before all of them have been specified. The order of the vertices is significant in lighting, and polygon rasterization is discussed later in this chapter.

A *triangle strip* is a series of triangles connected along shared edges. A triangle strip is specified by giving a series of defining vertices between a Begin/End pair when Begin is called with TRI-ANGLE-STRIP. In this case the first three vertices define the first triangle (and their order is significant, just as for polygons). Each subsequent vertex defines a new triangle, using that point along with two vertices from the previous triangle. A Begin/End pair enclosing fewer than three vertices, when TRIANGLE-STRIP has been supplied to Begin, produces no primitive. See Figure 13.4.

The state required to support triangle strips consists of a flag indicating whether the first triangle has been completed, two stored processed vertices, (called vertex A and vertex B), and a one-bit pointer indicating which stored vertex will be replaced with the next vertex. After a **Begin(TRIANGLE-STRIP)**, the pointer is initialized to point to vertex A. Each vertex sent between a **Begin/End** pair toggles the pointer. Therefore the first vertex is stored as vertex A, the second stored as vertex B, the third stored as vertex A, and so on. Any vertex after the second one sent forms a triangle from vertex A, vertex B, and the current vertex (in that order).

A *triangle fan* is the same as a triangle strip with one exception: Each vertex after the first always replaces vertex B of the two stored vertices. The vertices of a triangle fan are enclosed between Begin and End when the value of the argument to **Begin** is TRIANGLE_FAN.

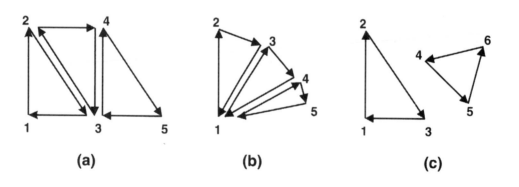

Figure 13.4 (a) Triangle strip; (b) Triangle fan; (c) Independent triangles. The numbers give the sequencing of the vertices between Begin and End. Note that in (a) and (b) triangle edge ordering is determined by the first triangle, whereas in (c) the order of each triangle's edges is independent of the other triangles.

Separate triangles are specified by placing vertices between **Begin** and **End** when the value of the argument to **Begin** is TRIAN-GLES. Otherwise, separate triangles are the same as a triangle strip. The rules given for polygons also apply to each triangle generated from a triangle strip, triangle fan, or separate triangles.

Quadrilateral (quad) strips generate a series of edge sharing quadrilaterals from vertices appearing between **Begin** and **End** when **Begin** is called with **QUAD_STRIP**. The state required is thus three processed vertices to store the last two vertices of the previous quad along with the third vertex (the first new vertex) of the current quad, a flag to indicate when the first quad has been completed, and a one-bit counter to count members of a vertex pair, as shown in Figure 13.5. The rules given for polygons also apply to each quad generated in a quad strip or from separate quads.

A quad strip with fewer than four vertices generates no primitive. If the number of vertices specified for a quadrilateral strip between **Begin** and **End** is odd, the final vertex is ignored.

Polygon Edges

Each edge of each primitive generated from a polygon, triangle strip, triangle fan, separate triangle set, quadrilateral strip, or separate

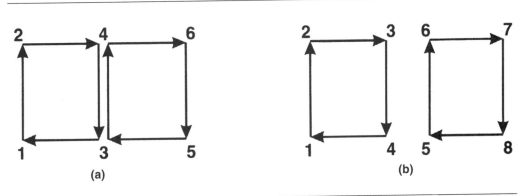

Figure 13.5 (a) Quad strip; (b) Independent quads. The numbers give the sequencing of the vertices between Begin and End.

quadrilateral set is flagged as either boundary or nonboundary. These classifications are used during polygon rasterization. Some modes affect the interpretation of polygon boundary edges, as discussed later in the chapter. By default, all edges are boundary edges.

But the default flagging of polygons, separate triangles, or separate quadrilaterals may be altered by calling either of the following to change the value of a flag bit:

```
void EdgeFlag( boolean flag ) ;
void EdgeFlagv( boolean *flag )
```

If flag is 0 the flag bit is set to FALSE. If flag is nonzero, the flag bit is set to TRUE.

When Begin is supplied with one of the argument values **POLYGON, TRIANGLES,** or **QUADS,** each vertex specified within a **Begin** and **End** pair begins an edge. If the edge flag bit is **TRUE,** each specified vertex begins an edge that is flagged as boundary. If the bit is **FALSE,** induced edges are flagged as nonboundary.

The state required for edge flagging consists of one current flag bit. Initially the bit is TRUE. In addition, each processed vertex of an assembled polygonal primitive must be augmented with a bit indicating whether the edge beginning on that vertex is boundary or nonboundary.

GL Commands within Begin/End

The only GL commands that are allowed within any **Begin/End** pairs are the commands for specifying vertex coordinates, vertex color, normal coordinates, and texture coordinates (**Vertex, Color, Index, Normal, TexCoord), EvalCoord,** and **EvalPoint** commands. Commands for specifying lighting material parameters (**Material** commands) are discussed later in the chapter, as well as display list invocation commands (**CallList** and **CallLists**) and the **EdgeFlag** command. Executing **Begin** after **Begin** has already been executed but before an **End** is issued generates the **INVALID_OPERATION** error, as does executing **End** without a previous corresponding **Begin**. Executing any other GL command within **Begin/End** results in the error **INVALID-OPERATION.**

Vertex Specification

Vertices are specified by giving their coordinates in two, three, or four dimensions. This is done by using one of several versions of the Vertex command:

```
void Vertex{1234}{sifd}( T coords ) ;
void Vertex{1234}{sifd}v( T coords ) ;
```

A call to any **Vertex** command specifies four coordinates: x, y, z, and w. The x coordinate is the first coordinate, y is second, z is third, and w is fourth. A call to *Vertex2* sets the x and y coordinates. The z coordinate is implicitly set to 0 and the w coordinate to 1. **Vertex3** sets x, y, and z to the provided values and w to 1. **Vertex4** sets all four coordinates, allowing the specification of an arbitrary point in projective three-space. Invoking a **Vertex** command outside of a **Begin/End** pair results in undefined behavior.

Current values used in associating auxiliary data with a vertex are discussed later in the chapter. A current value may be changed at any time by issuing an appropriate command.

The following commands specify the current homogeneous texture coordinates named s, t, r, and q:

```
void TexCoord{1234}{sifd}( T coords ) ;
void TexCoord{1234}{sifd}v( T coords)
```

The **TexCoord1** family of commands set the s coordinate to the provided single argument while setting t and r to 0 and q to 1. Similarly **TexCoord2** sets s and t to the specified values, r to 0, and q to 1. **TexCoord3** sets s, t, and r, with q set to 1; **TexCoord4** sets all four texture coordinates.

The current normal is set using the following:

```
void Normal3{bsifd}( T coords ) ;
void Normal3{bsifd)v( T coords ) ;
```

The current normal is set to the given coordinates whenever one of
these commands is issued. Byte, short, or integer values passed to
Normal are converted to floating-point values as indicated for the
corresponding (signed) type in Table 13.4.

Finally, there are several ways to set the current color. The GL
stores both a current single-valued *color index* and a current four-
valued RGBA color. One or the other of these is significant,
depending on whether the GL is in *color index mode* or *RGBA mode*.
The mode selection is made when the GL is initialized.

The command to set RGBA colors is:

```
void Color{34}{bsifd ubusui}( T components ) ;
void Color{34}{bsifd ubusui}v( T components ) ;
```

Table 13.4 Component Conversions. Color, normal, and depth components (*c*)
are converted to an internal floating-point representation (*f*), using the equations in this table. All arithmetic is done in the internal floating-point format.
These conversions apply to components specified as parameters to GL commands and to components in pixel data. The equations remain the same even
if the implemented ranges of the GL data types are greater than the minimum
required ranges. (Refer to Table 13.2)

GL Type	Conversion
ubyte	$c/(2^8 - 1)$
byte	$(2c + 1)/(2^8 - 1)$
ushort	$c/(2^{16} - 1)$
short	$(2c + 1)/(2^{16} - 1)$
uint	$c/(2^{32} - 1)$
int	$(2c + 1)/(2^{32} - 1)$
float	c
double	c

The **Color** command has two major variants: **Color3** and **Color4**. The four-value versions set all four values. The three-value versions set **R**, **G**, and **B** to the provided values. A is set to 1.0. The conversion of integer color components (R, G, B, and A) to floating-point values is discussed later in this chapter.

Versions of the **Color** command that take floating-point values accept values nominally between 0.0 and 1.0; 0.0 corresponds to the minimum, and 1.0 corresponds to the maximum (machine-dependent) value that a component may take on in the frame buffer. Values outside [0, 1] are not clamped.

The command

```
void Index{sifd}( T index ) ;
void Index{sifd}v( T index ) ;
```

Index updates the current (single-valued) color index. It takes one argument, the value to which the current color index should be set. Values outside the (machine-dependent) representable range of color indices are not clamped.

The state required to support vertex specification consists of four floating-point numbers to store the current texture coordinates s, t, r, and q; three floating-point numbers to store the three coordinates of the current normal; four floating-point values to store the current RGBA color; and one floating-point value to store the current color index. There is no notion of a current vertex, so no state is devoted to vertex coordinates. The initial values of s, t, and r of the current texture coordinates are 0. The initial value of q is 1. The initial current normal has coordinates (0, 0, 1). The initial RGBA color is (R, G, B, A) = (1, 1, 1, 1). The initial color index is 1.

A set of GL commands supports efficient specification of rectangles as two corner vertices:

```
void Rect{sifd}( T x1, T y1, T x2, T y2 ) ;
void Rect{sifd}v( T v1[2], T v2[2] ) ;
```

Each command takes either four arguments organized as two consecutive pairs of (x, y) coordinates or two pointers to arrays, each of which contains an x value followed by a y value.

The effect of the **Rect** command—**Rect** (x_1, y_1, x_2, y_2) ;—has exactly the same effect as the following sequence of commands:

```
Begin(POLYGON)  ;
     Vertex2  (x₁, y₁);
     Vertex2  (x₂, y₁);
     Vertex2  (x₂, y₂);
     Vertex2  (x₁, y₂);
End();
```

The appropriate **Vertex2** command would be invoked, depending on which of the **Rect** commands is issued.

Coordinate Transformations

Vertices, normals, and texture coordinates are transformed before their coordinates are used to produce an image in the frame buffer. Let's begin with a description of how vertex coordinates are transformed and how this transformation is controlled.

Figure 13.6 diagrams the sequence of transformations applied to vertices. The vertex coordinates that are presented to the GL are termed *object coordinates*. The *model-view* matrix is applied to these coordinates to yield *eye* coordinates. Then another matrix, called the *projection* matrix, is applied to eye coordinates to yield *clip* coordinates. A perspective division is carried out on clip coordinates to yield *normalized device* coordinates. A final *viewport* transformation is applied to convert these coordinates into *window coordinates*.

Object coordinates, eye coordinates, and clip coordinates are four-dimensional, consisting of $x, y, z,$ and w coordinates (in that order). The model-view and perspective matrices are thus 4×4.

Current Raster Position

The *current raster position* is used by commands that directly affect pixels in the frame buffer. These commands, which bypass vertex

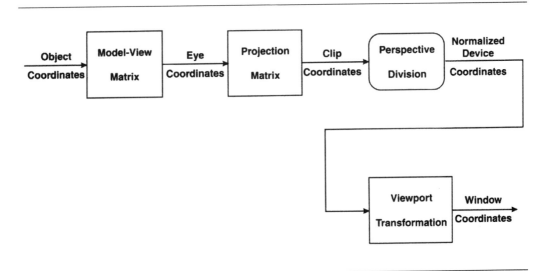

Figure 13.6 Vertex transformation sequence.

transformation and primitive assembly, are described later in the chapter. The current raster position, however, shares some of the characteristics of a vertex.

The current raster position consists of three window coordinates (x_w, y_w, and z_w), a clip coordinate (w_c) value, an eye coordinate distance, a valid bit, and associated data consisting of a color and texture coordinates. The current raster position is set by using one of the *RasterPos* commands:

```
void RasterPos{234}{sifd}( T coords ) ;
void RasterPos{234}{sifd}v( T coords ) ;
```

RasterPos4 takes four values indicating x, y, z, and w. **RasterPos3** (or **RasterPos2**) is analogous but sets only x, y, and z, with w implicitly set to 1 (or only x and y, with z implicitly set to 0 and w implicitly set to 1).

The coordinates are treated as if they were specified in a **Vertex** command. The x, y, z, and w coordinates are transformed by the current model-view and perspective matrices. These coordinates, along with current values, are used to generate a color and texture coordinates, just as is done for a vertex. The color and texture coordinates so produced replace the color and texture coordinates stored in the current raster position's associated data. The distance from the origin of the eye coordinate system to the vertex—as transformed by only the current model-view matrix—replaces the current raster distance. This distance can be approximated.

The transformed coordinates are passed to clipping as if they represented a point. If the point is not culled, the projection to window coordinates is computed and saved as the current raster position, and the valid bit is set. If the point is culled, the current raster position and its associated data become indeterminate, and the valid bit is cleared. Figure 13.7 summarizes the behavior of the current raster position.

The current raster position requires five single-precision floating-point values for its x_w, y_w, and z_w window coordinates; its w_c clip coordinate; its eye coordinate distance; a single valid bit; a color (RGBA and color index); and texture coordinates for associated data. In the initial state the coordinates and texture coordinates are both $(0, 0, 0, 1)$, the eye coordinate distance is 0, the valid bit is set, the associated RGBA color is $(1, 1, 1, 1)$, and the associated color index color is 1. In RGBA mode the associated color index always has its initial value. In color index mode the RGBA color always maintains its initial value.

Colors and Coloring

Figure 13.8 diagrams the processing of colors before rasterization. Incoming colors arrive in one of several formats. Table 13.4 summarizes the conversions that take place on R, G, B, and A components, depending on which version of the **Color** command was invoked to specify the components. As a result of limited precision, some converted values will not be represented exactly. In color index mode a single-valued color index is not mapped.

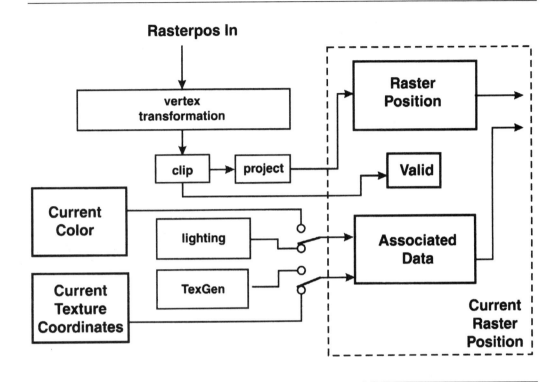

Figure 13.7 The current raster position and how it is set.

Next, lighting, if enabled, produces a color. If lighting is disabled, the current color is used in further processing. After lighting, RGBA colors are clamped to the range [0, 1]. A color index is converted to fixed-point, and then its integer portion is masked. After being clamped or masked, a primitive may be flatshaded, indicating that all vertices of the primitive are to have the same color. Finally, if a primitive is clipped, colors (and texture coordinates) must be computed at the vertices introduced or modified by clipping.

Lighting

GL lighting computes a color for each vertex sent to the GL. This is accomplished by applying an equation defined by a client-specified lighting model to a collection of parameters that can include the

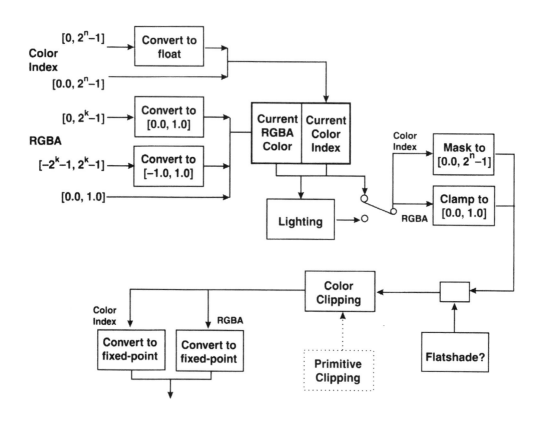

Figure 13.8 Processing of colors: n is the number of bits in a color index; m is the number of bits in an R, G, B, or A component. See Table 14.4 for the interpretation of k.

vertex coordinates, the coordinates of one or more light sources, the current normal, and parameters defining the characteristics of the light sources and a current material. The following discussion assumes that the GL is in RGBA mode. Color index lighting is described later in the chapter.

Lighting may be in one of two states: on or off. If lighting is off the color assigned to a vertex is the current color. If lighting is on, a vertex's color is found by computing a value given the current lighting parameters. Lighting is turned either on or off by using the generic **Enable** or **Disable** commands with the symbolic value **LIGHTING**.[3]

A lighting parameter is of one of five types: color, position, direction, real, or Boolean. A color parameter consists of four floating-point elements, one for each of R, G, B, and A, in that order. There are no restrictions on the allowable values for these parameters. A position parameter consists of four floating-point coordinates (x, y, z, and w) that specify a position in object coordinates (w may, in some cases, be 0, indicating a point at infinity in the direction given by x, y, and z). A direction parameter consists of three floating-point coordinates (x, y, and z) that specify a direction in object coordinates. A real parameter is one floating-point value. The various values and their types are summarized in Table 13.5. The result of a lighting computation is undefined if a value specified for a parameter is outside the range given for that parameter in the table.

Table 13.5 Summary of Lighting Parameters. The range of individual color components is (-•, +•).

Parameter	Type	Default Value	Description
Material Parameters			
a_{cm}	Color	(0.2,0.2,0.2,1.0)	Ambient color of material
d_{cm}	Color	(0.8,0.8,0.8,1.0)	Diffuse color of material
s_{cm}	Color	(0.0, 0.0, 0.0, 1.0)	Specular color of material
e_{cm}	Color	(0.0, 0.0, 0.0, 1.0)	Emissive color of material
s_{rm}	Real	0.0	Specular exponent (range: [0.0,128.0])
a_m	Real	0.0	Ambient color index
d_m	Real	1.0	Diffuse color index
s_m	Real	1.0	Specular color index

Continued

Table 13.5 Continued.

Parameter	Type	Default Value	Description
Light Source Parameters			
$\mathbf{a}cli$	Color	(0.0, 0.0, 0.0, 1.0)	Ambient intensity of light i
$\mathbf{d}cl_i(i = 0)$			
$\mathbf{d}_{cli}(i > 0)$	Color		
	Color	(1.0, 1.0, 1.0, 1.0)	
		(0.0, 0.0, 0.0, 1.0)	Diffuse intensity of light 0
			Diffuse intensity of light i
$\mathbf{s}cli(i = 0)$			
$\mathbf{s}cli(i = 0)$	Color		
	Color	(1.0, 1.0, 1.0, 1.0)	
		(0.0, 0.0, 0.0, 1.0)	Specular intensity of light
			Specular intensity of light i
$\mathbf{P}pli$	Position	(0.0, 0.0, 1.0, 0.0)	Position of light i
$\mathbf{s}dli$	Direction	(0.0, 0.0, -1.0)	Direction of spotlight for light
$srli$	Real	0.0	Spotlight exponent for light i (range: [0.0, 128.0])
$crli$	Real	180.0	Spotlight cutoff angle for light i (range: [0.0,90.0],180.0)
koi	Real	1.0	Constant attenuation factor for light i (range: [0.0,∞])
$k1i$	Real	0.0	Linear attenuation factor for light i (range: [0.0,∞])
$k2i$	Real	0.0	Quadratic attenuation factor for light i (range: [0.0,∞])

Table 13.5 Continued.

Parameter	Type	Default Value	Description
Lighting Model Parameters			
a*cs*	Color	(0.2, 0.2,0.2,1.0)	Ambient color of scene
vbs	Boolean	**FALSE**	Viewer assumed to be at (0,0,0) in eye coordinates (**TRUE**) or (0, 0,∞) (**FALSE**)
tbs	Boolean	**FALSE**	Use two-sided lighting mode

Lighting Parameter Specification

Lighting parameters are divided into three categories: material parameters, light source parameters, and lighting model parameters (see Table 13.5). Sets of lighting parameters are specified with the following:

```
void Material{if}( enum face, enum pname, T param ) ;
void Material{if}v( enum face, enum pname, T params ) ;
void Light{if}( enum light, enum pname, T param ) ;
void Light{if}v( enum light, anum pname, T params ) ;
void LightModel{if}( enum pname, T param ) ;
void LightModel{if}v( enum pname, T params ) ;
```

Pname is a symbolic constant indicating which parameter is to be set (see Table 13.6). In the vector versions of the commands, *params* is a pointer to a group of values to which to set the indicated parameter. The number of values pointed to depends on the parameter being set. In the nonvector versions *param* is a value to which to set a single-valued parameter. If *param* corresponds to a multivalued parameter, the error **INVALID_ENUM** results. For the **Material** command, *face* must be one of **FRONT, BACK,** or **FRONT_AND_BACK_,** indicating that the property *name* of the front or back material, or both, respectively, should be set. In the case of **Light,** *light* is a symbolic constant of the form **LIGHT***i,* indicating that light *i* is to have the specified parameter set. The constants obey **LIGHT***i* = **LIGHT0** + *i.*

Table 13.6 gives, for each of the three parameter groups, the correspondence between the predefined constant names and their names in the lighting equations, along with the number of values that must be specified with each. Color parameters specified with Material and Light are converted to floating-point values (if specified as integers), as indicated in Table 13.4, for signed integers. The error INVALID-VALUE occurs if a specified lighting parameter lies outside the allowable range given in Table 13.5. The symbol {I} indicates the maximum representable magnitude for the indicated type.

ColorMaterial

One or more material properties can be attached to the current color, so that they continuously track its component values. This behavior is enabled and disabled by calling **Enable** or **Disable** with the symbolic value **COLOR_MATERIAL**. (See Figure 13.9.)

The command that controls which of these modes is selected is

```
void ColorMaterial( enum face, enum mode ) ;
```

Face is one of **FRONT, BACK,** or **FRONT_AND_BACK,** indicating whether the front material, back material, or both are affected by the current color. *Mode* is one of **EMISSION, AMBIENT, DIFFUSE, SPECULAR,** or **AMBIENT_AND_DIFFUSE** and specifies which material property or properties track the current color. If *mode* is **EMISSION, AMBIENT, DIFFUSE,** or **SPECULAR,** the value of e_{cm}, a_{cm}, d_{cm}, or s_{cm}, respectively, will track the current color. If *mode* is **AMBIENT_AND_DIFFUSE,** both a_{cm} and d_{cm}, track the current color.

The replacements made to material properties are permanent. The replaced values remain until changed by either sending a new

Table 13.6 Correspondence of Lighting Parameter Symbols to Names. AMBIENT_AND_DIFFUSE is used to set acm and dcm to the same value.

Parameter	Name	Number of Values
Material Parameters (Material)		
acm	AMBIENT	4
dcm	DIFFUSE	4
acm dcm,	AMBIENT_AND_DIFFUSE	4
scm	SPECULAR	4
ecm	EMISSION	4
srm	SHININESS	1
a_m d_m, s_m	COLOR_INDEXES	3
Light Source Parameters (Light)		
acli	AMBIENT	4
dcli	DIFFUSE	4
scli	SPECULAR	4
Ppli	POSITION	4
sdli	SPOT_DIRECTION	3
srli	SPOT_EXPONENT	1
crli	SPOT_CUTOFF	1
koi	CONSTANT_ATTENUATION	1
$k1i$	LINEAR_ATTENUATION	1
$k2i$	QUADRATIC_ATTENUATION	1
Lighting Model Parameters		
acs	LIGHT_MODEL_AMBIENT	4
vbs	LIGHT_MODEL_ LOCAL_VIEWER	1
tbs	LIGHT_MODFEL_TWO_SIDE	1

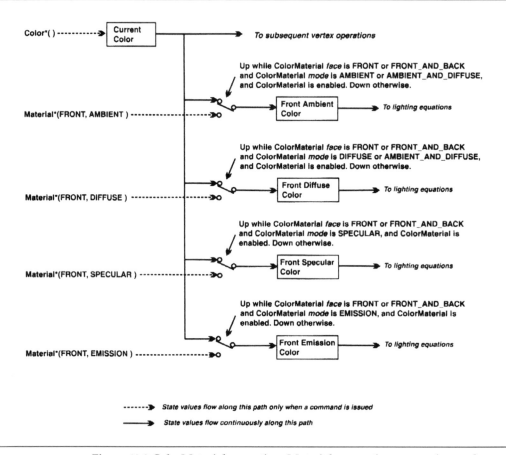

Figure 13.9 ColorMaterial operation. Material properties are continuously updated from the current color while ColorMaterial is enabled and has the appropriate mode. Only the front material properties are included in this figure. The back material properties are treated identically.

color or by setting a new material value when **ColorMaterial** is not currently enabled to override that particular value. When **COLOR_MATERIAL** is enabled, the indicated parameter or parameters always track the current color. For instance, calling the following while **COLOR_MATERIAL** is enabled sets the front material, a_{cm}, to the value of the current color:

```
ColorMaterial(FRONT, AMBIENT)
```

Lighting State

The state required for lighting consists of all of the lighting parameters (front and back material parameters, lighting model parameters, at least eight sets of light parameters), a bit indicating whether a back color distinct from the front color should be computed, at least eight bits to indicate which lights are enabled, a five-valued variable indicating the current **ColorMaterial** mode, a bit indicating whether **COLOR_MATERIAL** is enabled, and a single bit to indicate whether lighting is enabled or disabled. In the initial state all lighting parameters have their default values. Back-color evaluation does not take place. **ColorMaterial** is **FRONT_AND_BACK** and **AMBIENT_AND_ DIFFUSE**; both lighting and **COLOR_MATERIAL** are disabled.

Clamping or Masking

After lighting, RGBA colors are clamped to the range [0, 1]. For a color index the index is first converted to fixed point, with an unspecified number of bits to the right of the binary point. The nearest fixed-point value is selected. Then the bits to the right of the binary point are left alone while the integer portion is masked (bitwise ANDed) with $2n - 1$, where n is the number of bits in a color in the color index buffer. Buffers are discussed later in this chapter.

Flatshading

A primitive may be *flatshaded*, meaning that all vertices of the primitive are assigned the same color. This color is the color of the vertex that spawned the primitive. For a point this is the color associated with the point. For a line segment it is the color of the second (final) vertex of the segment. For a polygon the selected color depends on how the polygon was generated. Flatshading is controlled by:

```
void ShadeModel( enum mode ) ;
```

Mode value must be either of two symbolic constants. If node is **SMOOTH** (the initial state), vertex colors are treated individually.

If mode is **FLAT**, flatshading is turned on. **ShadeModel** thus requires one bit of state.

Final Color Processing

For an RGBA color, each color component (which lies in [0,1]) is converted by rounding to the nearest fixed-point value with m bits; m must be at least as large as the number of bits in the corresponding component of the frame buffer. If the frame buffer does not contain an A component, m must be at least 2 for A. A color index is converted by rounding to the nearest fixed-point value with at least as many bits as there are in the color index portion of the frame buffer.

Suppose that lighting is disabled, the color associated with a vertex has not been clipped, and one of Colorub, Colorus, or Colorui was used to specify that color. When these conditions are satisfied, an RGBA component must convert to a value that matches the component as specified in the Color command. If m is less than the number of bits (b) with which the component was specified, the converted value must equal the most significant m bits of the specified value. Otherwise, the most significant b bits of the converted value must equal the specified value.

Rasterization

Rasterization is the process by which a primitive is converted to a two-dimensional image. Each point of this image contains such information as color and depth. Thus rasterizing a primitive consists of two parts. The first is to determine which squares of an integer grid in window coordinates are occupied by the primitive. The second is to assign a color and depth value to each square. The results of this process are passed on to the next stage of the GL (per fragment operations), which uses the information to update the appropriate locations in the frame buffer. Figure 13.10 diagrams the rasterization process.

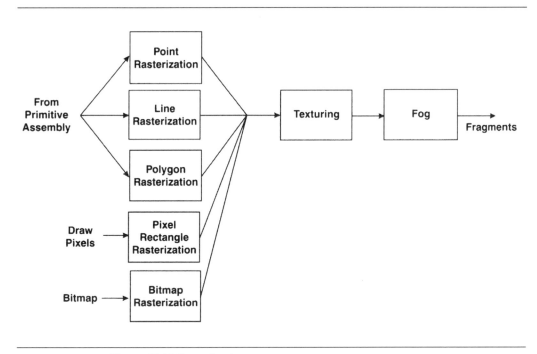

Figure 13.10 Rasterization.

A grid square along with its parameters of assigned color, z (depth), and texture coordinates is called a *fragment*. The parameters are collectively dubbed the fragment's *associated data*. A fragment is located by its lower-left corner, which lies on integer grid coordinates. Rasterization operations also refer to a fragment's *center*, which is offset by $(1/2, 1/2)$ from its lower-left corner (and so lies on half-integer coordinates).

Grid squares need not actually be square in the GL. Rasterization rules are not affected by the actual aspect ratio of the grid squares. Display of nonsquare grids, however, will cause rasterized points and fine segments to appear fatter in one direction than in the other. Assume that fragments are square, since it simplifies antialiasing and texturing.

Several factors affect rasterization. Lines and polygons may be stippled. Points may be given differing diameters and line segments differing widths. A point, line segment, or polygon may be antialiased.

Invariance

Consider a primitive p' obtained by translating a primitive p through an offset (x,y) in window coordinates, where x and y are integers. As long as neither p' nor p is clipped, it must be the case that each fragment f' produced from p' is identical to a corresponding fragment f' from p' except that the center of f' is offset by (x, y) from the center of f.

Antialiasing of a point, line, or polygon is affected in one of two ways, depending on whether the GL is in RGBA or color index mode. In RGBA mode the R, G, and B values of the rasterized fragment are left unaffected, but the A value is multiplied by a floating-point value in the range [0, 1] that describes a fragment's screen pixel coverage. The per fragment stage of the GL can be set up to use the A value to blend the incoming fragment with the corresponding pixel already present in the frame buffer.

In color index mode the least-significant b bits (to the left of the binary point) of the color index are used for antialiasing, where $b = \min(4,m)$, and m is the number of bits in the color index portion of the frame buffer. The antialiasing process sets these b bits based on the fragment's coverage value: the bits are set to 0 for no coverage and to all 1s for complete coverage.

The details of how antialiased fragment coverage values are computed are difficult to specify in general. The reason is that high-quality antialiasing may take into account not only perceptual issues but also as characteristics of the monitor on which the contents of the frame buffer are displayed. Such details cannot be addressed within the scope of this chapter. Further, the coverage value computed for a fragment of some primitive may depend not just on the fragment's grid square but also on the primitive's relationship to a number of grid squares neighboring the one corresponding to the fragment. Another consideration is that accurate calculation of coverage values may be computationally expensive. Consequently a given GL implementation is allowed to approximate true coverage values by using a fast but not entirely accurate coverage computation.

A GL implementation may use other methods to perform antialiasing, subject to the following conditions:

- If f_1 and f_2 are two fragments and the portion of f_1 covered by some primitive is a subset of the corresponding portion of f_2 covered by the primitive, the coverage computed for f_1 must be less than or equal to that computed for f_2.
- The coverage computation for a fragment f must be local. It may depend only on f's relationship to the boundary of the primitive being rasterized. It may not depend on f's x and y coordinates.
- Desirable but not required is the sum of the coverage values for all fragments produced by rasterizing a particular primitive must be constant, independent of any rigid motions in window coordinates, as long as none of those fragments lies along window edges.[4]

In some implementations varying degrees of antialiasing quality may be obtained by providing GL hints, thus allowing a user to make an image quality versus speed tradeoff.

Points

Point antialiasing is enabled or disabled by calling **Enable** or **Disable** with the symbolic constant **POINT_SMOOTH**. The default state is for point antialiasing to be disabled.

The rasterization of points is controlled with

```
void PointSize( float size ) ;
```

where *size* specifies the width or diameter of a point. The default value is 1.0. A value less than or equal to 0 results in the error **INVALID_VALUE**.

In the default state a point is rasterized by truncating its x_w and y_w coordinates (recall that the subscripts indicate that these are x and y window coordinates) to integers. This (x, y) address, along with the data associated with the vertex corresponding to the point, is sent as a single fragment to the per fragment stage of the GL.

All fragments produced in rasterizing a nonantialiased point are assigned the same associated data, which are those of the vertex corresponding to the point, as shown in Figure 13.11. If antialiasing is enabled, point rasterization produces a fragment for each fragment square that intersects the region lying within the circle having the diameter equal to the current point width and centered

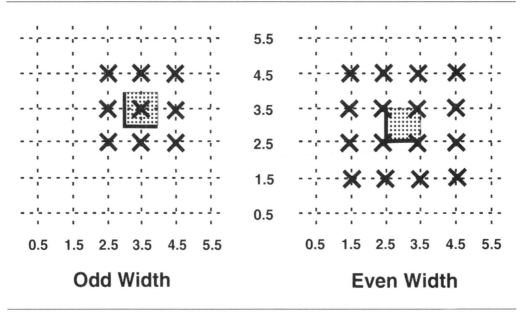

Odd Width   **Even Width**

Figure 13.11 Rasterization of nonantialiased wide points. The crosses show fragment centers produced by rasterization for any point that lies within the shaded region. The dotted grid lines lie on half-integer coordinates.

at the point's (x_w, y_w), as shown in Figure 13.12. The coverage value for each fragment is the window coordinate area of the intersection of the circular region with the corresponding fragment square. This value is saved and used in the final step of rasterization. The data associated with each fragment is otherwise the data associated with the point being rasterized.

Not all widths need be supported when point antialiasing is on, but the width 1.0 must be provided. If an unsupported width is requested, the nearest supported width is used instead. The range of supported widths and the width of evenly spaced gradations within that range are implementation dependent. If, for instance,

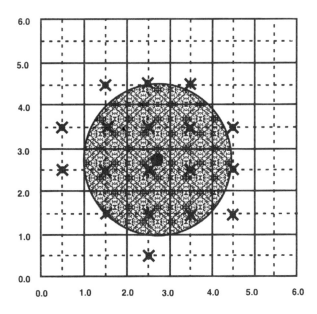

Figure 13.12 Rasterization of antialiased wide points. The black dot indicates the point to be rasterized. The shaded region has the specified width. The X marks indicate those fragment centers produced by rasterization. A fragment's computed coverage value is based on the portion of the shaded region that covers the corresponding fragment square. Solid lines lie on integer coordinates.

the width range is from 0.1 to 2.0 and the gradation width is 0.1, the widths 0.1, 0.2, . . . , 1.9, 2.0 are supported.

The state required to control point rasterization consists in part of the floating-point point width. It also consists of a bit indicating whether antialiasing is enabled.

Line Segments

A line segment results from a line strip Begin/End object, a line loop, or a series of separate line segments. Line-segment rasterization is controlled by several variables.

Line width may be set by calling

```
void LineWidth( float width ) ;
```

with an appropriate positive floating-point width. Line width controls the width of rasterized line segments.

The default width is 1.0. Values less than or equal to 0.0 generate the error **INVALID_VALUE**. Antialiasing is controlled with **Enable** and **Disable,** using the symbolic constant **LINE_SMOOTH**. Finally, line segments may be stippled. Stippling is controlled by a **GL** command that sets a *stipple* pattern.

Antialiasing

Rasterized antialiased line segments produce fragments whose fragment squares intersect a rectangle centered on the line segment. Two of the edges are parallel to the specified line segment. Each is at a distance of one-half the current width from that segment: one above the segment and one below it. The other two edges pass through the line endpoints and are perpendicular to the direction of the specified line segment. Coverage values are computed for each fragment by computing the area of the intersection of the rectangle with the fragment square, as shown in Figure 13.13.

For purposes of antialiasing, a stippled line is considered to be a sequence of contiguous rectangles centered on the line segment.

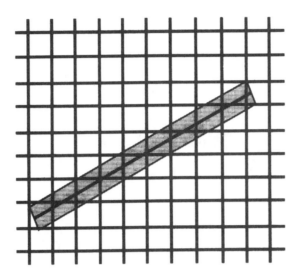

Figure 13.13 Region used in rasterizing and finding corresponding coverage values for an antialiased line segment (an *x*-major line segment is shown).

Each rectangle has width equal to the current line width and length equal to one pixel (except the last, which may be shorter). These rectangles are numbered from 0 to n, starting with the rectangle incident on the starting end point of the segment. Each of these rectangles is either eliminated or produced according to the procedure given under **Line Stipple**, above, where fragment is replaced with rectangle. Each rectangle so produced is rasterized as if it were an antialiased polygon, described later (but culling, nondefault settings of **PolygonMode** and polygon stippling are not applied).

Line Rasterization State

The state required for line rasterization consists of the floating-point line width, a 16-bit line stipple, the line stipple repeat count, a bit indicating whether stippling is enabled or disabled, and a bit indicating whether line antialiasing is on or off. In addition, during rasterization an integer stipple counter must be maintained to implement line stippling. The initial value of the line width is 1.0. The initial value of the line stipple is *0xFFFF* (a stipple of all 1s). The initial value of the line stipple repeat count is 1. The initial state of line stippling is disabled. The initial state of line segment antialiasing is disabled.

Polygons

A polygon results from a polygon **Begin/End** object. A triangle results from a triangle strip, a triangle fan, or a series of separate triangles or a quadrilateral arising from a quadrilateral strip, series of separate quadrilaterals, or a **Rect** command. Like points and line segments, polygon rasterization is controlled by several variables. Polygon antialiasing is controlled with **Enable** and **Disable** with the symbolic constant **POLYGON_SMOOTH**. The analog to line segment stippling for polygons is polygon stippling.

Stippling

Polygon stippling works much the same way as line stippling, masking out certain fragments produced by rasterization so that they are not sent to the next stage of the GL. This is the case regardless of the state of polygon antialiasing.

Stippling is controlled with

```
void PolygonStipple( ubyte pattern [] ) ;
```

The *pattern* is a pointer to memory into which a 32 x 32 pattern is packed. The pattern is unpacked from memory according to the procedure given later in the chapter for **DrawPixels**. It is as if the *height* and *width* passed to that command were both equal to 32, the *type* were **BITMAP**, and the *format* were **COLOR_INDEX**. The unpacked values (before any conversion or arithmetic would have been performed) are bitwise ANDed with 1 to obtain a stipple pattern of 0s and 1s.

Polygon stippling may be enabled or disabled with **Enable** or **Disable,** using the constant **POLYGON_STIPPLE**. When disabled, it is as if the stipple pattern were all 1s.

Antialiasing

Polygon antialiasing rasterizes a polygon by producing a fragment wherever the interior of the polygon intersects that fragment's square. A coverage value is computed at each such fragment, and this value is saved to be applied later. Associated data is assigned to a fragment by integrating the data's value over the region of the intersection of the fragment square with the polygon's interior and dividing this integrated value by the area of the intersection. For a fragment square lying entirely within the polygon, the value of the data at the fragment's center may be used instead of integrating the value across the fragment.

Options Controlling Polygon Rasterization

Face is one of **FRONT**, **BACK**, or **FRONT_AND_BACK**, indicating that the rasterizing method described by *mode* replaces the rasterizing method for front-facing polygons, back-facing polygons, or both front- and back-facing polygons, respectively. *Mode* is one of the symbolic constants **POINT**, **LINE**, or **FILL**. Calling **PolygonMode** with **POINT** causes certain vertices of a polygon to be treated, for rasterization purposes, just as if they were enclosed within a **Begin(POINT)** and **End** pair. The vertices selected for this treatment are those that have been tagged as having a polygon boundary edge beginning on them. **LINE** causes edges that are tagged as boundary to be rasterized as line segments. The line stipple counter is reset at the beginning of the first rasterized edge of the polygon but not for subsequent edges. **FILL** is the default mode of polygon rasterization. Note that these modes affect only the final rasterization of polygons. In particular a polygon's vertices are lit, and the polygon is clipped and possibly culled before these modes are applied.

The interpretation of polygons for rasterization is controlled by using

```
void PolygonMode( enum face, enum mode ) ;
```

Polygon antialiasing applies only to the **FILL** state of **PolygonMode**. For **POINT** or **LINE**, point antialiasing or line segment antialiasing, respectively, apply.

Polygon Rasterization State

The state required for polygon rasterization consists of a polygon stipple pattern, whether stippling is enabled or disabled, the current state of polygon antialiasing (enabled or disabled), and the current values of the **PolygonMode** setting for each of front- and back-facing polygons. The initial stipple pattern is all 1s. Initially stippling is disabled. The initial setting of polygon antialiasing is disabled. The initial state for **PolygonMode** is **FILL** for both front- and back-facing polygons.

Pixel Rectangles

Rectangles of color, depth, and certain other values may be converted to fragments by using the **DrawPixels** command. Some of the parameters and operations governing the operation of **DrawPixels** are shared by **ReadPixels** (used to obtain pixel values from the frame-buffer) and **CopyPixels** (used to copy pixels from one frame buffer location to another). The discussion of **ReadPixels** and **CopyPixels**, however, is deferred until later in the chapter after the frame buffer has been discussed in detail. Nevertheless, it is noted here when parameters and state pertaining to **DrawPixels** also pertain to **ReadPixels** or **CopyPixels**.

A number of parameters control the encoding of pixels in client memory (for reading and writing) and how pixels are processed before being placed in or after being read from the frame buffer (for reading, writing, and copying). These parameters are set with three commands: **PixelStore**, **PixelTransfer**, and **PixelMap**.

Pixel Storage Modes

Pixel storage modes affect the operation of DrawPixels and ReadPixels (as well as other commands) when one of these commands is issued. This may differ from the time that the command is executed if the command is placed in a display list.

Pixel storage modes are set with

```
void PixelStore{if}( enum pname, T param ) ;
```

The *pname* is a symbolic constant indicating a parameter to be set, and *param* is the value to set it to. Table 13.7 summarizes the pixel storage parameters, their types, their initial values, and their allowable ranges. Setting a parameter to a value outside the given range results in the error **INVALID_VALUE**.

The version of **PixelStore** that takes a floating-point value may be used to set any type of parameter. If the parameter is Boolean, it is set to **FALSE** if the passed value is 0.0 and **TRUE** otherwise. If the parameter is an integer, the passed value is rounded to the nearest integer. The integer version of the command may also be used to set any type of parameter. If the parameter is Boolean, it is set to **FALSE** if the passed value is 0 and **TRUE** otherwise; if the parameter is a floating-point value, the passed value is converted to floating point.

Pixel Transfer Modes

Pixel transfer modes affect the operation of **DrawPixels**, **ReadPixels**, and **CopyPixels** at the time when one of these commands is executed (which may differ from the time the command is issued).

Some pixel transfer modes are set with

```
void PixelTransfer{if}( enum param, T value ) ;
```

Table 13.7 *PixelStore* **Parameters Pertaining to** *DrawPixels*

Parameter Name	Type	Initial Value	Valid Range
UNPACK_SWAP_BYTES	Boolean	**FALSE**	**TRUE/FALSE**
UNPACK_LSB_FIRST	Boolean	**FALSE**	**TRUE/FALSE**
UNPACK_ROW_LENGTH	Integer	0	$(0, \infty)$
UNPACK_SKIP_ROWS	Integer	0	$(0, \infty)$
UNPACK_SKIP_PIXELS	Integer	0	$(0, \infty)$
UNPACK_ALIGNMENT	Integer	4	1,2,4,8

The *param* is a symbolic constant indicating a parameter to be set; *value* is the value to set it to. Table 13.8 summarizes the pixel transfer parameters that are set with **PixelTransfer**, their types, their initial values, and their allowable ranges. Setting a parameter to a value outside the given range results in the error **INVALID_VALUE**. The same versions of the command exist as for **PixelStore**, and the same rules apply to accepting and converting passed values to set parameters.

The other pixel-transfer modes are the various look-up tables used by **DrawPixels**, **ReadPixels**, and **CopyPixels**. These are set with

```
void PixelMap{ui us f}v( enum map, sizei size, T values[] ) ;
```

Table 13.8 Pixel Transfer Parameters

Parameter Name	Type	Initial Value	Valid Range
MAP_COLOR	Boolean	**FALSE**	**TRUE/FALSE**
MAP_STENCIL	Boolean	**FALSE**	**TRUE/FALSE**
INDEX_SHIFT	Integer	0.0	$(-\infty, \infty)$
INDEX_OFFSET	Integer	0.0	$(-\infty, \infty)$
RED_SCALE	Float	1.0	$(-\infty, \infty)$
GREEN_SCALE	Float	1.0	$(-\infty, \infty)$
BLUE_SCALE	Float	1.0	$(-\infty, \infty)$
ALPHA_SCALE	Float	1.0	$(-\infty, \infty)$
DEPTH_SCALE	Float	1.0	$(-\infty, \infty)$
RED_BIAS	Float	0.0	$(-\infty, \infty)$
GREEN_BIAS	Float	0.0	$(-\infty, \infty)$
BLUE_BIAS	Float	0.0	$(-\infty, \infty)$
ALPHA_BIAS	Float	0.0	$(-\infty, \infty)$
DEPTH_BIAS	Float	0.0	$(-\infty, \infty)$

The *map* is a symbolic map name, indicating the map to set *size* indicates the size of the map, and *values* is a pointer to an array of *size* map values.

The entries of a table may be specified by using one of three types: single-precision floating-point, unsigned short integer, or unsigned integer. This all depends on which of the three versions of **PixelMap** is called. A table entry is converted to the appropriate type when it is specified. An entry giving a color-component value is converted according to Table 13.4. An entry giving a color index value is converted from an unsigned short integer or unsigned integer to floating point. An entry giving a stencil index is converted from single-precision floating point to an integer by rounding to nearest. The various tables and their initial sizes and entries are summarized in Table 13.9. A table that takes an index as an address must have $size = 2n$ or the error **INVALID_VALUE** results. The maximum allowable size of each table is implementation dependent but must be at least 32 (a single maximum applies to all tables). The error

Table 13.9 *PixelMap* Parameters

Map Name	Address	Value	Init. Size	Init. Value
PIXEL_MAP_I_TO_I	color idx	color idx	1	0.0
PIXEL_MAP_S_TO_S	stencil idx	stencil idx	1	0.0
PIXEL_MAP_I_TO_R	color idx	R	1	0.0
PIXEL_MAP_I_TO_G	color idx	G	1	0.0
PIXEL_MAP_I_TO_B	color idx	B	1	0.0
PIXEL_MAP_I_TO_A	color idx	A	1	0.0
PIXEL_MAP_R_TO_R	R	R	1	0.0
PIXEL_MAP_G_TO_G	G	G	1	0.0
PIXEL_MAP_B_TO_B	B	B	1	0.0
PIXEL_MAP_A_TO_A	A	A	1	0.0

INVALID_VALUE is generated if a size larger than the implemented maximum, or less than zero, is given to PixelMap.

Rasterization of Pixel Rectangles

The process of drawing pixels encoded in host memory is diagrammed in Figure 13.14. The stages of this process are described in the order in which they occur.

Pixels are drawn by using

```
void DrawPixels( sizei width, sizei height, enum
format, enum type,
void *data ) ;
```

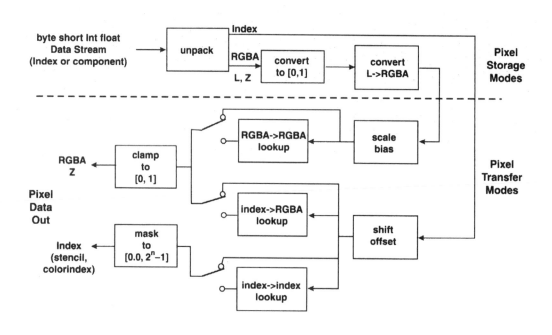

Figure 13.14 Operation of DrawPixels. The parameters controlling the stages above the dotted line are set with PixelStore; those controlling the stages below the line are set with PixelTransfer or PixelMap.

The *format* is a symbolic constant indicating what the values in memory represent; *width* and *height* are the width and height, respectively, of the pixel rectangle to be drawn; *data* is a pointer to the data to be drawn. The data is represented with one of seven GL data types, specified by *type*. The correspondence between the eight *type* token values and the GL data types they indicate is given in Table 13.10. If the GL is in color index mode and *format* is not one of **COLOR_INDEX**, **STENCIL_INDEX**, or **DEPTH_COMPONENT**, the error **INVALID_OPERATION** occurs.

Unpacking: Data is taken from host memory as a sequence of signed or unsigned bytes (GL data types byte and ubyte), signed or unsigned short integers (GL data types short and ushort), signed or unsigned integers (GL data types int and uint), or floating-point values (GL data type float). These elements are grouped into sets of one, two, three, or four values, depending on the *format*, to form a group. Table 13.11 summarizes the format of groups obtained from memory and also indicates those formats that yield indices and those that yield components.

Table 13.10 *DrawPixels* and *ReadPixels* Type Parameter Values and the Corresponding GL Data Types. Refer to Table 14.2 for definitions of GL data types.

Type Parameter Token Name	Corresponding GL Data Type
UNSIGNED_BYTE	ubyte
BITMAP	ubyte
BYTE	byte
UNSIGNED_SHORT	ushort
SHORT	short
UNSIGNED_INT	uint
INT	32-bit integer
FLOAT	float

Table 13.11 DrawPixels and ReadPixels Formats. The second column gives a description of and the number and order of elements in a group.

Format Name	Element Meaning and Order	Target Buffer
COLOR_INDEX	Color index	Color
STENCIL_INDEX	Stencil index	Stencil
DEPTH_COMPONENT	Depth component	Depth
RED	R component	Color
GREEN	G component	Color
BLUE	B component	Color
ALPHA	A component	Color
RGB	R, G, B components	Color
RGBA	R, G, B, A components	Color
LUMINANCE	Luminance component	Color
LUMINANCE_ALPHA	Luminance, A components	Color

By default, the values of each GL data type are interpreted as they would be specified in the language of the client's GL binding. If UNPACK_SWAP_BYTES is set to **TRUE**, however, the values are interpreted with the bit orderings modified as per Table 13.12. The modified bit orderings are defined only if the GL data type ubyte has eight bits and then for each specific GL data type only if that type is represented with 8, 16, or 32 bits.

Table 13.12 Bit Ordering Modification of Elements When UNPACK_SWAP_BYTES IS TRUE. These reorderings are defined only when GL data type ubyte has 8 bits and then only for GL data types with 8, 16, or 32 bits.

Element Size	Default Bit Ordering	Modified Bit Ordering
8 bit	[7..0]	[7..0]
16 bit	[15..0]	[7..0][15..8]
32 bit	(31..0)	[7..0][15..8][23..16][31..24]

The groups in memory are treated as being arranged in a rectangle. This rectangle consists of a series of rows, with the first element of the first group of the first row pointed to by the pointer passed to **DrawPixels**. If the value of **UNPACK_ROW_LENGTH** is not positive, the number of groups in a row is width. Otherwise, the number of groups is UNPACK_ROW_LENGTH.

Conversion to floating-point: This step applies only to groups of components. It is not performed on indices. Each element in a group is converted to a floating-point value according to the appropriate formula in Table 13.4.

Conversion to RGB: This step is applied only if the *format* is **LUMINANCE** or **LUMINANCE_ALPHA**. If the *format* is **LUMINANCE**, each group of one element is converted to a group of R, G, and B (three) elements by copying the original single element into each of the three new elements. If the *format* is LUMINANCE_ALPHA, each group of two elements is converted to a group of R, G, B, and A (four) elements. This is done by copying the first original element into each of the first three new elements and copying the second original element to the A (fourth) new element.

Final expansion to RGBA: This step is performed only for nondepth component groups. Each group is converted to a group of four elements as follows: If a group does not contain an A element, A is added and set to 1.0. If any of R, G, or B is missing from the group, each missing element is added and assigned a value of 0.0.

Arithmetic on Components: This step applies only to component groups. Each component is multiplied by an appropriate signed scale factor: **RED_SCALE** for an **R** component, **GREEN_SCALE** for a **G** component, **BLUE_SCALE** for a **B** component, **ALPHA_SCALE** for an **A** component, or **DEPTH_SCALE** for a depth component. Then the result is added to the appropriate signed bias: **RED_BIAS**, **GREEN_BIAS**, **BLUE_BIAS**, **ALPHA_BIAS**, or **DEPTH_BIAS**.

Arithmetic on Indices: This step applies only to indices. If the index is a floating-point value, it is converted to fixed point, with an unspecified number of bits to the right of the binary point. Indices that are already integers remain so; any fraction bits in the resulting fixed-point value are 0.

The fixed-point index is then shifted by | INDEX_SHIFT | bits, left if **INDEX_SHIFT** > 0 and right otherwise. In either case the shift is zero-filled. Then the signed integer offset INDEX_OFFSET is added to the index.

RGBA-to-RGBA lookup: This step applies only to RGBA component groups and is skipped if MAP-COLOR is FALSE. First, each component is clamped to the range [0, 1]. A table is associated with each of the R, G, B, and A component elements: PIXEL-MAP-R-TO-R for R, PIXEL-MAP-G-TO-G for G, PIXEL-MAP-B-TO-B for B, and PIXEL-MAP-A-TO-A for A. Each element is multiplied by an integer one less than the size of the corresponding table, and for each element, an address is found by rounding this value to the nearest integer. For each element the addressed value in the corresponding table replaces the element.

Index lookup: This step applies only to indices. If the GL is in RGBA mode, the integer part of the index is used to reference four tables of color components: **PIXEL_MAP_I_TO_R**, **PIXEL_MAP_I_TO_G**, **PIXEL_MAP_I_TO_B**, and **PIXEL_MAP_I_TO_A**. Each of these tables must have $2n$ entries for some integer value of n (n may be different for each table). For each table the index is first rounded to the nearest integer; the result is ANDed with $2n - 1$, and the resulting value used as an address into the table. The indexed value becomes an R, G, B, or A value, as appropriate. The group of four elements so obtained replaces the index, changing the group's type to component.

If the GL is in color index mode and if **MAP_COLOR** is **TRUE**, the index is looked up in the **PIXEL_MAP_I_TO_I** table (otherwise, the index is not looked up). Again, the table must have $2n$ entries for some integer n, and the integer part of the index is ANDed with $2n - 1$, producing a value. This value addresses the table, and the value in the table replaces the index. The floating-point table value is first rounded to a fixed-point value with unspecified precision. Finally, if *format* is **STENCIL_INDEX** and if **MAP_STENCIL** is **TRUE**, the index is looked up as described in the preceding paragraph but using the **PIXEL_MAP_S_TO_S** table.

Texturing

Texturing maps a portion of a specified image onto each primitive for which texturing is enabled. This mapping is accomplished by using the color of an image at the location indicated by a fragment's (s, t) coordinates to modify the fragment's RGBA color (r is currently ignored). Texturing is specified only for RGBA mode. Its use in color index mode is undefined.

The GL provides a means to specify the details of how texturing of a primitive is effected. These details include specification of the image to be texture mapped, the means by which the image is filtered when applied to the primitive, and the function that determines what RGBA value is produced given a fragment color and an image value.

The command used to specify a texture image is:

```
void TexImage2-D( enum target, int level, int components,
sizei width, sizei height, int border, enum format, enum
type, void *data ) ;⁵
```

Currently *target* must be **TEXTURE_2-D**. The arguments *width*, *height*, *format*, *type*, and *data* correspond precisely to the corresponding arguments to **DrawPixels**. They specify the image's *width* and *height*, a *format* of the image data, the *type* of the data, and a pointer to the image data in memory. The image is taken from memory exactly as if these arguments were passed to **DrawPixels**, but the process stops just before final conversion. Each R, G, B, and A value so extracted is clamped to [0, 1]. The *formats* **STENCIL_INDEX** and **DEPTH_COMPONENT** are not allowed. Components are selected from the R, G, B, and A values to obtain a texture with *components* (the significance of the number of components is described later). Table 13.13 summarizes the mapping of R, G, B, and A values to texture components. Specifying a number of components other than 1, 2, 3, or 4 generates the error **INVALID_VALUE**.

The image itself (pointed to by *data*) is a sequence of groups of values. The first group is the lower-left corner of the texture image. Subsequent groups fill out rows of *width* from left to right. *Height* rows are stacked from bottom to top.

The *level* argument to **TexImage2-D** is an integer *level-of-detail* number. Levels of detail are discussed later. The main texture image has the number 0 for level of detail.

The *border* argument to **TexImage2-D** is a border width. The significance of borders is described later. If *width* and *height* do not satisfy these relationships, the error **INVALID_VALUE** is generated. Currently if *b* is not either 0 or 1, the error **INVALID_VALUE** is generated. The maximum allowable width or height of an image is implementation dependent but must be at least 64. An excessive width or height or a width or height less than 0 generates the **INVALID_VALUE** error.

Another command is used to specify one-dimensional texture images:

Table 13.13 Correspondence of Texture Components to Extracted R, G, B, and A Values.

Components	RGBA Values	Texture Components
1	R	*L*
2	R, A	*L, A*
3	R, G, B	*C*
4	R, G, B, A	*C, A*

```
void TexImage1D( enum target, int level, int
components, sizei width,
int border, enum format, enum type, void *data ) ;
```

Currently *target* must be the texture target **TEXTURE_1D**. For the purposes of decoding the texture image, **TexImage1D** is equivalent to calling **TexImage2-D** with corresponding arguments and a *height* argument of 1, except that the height of the image is always 1, regardless of the value of *border*.

An image with zero height or width (or zero width, for **TexImage1D**) indicates the null texture. If the null texture is specified for level-of-detail zero, it is as if texturing were disabled.

The image indicated to the GL by the image pointer is decoded and copied into the GL's internal memory. This copying places the decoded image inside a border of the maximum allowable width (currently 1), whether or not a border has been specified (see Figure 13.15). If no border or a border smaller than the maximum allowable width has been specified, the image is still stored as if it were surrounded by a border of the maximum possible width. Any excess border (which surrounds the specified image, including any border) is assigned unspecified values. A one-dimensional texture has a border only at its left and right ends.

An element (i, j) of the texture array is called a *texel* (for a one-dimensional texture, j is irrelevant). The *texture value* used in texturing a fragment is determined by that fragment's associated (s, t) coordinates but may not correspond to any actual texel. See Figure 13.15.

Various parameters control how the texture array is treated when applied to a fragment. Each parameter is set by calling

```
void TexParameter{if}( enum target, enum pname, T param ) ;
void TexParameter{if}v( enum target, enum pname, T params ) ;
```

The target is *Target*. Either **TEXTURE_1D** or **TEXTURE_2-D**, *pname* is a symbolic constant indicating the parameter to be set.

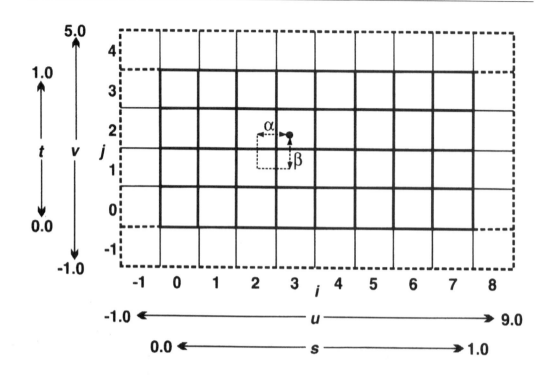

Figure 13.15 A texture image and the coordinates used to access it. This is a two-dimensional texture with $n = 3$ and $m = 2$. A one-dimensional texture would consist of a single horizontal strip. The α and β values used in blending adjacent texels to obtain a texture value are also shown.

The possible constants and corresponding parameters are summarized in Table 13.14. In the first form of the command, *param* is a value to which to set a single-valued parameter; in the second form of the command, *params* is an array of parameters whose type depends on the parameter being set. If the values for **TEXTURE_BORDER_COLOR** are specified as integers, the conversion for signed integers from Table 13.14 is applied to convert the values to floating point. Each of the four values set by **TEXTURE_BORDER_COLOR** is clamped to lie in [0, 1].

Table 13.14 Texture Parameters and Their Values

Name	Type	Legal Values
TEXTURE_WRAP_S	Integer	**CLAMP, REPEAT**
TEXTURE_WRAP_T	Integer	**CLAMP, REPEAT**
TEXTURE_MIN_FILTER	Integer	**NEAREST, LINEAR, NEAREST_MIPMAP_ NEAREST, NEAREST_ MIPMAP_LINEAR, LINEAR_MIPMAP_ NEAREST, LINEAR_ MIPMAP_LINEAR**
TEXTURE_MAG_FILTER	Integer	**NEAREST, LINEAR**
TEXTURE_BORDER_COLOR	Four Floats	any four values in [0, 1]

Texture Wrap Modes

If **TEXTURE_WRAP_S** or **TEXTURE_WRAP_T** is set to **REPEAT**, the GL ignores the integer part of s or t coordinates, respectively, using only the fractional part. For a number r, the fractional part is $r - \lfloor r \rfloor$, regardless of the sign of r; recall that the *floor* function truncates toward $-\infty$. **CLAMP** causes s or t coordinates to be clamped to the range [0, 1]. The initial state is for both s and t behavior to be that given by **REPEAT**.

Texture Magnification

When λ indicates magnification, the value assigned to **TEXTURE_ MAG_FILTER** determines how the texture value is obtained. There are two possible values for **TFXTURE_MAG_FILTER_ NEAREST** and LINEAR. **NEAREST** behaves exactly as **NEAREST** for **TEXTURE_ MIN_FILTER**. **LINEAR** behaves exactly as **LINEAR** for **TEXTURE_ MIN_FILTER**. The level-of-detail 0 texture array is always used for magnification.

Finally, there is the choice of c, the minification versus magnification switchover point. If the magnification filter is given by **LINEAR** and the minification filter is given by **NEAREST_MIPMAP_**

NEAREST or **LINEAR_MIPMAP_NEAREST**, $c = 0.5$. This is done to ensure that a minified texture does not appear sharper than a magnified texture. Otherwise, $c = 0$.

The state necessary for texture can be divided into two categories. First are the two sets of mipmap arrays (one-dimensional and two-dimensional) and their number. Each array has associated with it a width and height (two-dimensional only), a border width, and a four-valued integer describing the number of components in the image. Each initial texture array is null (zero width and height, zero border width, one component). Next are the two sets of texture properties. Each consists of the selected minification and magnification filters, the wrap modes for s and t, and the **TEXTURE_BORDER_COLOR**. In the initial state the value assigned to **TEXTURE_MIN_FILTER** is NEAREST_MIPMAP_LINEAR, and the value for **TEXTURE_MAG_FILTER** is **LINEAR**. Both s and t wrap modes are set to **REPEAT**. **TEXTURE_BORDER_COLOR** is (0,0,0,0).

Texture Environments and Texture Functions

Currently *target* must be the symbolic constant **TEXTURE_ENV**; *pname* is a symbolic constant indicating the parameter to be set. In the first form of the command, *param* is a value to which to set a single-valued parameter. In the second form, *params* is a pointer to an array of parameters: either a single symbolic constant or a value or group of values to which the parameter should be set. The possible environment parameters are **TEXTURE-ENV-MODE** and **TEXTURE_ENV_COLOR**. **TEXTURE_ENV_MODE** may be set to one of **MODULATE**, **DECAL**, or **BLEND**; **TEXTURE_ENV_COLOR** is set to an RGBA color by providing four single-precision floating-point values in the range [0, 1] (values outside this range are clamped to it). If integers are provided for **TEXTURE_ENV_COLOR**, they are converted to floating-point, as specified in Table 13.14 for signed integers.

The following command sets parameters of the *texture environment* that specifies how texture values are interpreted when texturing a fragment:

```
void TexEnv{if}( enum target, enum pname, T param ) ;
void TexEnv{if}v( enum target, enum pname, T params ) ;
```

Texture Application

Texturing is enabled or disabled by using the generic **Enable** and **Disable** commands, respectively, with the symbolic constant **TEXTURE-1D** or **TEXTURE_2-D** to enable the one-dimensional or two-dimensional texture. If both one- and two-dimensional textures are enabled, the two-dimensional texture is used. If all texturing is disabled, a rasterized fragment is passed on unaltered to the next stage of the GL (although its texture coordinates may be discarded). Otherwise, a texture value is found according to the parameter values of the currently bound texture image of the appropriate dimensionality. This texture value is used along with the incoming fragment in computing the texture function indicated by the currently bound texture environment. The result of this function replaces the incoming fragment's R, G, B, and A values. These are the color values passed to subsequent operations. Other data associated with the incoming fragment remains unchanged, except that the texture coordinates may be discarded.

The required state is two bits indicating whether each of one- or two-dimensional texturing is enabled or disabled. In the initial state all texturing is disabled.

Finally, if antialiasing is enabled for the primitive from which a rasterized fragment was produced, the computed coverage value is applied to the fragment. In RGBA mode the value is multiplied by the fragment's alpha (A) value to yield a final alpha value. In color index mode the value is used to set the low-order bits of the color index value.

Per Fragment Operations and the Frame Buffer

The frame buffer consists of a set of pixels arranged as a two-dimensional array. The height and width of this array may vary from one GL implementation to another. For purposes of this discussion, each pixel in the frame buffer is simply a set of some number of bits. The number of bits per pixel may also vary, depending on the particular GL implementation or context.

Corresponding bits from each pixel in the frame buffer are grouped together into a bit plane, each containing a single bit from each pixel. These bit planes are grouped into several logical buffers: the color, depth, stencil, and accumulation buffers. The color buffer consists of a number of buffers: the front left buffer, the front right buffer, the back left buffer, the back right buffer, and some number of auxiliary buffers. Typically the contents of the front buffers are displayed on a color monitor, and the contents of the back buffers are invisible. Monoscopic contexts display only the front left buffer. Stereoscopic contexts display both the front left and the front right buffers. The contents of the auxiliary buffers are never visible. AU color buffers must have the same number of bit planes, although an implementation or context may choose not to provide right buffers, back buffers, or auxiliary buffers at all. Further, an implementation or context may not provide depth, stencil, or accumulation buffers.

Color buffers consist of either unsigned integer color indices or R, G, B, and, optionally, A unsigned integer values. The number of bit planes in each of the color buffers, the depth buffer, the stencil buffer, and the accumulation buffer is fixed and window dependent. If an accumulation buffer is provided, it must have at least as many bit planes per R, G, and B color component as do the color buffers.

The initial state of all provided bit planes is undefined.

Per Fragment Operations

A fragment produced by rasterization with window coordinates of (x_w, y_w) modifies the pixel in the frame buffer at that location, based on a number of parameters and conditions. These modifications and tests are described and diagrammed in Figure 13.16, in the order in which they are performed.

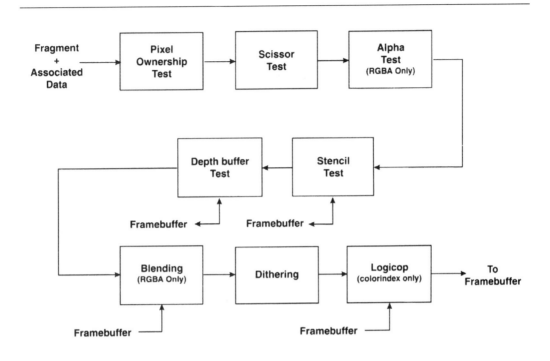

Figure 13.16 Per fragment operations.

Pixel Ownership Test

The first test is to determine whether the pixel at location (xw, yw) in the frame buffer is currently owned by the GL (more precisely, by this GL context). If it is not, the window system decides the fate of the incoming fragment. Possible results are that the fragment is discarded or that some subset of the subsequent per fragment operations is applied to the fragment. This test allows the window system to control the GL's behavior—for instance, when a GL window is obscured.

Scissor Test

If $left < xw < left + width$ and $bottom < yw < bottom + height$, the scissor test passes. Otherwise, the test fails and the fragment is discarded. The test is enabled or disabled by using **Enable** or **Disable,** using the constant **SCISSOR_TEST**. When disabled, it is as if the scissor test always passes. If either *width* or *height* is less than 0, the error **INVALID_VALUE** is generated. The state required consists of four integer values and a bit indicating whether the test is enabled or disabled. In the initial state *left* = *bottom* = 0. Both *width* and *height* are determined by the size of the GL window. Initially the scissor test is disabled.

The scissor test determines whether *(xw, yw)* lies within the scissor rectangle defined by four values. These values are set with

```
void Scissor( int left, int bottom, sizei width,
sizei height ) ;
```

Alpha Test

This step applies only in RGBA mode. In color index mode proceed to the next step. The alpha test discards a fragment conditional on the outcome of a comparison between the incoming fragment's alpha value and a constant value. The comparison is enabled or disabled with the generic **Enable** and **Disable** commands, using the symbolic constant **ALPHA_TEST**. When disabled, it is as if the comparison always passes. The test is controlled with

```
void AlphaFunc( enum func, clampf ref ) ;
```

The *func* is a symbolic constant indicating the alpha test function; *ref* is a reference value clamped to lie in [0, 1], and then converted to a fixed-point value according to the rules given earlier in the chapter for an A component. For purposes of the alpha test, the fragment's alpha value is also rounded to the nearest integer. The possible constants specifying the test function are **NEVER, ALWAYS, LESS, LEQUAL, EQUAL, GEQUAL, GREATER,** or **NOTEQUAL,** or pass the fragment never, always, if the fragment's alpha value is less than, less than or equal to, equal to, greater than or equal to, greater than, or not equal to the reference value, respectively.

The required state consists of the floating-point reference value, an eight-valued integer indicating the comparison function, and a bit indicating whether the comparison is enabled or disabled. The initial state is for the reference value to be 0 and the function to be **ALWAYS.** Initially the alpha test is disabled.

Stencil Test

The test is enabled or disabled with the **Enable** and **Disable** commands, using the symbolic constant **STENCIL_TEST.** When disabled, the stencil test and associated modifications are not made, and the fragment is always passed.

The stencil test conditionally discards a fragment, based on the outcome of a comparison between the value in the stencil buffer at location (xw, yw) and a reference value. The test is controlled with

```
void StencilFunc( enum func, int ref, uint mask ) ;
void StencilOp( enum sfail, enum dpfail, enum
dppass ) ;⁶
```

The *ref* is an integer reference value that is used in the unsigned stencil comparison. It is clamped to the range [0, $2s - 1$], where s is the number of bits in the stencil buffer. The *func* is a symbolic constant that determines the stencil comparison function. The eight symbolic constants are **NEVER, ALWAYS, LESS, LEQUAL, EQUAL, GEQUAL, GREATER,** or **NOTEQUAL.** Accordingly the stencil test passes never, always, if the reference value is less than, less than or equal to, equal to, greater than or equal to, greater than, or not equal to the masked stored value in the stencil buffer. The s least-significant bits of *mask* are bitwise ANDed with both the reference and the stored stencil value. The ANDed values are those that participate in the comparison.

StencilOp takes three arguments that indicate what happens to the stored stencil value if this or certain subsequent tests fail or pass; *sfail* indicates what action is taken if the stencil test fails. The symbolic constants are **KEEP, ZERO, REPLACE, INCR, DECR,** and **INVERT.** These correspond to keeping the current value, setting it to 0, replacing it with the reference value, incrementing it, decrementing it, or bitwise inverting it. For purposes of increment and decrement, the stencil bits are considered as an unsigned integer. Values clamp at 0 and the maximum representable value. The same symbolic values are given to indicate the stencil action if the depth buffer test fails *(dpfail)* or if it passes *(dppass)*. If the stencil test fails, the incoming fragment is discarded. The state required consists of the most recent values passed to **StencilFunc** and **Stencil0p** and a bit indicating whether stencil testing is enabled or disabled. In the initial state stenciling is disabled the stencil reference value is 0, the stencil comparison function is **ALWAYS,** and the stencil *mask* is all 1s. Initially all three stencil operations are **KEEP.** If there is no stencil buffer, no stencil modification can occur, and it is as if the stencil tests always pass, regardless of any calls to **StencilOp.**

Depth Buffer Test

The depth buffer test discards the incoming fragment if a depth comparison fails. The comparison is enabled or disabled with the generic **Enable** and **Disable** commands, using the symbolic constant **DEPTH_TEST.** When disabled, the depth comparison and subsequent possible updates to the depth buffer value are bypassed, and the fragment is passed to the next operation. The stencil value, however, is modified, as if the depth buffer test passed. If enabled, the comparison takes place, and the depth buffer and stencil value may subsequently be modified. The comparison is specified with

```
void DepthFunc( enum func ) ;
```

This command takes a single symbolic constant: one of **NEVER, ALWAYS, LESS, LEQUAL, EQUAL, GREATER, GEQUAL, NOTEQUAL.** Accordingly, the depth buffer test passes never, always, if the incoming fragment's zw value is less than, less than or equal to, equal to, greater than, greater than or equal to, or not equal to the depth value stored at the location given by the incoming fragment's (xw, yw) coordinates.

If the depth buffer test fails, the incoming fragment is discarded. The stencil value at the fragment's (xw, yw) coordinates is updated according to the function currently in effect for depth buffer test failure. Otherwise, the fragment continues to the next operation, and the value of the depth buffer at the fragment's *(xw, yw)* location is set to the fragment's *zw* value. In this case the stencil value is updated according to the function currently in effect for depth buffer test success.

The necessary state is an eight-valued integer and a single bit indicating whether depth buffering is enabled or disabled. In the initial state the function is **LESS** and the test is disabled. If there is no depth buffer, it is as if the depth buffer test always passes.

Blending

Blending combines the incoming fragment's R, G, B, and A values with the R, G, B, and A values stored in the frame buffer at the incoming fragment's *(xw, yw)* location. This blending is dependent on the incoming fragment's alpha value and that of the corresponding currently stored pixel. Blending applies only in RGBA mode. In color index mode it is bypassed. Blending is enabled or disabled, using **Enable** or **Disable** with the symbolic constant **BLEND.** If it is disabled, proceed to the next stage.

The command that controls blending is

void **BlendFunc**(enum *src*, enum *dst*) ;

The *src* indicates how to compute a source blending factor, and *dst* indicates how to compute a destination factor. The possible arguments and their corresponding computed source and destination factors are summarized in Tables 13.15 and 13.16. In these tables *A* is a single alpha value, and *C* is a quadruplet of R, G, B, and A values. A subscript of *s* indicates a value from an incoming fragment; one of *d* indicates the corresponding current frame buffer value. Division of a quadruplet by a scalar means dividing each element by that value. Addition or subtraction of quadruplets or triplets means adding or subtracting them componentwise.

The computations in Tables 13.15 and 13.16 are carried out in floating point and yield floating-point blending factors. Destination (frame buffer) components referred to in the tables are taken to be fixed-point values represented according to the scheme given earlier in the chapter, as are source (fragment) components. Any implied conversion to floating-point must leave 0 and 1 invariant.

The state required is two integers indicating the source and destination blending functions and a bit indicating whether blending is enabled or disabled. The initial state of the blending functions is **ONE** for the source function and **ZERO** for the destination function. Initially blending is disabled.

Blending occurs once for each color buffer currently enabled for writing using each buffer's color for Cd. If a color buffer has no A value, then it is as if the destination A value is 1.

Dithering

Dithering selects between two color values or indices. In RGBA mode consider the value of any of the color components as a fixed-point value with m bits to the left of the binary point, where m is the number of bits allocated to that component in the frame buffer.

Table 13.15 Values Controlling the Source Blending Function and the Source Blending Values They Compute $f = min(As, 1 - Ad)$

Value	Blend Factors
ZERO	$(0, 0, 0, 0)$
ONE	$(1,1,1,1)$
DST_COLOR	Rd, Gd, Bd, Ad
ONE_MINUS_DST_COLOR	$(1, 1, 1, 1) - (Rd, Gd, Bd, Ad)$
SRC_ALPHA	(As, As, As, As)
ONE_MINUS_SRC_ALPHA	$(1, 1, 1, 1) - (As, As, As, As)$
DST_ALPHA	(Ad, Ad, Ad, Ad)
ONE_MINUS_DST_ALPHA	$(1, 1, 1, 1) - (Ad, Ad, Ad, Ad)$
SR_ALPHA_SATURATE	$(f, f, f, 1)$

Table 13.16 Values Controlling the Destination Blending Function and the Destination Blending Values They Compute

Value	Blend Factors
ZERO	(0,0,0,0)
ONE	(1,1,1,1)
SRC_CCLOR	Rd, Gd, Bd, Ad
ONE_MINUS_SRC_COLOR	$(1, 1, 1, 1) - (Rd, Gd, Bd, Ad)$
SRC_ALPHA	(As, As, As, As)
ONE_MINUS_SRC_ALPHA	$(1, 1, 1, 1) - (As, As, As, As)$
DST_ALPHA	(Ad, Ad, Ad, Ad)
ONE_MINUS_DST_ALPHA	$(1, 1, 1, 1) - (Ad, Ad, Ad, Ad)$

Call each such value c. In color index mode the same rule applies, with c being a single color index. The c value must not be larger than the maximum value representable in the frame buffer for either the component or the index, as appropriate.

Many dithering algorithms are possible, but a dithered value produced by any algorithm must depend only on the incoming value and the fragment's x and y window coordinates. If dithering is disabled, each color component is truncated to a fixed-point value with as many bits as there are in the corresponding component in the frame buffer. A color index is rounded to the nearest integer representable in the color index portion of the frame buffer.

Dithering is enabled with **Enable** and is disabled with **Disable,** using the symbolic constant **DITHER.** The state required is thus a single bit. Initially dithering is enabled. In RGBA mode this is the last operation, and the result goes into the frame buffer. In color index mode continue on to the last operation.

Logical Operation

Finally, a logical operation is applied between the incoming fragment and the value stored at the corresponding location in the frame buffer. The result replaces the current frame buffer value. The logical operation is enabled or disabled with **Enable** or **Disable**, using the symbolic constant **LOGIC-OP**. The logical operation is selected by

```
void LogicOp( enum op ) ;
```

The *op* is a symbolic constant. The possible constants and the corresponding logical operations are enumerated in Table 13.17. In this table *s* is the value of the incoming fragment, and *d* is the value stored in the frame buffer.

Table 13.17 Arguments to LogicOp and Their Corresponding Operations

Argument Value	Operation
CLEAR	0
AND	$s \wedge d$
AND_REVERSE	$s \wedge \varnothing \, d$
COPY	s
AND_INVERTED	$\neg s \wedge d$
NOOP	d
XOR	$s \text{ xor } d$
OR	$s \vee d$
NOR	$`\neg (s \vee d)$
EQUIV	$\neg (s \text{ xor } d)$
INVERT	$\neg d$
OR_REVERSE	$s \vee \neg d$
COPY_INVERTED	$\neg s$
OR_INVERTED	$\neg s \, v \, d$
NAND	$\neg (s \wedge d)$
SET	1

Note that the **SET** operation sets all bits of the result to 1. The result replaces the value in the frame buffer at the fragment's (x, y) coordinates. The numeric values assigned to the symbolic constants are the same as those assigned to the corresponding symbolic values in the X window system.

LogicOp applies only in color index mode. In RGBA mode it does not occur, and the previous operation is the last one applied to incoming fragments. **LogicOp** occurs once for each color buffer selected for writing. The required state is an integer indicating the logical operation and a bit to indicate whether the logical operation is enabled or disabled. The initial state is for the logic operation to be given by **COPY**, and it is disabled.

Whole Frame Buffer Operations

Earlier this chapter described the operations that occur as individual fragments are sent to the frame buffer. We now turn to operations that control or affect the whole frame buffer.

Selecting a Buffer for Writing

The symbolic constant *buf* specifies zero, one, two, or four buffers for writing. The constants are **NONE, FRONT_LEFT, FRONT_RIGHT, BACK_LEFT, BACK_RIGHT, FRONT, BACK, LEFT, RIGHT, FRONT_AND_BACK,** and **AUX0** through **AUXn**, where n +1 is the number of available auxiliary buffers.

The first such operation is controlling the buffer into which color values are written. This is accomplished with

```
void DrawBuffer( enum buf ) ;
```

The constants refer to the four potentially visible buffers *front_left*, *front_right*, *back_left*, and *back_right* and to the *auxiliary* buffers. Arguments other than **AUXi** that omit reference to **LEFT** or **RIGHT** refer to both left and right buffers. Arguments other than **AUXi** that omit reference to **FRONT** or **BACK** refer to both front and back buffers. **AUXi** enables drawing only to auxiliary buffer i.

Each **AUX***i* adheres to **AUX***i* = *AUX*0 + *i*. The constants and the buffers they indicate are summarized in Table 13.18. If **DrawBuffer** is supplied with a constant (other than **NONE**) that does not indicate any of the color buffers allocated to the GL context, the error **INVALID_OPERATION** results.

Indicating a buffer or buffers using **DrawBuffer** causes subsequent pixel color value writes to affect the indicated buffers. If more than one color buffer is selected for drawing, blending and logical operations are computed and applied independently for each buffer. Calling **DrawBuffer** with a value of **NONE** inhibits the writing of color values to any buffer.

Monoscopic contexts include only left buffers, whereas stereoscopic contexts include both left and right buffers. Likewise, single-buffered contexts include only front buffers, whereas double-buffered contexts include both front and back buffers. The type of context is selected at GL initialization.

Table 13.18 Arguments to DrawBuffer and the Buffers They Indicate

Symbolic Constant	Front Left	Front Right	Back Left	Back Right	Aux *i*
NONE					
FRONT_LEFT	•				
FRONT_RIGHT		•			
BACK_LEFT			•		
BACK_RIGHT				•	
FRONT	•	•			
BACK			•	•	
LEFT	•		•		
RIGHT		•		•	
FRONT_AND_BACK	•	•	•	•	
AUX*i*					•

The state required to handle buffer selection is a set of up to $4 + n$ bits. Four bits indicate whether the front left buffer, the front right buffer, the back left buffer, or the back right buffer are enabled for color writing. The other n bits indicate which of the auxiliary buffers is enabled for color writing. In the initial state the front buffer or buffers are enabled if there are no back buffers. Otherwise, only the back buffer or buffers are enabled.

Fine Control of Buffer Updates

Four commands are used to mask the writing of bits to each of the logical frame buffers after all per fragment operations have been performed.

The commands control the color buffer or buffers (depending on which buffers are currently indicated for writing):

```
void IndexMask( uint mask)
void ColorMask( boolean r, boolean g, boolean b, boolean a ) ;
```

The least-significant n bits of mask, where n is the number of bits in a color index buffer, specify a mask. Where a 1 appears in this mask, the corresponding bit in the color index buffer (or buffers) is written. Where a 0 appears, the bit is not written. This mask applies only in color index mode. In RGBA mode **ColorMask** is used to mask the writing of R, G, B, and A values to the color buffer or buffers; r, g, b, and a indicate whether R, G, B, or A values, respectively, are written (a value of **TRUE** means that the corresponding value is written). In the initial state all bits (in color index mode) and all color values (in RGBA mode) are enabled for writing.

The depth buffer can be enabled or disabled for writing z. values, using

```
void DepthMask( boolean mask ) ;
```

If *mask* is nonzero, the depth buffer is enabled for writing; otherwise, it is disabled. In the initial state the depth buffer is enabled for writing.

The command controls the writing of particular bits into the stencil planes:

```
void StencilMask( uint mask ) ;
```

The least-significant *s* bits of *mask* comprise an integer mask (*s* is the number of bits in the stencil buffer), just as for **IndexMask.** The initial state is for the stencil plane mask to be all 1s.

The state required for the various masking operations is two integers and a bit: an integer for color indices, an integer for stencil values, and a bit for depth values. A set of four bits is also required, indicating which color components of an RGBA value should be written. In the initial state the integer masks are all 1s as are the bits controlling depth value and RGBA component writing.

Clearing the Buffers

The GL provides a means for setting portions of every pixel in a particular buffer to the same value.

The following command takes as an argument the bitwise OR of a number of values indicating which buffers are to be cleared:

```
void Clear(bitfield buf ) ;
```

The values are **COLOR_BUFFER_BIT, DEPTH_BUFFER_BIT, STENCIL_BUFFER_BIT,** and **ACCUM_BUFFER_BIT,** indicating the buffers currently enabled for color writing, the depth buffer, the stencil buffer, and the accumulation buffer respectively. The value to which each buffer is cleared depends on the setting of the clear value for that buffer.

If the mask is not a bitwise OR of the specified values, the error **INVALID_VALUE** is generated. The following command sets the clear value for the color buffers in RGBA mode:

```
void ClearColor( clampf r, clampf g, clampf b, clampf a)
```

Each of the specified components is clamped to [0, 1] and convert-ed to fixed-point according to the rules discussed earlier in the chapter. The following command sets the clear color index:

```
void ClearIndex( float index ) ;
```

The *index* is converted to a fixed-point value with unspecified pre-cision to the left of the binary point. The following command takes a floating-point value that is clamped to the range [0, 1] and con-verted to fixed-point according to the rules for a window z value:

```
void ClearDepth( clampd d ) ;
```

Similarly, the following command takes a single integer argument that is the value to which to clear the stencil buffer. s is masked to the number of bitplanes in the stencil buffer:

```
void ClearStencil( int s ) ;
```

The following command takes four floating-point arguments that are the values, in order, to which to set the R, G, B, and A values of the accumulation buffer:

```
void ClearAccum( float r, float g, float b, float a ) ;
```

These values are clamped to the range [–1,1] when they are speci-fied.[7]

When **Clear** is called, the only per fragment operations that are applied (if enabled) are the pixel ownership test, the scissor test, and dithering. The masking operations described earlier are also effective. If a buffer is not present, a **Clear** directed at that buffer has no effect.

The state required for clearing is a clear value for each of the color buffer, the depth buffer, the stencil buffer, and the accumulation buffer. Initially the RGBA color clear value is (0,0,0,0), the clear color index is 0, and the stencil buffer and accumulation buffer clear values are all 0. The depth buffer clear value is initially 1.0.

The Accumulation Buffer

The symbolic constant *op* indicates an accumulation buffer operation, and *value* is a floating-point value to be used in that operation. The possible operations are **ACCUM, LOAD, RETURN, MULT,** and **ADD.**

Each portion of a pixel in the accumulation buffer consists of four values: one for each of R, G, B, and A. The accumulation buffer is controlled exclusively through the use of

```
void Accum ( enun op, float value ) ;
```

(except for clearing it).

The accumulation buffer operations apply identically to every pixel, so the effect is described of each operation on an individual pixel. Accumulation buffer values are taken to be signed values in the range [–1, 1]. Using **ACCUM** obtains R, G, B, and A components from the buffer currently selected for reading. Each component, considered as a fixed-point value in [0, 1], is converted to floating-point. Each result is then multiplied by *value*. The results of this multiplication are then added to the corresponding color component currently in the accumulation buffer. The resulting color value replaces the current accumulation buffer color value. The **LOAD** operation has the same effect as **ACCUM,** but the computed values replace the corresponding accumulation buffer components rather than being added to them.

The **RETURN** operation takes each color value from the accumulation buffer and multiplies each of the R, G, B, and A components by *value*. The resulting color value is placed in the buffers currently enabled for color writing, as if it were a fragment produced from rasterization. The exception is that the only per-fragment operations applied are the pixel ownership test. If enabled, dithering is also applied. Color masking is applied as well.

The **MULT** operation multiplies each R, G, B, and A in the accumulation buffer by *value* and then returns the scaled color components to their corresponding accumulation buffer locations. **ADD** is the same as **MULT,** except that *value* is added to each of the color components.

The color components operated on by **Accum** must be clamped only if the operation is **RETURN.** In this case a value sent to the enabled color buffers is first clamped to [0, 1]. Otherwise, results are undefined if the result of an operation on a color component is too large (in magnitude) to be represented by the number of available bits. When the scissor test is enabled, only those pixels within the current scissor box are updated by any **Accum** operation; otherwise, all pixels in the window are updated. If there is no accumulation buffer or if the GL is in color index mode, **Accum** generates the error **INVALID_OPERATION.** No state (beyond the accumulation buffer itself) is required for accumulation buffering.

Drawing, Reading, and Copying Pixels

Pixels may be written to and read from the frame buffer by using the *DrawPixels* and **ReadPixels** commands. **CopyPixels** can be used to **copy** a block of pixels from one portion of the frame buffer to another.

Writing to the Stencil Buffer

The operation of **DrawPixels** was described earlier. One exception would be if the format argument was **STENCIL_INDEX.** In this case all operations described for **DrawPixels** take place. But window (x, y) coordinates, each with the corresponding stencil index, are produced in lieu of fragments. Each coordinate stencil index pair is sent directly to the per fragment operations, bypassing the texture, fog, and antialiasing application stages of rasterization. Each pair is then treated as a fragment for purposes of the pixel ownership and scissor tests. All other per fragment operations are bypassed. Finally, each stencil index is written to its indicated location in the frame buffer, subject to the current setting of **StencilMask.** The error **INVALID_OPERATION** results if there is no stencil buffer.

Reading Pixels

The method for reading pixels from the frame buffer and placing them in client memory is diagrammed in Figure 13.17. The stages of the pixel-reading process are discussed in the order in which they occur.

Pixels are read by using

```
void ReadPixels( int x, int y, sizei width,
sizei height, enum format,
enum type, void *data ) ;
```

The arguments after x and y to **ReadPixels** correspond to those of **DrawPixels.** The pixel storage modes that apply to **ReadPixels** are summarized in Table 13.19.

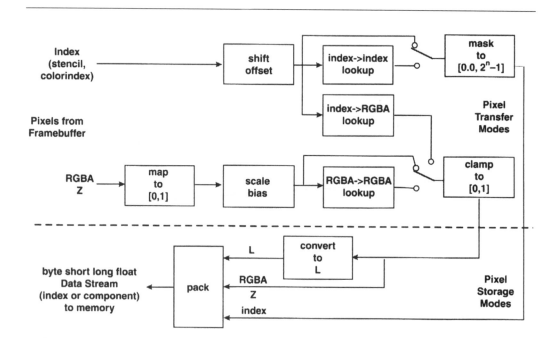

Figure 13.17 Operation of ReadPixels. The parameters controlling the stages above the dotted line are set with PixelTransfer or PixelMap; those controlling the stages below the line are set with PixelStore.

Table 13.19 PixelStore Parameters Pertaining to ReadPixels

Parameter Name	Type	Initial Value	Valid Range
PACK_SWAP_BYTES	Boolean	FALSE	TRUE/FALSE
PACK_LSB_FIRST	Boolean	FALSE	TRUE/FALSE
PACK_ROW_LENGTH	Integer	0	$(0,\infty)$
PACK_SKIP_ROWS	Integer	0	$(0,\infty)$
PACK_SKIP_PIXELS	Integer	0	$(0,\infty)$
PACK_ALIGNMENT	Integer	4	1,2,4,8

1. *Obtaining pixels from the frame buffer*

If the format is **DEPTH_COMPONENT,** values are obtained from the depth buffer. If there is no depth buffer, the error **INVALID_OPERATION** occurs. If the format is **STENCIL_INDEX,** values are taken from the stencil buffer; again, if there is no stencil buffer, the error **INVALID_OPERATION** occurs. For all other formats, the buffer from which values are obtained is one of the color buffers. The selection of color buffer is controlled with **ReadBuffer.**

The following command

```
void ReadBuffer( enum src ) ;
```

takes a symbolic constant as argument.

The possible values are **FRONT_LEFT, FRONT_RIGHT, BACK_LEFT, BACK_RIGHT, FRONT, BACK, LEFT, RIGHT,** and **AUXO** through **AUXN. FRONT** and **LEFT** refer to the front left buffer, **BACK** refers to the back left buffer, and **RIGHT** refers to the front right buffer. The other constants correspond directly to the buffers they name. If the requested buffer is missing, the error **INVALID_OPERATION** is generated. The initial setting for **ReadBuffer** is **FRONT** if there is no back buffer and **BACK** otherwise.

The number of values obtained from the selected buffer depends on the *format*. If the *format* is **LUMINANCE**, R, G, and B values are

obtained. If it is **LUMINANCE_ALPHA,** R, G, B, and A values are
obtained. If the frame buffer does not support alpha values then the
A that is obtained is 1.0. If the *format* is one of **RED, GREEN, BLUE,
ALPHA, RGB, RGBA, LUMINANCE,** or **LUMINANCE_ALPHA**
and if the GL is in color index mode, the color index is obtained.
Otherwise, the type and number of values that are obtained from
the selected buffer for each pixel are as shown in Table 13.11.

2. *Conversion of RGBA values*

This step applies only if the GL is in RGBA mode and then only if
format is neither **STENCIL_INDEX** nor **DEPTH_COMPONENT.**
The error **INVALID_OPERATION** results (in RGBA mode) if *format* is **COLOR_INDEX.** The R, G, and B (and possibly A) values
form a group of elements. Each element is taken to be a fixed-point
value in [0, 1] with m bits, where m is the number of bits in the corresponding color component of the selected buffer.

3. *Conversion to L*

This step applies only to RGBA component groups and only if the
format is either **LUMINANCE** or **LUMINANCE_ALPHA.** A value
L is computed as

$$L = R + G + B$$

where R, G, and B are the values of the R, G, and B components.
The single computed L component replaces the R, G, and B components in the group.[8]

4. *Final conversion*

For an index, if the *type* is not **FLOAT,** final conversion consists of
masking the index with the value given in Table 13.20. If the *type*
is **FLOAT,** the integer index is converted to a GL float data value.
For a component, each component is first clamped to [0, 1]. Then
the appropriate conversion formula from Table 13.21 is applied to
the component.

Groups of elements are placed in memory in the same way that
they are taken from memory for **DrawPixels.** That is, the ith group

Table 13.20 Index Masks Used by ReadPixels. Floating point is data that are not masked.

Type Parameter	Index Mask
UNSIGNED_BYTE	28 - 1
BITMAP	1
BYTE	27 - 1
UNSIGNED_SHORT	2^{16} - 1
SHORT	2^{15} - 1
UNSIGNED_INT	2^{32} - 1
INT	2^{31} - 1

Table 13.21 Reversed Component Conversions Used with Component Data.

Type Parameter	GL Data Type	Component Conversion Formula
UNSIGNED_BYTE	ubyte	$c = (28 - 1)f$
BYTE	byte	$c = [(28 - 1)f - 1]/2$
UNSIGNED_SHORT	u hort	$c = (2^{16} - 1)f$
SHORT	short	$c = (2^{16} - 1)f - 1]/2$
UNSIGNED_INT	uint	$c = (2^{32} - 1)f$
INT	*int*	$c = (2^{32} - 1)f - 1]/2$
FLOAT	float	$c = f$

These are/is being returned to client memory. Color, normal, and depth components are converted from the internal floating-point representation (f) to a datum of the specified GL data type (c), using the equations in this table. All arithmetic is done in the internal floating-point format. These conversions apply to component data returned by GL query commands and to components of pixel data returned to client memory. The equations remain the same, even if the implemented ranges of the GL data types are greater than the minimum required ranges. (Refer to Table 13.2) of the *j*th row (corresponding to the *i*th pixel in the *j*th row) is placed in memory just where the *i*th group of the *j*th row would be taken from for **DrawPixels.** The only difference is that the storage mode parameters whose names begin with **PACK_** are used instead of those whose names begin with **UNPACK_.**

Copying Pixels

CopyPixels transfers a rectangle of pixel values from one region of the frame buffer to another. Pixel copying is diagrammed in Figure 13.18.

This command has the form

void **CopyPixels**(int *x*, int *y*, sizei *width*, sizei *height*, enum *type*) ;

The *type* is a symbolic constant that must be one of **COLOR, STENCIL,** or **DEPTH,** indicating that the values to be transferred are colors, stencil values, or depth values, respectively. The first four arguments have the same interpretation as the corresponding arguments to **ReadPixels.** Values are obtained from the frame buffer, converted (if appropriate), subjected to arithmetic operations, and looked up in tables, just as if **ReadPixels** were called with the corresponding arguments. If the *type* is **STENCIL** or **DEPTH,** it is as if the *format* for **ReadPixels** were **STENCIL_INDEX** or **DEPTH_COMPONENT,** respectively. If the

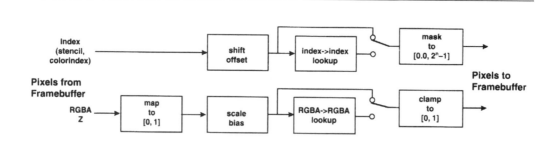

Figure 13.18 Operation of CopyPixels. All parameters affecting pixel copying are set with PixelTransfer or PixelMap.

type is **COLOR,** the GL is in RGBA mode. If the *format* were **RGBA** while the GL is in color index mode, it is as if the *format* were **COLOR INDEX.** The groups of elements so obtained are then written to the frame buffer just as if **DrawPixels** had been given width and height, beginning with final conversion of elements. The effective format is the same as that already described.

Pixel Draw/Read State

The state required for pixel operations consists of the parameters that are set with **PixelStore, PixelTransfer,** and **PixelMap.** This state has been summarized in Tables 13.7, 13.8, and 13.9. The current setting of **ReadBuffer,** a 12-valued integer, is also required, along with the current raster position. State set with **PixelStore** is GL client state.

Special Functions

Some GL functionality does not fit easily into any of the preceding chapters. This functionality consists of evaluators (used to model curves and surfaces), selection (used to locate rendered primitives on the screen), feedback (which returns GL results before rasterization), display lists (used to designate a group of GL commands for later execution by the GL), flushing and finishing (used to synchronize the GL command stream), and hints.

Evaluators

Evaluators provide a means to use a polynomial or rational polynomial mapping to produce vertex, normal, and texture coordinates and colors. The values so produced are sent on to further stages of the GL as if they had been provided directly by the client. Transformations, lighting, primitive assembly, rasterization, and per-pixel operations are not affected by the use of evaluators.

```
void Map1{fd}( enum type, T u1, T u2, int
stride, int order, T points ) ;
```

The *type* is a symbolic constant indicating the range of the defined polynomial. Its possible values, along with the evaluations that each indicates, are given in Table 13.22. The *order* is equal to $n + 1$. The error **INVALID_VALUE** results if *order* is less than 1 or greater than **MAX_EVAL_ORDER**. The value *points* is a pointer to a set of $n + 1$ blocks of storage. Each block begins with k single-precision floating-point or double-precision floating-point values, respectively. The rest of the block may be filled with arbitrary data. Table 13.22 indicates how k depends on *type* and what the k values represent in each case.

The number of single- or double-precision values (as appropriate) in each block of storage is stride. The error **INVALID_VALUE** results if *stride* is less than k. The order of the polynomial, *order*, is also the number of blocks of storage containing control points.

Figure 13.19 describes map evaluation schematically. An evaluation of enabled maps is affected in one of two ways. The first way is to use:

Table 13.22 Values Specified by the Target to Map1. Values are given in the order in which they are taken.

Target	k	Values
MAP1_VERTEX_3	3	x, y, z vertex coordinates
MAP1_VERTEXA	4	x, y, z, w vertex coordinates
MAP1_NDEX	1	Color index
MAPI_COLORA	4	R, G, B, A
MAP1_NORMAL	3	x, y, z normal coordinates
MAP1_TEXTURE_COORD_1	1	s texture coordinate
MAP1_TEXTURE_COORD_2	2	s, t texture coordinates
MAP1_TEXTURE_COORD_3	3	s, t, r texture coordinates
MAP1_TEXTURE_COORD_4	4	s, t, r, q texture coordinates

```
void EvalCoord{12}{fd}( T arg ) ;
void EvalCoord{12}{fd}v( T arg ) ;
```

EvalCoord1 causes evaluation of the enabled one-dimensional maps. The argument is the value (or a pointer to the value) that is the domain coordinate, u'. **EvalCoord2** causes evaluation of the enabled two-dimensional maps. The two values specify the two domain coordinates, u' and v', in that order.

When one of the **EvalCoord** commands is issued, all currently enabled maps of the indicated dimension are evaluated. Then, for each enabled map, it is as if a corresponding GL command were issued with the resulting coordinates, with one important difference. The difference is that when an evaluation is performed, the GL uses evaluated values instead of current values for those evaluations that are enabled (otherwise, the current values are used). The order of the effective commands is immaterial, except that **Vertex** (for vertex coordinate evaluation) must be issued last. Use of evaluators has no effect on the current color, normal, or texture coordinates.

No command is effectively issued if the corresponding map (of the indicated dimension) is not enabled. If more than one evaluation is enabled for a particular dimension (**MAP1_TEXTURE_COORD_1**

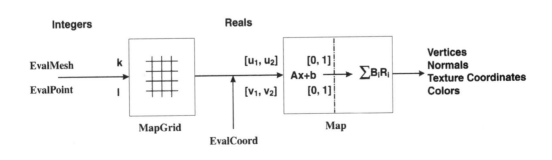

Figure 13.19 Map evaluation.

and **MAP1_TEXTURE_COORD_2**), only the result of the evaluation of the map with the highest number of coordinates is used.

Finally, if either **MAP2_VERTEX_3** or **MAP2_VERTEX_4** is enabled, the normal to the surface is computed analytically. If automatic normal generation is enabled, this computed normal is used as the normal associated with a generated vertex. Automatic normal generation is controlled with **Enable** and **Disable** and the symbolic constant **AUTO_NORMAL**. If automatic normal generation is disabled, a corresponding normal map, if enabled, is used to produce a normal. If neither automatic normal generation nor a normal map is enabled, no normal is sent with a vertex resulting from an evaluation (the effect is that the current normal is used).

The state required for evaluators potentially consists of nine one-dimensional map specifications and nine two-dimensional map specifications, as well as corresponding flags for each specification indicating which are enabled. Each map specification consists of one or two orders, an appropriately sized array of control points, and a set of two values (for a one-dimensional map) or four values (for a two-dimensional map) to describe the domain. The maximum possible order, for either u or v, is implementation dependent (one maximum applies to both u and v) but must be at least eight. Each control point consists of between one and four floating-point values (depending on the type of the map). Initially all maps have order 1 (making them constant maps). AD vertex coordinate maps produce the coordinates (0, 0, 0, 1) (or the appropriate subset). All normal coordinate maps produce (0, 0, 1). RGBA maps produce (1,1,1,1). Color index maps produce 1.0. In the initial state all maps are disabled. A flag indicates whether automatic normal generation is enabled for two-dimensional maps. In the initial state automatic normal generation is disabled. Also required are two floating-point values, an integer number of grid divisions for the one-dimensional grid specification, four floating-point values, and two integer grid divisions for the two-dimensional grid specification. In the initial state the bounds of the domain interval for 1-D is 0 and 1.0, respectively. For 2-D, they are (0, 0) and (1.0, 1.0), respectively. The number of grid divisions is one for 1-D and one in both directions for 2-D. If any evaluation command is issued when no vertex map is enabled, nothing happens.

Selection

A programmer uses selection to determine which primitives are drawn into some region of a window. The region is defined by the current model-view and perspective matrices.

Selection works by returning an array of integer-valued *names*. This array represents the current contents of the *name stack*. This stack is controlled with the commands

```
void InitNames( void ) ;
void PopName( void ) ;
void PushName( uint name ) ;
void LoadName( uint name ) ;
```

InitNames empties (clears) the name stack. **PopName** pops one name off the top of the name stack. **PushName** causes *name* to be pushed onto the name stack. **LoadName** replaces the value on the top of the stack with *name*. Loading a name onto an empty stack generates the error **INVALID_OPERATION**. Popping a name off of an empty stack generates **STACK_UNDERFLOW**. Pushing a name onto a full stack generates **STACK_OVERFLOW**. The maximum allowable depth of the name stack is implementation dependent but must be at least 64.

In selection mode no fragments are rendered into the frame buffer. The GL is placed in selection mode with

```
int RenderMode( enum mode ) ;
```

The *mode* is a symbolic constant: one of **RENDER, SELECT,** or **FEEDBACK. RENDER** is the default, corresponding to rendering as described until now. **SELECT** specifies selection mode, and **FEEDBACK** specifies feedback mode. Use of any of the name stack manipulation commands while the GL is not in selection mode has no effect.

Selection is controlled by using

```
void SelectBuffer( sizei n, uint *buffer ) ;
```

The *buffer* is a pointer to an array of unsigned integers (called the selection array) to be potentially filled with names and *n* is an integer indicating the maximum number of values that can be stored in that array. Placing the GL in selection mode before **SelectBuffer** has been called results in an error of **INVALID_OPERATION**, as does calling **SelectBuffer** while in selection mode.

In selection mode if a point, line, polygon, or the valid coordinates produced by a **RasterPos** command intersect the clip volume, then this primitive (or **RasterPos** command) causes a selection *hit*. In the case of polygons, no hit occurs if the polygon would have been culled. But selection is based on the polygon itself, regardless of the setting of **Polygonmode**. In selection mode whenever a name stack manipulation command is executed or **RenderMode** is called and there has been a hit since the last time the stack was manipulated or **RenderMode** was called a *hit record* is written into the selection array.

A hit record consists of the following items in order: a nonnegative integer giving the number of elements on the name stack at the time of the hit, a minimum depth value, a maximum depth value, and the name stack with the bottom-most element first. The minimum and maximum depth values are the minimum and maximum taken over all the window coordinate z values of each (postclipping) vertex of each primitive that intersects the clipping volume since the last hit record was written. The minimum and maximum (each of which lies in the range [0, 1]) are each multiplied by $2^{32} - 1$ and rounded to the nearest unsigned integer to obtain the values that are placed in the hit record.

Hit records are placed in the selection array by maintaining a pointer into that array. When selection mode is entered, the pointer is initialized to the beginning of the array. Each time a hit record is copied, the pointer is updated to point at the array element after the one into which the topmost element of the name stack was stored. If copying the hit record into the selection array would cause the total number of values to exceed n, as much of the record as fits in the array is written, and an overflow flag is set.

Selection mode is exited by calling **RenderMode** with an argument value other than **SELECT.** Whenever **RenderMode** is called in selection mode, it returns the number of hit records copied into the selection array and resets the **SelectBuffer** pointer to its last specified value. Values are not guaranteed to be written into the selection array until **RenderMode** is called. If the selection array overflow flag was set, **RenderMode** returns –1 and clears the overflow flag. The name stack is cleared and the stack pointer reset whenever **RenderMode** is called.

The state required for selection consists of the address of the selection array and its maximum size, the name stack and its associated pointer, a minimum and maximum depth value, and several flags. One flag indicates the current **RenderMode** value. In the initial state the GL is in the **RENDER** mode. Another flag is used to indicate whether a hit has occurred since the last name stack manipulation. This flag is reset entering selection mode and whenever a name stack manipulation takes place. One final flag is required to indicate whether the maximum number of copied names would have been exceeded. This flag is reset entering selection mode. This flag, the address of the selection array, and its maximum size are GL client state.

Feedback

Feedback, like selection, is a GL mode. The mode is selected by calling **RenderMode** with **FEEDBACK**. When the GL is in feedback mode, no fragments are written to the frame buffer. Instead, information about primitives that would have been rasterized is fed back to the application, using the GL.

Feedback is controlled by using

```
void FeedbackBuffer( sizei n, enum type, float
*buffer ) ;
```

The *buffer* is a pointer to an array of floating-point values into which feedback information will be placed; *n* is a number indicating the maximum number of values that can be written to that array; and *type* is a symbolic constant describing the information to be fed back for each vertex. The error **INVALID_OPERATION** results if the GL is placed in feedback mode before a call to **FeedbackBuffer** has been made or if a call to **FeedbackBuffer** is made while in feedback mode.

While in feedback mode, each primitive that would be rasterized (or bitmap or call to **DrawPixels** or **CopyPixels,** if the raster position is valid) generates a block of values that get copied into the feedback array. If doing so would cause the number of entries to exceed the maximum, the block is partially written so as to fill the array (if any room is left at all). The first block of values generated after the GL enters feedback mode is placed at the beginning of the feedback array, with subsequent blocks following. Each block begins with a code indicating the primitive type, followed by values that describe the primitive's vertices and associated data. Entries are also written for bitmaps and pixel rectangles. Feedback occurs after polygon culling and **PolygonMode** interpretation of polygons have taken place. It may also occur after polygons with more than three edges are broken up into triangles (if the GL implementation renders polygons by performing this decomposition). The *x, y,* and *z* coordinates returned by feedback are window coordinates. If *w* is returned, it is in clip coordinates. In the case of bitmaps and pixel rectangles, the coordinates returned are those of the current raster position. The texture coordinates and colors returned are those resulting from the clipping operations.

The ordering rules for GL command interpretation also apply in feedback mode. Each command must be fully interpreted and its effects on both GL state and the values to be written to the feedback buffer completed before a subsequent command may be executed.

The GL is taken out of feedback mode by calling **RenderMode** with an argument value other than **FEEDBACK**. When called while in feedback mode, **RenderMode** returns the number of values placed in the feedback array and resets the feedback array pointer to be *buffer*. The return value never exceeds the maximum number of values passed to **FeedbackBuffer.** If writing a value to the feedback buffer would cause more values to be written than the specified maximum number of values, then the value is not written and an overflow flag is set. In this case **RenderMode** returns –1 when it is called, after which the overflow flag is reset. While in feedback mode, values are not guaranteed to be written into the feedback buffer before **RenderMode** is called.

Table 13.23 gives the correspondence between feedback buffer and the number of values returned for each vertex.

The following command may be used as a marker in feedback mode:

```
void PassThrough( float token ) ;
```

The value of *token* is returned as if it were a primitive. It is indicated with its own unique identifying value. The ordering of any **PassThrough** commands with respect to primitive specification is maintained by feedback. **PassThrough** may not occur between **Begin** and **End**. It has no effect when the GL is not in feedback mode.

The state required for feedback is the pointer to the feedback array, the maximum number of values that may be placed there, and the

Table 13.23 Correspondence of Feedback Type to Number of Values per Vertex. Note that k is 1 in color index mode and 4 in RGBA mode.

Type	Coordinates	Color	Texture	Total Values
2-D	x,y	—	—	2
3-D	x,y,z	—	—	3
3-D COLOR	x, y, z	k	—	$3 + k$
3-D COLOR_TEXTURE	x, y, z	k	4	$7 + k$
4-D_COLOR_TEXTURE	x, y, z, w	k	4	$8 + k$

feedback type. An overflow flag is required to indicate whether the maximum allowable number of feedback values has been written. Initially this flag is cleared. These state variables are GL client state. Feedback also relies on the same mode flag as selection to indicate whether the GL is in feedback, selection, or normal rendering mode.

Display Lists

A display list is simply a group of GL commands and arguments stored for subsequent execution. The GL may be instructed to process a particular display list (possibly repeatedly) by providing a number that uniquely specifies it. Doing so causes the commands within the list to be executed just as if they were given normally. The only exception pertains to commands that rely on client state. When such a command is accumulated into the display list (that is, when issued, not when executed), the client state in effect at that time applies to the command. Only server state is affected when the command is executed. As always, pointers passed as arguments to commands are dereferenced when the command is issued.

A display list is begun by calling

```
void NewList( uint n, enum mode ) ;
```

n is a positive integer to which the display list that follows is assigned, and *mode* is a symbolic constant that controls the behavior of the GL during display list creation.[9]

If *mode* is **COMPILE,** commands are not executed as they are placed in the display list. If *mode* is **COMPILE_AND_EXECUTE,** commands are executed as they are encountered, then placed in the display list. If $n = 0$, the error **INVALID_VALUE** is generated. If the size of the display list exceeds the available memory, an **OUT_OF_MEMORY** error is generated.

After calling **NewList,** all subsequent GL commands are placed in the display list (in the order the commands are issued) until a call to

```
void EndList( void ) ;
```

After that occurs the GL returns to its normal command execution state.

It is only when **EndList** occurs that the specified display list is associated with the index indicated with NewList. The error **INVALID_OPERATION** is generated if EndList is called without a previous matching NewList or if **NewList** is called a second time before calling **EndList.** Once defined, a display list is executed by calling

void **CallList**(uint *n*) ;

n gives the index of the display list to be called.

This causes the commands saved in the display list to be executed, in order, just as if they were issued without using a display list. If n = 0, the error **INVALID-VALUE** is generated.

The command provides an efficient means for executing a number of display lists:

void CallLists(sizei n, enum *type*, void **lists*) ;

n is an integer indicating the number of display lists to be called, and *lists* is a pointer to an array of offsets.

Each offset is constructed as determined by *lists,* as follows. First, *type* may be one of the constants **BYTE, UNSIGNED_BYTE, SHORT, UNSIGNED_SHORT, INT, UNSIGNED_INT,** or **FLOAT.** This indicates that the array pointed to by *lists* is an array of bytes, unsigned bytes, shorts, unsigned shorts, integers, unsigned integers, or floats, respectively. In this case each offset is found by simply converting each array element to an integer (floating-point values are truncated).

Indicating a display list index that does not correspond to any display list has no effect. **CallList** or **CallLists** may appear inside a display list. If the *mode* supplied to **NewListCOMPILE_AND_EXECUTE,** the appropriate lists are executed. But the **CallList** or **CallLists,** rather than those lists' constituent commands, is placed in the list under construction. To avoid the possibility of infinite recursion resulting from display lists calling one another, an implementation, dependent limit is placed on the nesting level of display lists during display list execution. This limit must be at least 64.

Two commands are provided to manage display list indices. One is

```
uint GenLists( sizei s ) ;
```

This command returns an integer n such that the indices $n, \ldots, n + s - 1$ are previously unused (that is, there are s previously unused display list indices starting at n).

GenLists also has the effect of creating an empty display list for each of the indices $n, \ldots, n + s - 1$, so that these indices all become used. **GenLists** returns 0 if there is no group of s contiguous previously unused display list indices or if $s = 0$.

The second command is top here

```
boolean IsList( uint list ) ;
```

This command returns **TRUE** if *list* is the index of a display list.

A contiguous group of display lists may be deleted by calling

```
void DeleteLists( uint list, sizei range ) ;
```

Here *list* is the index of the first display list to be deleted, and *range* is the number of display lists to be deleted.

All information about the display lists is lost, and the indices become unused. Indices to which no display list corresponds are simply ignored. If range = 0, nothing happens.

Certain commands, when made within a display list, are not compiled into the display list but are executed immediately. These are **IsList, GenLists, DeleteLists, FeedbackBuffer, SelectBuffer,**

RenderMode, ReadPixels, PixelStore, Flush, Finish, IsEnabled, and all of the **Get** commands.

Display lists require one bit of state to indicate whether a GL command should be executed immediately or placed in a display list. In the initial state commands are executed immediately. If the bit indicates display list creation, an index is required to indicate the current display list being defined. Another bit indicates, during display list creation, whether commands should be executed as they are compiled into the display list. One integer is required for the current **ListBase** setting. Its initial value is 0. Finally, state must be maintained to indicate which integers are currently in use as display list indices. In the initial state no indices are in use.

Flush and Finish

The following command

```
void Flush( void ) ;
```

indicates that all commands that have previously been sent to the GL must complete in finite time:

The following command forces all previous GL commands to complete:

```
void Finish( void ) ;
```

Finish does not return until all effects from previously issued commands on GL client and server state and the frame buffer are fully realized.

Hints

The symbolic constant *target* indicates the behavior to be controlled, and *hint* is a symbolic constant indicating what type of behavior is desired. The *target* may be one of **PERSPECTIVE_CORRECTION_HINT.** This indicates the desired quality of parameter interpolation. **POINT_SMOOTH_HINT** indicates the desired sampling quality of points. **LINE_SMOOTH_HINT** indicates the desired sampling quality of lines. **POLYGON_SMOOTH_HINT** indicates the desired sampling quality of polygons. **FOG_HINT** indicates whether fog calculations are done per pixel or per vertex. *Hint* must be one of **FASTEST** (indicating that the most efficient option should be chosen), **NICEST** (indicating that the highest quality option should be chosen), or, **DONT_CARE** (indicating no preference in the matter).

Certain aspects of GL behavior, when there is room for variation, may be controlled with hints. A hint is specified by using

```
void Hint( enum target, enum hint ) ;
```

The interpretation of hints is implementation dependent. An implementation may ignore them entirely.

State and State Requests

The commands obtain Boolean, integer, floating-point, or double-precision state variables. The symbolic constant *value* indicates the state variable to return, and *data* is a pointer to an array of the indicated type in which to place the returned data.

In addition, the following can be used to determine whether value is currently enabled (as with **Enable**) or disabled:

```
boolean IsEnabled( enum value ) ;
```

The values of most GL state variables can be obtained by using a set of **Get** commands. There are four commands for obtaining simple state variables:

```
void GetBooleanv( enum value, boolean *data ) ;
void GetIntegerv( enum value, int *data ) ;
void GetFloatv( enum value, float *data ) ;
void GetDoublev( enum value, double *data ) ;
```

If a **Get** command is issued that returns value types different from the type of the value being obtained, a type conversion is performed. If **GetBooleanv** is called, a floating-point or integer value converts to **FALSE** if and only if it is 0 (otherwise it converts to **TRUE).** If **GetIntegerv** (or any of the **Get** commands following) is called, a Boolean value is interpreted as either 1 or 0, and a floating-point value is rounded to the nearest integer, unless the value is an RGBA color component, a **DepthRange** value, a depth buffer clear value, or a normal coordinate. In these cases, the **Get** command converts the floating-point value to an integer according the **INT** entry of Table 13.21. A value not in [−1, 1] converts to an undefined value.

If **GetFloatv** is called, a Boolean value is interpreted as either 1.0 or 0.0; an integer is coerced to floating point, and a double-precision floating-point value is converted to single precision. Analogous conversions are carried out in the case of **GetDoublev.** If a value is so large in magnitude that it cannot be represented with the requested type, the nearest value representable using the requested type is returned.

Other commands exist to obtain state variables that are indexed by a target:

```
void GetClipPlane( enum plane, double eqn[4] ) ;
void GetLight{if}v( enum light, enum value, T data ) ;
void GetMaterial{if}v( enum face, enum value, T data ) ;
void GetTexEnv{if}v( enum env, enum value, T data ) ;
void GetTexGen{if}v( enum coord, enum value, T data ) ;
void GetTexParameter{if}v( enum target, enum value, T data ) ;
void GetTexLevelParameter{if}v( enum target, int lod, enum
value, T data ) ;
void GetPixelMap{ui us f}v( enum map, T data ) ;
void GetMap{ifd}v( enum map, enum value, T data ) ;
```

GetClipPlane always returns four double-precision values in *eqn*. These are the coefficients of the plane equation of *plane* in eye coordinates (these coordinates were computed when the plane was specified).

GetLight places information about *value* (a symbolic constant) for *light* (also a symbolic constant) in *data*. **POSITION** or **SPOT_DIRECTION** returns values in eye coordinates (again, these coordinates were computed when the position or direction was specified).

GetMaterial, GetTexGen, GetTexEnv, and **GetTexParameter** are similar to **GetLight,** placing information about *value* for the target indicated by their first argument into *data*. The *face* argument to **GetMaterial** must be either **FRONT** or **BACK,** indicating the front or back material, respectively. The *env* argument to **GetTexEnv** must currently be **TEXTURE_ENV.** The *coord* argument to **GetTexGen** must be one of **S, T, R,** or **Q.** For GetTexGen, **EYE_LINEAR** coefficients are returned in the eye coordinates computed when the plane was specified. **OBJECT_LINEAR** coefficients are returned in object coordinates.

For **GetTexParameter** and **GetTexLevelParameter,** *target* must currently be either **TEXTURE_1D** or **TEXTURE_2-D,** indicating the target from which information is to be obtained. *Value* is a symbolic value indicating which texture parameter is to be obtained. The *lod* argument to **GetTexLevelParameter** determines which level-of-detail's state is returned. If the *lod* argument is less than 0 or if it is larger than the maximum allowable level of detail, the error **INVALID_VALUE** occurs.

For **GetPixelMap,** the map must be a map name from Table 13.9. For **GetMap,** *map* must be one of the map types described earlier, and *value* must be one of **ORDER, COEFF,** or **DOMAIN** .**GetTexImage** is used to obtain texture images.

```
void GetTexImage( enum tex, int lod, enum
format, enum type,
      void *img ) ;
```

It is somewhat different from the other get commands; *tex* is a symbolic value indicating which texture is to be obtained. **TEX-TURE_1D** indicates a one-dimensional texture, whereas **TEXTURE_2-D** indicates a two-dimensional texture. *Lod* is a level-of-detail number; *format* is a pixel format from Table 13.11; *type* is a pixel type from Table 13.10; and *img* is a pointer to a block of memory. **GetTexImage** obtains component groups from a texture image with the indicated level of detail, starting with the first group in the first row, and continuing by obtaining groups in order from each row and proceeding from the first row to the last. The number of components in a group is the number of components of the texture. The components are assigned among R, G, B, and A according to Table 13.13. These groups are then packed and placed in client memory as described earlier in the chapter. The row length and number of rows are determined by the size of the texture image (including any borders). Calling **GetTexImage** with *lod* less than 0 or larger than the maximum allowable causes the error **INVALID_VALUE.** Calling **GetTexImage** with format of **COLOR_INDEX, STENCIL_INDEX,** or **DEPTH_COMPONENT** causes the error **INVALID_ENUM.** The following command obtains the polygon stipple:

```
void GetPolygonStipple( void *pattern ) ;
```

The pattern is packed into memory according to the procedure given earlier for **ReadPixels.** It is as if the *height* and *width* passed to that command were both equal to 32, the *type* were **BITMAP,** and the format were **COLOR_INDEX.** Finally, a pointer to a static string describing some aspect of the current GL connection is returned by:

```
ubyte *GetString( enum name ) ;
```

The possible values for name are **VENDOR, RENDERER, VERSION,** and **EXTENSIONS.** The format of the **RENDERER** and **VERSION** strings is implementation dependent. The **EXTENSIONS** string contains a space-separated list of extension names The extension names themselves do not contain any spaces. The **VERSION** string is laid out as follows:

```
<version number><space><vendor-specific informa-
tion>
```

The version number is either of the form *major-number.minor-number* or *major-number.minor-number.release-number*, where the numbers all have one or more digits. The vendor-specific information is optional. However, if it is present, it pertains to the server, and the format and contents are implementation dependent.

GetString returns the version number (returned in the **VERSION** string) and the extension names (returned in the **EXTENSIONS** string) that can be supported on the connection. Thus if the client and server support different versions or extensions, a compatible version and Est of extensions is returned.

Tables 13.24 and 13.25 indicate which state variables are obtained with what commands. State variables that can be obtained using any of **GetBooleanv, GetIntegerv, GetFloatv,** or **GetDoublev** are listed with just one of these commands—the one that is most appropriate given the type of the data to be returned. These state variables cannot be obtained using **IsEnabled**. However, state variables for which **IsEnabled** is listed as the query command can also be obtained by using **GetBooleanv, GetIntegerv, GetFloatv,** and **GetDoublev**. State variables for which any other command is listed as the query command can be obtained only by using that command.

Unless otherwise indicated, multivalued state variables return their multiple values in the same order as they are given as arguments to the commands that set them. For instance, the two **DepthRange** parameters are returned in the order n followed by f. Similarly, points for evaluator maps are returned in the order that they appeared when passed to **Map1**. **Map2** returns R_{ij} in the $[(uorder)i + j]$th block of values.

Besides providing a means to obtain the values of state variables, the GL also provides a means to save and restore groups of state variables. The **PushAttrib** and **PopAttrib** commands are used for this purpose.

The following command takes a bitwise OR of symbolic constants indicating which groups of state variables to push onto an attribute stack:

void **PushAttrib**(bitfield *mask*) ;

Each constant refers to a group of state variables. The classification of each variable into a group is indicated in the following tables of state variables.

The following command resets the values of those state variables that were saved with the last **PushAttrib:**

void **PopAttrib**(void) ;

Those not saved remain unchanged. It is an error to pop an empty stack or to push onto a full one. Table 13.24 shows the attribute groups with their corresponding symbolic constant names.

The depth of the attribute stack is implementation dependent but must be at least 16. The state required is potentially 16 copies of each state variable, 16 masks indicating which groups of variables are stored in each stack entry and an attribute stack pointer. In the initial state the attribute stack is empty.

In Tables 13.24 and 13.25, a type is indicated for each variable. Table 13.25 explains these types. The type identifies all states associated with the indicated description. In certain cases only a portion of this state is returned. This is the case with all matrices, where only the top entry on the stack is returned; with clip planes, where only the selected clip plane is returned; with parameters describing lights, where only the value pertaining to the selected light is returned; with textures, where only the selected texture or texture parameter is returned; and with evaluator maps, where only the selected map is returned. Finally, a "-" in the attribute column indicates that the indicated value is not included in any attribute group (and thus cannot be pushed or popped with **PushAttrib** or **PopAttrib).**

Table 13.24 Attribute Groups

Attribute	Constant
accum-buffer	ACCUM_BUFFER_BIT
color-buffer	COLOR_BUFFER_BIT
current	CURRENT_BIT
depth-buffer	DEPTH_BUFFER_BIT
enable	ENABLE_BIT
eval	EVAL_BIT
fog	FOG_BIT
hint	HINT_BIT
lighting	LIGHTING_BIT
line	LINE_BIT
list	LIST_BIT
pixel	PIXEL_MODE_BIT
point	POINT_BIT
polygon	POLYGON_BIT
polygon-stipple	POLYGON_STIPPLE_BIT
scissor	SCISSOR_BIT
stencil-buffer	STENCIL_BUFFER_BIT
texture	TEXTURE_BIT
transform	TRANSFORM_BIT
viewport	VIEWPORT_BIT ALL_ATTRIB_BITS
client	can't be pushed or pop'd

Invariance

The OpenGL specification is not pixel exact. It therefore does not guarantee an exact match between images produced by different

Table 13.25 State Variable Types

Type Code	Explanation
B	Boolean
C_-	Color (floating-point R, G, B, and A values)
CI	Color index (floating-point index value)
T	Texture coordinates (floating-point s, t, r, q values)
N	Normal coordinates (floating-point x, y, z values)
V	Vertex, including associated data
Z	Integer
$Z+$	Non-negative integer
$Z_k,\ \_Z_{k*}$	k-valued integer ($k*$ indicates that k is minimum)
R	Floating-point number
$R+$	Non-negative floating-point number
Rk	k-tuple of floating-point numbers
P	Position (x, y, z, w floating-point coordinates)
D	Direction (x, y, z floating-point coordinates)
$M4$	4 * 4 *floating-point matrix*
I	Image
A	Attribute stack entry, including mask
$n\ x\ type$	n copies of type *type* ($n*$ indicates that n is minimum)

GL implementations. However, the specification does specify exact matches, in some cases, for images produced by the same implementation. This part of the chapter identifies and provides justification for those cases that require exact matches.

Repeatability

The obvious and most fundamental case is repeated issuance of a series of GL commands. For any given GL and frame buffer state vector, and for any GL command, the resulting GL and frame buffer state must be identical whenever the command is executed on that initial GL and frame buffer state.

One purpose of repeatability is avoidance of visual artifacts when a double-buffered scene is redrawn. If rendering is not repeatable, swapping between two buffers rendered with the same command sequence may result in visible changes in the image. Such false motion is distracting to the viewer. Another reason for repeatability is testability.

Repeatability, although important, is a weak requirement. Given only repeatability as a requirement, two scenes rendered with one (small) polygon changed in position might differ at every pixel. Such a difference may be within the law of repeatability but is certainly not within its spirit. Additional invariance rules are desirable to ensure useful operation.

Multipass Algorithms

Invariance is necessary for a whole set of useful multipass algorithms. Such algorithms render multiple times, each time with a different GL mode vector, to eventually produce a result in the frame buffer. Examples of these algorithms include:

- erasing a primitive from the frame buffer by redrawing it, either in a different color or using the XOR logical operation; and
- using stencil operations to compute capping planes.[10]

On the other hand, invariance rules can greatly increase the complexity of high-performance implementations of the GL. Even the weak repeatability requirement significantly constrains a parallel implementation of the GL. Because GL implementations are required to implement *all* GL capabilities, not just a convenient subset, those that use hardware acceleration are expected to alternate between hardware and software modules based on the current GL mode vector. A strong invariance requirement forces the behavior of the hardware and software modules to be identical. This is something that may be very difficult to achieve if, for example, the hardware does floating-point operations with different precision than the software. What is desired is a compromise that results in many compliant, high-performance implementations and in many software vendors' choosing to port to OpenGL.

Invariance Rules

For a given instantiation of an OpenGL rendering context, three rules apply.

Rule 1 *For any given GL and frame buffer state vector and for* **any** *given GL command, the resulting GL and frame buffer state must be identical each time the command is executed on that initial GL and frame buffer state.*

Rule 2 *Changes to the following state values have no side effects (the use of* **any** *other state value is not affected by the change):*

The following are required:

- ◆ frame buffer contents (all bit planes);
- ◆ the color buffers enabled for writing;
- ◆ the values of matrices other than the top-of-stack matrices;
- ◆ scissor parameters (other than enable);
- ◆ writemasks (color, index, depth, stencil);
- ◆ clear values (color, index, depth, stencil, accumulation);
- ◆ *current values (color, index, normal, texture coords, edgeflag);*
- ◆ *current raster color, index and texture coordinates;*
- ◆ material properties (ambient, diffuse, specular, emission, shininess).

Strongly suggested:

- ◆ *matrix mode;*
- ◆ *matrix stack depths;*
- ◆ *alpha test parameters (other than enable);*
- ◆ *stencil parameters (other than enable);*

+ *depth test parameters (other than enable);*
+ *blend parameters (other than enable);*
+ *logical operation parameters (other than enable);*
+ *pixel storage and transfer state; and*
+ *evaluator state (except as it affects the vertex data generated by the evaluators).*

Corollary 1 *Fragment generation is invariant with respect to the state values marked with **bullets** in Rule 2.*

Corollary 2 The window coordinates (x, y, and z) of generated fragments are also invariant with respect to the following requirements:

+ *current values (color, color index, normal, texture coordinates, edge flag);*
+ *current raster color, color index, and texture coordinates; and*
+ *material properties (ambient, diffuse, specular, emission, shininess).*

Rule 3 *The arithmetic of each per fragment operation is invariant except with respect to parameters that directly control it (the parameters that control the alpha test, for instance, are the alpha test enable, the alpha test function, and the alpha test reference value).*

Corollary 3 *Images rendered into different color buffers, either simultaneously or separately using the same command sequence, are pixel identical. (Note that this does not hold between X * pirmaps and color buffers, however.)* Hardware-accelerated GL implementations are expected to default to software operation when some GL state vectors are encountered. Even the weak repeatability requirement means, for example, that OpenGL implementations cannot apply hysteresis to this swap. It must instead guarantee that a given mode vector implies that a subsequent command is *always* executed in either the hardware or the software machine.

The stronger invariance rules constrain when the switch from hardware to software rendering can occur, given that the software and hardware renderers are not pixel identical. For example, the switch can be made when blending is enabled or disabled, but it should not be made when a change is made to the blending parameters.

Because floating-point values may be represented using different formats in different renderers (hardware and software), many OpenGL state values may change subtly when renderers are swapped. This is the type of state value change that Rule 1 seeks to avoid.

From Here

The intense interest expressed within the WWW community during 1997 (especially the last six months) for a visualized interface to bring virtual reality to the Internet and the Web has exploded beyond all expectations. Part III and following chapters will present those visions as to what the Web community wants to be able to do with VRML. Chapter 14 will begin Part III by taking a look at Distributed Virtual Environments (DVEs): The sharing of virtual worlds and the new Internet technologies that promise even richer forms of interpersonal interactions.

Endnotes

1 Mark Segal and Kurt Akeley, OpenGL Specification, *Utility Library Specification and GLX Protocol*, Silicon Graphics, Inc., January 16, 1995.

2 Ibid., pp. 15–16.

3 Ibid., pp. 38–39.

4 Ibid., p. 53.

5 Ibid., p. 81.

6 Ibid., p. 98.

7 Ibid., pp. 106–107.

8 Ibid., p. 113.

9 Ibid., p. 128.

10 Ibid., p. 158.

Part Three

Distributed Virtual Environments

14

Sharing Distributed Virtual Worlds

For much of the history of computers, the dominant mode of computer use was batch processing. You prepared a program, submitted it to a computer center, and got an answer hours or days later. Now, however, the dominant mode of computer use is single-user, real-time interaction. You make a change with a spreadsheet program, word processor, or computer-aided design tool and see the effect of this change in a second or less. Over the next decade, multiuser real-time interaction will become a major mode of computer use. Logged into a session including many other people, you will interact with these people and various computer tools in real time. In particular, so-called *Distributed Virtual Environments*, or *DVEs*, will have a significant impact on the way we work, learn, and play.

Distributed Virtual Environments are emerging as an important new kind of computer system in which multiple geographically separated users interact in real time. This chapter summarizes the current state of the art of DVEs and illustrates some of the directions future developments may take.

Worldwide Interactions

In the very near future, people using a microcomputer-based system may routinely log on to an intranet and find themselves in a highly graphical environment. Many people would end up populating this computer-generated world. Helped by various computer tools they could pick up and use intuitively (like a hammer), they would be able to interact in real time. As previously mentioned, these shared, computer-resident worlds are called DVEs.

For example, imagine architects in Rome, structural engineers in Houston, and a developer in Copenhagen participating in a joint virtual "walkthrough" of a building's design. Each would be represented on screen by a three-dimensional icon—a so-called *avatar*. The participants could then move through the virtual environment and open doors and rearrange tables, chairs, windows, walls, and other objects. As they view the building from various exterior and interior vantage points, they discuss alternatives and experiment in real time with potential changes and how the changes affect the structural integrity of the building. They meet in this collaborative design DVE not only during the design of the building, but also during later construction, to review progress and plan necessary changes.

An important feature of this DVE is that the participants meet early and often during design and construction. In other words, the group might meet in this collaborative DVE many times to review progress and plan changes necessitated by altered economic conditions or corporate objectives during the lifetime of the project. This allows the kind of repeated interaction that is essential for them to become fully aware of each other's concerns and arrive at a joint solution that works better than could have been created by any one party.

A DVE could also reshape the educational process in a similar manner. For example, imagine a virtual street in Florence lined with apartments, shops, restaurants, a church, and a small park. The street is populated with residents, shopkeepers, patrons, waiters, pedestrians, and tourists. You and other people join this world by taking on the roles of some of these characters. The remaining characters are played by native speakers or are computer simulated. By participating in this foreign language practice DVE, you practice speaking Italian with other people in a non-threatening environment and learn about Italian culture. This is vastly different from current computer-assisted language learning tools, almost all of which boil down to rote drills with little or no spoken language production on your part, let alone any interaction with other people.

An important feature of this DVE is that tens of thousands of people from around the world participate from time to time. In other words, interactivity is the outstanding advantage for this DVE. As a result, you can join with other people who are interested in practicing Italian almost any time you want.

The way in which people make purchases and purchasing decisions could also be recast by DVEs. For example, imagine that you are planning (or just daydreaming about planning) a trip to Australia. Using a virtual tourism marketplace DVE, you explore various tourist sites and talk with people from the government travel bureau. You also visit various hotels and resorts, touring rooms you might rent, and discussing alternatives with hotel staff. During your virtual tour, you speak with other people who are planning trips to Australia, swapping information about what is new and interesting.

An important feature of this DVE is that the environment is continually evolving even as it is being used. In other words, this DVE's strong point is constant updating. Virtual models of cultural sites and accommodations are continually refined and added, without the system ever having to be shut down.

Now let's explore the possibilities of using DVEs for work, leisure, and learning.

Exploring Possible Uses of DVEs

A group of researchers and artists at MERL (Mitsubishi Electric Research Laboratories), Cambridge, Massachusetts, created a prototype DVE called Diamond Park using the *Scalable Platform for Large Interactive Networked Environments* (SPLINE) and VRML in order to explore possible uses of a distributed virtual environment for leisure, learning, and work. The DVE was designed as an amalgam of landscape, park, village, and World's Fair covering an area exactly one mile square, accommodating both bicycling and social interaction. The park encourages live conversation and is rich in audio effects, including bird song, music, and sound effects cued by particular actions in addition to its visual details. Most of the figures in this part of the chapter are screen captures of live action from Diamond Park, as shown in Figure 14.1.[1]

A colonnaded structure is one of the first things a visitor sees when entering the park, as shown in Figure 14.2.[2] Its three-dimensional

Figure 14.1 Diamond Park.

tabletop map (situated high on a virtual hill) helps orient park visitors, who can move about the park in two ways. The park is seen on a wide screen by those who ride an actual computer-controlled stationary bike where they are represented by avatars riding bicycles. Others use a regular computer monitor and mouse-keyboard inputs. They appear as avatars on unicycles. The park's audio effects can be heard by both groups using a headset to talk with each other. The groups then come to an open-air café (see Figure 14.3) as they move into the park, whose ambient noises include jazz and the clink of china.[3] There they can practice a foreign language with a visitor from another country or just stop to chat.

As shown in Figure 14.4, two visitors on unicycles overlook the park from one of the peaks surrounding it.[4] Added by the designers

Figure 14.2 Orientation Center.

Figure 14.3 The Plaza.

is a 3-D model of a standing figure that lends a populated feeling to the park even when visitors are widely scattered.

The round-shaped building shown in Figure 14.5 is a velodrome, which can be reached by hover bus.[5] The bus driver is a *bot*—a character controlled by a simple program. The driver delivers a patter about the park's sights, all the while stopping the vehicle to take on and let off passengers.

A sports-official bot in a black-and-white striped shirt asks entering bicyclists inside the velodrome (see Figure 14.6) if they would like to race on the Olympic-sized track.[6] This bot could also be pro-

Figure 14.4 Panorama.

grammed with VRML Script to be made to act as the starter (once he has assembled a group of competitors), keep track of each racer's time, and declare a winner. The scoreboard on the wall could also be used to keep track of race statistics as well.

Visitors on the customized stationary bikes can simply ride one of the many paths through the park if they decline to race (see Figure 14.7), all the while talking with each other and enjoying the park's other sights.[7] Or, they can tackle an obstacle course as shown in Figure 14.8. Here the obstacles can be repositioned to suit the rider. Leaning to the left or right on the stationary bike steers the on-screen rider around the pylons.[8]

Figure 14.5 Velodrome.

Figure 14.6 Velodrome interior.

Figure 14.7 Bike paths.

Figure 14.8 Obstacle course.

Visitors can enter the Desert House, as shown in Figure 14.9, if more vigorous exercise is wanted. The glass structure seen from afar is the image at the top.[9] Although only virtual, realistic physical effects for bicyclists are created by the Desert House's steep hills. As the pedal resistance on the visitors' computer-controlled stationary bikes increases (as they ride up a hill), the riders are given a thorough workout.

Several "entertainers" may be encountered by those touring Diamond Park. Figure 14.10 shows an automated acrobat in the form of a checkered fellow standing on his hands.[10] Also common in the park are software-based joggers and baseball players. Visitors are encouraged to bring similar "friends."

The park's authors also created the futuristic Outer Space Building, as shown in Figure 14.11 (which from the outside seems relatively small), in order to explore some of the non-Euclidean possibilities of virtual space.[11] Visitors entering the building find themselves on an observation platform (Figure 14.12). They look out at a vast universe of orbiting, rotating planets, complete with astronauts who drift weightlessly through space. A finishing touch here is cosmic electronic music.[12]

Figure 14.9 The Desert House.

Figure 14.10 "Live" entertainment in Diamond Park.

DVE Attributes

The previous examples are only but a few out of a multitude of possible DVE features. For example, a group of geographically separated users can interact in real time through a DVE. This means not just small groups of users, but also scalability to thousands of users or more. For instance, in a packed auditorium, it should be possible for musicians in a studio to move seamlessly into an orchestra.

A DVE user is immersed in an environment that is three-dimensional to the eye and ear. The user's visual and auditory perspectives

Figure 14.11 Outer Space Building.

are changed as he or she moves in the environment. In contrast to
a videoconferencing system where the users see each other in each
other's videoconference rooms on an array of TV screens, the
users of a DVE are gathered together in a virtual world (they are
seated around a conference table in one conference room), or
walking together in a virtual building. Thus, every user of a DVE
appears in the computer environment as an avatar. This is where
the avatar can be either a customized graphical representation, a
video of the user, or some combination of both, which the user
controls.

Figure 14.12 Inside the Outer Space Building.

Besides interacting with one another, users also deal with multiple computer simulations. One of the most powerful features of a virtual world is to go beyond merely imitating the real world by including computer simulations that support things that cannot, or at least do not, exist in the real world.

Users speak to computer-generated beings or objects or to each other, which then respond in context. Words are basic to human interaction. Therefore, verbal communication is one of the most necessary features of DVEs.

In every aspect, a DVE can change continually while in use. As an analogy with the World Wide Web, someone new can enter and share a computer "space" by simply downloading the space's current content. Furthermore, this allows a DVE to grow based on contributions from many sources.

The system operates on inexpensive hardware over standard intranets. This is not necessary for a DVE to work; however, it is necessary for a DVE to have a wide impact on the public at large.

Back to the Future

DVE research has been underway for over 25 years. Until recently, interest in DVEs has been held in check by two key problems: very few people could afford to buy a computer capable of generating images of a virtual world in real time, and even fewer people could get access to wide area computer networks capable of the high-bandwidth, low-latency communication needed by DVEs. However, multiuser virtual worlds are on the brink of widespread availability now that these obstacles are beginning to disappear.

Furthermore, DVE computations can now be done by high-end PCs, especially with the arrival of powerful graphics accelerator cards, combined with the ever-growing power of PC processors. Thus, the networking needs of some simple DVEs can be met by 28.8-kb/s modems, which became common in 1996. In addition, modems almost twice as fast as that are now on the market. And, in a short while, several developing technologies such us *Asymmetric Digital Subscriber Line* (ADSL) and *cable modems* (to name but two) should be able to provide affordable multi-megabit-per-second network connections to the home. So, when this occurs, the pipeline to the home or office will then offer enough bandwidth for just about any DVE.

The results of research that has been going on for many years will soon appear in the home and office, now that the hardware needed for DVEs exists. This research has been conducted in two separate communities: the Internet world (paced by commercial developers), and *the Distributed Interactive Simulation* (DIS) world (pushed by developers of military simulators). Both efforts have the same long-range goal: a complex yet flexible cyber-environment fully shared by many users. But, the Internet and DIS camps have made diametrically opposed decisions as to which path leads there. Both camps have disagreed about which DVE features are essential now and which can be deferred. In essence, each group has attacked the aforementioned list of attributes from opposite ends: the DIS camp working on multimillion-dollar environments, while the Internet camp focused on affordability.

The Internet Group's Perspective

From the Internet camp's view, a DVE must run over the kind of network connections that most people have and on the kinds of computers most people own. Until just recently, this goal meant sacrificing the sense of 3-D immersion in a DVE on the altar of mass access and voice communication.

Before looking at current developments in DVEs, it is instructive to consider two key forerunners of current systems: *Adventure* and *Dungeons and Dragons*. This in turn sets the stage for Internet DVE work in the mid-1970s.

The first of the two key forerunners was a new kind of computer game developed in the early 1970s called Adventure (created by Will Crowther and Donald Woods of Xerox Palo Alto Research Center, California). It ran on a Digital Equipment Corp. PDP-10 mainframe computer. Since computers of the time did not permit longer filenames, the game was also known by the truncated name *Advent*.

Adventure was inspired at least in part by Crowther's love of exploring caves (in particular, the Mammoth Cave system in

Kentucky). It was also inspired by Dungeons and Dragons, a fantasy adventure simulation game created by Dave Arneson and published by TSR Inc., Lake Geneva, Wisconsin, in 1973. Dungeons and Dragons was the first role-playing game played with pencil and paper. And, it was also the rage among teens, preteens, and college students worldwide.

In Dungeons and Dragons, a group of players gather to act out roles as knights and sorcerers in a virtual world designed by a dungeon master. A determination of how the rooms and other environments in the game would look and be connected, and what objects would be in them was made by the dungeon master. At first, only written descriptions were used. Later on, however, a painted metal figurine represented each player amid scale models of props and rooms.

A player was free to ask the dungeon master questions about the room. If a player picked up an object (perhaps a sword), he or she would be told by the dungeon master of its special properties (maybe a magic ability to heal wounds). The rolling of a special die (often one with 8 or 12 sides) usually determined the movement through the world and the outcome of battles. Play could last for days. The game would terminate only when all the players "died" or a goal defined by the dungeon master was reached.

In Adventure, a single user interacts in real time with a virtual world, exploring, fighting demons, and finding treasure. The game was entirely text based, relying on the imagination of the user to create mental images from textual descriptions. The descriptions of environments, objects, and possible actions appeared as text on the computer's display. Players typed simple commands like UP or DOWN on a computer keyboard in order to proceed through the space.

Needless to say, Adventure spawned a whole genre of computer-based fantasy games. These games continue to be popular to this day.

A key development in Adventure-type games (from the DVE perspective) was the addition of multiuser interaction, leading to so-called *Multiuser Dungeons* (MUDs). Considered to be the earliest of these multiuser games, MUD was a text-based game written by Roy Trubshaw and Richard Bartle of the University of Essex, Colchester, England, in 1980 to run on a Digital Equipment DEC station. Thus, the term *MUD* became a generic description for multiuser computer games because of the popularity of this game and its successors.

Subsequent development of MUDs led in several interesting directions. One direction focused on person-to-person interaction rather than gaming. In the form of Internet chat rooms, this kind of MUD has become a staple of online service providers. Another direction focused on the ability of a dungeon master to design a game setting. This kind of MUD is often referred to as a *MUD Object Oriented* (MOO) and supports a high degree of extendibility. In general, the ability for many users to collaboratively and synergistically extend and evolve a MUD is a key factor in their popularity.

It is safe to say that the developers of the first MUD dreamed of having pictures and sound instead of just text. An important early step in this direction was Lucasfilm's *Habitat* and its successor *WorldsAway* (http://worldsaway.com), which added 2-D graphics, but not sound.

The line of development that led to MUDs was a grassroots effort that at each stage focused on using readily available technology to fashion systems that embody some of the key features of DVEs. In the same time frame, the U.S. Department of Defense (DOD) took a very different route; they chose to spend whatever it took to create a large-scale, high-fidelity DVE. By doing so, they deserve a lot of the credit for bringing DVEs to life.

Military Virtual Simulations

By the 1970s, the DOD had simulators for various fighting vehicles such as tanks, planes, and helicopters. These simulators were single-user, virtual-reality systems, using multimillion-dollar, special-purpose, real-time graphics hardware for generating images of the simulated world surrounding the vehicles. Starting with the SIMNET program in the early 1980s, the DOD sponsored research to link groups of simulators together over dedicated, high-speed intranets so that trainees in separate simulators could interact in group exercises. This research led to the IEEE (Institute of Electrical and Electronics Engineers) *Distributed Interactive Simulation* (DIS) standard and various highly successful group training systems (see Chapter 17, *Virtual Battlefields*, for a thorough examination of DIS in the military). Thus, the sole focus of DIS is on how simulators in the course of a training session can communicate dynamic information, such as the position of objects like virtual troops, tanks, and helicopters. Also, DIS has created a prosperous simulation industry and several highly successful military training systems. These are systems that support thousands of users simultaneously in rich, 3-D visual and auditory worlds.

There is no system in existence today that satisfies all of the key DVE criteria previously listed. However, system developers are driving rapidly toward this goal from several different directions.

Military training systems based on DIS are the closest things to full-scale DVEs that are in regular use today. They support thousands of simultaneous users in 3-D visual and audio worlds. In addition, DIS is a proven commercial success, backed by scores of military contractors, its own standards committee, and a series of yearly conferences.

Unfortunately, DIS-based systems have a number of key weaknesses. They provide very little support for spoken interaction (the emphasis being on people shooting at each other from a distance rather than talking to each other). They are difficult to extend in general and impossible to extend at run time (the emphasis being on preplanned exercises). Furthermore, most DIS-based systems are hosted on extremely expensive hardware.

In other words, DIS systems lack any standards for moving virtual objects and environments from one simulator to another (portable content standards), and so are awkward to extend. For example, simulator manufacturers must each construct a 3-D model of the new object and link it into their proprietary simulator software in order to add a new visual object, such as a new tank or aircraft to a multi-simulator system of this kind.

Continual improvements in DIS are being made, as exemplified by the work on NPSNET at the Naval Post Graduate School. However, precisely because DIS is already big business and a formal standard, forward progress has been somewhat ponderous. Therefore, despite DIS's early lead in the field of DVEs, it is likely that other developments will pass it by.

Nevertheless, DIS does a good job of minimizing the constraints on how a simulator is constructed. DIS however, gives little help for reusing simulator software. Major standards efforts are underway to develop a run-time software infrastructure needed to build a common platform form implementing simulators and a high-level system architecture. System procurement and maintenance costs would be reduced by this approach.

Can the Internet and DIS Meet?

Despite being ignorant of each other's achievements, the worlds of DIS and the Internet are advancing. This is quite unfortunate, because each has a great deal to learn from the other.

For instance, the Internet world wants to be home to DVEs with large numbers of users. They are unlikely to succeed, however, until they incorporate what the DIS world has learned about how to scale up in users.

Contrary to popular belief, various government and subcontractor groups are trying to move DIS beyond the military training realm to a more general commercial arena. Nevertheless, until they incorporate key features such as the ability to quickly move content pioneered on the Internet from system to system, they are unlikely to succeed. Rather than competing and condemning each other's weaknesses, DVEs with a full range of features will become available much sooner if the Internet and DIS worlds pool their respective strengths.

New Kid on the Block

The Internet world is now free to experiment with building virtual environments that provide 3-D immersion and spoken interaction, especially since more capable PCs and intranets are proliferating. The effort includes proprietary systems, but there is also a strong movement toward open standards. Central to this movement is the *Virtual Reality Modeling Language* (VRML) 97 standard for portable VR content.

As previously discussed, VRML first appeared as a standard for static 3-D models (VRML 1.0). Subsequently, it grew into a standard for content that can interact in real time with a single user (VRML 2.0). Currently, efforts such as the proposed Living Worlds and Open Community standards (see Chapter 15, *Virtual Worlds for Social Interaction*) are attempting to expand VRML (now VRML97) into a standard for DVEs.

Prompted by the increasing ability of PCs to support 3-D graphics and the explosive growth of interest in the Internet, there has been a rush over the past couple of years toward MUDs that incorporate 3-D graphics. This has lead to a whole category of MUDs that continue to use text for conversation between the users, but represent the users by 3-D avatars in a 3-D setting. These systems include Black Sun Interactive's *Passport* (see Figure 14.13);[13] Chaco Communications' *Pueblo* (see Figure 14.14);[14] Sony's *Community Place* (see Figure 14.15);[15] and The Palace Inc.'s *The Palace*, as shown in Figure 14.16.[16]

Figure 14.13 Passport's avatars and chat in action.

At the time of this writing, very few Internet MUDs have taken the critical next step of supporting spoken interaction between users instead of typed interaction. Two that have are Intel Inc.'s *Distributed Moo* (see Figure 14.17)[17] and OnLive! Technologies Inc.'s *OnLive! Traveler* (see Figure 14.18).[18] These MUDS use Internet phone software to transmit highly compressed live sound between users. Unfortunately, the latency of the current Internet is

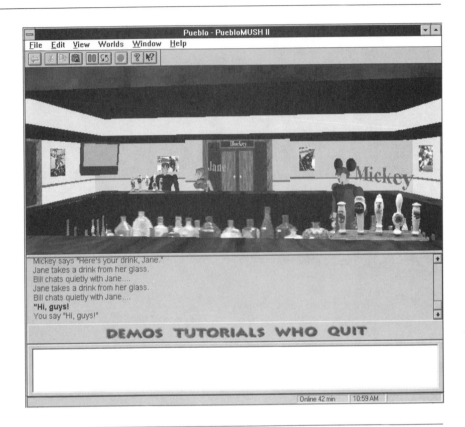

Figure 14.14 Pueblo.

so high (sometimes approaching a round-trip delay of a second or more) that conversation is stilted at best. However, Moondo and OnLive! Traveler point toward what will be possible as the quality of the Internet improves.

Faithful to their historical roots, the MUDs just previously discussed focus on practicality over features so that they can operate on inexpensive computers and the current Internet. This limits the extent to which they can be full-scale DVEs. However, because of

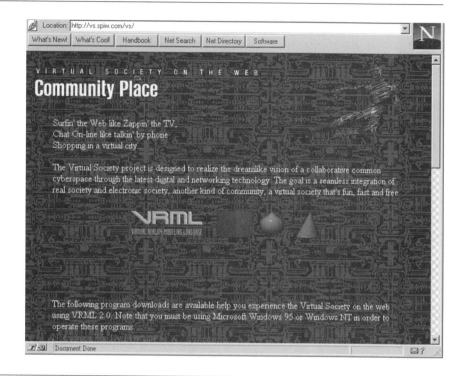

Figure 14.15 Community Place.

their low hardware demands, these MUDs are the closest thing to full-scale DVEs that are readily available to the general public.

Two additional developments in MUDs are particularly worthy of note. At the Xerox Palo Alto Research Center, a MUD called *Jupiter* has been created to explore the use of MUDs to support cooperative work. Jupiter is a MOO with support for live audio and video, but not 3-D graphics. Jupiter operates over a high-quality intranet between a small number of fixed sites. Each "room" in the Jupiter MUD can display slow-rate video of each of the participants in the room, much like a videoconferencing system, and share live audio between the participants.

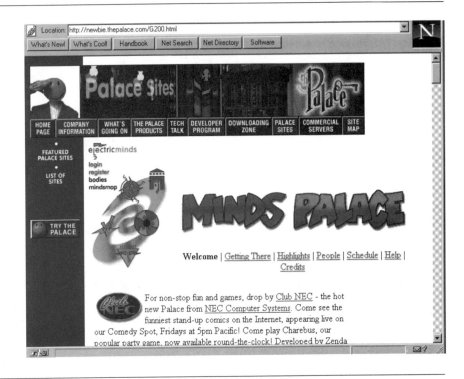

Figure 14.16 The Palace.

NTT Software's *CyberCampus* as shown in Figure 14.19,[19] combines 3-D graphics, limited video, and live sound. In CyberCampus, users can speak to each other and interact in a simple 3-D world featuring avatars with faces that are communicated by 2-Hz video. A particularly interesting feature of CyberCampus is that rather than using the Internet, video and audio is communicated over the phone network. Sending all the data relevant to a MUD over a single intranet is attractive; however, until the latency and reliability of the Internet improves markedly, the phone network may well be a better option for transmitting sound.

A final line of development is in the videogame industry. For a number of years, there have been multiplayer games in arcades.

Figure 14.17 Distributed Moo.

But these arcade games can only support a small number of users at one site through dedicated wires. The players can talk to each other only because they are sitting side by side.

Recently, more and more games are beginning to appear with remote multiplayer capabilities. Among the most popular are *Marathon* by Bungie Software Products Inc. (see Figure 14.20);[20] *Doom and Quake* from Id Software Inc. (see Figure 14.21);[21] and the *Warcraft* series and *Battle.net* by Blizzard Entertainment (see Figure 14.22).[22] These games typically allow a few players to interact in the same game space. This is typically supported using 28.8 modems either directly connected to a server or connected via the Internet. Sometimes, all the players can do is race each other or

Figure 14.18 OnLive! Traveler.

shoot at each other. However, sometimes the players can communicate using textual messages as in a standard MUD. It is interesting to note that by using a conference call in conjunction with a game, the players can achieve the effect of a much more powerful DVE. Special Internet service providers, such as Mpath Interactive Inc., Cupertino, California (see Figure 14.23), are emerging to provide low-latency multiuser interaction and audio communication specifically for use in Internet games.[23]

A key thing to bear in mind with videogames is that they have had a history of producing amazingly good graphics and background sound with very inexpensive hardware. If the game manufacturers focus on the addition of live audio and have anywhere near as

Figure 14.19 CyberCampus.

much success with it as they have had with graphics, they may have a very strong impact on DVEs.

Multiuser VR Applications

Until quite recently, *Virtual Reality* (VR) research has focused on single-user applications. However, research on multiuser

Figure 14.20 Marathon.

applications is growing rapidly. A key difference between this research and MUDs is that VR research focuses on features over practicality, using high-end graphics machines and special input devices to create higher-quality environments.

One line of development has been the extension of single-user VR toolkits to encompass multiuser operation. This is typified by the tools developed by Division Ltd. (http://www.division.com) and Sense8 Inc. (http://www.sense8.com). In the past, these tools have been limited to only a few simultaneous users because they relied on maintaining an exactly replicated database. In addition, support for live audio has been weak, requiring the use of separate phone connections. However, these tools are evolving rapidly with the goal of eliminating these problems.

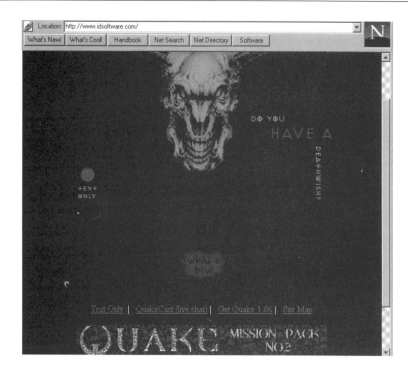

Figure 14.21 Quake.

A notable example of a system built from the ground up for multi-user VR is the Swedish Institute of Computer Science's *Distributed Interactive Virtual Environment* (DIVE) system as shown in Figure 14.24.[24] DIVE supports 3-D visual and audio worlds. Initially, DIVE was limited in its scalability because it relied on standard replicated database technology (see Chapter 23, *Other VR Research*). However, DIVE has recently been improved to the point where dozens of users can be supported over a local area network. Nevertheless, due to the high-bandwidth requirements of transmitting sound, only a few users can be supported over a wide area network.

Figure 14.22 Warcraft.

As previously discussed, in order to achieve a high degree of scalability, the *Scalable Platform for Large Interactive Networked Environments* (SPLINE) developed by Mitsubishi Electric's MERL research lab incorporates the approximate database replication idea that is the foundation of DIS. In addition, it adds flexible support for all kinds of audio and complete run-time extendibility. The first major use of SPLINE has been an application called Diamond Park as shown in Figure 14.25 and previously shown in Figure 14.1.[25]

For instance, SPLINE builds on the "approximate database replication" idea on which DIS is founded in order to scale the system to

Figure 14.23 Mpath Interactive Inc.

numerous users. The platform's design lets a world's content be ported to a wide variety of computer systems all at the same time. Also, the world can be changed and added to at run time.

Because they rely on high-end graphics hardware and relatively high-speed intranets, multiuser VR systems are not appropriate for use on current PCs over the Internet. Rather, they look forward a year or two to the point where PCs with plug-in graphics cards will be as powerful as current high-end graphics hardware, and the Internet will have lower latency and much greater capacity. MERL is currently implementing a revised version of SPLINE that will run on high-end PCs. In the short term, multiuser VR systems

Figure 14.24 A conferencing application built using DIVE.

are most suitable for specially tailored situations such as corporate intranets and location-based entertainment. As with VR in general, it is quite likely that location-based entertainment will be an early adopter of multiuser VR.

We are approaching a threshold where full-scale DVEs will become practical for widespread use. DVEs are so new that no one can say with any confidence what the most important use of DVEs will be. However, their significant success in the guise of MUDs

Figure 14.25 Diamond Park.

and military training systems suggests that there are many possibilities. The most important thing now is to let many flowers bloom (for a wide range of people to create many different kinds of DVEs). We will not have plumbed the depths of this new medium until many experiments have been tried and many have failed.

Communication standards are an essential underpinning of DVEs, because the whole idea is for lots of people to be able to interact with each other in many different DVEs. This cannot work if DVE clients and servers are divided into a multitude of competing camps that cannot communicate. However, standards must follow practice. For the immediate future, there must be many experiments and we must resist freezing standards until we are sure they can support real needs.

From Here

This chapter has shown how DVEs could enable individuals around the world to meet as never before in (somewhat) realistic digital settings with their "selves" represented as avatars—three-dimensional images under direct control. It has also discussed how many people can now share virtual environments simultaneously in a commercial reality.

Chapter 15 will describe how virtual worlds present programmers with unprecedented problems. It will also discuss how vendors will need a common platform customized for social interaction in order to develop a true mass market.

Endnotes

1 Waters, Richard C. and Barrus, John W. "Distributed Virtual Environments," MERL (Mitsubishi Electric Research Laboratory), Cambridge, MA (http://www.merl.com), 1996.

2 Ibid.

3 Ibid.

4 Ibid.

5 Ibid.

6 Ibid.

7 Ibid.

8 Ibid.

9 Ibid.

10 Ibid.

11 Ibid.

12 Ibid.

13 Black Sun Interactive, Inc., 50 Osgood Place, Suite 100, San Francisco, CA 94133.

14 Chaco Communications, Inc., 10164 Parkwood Dr., Suite 8, Cupertino, CA 95014-1533.

15 Sony Corporation, 550 Madison Ave., New York, NY 10022.

16 The Palace Inc., 9401 SW Nimbus Ave., Beaverton, OR 97008.

17 Intel Corporation, 2200 Mission College Blvd., Santa Clara, CA 95052-8119.

18 OnLive! Technologies, 10131 Bubb Road, Cupertino, CA 95014.

19 Nippon Telegraph and Telephone Corporation, San Francisco, CA and Japan.

20 Bungie Software Products Inc., 1925 S Halsted, Suite 204, Chicago IL 60608.

21 Id Software Inc., Mesquite, TX.

22 Blizzard Entertainment, P.O. Box 18979, Irvine, CA 92623.

23 Mpath Interactive Inc., 665 Clyde Ave. Mountain View, CA 94043.

24 Waters, Richard C. and Barrus, John W. "Distributed Virtual Environments," MERL (Mitsubishi Electric Research Laboratory), Cambridge, MA (http://www.merl.com), 1996.

25 Ibid.

Virtual Worlds for Social Interaction

Over the past decade, experimental work on distributed virtual environments has achieved some astonishing results. For the most part, this work has been exclusively in the province of military and major corporate R&D. Very recently, however, a more populist variety has emerged, in pursuit of quite a different kind of result. Developers of these new, low-cost variants have as their goal not ever-more realistic simulations of real-world situations, but a new technology for online social interaction.

Exploiting the emergence of the Internet as a platform for commercial applications are start-up ventures such as Black Sun Interactive, Chaco Communications, OnLive!, ParaGraph International, and OZ Virtual (see Figure 15.1 for an example of one of these start-up companies).[1] They are developing *distributed virtual environments* (DVEs) for the mass market—and attracting investment (and competition) from the likes of computing giants Fujitsu, IBM, Intel, Mitsubishi, Softbank, and Sony. The start-ups are insisting (and increasingly, demonstrating) that people from around the world can meet effectively and satisfyingly in virtual social settings ranging from interactive multiplayer adventures to international trade fairs. Quite suddenly, it seems that the infant technology of DVE is about to leave the sheltered garden of big-

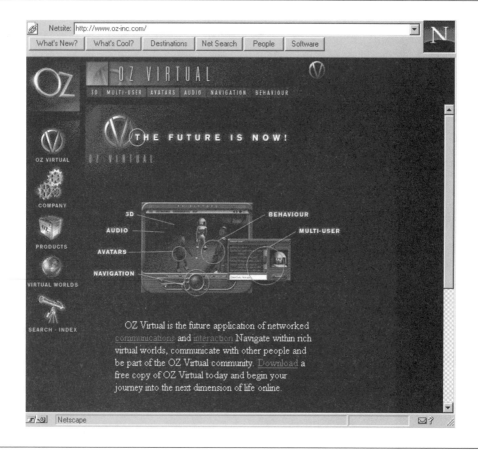

Figure 15.1 OZ Virtual.

budget R&D for the 50 million offices, hotels, and living rooms around the world with access to the Internet.[2]

Social Interaction

In the physical world, complex social interactions are usually made manageable by facilities, rules, and service providers that guide and support the participants. Consider what goes on at trade fairs, legislative hearings, conferences, and in shopping malls. People must get from one place to another, meeting rooms must be allocated, agendas prepared and results published, and the general logistics must be managed concerning who deals with whom—and where, when, and how those interactions take place. In situations where the facilities are inadequate or the rules are not codified, the services of tour guides and administrative assistants, brokers and agents, couriers, and consultants may supply the missing social structures.

In a virtual world (as the DVE applications themselves are often called), this kind of logistical support must be supplied by software. As the range of DVE applications expands, they will need software support of a kind rarely envisioned by previous generations of programmers. A new breed of programs is required: social software.

The overriding point of social software is not simulation but conversation. Its applications are not substitutes for real-world interaction, but extensions of it. Its worlds are not virtual in the customary sense; they are real media for meeting others on line. Designers of social software are less concerned with how well their on-screen objects mimic real-world objects than with how well they connect their users to each other.

Simulation environments can be thought of as being like the "preview" mode of a word processor, designed to match the look of a printed document. Social environments, by comparison, are like hypertext, opening up avenues of communication that were unforeseen in the media that preceded them.[3]

Mass-Market DVEs

The mass-market DVEs will be social software in another sense as well. Being complex assemblies of subtly interacting hardware and software, they will require the cooperation of an entire industry of component suppliers, subsystem integrators, testing and certification agencies, and upgrade and customization experts. And that's just on the manufacturing and supply side. No doubt product planning, marketing, sales, and customer care will require a similarly complex integration of providers.

Mass-market DVEs will support and require a small army of suppliers. In this aftermarket will be specialist firms to design and charge the real-world customers for virtual trade-fair booths and fantasy armor, online department store displays, virtual academy curricula, and fashion accessories for avatars.

Like small firms anywhere, each of these suppliers will satisfy its customers—and keep itself alive as a business—by focusing on particular problems, relying on a network of other suppliers to provide the rest of the structure into which they fit. Only when this kind of mature network of secondary and tertiary suppliers has been established will DVEs acquire the simplicity and flexibility needed to deliver valuable real-world services at mass-market prices.

The key technical prerequisite for achieving a mature market for components is what software engineers call a *common platform*—a set of basic software services and standard interfaces that enable independently developed programs to work together effectively. To borrow a term from city planning, what is needed is an infrastructure for social software.[4]

Mass-Market Technology Standards

If DVEs are to move from experiment to consumer service, the supplier of the technology must divide its many software and hardware functions into interchangeable components. Component-based production will lead to lower costs, and market forces will naturally lead to lower prices and wider distribution.

By definition, mass-market technology must be ubiquitous and low priced, which is why the new DVEs avoid special-purpose hardware. Instead, they use the standard monitors and mice of current mass-market personal computers. Users need not buy special computer displays or fancy goggles and data gloves (which help the simulation experience).

In the same way, the new DVE developers accept the fact that few users have dedicated high-performance network connections. Their products can be used with public Internet hookups and standard 14.4- or 28.8-kb/s telephone modems (the torrent of data in DVEs is discussed in Chapter 16, *Object Filtering Data Swamped Virtual Worlds*).

Initially, each of the pioneer DVE vendors found its own proprietary solution to the challenges of the consumer marketplace. But they are now cooperating on a set of common interfaces for DVE-based applications. These emerging standards are intended to encourage the emergence of a layered industry of DVE component suppliers and application developers.[5]

Common Languages Are Not Enough

Some may argue that the essential standards are already in place for developing consumer-grade DVEs on the Internet. The reigning browsers from Netscape Communications Corp., Mountain View, California, and Microsoft Corp., Redmond, Washington, support the new Virtual Reality Modeling Language (VRML) 2.0, which provides a basic vocabulary for describing the content of three-dimensional virtual scenes delivered over the Internet. VRML 2.0 (a.k.a. VRML97) is already well on its way to ISO standardization.

There is even broader support for Java, a language and set of run-time mechanisms for creating programs that grab whichever functional modules they need from the Internet. Introduced only a couple of years ago by Sun Microsystems Inc., Mountain View, California, Java seems slated to become the lingua franca for designing and sharing simple DVE application modules.

Nevertheless, agreeing to use common languages is just a beginning, analogous perhaps to agreeing on standards for the transmission and display of television images. As yet, there are no DVE equivalents for the huge array of creative, technical, and organizational structures that enable television programs, for instance, to be conceived, produced, distributed, and, of course, paid for.

VRML and Java provide a vocabulary and syntax for defining structures and behaviors in programs. But they provide no hint as to what constitutes a workable virtual environment, any more than special-purpose languages for database design and information retrieval contain instructions on how to run a warehouse or balance accounts. When people use languages to create something, be it sonnet or software, they need more than a vocabulary and a syntax. For capturing their thoughts in a recognizable form, they need models that are widely shared. The key word here is "recognizable": ideas captured in languages will be imprisoned unless their intended audience can interpret them correctly.[6]

Ensuring DVE Component Recognizability

Ensuring recognizability is especially critical in DVE applications, where components come together in what at times seems less like an engineered construct than a software cocktail party. Increasingly, DVE components will be designed and constructed by different authors—in most cases, even by different organizations. What's more, they will be written in different computer programming languages. No matter how quickly a consensus builds on the use of the Internet-specific languages VRML and Java, some DVE components no doubt will continue to be programmed in other languages, for reasons of efficiency, secrecy, or organizational inertia.

In addition, DVE components will not always operate under any central control. Internet applications are more than just distributed. Often they are wholly peer-to-peer, that is, they consist of connections among individual desktop systems, entered into and terminated at will, with no recourse to any central management facility. This situation makes it hard to apply the classical disciplines of software engineering to their design.

Conventional client-server applications are typically assembled by professional system integrators, organizations that carefully select application components for their mutual compatibility. Each one is then tested and tweaked as necessary until it operates correctly with all the other components. The new DVE applications are constructed more like the conversations they support: Within a generic framework, independently developed components will appear over the network, introduce themselves into the flow of the application for a while, and depart when they have done their job.

In daily operation, DVEs thus will involve continual negotiations among more or less autonomous, independently developed software objects, many of which will encounter each other for the first time only at run time. This unpredictability is compounded because these objects may invoke input from multiple third-party programs, or, even worse, from live users, who probably don't care about the run-time problems of the component designer (nor should they).[7]

When DVEs Converge

For existing DVE efforts to converge, a common infrastructure founded on VRML, Java, and some of the principles outlined here is vital. Working together, some of the early pioneers of the DVE community—among them Black Sun Interactive, ParaGraph

International, and Sony, along with over 30 other companies as supporters—are searching for an "open VRML" solution to the compatibility problem. Under the name Living Worlds (previously discussed in Chapter 9, *Living Worlds*), this initiative is seeking to exploit the extensibility features of VRML 2.0 in order to build an application framework for use with open, consumer-grade DVEs.

Of course, a VRML interface is only one part of what is needed. The work at Living Worlds dovetails nicely into the Open Communities proposal of several companies and researchers led by Mitsubishi Electric Research Laboratories, Cambridge, Massachusetts. Open Communities offers an application programming interface that is focused on world-to-world communication and is designed to be independent of whatever language is employed to implement the visualization of the community. The combined efforts of these groups represent the first steps toward a genuinely public infra-structure for cyberspace.[8]

Their shared theme is the establishment of real-world DVEs, where the goal is to make everyday social interactions possible across the Web. Their goal is not to simulate the physical world but to create a digital one no less real. Even if only a small part of that goal is achieved, the result will be not so much a new technology as a new place to be.

From Here

In this chapter we've discussed that in order to establish a true mass market for their social software, commercial DVE vendors must recognize that the old rules of programming just don't apply. The next chapter shows how the careful filtering of objects on a moment-by-moment basis, with networking schemes to match, can prevent virtual worlds from being swamped by their own data.

Endnotes

1 OZ Interactive (U.S. Headquarters), 525 Brannan Street, Suite 400, San Francisco, CA 94107.

2 Rockwell, Robert. "An Infrastructure for Social Software," IEEE SPECTRUM (March, 1997), p. 26.

3 Ibid.

4 Ibid., p. 27.

5 Ibid., p. 28.

6 Ibid.

7 Ibid.

8 Ibid., p. 31.

16

Object Filtering Data Swamped Virtual Worlds

One of the hottest topics in *Virtual Reality* (VR) research is the idea of *Distributed Virtual Environment* (DVE). Programmers and users of virtual worlds—when using DVEs—must fall back on base material with which to ply their craft. They must rely on the Distributed Virtual Environment and intranet software that can provide a simulated environment in which two or more participants interact with each other and with their surroundings. A lot of ideas about DVEs have been tossed around in various newsgroups and mailing lists; this chapter attempts to bring together some of the more interesting concepts and organize them in a way that's easy to follow. This chapter also attempts to gather and organize some ideas related to the idea of "behavior" in VR systems, particularly distributed (intranet) VR systems.

As discussed in Chapter 14, *Sharing Distributed Virtual Worlds*, and Chapter 15, *Virtual Worlds for Social Interaction*, the idea behind distributed VR is very simple: A simulated world runs not on one computer system but on several. The computers are connected over an intranet (possibly the global Internet) and people using those computers are able to interact in real time, sharing the same virtual world. In theory, people can be sitting at home in London, Paris, New York, and Edmonton, all interacting in a meaningful way in VR.

It's clear that there are a number of obstacles to be overcome in achieving this goal. The fact that we (as developers) want people to be able to access it from their homes means that we have to be able to run over relatively limited-bandwidth links, such as 28.8k modems. The fact that we want to run over the Internet means that we have to tolerate a certain amount of latency in the delivery of update information. Finally, the fact that people are running on different computer systems with different hardware and software means that we must design the system for portability.

The Naïve Approach to DVE

The simplest approach, and the one that some multiplayer computer game systems use, is to simply have each host broadcast the location of each entity that it maintains. These broadcasts are received by every host in the simulation, and are used to update their local copy of the *world database*.

The first networked version of the computer game *Doom* worked in a *broadcast* mode; each participant constantly broadcasted the current state of their *avatar*. Most multiplayer arcade games work the same way.

This approach works acceptably on small, dedicated intranets; however, there are a number of problems with it. The most important problem with broadcasting is that every machine on the subnet must receive and process every update packet; this includes machines that aren't participating in the simulation! That's not a problem on a dedicated LAN, but intranets that are being used for other things can't have huge amounts of broadcast traffic on them; this is why so many companies and universities adopted a *no network DOOM* policy. DOOM, incidentally, switched to point-to-point messages for subsequent releases in order to be more friendly to nondedicated intranets.

The other problem is that simply broadcasting your current location and orientation requires a lot of bandwidth, since those (potentially) change every time through your simulation loop. When you're dealing with a large number of entities and limited bandwidth, the system just stops working.

In short, the naïve approach doesn't scale up. What about a technological approach?

The Technological Approach to DVE

In working with DVE and intranet software, programmers and users face great technological problems. The biggest of these problems are: managing the enormous data loads involved; negotiating the interplay of all the virtual objects, including the virtual people; and creating the most-efficient intranet topologies possible for users' machines. Each occupant of a DVE system uses a computer that is connected to a local- or wide-area network (LAN or WAN) at the intranet level. At this level, information is provided on the changing state of the virtual environment and its contents. In DVE jargon, each of the computers participating in the simulation is called a *host*. On each host there are a number of *entities* (things in the virtual environment) that communicate their changing state by sending *update messages*. The specific entity that corresponds to a human participant's virtual body is called an *avatar*. Sometimes entities operate relatively autonomously, in which case they are commonly known as *agents* or *bots* (from *robots*) For an example of this, let's look at Figure 16.1.

In other words, an entity is any object in a virtual world that can change its state in some way. The scene in Figure 16.1 is inhabited by the basic entity types: avatars, controlled by real people; autonomous entities, or agents, controlled to a greater or lesser extent by software alone; and, static entities, which are part of the scene design.[1]

Thus, *dynamic state*, or *dynamic state vector*, is the collection of information that describes an entity in full. For instance, the state of an object is considered to be its current location and orientation. In addition, the state of an object can also be its color, size, and any other property that is subject to change over time.

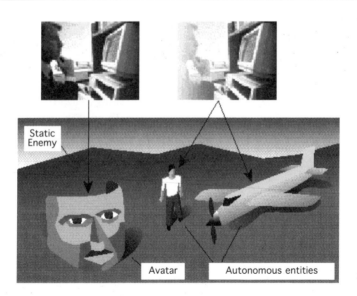

Figure 16.1 Autonomous agents.

Data Timing and Spacing

The mediation of the exchange of an entity's dynamic state information among hosts on the intranet is the job of a DVE system. State changes must be communicated to other hosts on the intranet as soon as they are invoked by a user on another system (such as making an avatar open a door). This *updating* allows hosts/users to have a consistent view of the world. In other words, when a user opens a particular door, all of the others with an unobstructed view should see it open.

In order to convey the current state of the entities in the system, a DVE system will typically send packets of information over an intranet. For instance, the system might send out a packet containing data about a door's angle of rotation around its hinge when the door starts to open. So that a DVE system could update the door's degree of rotation in the virtual world it is presenting to its users, the information would have to be received on all the other systems.

Now let's look at how others are solving DVE system problems.

How Have Other People Solved These Problems?

In designing a standard for representing scene geometry, the VRML Consortium (discussed in Chapter 8) chose to use a subset of an existing format as their jumping-off point, rather than create yet another new format. This approach has worked well; maybe users and developers can do the same thing in selecting standards for distributed VR?

The largest, best-known, and most successful standard for distributed VR has been the *Distributed Interactive Simulation* (DIS) protocol. As its name suggests, it addresses the very issues developers and users are concerned about. Perhaps they could simply adopt it, and declare their task complete?

Well, as it turns out, it's not quite that simple. DIS, like its predecessor SIMNET, is designed for a very specific application domain: military simulations. As developers and users will tell you, it's extremely well-optimized for that application, but is not an ideal choice for their needs. However, they can benefit from a lot of the work done on DIS; the military designers have already encountered and dealt with a lot of the same challenges developers will be facing in designing a distributed VR standard. More information about DIS in military simulations is available in Chapter 17, *Virtual Battlefields*.

The Basic Ideas of DIS—PDUs and Dead Reckoning

As mentioned earlier, among the key challenges in implementing a DVE system are maintaining a virtual world consistent (compatibility) for all its inhabitants, dealing with limited intranet communications bandwidth, and working with high and variable latency (delay in sending messages).

DIS addresses the first of these problems, compatibility, by defining a standard message format for interchanging information between simulation hosts. This standard format is called a *Protocol Data Unit* (PDU). There are many different types of PDUs, most of which (like requests for resupply of munitions) are not applicable to a developer's needs. However, one of the formats, the *Entity State PDU* (ESPDU), contains information very similar to what developers and users need to send between hosts.

The second and third problems, limited bandwidth and update latency, are dealt with in DIS using a technique called *dead reckoning*, which was pioneered in the 1980s in the U.S. Army's Simulation Networking (SIMNET) protocol. SIMNET has been extended into the *Distributed Interactive Simulation* (DIS) protocol and, more recently, the *High-Level Architecture* (HLA) protocol (see Chapter 17, *Virtual Battlefields*).

The idea behind dead reckoning is simple: Instead of just sending an entity's location, a host sends a message (an ESPDU) that contains the entity's location, a timestamp, and a velocity vector. Using that information, each host in the intranet can then extrapolate the entity's location without additional updates. This can be done for entity orientation as well as location.

Each entity runs its own full-up simulation, and also runs the simple dead-reckoning model for itself. It keeps track of the actual location predicted by the two models; when they diverge by more than a certain amount, it sends out another update to bring everyone's model of the entity back in line with what the entity is actually doing.

In addition, each entity sends out periodic update messages (say once every five seconds or so) that act as *keep-alives*. These keep-alives actually serve three purposes: If someone enters the simulation after it's started, they'll get caught up with every entity's state within a few seconds. If update messages get missed for any reason, the system recovers gracefully; within a few seconds, a new update message will arrive and bring the host up to date. If no updates are received from an entity within a certain period of time, the other hosts on the intranet can assume the entity is no longer around.

Dead reckoning produces impressive results. Since updates are sent only when needed, the amount of traffic is greatly reduced. The system works particularly well for the problem domain it's designed for: military simulation. Since every entity is either a vehicle or projectile, the dead-reckoning approach works nicely.

Limitations of DIS

However, a more general distributed VR system doesn't work nearly as well with standard DIS. Let's say we want to simulate a park; we want to have birds fluttering around overhead, squirrels foraging for nuts, and so on. Despite the fact that birds do occupy airspace, their behavior is surprisingly unlike that of a jet-fighter aircraft. And despite the fact that squirrels are land-based, they're not very much like tanks.

Perhaps more importantly, people don't move anything like vehicles, nor do they behave like projectiles (unless you fire them out of a cannon, which is an exceptional case). People are considered to be more like dismounted infantry. Here, information is sent about their configuration: Small packets of information giving the rotation angles of each limb are sent as part of the PDU.

This works well, but is (by design) highly anthropomorphic. The packet format actually stores information about the rotation of each hip joint; it has no provision for body configurations other than human. In terms of our park example, the data structures they propose make no provision for a bird's wings or a squirrel's big fluffy tail. Treating birds and squirrels as *dismounted infantry* isn't really the best approach.

This is not meant as a criticism of the work done on dismounted infantry or the *Dismounted Infantry Virtual Environment* (DIVE) system; it's certainly better than the standard DIS approach that would require us to treat each of the squirrel's legs as a tiny gun turret! See Chapter 17, *Virtual Battlefields*, and Chapter 23, *Other VR Research*, for in-depth discussions about the DIVE system—specially designed gateways to instrumented rooms or chambers that allow soldiers to immerse themselves in a virtual environment.

Transmitting Vectors and Packets

Designing a DVE system with no concern for bandwidth or latency is relatively easy. The entire state vector from each entity would be transmitted. Packets containing this set of values would be sent at an update rate sufficient to provide visual realism. Currently, DVEs used with home modems provide a fairly jerky frame rate of 4 to 10 frames a second.

In reality, even with a modest number of users, bandwidth would quickly run out. For example, suppose that a toy airplane is flying around a room under the control of a user. An update for the plane would include its current location in x, y, and z coordinates. Each of the coordinates might be a 4-byte, floating-point number, making 12 bytes in total.

Another example (for another 12 bytes) would be a set of three floating-point numbers for the orientation of the airplane around the x, y, and z axes. Also, by adding on another 4 bytes, requires some kind of identification in order to distinguish the airplane from other entities.

So, per state vector, that adds up to a total of 28 bytes. However, the total jumps to 840 bytes per second (not including any overhead imposed by the lower-level intranet protocols) if each vector is sent 30 times per second. Therefore, the total bandwidth requirement is 5040 bytes per second, or roughly 50 kilobaud (10 bits sent for each byte), with just half a dozen such entities in the world at once. This is more than twice the data rate of the fastest modem most people have today.

The need for bandwidth goes up as more entities arrive in the simulated world. Also, as the complexity of the entities grows, bandwidth increases even faster. For instance, the update packets might double or triple in size (with a corresponding increase in the necessary bandwidth) if the airplane had movable wing surfaces. Nevertheless, a call for even more bandwidth may be needed, if various sounds are incorporated in these environments (but see Chapter 18, *Virtual Acoustics*).

Bandwidth Compression

Bandwidth requirements can be reduced by using *compression* when streaming media such as audio or video are sent. For example, *video compression* takes advantage of the fact that one frame changes very little from its neighbor. This makes it possible to send only the differences between the frames.

The bandwidth required for DVEs can be reduced, however, through a related approach. Here, the whole idea is to take advantage of the similarity of the current state of an entity to its previous state. Given the predictability of events though, many data packets are more or less *superfluous*.

For instance, consider a virtual ball rolling across a pool table using a DVE protocol with continuous updates as shown in Figure 16.2.[2] Initially, what are known are the coordinates, speed, and direction of the ball. Here, the equations of motion are stored. They're probably stored at the host.

Vastly different data loads impose different DVE techniques or vice versa. In other words, all interested parties are made aware of the initial coordinates and starting time of the ball entity on a pool table with regard to continuous updates. Thus, the system calculates the path for the ball once the force of the pool cue is applied. The simulation update rate is also taken into account by the computer. In addition, the entity sends out a packet giving its coordinates at every clock tick of that rate.

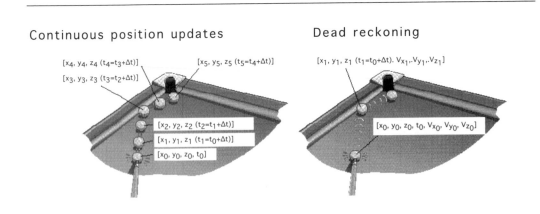

Continuous position updates

$[x_4, y_4, z_4 \ (t_4=t_3+\Delta t)]$

$[x_3, y_3, z_3 \ (t_3=t_2+\Delta t)]$

$[x_5, y_5, z_5 \ (t_5=t_4+\Delta t)]$

$[x_2, y_2, z_2 \ (t_2=t_1+\Delta t)]$

$[x_1, y_1, z_1 \ (t_1=t_0+\Delta t)]$

$[x_0, y_0, z_0, t_0]$

Dead reckoning

$[x_1, y_1, z_1 \ (t_1=t_0+\Delta t). \ V_{x_1}, V_{y_1}, V_{z_1}]$

$[x_0, y_0, z_0, t_0, V_{x_0}, V_{y_0}, V_{z_0}]$

Figure 16.2 DVE protocol with continuous updates.

The ball does receive an initial impetus, even though it is not guided by the user. The equations are applied to the pool-ball entity. Its final position is then calculated. Calculations of where the ball should appear at each moment are made by the software. The entity is then sent on its way. Finally, at each clock tick of the simulation, the pool ball entity sends out a packet giving its location.

Nevertheless, the behavior of an entity is predictable in many cases. Few entities change state continuously. Even then they tend to behave fairly consistently.[3] The path is easily extrapolated in the pool-ball example. Unless some other event affects it, a change is not likely. Thus, the equations of motion are simple. That raises a couple of questions though: Couldn't any other entity, if it wanted to, figure out where the pool-ball entity is and what it's doing? Why does the pool-ball entity have to keep sending updates about its location?

The answer to both questions is that it doesn't have to. Rather, some DVEs make use of *dead reckoning*.

DIS includes not only position, but velocity and rotational velocity as well when it transmits entity state information. Thus, only one packet would be required for a roll of a pool ball. A determination by all the hosts of the ball's location and orientation at any point in the future (until it reached the edge of the table or hit another ball as shown in Figure 16.2) could then be made.

However, a far more efficient method is to use dead reckoning as shown in Figure 16.2 when the trajectories of an entity are fairly predictable, as these are. Here the velocity (V) in each spatial dimension is given, as well as the initial coordinates. Fewer packets need be sent at this point. Thus, the other entities can infer the information by examining the original packet and performing the calculations, especially when they need to know the location and heading of the ball.

The decision-making for a particular entity is usually the responsibility of one specific host somewhere in the intranet. One computer controls the plane in the case of the toy airplane. That computer is operated by one person. Thus, the relationship of the thing being controlled and the human controller can be thought of as a relationship between *pilot* (human) and *drone* (entity). Guided entirely by dead reckoning based on updates received from the pilot, most of the machines in the DVE intranet will have only a drone version of the airplane.

Every aspect of the aircraft's flight is run by the flight simulation algorithm operated by the pilot host for the plane. Whether the input is by joystick, mouse, or whatever, the plane runs in response to its (human) controller's wishes. The simpler dead-reckoning algorithm is also handled by the same host.

A new update is sent out to all the drones on other people's machines only when the results of the two algorithms differ by more than a certain threshold value. Actually, the entity periodically sends out updates on its own status to let the system know that it is still around, even if there is no divergence. These updates are engagingly known as *heartbeats* or *keep-alives*. In crowded environments, even the constant throb of heartbeats can seriously clog the intranet. Dead reckoning not only makes the system less vulnerable to latency, but also saves bandwidth. For example, the timestamp can be used to compute the current position of the ball on the table if the pool ball's packet arrives late, especially since every update message is marked with the time it was sent.

Beyond Bandwidth Compression

Dead reckoning by itself, even when supplemented by anthropomorphic joint information, isn't enough. Does that mean we should be looking for a completely different approach? Not necessarily.

After a little thought, it becomes clear that dead reckoning is just a special case of a more general idea: Instead of sending location and orientation updates, we should be sending updates about an entity's *behavior*. In a sense, we're generalizing dead reckoning, and extending it to meet our needs.

The update messages an entity sends out will specify a "behavior" and some behavior parameters; the dead-reckoning approach then becomes just one of a repertoire of behaviors, which might be arbitrarily complex. In the case of the dead-reckoning behavior, the parameters are the initial time, initial location, and initial velocity vector (direction and magnitude).

The set of behaviors available to an entity should be extensible, so that developers and users don't have to anticipate every possible behavior ahead of time. The behavior scripts are complex enough that they don't want to try to squeeze them into their equivalent of a PDU; instead, they want them to be distributed in much the same way that geometry or texture-map information is.

Clearly, we need a standard way of describing behavior. More on this next.

From Velocity Vectors to High-Level Behaviors

Sending higher- (rather than lower-) level behavior information is in essence a special case of a more general technique known as dead reckoning. In other words, with regards to dead reckoning, the higher-level information is the entity's velocity vector. The lower-level information, on the other hand, is the result of the equations of motion employing that vector. Originally, if you recall, this technique was used in the combat simulation example. Velocity vectors are usually fine for simple trajectories. However, for more subtle forms of interaction (particularly with jointed entities like people), it is possible to define other high-level behaviors, such as walking, jumping, or dancing.

For instance, suppose an avatar walks across a room. Initially, the avatar might send a packet of information marked *walk*. This packet gives its starting location, start time, and velocity vector. Here the host is equipped with knowledge of how joints, bones, and muscles move in relation to one another (an active area of research, by the way).

This packet of information is inferred by, and simulated on, all the other machines in the DVE that base their calculations on the *walk* message and the location and orientation of the avatar. This is in sharp contrast, however, to having the host send a list of joint angles (to describe the motion of the avatar's arms and legs). A method of this type is kind of like data compression. In order to transmit less data, the packet exploits prior knowledge of the entity's hierarchical structure (feet attached to calves, calves to thighs, thighs to pelvis, and so on). Sending the x, y, or z location of each foot is not necessary because it can be computed from the known lengths of the body segments and joint angles.

Also note that this DVE software design is strongly object oriented. This approach tends to be cleaner and easier to maintain. In other words, each entity is an object to which messages are sent. In addition, each class of entity is able to respond to messages via a repertoire of behaviors.

The entity itself is designed at the same time that the entity's repertoire is created. As a general guideline, however, there should be nothing preventing other behaviors from being added, from hopping and waving the arms to tap dancing.[4]

A Consistent Representation of the World

Maintaining a consistent view of the world on all the different hosts is one of the trickiest tasks in designing a DVE system. So, who *wins* if multiple users try to interact with the same entity at the same time?

In order to solve this problem, a number of approaches can be used. The simplest way is to use the real-life social protocols everyone is familiar with. Users of a DVE usually stay aware of what other users are doing. DVE users are also very polite and allow other users to go ahead. No one else interferes, especially if someone indicates that he or she is going to open a door. In most situations, this arrangement works fine. However, there are some application areas in which users cannot be relied upon to follow this sort of protocol. Combat simulations or online gaming for instance, would be a couple of examples where this protocol could not be used—nor would anyone want them to be.

Nevertheless, with other approaches, the software negotiates conflicts. Arbitration with regard to access could come from the entity itself. For example, a user wanting to pick up a suitcase sends it a message. The suitcase agrees to respond. However, if multiple users grab for the suitcase simultaneously, the suitcase itself decides who got there first.

Even though this approach works well, it can slow down the whole system. In other words, if a user wants to carry the suitcase across the room, she or he needs to constantly get its permission. For instance, there will be an annoying half-second of delay whenever the entity is manipulated. This happens if it takes 250 milliseconds for a message to get from the user to the suitcase entity, and another 250 ms for a response to come back.

Locking is another approach. For example, if an object is picked up by a user, the object announces to anyone else attempting to manipulate it that it is *locked* by that user. Change must come from its owner/user. This causes the object to change state in any way (be moved or recolored, say).

Since the entity would in effect be *orphaned* if a user abruptly goes off line without releasing the lock, difficulties with locking could arise. One solution to this problem is to have the entity's user/owner periodically send packets. These packets of information would verify to the locked entity that its owner is still there and in control. The entity unlocks itself, however, especially if these packets are not received.

Attachment is still another technique. Here, an entity announces that it is *attached* to the user if a user picks up the entity. The entity retains control over itself. It also may detach itself from the user at any time. The entity's position and orientation, however, are all relative to the user. So, carrying the object across the room does not add to intranet traffic.

Update Filtering

The technique of sending just higher-level behaviors is still not enough to allow for the data that must be passed around, although it does use less bandwidth.[5] Hundreds or thousands of active entities are contained in a large-scale DVE. Thus, the available bandwidth will be quickly exhausted if each entity sends out a packet only every couple of seconds.

For instance, the packet still ends up 32 bytes long, even if each update message contains the x, y, and z coordinates to which an object is moving, as well as the rotation around x, y, and z axes; a timestamp giving the desired arrival time; and, a 4-byte identifier. Thus, the bandwidth averages out to 16 bytes per second per entity, even if a packet is sent only every other second. That means the available 28.8-kilobaud data rate is again exceeded, especially if there are a couple of hundred entities.

Useless information can be filtered out of the update stream for further reductions of data. Calculating the distance that a user could *see* is one filtering technique. Thus, an entity's status to a user's avatar need not be sent if it is beyond that (simulated) distance.

Note: A *far-away* entity cannot stop sending packets. However, it may still be perfectly visible to other entities, as shown in Figure 16.3.[6] So, what must be done between each pair of entities is to calculate whether entities are in range of each other, and if so, whether they are visible. This example uses models of human vision and visible light. However, the same principle would equally apply with different parameters: in a military DVE to an infrared seeker, or in a gaming DVE to a Superman that sees through walls. The technique bears some relation to what in computer graphics research is known as *level-of-detail* (LOD). LOD refers to the number of polygons representing an object (the amount of detail), which varies with the viewer's position.

In other words, many DVEs use filtering techniques to analyze the relevance of data before passing it on in order to contain the flood of data packets. The system of one type of *distance-based filtering* calculates on the basis of stored information of whether a particular entity will be in view. From Amy's point of view (deduced from real-world experience) as shown in Figure 16.3, data packets are exchanged between her and everyone but David (who is too far away for her to see). However, the calculations must be performed for each pair of entities; thus, David is still very much an active entity. He still sends packets to people he can *see*.

The simplest filtering technique of this kind is based on distance. An entity's actions are not currently relevant to the user, especially if the ratio of an entity's size to its distance from the user is less

Distance Filtering

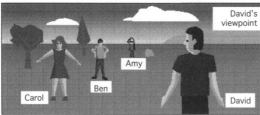

Figure 16.3 Distance-based filtering.

than some predetermined threshold value. For example, it becomes unnecessary for a user to send a bird's update packets down the wire if the bird is in flight 20 kilometers away and cannot be seen.

Some other entities may be obscured by the presence of certain environmental effects (fog or clouds) in the modeling software, or by fixed features in the environment. For example, updates for such entities would not be sent to the user's machine if a technique known as *occlusion filtering* is used. Occlusion filtering would use up precious bandwidth and processing cycles.

Spatial subdivision for instance, is used in another form of relevance filtering. The virtual environment can be divided into zones. Zone-to-zone visibility can be precomputed. Suppose an avatar is in the bedroom of its virtual home. The avatar will thus be unable to see anything in the kitchen, garage, or den. If the DVE system is aware of this, it will not send it any updates for entities contained entirely in those regions. Sound occlusion is not so clear cut a process because the user may be able to hear events in the kitchen, as shown in Figure 16.4.[7]

In other words, another way to lessen the amount of data flowing through a distributed virtual environment is by using occlusion fil-

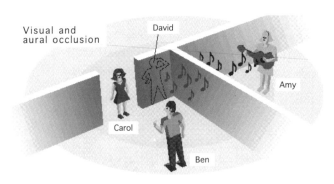

Figure 16.4 Optical and sound occlusion.

tering. It builds on the fact that people ordinarily cannot clearly hear or see through solid objects. When a host computer analyzes the location of the walls and the position of the figures, it notes that David, like Amy, is visually cut off from everyone else. So the two do not need to send visual data at all. On the other hand, Ben and Carol need to send visual data only between themselves. Occasionally, David does send *keep-alives*, data sent to the system signaling that he is still in the scene. Amy sends sonic data packets to all.

Distance-based filtering is useful for outdoor environments for the most part. Occlusion-based filtering, on the other hand, is useful for indoor ones.

System Decentralization

In DVE design, choosing the high-level intranet protocol is important—on any kind of intranet, and not just the Internet. The choice is between a connection-oriented approach (such as *Transmission Control Protocol* (TCP)), or a connectionless approach, such as *User Datagram Protocol* (UDP) (see the sidebar "A Brief Digression: TCP/IP"). At the cost of high latency, TCP provides guaranteed packet transmission. However, in order to ensure that none of the hosts lacks crucial information with UDP, state information must be re-sent periodically. Each has its pros and cons. And, most DVEs use some combination of connection-oriented (TCP-like) and connectionless (UDP-like) protocols.

Why Broadcasting Doesn't Scale

The broadcast approach works for DIS because it has its own dedicated intranet. Unlike DOOM though, there's no need to be concerned about the broadcast activity playing havoc with other users of the intranet.

However, the broadcast approach still doesn't scale. Even with dead reckoning, the problem of limited bandwidth is still there; as the number of entities grows larger, the slower-speed links become

A Brief Digression: TCP/IP

As mentioned earlier, broadcasting update messages is a bad idea. In order to understand the alternatives, it's worth taking a quick look at the underlying intranet infrastructure that's available to us.

The Internet is based around a family of protocols called *TCP/IP*. The *IP* (Internet Protocol) part is the lowest level; it handles addressing and routing. IP packets can be sent over Ethernet, fiber optics, telephone lines, radio links, tin cans and string, or any other medium that can move bits.

Above IP are two other protocols: *TCP* and *UDP*. *TCP* (Transmission Control Protocol) provides a connection-oriented, reliable byte-stream form of communication. Applications can use TCP to open a logical connection to another host on the Internet, send data down that connection, and receive data back. TCP handles the complex chores of breaking the stream of data into smaller pieces, doing checksums on the data to make sure it arrives intact, sorting the packets as they arrive to make sure they're in the correct order, requesting retransmission when needed, handling flow control, and lots more. TCP uses IP to actually move the packets to other hosts.

TCP is the protocol on which most Internet applications run. The Web uses *Hypertext Transport Protocol* (HTTP), which runs over TCP; when you click on a link, a connection is opened to another host using TCP, the URL is sent down the wire, the data is received back and the connection is closed. Similar techniques are used for Finger, SMTP (electronic mail), and NNTP (USENET news). In all cases, the hard parts are handled transparently by TCP.

User Datagram Protocol (UDP) is quite different from TCP. It provides a connectionless, unreliable way of sending *datagrams* from one host to another. The word *unreliable* in this context doesn't mean that UDP is somehow flakey or error prone; it just means that there's no guarantee that a specific packet will arrive. However, if a packet *does* arrive, it will arrive intact. UDP is used by Network File System (NFS), Network Time Protocol (NTP), and several others.

There are some important advantages in using UDP instead of TCP. The problem with TCP lies in its strengths. The fact that it does all kinds of flow control, error checking, and sequencing means that it has a fair amount of overhead; this translates into *lag*, which is one of our enemies.

UDP packets are relatively *lightweight*. Although they get lost occasionally, there'll never be any congestion; they won't clog things up, they'll just be discarded. Also, unlike TCP, UDP packets can be broadcasted on subnets (since there's no *logical connection* involved).

However, because UDP is *unreliable*, it requires the use of *stateless* protocols; in other words, each message must be complete and self-contained, and make no assumptions about previous messages having been received. NFS is an example of a stateless protocol; so is DIS.

DIS uses UDP broadcast packets to send its PDUs to other hosts. Each ESPDU has the complete state of the entity, and they're rebroadcast every few seconds (or more often, if the entity determines that more frequent updates are needed).[8]

saturated. Even if bandwidth weren't an issue, the processing of updates for a large number of entities begins to exceed the capacity of the slower hosts, especially since they must also do all the rendering, input device processing, and so on.

The designers of DIS are well aware of these problems, and they're looking at solutions. The central idea, common to DIS and many other approaches as well, is the use *of update filtering* (as previously discussed).

The basic idea is again very simple. The virtual world is divided up into a large number of *cells*, much like the way the cellular telephone system works. These cells are used as the basis for filtering update messages.

Each host participating in the simulation determines an *Area of Interest* (AOI), consisting of a number of cells within its range of vision. Here the cells are hexagonal, somewhat like a strategy board game or certain types of military simulation computer games. This hex grid is well-suited to military simulations, and is a closer model for circular Areas of Interest than a square grid would be.

As a participant moves around, cells will enter and leave their Area of Interest; at any given time, they're only receiving updates for cells they can see, resulting in a small, manageable number of updates. The combination of AOI filtering and dead reckoning produces significant bandwidth savings.

Now clearly, hexagonal grid cells are better-suited for military simulations than for real-world VR. The cells (perhaps better described as *zones*) wouldn't necessarily be hexagonal grid cells; they would probably be defined by other criteria. For example, a virtual mansion might be divided up into a large number of rooms, each of which would be its own zone. Since no regular grid would be used, there would need to be some way to specify zone-to-zone visibility (as previously discussed).

Other than that, the basic idea is sound. Just as the idea of dead reckoning has been extended to the more general concept of behavior, extending the idea of update filtering from hexagonal grid cells to arbitrarily-shaped volumes of space is just as sound.

Intranet Topology

The topology the intranet uses is another cardinal aspect of DVE design. Thus, a naive intranet might have a single central server to which all the client hosts connect. As shown in Figure 16.5, the server at the hub would relay packets between hosts and doing relevance filtering as needed.[9]

In other words, as the number of users (hosts) steadily increases, a simple intranet with a central server would probably fail as shown

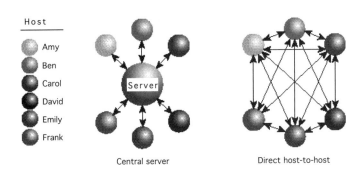

Figure 16.5 Intranet topology.

in Figure 16.5. So, even if unlimited power were available, the bandwidth would be saturated, and the processing power of the server would be unable to handle the load.

Such a system works fine for toy worlds with a couple of dozen participants. Clearly though, that world will not scale up. The central host will become overburdened as the number of simultaneous users rises. The reason for this is because more memory and *Central Processing Unit* (CPU) cycles would be needed to cope with the additional entities.

Using a more powerful computer for the central host is possible; however, the available computing power will never increase as rapidly as the peak number of simultaneous users does. Thus, the central server will no longer be able to handle the load. The sheer volume of data flowing into the hub will unfortunately start to saturate the available bandwidth, even if unlimited quantities of memory and boundless CPU power were available.

Nevertheless, the establishment of a direct TCP connection that links every host to every other host is an alternative approach. It eliminates the need for a central server as shown in Figure 16.5.

But a new problem arises: Each host must send every update n–1 times (once for each of the other n hosts it's connected to in the simulation). This setup also does not scale, the reason being that sending the same update message several times is a waste of bandwidth.

However, all of this has led to another new problem: an alternative configuration that eliminates the central server as shown in Figure 16.5. Here there exists a direct connection between each of the hosts. Nevertheless, the connections are clogged with duplicates (and much of the bandwidth is wasted), since each update must be sent n–1 times (where n is the number of hosts).

The direction this technology takes will be determined by market considerations and not solely by technical criteria. Many commercial DVE firms are creating server-oriented systems in spite of the technical advantages of decentralized, highly distributed virtual environments. The reason is simple: Their business model is based on giving away the client (host) software to users. It's also based on selling the server software to those who want to create their own DVEs. In other words, DVE firms have no revenue-producing product, unless they have large central servers for their clients to connect to.

Still, there may well be ways of generating revenue from a fully distributed virtual environment. The World Wide Web is entirely decentralized after all, yet it remains to be seen whether a decentralized or centralized approach becomes prevalent.

Multicasting

Given that users want to filter messages, what mechanism should they use for doing so? The DIS system uses *multicasting*, and that approach seems promising for more general distributed VR applications as well.

Multicasting is an attempt to have the best of two worlds: broadcasting and point-to-point links. The idea is that any given host, in addition to having its own Internet address, can belong to a number of *multicast groups*. Each multicast group has its own special Internet address; IP addresses in a certain range have been set aside for this purpose. When any host sends a message to a multicast address, that message is sent to all the hosts that belong to that multicast group. In effect, it's like broadcasting to a subnet that spans continents.

Sending a multicast message is better than having to send point-to-point messages to every host in the simulation, so it's easier on the sender. Hosts that aren't in a particular multicast group will ignore the packet at a very low level, with minimal overhead; this makes it easier on every host on the intranet.

Multicasting has a number of other pluses. It scales well, requires no central host, and has no need for a host to send an update packet more than once.

Perhaps most importantly, it also maps well to occlusion-based filtering, as described earlier. Here, each occlusion zone (comprising a set of entities in virtual contact with each other) corresponds to a multicast group address created on the fly whenever it changes. As shown in Figure 16.6, a host joins or leaves only those multicast groups that contain data based on which subsets of the overall environment it can see.[10]

In other words, multicasting is an efficient protocol for DVEs. This is because only the data needed for particular hosts at any one time are made commonly available to those hosts. The data are sent by way of an Internet group address. The address is created on the fly by the system software as the data needs of the users change. At this moment (also depicted in Figure 16.4), Ben and Carol are in sight of each other but no one else, and both can hear Amy's music; the three hosts need to send visual and sonic data packets to each other only, doing so by way of an Internet group address 1.

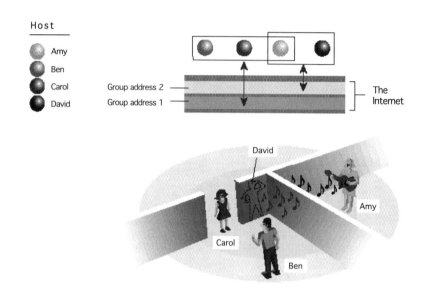

Figure 16. 6 Multicast groups.

Concurrently, although he is visually occluded from everyone, David can hear Amy's guitar. The specific data necessary for just these two users are made mutually available by way of Internet group address 2.

There are some problems with multicasting however; the most important is that it's not universally implemented. Some systems have it, some don't. An effort is underway to link small pockets of multicast-capable machines to each other over the Internet; the result is a *multicast backbone* or *MBONE*. The MBONE system uses *tunneling*; it wraps the IP packets destined for a multicast address inside of another IP packet, which travels through the regular Internet from one MBONE subnet to another.

Multicasting and Zones

How does multicasting fit in with Area of Interest management? In the DIS system, each cell has its own multicast group address; in other words, there's a one-to-one correspondence between cells and multicast addresses.

As participants move around, they enter and leave cells; this corresponds to entering and leaving multicast groups. Since participants only receive messages for multicast groups they're in, the multicast system itself does our message filtering for us.

The implementation of multicasting for DIS also does away with the *keep-alive* messages, which (according to their figures) account for a high percentage of the total traffic. Instead, a *group leader* is chosen for every group (cell); the group leader is the simulation host that has been in the cell the longest. When a host first enters a cell, it sends a message to the multicast address for that cell asking the group leader to identify itself. The response is a message informing the newly arrived host where they might obtain the complete current set of Entity State PDUs for this zone. The newcomer then requests and receives that set.

Another, simpler approach might be to send an *identify yourself* message to the multicast address. Here, all the hosts would respond by sending their most recent update message, and perhaps (in the absence of any kind of *registry*) a message containing the URI of a file containing more detailed information about them.

Multicasting is not the only approach to filtering, a *hybrid system* that is the basis of the next discussion is another one. Nevertheless, multicasting is a good one; it doesn't involve any higher-level functionality to do the filtering, and therefore imposes minimal overhead.

A Hybrid System

An intranet approach that has undergone a good deal of research and looks promising is a *hybrid system*. As shown in Figure 16.7, users would connect to a DVE server, which would handle relevance filtering and similar chores.[11] Each DVE server would be connected to other DVE servers using multicasting in this particular setup. In order to ensure compatibility among various systems, these servers would guarantee that the software running in the client machine neither knows nor cares what technology is being used between servers, All of the clients need not have the same local networking technology. Some users could connect to the server through dial-up modems, others might use direct *Integrated Services Digital Network* (ISDN) connections.

In other words, direct host-to-host intranet topologies and the central server are combined. In this case, DVE servers themselves are considered hosts. The example shown here depicts the DVE servers scattered around the world as being directly connected by multicasting (only two multicast data highways are shown for simplicity). In order to lessen the number of hops the connections must make, each user (such as Amy and her physical neighbors) would normally connect to the central server that is geographically closest. Users could then connect to the server with ISDN lines, dial-up modems, or whichever technology they choose. As an added benefit, the DVE server to which the user connects might

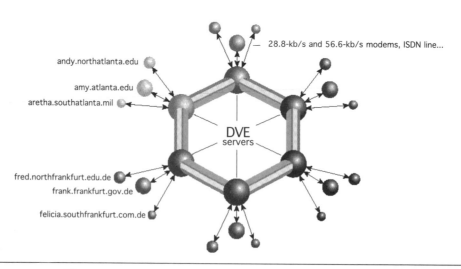

Figure 16.7 Hybrid system.

well be co-located with his or her *Internet Service Provider* (ISP). Here, the ISP need only send relevant updates down the relatively low-bandwidth link to the user's machine.

Note that none of the topologies described previously has necessarily any relationship to low-level intranet topology. Each of the previously discussed models can be applied at a higher level, regardless of whether the underlying intranet is Ethernet-based, token ring, or some other approach altogether.

Placing Standards

Clearly, in most cases, solutions seem to be close for DVE systems, but challenges still lie ahead. Bandwidth and latency problems can be resolved by sending higher-level behaviors, doing relevance filtering, using connectionless protocols, and working with a decentralized architecture.[12] Also, in order to maintain consistency across hosts, a variety of approaches are also available.

But what is clearly needed, and needed soon, is a set of standards. The *Virtual Reality Modeling Language* (VRML) deals with how three-dimensional virtual objects can be designed for transmission on the Internet. Now at version 2.0, it is soon to be an ISO standard. It then will be extended so that objects in those environments, and the environments themselves, can be shared in real time.

A working group called *Living Worlds* (as discussed in Chapter 9, *Living Worlds*) is putting together a proposal for multiuser standards for VRML (a.k.a. VRML97). A related proposal as discussed in Chapter 10, called *Open Community* (for an application programmer's interface for multiuser technology), has been announced by Mitsubishi Electric Research Laboratory and a number of other companies (the complex issues in providing support for DVE developers are detailed in Chapter 15, *Virtual Worlds for Social Interaction*).

Once these standards are adopted (not to be overstating the case in any way), this new version of VRML will have the same impact that *HyperText Markup Language* (HTML) had on the Internet!

From Here

This chapter discussed how well DVEs can hold up when everyone's data is clamoring for attention. The next chapter discusses how some soldiers are driven by guts, others by computers. It shows how military trainees can fight virtual battles against software foes without knowing who's real and who isn't.

Endnotes

1 Roehle, Bernie. "Distributed Virtual Reality," Electrical and Computer Engineering Department, University of Waterloo, Ontario, Canada, June, 1995.

2 Ibid.

3 Roehle, Bernie. "Some Thoughts on Behavior in VR Systems," Electrical and Computer Engineering Department, University of Waterloo, Ontario, Canada, August, 1995.

4 Ibid.

5 Ibid.

6 Roehle, Bernie. "Distributed Virtual Reality," Electrical and Computer Engineering Department, University of Waterloo, Ontario, Canada, June, 1995.

7 Ibid.

8 Ibid.

9 Ibid.

10 Ibid.

11 Ibid.

12 Roehle, Bernie. "Some Thoughts on Behavior in VR Systems," Electrical and Computer Engineering Department, University of Waterloo, Ontario, Canada, August, 1995.

17

Virtual Battlefields

Out of my M2 infantry fighting vehicle's viewport, I can see the three other M2s in my platoon. We're driving in column formation up Tanner Highway through rolling country hills following another platoon of tanks. On either side of the road are clusters of trees; periodically dirt roads veer off the main road. It's a clear day under a cloudless blue sky. The low boom of artillery explosions in the distance to the left reminds me that this is a dangerous battle zone.

"Stay alert." The radio crackles at the end of the vehicle commander's message. Dismounted soldiers are hard to spot in this rural area, but failing to detect and neutralize them can be deadly.

I see the flash from a missile launch out of the corner of my eye. An enemy missile hits the lead tank. Apparently, there are enemy soldiers hiding in the trees to the right of the road ahead. Boom, boom. I hear my platoon firing at the launch point to keep them from launching another missile. Quickly, my platoon scatters off the road while firing. As we turn away, I glimpse flames leaping from the destroyed tank. I feel a surge of adrenaline in anticipation of battle.

557

The speaker in this passage is one of a crew of four human trainees in a battlefield simulation exercise. All of the other vehicles and soldiers described are *Computer Generated Force* (CGF) entities created and controlled by a computer.

A battlefield is a vastly complicated and dynamic environment with numerous vehicles and people interacting in complex ways. To successfully train soldiers, the military must simulate this complex and dynamic environment, and employ *Virtual Reality* (VR) as one approach to simulating the battlefield. The U.S. military (the Army in particular) is perhaps the largest user of VR in training. The U.S. Army SIMNET training sites at Ft. Knox, Kentucky, Ft. Benning, Georgia, and Ft. Rucker, Alabama, train hundreds of M1 tank, M2 Bradley fighting vehicle, and helicopter crews each year. Soldiers enter simulations of their equipment (simulators) and fight in a synthetic world that is populated by other simulators and computer-generated vehicles and soldiers. In fact, the enemy (opposing force or OPFOR) is entirely computer generated, while friendly forces (blue force or BLUFOR) can be a mixture of simulators and computer-generated entities. Computer Generated Force (CGF) systems supply the numerous entities on the VR battlefield that are not human participants. The challenge for CGF systems is to provide a realistic and accurate portrayal of human behavior on the battlefield.

CGF systems come in two basic flavors: *aggregate* and *entity level*. Aggregate simulations (war games) portray military units as single objects, while entity-level simulations represent each vehicle or soldier as an individual object. For example, a tank company might be a single *piece* in an aggregate simulation, while being represented by 14 individual tanks in an entity-level simulation.

Training Simulations:
Live, Virtual, and Constructive

Training simulations are categorized by how the simulation interacts with a human. *Live* simulation attaches simulation equipment to real equipment (replacing a gun sight with a computer screen). The trainee manipulates his or her real equipment while interacting with the simulation. *Virtual* simulation immerses a human in the synthetic environment. Typically, the trainee (called a *Man in the Loop* or MITL) operates a simulation of his or her equipment. This simulated equipment is called a *simulator* (an aircraft simulator). A MITL in a simulator is a participant in VR (events in VR are considered to happen to the participant). *Constructive* simulations either do not have a MITL, or the MITL is an *operator* rather than a participant. Events in the VR are not considered to have happened to the operator. The operator simply supplies guidance to the computer to supplement its automated decision making. For example, CGF systems currently do not model fear, self-preservation, or fatigue well. In fact, CGF units typically *fight to the last man* with little or no performance degradation of survivors as casualties. The CGF operator will intervene to give a heavily attrited (worn down by attrition) CGF unit an order to retreat and keep the battle realistic. CGF systems are constructive simulations guided by a human operator, and hence are sometimes called *Semi-Automated Force* (SAF) systems. The typical SIMNET training exercise is a mixture of simulators and CGF simulations. A SIMNET battle may pit trainees in M1 tank and M2 Bradley simulators against opponents generated by CGF systems. The trainees *die* when their vehicles are destroyed, unlike the CGF operator who continues to control his or her forces to the last man or woman.

Because CGF systems in general represent many types of vehicles (tanks, trucks, helicopters, aircraft, boats, artillery) and weapons (missiles, artillery rounds, armor-piercing rounds, high-explosive shells), they provide an inexpensive mechanism for introducing a wide variety of vehicles and weapons into virtual environments. A variety of databases support each CGF system; for example, there are tables of *Probability of Hit* (pH) and *Probability of Kill* (pK) for each weapon against each vehicle.

This chapter discusses CGF systems that operate in a particular type of VR called *Distributed Interactive Simulation* (DIS). DIS allows different simulations to interact over an intranet. Over the years, live, virtual, and constructive simulations have been developed for a variety of purposes. Linking these simulations in a DIS environment is an appealing method of gaining the benefits of different types of simulation. A representative Army DIS CGF known as *ModSAF* (Modular Semi-Automated Forces) is under concurrent development by many universities, companies, and government agencies. ModSAF is a medium-cost, workstation-based CGF capable of simulating dozens of vehicles per workstation. Its cost makes it acceptable for widespread research—where low cost is frequently critical. ModSAF's capabilities, on the other hand, make it suitable for small- and medium-sized (less than 500 vehicles) training engagements. For example, forces generated by the same CGF system used in visually realistic, man-in-the-loop exercises can also be used against each other in a different environment for planning of tactics, as shown in Figure 17.1.[1]

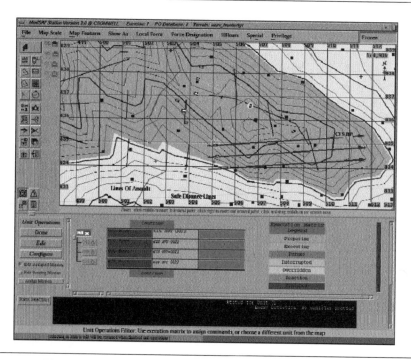

Figure 17.1 Army CGF system.

Among the many companies that develop ModSAF are Lockheed-Martin Corporation and Science Applications International Corporation. STRICOM (Simulation, Training, and Instrumentation Command) is the Army command responsible for managing ModSAF.

Distributed Interactive Simulation

Interactive simulations involve one or more humans as participants in VR. Typical computer games are interactive simulations. *Distributed* simulations spread the simulation over multiple computers. *Distributed Interactive Simulations* (DIS) combine interactivity and distributed processing. Some computer games allow several players (each on their own machine) to play in the same game and interact with one another. These DIS games gain the advantages of distributed processing (multiple inexpensive systems versus one expensive system and participation from separate locations).

The Department of Defense and the U.S. Army have pioneered the use of DIS environments in training. In the 1980s, the *Defense Advanced Research Projects Agency* (DARPA) created the first large-scale DIS training system called *Simulation Networking* (SIMNET). SIMNET demonstrated the feasibility and efficacy of training in DIS-type environments, but had limitations. Only a few types of vehicles were well represented (tanks and infantry fighting vehicles). The interaction among vehicles was limited (only line-of-sight sensors (no radar)). Since 1989, industry, academia, and government have been defining and refining an IEEE DIS protocol to replace and extend the experimental SIMNET protocol. Thousands of people representing hundreds of companies, government agencies, and universities attend the semiannual DIS workshops. IEEE Standard 1278 (*IEEE Standard for Information Technology—Protocols for Distributed Interactive Simulation Applications—Entity Information and Interaction*) was approved on March 18, 1993, and published by IEEE on May 12, 1993. Since then, semiannual DIS workshops have refined and extended the

IEEE DIS protocol. IEEE 1278.1 was released on March 26, 1996. As of this writing, addendum (IEEE 1278.1A) is still under review.

In parallel with the development of SIMNET and IEEE DIS, efforts to link aggregate simulations resulted in the *Aggregate Level Simulation Protocol* (ALSP). Today, under the sponsorship of the *Defense Modeling and Simulation Office* (DMSO), a series of experiments are under way to create a new distributed architecture (the *High Level Architecture* (HLA)) that combines and improves DIS and ALSP capabilities into one architecture for linking all different types of simulations. HLA fosters the formation of *federations* of different simulations to more correctly simulate the battlefield in all its complexity.

Use of CGF Systems in Training

All branches of the U.S. military use VR in training to various degrees. This section presents some U.S. Army and U.S. Marine Corps uses of CGF in VR training.

U.S. Army

SIMNET began as an armor training environment and was extended to helicopter training. The typical SIMNET site consists of a large building housing as many as 60 vehicle simulators, CGF systems, and other equipment connected to an intranet. For training exercises, each tank crew of a tank company would be assigned to a simulator. The company would conduct a training exercise against a CGF OPFOR in the SIMNET VR. CGFs also provide supplementary friendly forces. If, for example, the training plan calls for the tank trainees to cooperate with infantry, CGF infantry fills the bill.

A member of a tank crew (in a SIMNET M1 simulator), looking through the simulator's gun sight or vision block, would see a three-dimensional recreation of real terrain (perhaps Ft. Knox, Kentucky) populated by vehicles controlled by other crews in his or her unit, or by CGF systems. Enemy and friendly tanks, helicopters, planes, trucks, artillery, air defense vehicles, and more, are all available for inclusion in SIMNET training exercises.

The SIMNET and IEEE DIS intranet protocols allow widely separated VR training sites to participate in the same VR exercise, as shown in Figure 17.2.[2] The 1994 *Synthetic Theater of War—Europe* (STOW-E) experiment linked CGFs and manned simulators in the United States and Europe in a real-time training exercise. The simulators were located at Hohenfels Training Area (Germany), Grafenwoehr Training Area (Germany), and Fort Rucker Alabama (U.S.). These sites were connected via a transatlantic cabling mechanism. Over 3000 entities participated in the battle, including helicopter and tank units.

U.S. Marine Corps (USMC)

The USMC is using CGF and the DIS protocol in two new systems that are focused on training the *individual combatant* (IC—the soldier on the ground carrying a rifle). This focus comes naturally from the USMC's emphasis on the dismounted soldier, as opposed to mounted troops, armor, aircraft, or ships.

Figure 17.2 The virtual battlefield.

LeatherNet is a USMC project aimed at inserting Marines into large, multiservice training exercises. Since the USMC fights with much less emphasis on armor than the U.S. Army, LeatherNet focuses on dismounted infantry units. The exercises use a high-resolution terrain database of the California desert, and involve battalion and smaller Marine units. Marine trainees will probably be battalion and company commanders, although the technology is applicable at the platoon- and squad-commander level as well. The Marine commander will stand in front of a bank of television screens or use a Head Mounted Display that gives a view into the 3-D battlefield. He or she gives orders verbally to his or her CGF troops. The orders are in a stylized, limited vocabulary English called *CommandTalk*. Thus, the orders are understood and executed by the CGF system. Company-level orders, for example, are decomposed into platoon, squad, and team orders, and ultimately into the actions of individual CGF Marines on the synthetic battlefield. The commander gets to observe results in the actions of individual soldiers of his or her high-level commands. In addition, the commander can then use the system to plan, replan, and rehearse missions. In other words, it's almost like playing 3-D chess where the pieces move themselves to follow the plan.

The CGF for LeatherNet, called *IC SAF*, is being developed by the Information Sciences Laboratory of Hughes Research Laboratories. IC SAF is a semi-automated force that represents the behavior of each individual Marine. The individuals move and fight together in four man teams; three teams form a squad. An IC SAF operator typically plans a squad's mission and assigns tasks to each team. The teams accomplish their tasks autonomously. For example, given a squad order to attack, the teams plan and follow covered routes in formation to fire support and assault positions; then fire and maneuver to the objective. Automated planning is done through a variety of Artificial Intelligence and computer-aided techniques (see *Mental Models* later in the chapter for more detail). Eventually, operators will give orders to entire companies, and simulated commanders will generate tasks for their platoons and squads. For example, an operator may command a CGF company to assault an objective. The CGF company commander analyzes the terrain to determine good battle positions and routes. The commander then generates orders to his or her squad commanders. During the assault, the CGF company, squad, and team commanders monitor their subordinates, the events on the battlefield, and the progress of the assault. The CGF commanders give orders to their subordinates to change their actions as the assault progresses as necessary. For example, the CGF company commander when faced with heavy resistance will order his platoons to change their method of movement to one maximizing the cover and concealment of the CGF soldiers.

IC SAF represents individuals in a squad with far more detail than the typical CGF represents tanks. Individual infantrymen and even whole teams can carry different weapons and equipment. Thus, each soldier is given a different role (rifleman, automatic-weapon gunner, team leader); and he or she may behave differently as the team undertakes its task. Special teams such as mortar or machine-gun sections behave differently than other teams in the squad. This system like other CGFs uses predefined metrics of wound effects and equipment damage.

Another USMC project is called the *Team Tactical Engagement Simulator*. Unlike LeatherNet, the primary purpose of this project is to immerse individual soldiers—a team at a time—in a virtual battlefield to train them in team tactics. Each trainee stands in front of a wall-sized, back-projection television screen. He or she has a position tracker, so the computers know his or her posture and location in front of the screen. The real M16 rifle the trainee carries is also instrumented, so the computers know where its aimed and when the trigger is pulled. The trainee has a foot pedal that allows him or her to move forward and backward in the scene. The trainee causes the scene to change left or right by looking left or right (the computers detect the direction the head is turned and move the scene that direction). The trainee can leave the foot pedal and move around in an 8-foot-by-8-foot square. In fact, the trainee can move up close to the screen, kneel down, and *peek* around a corner of a building. To provide realism, all people (CGF and other trainees) appear as smoothly animated figures. A trainee may move forward by pressing on the foot pedal, but other trainees see a smoothly walking soldier. The primary use of TTES is for operations in urban areas. So, the terrain is a high-resolution database of a Marine training village located at their base in Quantico, Virginia. This database includes multi-story buildings with doors, windows, small loopholes, and even rubbled walls. TTES will allow Marine teams or squads to practice tactics together, possibly on board ships bound for world hotspots. The system could also evolve for use by Special Forces, hostage rescue units, or civilian SWAT teams. The Marine Corps Systems Command at Quantico, Virginia, is the funding agency. The *Naval Air Warfare Center Training Systems Division* (NAWC-TSD) in Orlando, Florida, is the system developer and integrator. And, the *Institute for Simulation and Training* (IST) is the subcontractor responsible for the CGF system and for dynamic terrain. Finally, Boston Dynamics, Inc., is the subcontractor responsible for visually rendering an animated human figure.

The CGF for this project, called *Computer Controlled Hostiles* (see sidebar, "Computer Controlled Hostiles (CCH)," is being built by the Institute for Simulation and Training at the University of Central Florida. The emphasis for the CCH/N is to simulate realistically the movement, perception, weapon use, and behaviors of humans. Assessing the situation to select an action is often very difficult because of the reasoning behind the complex terrain. Behavior often consists of reacting to detected Marines by firing or running for cover behind a corner. The CCH then may move from position to position, and fire at the trainees, as the Marine fireteam attempts to suppress and kill them. *Neutrals* or civilians normally wander about the village, sometimes congregating, but run away or cower when shots are fired. This behavior has supported a number of free-play exercises in which the Marines played offensive roles. Additional behavior is envisioned that will allow more complex situations for the Marine trainees.

Computer Controlled Hostiles (CCH)

The CCH system for the TTES project includes a cognitive architecture for developing intelligent agent behavior. In particular, it is used to model a human soldier. The CCH architecture comprises three main levels: a problem-solving level, an action-selection level, and a feedback-control level. The action selection component determines what the agent is doing at any moment. It triggers problem-solving functions that require significant time to complete, and keeps track of controllers that govern continuous variables that require rapid updates from sensors. Problem solving includes, for example, mission planning, route planning, or tactical position selection. Controllers can move the agent toward a goal without hitting obstacles or rotate the entity to track a target.

In the action-selection level, knowledge of what to do on the battlefield is represented in a hierarchy of tasks and subtasks. The agent repeatedly—with a period of a second or less—reviews the conditions and determines what subtasks best accomplish their parent tasks. A subtask at the bottom of the hierarchy describes an action that involves keeping track of controllers or starting problem-solving functions. These actions continue in parallel with action selection, until they are completed or a different action is selected.

Multiple tasks may be active simultaneously, especially at the top of the hierarchy. For example, top-level tasks may include *avoid threats*, *kill enemy*, *stay informed on the situation*, and *accomplish mission*. Each of these has a priority weight. Within each task, fuzzy rules test conditions and propose alternative subtasks to accomplish the task. Each of these subtasks is given a priority that depends on the strength of the conditions, the weight of the rules, and the priority of the parent task. At the bottom of the task hierarchy, all of the actions that have been proposed are evaluated to determine what combination offers the best net priority weight. All actions that do not conflict by using the same resources can be performed simultaneously. Thus, a infantryman could move toward cover as part of *avoid threats*, while at the same time fire at a threat (albeit inaccurately) as part of *kill enemy*.

These three U.S. Army and USMC systems illustrate the range of the training audience. SIMNET was developed to train armor crews in cooperative action on the battlefield. LeatherNet is being developed to help train the Marine commander in planning and monitoring the battlefield. TTES is designed to train the individual soldier on the ground in urban combat skills.

CGF Systems in Analysis

While training uses have pushed the development of CGF, opportunities for using CGFs in analysis have been recognized. Two examples are the U.S. Army's *Anti-Armor Advanced Technology Demonstration* (A2ATD) and the *Joint Precision Strike Demonstration* (JPSD).

A goal of the A2ATD program is to conduct weapon systems effectiveness analysis studies using VR. To date, much work on this program has been put into upgrading CGF systems' physical and behavioral models to match U.S. Army doctrine. Ultimately, the upgraded CGFs will be used to answer questions like: What is the effect of increasing the range of the M1 tank's main gun?

The goal of the JPSD program is to develop a simulation system to allow tactic improvements in precision artillery strikes. This project links simulators, live equipment, entity-level CGFs, and aggregate CGFs. The aggregate CGF populates the battlefield with hundreds of enemy units. A simulation of an airborne intelligence system shows it relaying information to simulated ground stations. Real soldiers select targets and pass orders to the entity-level CGF, which attacks the targets with precision artillery. With his or her units being destroyed, the aggregate CGF OPFOR commander is forced to alter his or her plans.

CGF Systems in Acquisition

Although a variety of simulations are available for analyzing the design of a new weapon system from the engineering-level simulation to force-on-force war games, only recently has the use of DIS CGF systems been considered for testing and evaluating new designs in a VR. The idea is that designs and tactics can be tested in VRs throughout the design process. Observation of performance of a design in a VR could reveal problems and strengths from designs created earlier in the design process, rather than current methods.

The U.S. Marine Corps is in the process of designing a new *Advanced Amphibious Assault Vehicle* (AAAV). The USMC AAAV office sponsored a 1995 experiment to develop a method for using DIS CGF systems for *virtual test and evaluation*. The experiment compared two AAAVs as being identical, except that one was armed with a Javelin antitank missile launcher. Two VR scenarios were developed: a raid on a shore to destroy a SCUD missile, and a rescue of a group of noncombatants. The AAAV variants were tested in the scenarios and then statistically evaluated. The experiment showed that DIS CGF systems can be used for virtual test and evaluation. In this experiment, all the vehicles were CGF generated. One of the challenges was to model the cognitive activity of a crew of a nonexistent vehicle.

CGF Implementation

In order to simulate a human-controlled platform or another animated agent in a DIS, a designer must model both physical and mental parts of the agent. In general, the more detailed and realistic the models are, the more difficult the computations. In addition, detailed and realistic models translate into fewer entities that can be simulated on a host computer. While coarse models can provide videogame-like performance, they will ultimately fail to provide the desired intelligence and realism as the overall simulation gets more realistic.

Physical Models

A CGF system must model physical aspects of both the environment and the vehicle or body of the entity. Realistic physical models play an important part in making the overall simulation realistic. In addition, the physical models constrain what the entity can do in the virtual world and thus have a big effect on entity behavior.

A CGF system must model the environment in a way that allows easy access to information the entity or agent in *Artificial Intelligence* (AI) parlance (discussed in more detail later in the chapter) needs.

For example, a *CGF environment* is often entirely different from the environment representation used by simulators. Why? Because CGF must reason about the terrain rather than just display it on a view screen. Typically, a display database is composed of polygons representing the surface of the ground, water, building walls, and even stands of trees. A visual system will use the polygons in the database to determine which polygons to display and what their size should be. But, there is little associated meaning to what the polygons are. For example, a nearby polygon could be part of a wall, the floor, ground, road, or the surface of some water. The visual system is only concerned with that polygon's position in space and surface texture (appearance). A CGF system, in contrast, needs to know about the topology of roads on the surface of the ground and about the geometry of rooms between the walls of a building. Like manned simulators, the CGF environment includes models for light and sound propagation, motion of accelerating objects subject to terrain constraints, detection of collisions between objects, and the ballistics of munitions. Many of these models are simple for general CGF systems, but some may be highly detailed. For example, an aircraft simulation may have a high-fidelity flight dynamics model.

The physical simulation of an *agent* includes at least four general components: *action*, *perception*, *fatigue*, and *damage*. The action component describes the agent's ability to move, fire, and perform other tasks. This description may include parameters such as acceleration rates and constraints (such as whether the agent can move and fire at the same time). The perception component model shows how an agent detects events and objects in the simulated world. Of particular importance is how quickly the agent notices enemy entities. For CGF agents to act realistically, they must have the same capabilities and limitations that humans have to detect and identify enemies. Perception by CGF agents is a particularly challenging area. First, to determine if an agent can see another object, the existence of a *line of sight* (LOS) between the two must be determined. Modeling soldiers scanning the battlefield requires frequent LOS determinations, each of which involves tracing a line (like a ray of light) across the terrain looking for objects that block visibility. Since every CGF entity could potentially see every other entity, these LOS checks have to be done between all pairs of entities. And, to make matters worse, the LOS checks have to be done frequently in battle situations. Once a LOS determination reveals that it's possible for an agent to see an object, models of perception determine if the object is detected and, if so, identified. The complexity and computational expense of these relatively simple visual models prevents the use of high-fidelity visual models. The CGF systems would spend all their time *looking* and have little time for anything else. Research is under way to incorporate nonvisual perception (aural and radar). The third component, fatigue, means different things for different kinds of entities. For tanks, fatigue may include ammunition and fuel use, gun barrel wear, and engine overheating. Individual humans suffer from aerobic limits, muscular fatigue, heat stress, and hunger, among other things. The final major component of the physical simulation is damage. Damage—or for humans, wounding—affects the agent's ability to perform actions and perceive. Although high-fidelity models of wounds and weapons effects are available, CGF systems currently use simplified models. In addition to these four general components, the physical simulation of the agent may include other capabilities. These capabilities may be simplifications of cognitive actions that are not modeled in detail. For example, if the control of individual limbs of a human is not modeled in detail, then aiming a weapon could be modeled abstractly as a physical action that yields a hit probability.

Mental Models

On top of a physical model, the CGF implementers build a mental model that determines what the agent does. This mental model could be an unstructured computer program for simple applications—zombie-like bad guys in a videogame with a static environment, perhaps. But, to achieve more flexible, intelligent, robust, and human-like behavior, CGF implementers use a variety of *software engineering* (SE) and AI techniques. These techniques serve to provide several capabilities. The first capability represents knowledge, including military doctrine, standard procedures for doing things, background facts about the agent, his or her unit, his or her equipment, the terrain, the mission, and, a dynamic model of the current threat situation. The second desirable capability is to reason about how to accomplish a mission given the agent's knowledge (which will be incomplete and uncertain) and an enemy who behaves unpredictably. The third capability is to decide quickly what to do next (be able to respond to the changing threat situation even while planning how to accomplish a mission task). A fourth capability is to reflect the limitations of humans, especially in terms of degraded performance from battlefield stress (dangerous threats, nearby explosions, etc.). Finally, the mental model should ideally learn from what it observes on the battlefield, and adapt the agent's behavior to accommodate the new situations. SOAR and the CCH component of TTES are examples of software architectures for providing these capabilities in principled ways (see "SOAR" and "CCH" sidebars).

One common way to structure the mental agent model is to divide the functions into processes according to their time criticality. CGF agents live in a dynamic, real-time environment and must be able to respond to changing situations even while they perform complex analyses or make detailed plans. Smooth tracking or following motions, such as when a gunner lays his or her gun sight on a target, can be performed by manned simulators; but it requires feedback control processes running at a relatively high update rate. CGF designers must encode reactions to new threats, or they must encode them to significant events in processes that execute frequently or are triggered directly by the events. Mission planning, on the other hand, may run in a lower-priority process. In other words, the agent may interrupt this process with control or reaction processes.

Feedback control processes are used for behavior (such as target tracking or path following) that requires frequent sensing and correction. These processes generally perform continuous numerical calculations rather than manipulating discrete symbolic data. Several intelligent agent designs implement a control system as an intranet of modules that sense, process, and combine data in a variety of ways to perform different functions. The intranets are created and modified at run time to accomplish tasks selected by the symbolic decision-making processes.

The decision-making process of a CGF agent can be designed in many ways. CGF agents have used finite state machines (see sidebar, "Finite State Machine"), Petri nets, neural networks, production rules, fuzzy logic, game theory, simulation-based look-ahead search, and other techniques to decide what to do. Many of the agent designs have two basic parts: an action selection mechanism, and a set of modules or library functions that process input data to assess the current situation. Fuzzy logic, for example, could be used to select an action based partly on the presence of *nearby cover*. On the other hand, nearby cover is determined by functions that analyze the terrain and currently known threats.

Finite State Machine

One of the techniques for encoding behavior is through a *Finite State Machine* (FSM). An FSM tracks the *state* of a process, handling *events* that may cause the process to change state. Consider a simple candy vending machine that dispenses candy when exactly 15 cents in nickels and dimes are deposited. The FSM for this vending machine is shown in Figure 17.3.[3]

Let's see how the FSM works. The FSM has four states: 0¢, 5¢, 10¢, and 15¢, corresponding to how much has been deposited. There are three events: <5¢>, <10¢>, and <dispense>, corresponding to *nickel deposited*, *dime deposited*, and *start dispensing*. The dispensing of the candy is accomplished by the DispenseCandy operation. Initially, the vending machine is in state of 0¢ which will accept either a nickel or a dime deposit (no quarters, please). If a nickel is deposited, the FSM transitions to the 5¢ state. The 5¢ state will also accept a nickel or dime deposit. If a second nickel is deposited, the FSM transitions to the 10¢ state that will accept only a nickel. When the third nickel is deposited, the FSM transitions to the 15¢ state and a <dispense> event is sent. The 15¢ state receives the <dispense> event, dispenses the candy with the DispenseCandy operation, and transitions the FSM back to the 0¢ state.

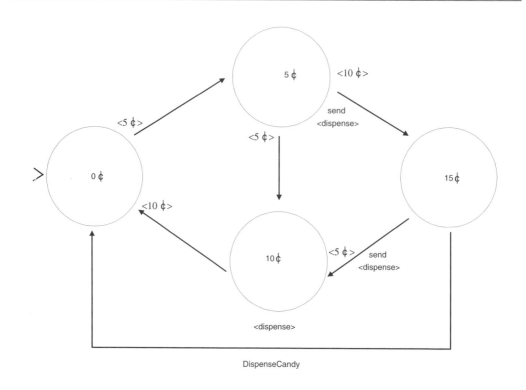

Figure 17.3 FSM for a coin-operated candy dispenser.

This example is quite simple, but illustrates some points about FSMs. First, the FSM is in exactly one state at a time. Second, the FSM's state and the event determine the next state. Third, FSMs can issue events to themselves. Fourth, the *work* is done in transitioning between states; in this case, by the DispenseCandy operation.

FSMs can be used to describe behavior. Consider *bounding overwatch* (see Figure 17.4), where one vehicle moves forward a short distance (the bound), while another watches (the overwatch), and then they switch roles.[4] A simple FSM can describe this behavior. The FSM needs three states (Waiting, Move, and Overwatch) and three events (<startmove>, <startwatch>, and <stop>). The vehicles start in the Waiting state. To start the bounding overwatch, one vehicle is sent a <startmove> and the other a <startwatch>. When the bounding vehicle stops, it sends a <startwatch> event to itself and a <startmove> to the other vehicle. To end the bounding overwatch behavior, <stop> events are sent to each vehicle.

But what happens if something not covered by the FSM happens? If the vehicles executing the bounding overwatch FSM were attacked by artillery, another behavior (scatter) might be appropriate. If a *scatter* FSM were started in response to the artillery attack, the scatter and bounding overwatch FSMs could start competing for control of the vehicle. Furthermore, when finished, the winning FSM might not leave the vehicle in an activity compatible with the other FSM. Mechanisms for adjudicating between FSMs, selecting

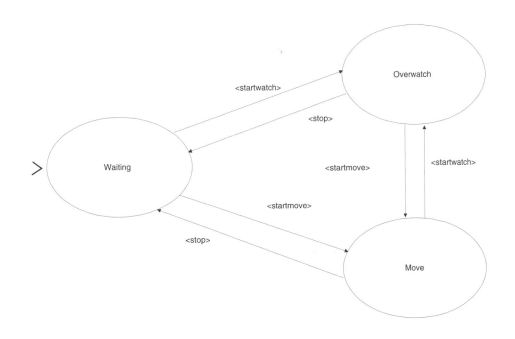

Figure 17.4 FSM for bounding overwatch.

the FSM to the executed, and transitioning between FSMs are required to effectively model human behavior in complex situations.

One of the simplest and most common approaches to action selection is to decompose military tasks into a set of subtasks. Subtasks of a task are encoded as states in a finite state machine (see "Finite State Machine" sidebar) and condition statements determine whether a transition can be made to the next task in the current situation. In a variation of this, production rules (see sidebar, "SOAR") associated with the task are evaluated to decide which of many subtasks should be performed next to accomplish the task. When a subtask is selected, it may represent a primitive action or it may itself be implemented with subtasks. CGF systems often allow multiple subtasks to be active simultaneously, although in this case an arbitration mechanism must be implemented to handle conflicts between the subtasks.

SOAR

SOAR is a software system architecture that was designed to model all types of human cognitive activity. It was developed at Carnegie Mellon University in the 1980s by researchers led by Allen Newell. SOAR is based on a production system with additional architectural structure added to manage a goal stack. In the AI world, *if-then* rules are called *productions* and rule-based reasoning systems are called *production systems*. The premise of SOAR is that all cognitive activity can be viewed as problem solving, and problem solving involves searching through the states of a *problem space*. *Operators* in a problem space cause the state to change, reflecting some (mental or physical) action the agent takes. The production rules associated with a given goal and problem space propose operators that can be applied to move from one state to another in the space. Rules can also express preferences for one operator over another, or describe how an operator is to be implemented. When conditions allow rules to *fire* to propose operators and specify an unambiguous preference for one, SOAR applies the operator and moves to a new state. If there isn't a preference for one rule (this is where SOAR goes beyond simple production systems), then the SOAR architecture automatically creates a subgoal and a new problem space to resolve the ambiguity.

For example, suppose in a combat situation (a problem space) two rules propose the operators *withdraw* and *attack*. Suppose that the goal is to reach an objective. Without a rule that expresses a preference, SOAR would come to an impasse and automatically create a *selection* subgoal (decide which operator to use) and problem space. Here, using a copy of the original problem state, both operators may be evaluated. For instance, they may be evaluated by trying them both and seeing which one leads to the goal more quickly. When the evaluation is complete, a rule in the selection problem space will create a preference in the parent problem space for one of the two operators. SOAR then pops the subgoal from the goal stack leaving the original goal (reach objective) on the top of the goal stack. Now SOAR has a preference for one of the operators and chooses it.

SOAR has been used to create CGF aircraft pilot agents. The main problem space is used to determine what the agent should do at any moment. Operators describe possible actions (turn left/right, fire missile, execute f-pole maneuver). Some actions may be executed immediately, providing a rapid response to a stimulus. However, many of the military tasks for the agent are described hierarchically. Thus, when an operator is selected in the main problem space, the operator's implementation may involve creating a subgoal and a new problem space to select a component action to help implement the main one. This operator selection and subgoaling process continues recursively until a physical action is selected. At any moment though, conditions (reflected by changing facts in the fact memory) may dictate a new action at any level of the hierarchy. The agent thus stays responsive during the time it figures out how to decompose complex tasks.

Command and Control

Like real soldiers, CGF entities known as agents must cooperate with one another. In a sense, agents, whether they are embodied graphically in soldiers or in vehicles driven by them, are avatars for a computer as shown in Figure 17.5.[5]

There are two approaches to CGF cooperation: *centralized* and *decentralized*. With centralized control, a CGF entity makes all the decisions for its subordinates. In contrast, decentralized control allows each entity to control itself. Entities cooperate with one another either explicitly by sending and receiving messages or implicitly by observing one another. CGF commanders send orders to CGF subordinates and allow them to follow the orders while reacting to the battlefield situation.

To date, most entity-level CGF systems are not fully autonomous; they still need some guidance. Two approaches to replacing human CGF controllers are being investigated. First, the *Command Forces* (CFOR) project jointly sponsored by the *United States*

Figure 17.5 Virtual soldiers.

Atlantic Command (USACOM) and DARPA combines decentralized with distributed command and control. CFOR CGF systems are being developed to simulate just the commander. The CFOR commander and his or her subordinate CGF entities are simulated by different CGF systems but communicate using orders and reports expressed in *Command and Control Simulation Interface Language* (CCSIL) messages. Second, linkages between entity level and existing aggregate CGFs are being developed. The aggregate CGF simulates the higher command levels and simulates a larger battle in parallel with the entity-level CGF. This situates the entity training exercise in the context of a larger battle.

While aggregate and entity-level CGF linkages benefit from significant investments in these distinct simulations, they do have limitations caused by different underlying designs. For example, terrain models in an aggregate CGF are often two dimensional like a chess board; the terrain is divided into squares with attributes describing the square. Because an aggregate CGF represents a low level of resolution, it has little need for detailed geometric terrain information. In DIS, however, terrain is three dimensional. The vehicles represented by an entity CGF require high-resolution terrain information to allow realistic movement, cover, and concealment. These different representations create a correlation problem when information is passed between the two types of CGFs. A location that is perfectly passable in an aggregate terrain model may be blocked by a river in an entity terrain model.

Technical Challenges

Although there has been tremendous progress in CGF development, many technical challenges remain. In some cases, partial solutions were developed because complete solutions were unknown or too expensive to implement. In other cases, advancing demands have outdated previously acceptable solutions. Understanding CGF performance tradeoffs in terms of cost, number of entities simulated, and the validity of the simulation is critical for determining how

CGFs can be used in future simulations. For example, it is not clear how to build terrain representations for efficient terrain reasoning that also correlate well with visual terrain representations. Because CGF technology depends on AI, unsolved AI problems (for example, planning unit operations such as an assault) are also open areas for CGF research. Introducing fear and human variation are open issues. CGF entities currently are fearless, with little variation in responses to similar situations. Allowing natural forms of human communication with CGFs (for example, via natural language or gestures) is needed to diminish the existing artificial operator to CGF interface (keyboard input).

A central challenge for the CGF community is *verification* and *validation*. Verification ensures that the computer program is doing what the programmers want it to do; validation ensures that the computer program is modeling reality correctly. Verification and validation of CGFs is challenging because it is not clear how to ensure that algorithms modeling human behavior are realistic, as shown in Figure 17.6.[6] Figure 17.6 shows how CGF systems can be used to study how equipment still being designed would be used in battle.

The *Close Combat Tactical Trainer* (CCTT) program is attacking this problem by building a CGF with its behaviors based on well-defined *Combat Instruction Sets* (CISs). CISs are systematic descriptions of behaviors as specified in Army training and tactics

Figure 17.6 Computer Generated Force systems.

manuals. This approach allows behaviors to be traced from the CGF back to doctrine.

Future of CGF Systems

CGF systems are making the transition from research tools and experimental systems to production systems. The U.S. Army is building a new set of DIS training simulators under the *Combined Arms Tactical Trainer* (CATT) program. The first CATT training system is the CCTT, which will replace SIMNET armor training systems. Integrated into the CCTT architecture is the CCTT-SAF, a new CGF capable of processing the vastly increased realism of the CCTT VR.

Because CGF systems simulate human behavior in complex environments, they have applicability to and are being evaluated for use in nonmilitary domains. Among these domains are emergency management, drug interdiction, medical simulation (virtual surgical suites), and entertainment.

From Here

This chapter discussed how big-budget military simulations are now being joined by artificial-intelligence-driven comrades. The next chapter discusses how users need information about the locations of objects in a virtual environment if it is to function well. Their ears, not only their eyes, must have it.

Endnotes

1 Karr, Clark R.; Reece, Douglas; and Franceschini, Robert. "Computer Generated Forces," Institute for Simulation and Training, Orlando, Florida, March, 1997.

2 Ibid.

3 Ibid.

4 Ibid.

5 Ibid.

6 Ibid.

18

Virtual Acoustics

Although the spotlight of virtual reality research has been on providing views of simulated scenes and objects, some researchers have chosen to study how to fool other senses—hearing, touch, and even smell—into perceiving what is not there. They have good reason: The virtual environments that are best at stimulating multiple senses are also best at evoking a feeling of presence and immersion.

Next to sight, hearing is the sense on which people rely the most. So sounds, too, can play an extremely critical role in a *Distributed Virtual Environment* (DVE). The *virtual reality* (VR) experience is more satisfying when sound adds to or reinforces other DVE information.

The extra cues present with sound can help orient the user in a virtual environment, as well as add a pleasing quality to an otherwise eerily silent artificial world. For example, when a friend's virtual representation (avatar) speaks to you, the sound should seem to come from the avatar, wherever it is in the environment. When an object is behind you in the virtual environment, it should sound as if it were behind you. Not only should sound be localized, but it should also be affected by the acoustics expected of the environment: Footsteps in a cathedral should sound different from footsteps in the open.

In short, sound can compensate somewhat for the visual shortcomings of virtual environments, often impoverished compared to the real thing. Whereas in the real world, the perception of a bouncing ball is confirmed by the sight of its tag-along shadow, in a DVE, rendering those shadows in real time is technically costly or even prohibitive, and frame rates may be so low that a frame in which the ball is seen striking the floor may not be rendered. Making the right sound at the right time goes far to masking these defects as well as adding character to the dynamics of objects in the environment.

Sound Comes in Different Flavors

The three types of sound sources in distributed VR systems are live, Foley, and ambient as shown in Figure 18.1.[1] Live sounds (speech from a user's microphone, say) cannot be precomputed, but must be transmitted to the other users as they occur.

Foley sounds—such as doors closing, surfaces colliding, or objects changing state—are associated with events in the environment. Their name commemorates the radio and movie pioneer Jack Foley, who, as a Universal Studios technician in the 1950s, became known for his synchronized sound effects, such as the reverberating footsteps of an actor moving down a hallway. Unlike live sounds, Foley sounds are predictable and thus precomputable, but they can be triggered by unpredictable events; the sound of a ball hitting a tennis racket, while predictable, depends on whether the player's racket comes in contact with the ball.

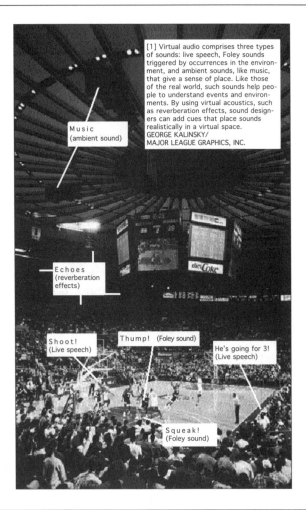

Figure 18.1 Sound types.

Ambient sounds comprise looped (that is, continuously repeated) sounds and music that evoke an atmosphere or sense of place, thereby heightening the overall feeling of immersion in the virtual environment. Like Foley sounds, they can be precomputed. But they are not triggered by unique events; rather, they are associated with the environment and run when it runs.

When implementing audio for DVEs, it is often useful to relax the constraints of the real world and present sounds the user would not hear in a strict imitation of reality. In large virtual environments, for example, users can be helped by being made to hear certain sounds, such as speech, over much greater distances than would really be possible. Similarly, sound that would be unavailable in the real world may be used to provide feedback about actions and events in the virtual setting. For example, a door chime could signal someone's entry into the virtual environment.

Music is an often overlooked but extremely useful aspect of VR environments. For example, videogames use music to lend an emotional charge or suggest repose during the course of the action. So-called isolation-tank VR systems, meant for meditation and relaxation, use quiet ambient music to immerse the subject aurally as well as visually in peaceful surroundings. Some VR systems are designed so that the music responds to changes in the action; a musical-instrument digital interface (MIDI) controls specialized music hardware and software in real time.

MERL's Diamond Park DVE (see Chapter 14, *Sharing Distributed Virtual Worlds*) has an elaborate sound design. It includes many Foley sound effects—bicycle noises, doors opening, and a hover-bus starting up and running—plus about 50 loops of birds, wind, water, insects, and music. Typically five or six of those sounds are heard at once, rendered by software on the same Silicon Graphics workstation that is rendering the graphics. Monaural sounds are manipulated to give some sense of direction and distance to each sound source. Users entering the environment wear a microphone, in a fixed position near the mouth, and headphones, rather than rely on loudspeakers, so as to simplify the experimental interface setup and to avoid such problems as feedback and echo.

Viewpoint and Dimensionality

Sound can tell a lot about the environment. It reaches its full potential when used to exploit the listener's ability to locate its source accurately. To achieve this, artificial spatial location cues must be added to the sounds in the virtual environment. These cues vary with both the object's position and the listener's *point of view* (POV). The type of audio-image rendering chosen depends on the specifics of a VR system, but generally falls into one of two classes: stereo and three-dimensional audio imaging.

Like home stereo equipment, stereo imaging uses two audio channels. Unlike home systems, the source sounds are monaural (one channel). The intensity of the sound (volume) is varied (panned) between the two channels to give a relative left-right balance that will aid the listener in locating its source.

Three-dimensional audio imaging also transforms a monaural source sound, but goes much further than merely varying the volume between channels. More sophisticated techniques alter the sound so that it is perceived to be emanating from the source, no matter where that source is in the virtual world, even behind or above the listener's head.

The brain's ability to extract psychophysical cues from a binaural signal (one signal per ear) is key. The 3-D audio systems emulate these cues to trick the auditory perceptual mechanisms into believing the source sounds are localized in 3-D space. The main cues to a sound's point of origin are any frequency-dependent differences between the sounds arriving at the two ears. Time (phase) differences are caused by differing path lengths from the source to the two ears, and amplitude differences, by the diffraction of the sound by the torso, head, and external ear.

The transformation of a sound from a specific point of origin to a listener's ears is described by a *head-related transfer function* (HRTF). Each HRTF has two components: the effect of the sound on the ear canals of both the left and right ear. To place a monaural sound source in a 3-D sound field, it is convolved with the binaural HRTF for the given location as shown in Figure 18.2.[2] The effect simulates the pressure at each ear of the sound waves arriving from the specified direction. The results can be startlingly realistic.

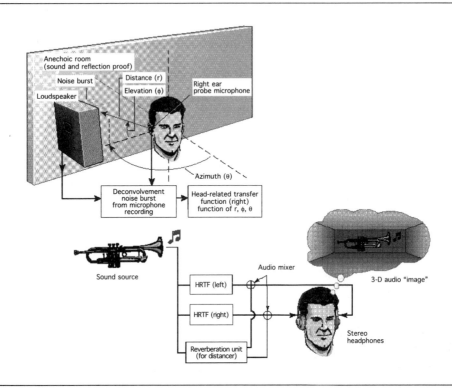

Figure 18.2 Head-related transfer function.

In other words, three-dimensional audio modeling emulates the acoustics of a sound originating from a particular point in free space (localized sound) by simulating the ears' responses to such sounds. The binaural responses, known as *head-related transfer functions* (HRTFs), are measured in an anechoic chamber or other dead space. Probe microphones are placed in a listener's or a dummy-head's ears (left) to pick up a test sound having known spectral characteristics. Readings are made with the sound source in many different locations, given in spherical coordinates. As the test sound's spectrum is known, it is easily **deconvolved** from the microphone recordings, yielding the location-dependent HRTFs. They are then used to add dimension to pure sound as shown in Figure 18.2.

Headphones are often used to deliver binaural audio because they send the left and right channels separately to the listener's ears, thus avoiding the cross talk associated with ordinary stereo systems that would destroy the 3-D audio illusion. However, if the listener turns her or his head, the HRTFs must be updated because the HRTF location measurements are relative to the position of the head, and that means position tracking must be incorporated.

Although reasonable for body-mounted VR systems in which a headset is used for visuals, headphones are impractical in many situations. Instances are home systems whose users sit before a computer display, or applications where headphones would become fatiguing because of regular or lengthy immersion. Those situations need transaural systems, which produce 3-D audio from a pair of ordinary stereo speakers plus, to cancel cross talk between the two speakers, the addition of another filtering stage to the binaural HRTF signals. As a result, only the intended HRTF signals are delivered to each of the ears, producing the 3-D audio illusion.

The advantage transaural audio has over 3-D audio with headphones is that the user is unencumbered by body-mounted equipment. The chief disadvantage is that the 3-D illusion works for only a small area; this "sweet spot" and its size and position are controlled by the location of the speakers and the details of the underlying transaural model. Current research directions in transaural audio include methods for steering the sweet spot as the user's head moves. As with headphone-presented 3-D audio, the user's head movements must be tracked in order to update the HRTFs correctly. This can be done with a remote sensing device, such as a video camera, plus a software tracking system so that the user remains free of body-mounted equipment.

Some experimental so-called free-field VR systems even let a user experience the virtual world while moving freely, without body-mounted equipment. For instance, the Alive system created by the Massachusetts Institute of Technology's Media Laboratory in Cambridge presents visuals on a large projection display and delivers 3-D sound using a transaural audio system with two loudspeakers. Speech is captured by microphones arrayed along the bottom of the display and steered electronically to respond maximally in the user's direction. The user's position is tracked with a video camera and a custom vision system developed at the Media Lab. As such systems make great demands on audio and visual technologies, they are the subject of ongoing research into the next generation of VR display systems.

Sound in the Real World

So far, the focus has been on methods for placing a sphere of sound around a listener's head. But what of sound in the real world? There, it reflects off surfaces in the environment, rising to a wash of diffuse dense echoes as it is bounced around many hundreds of times before settling below the audible threshold. These effects are due to the acoustics of the environment, and they act as subtle but effective cues to its size, shape, and surface materials. The process of synthetically generating these cues is called *virtual acoustics* as shown in Figure 18.3.[3]

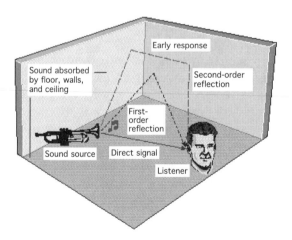

Figure 18.3 Virtual acoustics.

Virtual acoustics add the information present in the real world—but often lacking in virtual ones—that reflects the size, shape, and material properties of the environment. For example, the acoustic response of the floor, walls, and ceiling of a wood-paneled room is quite different from that of a stone cathedral. This data is most evident in first- and second-order reflections.

The main approaches to virtual acoustics modeling are called *auralization* and *perceptual acoustic modeling*. Auralization systems start with a description of the geometry and surface properties of a virtual room and the listener's position in it. From this information the systems calculate a huge number of filter coefficients that approximate the impulse response heard at that point in that room. A real room's impulse response can be heard by clapping; the sound reflected contains all the information that matters about the room's response to sound at a given location. The approximated response is convolved with source sounds to simulate the virtual room's acoustics. For example, a recording of a string quartet can be processed to sound as if the performers are on stage and the listener is in her or his favorite seat in her or his favorite concert hall. Such systems have until now been mainly of interest to architects whose work is constrained by the need to enhance or deaden sound levels in, for instance, concert hall design.

Auralization is the most accurate technology available for hearing how a building will sound as people walk through it, talking to others and producing assorted noises in the shared virtual space. The approach can, on the one hand, derive a simulation of the acoustics of any space from a description of its geometry. On the other hand, the process of approximating the impulse response for each new position of the listener or source sound requires a great deal of computation.

Perceptual acoustic modeling has a different starting point—a relatively simple but efficient acoustical model that generates reverberant signals. A room's impulse response typically comprises a short group of sparse echoes, called the early response, immediately followed by a very diffuse, dense set of echoes that decay with time, called the late response. This general behavior encompasses much of the detail relevant to approximating the acoustical effect of many simulated rooms. Most commercial reverberation units used in the music and film industries are of this type, and they capture the most perceptually salient features of virtual acoustics with a few carefully chosen parameters, such as reverberation decay time, early reflection delay times, and the spatial diffuseness of the late response.

In perceptual acoustic modeling, the efficiency of the algorithms is offset by the lack of an easy way of relating the perceptual parameters to the geometric properties of the virtual space. That makes reverberation control very much a matter of trial and error.

Distance is an important parameter in virtual acoustic modeling. Its perception is facilitated by the fact that, as a sound moves away from the listener, the direct signal level falls off but the reverberant response level does not. Sound recording engineers have profited from this knowledge for years. They create an impression of distance by sending a constant level of the source sound to a reverberation device, fixing the latter's output at a constant level but adjusting the relative level of the unprocessed source sound in the listener's final sound mix.

The impression of speed can be created by simulating the Doppler shift—the change in frequency, and therefore pitch, that occurs when a source is traveling toward and then away from a listener. The greater the velocity of the moving sound source, the more pronounced the Doppler shift becomes.

Designing and Selecting Sound Software

Designing and selecting software and hardware for these uses of audio in large-scale DVE systems is not simple. The numerous technical issues that have to be resolved for DVE databases (see Chapter 16, *Object Filtering Data Swamped Virtual Worlds*) also affect how DVEs handle the sound. The primary distributed system concerns here are the delivery of live sounds and the synchronization of the control of the sound sources with the graphics.

For delivery of live sound, managing the end-to-end latency (or delay) is the most crucial issue as shown in Figure 18.4.[4] Audio is a continuous stream ideally played back without dropouts; hence, enough end-to-end buffering must be available to cover the worst-case delay. Fortunately, conversational delays of under 100 ms are seldom too noticeable, and delays in the 200–400-ms range are tolerable.

In other words, each step in the path taken by live speech sounds introduces some delay that, for the most part, is constant and

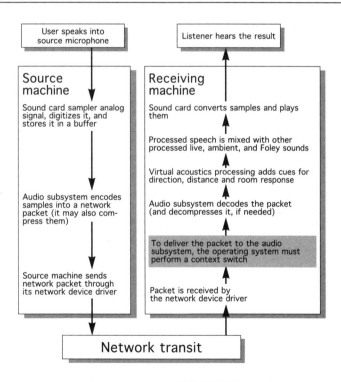

Figure 18.4 Managing delay.

hence easy to compensate for. But delays introduced by the high-lighted areas (as shown in Figure 18.4)—the operating system of the receiving machine and network transit—is randomly variable. This so-called delay *jitter* makes it much more difficult to play back the sound without interruption and to maintain synchronization between sound and image.

It is variations in delay, or jitter, that most hamper system design. The major causes of jitter are irregularities in wide-area network routing and the fact that few popular operating systems support prompt delivery of every incoming packet to the sound-processing part of the DVE system.

Choosing the optimum size for the chunks of speech, or packets, to be sent over the intranet is a delicate balancing act. Today, packet lengths typically range from 20 to 80 ms. While the smaller packets reduce the delay inherent in buffering and if lost have less of an impact on intelligibility, they are more numerous, increasing intranet congestion and raising the processing overhead at the receivers. Compression will reduce congestion and handling costs, but at the price of reduced fidelity and increased central-processor loading for decompression.

The demands of supporting audio chat and a rich aural environment while rendering a 3-D scene and providing an interactive user interface, with all the real-time scheduling it entails, are a strain on any PC or workstation. Consequently, sound processing in DVE systems is often offloaded to a second computer (or extra processor in a multiprocessor computer) or to dedicated digital signal-processing hardware.

The requirements for supporting speech in DVEs resemble those for audio/videoconferencing systems. Builders of DVE systems are turning to new standards for encoding and routing speech data on the Internet, but still face a few challenges, due to differences in the application domains. Whereas audio/videoconferencing systems have no use for virtual acoustics processing, DVE systems need it to situate users' speech within a virtual scene, as well as synchronize and mix live speech with other sound sources and with graphics. Also, many of the more scalable DVE systems use different communication channels (for example, different multicast addresses) for different regions within larger spaces, fluidly assigning users to new addresses as they move about the virtual environment. Though most conferencing and session management tools at present are not flexible enough for those needs, the relevant standards are changing in ways that give some hope for better convergence in the future.

Traditionally, audio/videoconferencing has been done over circuit-switched networks, like the phone network, where bandwidth and quality of service are usually guaranteed. But interest has grown in doing conferencing over packet-switched networks, like the Internet. This interest is driving the development of new standards. Examples are the *Real Time Transport Protocol* (RTP) for delivering continuous streams of data packets; the *Resource Reservation Setup Protocol* (RSVP) for bandwidth reservation; and the H.323 standard for audio/videoconferencing over the Internet.

Recently, a group of companies led by Progressive Networks Inc., Seattle, Washington, and Netscape Communications Corp., Mountain View, California, proposed a *Real Time Streaming Protocol* (RTSP) to control and deliver real-time streaming media over the Internet. RTSP is a higher-level protocol intended to help smooth the present transition period while the new lower-level services, such as RTP and RSVP, are being deployed.

Prerecorded ambient and Foley sounds that belong to objects in a DVE must also be delivered to the user's machine. These sounds are automatically retrieved over the World Wide Web by some systems, such as the SPLINE system (Spline stands for Scalable Platform for Large Interactive Networked Environments) developed by MERL's David Anderson and Richard Waters, and the *DIVE* (Distributed Interactive Virtual Environment) system developed by Olof Hagsand at the Swedish Institute of Computer Science (SICS). As these kinds of sounds change infrequently, Web retrieval and local caching do a fine job of supplying them.

Generating Synthetic Sound through Models

A new direction in DVE sound research is the use of model-based representations for generating sound synthetically. Foley sounds today are stored as samples—short digital recordings that are played back when an event in the environment triggers a sound. One drawback of sampling is its expensive storage and transmission. Another is inflexibility; a sampled sound cannot be changed in a meaningful manner (the sampled sound of a door closing cannot be varied on-the-fly to reflect whether it is slammed or closed softly).

In contrast, model-based audio methods convey a sound's latent structure by either algorithmic or perceptual encoding, and sounds are synthesized from these structured descriptions as shown in Figure 18.5.[5] One approach to model-based sound synthesis is physical modeling, in which a sound is generated by efficiently solving the wave equation for the acoustical model of an object. When a physical model's parameters change, the synthesized sound changes, too, reflecting the object's new state. Alternatively, perceptual approaches to model-based audio identify the salient features of an object's sounds, offering control over the audible structure. These features can be variously combined to render a multitude of sounds representative of an object's different physical states.

In other words, rather than relying on digital recordings, model-based audio techniques use a structured representation (model) of the physical or perceptual constituents of sound to synthesize the sound. In virtual space, this approach lets physical properties attributed to objects—their size, dimensions, and constituent materials, say—control the sounds.

The main attraction of model-based synthesis is that sounds are based on descriptions of their desired properties. Consequently, changes in an object's material makeup, dimensions, or other physical attributes can be heard in the sounds the object gives off. Another plus is data reduction, because the descriptions are more compact than the audio bit-streams synthesized. Several model-

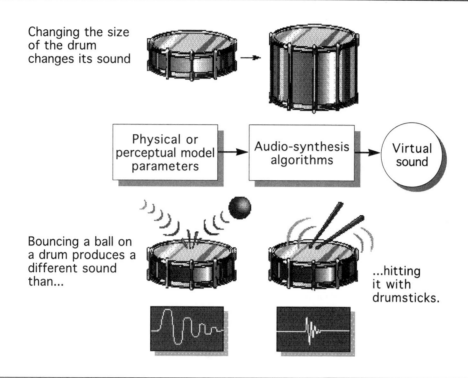

Changing the size
of the drum
changes its sound

Physical or
perceptual model
parameters → Audio-synthesis
algorithms → Virtual
sound

Bouncing a ball on
a drum produces a
different sound
than...

...hitting
it with
drumsticks.

Figure 18.5 Model-based audio methods.

based techniques are currently being weighed for the MPEG-4 audio encoding standard; such standards are essential to the efficient transmission of audio over intranets for DVE and comparable applications.

So, What's Next?

With its support for stereo-panned point and ambient sound sources, as well as for voice chat with lip-synch animation, OnLive! Traveler from OnLive! Technologies Inc., Cupertino, California (as shown in Figure 18.6), is a good example of what

Figure 18.6 Model-based audio methods.

today's technology can do.[6] More sophisticated audio technologies, such as model-based synthesis, 3-D sound, and virtual room acoustics, will only see widespread use after improvements in the price-performance ratio of new computer systems.

As central processor performance increases, implementation of the algorithms described earlier is likely to shift from specialized hardware to software. When that happens, advanced audio techniques will become available for general use, and their performance features, like fidelity and number of simultaneous 3-D sound sources, will be scaled to the capabilities of the end-user's equipment. At the same time, improvements in compression techniques and networking protocols will lead to more natural, and more comprehensible, conversations in this new medium.

From Here

This chapter discussed the use of three-dimensional sound. The next chapter will begin with a visionary journey by taking a brief tour of proposed VRML research projects and systems. Other chapters will follow with a discussion of VRML applications and other futuristic related research projects and proposals.

Endnotes

1 Anderson, David B. and Casey, Michael A. "The Sound Dimension," IEEE SPECTRUM (March, 1997), p. 46.

2 Ibid., p. 47.

3 Ibid., p. 48.

4 Ibid., p. 49.

5 Ibid., p. 50.

6 OnLive! Technologies, 10131 Bubb Road, Cupertino, CA 95014.

Part Four

Results and Future Directions

19

Proposed VRML Systems

This chapter begins the visionary quest of briefly visiting the numerous proposed VRML research projects and systems. The chapter guides you through the development of ongoing realistic VRML research projects and proposals from VRML97 to VRML behaviors. Keep in mind, though, that the VRML technology is still not yet stable. Therefore, some of these research projects and proposals could drastically change in design and functionality at any time.

Adding Behavior to VRML

The *German National Research Center for Information Technology* (GMD) agrees with most other writers of proposals that interaction and behavior are essential for the future of VRML, since without them, real VRML applications will not be possible. However, the GMD thinks that most existing approaches are not flexible enough. Most of them provide mechanisms that are either specialized or not powerful enough to support complex behavior.

GMD's Goals

On first sight, the GMD approach seems to be much more complex than the existing ones. Nevertheless, it is just the formal specification that is more complicated. If you look at the examples, you will realize that the behavior specifications are actually very short and simple.

Simplicity

The designer of a VRML world should be able to add behavior to virtual world objects without any knowledge of programming. It should be possible to define even complex behaviors with simple mechanisms.

Reusability

One major goal of GMD's approach is to support reusability. Behaviors (especially complex ones) once realized should be easily applied to new artifacts (virtual world objects).

Dynamics

The behavior mechanism should be flexible enough to apply a single behavior to several artifacts at the same time. It should even be possible to apply existing behaviors to new entities joining the virtual world dynamically.

Authoring

GMD's approach supports the interactive modeling of interactions and behavior. Even complex interactions or interaction hierarchies can easily be applied to virtual worlds, or parts of them. In the future this could even be done by using an interactive tool.

Scripting

GMD thinks that scripting languages are necessary to realize VRML applications, but they are not needed for most (more than 90 percent) of the object behaviors. However, the GMD model also provides the possibility of including arbitrary scripting languages.

Sharing

In a distributed multiuser virtual world, special mechanisms to support shared interactions and behavior are required. The GMD approach can easily be extended to support multiuser interactions, as well as synchronized shared behavior. Sharing behavior is performed by using a generalized dead-reckoning mechanism.

This approach is based on an interaction model GMD developed for collaborative distributed virtual environments, not in particular for VRML. The model was presented at the ACM SIVE95 (Iowa City) and was adapted for VRML, which is used as an evaluation platform.

Artifacts

GMD proposes to add a new node type, which is guaranteed to be kept by the internal representation of the browser. Thus it can be addressed during the life time of the world. An Artifact node will traverse its children similarly to the new-style Separator node.

An Artifact node (like a Separator node) may have arbitrary children; however, all transformations are combined into a single child. Only the last property node of each type is traversed. Transformations and properties apply before shape nodes and subgroups. Subgroups are traversed after all other nodes. Thus, property changes within subgroups do not influence the nodes of the Artifact node or any node above it. We could also think of a more restrictive Artifact node, where children will be forced to meet the required order, and only one child of each property node will be allowed

Subclassing

Subclassing provides the possibility of creating new classes within a VRML file and using them later as if they were built-in nodes. GMD's main purpose here was to provide a possibility of realizing new behavior classes and inheriting new classes from existing ones. There are some differences to the prototyping mechanism proposed by SGI, but GMD can also think of extending its approach in this direction.

Events

GMD's behavior approach is based entirely on an object-oriented event model. It achieved high flexibility by providing the user with built-in event objects and the additional possibility of adding arbitrary user-defined events within a VRML file. GMD is aware of the fact that many people do not like the idea of having an additional type of objects that have to be specified within VRML. But it gives GMD the possibility of specifying behavior in a much more flexible and artifact-independent way.

Behavior

GMD's behavior model is based on the subclassing mechanism. It allows the user to define arbitrary new behavior nodes (classes) by combining behavior components. Behavior nodes, whether used to compute user interactions or independent artifact behavior, can always be assembled from a basic set of components. These basic components can be subdivided into the classes triggers, actions, engines, semantic, activate, deactivate, scripts, and sensors.

By providing specialized or preconfigured realizations of certain components, most common behaviors can be realized with minimal effort. However, more complex behavior can still be realized by assembling those components but will usually be based on more powerful, configurable ones.

Distributed Behavior

These are some very rough ideas to extend the behavior model to support multiuser interactions (several users interact with the same artifact concurrently), as well as synchronized distributed behavior. Support for shared distributed multiuser worlds can easily be integrated within GMD's approach by adding two modified components types: *shared trigger* and *synchronized engines*.[1]

Multiuser Representation of Virtual Worlds to Support VRML

In a cooperative, virtual organization teams of users can be formed at will to share and interact with abstract artifacts and to communicate with one another through these artifacts. In such a world, users can be aware of one another's activities, interact with shared objects, and have their own 3-D representation (or embodiment). This part of the chapter shows how multiple users can be supported by using VRML/HTTP. The GMD describes how VRML can be extended and supported with extended clients and servers to provide mechanisms for awareness, embodiment, and access control.

The key distinction between CSCW (Computer Support for Cooperative Work) systems and applications aimed at individual computer users is that CSCW systems allow users to coordinate their activities around a group of tasks. The form of coordination is very loose. Users might use social protocols or a model, as in work-flow systems. Social protocols are currently the most popular way of supporting user coordination, as they allow users to develop methods of cooperation and coordination that can be tailored to their specific tasks. The goal of the work at GMD is to show how virtual reality and VRML can be used to enhance CSCW applications. GMD research shows how VRML/HTTP can be used as a basis for this aim by supporting multiple users. GMD wants to establish the cooperative context in which a multiple-user VRML/HTTP architecture would be used.

What are the artifacts that GMD might wish to model in VRML to support cooperating users? Many CSCW systems attempt to provide analogs of the features of real-world organizations. However, to adequately support social and organizational protocols, GMD needs to provide some underlying mechanisms with which users can establish their own cooperation environment. GMD needs to provide mechanisms that support important concepts, such as:

♦ Awareness,
♦ Access control,
♦ Group membership, and
♦ Version control.[2]

Most existing work on multiuser virtual reality has concentrated on visualizing the first two items. In virtual reality, awareness is more graphic: Users are present as visual objects, or embodiments. We can actually see who is around, what they are doing, and which artifacts they are working on (see Figure 19.1). The spatial model takes this further and allows users to control what they see and how they are seen. Users can set a focus on vision and sound, and they can also set an aura, which defines when they become visible (or audible) to others. In conventional systems, access control is usually displayed by showing that objects or commands are either available or not. Commonly unavailable commands are grayed out. The idea of boundaries in VR takes the idea of graying out further by representing the access state of objects by different graphical properties. So, for example, a completely inaccessible object may be hidden behind a wall. An object that is visible but not accessible may be shown behind a window. When GMD wants a user to be aware of the existence of an object but not its details, it may hide the object behind frosted glass. The boundaries idea mixes access control and awareness. This demonstrates one of the benefits of VR for CSCW. GMD can combine (with careful design) many properties and mechanisms in the visualization of one object and thus give more information to users.

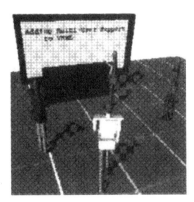

Figure 19.1 Multiuser virtual world.

VRML provides an additional medium for visualizing awareness and access control. Visualizations can, of course, be provided in two dimensions, but they produce greater clutter of limited display space. The third dimension and the dimension of time provide the means for viewing more attributes simultaneously. For example, suppose we have a virtual library in which the users are embodied and the query from shared bibliographic searches is visualized. In such a scenario, GMD can spread the results of the query into, for example, a pyramid. Users can be seen moving about this pyramid and you can watch them as they choose individual artifacts returned by the query. Different users, librarian and readers, may have different styles of embodiment. Readers may find that some artifacts are not accessible to them; their visualization represents the state of their accessibility (by boundary objects). Another user might make a further refining query that changes the population of the data landscape. Other users may come in and out of the system and become visible to their co-workers.

However, before GMD can provide VRML models that visualize awareness and access features, it first needs to examine the existing model of distribution. In the current vision of the World Wide Web, information is shared only in that multiple users are able to simultaneously view pages put up by many providers. The users are just browsers of the information provided, and interaction is limited to following links or completing forms. The control of information remains largely with the information provider. The traditional client-server model of distribution supports this type of information exchange well. However, for truly cooperative work, such as that researched at GMD, researchers need to support awareness and access control as described earlier. Some Web products, such as Virtual Places for Windows, from Ubique, provide a crude notion of awareness, but this is not adequate. In addition, there are requirements for the consistency of views on a virtual world that cannot be met by the current WWW architecture.

GMD is examining how VRML could be extended to support cooperative, multiuser worlds on the Internet. GMD stresses cooperative in addition to multiuser worlds, as shown in Figure 19.1.[3] Many systems are multiuser but not cooperative; that is, users cannot coordinate their activities through the system. GMD is also examining how cooperation can be supported without radically altering VRML. Radical changes are unacceptable for an emerging standard. Ideally, GMD feels, it should be able to provide a smooth transition from the existing, isolated-client model to a communicating-clients model.

What are the functional requirements for a VRML/HTTP basis for GMD's virtual library world? First, it needs to be able to create a VRML scene graph of the preceding query result. This can be done with current technology. Individual users could then view the scene graph. However, as VRML objects (currently) have no behavior they could not interact with the objects (unless they were links). The addition of behaviors to VRML would support interaction with the artifacts and the representation of access to artifacts, which could be given different behaviors when chosen by different users. As users joined the system, GMD could create a VRML scene graph of their embodiment and add that to the query scene graph. However, this updated scene graph would be visible only to the user currently joining and to later users. For existing users to be made aware of the new user would require the server (or other clients in a peer-to-peer approach) to notify the connected clients.

This is not part of the WWW architecture. However, work at GMD by the BSCW project (*Basic Support for Cooperative Work*) shows how this might be done by modifying servers and clients so that server-to-client notification is possible. Now as users move about the virtual world, other users would need to be made aware of their changes in position. Again, GMD would need some form of server-to-client notification of these changes.

The problem of the distribution of artifacts in virtual worlds can be tackled at two levels. First, there are problems of multiuser access to documents and how changes to shared documents might be managed. Second, there is the question of how the visualization of objects in a shared space might be kept consistent. Some existing work has looked at the problems of distributed virtual environments. For example, the DIS (*Distributed Interactive Simulation)* protocol has been used to support distributed applications with more than 300 participants. However, this requires the use of a dedicated intranet. In further enhancements to NPSNET (based on DIS), it is shown how multicasting can be used to reduce intranet and computing requirements. In this part of the chapter we will discuss GMD's use of multicasting to support multiuser VRML. NPSNET is limited to military simulations, and this limitation is most evident in its restriction to the use of dead reckoning for propagate changes. For the wider spectrum of VR applications, GMD needs to move toward distributing behaviors.

In the rest of this chapter we will look in more detail at GMD's approaches to distributing changes to user representations, and how interactions on artifacts may be distributed. The focus here is on the topology and protocol of communications between server and clients. Finally, we will look at some proposals for further extension to VRML in terms of object naming and multiuser interactions.

Multiuser Representation

Let's look at GMD's two approaches to supporting several users using VRML, based on slight extensions to the existing HTTP protocol and servers. The two approaches are very different.

Minimal-Changes Approach

GMD's first approach requires only minimal changes to VRML clients/browsers, such as WebSpace or WorldView, and slight extension to the HTTPD server. Most of the server extensions might even be realized by CGI scripts. All clients communicate directly with the server.

Each user can define his or her own representation within a local VRML file (myBody.wrl). The browser will use this file or even several files for different user representations (see Figure 19.2).[4] A user might be presented by a human model within an office environment but a spaceship representation when in a solar-system world. However, multiuser-capable browsers should also provide at least one default user representation.

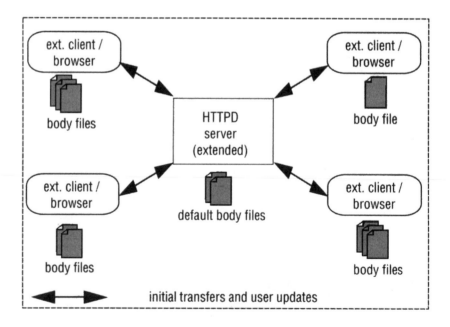

Figure 19.2 Multiuser support using direct client/server connections.

The protocol extensions used to distribute user representations and to update their locations (or even other attributes) will be described later (see Figure 19.3).[5]

The browser first sends a request for the world description to the server. The server returns the VRML file. This is the standard mechanism used to transmit VRML files by HTTP. If the browser supports user representations, it sends a request for the representations of the other users along with the location (position/direction) and, if available, local representation of the user. The multiuser-capable server will return the current locations of other users in the same world, followed by their individual representations. User representations for a specific world might be provided by the author of the world. The server will send the data received from the browser to all other participants of the world. The local browser then adds the incoming user representations to the local scene graph. It sends any updates on the location of the local user to the server (using some kind of threshold or a dead-reckoning mechanism to reduce

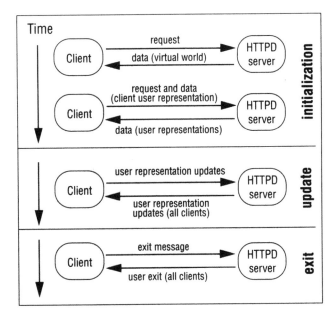

Figure 19.3   Extended protocol for multiuser support.

intranet load) and listens for updates on other user locations from the server. As soon as the local browser moves to another virtual world location (VRML file), it sends a quit message to the server. The server eliminates the user from the world and distributes this information among the participants. The server should also realize a time-out mechanism to eliminate users who have not updated their positions for a certain time. Additionally, the server may limit the total number of displayed user embodiments or the number of users participating in the world.

Caching might be used to reduce the amount of transmitted data. Servers (or even browsers) may keep user representations for a certain time to reduce retransmission when the user returns to a previous page. Servers might also use the transmitted user representation if the browser switches to another document on the same server.

The approach allows arbitrary user representations of a theoretically unlimited number of users for each world. However, servers of popular sites will very quickly become a bottleneck, since they have to handle the communication of all participants of all provided multiuser worlds.

It would be preferable if the server could also add user representations to pages requested by clients not capable of multiuser support. Currently, the user description cannot be included within the virtual world description, since the naming mechanism used in VRML is not general enough to identify different users and different types of user representations. Thus, VRML could be extended to allow the identification of a subtree of the scene graph as a user or the server distinguishes between the different clients; it would include the user embodiments as parts of the scene graph by default (this can be realized within a simple CGI script). Or VRML could send those embodiments separately on request to multiuser-capable clients.

Multicast Approach

GMD's second approach, very different from the first one, moves many tasks from the server to decentralized components. As shown earlier, central servers can very quickly become a bottleneck of a distributed system, especially when adding further enhancements, such as interaction within shared worlds. The central-server approach is no longer suitable, since it is not scalable. The second approach uses the multicast mechanism, which has already proved to be suitable for large-scale interactive multiuser virtual environments, such as NPSNET and DIVE.

The initial setup of the connections is the same as in the first approach: The browser contacts the server to receive the VRML page. Afterward, the client will introduce itself as a user to the server, and the server will respond by sending the user embodiment files of the current users. Along with this, the client receives a multicast address and port number. The multicast address will usually refer to the server; the port number to the individual world. However, in large virtual worlds or when separating groups of users by replicated worlds, different relations might be used. The browser now sends its current user description, including the location, to the multicast address. All participants, as well as the server, get the new user information from the multicast address. The browser now listens to the multicast address for updates of other user representations, for new users, and for quit messages of existing users. A time-out mechanism can be provided by the server as in the first approach. In this case, the server sends the quit message to the multicast address instead of to the client.

This approach reduces server communication dramatically, since the update messages are sent by clients. Thus they are reduced to necessary updates only. Additionally, sending the messages directly via the multicast address increases the average update time significantly, since the messages need not be redistributed by the server (see Figure 19.4).[6]

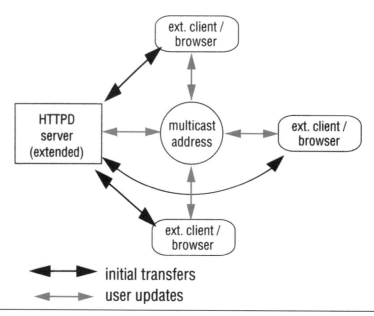

Figure 19.4 Multiuser support using multicast groups.

Compared to the average intranet load based on browsing through VRML pages, or even HTML pages, the number of messages in a multiuser virtual world will be significantly higher. Instead of loading a new page every few minutes, updates will be necessary at least every few seconds.

Using the using traditional client/server connections, a small number of participants in a multiuser virtual world would make it impossible for the server to realize realistic (almost real-time) updates of user representations. Multicast has been proved to be suitable for this task. In contrast to symmetrical (nonserver-based, systems without any central components) distributed multiuser VR systems, GMD's second approach still includes a central server. But this server is used to provide a uniform address to "dial in" the world (to get the multicast address) and to provide all participants with the same set of virtual world contents. These services cannot be provided for frequently changing (connecting, disconnecting) hosts. Within specialized systems, such as NPSNET, such problems do not occur, since they are limited to a certain kind of application. Within its limited world (military simulation), all entities are well defined, so each participating site can use a fixed database to set up the world. But this approach is not to be suitable for general-purpose virtual environments, especially when sites participate at worlds for a rather short period.

Sharing and Distributed Interactions

Real distributed, multiuser, virtual environments require sharing of not only a static world and dynamic user representations but also interactions. So users should be able to change the virtual world or parts of it and have these modifications distributed among all current and future participants of the specific world. Other users should realize who is participating in the shared world and what the participants are doing. This was referred to earlier as *awareness*.

One problem, well known from distributed databases and from existing distributed VR systems, is that of providing consistency among the different sites. Another problem, specific to VRML, is the implementation of user movement between different worlds. Users should be able to move easily between different worlds. Portals seem to be a more adequate metaphor for that purpose than simple links. This issue was very controversial during the specification of VRML but was not resolved. Moving objects or entities (currently parts of the scene graph) from one world to another is an important issue, which has to be addressed within this topic.

Let's look at GMD's approach to handling the sharing of objects and interactions, and allowing users to exchange objects as well as their own representations between several worlds. The approach is an extension of the multicast approach.

Realizing Consistency of Virtual Worlds

Before we look at possible solutions to managing access in distributed, VRML-based systems and to keeping distributed virtual worlds consistent, let's look at GMD's answer to the question, "Why do we need access control at all?" There are several examples of multiuser applications in the VR context and in the CSCW context.

These examples show that access management can be solved on social rather than on technical mechanisms. Imagine a group of users standing in front of a virtual whiteboard: Only one user writes at the whiteboard at any time, so no access control is necessary. If you extend this to a large virtual world (or even a MUD), this world will be completely anarchistic but might still work.

However, another example that shows some problems that might occur when consistency among worlds or views of worlds is not supported. Imagine a user who wants to move an object (a picture in his or her virtual office). Thus he or she will grab the object, move it, and release it. The object should now be placed at the new location. If we allow several people to change and modify parts of the world, without any consistency control, a second user might also grab the object within his or her local copy of the world at the same time. When one of the users releases the object and the object's final position is distributed among all sites, the other user's view will certainly be distorted. The object will appear at a new location, while he or she is supposed to have grabbed it. Thus, it is sometimes very important to define and realize a certain level of access control. GMD has some possible solutions. Let's review their advantages and disadvantages.

No Access Management

If no access management is provided, each client is allowed to change the scene graph independently. All modifications are posted to the multicast address and distributed among the other clients and the server. This method is very fast, since no additional information other than the modifications of the scene graph has to be distributed. For that reason, it might be used for the modification of worlds, where reliability of modifications and consistency among the worlds is not a major requirement. Consistency cannot be guaranteed, since concurrent access is not detected. Additionally, modifications of the virtual world may arrive at the individual client sites in different orders.

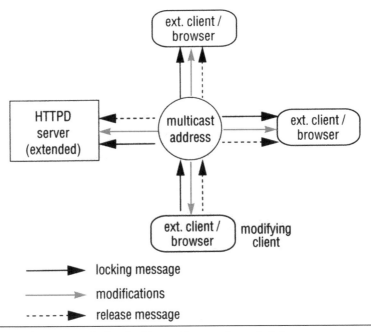

Figure 19.5 Active locking without acknowledging.

Active Locking without Acknowledge

Active locking without acknowledging requires at least three times as many messages as without any access management (see Figure 19.5).[7] Object modifications or a block of them have to be preceded by a locking message on the specific objects. After the distribution of the modifications, a release message has to be distributed. Locks are not acknowledged by the individual clients or by the server, but the server will manage multiple locks on the same object. Different kinds of locks might be used to support various kinds of reliability requirements. Locks should not be understood to guarantee absolute access to an object. This kind of lock has failed in most cooperative environments. GMD sees locks, rather, as a guarantee of achievable consistency, based on a prediction of the client's future activities. This mechanism provides a kind of soft locks, which may be broken for the price of a certain loss of consistency.

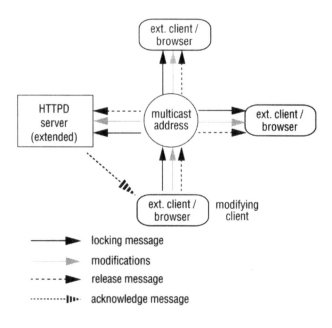

Figure 19.6 Active locking with acknowledge.

However, this scheme may lead to rejections of locking requests. Thus, an appropriate message can be sent to the client to reset its lock. Additionally, the client might send a request to the server to restore the object. The server will also distribute the current lock status to all new clients joining the world. Again, the server will be responsible for releasing a lock after a certain time-out and to achieve consistency.

Active Locking with Acknowledge

Active locking with acknowledgment requires only small extensions to the previous method. The main difference is that the server always sends an acknowledge message of the lock to the client (see Figure 19.6).[8] This is an improvement over sending an acknowledge message to every client. The latter would either cause an unnecessary heavy load on the multicast address or require that each client be able to communicate with all other clients directly (peer to peer).

This would then require the distribution of all client addresses and heavily increase the load on the locking client. Additionally, the locking phase would be extended to an unacceptable length, and clients not capable of locking or with slow intranet connections would slow down the whole process.

Decentralized Access Management

The mechanisms discussed are based on a central access management provided by the server. In a large-scale virtual environment including a large number of participants, the server will again become a bottleneck. System performance will decrease, even when using the multicast distribution mechanism, since access control is performed entirely on the server.

Decentralized mechanisms to manage access control include migration and master entities. Migration does not seem to be very useful in the VRML context, since the graphical representation of all virtual world contents has to be locally available. Also, VRML does not provide any additional object representation. Nevertheless, migration has proved suitable even for distributed VR (in the AVIARY system). It might be a solution, as soon as object identification and naming are solved within VRML in an appropriate way, and objects may hold more information than just a graphical representation.

Master entities provide a mechanism for flexible access in a distributed system. Access control for each part of the virtual world (objects, artifacts, or just subtrees of the scene graph) is located at potentially different sites. The object copy at the managing site (also called the *owner* of the object) is called *master entity*. When changes to certain objects are closely related to their owners, this method provides a very fast mechanism, even in distributed systems. If access has to be provided for different sites (clients), but it's concentrated at each time to one of them, master entities (object ownership) can be migrated.

In a central server system, pure master-entity mechanisms are not appropriate. As there might not be any clients at all, the server has to be the owner of all master entities, at least at startup time. Clients can request ownership from the server. The server keeps track of the current owner and gets the master entity back by migration, disconnection of the client, or after a time-out. So far, there is almost no difference to the locking schemes described earlier. But master entities might also be transferred directly from one client to another. This can be done by using the multicast connection, since all clients and the server always have to know the current owner of the object.

When supporting multiple locks for each object, migration cannot be used as a general mechanism to provide access for sites other than the current owner. For that reason, the owner has to provide server functionality for access management. This can be achieved either by direct (peer-to-peer) connections between the two sites or via the multicast address. Both solutions raise some problems. Direct connections require the distribution of all participants' addresses and may cause a heavy load on some participating sites (especially when they own several master entities). Using the multicast address will increase the load of all participants, even those for which the access for this particular object is not of any interest. The main problem with this kind of decentralized access management is to find an appropriate algorithm to decide under which conditions master entities (rights) are relocated to achieve a good performance.

Beyond the access mechanisms shown here, there exist several more. These could be applied to support multiuser virtual worlds, but they do not seem to be suitable for smooth VRML/HTTP extensions.

GMD will now try to review the different approaches to get an idea of the final approach, which may be used for future VRML97 extensions.

On the one hand, many virtual worlds will not need any kind of access control, since consistency is not a major problem if users use social protocols. This allows the server to stay almost passive after the initialization phase, and for that reason reduces server and intranet load. On the other hand, at least for some objects of the world (including avatars) or for certain kinds of interactions (grabbing, moving), consistency is important. Thus, it should be possible to specify consistency either on an object (subgraph) level or on an interaction level. This will require extensions to the VRML specification or will have to be included in the interaction and behavior specifications, respectively.

As long as GMD distinguishes between servers and clients (a more or less centralized system), decentralized access mechanisms do not seem to be advantageous, especially since all virtual world contents are originally located at the server. However, this may change if all users have a basic common library of objects on their local system. Thus, a participating site (server/client) would have to supply only some special objects.

For the central server architecture, a rather simple approach should be used. GMD thinks that access should not be restricted by default, but it should be possible to manage access on a soft lock mechanism, if required.

Moving Objects and Users through Multiple Worlds

Another important issue to the realization of multiple users and interactions is the question, "How can users and object move among several worlds?" Currently, VRML uses hyperlinks realized by Anchor nodes to switch to other virtual worlds. With some late extensions of the specification, it is possible to specify the destination location in the new world, if it is another VRML page. The term *portal* is used to specify a special kind of link, potentially bidirectional, and also capable of connecting points within the same world. However, a portal can always be realized by a pair of hyperlinks specifying the world and the position in the appropriate counterpart. It has to be part of the client realization to provide mechanisms to avoid unnecessary reloading of pages.

Since portals and links connect different worlds or parts of them, they are closely related to the movement of user representations and objects among such worlds. In GMD's approach, user representation is provided by the client and sent to the server for each page separately. However, as mentioned earlier, user movements among several worlds on the same server should be cached to reduce intranet transfers.

Moving objects can be realized by the same mechanism. The object, or even several objects, become parts of the user representation. They are distributed along with it but have to be identified as independent objects. The user needs to be able to drop objects in a world so that they can be manipulated or modified by other users. However, picking, grabbing, and dropping objects will require further extensions to VRML to realize interaction and behavior. This is not part of this chapter.

Additionally, some extensions are necessary to specify whether objects can be removed or just copied, and whether it is possible to add objects to a world. Authors of virtual worlds might also want to specify objects or parts of their worlds so that they can be neither removed nor copied. But since all transferred VRML data is accessible, restrictions could be applied only to the unexpected copying or removing of objects. This would not allow an author to restrict access to his or her virtual world data (although this might be useful for some commercial use of VRML in the future).

Distributed Interactive Virtual Environment (DIVE)

DIVE is an Internet-based multiuser VR system in which participants navigate in 3-D space and see, meet, and interact with other users and applications. The DIVE software is a research prototype covered by licenses. Binaries for noncommercial use, however, are freely available for a number of platforms. The first DIVE version appeared in 1991.

The SICS DIVE is an experimental platform for the development of virtual environments, user interfaces, and applications, based on shared 3-D synthetic environments. DIVE is especially tuned to multiuser applications, in which several networked participants interact over the Internet.

DIVE is based on a peer-to-peer approach with no centralized server, where peers communicate by reliable and nonreliable multicast, based on IP multicast. Conceptually, the shared state can be seen as a memory shared over an intranet, where a set of processes interact by making concurrent accesses to the memory.

Consistency and concurrency control of common data (objects) are achieved by active replication and reliable multicast protocols.

That is, objects are replicated at several nodes, where the replica is kept consistent by being continuously updated. Update messages are sent by multicast so that all nodes perform the same sequence of updates.

The peer-to-peer approach without a centralized server means that as long as any peer is active within a world, the world, along with its objects, remains alive. Since objects are fully replicated (not approximated) at other nodes, they are independent of any one process and can exist independently of the creator.

The dynamic behavior of objects may be described by interpretative scripts in DIVE/Tcl that can be evaluated on any node where the object is replicated. A script is typically triggered by events in the system, such as user interaction signals, timers, and collisions.

Users navigate in 3-D space and see, meet, and collaborate with other users and applications in the environment. A participant in a DIVE world is called an *actor* and is either a human user or an automated application process. An actor is represented by a body-icon (or avatar) to facilitate the recognition and awareness of ongoing activities. The body-icon may be used as a template on which the actor's input devices are graphically modeled in 3-D space.

A user *sees* a world through a rendering application called a *visualizer* (the default is currently called *Vishnu*). The visualizer renders a scene from the viewpoint of the actor's eye. Changing the position of the eye or changing the eye to an another object will change the viewpoint. A visualizer can be set up to accommodate a wide range of I/O devices, such as an HMD, wands, datagloves, and so forth. Further, it reads the user's input devices and maps the physical actions taken by the user to logical actions in the DIVE system. This includes navigation in 3-D space, clicking on objects, and grabbing objects.

In a typical DIVE world a number of actors leave and enter worlds dynamically. Additionally, any number of application processes (applications) exist within a world. Such applications typically build their user interfaces by creating and introducing necessary graphical objects. Thereafter, they listen to events in the world, so that when an event occurs, the application reacts according to some control logic.

The software is a research prototype and is therefore provided on an as-is basis, with no provisions for support or future enhancements.

High-Performance Rendering Capabilities of High-End VR Systems

This part of the chapter presents i3-D from the *Center for Advanced Studies, Research, and Development in Sardinia* (CASRDS). This system combines the 3-D input and high-performance rendering capabilities of high-end virtual reality systems with the data-fetching abilities of intranet browsers. Using a *spaceball*, the user can intuitively navigate inside the three-dimensional data while selecting 3-D objects. All of this is done with the mouse trigger's requests for access to remote media documents that can be text, still images, animations, or even other 3-D models. Time-critical rendering techniques allow the system to display complex 3-D scenes at high and constant frame rates, making it possible to use it in the context of large-scale projects. The system is currently being used at CERN as a visualization and data management tool for the design of the new Large Hadron Collider, and at CRS4 for the Virtual Sardinia project. The i3-D is available through anonymous FTP from various sites on the Internet.

The World Wide Web has rapidly become one of the fundamental structures of the Internet. It adds a universal organization to the data made available on the Internet. It allows a view of all hosts as a unique data source, as well as treating all of this data as parts of a single structured document. The HyperText Markup Language used to describe WWW documents has its roots in SGML, a format for printed media, and is therefore intrinsically suited for the composition of bi-dimensional documents composed of textual and pictorial data. Other types of media, such as digital video and sound, are accessible through the invocation of external specialized viewer applications.

The availability, at relatively low costs, of 3-D graphics workstations that are able to display scenes composed of thousands of polygons at interactive speeds has made it possible to bring 3-D data to the World Wide Web through specialized viewers for this new kind of media. However, it has been rapidly identified that the effectiveness of interactive 3-D viewers in communicating information about 3-D environments can be dramatically enhanced by attaching digital media annotations to the environment's models. By allowing users to interactively recall and view the attached information by selecting objects of interest during navigation, the interactive 3-D viewer becomes a natural front end for querying information about 3-D models. Annotations can refer to text, still images, animations, or even other 3-D models, thus exploiting all of the digital media capabilities of current workstations, as shown in Figure 19.7.[9]

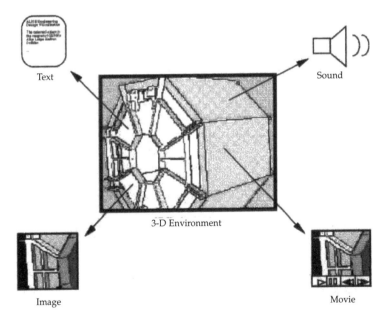

Figure 19.7 Annotated 3-D model.

As an example, in architectural CAD applications the virtual building representation could be augmented by linking to its various components the original drawings showing engineering details of the structure, photographs of the real site, and so on. The interactive 3-D model can therefore be used for data management purposes during the design phase. Information about the building can be presented to the client with maximum efficiency.

When exploring three-dimensional environments, navigation using interactive control of virtual camera motions is often the most important form of three-dimensional interaction. Multiple degree-of-freedom input devices, such as the spaceball and the 3-D mice, allows interactive 3-D viewing with continuous viewpoint control. Hence, providing visual cues are of invaluable help in understanding the structure of the three-dimensional data. It requires that images be rendered smoothly and quickly enough so that an illusion of real-time exploration of a virtual environment can be achieved as the simulated observer navigates through the model.

Characteristics of a 3-D Environment

To best perform its function, an interactive system for exploring annotated 3-D environments should combine the following characteristics:

- **Interactive 3-D viewing capabilities**. Effective exploration of a 3-D environment requires the ability to directly specify 3-D motions and the generation of enough depth cues to understand the structure of the 3-D world.
- **Time-critical rendering**. High feedback bandwidth and low response times are crucial for an interactive 3-D graphics system, where motion parallax is obtained only by means of high frame rates and continuous motion specification. In order to guarantee low response times when handling large datasets, the system must be able to adoptively trade rendering and computation quality with speed.
- **Distribution and sharing**. With the World Wide Web, two standard mechanisms for defining distributed

documents and sharing information over an intranet have been introduced: the *uniform resource locator* (URL) mechanism, for locating information residing anywhere within the Internet domain; and the *HyperText Transfer Protocol* (HTTP), for rapid file transfer. By using URLs to represent annotations on 3-D models and to fetch the documents on request, annotated 3-D environments can be distributed and shared over the Internet.

♦ **Multiple kinds of annotations**. Users should be given the possibility of attaching to 3-D models the kinds of digital media that are best suited to convey their ideas. The 3-D system should thus be able to recognize multiple kinds of annotation and to communicate with other viewers capable of handling the various digital media (images, hypertexts, movies). The hypertext transfer protocol HTTP uses the multipurpose Internet mail extensions (MIME), which describe a set of mechanisms for specifying and describing the format of Internet message bodies for request and response message formats. This allows servers to use a standard notation for describing document contents. When a client receives a MIME message, the content is used to invoke the appropriate viewer by analyzing the mailcap configuration file that describes the bindings between document types and viewer applications. That way, it is easy to add local support for a new format without changes to the Web browser.[10]

A number of systems currently have some of these capabilities, but none possesses them all. Visual simulation and virtual reality systems, such as dVISE and Performer, strive at providing support for high-performance rendering and multidimensional input, but do not permit the annotation of 3-D models with other digital media. Iris Annotator is a 3-D view-and-markup utility that allows users to attach digital media annotations to 3-D objects. However, Iris Annotator's documents are monolithic and cannot be shared over the intranet . WWW browsers, such as NCSA Mosaic or Netscape, are good at fetching many kinds of data over the Internet but are currently not able to deal with annotated 3-D objects. To overcome this limitation, 3-D geometry viewers, such as Geomview, have been connected to WWW browsers to permit the inclusion of 3-D models as elements of a hypertext document. The new language, VRML, has been defined to serve as a standard for defining 3-D scenes hyperlinked with the World Wide Web. VRML browsers, such as WebView from the San Diego Supercomputing Center and WebSpace from Silicon Graphics, are both based on Open Inventor and have been developed recently. The integration of a standard intranet browser with a 3-D geometry viewer offers an ideal basis for a system geared towards the exploration of annotated 3-D environments. However, the geometry viewers that have been integrated with the WWW to date, as well as available 3-D browsers, are limited to mouse-based interaction. They are also not able to ensure constant high frame rates when dealing with large datasets, thus limiting their appropriateness for large-scale projects.

The i3-D System

The i3-D system for the interactive exploration of annotated 3-D models described using VRML or a proprietary file format incorporates the 3-D input and high-performance rendering capabilities of a high-end VR system with the data-fetching abilities of intranet browsers. The system is currently being used at CERN as a visualization and data management tool for the design of the new Large Hadron Collider and at CRS4 for the Virtual Sardinia project. Beginning in June 1995, unsupported binaries of i3-D were also made publicly available by CRS4 through anonymous FTP at the addressftp//sgvenus.cern.ch/pub/I3-D. Mirror sites are listed in http://sgvenus.cern.ch/3-D/i3-D-install.html.

Future work will concentrate on improving the interaction with the system by providing additional navigation metaphors and by adding the capability to annotate the 3-D scene interactively. CAS-RDS finds it also necessary to widen the range of supported file formats for data importation. Improved visual cues for media annotations are planned so that the user can quickly identify the type of the annotation and determine whether it has already been accessed.

The i3-D tool allows the exploration of three-dimensional scenes annotated with any kind of media documents that can be accessed on the World Wide Web. It is implemented on top of XI I and OpenGL. It runs on Silicon Graphics' workstations. Using a 3-D device, the user can explore its three-dimensional data and request access to other documents. When retrieving and displaying media documents, i3-D handles directly the three-dimensional data and collaborates with Netscape for other types of media.

Application Overview

As shown in Figure 19.8, i3-D is composed of the following units:

- The *user manager* is responsible for sensing and analyzing the user's movements and actions in order to recompute the new viewpoint position and orientation; to trigger retrieval of media documents by the protocol manager; and to navigate among the stack of worlds that is maintained by the database manager.
- The *protocol manager* is responsible for the retrieval of media documents from the World Wide Web. Three-dimensional scenes as well as inlined worlds and textures are loaded locally and transmitted to the database manager. This is all happening while requests for other types of media documents are delegated to a WWW browser(Netscape) for retrieval and display by the most adequate viewer application.
- The *database manager* maintains the state of the 3-D scenes in order to provide the necessary geometrical information and visual attributes for the user and rendering managers to perform their tasks. It also maintains a stack of the scenes that have been visited to reach the current world and provides fast world switching on user manager's requests.
- The *rendering manager* is responsible for the generation of the visual representation of the current scene at a high and constant frame rate.[11]

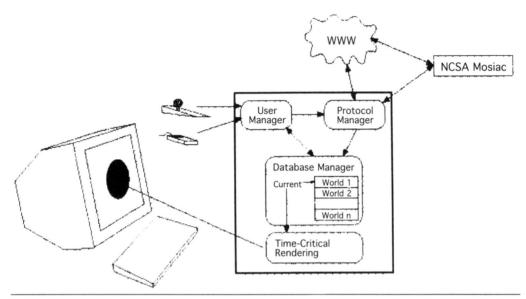

Figure 19.8 Application overview.

User Interaction

The i3-D's device configuration uses a spaceball and a mouse as input devices for the continuous specification of the camera's position and orientation to select objects and access media documents, respectfully. Both of a user's hands can therefore be employed simultaneously to input information (Figure 19.9).[12] Additionally, abstractions of the 2-D mouse motions into 3-D transformations are also provided so that navigation is possible when no spaceball is available. A popup menu and keyboard commands are used to control various visibility flags and rendering modes. The ability to continuously specify complex camera motions in an intuitive way, together with high visual feedback rates, provides an accurate simulation of motion parallax. This is one of the most important depth cues when dealing with large environments.

Figure 19.9 Device configuration i3-D.

To explore three-dimensional worlds, the user can either free-fly, using an eye-in-hand metaphor, or can inspect the scene or the currently selected object using a slide-on-ball, thus allowing the camera to rotate around its interest point, by placing it at the center of the object's (or scene's) bounding box. While navigating inside a three-dimensional scene, the user can request additional information by accessing media documents associated with geometrical data. Since annotated geometries are drawn with a blue silhouette, they can be easily identified. Selecting an annotated geometry by clicking on its visual representation with the mouse triggers the document retrieval and display. For three-dimensional scenes, i3-D maintains a stack of active worlds. Through keyboard commands, the previous or next world in the stack can be made current, thus providing a means to quickly navigate among active worlds.

Figure 19.10 A simple annotated 3-D scene.

Application Examples

Defining annotated three-dimensional scenes using the i3-D file format is made easy by the simple three-dimensional scene shown in Figure 19.10.[13] The scene is composed of three textured cubes. The material and the triangle list defining the cube's geometry are shared among the 3-D objects. Each cube is associated with a different texture image that is accessed through HTTP. Media annotations link the cubes to three documents: the cube on the left references an HTML document; the center cube references an MPEG movie; and the cube on the right references an alternative 3-D scene.

The CERN VENUS Project

The *European Laboratory for Particle Physics* (CERN) is currently involved in designing its next-generation particle accelerator, namely, the *Large Hadron Collider* (LHC). In any project of this scale, the design phase is probably the most delicate one, as this is when some critical choices are to be taken that might dramatically affect the final results, timing, and costs. The ability to visualize the model in depth is essential to a good understanding of the interrelationships among the parts. An iterative design-optimization process can remarkably improve issues of space management and ergonomics. However, with the visual capability of the present CAD tools, it takes a fair amount of time and imagination to isolate

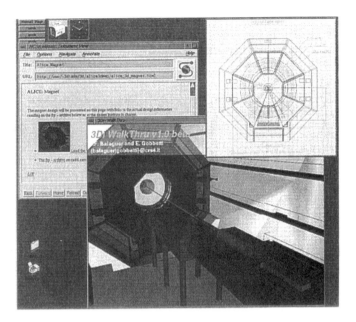

Figure 19.11 Exploring CERN alice.

eventual design faults. A pilot project, named VENUS (*Virtual Environment Navigation in the Underground Sites*) was started at CERN in January, 1994. Its mandate was to produce a detailed virtual prototype of the LHC premises and to allow navigation and access to engineering data in the form of fly-through by natural interaction. The i3-D system is being actively used for the exploration of the virtual prototype. Figure 19.11 shows a snapshot of a typical i3-D session.[14]

The VENUS virtual prototype is entirely extracted from the original EUCLID CAD database. As soon as engineers add new drawings, these are extracted and converted to the i3-D format in two steps: First, EUCLID data is converted to Wavefront OBJ format; second, the resulting Wavefront objects are converted to i3-D and assembled into a scene. Some minor manual treatment is necessary at the moment to compensate for lack of some features (color and textures) in the EUCLID-to-Wavefront converter utility supplied by Matra-Datavision. Annotations that refer to various sources of information are then added by associating URLs to relevant 3-D objects. A further step is necessary to optimize the geometry for interactive navigation. All the process is fairly automatic and does not require major efforts, since the data conversion and optimization are handled by software utilities. The entire conversion process should be completely automated in the near future, triggered from the EUCLID side on any significant changes to the geometry. This way the virtual prototype will always reflect the latest state of the design.

The i3-D is made available to all CERN users. This allows any CERN user with a Silicon Graphics' workstation to connect to the CERN server, to fly through the latest models of the detectors, and to inspect all the information attached to the three-dimensional model (latest CAD drawings, technical papers).

Objects in the scene are specified at one or two levels of detail. Perhaps the user specified an expected frame rate of 20 frames/second and a desired graphical load of 80 percent. This means that the user desired a constant frame duration of 50 ms, with 40 ms allocated to rendering and 10 ms for all other tasks. By combining hierarchical culling and level-of-detail selection, the system is able to adhere to the timing requirements.

The Virtual Sardinia Project

This project, under realization at CRS4, aims at providing on the Internet easily accessible information on the island of Sardinia, as shown in Figure 19.12.[15] Using i3-D, users can explore a 3-D model of the island, built from digital terrain model data textured with satellite images. Various 3-D markers are positioned on the surface of the terrain to indicate sites of interest. The interactive selection of one of these markers during navigation triggers the request for accessing a descriptive document. This occurs while the selection of a location on the terrain triggers the request to view a high-resolution version of the area surrounding the selected point.

Figure 19.12 Exploring Sardinia.

The possibilities of i3-D are exploited to allow the exploration of detailed terrain models on a range of machines. To produce the i3-D description of the terrain, the original terrain data (a regular grid) is subdivided into subregions that can be drawn and culled independently. Each subregion is described at various levels of detail by transforming the original regular grid into simpler irregular triangular meshes through a decimation process that iteratively groups nearly coplanar polygons and simplifies them. Different tolerances for planarity checks are used to produce the various levels of detail. To avoid cracking problems, small tolerances are used at the borders of the subregions. In addition to the optimization of the geometric model, images that are to be used as textures are clipped and rescaled so as to have them fit into texture memory. All these optimizations are done automatically by a tool that takes as input the original digital terrain model, the satellite images, and, a list of descriptions of geographical locations that have to be marked and associated to a hyperlink. Thanks to hierarchical culling and on-the-fly, level-of-detail selection, the resulting model can be explored at interactive speed (more than 10 frames per second) on a Silicon Graphics Onyx RE2.

MPh (Metaphysical Modeling Language)

MPh is a proposal for a language to describe the metaphysics of various models of reality. The basis of MPh is the concept of an interaction between objects as an object type itself. An interaction consists of a list of actors, the effects of the action on each of the actors, and whether each of the actors has a choice. A field called *mutability* determines whether subclasses of the actor classes will be able to alter the implementation of the interaction. Using this model, a wide range of phenomena and belief systems can be simulated.

The intent of this theoretical language description is to stimulate discussion in the field of reality modeling. This gets down to those essential nitty-gritty questions of what is reality and what is the basis of our models of reality.

Physics is the study of interactions between objects. Physics and biology can be modeled by using MPh.

VR Data Structures

In some of the previous HTML documents that the surfer may have browsed, there was mention of transport of graphical objects over the Web. Think about it. If you can transport a lamp over the Web, you can transport a room over the Net. If you can transport a room over the Net, you can transport a virtual environment over the Net—not just the picture or a set of pictures that can be pieced together to form a virtual reality scene, but the real unreal thing.

Many systems bring you VR data structures. Most CAD and architectural systems are examples. Brigham Young University has the RLE format.

So, what do we need that they don't have? Consider this. Animation is just a moving picture of a dynamic situation. So we need dynamic information. One easy way to think of the problem is to classify it as a simulation problem. So we need simulation information, such as position, motion, state information; connectivity information; lists of static architectural/terrain constraints; and models for motion, feeding, interaction and their data elements. One of the goals of the BOLTS group is to generate such a data structure.[16]

Virtual Society Project

The *Virtual Society Project* (VSP) is an umbrella for a set of research projects within Sony CSL. The overall goal of the project is to investigate how the future online community will evolve.

It is CSL's belief that future online systems will be characterized by a high degree of interaction, support for multimedia, and, most important, the ability to support shared 3-D spaces. Users will not simply access textual-based chat forums but will enter into 3-D worlds where they will be able to interact with the world and with other users in that world.

CSL is looking at several issues. These issues include the basic networking structure, distributed consistency, continuous media support, and support for many hundreds of users.

CSL's original work was based on the DIVE system from SICS. CSL is currently collaborating with SICS to investigate how to support a DIVE-like system in a wide area Internet-based environment. CSL is also experimenting with Apertos running on ATM networks to investigate resource-related issues. CSL will eventually port its shared 3-D platform to machines running Apertos.

CSL believes that the growth of the WWW and its open architecture is a perfect opportunity to further study a large-scale, shared 3-D space. To achieve this, CSL is investigating how to merge its shared 3-D infrastructure and the WWW. An initial draft proposal discusses an open architecture combining the WWW and the Virtual Society system.

Currently, CSL interfaces to its shared 3-D world by using traditional 2-D screens. NaviCam is an investigation into a hand-held access device that will free users from traditional desktop terminals.

CyberLab is a longer-term project that aims to pull together some of the other projects to investigate the use of shared 3-D spaces as support for CSCW. The main aim of CyberLab is to build a shared 3-D space that seamlessly integrates a virtual world and the real world.

There is considerable interest at CSL in agent-based computing. CSL is currently investigating how to apply A-Life techniques to create and evolve intelligent agents who inhabit the shared 3-D worlds.

Other Proposed VRML Systems

There are a number of other proposed VRML systems that are currently being developed or are in the process of being implemented. Let's take a brief look at some of these proposed systems:

- ◆ **ActiveVRML**: Microsoft's Active Virtual Reality Modeling Language (ActiveVRML). It is a descriptive (also known as a *declarative* or *modeling*) framework for constructing interactive animations. Using Active VRML, one can create simple or sophisticated animations without programming in the usual sense of the word.

- ◆ **Distributed virtual reality**: One of the hottest topics in virtual reality research. A lot of ideas have been tossed around in various newsgroups and mailing lists. This proposal is an attempt by the University of Waterloo to bring together some of the more interesting concepts and to organize them in a way that's easy to follow.
- ◆ **Division Ltd. products**: Including dVS, the virtual reality operating environment; dVISE, a ready-to-use VR application providing a virtual design environment for traditional CAD users; the fully integrated ProVision range of affordable virtual reality platforms; and Pixel-Planes, the massively parallel rendering engine that offers new levels of visual realism and supercomputer performance to virtual worlds.

Recently, there has been a great deal of discussion on the mailing lists about making VRML more object oriented. There has also been a lot of work done on adding behavior to VRML. However, there are still a number of unresolved issues that may prove to be sources of conflict. The University of Waterloo has a proposal to address some of these unresolved issues and to propose a way of making VRML more object oriented. This proposal is an attempt to gather and organize some ideas related to the idea of behavior in VR systems, particularly distributed (networked) VR systems. Many of these ideas have come from discussions on the Net.

The Virtual Environment Systems Protocol from the DEC Computer Lab, Utah State University, for a protocol to handle multiple streams and sockets via TCP/IP, is intended for use with integrating VRML into these systems. Also being proposed is virtual HTML, a modification of HTML in order to have it work in a stream rather than a document.

From Here

This chapter has presented proposals for many VRML systems that will be developed or are currently being implemented. The next chapter examines VRML concepts that would allow VR environments to be incorporated into the WWW, thereby allowing users to walk around and push through doors to follow hyperlinks to other parts of the Web. VRML is examined as a logical modeling format for nonproprietary platform-independent VR. The format describes VR environments as compositions of logical elements. Additional details are specified, using a universal resource-naming scheme supporting retrieval of shared resources over the intranet. The chapter closes with ideas on how to extend this to support virtual presence teleconferencing.

Endnotes

1   Wolfgang Broll, *Adding More Behaviors to VRML,* GMD—German National Research Center for Information Technology, wolfgang.broll@gmd.de, December 6, 1995.

2   Wolfgang Broll and David England, *Bringing Worlds Together: Adding Multiuser Support To VRML,* GMD—German National Research Center for Information Technology Institute for Applied Information Technology, (wolfgang.broll@gmd.de; david.england@gmd.de), D-53754 Sankt Augustin, Germany, 1995.

3   Ibid.

4   Ibid.

5   Ibid.

6   Ibid.

7   Ibid.

8   Ibid.

9   Jean-Francis Balaguer and Enrico Gobbetti, *A High-Speed 3-D Web Browser,* Center for Advanced Studies, Research and Development in Sardinia, Via Sauro, 10, I-09123 Cagliari, (balaguer@cern.ch and gobbetti@cs.umbc.edu), 1995.

10 Ibid.

11 Ibid.

12 Ibid.

13 Ibid.

14 Ibid.

15 Ibid.

16 *Virtual Reality Standard Data Structure,* VR Data Structure, richards@ marlin.nosc.mil, 1995.

20

VRML Concepts

This chapter describes preliminary ideas for extending the World Wide Web to incorporate *virtual reality* (VR), the primary focus of this book. By the end of this decade, the continuing advances in price/performance will allow affordable desktop systems to run highly realistic virtual reality models. VR will become an increasingly important medium, and the time is now ripe to develop the mechanisms for people to share VR models on a global basis.

VR systems at the low end of the price range show a 3-D view into the VR environment together with a means of moving around and interacting with that environment. At the minimum, you could use the cursor keys for moving forward and backward and turning left and right. Other keys would allow you to pick things up and put them down. A mouse improves the ease of control, but the realism is determined primarily by the latency of the feedback loop from control to changes in the display. Joysticks and spaceballs improve control but cannot compete with the total immersion offered by *head-mounted displays* (HMDs). High-end systems use magnetic tracking of the user's head and limbs, together with such devices as 3-D mice and datagloves, to yet further improve the illusion.

Sound can be just as important to the illusion as the visual simulation: The sound of a clock gets stronger as you approach it. An airplane roars overhead crossing from one horizon to the next. High-end systems allow for tracking of multiple moving sources of sound. *Distancing* is the technique whereby you get to see and hear more detail as you approach an object. The VR environment can include objects with complex behavior, just like their physical analogs in the real world (drawers in an office desk, telephones, calculators, and cars). The simulation of behavior is frequently more demanding computationally than updating the visual and aural displays.

The virtual environment may impose the same restrictions as in the real world (gravity and restricting motion to walking, climbing up/down stairs, and picking up or putting down objects). Alternatively, users can adopt superpowers and fly through the air or even through walls with ease! When using a simple interface (a mouse), it may be easier to learn whether the range of actions at any time is limited to a small set of possibilities (moving forward toward a staircase causes you to climb the stairs). A separate action is unnecessary, as the VR environment builds in assumptions about how people move around. Avatars are used to represent the user in the VR environment. Typically these are simple disembodied hands, which allow you to grab objects. This avoids the problems in working out the positions of the user's limbs and cuts down on the computational load.

Platform Independent VR

Is it possible to define an interchange format for VR environments that can be visualized on a broad range of platforms from

PCs to high-end workstations? At first sight there is little relationship between the capabilities of systems at either extreme. In practice, many VR elements are composed from common elements (rooms have floors, walls, ceilings, doors, windows, tables, and chairs). Outdoors there are buildings, roads, cars, lawns, and trees, and so forth.

The basic idea is to compose VR environments from a limited set of logical elements (chair, door, and floor). The dimensions of some of these elements can be taken by default. Others, such as the dimensions of a room, require lists of points (to specify the polygon defining the floor plan). Additional parameters give the color and texture of surfaces. A picture frame hanging on a wall can be specified in terms of a bitmapped image.

These elements can be described at a richer level of detail by reference to external models. The basic chair element would have a subclassification (office chair), which references a detailed 3-D model, perhaps in the DXF format.

Keeping such details in separate files has several advantages:

◆ High-level VR markup format can be simplified. This makes it easier to create and revise VR environments than with a flat representation.
◆ Models can be cached for reuse in other VR environments. Keeping the definition separate from the environment makes it easy to create models in terms of existing elements and saves resources.
◆ Models can be shared over the Net. Directory services can be used to locate and retrieve the model. In this way, a vast collection of models can be shared across the Net.
◆ Alternative models can be provided according to each browser's capabilities.[1]

Authors can model objects at different levels of detail according to the capabilities of low-, mid-, and high-end machines. The appropriate choice can be made when querying the directory service (by including machine capabilities in the request). This kind of negotiation is already in place as part of the World Wide Web's HTTP protocol.

Limiting VR environments to compositions of known elements would be overly restrictive. To avoid this, it is necessary to provide a means of specifying novel objects, including their appearance and behavior. The high-level VR markup format should therefore be dynamically extendible. The built-in definitions are merely a short-cut to avoid the need to repeat definitions for common objects.

Universal Resource Locators (URLs)

The World Wide Web uses a common naming scheme to represent hypermedia links and links to shared resources. It is possible to represent nearly any file or service with a URL.

The first part of the URL always identifies the method of access (or protocol). The next part generally names an Internet host and is followed by path information for the resource in question. The syntax varies according to the access method given at the start. Here are some examples:

- http://info.cern.ch/hypertext/WWW/TheProject. html: This is the CERN homepage for the World Wide Web project. The prefix http implies that this resource should be obtained by using the HyperText Transfer Protocol (HTTP).
- http://cui_www.unige.ch/w3catalog: This is the searchable catalog of WWW resources at CUI, in Geneva; it is updated daily.
- news:comp.infosystems.www: This is the Usenet news-group comp.infosystems.www. This is accessed via the NNTP protocol.
- ftp://ftp.ifi.uio.no/pub/SGML: This names an anony-mous FTP server: ftp.ifi.uio.no, which includes informa-

tion relating to the Standard Generalized Markup Language {SGML}.[2]

The URL notation can be used in a VR markup language for referencing wire frame models, image tiles, and other resources; for example, a 3-D model of a vehicle or an office chair. Resources may be defined intentionally and generated by the server in response to the user's request.

Major museums could provide educational VR models on particular topics. Hypermedia links (to other parts of the Web) would allow students to easily move from one museum to another by walking through links between the different sites.

One drawback of URLs is that they generally depend on particular servers. Work is continuing in the VRML community to provide widespread support for life-time identifiers that are location independent. This will make it possible to provide automated directory services akin to X.500 for locating the nearest copy of a resource.

Multipurpose Internet Mail Extensions (MIME)

MIME describes a set of mechanisms for specifying and describing the format of Internet message bodies. It is designed to allow multiple objects to be sent in a single message, to support the use of multiple fonts plus nontextual material, such as images and audio fragments. Although it was conceived for use with e-mail messages, MIME has a much wider applicability. The HyperText Transfer Protocol (HTTP) uses MIME for request and response message formats. This allows servers to use a standard notation for describing document contents (image/gif for GIF images and text/html for hypertext documents in the HTML format). When a client receives a MIME message, the content type is used to invoke the appropriate viewer. The bindings are specified in the mailcaps configuration file. This makes it easy to add local support for a new format without changes to your mailer or Web browser. You simply install the viewer for the new format and then add the binding into your mailcaps file.

VRML Issues

A major distinction appears to be indoor and outdoor scenes. Indoors, the scene is constructed from a set of interconnected rooms. Outdoors, you have a landscape of plains, hills, and valleys on which you can place buildings, roads, fields, lakes, and forests, and so forth. The following sketch is in no way comprehensive but should give a flavor of how VRML would model VR environments.

Indoor Scenes

The starting point is to specify the outlines of the rooms. Architects' drawings describe each building as a set of floors, each of which is described as a set of interconnected rooms. The plan shows the position of windows, doors, and staircases. Annotations define whether a door opens inward or outward and whether a staircase goes up or down. VRML directly reflects this hierarchical decomposition with separate modeling elements for buildings, floors, rooms, doors, staircases, and so forth. Each element can be given a unique identifier. The modeling for adjoining rooms uses this identifier to name interconnecting doors. Rooms are made up from floors, walls, and ceilings. Additional attributes define the appearance (the color of the walls and ceiling). This would be the kind of plaster covering used to join walls to the ceiling, as well as the style of windows. The range of elements and their permitted attributes are defined by a formal specification analogous to the SGML document type definition.

Rooms have fittings: carpets, paintings, bookcases, kitchen units, tables, and chairs, and so forth. A painting is described by reference to an image stored separately (like inlined images in HTML). The browser retrieves this image and then applies a parallax transformation to position the painting at the designated location on the wall. Wallpaper can be modeled as a tiling, where each point on the wall maps to a point in an image tile for the wallpaper. This kind of texture mapping is computationally expensive, and low-power systems may choose to employ a uniform shading instead. Views through windows to the outside can be approximated by mapping the line of sight to a point on an image acting as a back cloth and effectively at infinity. Kitchen units, tables, and chairs, and so on, are described by reference to external models. A simple hierarchical naming scheme can be used to substitute a simpler model when the more-detailed one would overload a low-power browser.

Hypermedia links can be represented in a variety of ways. The simple approach used in HTML documents for depicting links is almost certainly inadequate. A door metaphor makes good sense when transferring to another VR model or to a different location in the current model. If the link is to an HTML document, an obvious metaphor is opening a book (by tapping on it with your virtual hand?). Similarly, a radio or audio system makes sense for listening to a audio link, a television for viewing an MPEG movie.

Outdoor Scenes

A simple way of modeling the ground into plains, hills, and valleys is to attach a rubber sheet to a set of vertical pins of varying lengths and placed at irregular locations: x, y. The sheet is single-valued for any x and y, where $x<$ and y are orthogonal axes in the horizontal plane. Smooth terrain can be described by interpolating gradients specified at selected points. The process is applied only within polygons for which all vertices have explicit gradients. This makes it possible to restrict smoothing to selected regions as needed.

The next step is to add scenery onto the underlying ground surface by texture wrapping—mapping an aerial photograph onto the ground surface. This works well if the end user is flying across a landscape at a sufficient height that parallax effects can be neglected for surface detail such as trees and buildings. Realism can be further enhanced by including an atmospheric haze that obscures distant details, such as plants. These come in two categories: point-like objects, such as individual trees, and area-like objects, such as forests, fields, weed patches, lawns, and flower beds.

A tree can be placed at a given (x, y) coordinate and scaled to a given height. A range of tree types can be used (deciduous and coniferous). The appearance of each type of tree is specified in a separate model, so VRML needs only the class name and a means of specifying the model's parameters (in many cases, defaults will suffice). Extended objects, such as forests, can be rendered by repeating an image tile or generated as a fractal texture, using attributes to reference external definitions for the image tile or texture. Other examples of extended objects include:

- ♦ **Water:** streams, rivers, and waterfalls; ponds, lakes, and the sea. The latter involves attributes for describing the nature of the beach: muddy estuary, sandy, rocky, and cliffs.
- ♦ **Borders:** fences, hedges, walls, and so forth, which are fundamentally line-like objects.
- ♦ **Roads:** number of lanes, types of junctions, details for signs, traffic lights, and so forth.[3]

Each road can be described in terms of a sequence of points along its center and its width. Road lights and crash barriers can be generated by default according the attributes describing the kind of road. Road junctions could be specified in detail. But it seems possible to generate much of this locally on the basis of the nature of the junction and the end points of the roads it connects: freeway exit, clover-leaf junction, four-way stop, roundabout, and so forth. In general, VRML should avoid specifying detail where this can be inferred by the browsing tool. This reduces the load on the intranet and allows browsers to show the scene in the detail appropriate to the power of each platform.

Most buildings (houses, skyscrapers, factories, filling stations, barns, silos, and others) can be specified by using constructive geometry (as a set of intersecting parts, each of which is defined by a rectangular base and some kind of roof). This approach describes buildings in a compact style and makes it feasible for VRML to deal with a rich variety of building types. The texture of walls and roofs, as well as the style of windows and doors, can be defined by reference to external models.

A scene could consist of a number of parked vehicles (and other moving objects) and a number of vehicles moving along the road. Predetermined trajectories are rather unexciting. A more interesting approach is to let the behavior of the set of vehicles emerge from simple rules governing the motion of each vehicle. This could also apply to pedestrians moving on a sidewalk. The rules would be defined in scripts associated with the model and not part of VRML itself. The opportunities for several users to meet up in a shared VR scene are discussed later.

Distant scenery (a mountain range on the horizon) is effectively at infinity and can be represented as a backcloth hung in a cylinder around the viewer. It could be implemented by using bitmap images (in GIF or JPEG formats). One issue is how to make the appearance change according to the weather/time of day.

Outdoor scenes wouldn't be complete without a range of weather types (and sky)! Objects should gradually lose their color and contrast as their distance increases. Haze is useful for washing out details, as the browser can then ignore objects beyond a certain distance. The opacity of the haze will vary according to the weather and time of day. Fractal techniques can be used to synthesize cloud formations. The color of the sky should vary as a function of the angle from the sun and the angle above the horizon. For VRML, the weather would be characterized as a set of predetermined weather types.

The illusion will be more complete if you can see more detail the closer (distancing) you get. Unfortunately, it is impractical to explicitly specify VR models in arbitrary detail. Another approach is to let individual models reference more detailed models in a chain of increasingly fine detail. A model that defines a lawn as a green texture can reference a model that specifies how to draw individual blades of grass. The latter is needed only when the user zooms in on the lawn. The browser then runs the more detailed model to generate a forest of grass blade.

Actions and Scripts

Simple primitive actions, such as the ability of the user to change position/orientation and to pick up/put down or press objects, are part of the VRML model. Other behavior is the responsibility of the various objects and lies outside the scope of VRML. Thus, a virtual calculator would allow users to press keys and carry out calculations just like the real thing. This rich behavior is specified as part of the model for the calculator object class, along with details of its appearance. A scripting language (Java Script) is needed for this. But it will be independent of VRML; indeed, there could be a variety of languages. The format negotiation mechanism in HTTP seems appropriate to this, as it would allow browsers to indicate which representations are supported when sending requests to servers.

Achieving Realism

Another issue is how to provide realism without excessive computational demands. To date, the computer graphics community has focused on mathematical models for realism (ray tracing with detailed models for how objects scatter or transmit light). An alternative approach could draw on artistic metaphors for rendering scenes. Paintings are not like photographs, and artists don't try to capture all details; rather, they aim to distill the essentials with a much smaller number of brush strokes. This is akin to symbolic representations of scenes. As an example, consider the difficulty in modeling the folds of cloth on your shirt as you move your arm around. Modeling this computationally is going to be very expensive; perhaps a few rules can be used to draw in folds when you fold your arms.

Virtual Presence Teleconferencing

The price performance of computer systems currently doubles about every eight months. This has happened for the last seven years, and industry pundits see no end in sight. It therefore makes sense to consider approaches that today are impractical but will soon come within reach.

A world without people would be a dull place indeed! VRML allows us to define shared models of VR environments, so the next step is to work out how to allow people to meet in these environments. This comes down to two parts:

- ◆ The protocols needed to ensure that each user sees an up-to-date view of all the other people in the same virtual location, whether this is a room or somewhere outdoors; and
- ◆ A way of visualizing people in the virtual environment. This in turn begs the question of how to sense each user—the expressions, speech, and movements.[4]

For people to communicate effectively, the latency for synchronizing models must be on the order of 100 milliseconds or less. You can get by with longer delays, but it gets increasingly difficult. Adopting a formal system for turn taking helps, but you lose the ability for nonverbal communication. In meetings, it is common to exchange glances with a colleague to see how he or she is reacting to what is being said. The rapid feedback involved in such exchanges calls for high-resolution views of people's faces, together with very low latency.

A powerful technique will be to use video cameras to build real-time, 3-D models of people's faces. As the skull shape is fixed, the changes are limited to the orientation of the skull and the relative position of the jaw. The fine details in facial expressions can be captured by wrapping video images onto the 3-D model. This approach greatly reduces the bandwidth needed to project life-like figures into the VR environment. The view of the back of the head and the ears, and so forth, is essentially unchanging and can be filled in from earlier shots or, if necessary, synthesized from scratch to match visible cues.

In theory, the approach needs a smaller bandwidth than conventional video images, as head movements can be compressed into a simple change of coordinates. Further gains in bandwidth could be achieved at a cost in accuracy by characterizing facial gestures in terms of a composition of identikit stereotypes (shots of mouths that are open or closed, smiling or frowning). The face is then built up by blending the static model of the user's face and jaw with the stereotypes for the mouth, cheeks, eyes, and forehead.

Although head-mounted displays offer total immersion, they also make it difficult to sense the user's facial expressions. They are also uncomfortable to wear. Virtual presence teleconferencing is therefore more likely to use conventional displays, together with video cameras mounted around the user's workspace. Lightweight headsets are likely to be used in preference to stereo or quadraphonic loudspeaker systems, as they offer greater auditory realism and avoid trouble when sound spills over into neighboring work areas.

The cameras also offer the opportunity for hands-free control of the user's position in the VR environment. Tracking of hands and fingers could be used for gesture control without the need for 3-D mice or spaceballs. Another idea is to take cues from head movements. Moving your head from side to side could be exaggerated in the VR environment to allow users to look from side to side without needing to look away from the display being used to visualize that environment.

Where Next?

For workstations running the XI I windowing system, the PEX library for 3-D graphics is now available on most platforms. This makes it practical to start developing proof-of-concept platform-independent VR. The proposed VRML interchange format could be used within the World Wide Web or for e-mail messages. All users would need to do is to download a public domain VRML browser and add it to their mailcaps file. I am interested in getting in touch with people willing to collaborate in turning this vision into a reality.

From Here

As interest in computer graphics has grown, so has the desire to be able to write VRML applications that run on a variety of platforms—the premise of this chapter. The next chapter describes how VRML applications and other considerations have governed the selections and presentation of graphical operators in OpenGL.

Endnotes

1 David Raggett, *Extending WWW to Support Platform Independent Virtual Reality*, Hewlett Packard Laboratories (dsr@hplb.hpl.hp.com), 1995.

2 Ibid.

3 Ibid.

4 Ibid.

21

The OpenGL Graphics Interface Design

OpenGL is an emerging graphics standard that provides advanced rendering features while maintaining a simple programming model. Because OpenGL is only for rendering, it can be incorporated into any window system (and has been, into the X Window System and a soon-to-be-released version of Windows) or can be used without a window system. An OpenGL implementation can efficiently accommodate almost any level of graphics hardware, from a basic frame buffer to the most sophisticated graphics subsystems. It is therefore a good choice for use in interactive 3-D, and VRML applications.

This chapter describes how these and other considerations have governed the selection and presentation of graphical operators in OpenGL. Complex operations have been eschewed in favor of simple, direct control over the fundamental operations of 3-D and 2-D graphics. Higher-level graphical functions (such as virtual reality) may, however, be built from OpenGL's low-level operators. The operators have been designed with such layering in mind.

Computer graphics (especially 3-D graphics, and interactive 3-D graphics in particular) is finding its way into an increasing number of VRML applications, from simple graphing programs for personal computers to sophisticated modeling and visualization software on workstations and supercomputers. As the interest in computer graphics has grown, so has the desire to be able to write VRML applications that run on a variety of platforms with a range of graphical capabilities. A graphics standard eases this task by eliminating the need to write a distinct graphics driver for each platform on which the VRML application is to run.

To be viable, a graphics standard intended for interactive 3-D applications must satisfy several criteria. It must be able to be implemented on platforms with varying graphics capabilities without compromising the graphics performance of the underlying hardware and without sacrificing control over the hardware's operation. It must provide a natural interface that allows a programmer to describe rendering operations tersely. Finally, the interface must be flexible enough to accommodate extensions so that as new graphics operations become significant or available in new graphics subsystems, these operations can be provided without disrupting the original interface.

OpenGL meets these criteria by providing a simple, direct interface to the fundamental operations of 3-D graphics rendering. It supports basic graphics primitives, such as points, line segments, polygons, and images, as well as basic rendering operations, such as **affine** and projective transformations and lighting calculations. It also supports advanced rendering features such as texture mapping and antialiasing.

Several other systems provide an API (application program interface) for effecting graphical rendering. In the case of 2-D graphics, the PostScript page description language has become widely accepted, making it relatively easy to electronically exchange and, to a limited degree, manipulate static documents containing both text and 2-D graphics. Besides providing graphical rendering operators, PostScript is also a stack-based programming language.

The X window system has become standard for UNIX workstations. A programmer uses X to obtain a window on a graphics display into which either text or 2-D graphics may be drawn. X also provides a means for obtaining user input from such devices as keyboards and mice. The adoption of X by most workstation manufacturers means that a single program can produce 2-D graphics or obtain user input on a variety of workstations by simply recompiling the program. This integration even works across a network: The program may run on one workstation but display on and obtain user input from another, even if the workstations on either end of the network are made by different companies.

For 3-D graphics, several systems are in use. One relatively well-known system is *PHIGS* (Programmer's Hierarchical Interactive Graphics System). Based on *GKS* (Graphics Kernel System), PHIGS is an *ANSI* (American National Standards Institute) standard. PHIGS (and its descendant, PHIGS+) provides a means to manipulate and draw 3-D objects by encapsulating object descriptions and attributes into a *display list* that is then referenced when the object is displayed or manipulated. One advantage of the display list is that a complex object need be described only once even if it is to be displayed many times. This is especially important if the object to be displayed must be transmitted across a low-bandwidth channel (such as a network). One disadvantage of a display list is that it can require considerable effort to respecify the object if it is being continually modified as a result of user interaction. Another difficulty with PHIGS and PHIGS+ (and with GKS) is lack of support for advanced rendering features, such as texture mapping.

PEX extends X to include the ability to manipulate and draw 3-D objects. PEXlib is an API employing the PEX protocol. Originally based on PHIGS, PEX allows *immediate mode* rendering, meaning that objects can be displayed as they are described rather than having to first complete a display list. PEX currently lacks advanced rendering features (although a compatible version that provides such features is under design) and is available only to users of X. Broadly speaking, however, the methods by which graphical objects are described for rendering using PEX (or, rather, PEXlib) are similar to those provided by OpenGL.

Like both OpenGL and PEXlib, *Renderman* is an API that provides a means to render geometric objects. Unlike these interfaces, however, Renderman provides a programming language (called a shading language) for describing how these objects are to appear when drawn. This programmability allows for generating very realistic-looking images, but it is impractical to implement on most graphics accelerators, making Renderman a poor choice for interactive 3-D graphics.

Finally, some APIs provide access to 3-D rendering as a result of methods for describing higher-level graphical objects. Chief among these are *HOOPS* and *IRIS Inventor*. The objects provided by these interfaces are typically more complex than the simple geometry describable with PEXlib or OpenGL. They may comprise not only geometry but also information about how they are drawn and how they react to user input. HOOPS and Open Inventor free the programmer from tedious descriptions of individual drawing operations. But simple access to complex objects generally means losing fine control over rendering (or at least making such control difficult). In any case OpenGL can provide a good base on which to build such higher-level APIs.

Overview of OpenGL

OpenGL draws *primitives* into a frame buffer, subject to a number of selectable modes. Each primitive is a point, line segment, polygon, pixel rectangle, or bitmap. Each mode may be changed independently. The setting of one does not affect the settings of others, although many modes may interact to determine what eventually ends up in the frame buffer. Modes are set, primitives specified, and other OpenGL operations described by issuing *commands* in the form of function or procedure calls.

Figure 21.1 shows a schematic of OpenGL.[1] Commands enter OpenGL on the left. Most commands may be accumulated in a *display list* for processing at a later time. Otherwise, commands are effectively sent through a processing pipeline.

The first stage provides an efficient means for approximating curve and surface geometry by evaluating polynomial functions of input values. The next stage operates on geometric primitives described by vertices: points, line segments, and polygons. In this stage vertices are transformed and lit, and primitives are clipped to a viewing volume in preparation for the next stage, rasterization. The rasterizer produces a series of frame buffer addresses and values, using a two-dimensional description of a point, line segment, or polygon. Each *fragment* so produced is fed to the next stage which performs operations on individual fragments before they finally alter the frame buffer. These operations include conditional updates into the frame buffer, based on incoming and previously stored depth values (to effect depth buffering); blending of incoming fragment colors with stored colors; as well as masking and other logical operations on fragment values.

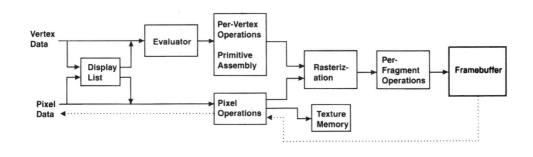

Figure 21.1 Block diagram of OpenGL.

Finally, pixel rectangles and bitmaps bypass the vertex-processing portion of the pipeline to send a block of fragments directly through rasterization to the individual fragment operations, eventually causing a block of pixels to be written to the frame buffer. Values may also be read back from the frame buffer or copied from one portion of the frame buffer to another. These transfers may include some type of decoding or encoding.

Design Considerations

Designing any API requires tradeoffs among a number of general factors such as simplicity in accomplishing common operations versus generality or many commands with few arguments versus few commands with many arguments. This part of the chapter describes considerations peculiar to 3-D API design that have influenced the development of OpenGL.

Performance

A fundamental consideration in interactive 3-D graphics is performance. Numerous calculations are required to render a 3-D scene of even modest complexity, and a scene in an interactive application must generally be redrawn several times per second. An API for use in interactive 3-D applications must therefore provide efficient access to the capabilities of the graphics hardware of which it makes use. But different graphics subsystems provide different capabilities, so a common interface must be found.

The interface must also provide a means to switch various rendering features on and off. Some hardware may not provide support for some features and so cannot provide those features with acceptable performance; also, even with hardware support, enabling certain features or combinations of features may decrease performance significantly. Slow rendering may be acceptable, for instance, when producing a final image of a scene, but interactive rates are normally required when manipulating objects within the scene or adjusting the viewpoint. In such cases the performance-degrading features may be desirable for the final image but unde-sirable during scene manipulation.

Orthogonality

Since it is desirable to be able to turn features on and off, it should be the case that doing so has few or no side effects on other fea-tures. If, for instance, it is desired that each polygon be drawn with a single color rather than interpolating colors across its face, doing so should not affect how lighting or texturing is applied. Similarly, enabling or disabling any single feature should not engender an inconsistent state in which rendering results would be undefined. These kinds of feature independence are necessary to allow a pro-grammer to easily manipulate features without having to generate tests for particular illegal or undesirable feature combinations that may require changing the state of apparently unrelated features. Another benefit of feature independence is that features may be combined in useful ways that may have been unforeseen when the interface was designed.

Completeness

A 3-D graphics API running on a system with a graphics subsys-tem should provide some means to access all the significant func-tionality of the subsystem. If some functionality is available but not provided, the programmer is forced to use a different API to get at the missing features. This may complicate the application because of interaction between the two APIs.

On the other hand, if an implementation of the API provides cer-tain features on one hardware platform, those features should, generally speaking, be present on any platform on which the API is provided. If this rule is broken, it is difficult to use the API pro-gram that is certain to run on diverse hardware platforms without remembering exactly which features are supported on which machines. In platforms without appropriate acceleration, some features may be poor performers (because they may have to be implemented in software), but at least the intended image will eventually appear.

Interoperability

Many computing environments consist of a number of computers (often made by different companies) connected together by a network. In such an environment it is useful to be able to issue graphics commands on one machine and have them execute on another (this ability is one of the factors responsible for the success of X). Such an ability (called *interoperability*) requires that the model of execution of API commands be *client-server.* The client issues commands, and the server executes them. Interoperability also requires that the client and the server share the same notion of how API commands are encoded for transmission across the network. The client-server model is just a prerequisite. Of course, the client and the server may be the same machine.

Since API commands may be issued across a network, it is impractical to require a tight coupling between client and server. A client may have to wait for some time for an answer to a request presented to the server (a *round-trip*) because of network delays, whereas simple server requests not requiring acknowledgment can be buffered up into a large group for efficient transmission to and execution by the server.

Extensibility

As was discussed earlier, a 3-D graphics API should, at least in principle, be extendible to incorporate new graphics hardware features or algorithms that may become popular in the future. Although attainment of this goal may be difficult to gauge until long after the API is first in use, steps can be taken to help to achieve it. Orthogonality of the API is one element that helps achieve this goal. Another is to consider how the API would have been affected if features that seem consciously omitted were added to the API.

Acceptance

It might seem that design of a clean, consistent 3-D graphics API would be a sufficient goal in itself. But unless programmers decide to use the API in a variety of applications, designing the API will have served no purpose. It is therefore worthwhile to consider the effect of design decisions on programmer acceptance of the API.

Design Features

This part of the chapter highlights the general features of OpenGL's design. Illustrations and justifications of each, using specific examples, are also provided.

Based on IRIS GL

OpenGL is based on Silicon Graphics' IRIS GL. Although a completely new API could have been designed, experience with IRIS GL provided insight into what programmers want and don't want in a 3-D graphics API. Further, making OpenGL similar to IRIS GL where possible makes OpenGL much more likely to be accepted. There are many successful IRIS GL applications, and programmers of IRIS GL will have an easy time switching to OpenGL.

Low-Level API

An essential goal of OpenGL is to provide device independence while still allowing complete access to hardware functionality. The API therefore provides access to graphics operations at the lowest possible level that still provides device independence. As a result, OpenGL does not provide a means for describing or modeling complex geometric objects. Another way to describe this situation is to say that OpenGL provides mechanisms to describe how complex geometric objects are to be rendered rather than mechanisms to describe the complex object themselves.

One benefit of a low-level API is that there are no requirements on how an application must represent or describe higher-level objects (since there is no notion of such objects in the API). Adherence to this principle means that the basic OpenGL API does not support some geometric objects that are traditionally associated with graphics APIs. For instance, an OpenGL implementation need not render concave polygons. One reason for this omission is that concave polygon-rendering algorithms are of necessity more complex than those for rendering convex polygons, and different concave polygon algorithms may be appropriate in different domains. In particular, if a concave polygon is to be drawn more than once, it is more efficient to first decompose it into convex polygons (or triangles) once and to then draw the convex polygons. Another reason for the omission is that to render a general concave polygon, all of its vertices must first be known. Graphics subsystems do not generally provide the storage necessary for a concave polygon with a (nearly) arbitrary number of vertices. Convex polygons, on the other hand, can be reduced to triangles as they are specified, so no more than three vertices need be stored.

Another example of the distinction between low level and high level in OpenGL is the difference between OpenGL evaluators and NURBS. The evaluator interface provides a basis for building a general polynomial curve and surface package on top of OpenGL. One advantage of providing the evaluators in OpenGL instead of a more complex NURBS interface is that applications that represent curves and surfaces as other than NURBS or that make use of special surface properties still have access to efficient polynomial evaluators (that may be implemented in graphics hardware) without incurring the costs of converting to a NURBS representation.

Concave polygons and NURBS are, however, common and useful operators. They were familiar (at least in some form) to users of IRIS GL. Therefore a general concave polygon decomposer is provided as part of the OpenGL utility library, which is provided with every OpenGL implementation. The library also provides an interface, built on OpenGL's polynomial evaluators, to describe and display NURBS curves and surfaces (with domain space trimming), as well as a means of rendering spheres, cones, and cylinders. The utility library serves both as a means to render useful geometric objects and as a model for building other libraries that use OpenGL for rendering.

In the client-server environment a utility library raises an issue: Utility library commands are converted into OpenGL commands on the client. If the server computer is more powerful than the client, the client-side conversion might have been more effectively carried out on the server. This dilemma arises not just with OpenGL but with any library in which the client and server may be distinct computers. In OpenGL the base functionality reflects the functions efficiently performed by advanced graphics subsystems, because no matter what the power of the server computer relative to the client, the server's graphics subsystem is assumed to efficiently perform the functions it provides. If in the future, for instance, graphics subsystems commonly provide full trimmed NURBS support, such functionality should likely migrate from the utility library to OpenGL itself. Such a change would not cause any disruption to the rest of the OpenGL API. Another block would simply be added to the left side in Figure 21.1.

Fine-Grained Control

In order to minimize the requirements on how an application using the API must store and present its data, the API must provide a means to specify individual components of geometric objects and operations on them. This fine-grained control is required so that these components and operations may be specified in any order and so that control of rendering operations is flexible enough to accommodate the requirements of diverse applications.

In OpenGL most geometric objects are drawn by enclosing a series of coordinate sets that specify vertices and, optionally, normals, texture coordinates, and a colon between glBegin/glEnd command pairs.

For example, to specify a triangle with vertices at (0, 0, 0), (0, 1, 0), and (1, 0, 1), one could write:

```
glBegin(GL_POLYGON);
    glVertex3i(0,0,0);
    glVertex3i(0,1,0);
```

```
    glVertex3i(1,0,1);
glEnd();²
```

Each vertex may be specified with two, three, or four coordinates (four coordinates indicate a homogeneous three-dimensional location). In addition, a *current normal, current texture coordinates*, and *current color* may be used in processing each vertex. OpenGL uses normals in lighting calculations. The current normal is a three-dimensional vector that may be set by sending three coordinates that specify it. Color may consist of red, green, blue, and alpha values (when OpenGL has been initialized to RGBA mode) or a single color index value (when initialization specified color index mode). One, two, three, or four texture coordinates determine how a texture image maps onto a primitive.

Each of the commands specifying vertex coordinates, normals, colors, or texture coordinates comes in several flavors to accommodate differing applications' data formats and numbers of coordinates. Data may also be passed to these commands either as an argument list or as a pointer to a block of storage containing the data. The variants are distinguished by mnemonic suffixes.

A procedure call is used to specify each individual group of data that together define a primitive; this means that an application may store data in any format and order that it chooses. Data need not be stored in a form convenient for presentation to the graphics API, because OpenGL accommodates almost any data type and format, using the appropriate combination of data-specification procedures. Another advantage of this scheme is that by simply combining calls in the appropriate order, different effects may be achieved. Figure 21.2 shows an example of a uniformly colored triangle obtained by specifying a single color that is inherited by all vertices of the triangle.³ A smooth-shaded triangle is obtained by respecifying a color before each vertex. Not every possible data format is supported (byte values may not be given for vertex coordinates, for instance) because it was found from experience with IRIS GL that not all formats are used. Adding the missing formats in the future, however, would be a trivial undertaking.

One disadvantage of using procedure calls on such a fine grain is that it may result in poor performance if procedure calls are costly. In such a situation an interface that specifies a format for a block of data that is sent all at once may have a performance advantage. The difficulty with specifying a block of data, however, is that it either constrains the application to store its data in one of the supported formats or requires the application to copy its data into a block structured in one of those formats, resulting in inefficiency. Allowing any format arising from an arbitrary combination of individual data types is impractical, because there are so many combinations.

In OpenGL the maximum flexibility provided by individual procedure calls was deemed more important than any inefficiency induced by using those calls. This decision is driven partly by the consideration that modem compilers and computer hardware have improved to the point where procedure calls are usually relatively inexpensive, especially when compared with the work necessary to process the geometric data contained in the call. This is one area in which OpenGL differs significantly from PEX, a primitive's vertices (and associated data) are generally presented all at

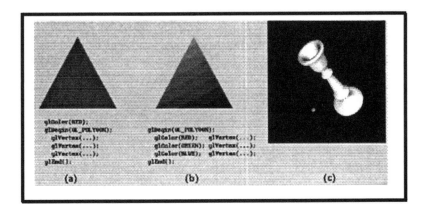

Figure 21.2 (a) A uniformly colored triangle; (b) Gouraud shaded triangle; (c) Scene consisting of many lit, shaded polygons.

once in a single array. If it turns out that fine-grained procedure calls are too expensive, it may be necessary to add a few popular block formats to the OpenGL API or to provide a mechanism for defining such formats.

Modal API

As a consequence of fine-grained control, OpenGL maintains considerable state, or modes, that determines how primitives are rendered. This state is present in lieu of having to present a large amount of information with each primitive that would describe the settings for all the operations to which the primitive would be subjected. Presenting so much information with each primitive is tedious and would result in excessive data being transmitted from client to server. Therefore essentially no information is presented with a primitive except what is required to define it. Instead a considerable proportion of OpenGL commands are devoted to controlling the settings of rendering operations.

One difficulty with a modal API arises in implementations in which separate processors (or processes) operate in parallel on distinct primitives. In such cases a mode change must be broadcast to all processors so that each receives the new parameters before it processes its next primitive. A mode change is thus processed serially, halting primitive processing until all processors have received the change, and reducing performance accordingly. One way to lessen the impact of mode changes in such a system is to insert a processor that distributes work among the parallel processors. This processor can buffer up a string of mode changes, transmitting the changes all at once only when another primitive finally arrives.

Another way to handle state changes relies on defining groups of named state settings, which can then be invoked simply by providing the appropriate name (this is the approach taken by X and PEX). With this approach a single command naming the state setting changes the server's settings. This approach was rejected for OpenGL for several reasons. Keeping track of a number of state vectors (each of which may contain considerable information) may be impractical on a graphics subsystem with limited memory. Named state settings also conflict with the emphasis on fine-grained control. In some cases changing the state of a single mode when transmitting the change directly is more convenient and efficient than first setting up and then naming the desired state vector. Finally, the named state–setting approach may still be used with OpenGL by encapsulating state-changing commands in display lists.

Matrix Stack

Three kinds of transformation matrices are used in OpenGL: the *model-view* matrix, which is applied to vertex coordinates; the *texture* matrix, which is applied to texture coordinates; and the *projection* matrix, which describes the viewing frustum and is applied to vertex coordinates after they are transformed by the model-view matrix. Each of these matrices is 4×4.

Any of one these matrices may be loaded with or multiplied by a general transformation. Commands are provided to specify the special cases of rotation, translations, and scaling (since these cases take only a few parameters to specify rather than the 16 required for a general transformation). A separate command controls a mode indicating which matrix is currently affected by any of these manipulations. In addition, each matrix type consists of a stack of matrices that can be pushed or popped. The matrix on the top of the stack is the one that is applied to coordinates and that is affected by matrix-manipulation commands.

The retained state represented by these three matrix stacks simplifies specifying the transformations found in hierarchical graphical data structures. Other graphics APIs also employ matrix stacks but often only as a part of more general attribute structures. But OpenGL is unique in providing three kinds of matrices that can be manipulated with the same commands. The texture matrix, for instance, can be used to effectively rotate or scale a texture image applied to primitive and, when combined with perspective viewing transformations, can even be used to obtain projective texturing effects, such as spotlight simulation and shadow effects using shadow maps.

State Queries and Attribute Stacks

The value of nearly any OpenGL parameter can be obtained by an appropriate get command. There is also a stack of parameter values that can be pushed and popped. For stacking purposes, all parameters are divided into 21 functional groups. Any combination of these groups can be pushed onto the attribute stack in one operation (a pop operation automatically restores only those values that were last pushed). The get commands and parameter stacks are required so that various libraries may make use of OpenGL efficiently without interfering with one another.

Frame Buffer

Most of OpenGL requires that the graphics hardware contain a frame buffer. This is a reasonable requirement, since nearly all interactive graphics applications (as well as many noninteractive ones) ran on systems with frame buffer. Some operations in OpenGL are achieved only through exposing their implementation using a frame buffer (transparency using alpha blending and hidden-surface removal using depth buffering are two examples). Although OpenGL may be used to provide information for driving such devices as pen plotters and vector displays, such use is secondary.

Multipass Algorithms

One useful effect of making the frame buffer explicit is that it enables the use of multipass algorithms, in which the same primitives are rendered several times. One example of a multipass algorithm employs an *accumulation buffer*: A scene is rendered several times, each time with a slightly different view, and the results are averaged in the frame buffer. Depending on how the view is altered on each pass, this algorithm can be used to achieve full-window antialiasing, depth-of-field effects, motion blur, or combinations of these. Multipass algorithms are simple to implement in OpenGL, because only a small number of parameters must be manipulated between passes. Changing the values of these parameters is both efficient and without side effects on other parameters that must remain constant.

Invariance

Consideration of multipass algorithms brings up the issue of how what is drawn in the frame buffer is or is not affected by changing parameter values. If, for instance, changing the viewpoint affected the way in which colors were assigned to primitives, the accumulation buffer algorithm would not work. For a more plausible example, if some OpenGL feature is not available in hardware, an OpenGL implementation must switch from hardware to software when that feature is switched on. Such a switch may significantly affect what eventually reaches the frame buffer, because of slight differences in the hardware and software implementations.

The OpenGL specification is not pixel exact. It does not indicate the exact values to which certain pixels must be set given a certain input. The reason is that such specification, besides being difficult, would be too restrictive. Different implementations of OpenGL ran on different hardware with different floating-point formats, rasterization algorithms, and frame buffer configurations. It should be possible, nonetheless, to implement a variety of multipass algorithms and expect to get reasonable results.

For this reason the OpenGL specification gives certain invariance rates that dictate under what circumstances one may expect identical results from one particular implementation given certain inputs (implementations on different systems are never required to produce identical results given identical inputs). These rates typically indicate that changing parameters that control an operation cannot affect the results due to any other operation, but that such invariance is not required when an operation is turned on or off. This makes it possible for an implementation to switch from hardware to software when a mode is invoked without breaking invariance. On the other hand, a programmer may still want invariance even when toggling some mode. To accommodate this case, any operation covered by the invariance rates admits a setting of its controlling parameters that cause the operation to act as if it were turned off even when it is on. A comparison, for instance, may be turned on or off, but when on, the comparison that is performed can be set to always (or never) pass.

Not Programmable

OpenGL does not provide a programming language. Its function may be controlled by turning operations on or off or specifying parameters to operations, but the rendering algorithms are essentially fixed. One reason for this decision is that, for performance reasons, graphics hardware is usually designed to apply certain operations in a specific order. Replacing these operations with arbitrary algorithms is usually unfeasible. Programmability would conflict with keeping the API close to the hardware and thus with the goal of maximum performance.

The model of command execution in OpenGL is that of a *pipeline* with a fixed topology (although stages may be switched in or out). The pipeline is meant to mimic the organization of graphics subsystems. The final stages of the pipeline, for example, consist of a series of tests on and modifications to fragments before they are eventually placed in the frame buffer. To draw a complex scene in a short amount of time, many fragments must pass through these final stages on their way to the frame buffer, leaving little time to process each fragment. Such high *fill rates* demand special-purpose hardware that can perform only fixed operations with minimum access to external data.

Even though fragment operations are limited, many interesting and useful effects may be obtained by combining the operations appropriately. Per-fragment operations provided by OpenGL include:

♦ Alpha blending: blend a fragment's color with that of the corresponding pixel in the frame buffer based on an alpha value.

♦ Depth test: compare a depth value associated with a fragment with the corresponding value already present in the frame buffer and discard or keep the fragment based on the outcome of the comparison.

♦ Stencil test: compare a reference value with a corresponding value stored in the frame buffer and update the value or discard the fragment based on the outcome of the comparison.[4]

Alpha blending is used to achieve transparency or to blend a fragment's color with that of the background when antialiasing. The depth test can effect depth buffering (and thus hidden-surface removal). The stencil test can be used for a number of effects, including highlighting interference regions and simple CSG (constructive solid geometry) operations. These (and other) operations may be combined to achieve, for instance, transparent interference regions with hidden surfaces removed or any number of other effects.

The OpenGL graphics pipeline also induces a kind of orthogonality among primitives. Each vertex, whether it belongs to a point, line segment, or polygon primitive, is treated in the same way. Its coordinates are transformed, and lighting (if enabled) assigns it a color. The primitive defined by these vertices is then rasterized and converted to fragments, as is a bitmap or image rectangle primitive. All fragments, no matter what their origin, are treated identically. This homogeneity among operations removes unneeded special cases (for each primitive type) from the pipeline. It also makes natural the combination of diverse primitives in the same scene without having to set special modes for each primitive type.

Geometry and Images

OpenGL provides support for handling both 3-D (and 2-D) geometry and 2-D images. An API for use with geometry should also provide support for writing, reading, and copying images, because geometry and images are often combined, as when a 3-D scene is laid over a background image. Many of the per fragment operations that are applied to fragments arising from geometric primitives apply equally well to fragments corresponding to pixels in an image, thus making it easy to mix images with geometry. For example, a triangle may be blended with an image, using alpha blending. OpenGL supports a number of image formats and operations on image components (such as lookup tables) to provide flexibility in image handling.

Texture mapping provides an important link between geometry and images by effectively applying an image to geometry. OpenGL makes this coupling explicit by providing the same formats for specifying texture images as for images destined for the frame buffer. Besides being useful for adding realism to a scene (Figure 21.3a), texture mapping can be used to achieve a number of other useful effects. Figures 21.3b and 21.3c show two examples in which the texture coordinates that index a texture image are generated from vertex coordinates.[5] OpenGL's orthogonality makes achieving such effects with texture mapping simply a matter of enabling the appropriate modes and loading the appropriate texture image, without affecting the underlying specification of the scene.

Immediate Mode and Display Lists

The basic model for OpenGL command interpretation is *immediate mode*, in which a command is executed as soon as the server receives it. Vertex processing, for example, may begin even before specification of the primitive (of which it is a part) has been completed. Immediate-mode execution is well suited to interactive applications in which primitives and modes are continually altered. In OpenGL the fine-grained control provided by immediate mode is taken as far as possible: Even individual lighting parameters (the diffuse reflectance color of a material, for instance) and texture

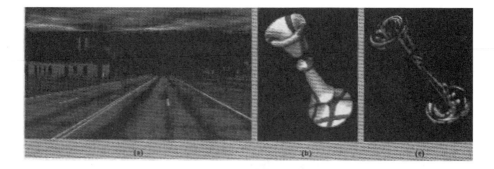

Figure 21.3 (a) A scene with a number of textures mapped onto primitives; (b) Contouring achieved with texture mapping and a texture coordinate generation function; (c) Reflectance mapping with a texture coordinate generation function.

images are set with individual commands that have immediate effect. Although immediate mode provides flexibility, its use can be inefficient if unchanging parameters or objects must be respecified. To accommodate such situations, OpenGL provides *display lists*. A display list encapsulates a sequence of OpenGL commands (all but a handful of OpenGL commands may be placed in a display list) and is stored on the server. The display list is given a numeric name by the application when it is specified. The application need only name the display list to cause the server to effectively execute all the commands contained within the list. This mechanism provides a straightforward, effective means for an application to transmit a group of commands to the server just once even when those same commands must be executed many times.

Display List Optimization

Accumulating commands into a group for repeated execution presents possibilities for optimization. Consider, for example, specifying a texture image. Texture images are often large, requiring a large, and therefore possibly slow, data transfer from client to server (or from the server to its graphics subsystem) whenever the image is respecified. For this reason some graphics subsystems are equipped with sufficient storage to hold several texture images simultaneously. If the texture image definition is placed in a display list, the server may be able to load that image just once when it is specified. When the display list is invoked (or reinvoked), the server simply indicates to the graphics subsystem that it should use the texture image already present in its memory, thus avoiding the overhead of respecifying the entire image.

Examples like this one indicate that display list optimization is required to achieve the best performance. In the case of texture image loading, the server is expected to recognize that a display list contains texture image information and to use that information appropriately. This expectation places a burden on the OpenGL implementor to make sure that special display list cases are treated as efficiently as possible. It also places a burden on the application writer to know to use display lists in cases where doing so could improve performance. Another possibility would have been to introduce special commands for functions that can be poor performers in immediate mode. But such specialization would clutter the API and blur the clear distinction between immediate mode and display lists.

Display List Hierarchies

Display lists may be redefined in OpenGL but not edited. The lack of editing simplifies display list memory management on the server, eliminating the penalty that such management would incur. One display list may, however, invoke others. An effect similar to display list editing may thus be obtained by building a list that invokes a number of subordinate lists and redefining the subordinate lists. This redefinition is possible on a fine grain: A subordinate display list may contain anything (even nothing), including just a single vertex or color command.

There is no automatic saving or restoring of modes associated with display list execution. If desired, such saving and restoring may be performed explicitly by encapsulating the appropriate commands in the display list. This allows the highest possible performance in executing a display list, since there is almost no overhead associated with its execution. It also simplifies controlling the modal behavior of display list hierarchies: Only modes explicitly set are affected.

Lack of automatic modal behavior in display lists also has a disadvantage: It is difficult to execute display lists in parallel, since the modes set in one display list must be in effect before a following display list is executed. In OpenGL display lists are generally not used for defining whole scenes or complex portions of scenes but rather for encapsulating groups of frequently repeated mode-setting commands (describing a texture image, for instance) or commands describing simple geometry (the polygons approximating aroms, for instance).

Depth Buffer

The only hidden-surface removal method directly provided by OpenGL is the depth (or z) buffer. This assumption is in line with that of the graphics hardware containing a frame buffer. Other hidden-surface removal methods may be used with OpenGL (a BSP tree coupled with the painter's algorithm, for instance), but it is assumed that such methods are never supported in hardware and thus need not be supported explicitly by OpenGL.

Local Shading

The only shading methods provided by OpenGL are local. That is, methods for determining surface color, such as ray tracing or radiosity, that require obtaining information from other parts of the scene are not directly supported. The reason is that such methods require knowledge of the global scene database. But so far, specialized graphics hardware is structured as a pipeline of localized operations and does not provide facilities to store and traverse the large amount of data necessary to represent a complex scene. Global shading methods may be used with OpenGL only if the shading can be precomputed and the results associated with graphical objects before they are transmitted to OpenGL.

Rendering Only

OpenGL provides access to rendering operations only. There are no facilities for obtaining user input from such devices as keyboards and mice, since it is expected that any system (in particular, a window system) under which OpenGL runs must already provide such facilities. Further, the effects of OpenGL commands on the frame buffer are ultimately controlled by the window system (if there is one) that allocates frame buffer resources. The window system determines which portions of the frame buffer OpenGL may access and communicates to OpenGL how those portions are structured. These considerations make OpenGL window system independent.

Integration in X

X provides both a procedural interface and a network protocol for creating and manipulating frame buffer windows and drawing certain 2-D objects into those windows. OpenGL is integrated into X by making it a formal X extension called *GLX*. GLX consists of about a dozen calls (with corresponding network encodings) that provide a compact, general embedding of OpenGL in X. As with other X extensions (two examples are Display PostScript and PEX), there is a specific network protocol for OpenGL rendering commands encapsulated in the X byte stream.

OpenGL requires a region of a frame buffer into which primitives may be rendered. In X such a region is called a *drawable*. A *window*, one type of drawable, has associated with it a *visual* that describes the window's frame buffer configuration. In GLX the visual is extended to include information about OpenGL buffers that are not present in unadorned X (depth, stencil, accumulation, front, back, etc.).

X also provides a second type of drawable, the *pixmap*, which is an off-screen frame buffer. GLX provides a GI-Y pixmap that corresponds to an X pixmap but with additional buffers as indicated by some visual. The GLX pixmap provides a means for OpenGL applications to render off screen into a software buffer.

To make use of an OpenGL-capable drawable, the programmer creates an OpenGL *context* targeted to that drawable. When the context is created, a copy of an OpenGL renderer is initialized with the visual information about the drawable. This OpenGL renderer is conceptually (if not actually) part of the X server, so that once created, an X client may *connect* to the OpenGL context and issue OpenGL commands (Figure 21.4).[6] Multiple OpenGL contexts may be created that are targeted to distinct or shared drawables. Any OpenGL-capable drawable may also be used for standard X drawing (those buffers of the drawable that are unused by X are ignored by X).

A GLX client that is running on a computer of which the graphics subsystem is a part may avoid passing OpenGL tokens through the X server. Such direct rendering may result in increased graphics performance, since the overhead of token encoding, decoding, and dispatching is eliminated. Direct rendering is supported but not required by GLX. Direct rendering is feasible, because sequentiality need not be maintained between X commands and OpenGL commands except where commands are explicitly synchronized.

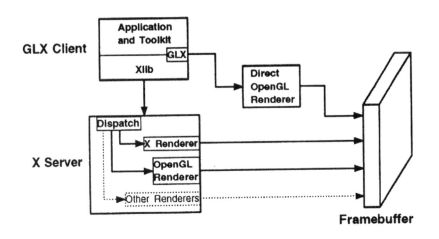

Figure 21.4 GLX client, X server, and OpenGL renderers.

Because OpenGL comprises rendering operations only, it fits well into existing window systems (integration into Windows is similar to that described for X) without duplicating operations already present in the window system (such as window control or mouse event generation). It can also make use of window system features, such as off-screen rendering, which among other uses can send the results of OpenGL commands to a printer. Rendering operations provided by the window system may even be interspersed with those of OpenGL.

API Not Protocol

PEX is specified primarily as a network protocol; PEXlib is a presentation of that protocol through an API. OpenGL, on the other hand, is specified primarily as an API. The API is encoded in a specified network protocol when OpenGL is embedded in a system (like X) that requires a protocol. One reason for this preference is that an applications programmer works with the API and not with a protocol. Another is that different platforms may admit different protocols (X places certain constraints on the protocol employed by an X extension, whereas other window systems may impose different constraints). This means that the API is constant across platforms even when the protocol cannot be, thereby making it possible to use the same source code (at least for the OpenGL portion) without regard for any particular protocol. Further, when the client and server are the same computer, OpenGL commands may be transmitted directly to a graphics subsystem without conversion to a common encoding.

Interoperability between diverse systems is not compromised by preferring an API specification over one for a protocol. Tests in which an OpenGL client running under one manufacturer's implementation was connected to another manufacturer's OpenGL server have provided excellent results.

Example: Three Kinds of Text

To illustrate the flexibility of OpenGL in performing different types of rendering tasks, three methods for the particular task of displaying text are outlined. The three methods are using bitmaps, using line segments to generate outlined text, and using a texture to generate antialiased text.

The first method defines a font as a series of display lists, each of which contains a single bitmap:

```
for i = start + 'a' to start + 'z' {
    glBeginList(i);
        glBitmap( ... );
glEndList();
```

glBitmap specifies both a pointer to an encoding of the bitmap and offsets that indicate how the bitmap is positioned relative to previous and subsequent bitmaps.[7]

In GLX the effect of defining a number of display lists in this way may also be achieved by calling glXUseXFont, which generates a number of display lists. Each display list contains the bitmap (and associated offsets) of a single character from the specified X font.

In either case the string Bitmapped Text whose origin is the projection of a location in 3-D is produced by:

```
glRasterPos3i(x, y, z);
glListBase(start);
glCallLists("Bitmapped Text",14,GL_BYTE);[8]
```

In Figure 21.5a glListBase sets the display list base so that the subsequent glCallLists references the characters just defined.[9] GlCallLists invokes a series of display lists specified in an array. Each value in the array is added to the display list base to obtain the number of the display list to use. In this case the array is an array of bytes representing a string. The second argument to glCallLists indicates the length of the string. The third argument indicates that the string is an array of 8-bit bytes (16- and 32-bit integers may be used to access fonts with more than 256 characters).

The second method is similar to the first but uses line segments to outline each character. Each display list contains a series of line segments:

```
glTranslate(ox, oy, 0);
glBegin (GL_LINES);
      glVertex( ... );
            . . .
glEnd ();
glTranslate(dx-ox, dy-oy, 0);
```

The initial glTranslate updates the transformation matrix to position the character with respect to a character origin. The final glTranslate updates that character origin in preparation for the following character. A string is displayed with this method just as in the previous example, but since line segments have 3-D position,

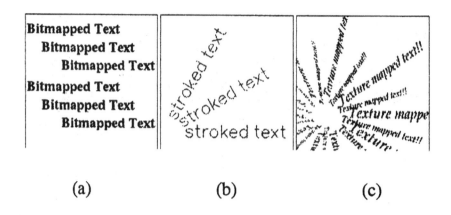

Figure 21.5 (a) Bitmap example; (b) Stroke font example; (c) Texture-mapped font example.

the text may be oriented as well as positioned in 3-D (Figure 21.5b).[10] More generally the display lists could contain both polygons and line segments, and these could be antialiased.

Finally, a different approach may be taken by creating a texture image containing an array of characters. A certain range of texture coordinates thus corresponds to each character in the texture image.

Each character may be drawn in any size and in any 3-D orientation by drawing a rectangle with the appropriate texture coordinates at its vertices:

```
glTranslate(ox, oy, 0);
glBegin(GL_QUADS)
     glTexCoord( ... );
     glVertex( ... );
          ...
glEnd ();
glTranslate(dx-ox, dy-oy, 0);
```

If each group of commands for each character is enclosed in a display list, and the commands for describing the texture image itself (along with the setting of the list base) are enclosed in another display list called TEX. Then, the string Texture mapped text!! may be displayed by:

```
glCallList(TEX);
glCallLists("Texture mapped text!!",21,GL_BYTE);
```

One advantage of this method is that, by simply using appropriate texture filtering, the resulting characters are antialiased (Figure 21.5c).

Summary

OpenGL is a 3-D graphics API intended for use in interactive applications. It has been designed to provide maximum access to hardware graphics capabilities, no matter at what level such capabilities are available. This efficiency stems from a flexible interface that provides direct control over fundamental operations. OpenGL does not enforce a particular method of describing 3-D objects and how they should appear but instead provides the basic means by which those objects, no matter how described, may be rendered. Because OpenGL imposes minimum structure on 3-D rendering, it provides an excellent base on which to build libraries for handling structured geometric objects, no matter what the particular structures may be.

The goals of high performance, feature orthogonality, interoperability, implementability on a variety of systems, and extensibility have driven the design of OpenGL's API. This chapter has shown the effects of these and other considerations on the presentation of rendering operations in OpenGL. The result has been a straightforward API with few special cases, which should be easy to use in a variety of applications.

Future work on OpenGL is likely to center on improving implementations through optimization and extending the API to handle new techniques and capabilities provided by graphics hardware. Likely candidates for inclusion are image-processing operators, new texture-mapping capabilities, and other basic geometric primitives, such as spheres and cylinders. If care is taken in the design of the OpenGL API, it will make these as well as other extensions simple and will result in OpenGL's remaining a useful 3-D graphics API for many years to come.

From Here

Now that we've discussed OpenGL graphics interface design considerations, let's look at behavior engine technology and its comparison to a behavior language protocol for VRML. These topics are discussed in the next chapter.

Endnotes

1 Mark Segal and Kurt Akeley, The Design of the OpenGL Graphics Interface, Silicon Graphics Computer Systems, 2011 N. Shoreline Blvd., Mountain View, CA 94039, 1994, p. 2.

2 Ibid., p. 4.

3 Ibid., p. 3.

4 Ibid., p. 6.

5 Ibid., p. 7.

6 Ibid., p. 8.

7 Ibid., p. 9.

8 Ibid., p. 9.

9 Ibid., p. 9.

10 Ibid., p. 9.

22

Virtual Behavior Engines

The technology underlying the *behavior engine* (BE) was developed during nearly 13 years of work in the domain of manufacturing simulation. This technology allows simulations, as well as the documents through which the reader accesses them, to be built by linking and embedding components distributed on the WWW. Thus, a repair manual for an automobile can be constructed by linking or embedding documents and simulations of its parts. Creation of the compound simulation includes specification of the behavioral interactions among the simulations of the parts.

The BE includes utilities supporting creation of a variety of behaviors, including motion of kinematic devices. At the same time, the authoring environment is fully open and allows description of arbitrarily complex behaviors in a programming formalism called *BEyond*. The power, efficiency, and completeness of this formalism are indicated by the fact that the behavior engine itself was implemented in BEyond.

Overview of BE

The basic technical idea underlying the behavior engine is the embedding of all of the varieties of information needed to describe objects and their behavior, including classes, algorithms, and specialized parametric behavioral forms, such as motion, into a unified structure with common methods for hierarchical assembly and hierarchical naming. This contrasts to conventional simulation and programming technology in which the realms of code and data are separated. Classes and behavior are on the code side, and code-side naming is of fixed depth (package/class/method).

As a result of the unified approach implemented by the behavior engine, behavior can be alloyed with other attributes of objects so that things, such as simulated mechanical devices, carry their behaviors within themselves. Assembly of systems and documents with associated behavior then goes very smoothly, because there is only one kind of glue needed to connect them—glue that works on behavioral and nonbehavioral elements alike.

BE products have three levels of technical content. The fundamental level supports creation of a kind of Web-distributed software component called a *BEing*, which is the external form of a BE object and implements the uniformities just described. In addition to embedding classes and their behavior, BEings support parameterization of their content, temporal modeling, versioning and configuration management, and object evolution; so objects can change class membership, as well as other properties, over their lifetimes.

The second level applies this general infrastructure to documents and three-dimensional objects and their behaviors. A BEing that incorporates these elements can serve as a parameterized document that embeds interactive 3-D simulations.

The third level adds support that is specifically useful to mechanical product modeling and simulation. For example, kinematic modeling, with associated user interfaces, allows creation of documented simulations of mechanisms.

Objects and Classes

As in most object systems, a BE class specifies a collection of typed fields. However, BE classes dictate the structure of their members less strictly than do conventional systems, such as C++, Smalltalk, or Java. BE objects can change their class membership over time and can have their own attributes in addition to those dictated by their classes.

Naming

A BE name (called a *reference*) is a kind of pathname that specifies a way to navigate to the named object through the object structure. References play all of the naming roles in the behavior engine; they serve as program variables, names of functions and classes, and pathnames of geometric objects in the hierarchically structured 3-D world model. References may appear as data embedded in any kind of object. They can be mentioned, as well as used, by programs.

BEings

A BEing is a BE object that is meaningful as a separate entity—an object that can be stored, sent as a message, or served on the WWW. A BEing, like any BE object, can serve as a programming context within which functions, classes, and global variables are defined. BEings can be assembled to form a hierarchically structured programming environment. All entities, including classes and functions, can appear at arbitrary depth in such a hierarchical structure and can be named by references. This contrasts to conventional programming formalisms (including C++, Smalltalk, CLOS, Java, etc.), in which classes and functions/methods must be organized in a structure of a fixed depth of 1, 2, or 3, and hierarchical assembly cannot be done directly but only via some kind of flattening. BEings are typically used to represent units of BE functionality, such as simulations of mechanical assemblies.

Assembly

The basic assembly operations are embedding or linking BEings into BEings at the next-larger scale. These operations use one uniform mechanism—resolution of references—to connect BEings. This uniformity is possible because references cover all varieties of symbolic naming.

Each level of a hierarchy is represented by a BEing with its own models, functions, behaviors, and classes. New levels are built by embedding, linking, or sharing BEings from the existing levels. A typical BEing is a simulation of a component of a system at a particular scale. For example, a mechanical assembly is modeled by a hierarchy of BEings mirroring the part-subpart structure of the assembly. BEings at each level fully encode the behavior and classes relevant at that level.

Time and Concurrency

The BE programming formalism includes a full complement of constructs for modeling time and concurrent activity. When modeling a temporal process using computation, some computations determine the state of a simulation at a particular instant of time, and other computations step through a duration of simulated time determining the sequence of events that will take place. For example, the computation that determines the gravitational forces acting on astronomical objects at a given instant of time in a planetary simulation is of the former kind. Of course, the computation takes time on the computer executing the simulation but should not be allocated any duration in the simulated world.

The behavior engine model posits that the state of the simulated world at any given moment consists of the following components:

- A real-valued clock whose state reflects the current time in the simulated world
- An ordered set of instantaneous computations, called *influences*, representing the conditions and constraints currently in force
- A current set of *temporal* behaviors—behaviors with nonzero duration in simulated time[1]

The influences are computations that update the state of the world, based on the current clock value. An influence can be sampled at any time while it is in force. Temporal behaviors are discrete threads of activity, including instantaneous acts interleaved with waits for events or semaphores, and delays in simulated time. Many temporal behaviors are effectively described by objects rather than directly by code. For example, there is a class motion whose subclasses are used to describe many varieties of motion in 3-D space, including articulated motions of kinematic mechanisms. Programmers are free to add their own temporal behavior classes to the existing hierarchy.

Programming the Behavior Engine

The programming formalism used in the BE is called *BEyond*. BEyond's syntax and semantics make it particularly suitable for use by people with an engineering or scientific background, who may not necessarily fit the profile of professional software developers. A programmer can get started and do useful work by treating BEyond as an interactive implementation of Pascal and pick up the more advanced features as needed.

Comparison to Other Simulation Technology

Many simulation systems exist, covering a wide variety of behaviors. But in traditional implementations of simulation software, the bulk of what it takes to describe and render complex behavior is rigidly fixed in the code that makes up the implementation. This makes it difficult or impossible to create kinds of behavior not contemplated by the architects of available simulators or to assemble disparate kinds of behavioral objects into a single system or document, even if each constituent of the system is addressed by one or another existing simulation product. The aim of the behavior engine is to provide an infrastructure for creation of simulation-enriched documents that does not place *a priori* constraints on the kinds of behavior that can be included.

Java is an adaptation of C++ that supports transmission of platform-independent executable code on the Internet. Java has been integrated with the WWW browser technologies HotJava (from Sun Microsystems) and Netscape Communicator. Those familiar with Java may wonder about how Java and BE technologies compare. Before embarking on a detailed discussion of this issue, it should be pointed out that the behavior engine is integrated with Netscape Communicator, which includes Java applets, enabling use of the two technologies in concert.

Like the behavior engine, Java-based technology exists at more than one level: at the fundamental level independent of applications, at the level of generic browser applications, and at the level of uses in particular industries. But Java and the behavior engine have several differences at the fundamental level.

First, Java, like the behavior engine, supports WWW distribution of software components. But in the current implementation, Java provides support for distribution only of classes, not instances. Although descriptions of instances can be encoded in classes (by constants or by algorithms that generate the instances), the classes still arise from source code. No generic support is available for saving or distributing an object that has been created or modified in the course of a Java session. To put it succinctly, Java technology in its current form supports distribution of code but not data. BE, on the other hand, supports saving any kind of structure, including those that mix classes, behaviors, and ordinary objects.

Of course, Java programmers, like programmers in any language, are free to design application-specific formats for transmitting their data, but the likely consequence is that multiple formats will prevent assembly of content from diverse sources. Also, generic support for persistent and distributable objects may well be added to Java in the future, but there is as yet no indication of what this support will look like or when it will arrive. The remaining differences between Java and BE are architectural and will not disappear with the addition of features to Java.

Second, BE, unlike Java, provides direct and generic support for hierarchical assembly of behavioral systems. In the BE classes, behaviors, and all other kinds of objects are embedded in a common hierarchy with a common naming scheme. Java takes a more conventional approach: All behavior is held in the methods of classes, and classes are effectively organized as a flat, not a hierarchical, structure (despite superficial appearance). The practical effect is that BE provides much more effective support for hierarchical assembly of systems and widespread distribution of components that can be used together freely at a later time than does Java. Here are the details.

In Java, behavior is defined by methods within classes, and any object gets all of its behavior from its class. Within Java code, a class is referenced by a simple name or a fully qualified name (package + name). Either way, by the time the Java compiler generates bytecodes, all such names have been resolved to fully qualified names. Although the programmer may have included dots or other symbols in the class and package names to represent a mental hierarchy, the name is treated as atomic by the time it is turned into bytecode. Thus in Java, as in C++, objective C, and Smalltalk, classes are organized in a flat name space. Behaviors appear as methods of classes. This leads to fundamental difficulties in the construction of hierarchical systems from distributed components.

For example, in BE it is commonplace to make a copy B of a system A and subsequently modify B, including internal classes and behaviors. Later on, A and the modified B might end up as parts of the same assembly. This might take place after a long separation and many previous assembly steps. None of this is problematic in BE. But in Java, under the same assumptions, A and B would have to remain forever separate. They could never end up together in the same assembly, because they include different classes with the same name. These names propagate upward arbitrarily through many levels of assembly. In Java, it is necessary to rename any class that is modified, especially if there is any chance of its bumping into its old self out on the Net. Java class names (and behavior names in the form of class.method), like IP addresses, must be unique on a planetary scale if all assembly dangers are to be avoided. But forcing uniqueness of names causes its own problems: Any code that mentioned an old version of a class by name and that is needed in a context where the new version is relevant must be not only recompiled but also rewritten.

Third, in the BE, objects can evolve. They can acquire new behaviors, lose old behaviors, and change class membership over time. This possibility for evolution is built into the structure of all objects. In Java, as in C++, objects are much more rigid; their class memberships, and thus their signatures (how their attributes are named), are frozen at creation time. The evolutionary features of BE objects are important both for simulation and for effectively supporting components that may have long lives traveling the Internet.

Finally, Java's reflective capabilities are better than C++ but still weak compared to BE. In Java, a class is an object, but the internal structure of classes is not available for manipulation; nor are the contents of an object accessible except by code, which has its class compiled in. In BE, all metadata, including the structure of classes and of behavior, is fully available. The practical effect is that general-purpose code can be developed in BE that applies to objects whose classes and interfaces are not known in advance. For example, generic user interfaces for browsing objects and metalevel facilities, such as systems for managing class repositories, can be developed within BE for dealing with its own content.

Other differences between Java and BE exist at the fundamental level, but an exhaustive list is beyond the scope of this chapter. There are also significant differences in the way that the two technologies are applied in the context of documents with active content. In Netscape Communicator and HotJava WWW browsers, Java serves as the implementation language for *applets*. An applet is a small application that presents itself to the user within a window allocated for it in an HTML document. In this approach, applets are elements of a document, not the other way around.

In contrast, BEings typically include documents as part of their content. Parameterized BEings may include document generators, which compute appropriate HTML from the values supplied for parameters. Three-dimensional content is treated the same way: as an element of a BEing that may be computed from parameters— often the same parameters as govern an associated document.

A BEing representing a complex set of data, such as assembly and maintenance methods for a mechanical system, should be viewed as a unified whole presented to the user by a collection of interactive documents. This approach allows both the content of the documents and the interpretation of user interactions with the document to be derived from a unified underlying model.

Example Applications

The behavior engine can be used to create owner's manuals for mechanical equipment that incorporate detailed simulations of the equipment's behavior. For example, Figure 22.1 shows an image of a radial arm saw as it would appear in the behavior engine's 3-D window.[2] Simulated operation of the saw is controlled by clicking on text or submitting forms from the associated document or, more directly, by manipulating the saw, using the mouse in the 3-D window. The details of how the saw works govern what can be done in the simulation.

Figure 22.1 Image of a Radial Arm Saw as it would appear in BE's 3-D Window.

The simulated world can also be affected by links or forms in the Web document. For example, clicking on a link called New Board in the document causes a 2×4 to appear on the saw table. Thereafter, dragging the blade over the 2×4 results in the simulated board being cut in two.

The BE edition of the owner's manual thus includes a working model of the thing it describes. The manual also includes step-by-step instructions for saw operations, which are illustrated by simulation and exercises in which operation of the saw by the reader is monitored and corrected.

Repositories of Parameterized Objects, Behaviors, and Documents

A central feature of BE technology is that it supports creation of repositories of software components, called BEings, that can be distributed on the World Wide Web and that serve as reusable building blocks for related applications. BEings include all of the varieties of data needed to represent an object, its behaviors, and the active documents via which the user interacts with the object. The next example illustrates the use of BEing repositories in creating online, simulation-based documentation for a line of related products. The same general points apply to many classes of products, but for the sake of simplicity and familiarity, the example described here will be assembly-required furniture kits.

There are three kinds of users in this scenario: repository builders, who add new BEings to the repository; document authors, who develop new individual documents by drawing on the repository; and the final customer, who learns how to assemble the furniture kit by interacting with an assembly document for that kit—that includes detailed 3-D simulations of the assembly steps. The repository builders may need some knowledge of BE technology, but neither the document author nor the final customer need any special expertise. Creating new documents for new kits is very efficient, because most of the elements of documentation, modeling, and simulation will be present already in parametric form in the repository.

Although this example is quite simple, exactly the same approach applies to the creation and use of simulation-based documentation for complex mechanical products, where the end user of the documentation is an engineer or maintenance person rather than a consumer. The objective in any case is to efficiently codify and reuse parametric descriptions of documents, mechanical parts, and mechanical behavior in the sharing of engineering knowledge.

The individual BEings in the repository for the furniture kit example hold the following varieties of information:

- *Classes*, that is, generic part descriptions. Examples are parameterized models of fasteners, such as screws and dowels; parameterized models of furniture elements, such as boards; parameterized models of tools, such as wrenches, screw drivers, and others.
- *Behaviors*, including mating behaviors (bringing furniture parts into correct relative position for an assembly

operation) and fastening behaviors, such as use of tools to perform a fastening operation. Behaviors are also parameterized and described by classes.

♦ *User interfaces* for assisting the designer in creating the particular parts, fasteners, and behaviors needed for a particular furniture assembly.

♦ *Parameterized documents* describing steps of assembly. A parameterized document in this case is a schematicized document and associated 3-D simulation describing an assembly step. Instances of such documents are used as parts of the final assembly instructions seen by the customer. So far, all the BEings have been of a parametric nature, and form a common base for designing and documenting many individual furniture kits.

From these parameterized BEings, the following concrete models and documents are created:

♦ Particular part and behavior models
♦ Particular assembly sequences
♦ Assembly instruction documents for particular kits[3]

Behavior Engine Products

The BEyond programming environment provides the tools necessary for developers to access behavior engine classes and to create new behaviors and behavior classes. BEyond is suitable for creating BEyond documents that do not include 3-D content or for developing simulation applications in which 3-D modeling is not appropriate. BEyond supports assembly of complex systems of behavior from components and is fully integrated with World Wide Web technology.

BE Designer

BE Designer extends the BEyond programming environment with behavior classes supporting three-dimensional simulations. It provides all of the facilities needed to create BEyond documents incorporating 3-D content, including utilities for creating simple kinematic mechanisms, and for basic temporal path planning and motion. The Open Inventor 3-D library supplies rendering and modeling functionality; 3-D models in any of the many formats convertible into Open Inventor format can be loaded into BE Designer as the starting point for creation of 3-D simulations. BEyond documents created with BE Designer can be served to the WWW by standard servers, such as Netscape Commerce Server.

BE Player

Finally, BE Player is the viewer or player for BEyond documents created with BE Designer. BE Player works with an HTML browser, such as Netscape Communicator. Like any browser, BE Player can access BEyond documents stored in the local file system or remotely on the WWW.

From Here

Now that I've thoroughly explored the intricacies of behavior engine technology as it relates to VRML, let's look at the numerous VRML applications that have been derived from this technology. The next chapter looks at numerous VR applications that have been developed and delivered via the Internet. They range from architectural models, to commercial (virtual banking and retailing), to military, space-related, medical, and last but not least, other miscellaneous applications. Now that I've thoroughly explored the intricacies of Behavior Engine Technology as it relates to VRML, the next chapter covers other ongoing VR research projects that will eventually be imported to the Internet.

Endnotes

1   *Behavior Engine Technology*, The BE Software Company, 1995.
2   Ibid.
3   Ibid.

23

Other VR Research

Chapter 19 presented numerous proposed VRML research projects and systems. This chapter will guide you through the development of ongoing realistic VR projects within the commercial, military, academic, and medical communities, and amusement for eventual importation to the Internet as possible VRML applications.

Commercial: Next Generation of Interactivity and Photorealism on the Web

Live Picture's RealSpace Imaging Solution is composed of tools and technologies that introduce a different look and feel for the Web, bringing a completely interactive experience to the desktop, across intranets, and on the Internet.[1] The RealSpace solution project combines visual realism, user-driven interactivity, and 3-D spatial navigation—while operating on standard network bandwidths. The project also offers methods for displaying and selecting information and products on the Web. It's also a scalable solution of products and technologies that can be integrated into existing Web environments.

In other words, RealSpace helps provide a comprehensive solution for visual interaction. The product line includes image viewers, server modules, and authoring software based on revolutionary imaging technologies. It is intended for Web designers, content creators, and pioneers of Internet and intranet solutions who want to create interactive 2-D and 3-D media-rich content. Web sites powered by this product offer a photospatial experience that goes well beyond the static page-based HTML metaphor. The product's methods and image-streaming technologies help advance the next generation of imaging on the Web. It lays the foundation for interactive television through video-quality and fully interactive content that can be manipulated with a remote control.

Advantages

The RealSpace solution project helps solve three of the fundamental problems that have prevented the broad adoption of new visual interactive techniques on the Web:

+ Printing and viewing high-resolution images on the Web
+ Displaying multiple media data types within one client
+ Incorporating spatial, 3D interactivity[2]

The project does the preceding all without increased bandwidth consumption. In each case, Live Picture has taken the technologies and incorporated them into the RealSpace solution project.

Printing and Viewing

RealSpace helps break the screen-resolution barrier by enabling high-resolution images to be used on the Web. Web designers can now use image sizes appropriate to the application and not be constrained by the resolution of the monitor. This is accomplished through active image-streaming technology, based on the recently introduced Internet Imaging Protocol. This protocol, co-defined by Live Picture, Hewlett-Packard, and Eastman Kodak, and endorsed by Netscape and Microsoft, lets a browser or viewer access selected areas of a FlashPix image that resides on a Web server. High-resolution images in the FlashPix file format (which will be discussed later in the chapter) can be used to represent individual 2-D images, image-based objects, and texture-mapped surfaces both in 3-D objects and panoramic images. The user can zoom in to an image and examine fine details and, for the first time, download sufficient image data to obtain high-quality print results. Web users are no longer limited to screen-resolution images. One of the key remaining problems on the Web is visual realism. While photographs and images have proliferated on the Web to some 100 million images, they are only available at screen resolution. Applications where higher-resolution print-quality images are beneficial, include:

♦ Promotion of high-ticket items such as automobiles, clothing, real estate, and travel
♦ Online publishing of print-quality documents such as magazines and stock photography
♦ Online technical support and training for efficient workflow[3]

One Browser for Mixed Media

RealSpace allows users to create, view, and combine multiple media formats within a single interactive viewing and browsing environment. They are based on core visual technologies designed specifically for the Web, including: high-resolution images incorporating the FlashPix technology and panoramic imaging that uses automatic image stitching to create:

♦ Photorealistic 3-D backgrounds
♦ Image-based objects that present products and objects in true photorealistic 3-D
♦ Industry-standard VRML 2.0 for dynamic 3-D rendered scenes and animation[4]

Most attempts to enhance the media experience on the Web have focused on combining multiple media types. As a result, there are separate browsers for audio, video, 3-D (based on VRML), and panoramic imaging. There is no comprehensive solution for creating a single interactive environment that combines multiple media data types.

Fully Immersed Photospatial Interactivity

RealSpace technologies push static page-based navigation to an advanced photospatial experience where users can manipulate images and objects on the Web. The photospatial experience offers familiar interactions, such as spatial navigation, that are commonplace in electronic games but nearly nonexistent on the Web. Users can zoom into 2-D images to view additional detail or content, and move freely through panoramic images with hotspots linking to different locations. In addition, users can select objects for interactive 3-D viewing.

Now, let's look at the FlashPix image file format as shown in Figure 23.1.[5] FlashPix is based on a multiple-resolution, tiled data structure that can be thought of as an image pyramid. The base of the pyramid represents the source image at its highest resolution. The other levels each represent another resolution.

Imaging Technologies

FlashPix can be thought of as an image file format designed as an open, cross-platform standard for the interchange and distribution of images—a *digital-film* format for imaging software and hardware from different vendors. Live Picture, in collaboration with Kodak, Hewlett-Packard, and Microsoft, jointly developed this format. In addition to the four initial developers, many other industry leaders have announced a commitment to delivering hardware and software solutions to support the FlashPix format, including Fuji, Canon, Intel, Apple, and IBM.

FlashPix also offers several features that are not available in mainstream image-file formats such as JPEG, PNG, TIFF, or GIFF:

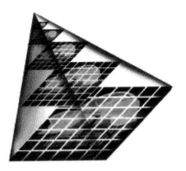

Figure 23.1 FlashPix pyramid.

♦ Multiresolution tiled image storage for rapid access to high-resolution data

♦ Extendible storage, based on Microsoft's OLE-structured storage, that makes it convenient to add application-specific data

♦ Standardized color space, called sRGB, that simplifies the interchange of color values between applications and systems

♦ Viewing parameters that define common image manipulations such as rotation, perspective adjustment, skewing, and cropping in a way that is nondestructive to the image data and that can be undone at any time[6]

In addition, FlashPix is a tiled, multiresolution image format supported in the mainstream applications arena. It enables applications to image data directly at any level of resolution and any spatial selection. This ability accelerates viewing, panning, zooming, rotating, and cropping, even when the image is stored on a relatively slow medium (such as a CD-ROM) or accessed across an intranet.

The Internet Imaging Protocol

In order to make the various features of FlashPix widely available across intranets and the Internet, a new active-streaming protocol has been defined by Live Picture, Hewlett-Packard, and Kodak. The protocol has been endorsed by Netscape and Microsoft and has been submitted to Internet standards bodies for public comment.

The *Internet Imaging Protocol* (IIP) enables a plug-in, Java applet, or other client application to interactively request image and property data from a Web server. IIP commands allow the client to request specific image tiles, a range of tiles, or download the entire FlashPix file. The image window becomes a viewing port for the underlying image that resides on an intranet server. Only the tiles necessary to fill the window are transferred across the intranet. The image can be viewed at any level of magnification with the desired cropping.

While IIP works most effectively with FlashPix image files, it is a general protocol that can be used to access other tiled-image formats. It can also be used to access existing formats, such as JPEG and TIFF.

The Internet Imaging Framework

The RealSpace Imaging Solution project is a commercial suite of applications based on Hewlett-Packard's Imaging for Internet Framework, a new architecture that enables end-to-end imaging applications on the Internet. Live Picture and Hewlett-Packard collaborated on the development of this framework and integrated core technologies of this architecture into the RealSpace Image Server and viewer modules. Live Picture will continue to work closely with Hewlett-Packard to develop a comprehensive, multi-platform, interactive imaging solution based on this framework. In addition, Microsoft, Netscape, Oracle, and Informix have endorsed their support for the framework and are developing customized Internet imaging applications that support it.

Panoramic Imaging

RealSpace also makes extensive use of *panoramic imaging*, a technique pioneered by Apple Computer's QuickTime VR. Panoramic imaging creates a photorealistic 3-D navigable environment by automatically stitching together photographs taken with ordinary cameras or digital cameras. Live Picture's patent-pending panoramic technology goes a step further by enabling Web designers to seamlessly blend in VRML 2.0 objects, audio and video, image-based objects, and high-resolution FlashPix images to create a 3-D multimedia browsing experience. In addition, RealSpace helps solve four limitations that are inherent to Apple's QuickTime VR and other systems based on the Apple technology:

- Panoramic images are streamed into the viewer—there's no waiting for the entire image to load.
- Panoramic image files are 3–10 times smaller than comparable QuickTime VR files.
- Panoramic technology supports 360- by 180-degree full spherical viewing.
- PhotoVista software can be used to automatically stitch photographs together to create panoramas in minutes, as shown in the companion CD-ROM.[7]

Image-Based Objects (IMOBs)

RealSpace IMOBs allow the use of images and video to represent 2-D or 3-D objects that can be placed in a virtual environment. They behave like 3-D objects and can be viewed from different directions. Since IMOBs are created with images or videos, they are photorealistic and showcase products in greater detail. They are typically created by placing an object on a turntable and photographing it from different directions.

3-D Objects and Scenes Based on VRML97

RealSpace includes full support for VRML97, the industry standard for describing 3-D virtual environments and displaying them on the Internet. VRML97 is the most recent release and is supported by major Internet browsers. The RealSpace Viewer supports both standard VRML97 as well as Live Picture's Image Worlds Specification. This specification extends standard VRML97 to include IMOBs and panoramic viewing. Using photographic images, the extension greatly enhances the display quality and applications of VRML.

Active-Image Streaming

Together, the FlashPix file format and the Internet Imaging Protocol offer a significantly improved approach for transmitting images across intranets. Table 23.1 compares the load times of JPEG and FlashPix images on a standard Ethernet connection.[8] The first image is a typical small, screen-resolution image on a Web page. The second is a full-page, 150-dpi image that would produce reasonable quality when printed on a standard home inkjet printer. The third is a full-page, 300-dpi color image suitable for high-quality printing.

The time to display the first image is slightly faster because it is supported natively by the Web browser. For the larger images, the RealSpace method is significantly faster because it is not necessary to retrieve the entire file; this only occurs when the image is downloaded or printed. The performance results for large files indicates clearly that it is impractical to load and print large JPEG images on the Web. RealSpace is able to provides this imaging solution when access to fine details, interactive panning and zooming, or printing is required. This is especially important for the new generation of home printers introduced by Hewlett-Packard, Epson, and Canon that print photographic quality, but the file sizes are typically 10MB uncompressed.

The Architecture

As previously mentioned, RealSpace is a client/server solution that establishes a standard for fast and easy transmission of high-resolution images, all within the framework of the HTTP protocol. Two free clients are available for accessing images on the RealSpace Image Server and both work with Netscape Navigator and Microsoft Internet Explorer. The FlashPix Viewer displays FlashPix images while the RealSpace Viewer displays 3-D images. Live Picture will soon combine the capabilities of both viewers and release the latest version of the RealSpace Viewer that is capable of both high-resolution 2-D and 3-D browsing.

Table 23.1 Active-Image Streaming Performance Comparison

Image Type & Size	Image Dimensions (pixels)	Image size Uncompressed/ Compressed	Load Time in Web Browser (JPEG files)	Load Time with RealSpace (FlashPix files)
Typical Web image	360 × 300	324KB/32KB	1.8 seconds	2.6 seconds
Typical consumer image 8≤ × 10≤ @ 150 dpi	1500 × 1200	5.4MB/500KB	15 seconds	3.2 seconds
Full-page color image 8≤ × 10≤ @ 300 dpi	24,000 × 3000	21.6MB/2.2MB	55 seconds	3.2 seconds

Imaging Products

The comprehensive RealSpace product line consists of the Image Server, client image viewers, and authoring tools. The solution is modular and scalable, enabling Web designers to combine and use different media types. For example, users can start by adding support for high-resolution viewing and printing, or advance to publishing virtual reality experiences on their Web sites.

The Image Server

The RealSpace Image Server is one solution for viewing, distributing, sharing, and printing photo-quality digital images on the Web. Based on the FlashPix image file format and IIP, the Image Server is a scalable solution for significantly enhancing image-based applications on the Internet, intranet, and extranet. It operates on the principle that only the image detail necessary for viewing is transmitted, not the entire image file. However, when the user zooms, pans, or prints, additional image data is streamed from the server. Both Netscape and Microsoft have announced that IIP will be supported in their future products, and Hewlett-Packard plans to support IIP in its future Internet servers.

In other words, the Image Server is a software module that runs on standard Web servers. It is currently available for Windows NT, Hewlett-Packard Unix (HP-UX), Sun Solaris, and Silicon Graphics IRIX platforms. Support for additional platforms is under development. All platforms feature a *Common Gateway Interface* (CGI). Fast CGI and *Netscape Server Application Programming Interface* (NSAPI) modules are available for selected platforms. The Image Server works in conjunction with the FlashPix and RealSpace client viewers that plug in to Netscape Navigator and Microsoft Internet Explorer. In addition, custom applications and viewers can be developed that operate with the Image Server.

Viewers

The FlashPix Viewer presents high-resolution FlashPix images quickly, even on 28.8K modems. Since only the image data necessary to view the current window is transferred, large image files can be efficiently transmitted.

The RealSpace Viewer brings photorealistic 3-D environments to the Web. Site designers can create rich multimedia scenes that combine panoramas, enhanced VRML97-rendered objects, 3-D photo objects, and streaming audio. RealSpace files are small; a typical panorama is less than 100K—3 to 10 times smaller than the current generation of QuickTime VR files. Both viewers are plug-ins for Netscape Navigator and Microsoft Internet Explorer, and are available for Macintosh and Windows platforms.

Authoring Tools

RealSpace also allows Web designers to work with their favorite multimedia software tools to create photospatial environments that can include 2-D and 3-D images, VRML 3-D objects, panoramic scenes, video, and audio. Because RealSpace is based on standards, designers can work with familiar 2-D imaging tools, 3-D modelers, or combine a range of media types to create a dynamic photospatial experience for the Web.

2-D Imaging

In addition, RealSpace works with standard GIF and JPEG images, as well as FlashPix images—the emerging and preferred file format for the Internet. The FlashPix Photoshop plug-in allows designers working in Photoshop to read and write FlashPix files quickly and easily. With this plug-in, users can save images to the FlashPix file format and add high-resolution images to their Web site.

Live Picture's FlashPix image-editing application delivers a variety of tools for masking, compositing, text handling, color correction, textures, gradients, and more. Designed to accelerate large-image handling, FlashPix is simply the fastest way to create high-quality photocomposites. Frequently used with Photoshop, FlashPix delivers new levels of creative freedom, image quality, and production speed.

Panoramic Imaging

Live Picture's new PhotoVista makes the complicated process of image stitching quick and easy with its point-and-click user interface. Users can take a series of photographs with virtually any camera, convert the photographs to digital format, and then import the digital images into PhotoVista, as shown in the companion CD-ROM. The software automatically aligns and pieces the images together by applying sophisticated edge detection and smoothing algorithms to create a seamless 360-degree panorama.

3-D Imaging

The RealSpace Viewer includes support for VRML97, the standard for 3-D on the Internet. VRML objects and scenes can be created with Macromedia Extreme 3-D, Fractal RayDream Designer, Autodesk 3D Studio, and other leading 3-D modelers. RealVR Xtra is a plug-in for Macromedia Director that adds photorealistic virtual worlds to the Director environment, enabling users to develop virtual-reality Web sites and CD-ROM titles. RealVR Xtra combines Director Lingo scripting and animation capabilities with RealSpace photospatial technologies to create an interactive experience blending multimedia and virtual reality.

Military: DIVE Technology

Until recently, no serious effort was under way to develop virtual environments to allow individual combatants access to the virtual battlefield. As new technologies allow the individual soldier to employ increasingly lethal smart weapons, the importance of the virtual soldier will be even greater on future battlefields.

Simulation and training systems currently under development, such as the *Close Combat Tactical Trainer* (CCTT), provide only a minimal ability to simulate the effects of dismounted infantry. Moreover, these systems do not provide any means to train infantry in even an approximately realistic setting.

Recent research conducted by the *United States Army Simulation Training and Instrumentation Command* (STRICOM) and Avatar Partners, Inc., Boulder Creek, California, attempts to enable the realistic simulation of combined arms combat, including dismounted infantry. The proposed approach will allow individual soldiers to enter the virtual battlefield through specially designed gateways known as *Dismounted Infantry Virtual Environment* (DIVE) chambers—instrumented rooms—that allow the soldiers to immerse themselves in a virtual environment, as shown in Figure 23.2. Within this environment, a soldier will be able to navigate through a variety of terrain, engage in combat, communicate with both real and synthetic forces, and train for a variety of combat scenarios. Moreover, the DIVE system will connect to the *Defense Simulation Internet* (DSI), allowing the dismounted soldier to participate in larger distributed interactive simulation (DIS) exercises (environments that permit mechanized units to fight on a simulated battlefield).

Figure 23.2 DIVE chamber.

Avatar Partners, Inc., was awarded a $1 million research and development contract a couple of years ago from STRICOM to develop the DIVE system.

This wireless unencumbered virtual reality system for infantry training applications represents a significant step forward in synthetic environment technology in terms of both immersion and realism. DIVE is the first step toward the creation of a holodeck-like virtual reality system.

The DIVE system consists of an intranet of up to 20 individual DIVE chambers, each of which generates a window into a shared synthetic environment. Each chamber generates a window into a shared synthetic environment: an immersive three-dimensional visual, audio, and tactile environment that allows individual participants to enter a shared virtual battlefield. Applications of the

DIVE system include hazardous-operations training and simulation for both military and civilian operations and location-based entertainment.

Technical Approach

Similar to the system seen in the popular movie *Disclosure*, the DIVE system combines unencumbered and immersive virtual reality technologies into a single full-body tracking system. This system allows the user's body to be tracked without encumbering cables or tethers. Within the virtual environment the user sees an animated character or virtual body that follows his or her body motions in real time. This virtual body enables natural navigation of the virtual environment when walking, climbing, and running or when manipulating virtual objects.

The DIVE technical approach focuses on minimum encumbrance, deep immersion (sensory and functional), and body-centered interaction. These goals are accomplished by using a variety of innovative technologies: video-based body tracking system, shared memory heterogeneous multiprocessing, physics-based modeling, synthetic agents, and speaker-independent voice recognition.[9]

Minimum Encumbrance

One of the goals of the DIVE system is to eliminate the perceivable interface between the participant and the equipment comprising the virtual environment. Optimally, the participant would wear no special equipment or devices to experience the synthetic environment.

Technology limits the degree to which the participant can be unencumbered. The current state of the art requires that the user carry various electronic devices, a portable computer, and other devices.

Deep Immersion

The degree of immersion is determined by the extent that the participant in a virtual environment feels that he or she is in the virtual space. Immersion is related to presence—the sensation of being located at a place—in this case, a location within the virtual environment. Immersion and presence can (and should) be measured.

Deep immersion occurs when the virtual environment becomes more real to the participant than the physical environment. Deep immersion produces suspension of disbelief. Immersion can be decomposed into two components: *sensory* and *functional*. Sensory immersion refers to the replacement of the normal sensory stimulus with artificially generated or synthetic sources. The majority of work in virtual environments has focused on sensory immersion (head-mounted display technology). Functional immersion refers to the operation of the virtual environment; that is, the physical simulation that lies behind the sensory stimuli (the simulation of gravitational properties of objects, weapons, effects, etc.). If either the sensory or functional immersion breaks, the illusion is disturbed and total immersion suffers.

Body-Centered Interaction

Experimental results indicate that there is a connection between the presence of a virtual body within a synthetic environment and the reported degree of presence in the environment. Presence refers to a measure of the participant's sense of being at a location within the virtual space rather than the physical space. Body-centered interaction focuses on developing interaction techniques that match sensory data (primarily visual) with proprioceptive feedback (sensed body position).

Video-Based Body Tracking

The eventual goal of the Avatar approach is to create a completely unencumbered system in which the participant wears only the normal battlefield equipment. Avatar has developed a proprietary video-based tracking methodology that is implementable with commercially available image processing systems. Multiple video cameras are arranged around the DIVE chamber, and positions of key body locations are triangulated to determine positions within the chamber.

Heterogeneous Multiprocessing

Reducing *system latency* (also referred to as *lag*) is one of the primary challenges in designing any virtual reality system. In addition to judicious design of the system, employing parallel processing and multiprocessing can greatly reduce system latency.

Avatar has developed a heterogeneous multiprocessing architecture, based on industry standard and COTS components, that implements a large-scale multiprocessing system. Each DIVE chamber includes approximately 12 processing systems that all act as a single shared-memory computer. The entire DIVE intranet (consisting of as many as 40 chambers) connects to the same fiber-optic LAN, effectively creating an enormous multiprocessing computer.

Physics-Based Modeling

The DIVE system architecture is concerned largely with the creation of an ultrarealistic physical environment. Multiple compute servers are dedicated to realistic modeling of gravitational effects, inertia, rigid and nonrigid body collision, weapons effect, fire simulation, and so forth. DIVE is a distributed real-time physics-based modeling environment.

Synthetic Agents

DIVE supports synthetic agents both to generate enemy forces and to fill out friendly forces. Agents have realistic sensory and cognitive limitations (they can't see behind them and can't do 10 things at once). Synthetic agents use a separately compiled map of the virtual environment to simplify sensing and navigation.

Agents use preprogrammed sequences of actions or scripts to implement specific activities, such as room entry and clearing. They communicate with one another and with human participants, using voice and hand signals. Agent body motion is then computed in real time using inverse kinematics and prerecorded motion sequences.

Voice Recognition

The system includes a capability for human participants to communicate with synthetic agents via voice and hand/arm gestures. A speaker-independent voice-recognition system, coupled with an English-like command syntax, allows the human participants to command a force of synthetic agents.

Additionally, agents can be communicated with via hand/arm signals. The outputs of the body-tracking system are interpreted as gestures, such as "come here," "get down," "halt," and so on. They also know how to respond to these commands.

Physiological and Psychological Requirements

In order to begin defining requirements for a dismounted-infantry training system, Avatar began by examining the ultimate system performance. The ultimate DIVE-type simulator would have the following properties:

- ◆ From the soldier's point of view, the virtual environment is indistinguishable from reality.
- ◆ From the trainer's point of view, the soldier's actions are indistinguishable from battlefield performance.
- ◆ Any mission can be simulated.[10]

Detailed requirements of the ultimate DIVE simulator are defined by examining each of the sensory channels available to the immersed soldier. People are used to talking about the five senses, but in fact, human sensory perception is much more complex. According to Avatar, the human sensory system includes the following categories: visual, auditory and vibratory, olfactory, tactile, temperature, pain, and propioceptive and kinesthetic.[11]

Most virtual reality research focuses on systems and technologies for supporting the visual channel. The ultimate performance of the visual channel is determined by examining the capabilities of the human eye. The instantaneous field of view of the eye is approximately 100 degrees in the horizontal and vertical axes. At the center of the field of view, the visual acuity of the human eye is about one arc minute. This rolls off approximately by 20 percent at 10 degrees from the center of the field of view. The eye can saccade rapidly +/–45 degrees shuts down for about 100 milliseconds. By combining the maximum motion about the center of the field of view and the instantaneous field of view, the system, the ultimate DIVE simulator, would also need to completely model the visual appearance of the world in such a way that the simulated world is indistinguishable from the real world. According to Avatar, this leads to the following set of requirements for the visual channel: resolution equivalent to performance of the human visual system, textures on everything, full color, complex lighting that includes shadows and reflections, and no perceivable lag.[12]

The second major sensory channel is the auditory channel. The frequency range of human hearing is typically quoted as ranging from 20–20,000 Hz, although lower-frequency vibrations can be experienced as tactile sensations. Avatar has been able to locate sounds fairly accurately within a range of 5–10 degrees. Localization is a complex function of time delays, frequency differences, and other cues.

Modeling the auditory environment is almost as complex as modeling the visual environment. The real world has a potentially infinite number of sound sources, which may be located arbitrarily and can be directional. Moving sources are subject to both atmospheric absorption and the Doppler effect. Reverberation and echoes can be very complex and are time varying.

The olfactory channel (smell) is perhaps the least explored of the human senses in current virtual environment research. The human olfactory system is very sensitive and capable of detecting minute amounts of chemical substances in the air. The human olfactory system is also capable of distinguishing individual odors in mixes, estimating the intensity of an odor and, to some extent, determining the direction or point of origin of an odor.

The human skin is capable of sensing a variety of stimuli, including touch, pain, and temperature. According to Avatar, three mechanical stimuli can produce the sensation of touch: step functions—a displacement of the skin for an extended time; impulse functions—transitory displacements of the skin, lasting only a few milliseconds; and periodic functions—repeat regular or irregular displacements of the skin.[13]

The frequency range over which the skin is sensitive to touch ranges from 0 to about 300Hz. Different frequency ranges activate different nerve fibers. Texture sensing occurs as a relative motion between the textured object and the skin receptors.

The skin can also sense temperature. The skin generally maintains a temperature of about 33 degrees Celsius; when in contact with a warmer or cooler medium, it changes temperature. These changes can be sensed and the location and extent determined.

Often overlooked, the sensation of pain is itself a separate and important sensory mechanism. In the case of the skin, pain generally occurs from damage to the skin from piercing, cutting, or burning. Pain sensations are localized but can become unlocalized in certain cases.

The propioceptive and kinesthetic sensory systems allow the body to sense its position and motion in the environment. The human being is extremely sensitive to differences in joint angles and forces exerted on the body. For example, specific joint angles can be easily duplicated accurately and remembered for extended periods. Joint-angle differences below one degree can be sensed, depending on the particular joint in question and the motion of the specific joint.

All of the sensory information received by the human being is processed in real time to produce high-level sensations, such as presence or immersion. These terms are often used in the VR literature to describe the effectiveness of VR simulations, but at best are poorly defined and understood.

Generally speaking, immersion refers to the feeling of being contained inside a space, whereas presence refers to the sensation of being at a place or part of an experience. Although there is little data available that would enable either of these terms to be quantified, some factors that impact immersion and presence have been identified and serve as pointers for further research.

Perceived presence in the virtual environment can contribute significantly to the training effectiveness of the system. For example, in the case of the proposed DIVE system, the participants' willingness to believe that they might be injured or killed by taking the wrong action, as well as the fear of being surprised, are important components of the simulation experience. If the participants do not seek to avoid injury, they may take actions that are unrealistic for a given situation. Additionally, fear and excitement cause the release of adrenaline into the participants, and that can alter the caloric consumption during the performance of a task.

Presence is defined as the degree to which, while immersed in the virtual environment, it becomes more "real" or "present" than everyday reality. Clearly, increasing the participants' perception of presence will also increase the likelihood that they will perform tasks as if they were actually performing them and will limit their willingness to take unrealistic risks.

As stated earlier, perceived presence can be decomposed into two components: *sensory* and *functional*. The sensory component refers to sensory immersion that is the focus of most virtual reality research. Functional presence refers to the behavioral and operational components of a virtual environment that contribute to presence. For example, if light switches do not operate, objects on a desk cannot be moved or picked up, and the participant will have a decreased sense of presence. Avatar refers to environments that exhibit both sensory and functional aspects of presence as deep, or immersive.

Body awareness, the ability to sense and see one's own body, contributes immensely to the sense of presence. Several controlled experiments have been conducted to determine the relationship among presence, the representation of a virtual body, and the method of navigation within the environment. Motion of the body in space is also related to the ability to remember directions and to navigate in an environment. The results of these studies indicate a very strong coupling between the degree of presence reported and the connection of a natural mode of navigation (walking) with a virtual body.

According to Avatar, participants in these experiments were asked to perform the degree of perceived presence under the following conditions: no virtual body, navigate by pointing; virtual body, navigate by pointing; and virtual body, navigate by walking.[14] According to Avatar, the results indicate that there was practically no difference in perceived presence between the first two conditions. However, the participants who navigated by walking reported a statistically significant increase in perceived presence.

High-resolution visual imagery over a wide field of view has been shown to contribute to the sensation of immersion, although a number of experiments have indicated that high-resolution imagery is necessary only over a small region of the field of view. The ability to look into any direction, and in particular to move the head while navigating, contributes to the feeling of immersion and aids the construction of an internal model of a space.

Appropriately placed and triggered audio cues can significantly enhance the overall realism of a virtual experience. Researchers have found that well-produced audio can cause users to report that graphics of videogames are of a higher quality than the same graphics presented without audio. The effective use of audio within a virtual environment is similarly important.

Unencumbered Virtual Reality Technology

Virtual reality technology provides a means by which members of the infantry can be immersed in a virtual environment and to participate in a DIS exercise. However, achieving this goal requires the development of new approaches and innovative combinations of these technologies.

Historically, the virtual reality community has been split between those who have favored total immersion and those favoring unencumbered approaches. By donning a head-mounted display with six degrees of freedom head tracking, the total immersion approach places the user inside of a three-dimensional synthetic environment.

The immersive approach requires the user to wear a variety of equipment, and this equipment (often weighing several pounds) is generally connected to one or more computers by a variety of cables. The combination of the equipment worn by the user and the cables connecting this equipment to computers encumbers the user, thus restricting his or her movement substantially. Usually the user of an immersive system is required to stand in a specific spot or sit to avoid tripping over the myriad of cables.

Head-mounted immersive systems also suffer from the fact that the user's body disappears when entering the virtual environment (you can't see your hands or feet). According to Avatar, with systems such as VPL's DataGlove, a portion of the user's body enters the virtual environment, but this experience is somewhat dissatisfying and unnatural for many applications. The loss of body awareness is particularly troubling when the user attempts to navigate in the virtual environment by using full body motion.

According to Avatar, the unencumbered approach to virtual environments uses video-based pattern recognition and tracking techniques to allow the user to interact with virtual (computer-generated) objects without wearing any specialized equipment or tracking systems. The user sees a graphical representation or video image of himself or herself projected inside of a virtual environment (second-person VR). Historically, these systems have been limited to two-dimensional videogame worlds. The existing unencumbered approaches allow the user to retain body awareness, but do not produce a total immersion experience.

Proposed Solution

The proposed effort will result in the development of a hybrid virtual reality interface combining total immersion with unencumbered body tracking to allow dismounted infantry people to engage directly in simulated exercises. DIVE will provide an interactive simulation environment that, for the first time, will allow people to be completely immersed in simulation exercises. By combining technology developed by both total immersion and unencumbered approaches, a system will be developed that allows for a total immersion experience in a virtual environment in which the user retains body awareness and can see his or her hands and feet. This capability will provide a major advance in the realism of infantry and combined infantry/mechanized training.

The DIVE project is more than the development of a single simulation system; it is also the development of an open system architecture that will be made available to other vendors to allow their equipment and software to interface with the DIVE intranet and eventually the Internet. An interface control document describing the DIVE system interfaces is now available from Avatar.

Academia: Computer Graphics and Immersive Technologies Laboratory

Over the past decade, user demands on intranets and databases have escalated from the bandwidth and storage requirements characteristic of text to those characteristic of both images and real-time, production-quality video and audio. As integrated media systems evolve to incorporate the advanced interfaces described in the Creator-Computer-Consumer Interfaces thrust, they will impose even greater demands on high-speed wired and wireless communication intranets. These enhanced visual and aural interfaces, as well as real-time digital video servers, integrated media databases, and distributed processing systems, will require the effective and efficient image and data compression methods, multi-Gb/s fiber-optic intranets, and high-bandwidth wireless intranets developed in this thrust.

Two cases illustrate how the need for such delivery fabrics arises depending on the number of connected users. In today's manufacturing environments with hundreds of untethered workers, or in video-on-demand intranets with thousands of consumers, each person requires of order 20 Mb/s of bandwidth over wireless or wired intranets to receive compressed video and graphics. On the other hand, in today's video production environment with dozens of users, each requires about 270 Mb/s for D1 digital video. A shared intranet is an efficient means for distributing data in both of these cases. One challenge for such a system with multi-Gb/s (2 to 50 Gb/s) aggregate throughput is to seamlessly support multiple data types such as D1, MPEG, text, and graphics. In addition, the interconnection and delivery fabric must be capable of satisfying future standards, such as video quality that is significantly superior to that of D1 or HDTV.

This thrust is focused on the development of technologies for shared integrated media intranets. Such delivery fabrics require high-capacity, fiber-optic intranets driven from real-time video database and graphics engines. These intranets can distribute high-quality, uncompressed video to a limited number of professional users with real-time media workstations, or compressed video to many more users via lower-bandwidth, possibly wireless, taps along the intranet. Achieving this extension of shared intranet capability to real-time media will permit the full integration of video, images, and text within common intranet, database, and workstation technologies, and foster a new unified view of interactive media applications and systems.

Interactive Media Applications

In the area of Interactive Media Applications, researchers at the *Integrated Media Systems Center* (IMSC) at the University of Southern California are integrating state-of-the-art, commercially available integrated media products into meaningful systems-level demonstrations in the near term.[15] As key IMSC milestones and system-level demonstrations successfully emerge from the three research thrusts, researchers will prove emerging IMSC technological and creative innovations through higher-level systems integration experiments in specific applications environments.

IMSC researchers are employing technologies that will emerge from the three research thrusts to enhance productivity and increase quality in the office and factory environments; will enable enriched, publicly accessible entertainment and artistic experiences; and, will add considerable flexibility to the repertoire of available teaching modalities. The researchers are leveraging IMSC advances in integrated media systems through similarly diverse applications; enriching the general educational objectives and missions of the academy; providing platforms to speed the development of cross-disciplinary applications; cutting across conventional lines of scholarly inquiry; facilitating the synergistic energy of experts sharing leading-edge information; and offering to students innovative cross-disciplinary combinations of science and the arts. On a more profound scale, the technological advances emerging from the Interactive Media Applications focus on new forums within which to examine the world's cultures, and to develop technology that would support and integrate communication—whether it be music, film, the written word, or the visual image—that can bridge the boundaries separating nations, classes, and individuals.

Integrated media systems applications span the fields of business and manufacturing to entertainment and the art. These systems will integrate technologies developed within IMSC with applications of interest to IMSC industrial partners and applications academically robust in multimedia content that address the needs of students of all ages and places. The researchers' objective is to demonstrate the utility of integrated media systems in real-world settings, for it is against the backdrop of end-user success and satisfaction that the ultimate value of IMSC technologies and innovations must be measured. The researchers' prototype systems are being developed within a common 3000-square-foot IMSC

Laboratory that will integrate professional video and audio production equipment; state-of-the-art computing and visualization systems; electronic systems integration and assembly areas; studios for multimedia performances; and the center Systems Integration Experiments.

Augmented Industrial Workplace

New multimedia technologies developed within IMSC will have a strong impact on engineering design and manufacturing. Modern notions of concurrent engineering and enterprise integration emphasize the importance of communication and cooperation at all levels of the corporate paradigm. These trends, supported in parallel by IMSC advances in interfaces, intranets, and databases, are having a strong impact on the business and manufacturing communities.

In collaborative efforts with the center's industrial partners, researchers at IMSC are developing application scenarios, implementing experimental systems, and assessing their industrial usefulness to the corporate sector at large. Their initial emphasis will be on the design and manufacture of mechanical and electromechanical systems, which are inherently three dimensional. The researchers are addressing issues of modeling, visualization, interaction, communication, cooperation, simulation (virtual execution), and remote (real) execution, in a media- and information-rich, distributed environment that supports concurrent engineering and agile manufacturing. Their first effort will focus on the application of augmented reality for guidance and instruction on the manufacturing floor. As Immersivision (which will be discussed later in the chapter) teleconference technology matures, they will develop a prototype for distributed workgroups in the automotive industry.

The flow of information between people and computers does not yet extend to the manufacturing floor to the degree that is possible and desirable. As such, the paradigm of engineering as cooperative interactivity has not yet reached the factory floor. The hurdles to be overcome are numerous and spread over many technical and human factors. The manufacturing workplace is one of the last frontiers to facilitate widespread adoption of computers for policy and procedure management and control. The need for portable displays renders crucial the wireless intranets and low-power compression developed in the MIDF (*Media Interconnection and Delivery Fabrics*) thrust discussed earlier. Guidance information is often complex and highly visual, requiring high-resolution displays and interactive modes of discourse. These needs argue for powerful CPUs and large storage subsystems as developed within the DMIM (*Distributed Multimedia Information Management*) thrust (which will be discussed later in the chapter) that must exist remotely and be shared by many untethered users that tap into a high-bandwidth network such as that developed in the MIDF Systems Integration Experiment. Augmented reality tracking and speech recognition/synthesis developed in the C3I (*Creator-Computer-Consumer Interfaces*) thrust (which will be discussed later in the chapter) support productive and intuitive interactions on the work floor without traditional mouse/keyboard input devices. And creative new ways of training, guiding, and coordinating manufacturing activities will reveal untapped potential for computers in the industrial domain.

IMSC researchers are developing representative components and capabilities that will be integrated in the future computer-augmented workplace. Components include personal portable displays and cameras, accurate tracking and alignment, wired and wireless intranet infrastructure, and data/media servers. These components support capabilities such as workpiece marking, animation and text annotation, virtual x-ray vision for seeing obstructed features, automatic verification and correctness assessment using camera images, virtual training and practice for assembly, disassembly, accessibility tests, online computer or human guidance, error and problem logging, and an information surround consisting of multiple information zones located anywhere in the work environment. IMSC industrial partners are providing application guidance, support, and field test opportunities. One such collaboration has identified several stages in the assembly of aircraft skin panels as operations that are expected to benefit from *Augmented Industrial Workplace* (AIW) technology, shown in Figure 23.3.[16] Researchers are currently considering trial applications in two areas: 1) stayout and drill instruction overlays during skin panel assembly, and 2) checking for *blown hole* clearance problems using virtual x-ray vision. These operations offer significant opportunities for time and cost savings through AIW technology.

In the assembly of aircraft skin panels, workers currently refer to large (up to 15 feet long) blueprints at a nearby table and attempt to relate the dozens of symbols marking hundreds or thousands of hole positions to determine the sequence of operations to be performed. A prototype Augmented Reality system could annotate the same skin panel with stayout instructions overlaid adjacent to the appropriate holes. Within one year, using off-the-shelf components, researchers intend to field a desktop, non-real time, closed-loop AR system based on a PC or workstation capable of displaying such annotation. This goal will focus their efforts on the essential system issues, and provide feedback on the utility and human factors encountered with AR systems in the workplace. Simplified or automatic system calibration methods are currently being researched and developed. Smart camera sensors will be pursued and integrated as they become available with expectations of reduced cost and higher-performance, closed-loop track-

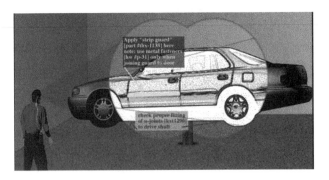

Figure 23.3 Augmented industrial workplace (AIW).

ing functionality. In the long term, the researchers envision workers with displays and cameras embedded in their safety glasses that use wrist-worn controls, and audio interfaces driven by belt-worn electronics and power packages that provide connections to the database and graphics server through a combination wireless/wired link.

Interactive Art Museum

Contemporary scholars increasingly rely on computer-based techniques and technologies to uncover the context and meaning of works of art. Meanwhile, museum curators and educators are striving to offer the richest possible art experience to the broadest range of patrons, whether onsite or networked.

At the same time, museum curators face increasing difficulties in exhibiting and preserving their collections in a time of decreasing funds. Due to a lack of space, some museums are forced to store as much as 90 percent of their collection. Technologies being studied within IMSC offer the potential to solve some of these problems, offering innovative ways to visit museums and radically new methods of viewing and studying the objects themselves.

IMSC's initial efforts in increasing museum access and interactivity through World Wide Web technologies will grow out of a collaboration with USC (*University of Southern California*) social scientists as well as museum scientists from USC's Fisher Gallery as shown in Figure 23.4.[17] A series of experimental Web sites designed to allow visitors to create and experience art are already under development at USC. These include an exploration of the USC-owned statue *Kneeling Girl* through a variety of stereoscopic viewing systems and an online exhibit of Japanese *shin-hanga* prints from the 1930s and 1940s. Future exhibitions will be structured so as to encourage participation and commitment and to facilitate dialog among visitors, artists, and museum personnel.

Future efforts will concentrate on developing more complex online interactive art exhibits on the World Wide Web incorporating 3-D

Figure 23.4 Interactive art museum.

modeling, remote tactile sensation, and Immersivision. Later extensions will incorporate pattern matching via networked databases. The exhibit will be based on Fisher Gallery collections of English snuff bottles and the Narramore teapots, allowing the user to *touch* the images of rare teapots made from porcelain, clay, wicker, or metal via a force-reflecting device that simulates the experience of contacting the actual solid objects. The work on networked database searches described in the DMIM thrust will let the user explore teapot collections from other museums to find matching patterns or similar designs. Manipulation of the 3-D items will be supported through both modeling and Immersivision.

As smart-camera-based head-tracking technology matures, IMSC researchers expect to extend these capabilities into the real museum through augmented reality techniques such as the untethered systems developed for the Augmented Industrial Workplace discussed earlier. Such a system could offer the museum visitor the capability to consult an audio track of the curator's analysis of any of the paintings, retrieve an annotated biography of the artist, zoom in on a selected portion of the canvas, view a work from vantage points not normally possible, alter the palette, and search a catalog for related works. The haptic enhancement feature will offer the chance to touch the surface of a painting or explore the texture of a sculpture.

Interactive Musical Instrument Database

The distinction between creator and consumer is sometimes blurred when personal expression is facilitated by powerful tools. In particular, musical expression has changed through technological enhancements. Music is sometimes considered the *universal language,* transcending all boundaries of time and space. It's the magic that sends chills up and down the spine, it's the model synthesis of intuition and expression, and the soothing therapeutic balm in the cloister of the car. Despite its reputation as a universal language, music from various cultures speaks many highly contrasting dialects, and most music enthusiasts around the world are familiar with only one or two of the hundreds of existing indigenous Western and non-Western musical systems. As a consequence, IMSC researchers are aiming at substantive bibliographic control and creative utilization of massive digital audio and video information resources that can be accessed at any time, by any user, anywhere in the world.

The researchers are creating a multimedia database that focuses on non-Western musical instruments, the sounds they make, the ensembles around the world in which they appear, and the socio-cultural performance contexts from which they emanate. Their interactive musical cultures audiofile/image database (see Figure 23.5) will incorporate a number of innovative features, including end-user ability to edit and utilize all onboard resources to create new sounds, new images, and even new musical instruments.[18] Language translation algorithms being developed in DMIM (discussed earlier) will be applied to scholarly dialog to provide for both scripted and spoken versions in the end-user's vernacular. Immersive virtual-reality ensemble and social context tours, as well as macro-imaging and haptic capabilities applied to individual instruments based on the work in C3I (discussed earlier), will be enhanced by computer-animated graphic modelings of instrument acoustics, performance techniques, and articulation nuances. Users will be able to simulate instrument construction by peeling away outer layers to access the instrument's inner anatomy, and they will be able to *play* the instrument pictured using tuning systems indigenous to the region(s), with the added capability of

East/West tuning and mode/scale comparison. The researchers have an interactive working model, based on the traditional music of Indonesia, that has been enthusiastically reviewed by several hundred USC students. This database incorporates a number of additional end-user capabilities including audile-visual-tactile contact, social-context virtual-reality tours, real-time intranet adaptation to end-user preference and expectation, and full provision for use of all onboard resources to produce new integrated digital *audio/video Gesamtkunstwerken* for performance in the IMSC researchers' next-generation wireless-stage MultiMedia Concert Demos in the United States and around the world.

Video and Audio Compression

Efficient transmission of real-time media in digital wired and wireless intranets presents an array of challenges that depend on the bandwidth and reliability of the system. Even though increased bandwidth has become available, aggregate throughput is still a serious system limitation. Furthermore, inefficiently used bandwidth represents an unwanted and unnecessary system-level cost. Hence, compression and decompression of audio and video streams (see Figure 23.6) have received increasing and deserved attention.[19] Even so, existing image and data compression technology is severely limited by relatively low compression ratios (requir-

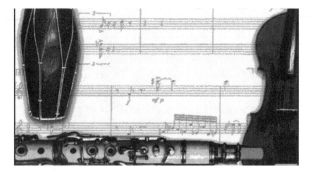

Figure 23.5 Interactive musical instrument database.

ing higher data transmission rates and more storage capacity), video and signal quality loss, and poor performance in the presence of transmission errors and intranet delays. The challenge IMSC researchers face in advancing compression technology is to define, simulate, and build compression systems that offer better image quality, higher compression ratios, increased functionality, and enhanced reliability transmission through noisy channels as compared with current standards such as JPEG, MPEG1, and MPEG2.

For video images, higher compression ratios can be achieved using new wavelet-based compression schemes. A major part of compression performance is determined by the choice of a quantization strategy. IMSC researchers are devising new techniques, putting an emphasis on adaptive algorithms that are also useful for modulating the compression ratio under changing channel conditions. Furthermore, an increased effort is being devoted to compression and delivery of graphics and other types of visual information.

Several alternatives exist for sending real-time media over high-bandwidth long-haul, local, or campus area intranets that support data of different classes, bit rates, quality, and delay requirements. Examples include ATM, intranets based on TCP/IP protocols such as the Internet, or high-speed fiber-optic solutions described in the

Figure 23.6 Video and audio compression.

systems integration experiment discussed later in the chapter. IMSC researchers are developing novel compression methods that take into account the common characteristics of these high-bandwidth intranets, including variable transmission rate, variable delay, and packet losses due to intranet congestion.

Intranets offer an attractive solution for real-time media delivery because they support simultaneous variable-rate connections that efficiently share transmission resources. By exploiting this statistical multiplexing gain, an increased number of communications can be accommodated. A key component necessary to achieve this gain is *rate control*. IMSC researchers are using rate control techniques to ensure that individual sources do not exceed certain transmission parameters, such as peak or average rate. They plan to demonstrate that these techniques allow source rates to adjust to changing conditions in the transmission system such as the number of users and degree of intranet congestion.

A daunting challenge unique to mobile systems is to provide untethered connection between continuous media sources and displays. Current wireless technology is plagued by low bandwidth and unreliable performance, which further necessitates the effective compression methods and efficient low-power implementations developed in this thrust. These methods are equally critical for smart cameras, Immersivision, and augmented reality applications in manufacturing and entertainment (as described in the Creator-Computer-Consumer Interfaces thrust). Current standards such as JPEG or MPEG are not sufficient for image and video transmission in low-bit-rate channels such as wireless intranets and existing telephone lines. The goal of the IMSC researchers is to devise novel compression techniques that achieve lower computational complexity, better energy compaction, and improved perceptual performance. They are examining pre- and post-processing techniques for image quality enhancement and fast motion field estimation algorithms, which can be directly applied to MPEG and H.263 (teleconferencing) standards.

The wireless transmission environment is characterized by changing channel conditions. Thus, a major function of the coding system will be to provide robust behavior in the presence of significant information losses. This can be accomplished by using multiresolution encoding schemes that divide the media information into classes according to their relative importance, providing higher protection to the most important information. The IMSC researchers are developing efficient and robust transmission techniques based on multiresolution representations and unequal protection with error-correcting codes. They are also exploring error concealment techniques that minimize the perceptual impact of information loss.

Robust real-time video compression requires processing power in the range of 20 MOPS for low-resolution applications to well over 1 GOPS for high-definition television and interactive media applications. These computing capabilities are beyond those of general-purpose processors and can only be met by specialized application-specific architectures. IMSC researchers have started with a specification of the compression scheme which will be followed by the development of parallel versions of the algorithms with the necessary processing power; and, their mapping onto architectures that minimize the area requirements in deep submicron VLSI circuits. Their VLSI designs will support heterogeneous intranets that have nonuniform bit rate channels. These features facilitate the integration of compression methods with high speed wired and wireless intranets in the heterogeneous visualization intranet Systems Integration Experiment within this thrust; as well as with high-capacity (terabyte) databases described in the Distributed Multimedia Information Management thrust.

Immersivision

Computer workstation displays, as well as current implementations of head-mounted displays, provide limited angular field of view, and hence, limited visual immersion. For augmented and virtual reality interfaces, as well as teleconference applications, visual immersion is considered crucial to both user acceptance and the visual suspension of disbelief.

For most of this century, visual media such as film and video have provided a *virtual eye* into times past and distant locations. One aspect of both content creation and delivery technology that has remained unchanged is the audience view, which is traditionally controlled at the source and is identical for all observers. The term *Immersivision* refers collectively to methods for transferring control of the view from the source acquisition cameras to the producer or viewer (see Figure 23.7).[20] IMSC researchers are developing technologies for applications in two domains. The first involves offline scene control and element manipulation for film and video production. Their goal is to increase the repertoire of techniques and capabilities for acquiring 3-D models of objects, merging scene elements from multiple image streams, modifying the viewpoint and other camera parameters, and altering individual elements within a scene. The second domain addresses immersive telepresence and teleconference systems that require real-time interaction and view control for all participants. They are also developing technology for such interactions through next-generation teleconference, collaborative work, tele-education, and telepresence systems. Furthermore, as core Immersivision technology is developed, it will be applied to enhanced design and manufacturing collaborative work systems.

The creation and mixing of synthetic and real images in post-production encounters numerous difficulties. These include: computation of proper occlusion for synthetic objects inserted into real 3-D backgrounds filmed with a moving camera, camera motion variations in image sequences produced by layering, or repeated filming against a blue screen, and hand-tuning of 2-D image

Figure 23.7 Immersivision.

sequences to compensate for the lack of 3-D information about an actor's movements relative to synthetic elements. Solutions to these and other related problems depend upon the ability to extract 3-D structure from 2-D images. Three-dimensional scene data permits correct occlusion computation, accurate determination and control of camera motion, and 3-D placement of real and synthetic elements.

Three-dimensional models of freely manipulated objects can be obtained with a range finder or an instrumented stylus. These methods are plagued by the large number of polygons required to faithfully model objects. Within a year, IMSC researchers expect to combine feature detection with surface fitting to reduce the number of polygons by an order of magnitude without sacrificing accuracy. Applying the same methodology to capture the structure of the general environment is not practical. The classical approach of inferring a 3-D model from a collection of 2-D images is plagued by numerical instability and lack of accuracy. Two new clear research trends have recently emerged: image-to-image alignment methods based on motion field computations, and implicit recovery of 3-D geometry in terms of affine and projective invariants. These two trends lead to new approaches toward the traditional *structure from motion* problem and overcoming previous limitations. The researchers are proposing to extend the existing and mature two-view invariants framework, and generalize it to multiple views so that reprojected images do not *jump* when the base images change. They will support moving objects in a scene, properly treating occlusion and motion such as waves and wind deformations. In addition, the researchers will attempt extensions for non planar statistically shaped objects such as trees and bushes.

In contrast to the offline production manipulations discussed earlier, approaches based on invariants are not suitable for real-time telepresence systems because correspondences are difficult to compute. More promising in the short term are motion field, or image mosaic, methods for capturing real-time panoramic scenes. Panoramic acquisition from multiple live images is feasible for approximately planar scenes. Acquisition of static nonplanar scenes is the basis for Apple's *QuickTime VR* (QT-VR). However, acquisition of live nonplanar scenes has proven difficult to achieve due to the need for coincident camera viewpoints.

IMSC researchers are developing a novel real-time nonplanar panoramic acquisition system based on a unique marriage of graphics and vision algorithms, optics, and smart camera VLSI technology. Their design goals include both scalable resolution and field of view. They envision eventual applications in teleconferencing and collaborative work environments in which the freedom of an individual's view of control may promote interactions and exploration of design alternatives. Their design incorporates a scalable camera array in which images are merged by a pixel processor into a seamless panoramic image. The panoramic image is resampled to create each user's unique view and to distribute it over a communications intranet. The seam regions can be precisely aligned by image resampling within bounded local regions using smart camera circuitry. A pyramidal scene representation will be employed to facilitate reconstruction of multiple output images.

Initial efforts will focus on development of a prototype immersivision system based on state-of-the-art components. Initially, the system will produce compressed images from a static panoramic image based on the cylindrical projection method used in QT-VR. Real-time updates will be incorporated into the prototype's static scene through motion detection and panoramic image updates. In a subsequent phase, collaboration with smart camera developers will attempt to incorporate real-time resampling and calibration functions into the camera processors.

Medical: VR Technology and Project ARCANA

Immersive Virtual Reality (IVR) is a mature technology to assist cognitive psychologists and therapists in their clinical work with brain-damaged patients. The rationale, the software, and the hardware of the first IVR system application—Advanced Research for the Computer-Based Assessment of Neuropsychological Ailments (ARCANA 1)—being developed by the Medical Division of CyberFunk Italy Srl, Signoressa, Italy (a subsidiary of CyberFunk, Inc., of Tucson, Arizona), provides a concrete example of what the role of IVR as a clinical tool will be. Although prospects are exciting, extensive research is needed to validate this new approach and reveal both its limits and advantages.

The Project ARCANA. has been promoted to develop IVR models to assist clinical psychologists, neurophyschologists, and cognitive therapists in their work with cognitively impaired patients. The main project is articulated into subprojects dealing with various aspects of IVR modeling and simulation. Each of the latter will have a completely worked-out rationale, evaluation protocol, and a specific cognitive model to which it is referred.

ARCANA 1 Project Description

The first subproject, termed ARCANA 1, started in October 1993 from a collaboration of the Medical Division of CyberFunk Italy. As a cognitive paradigm, ARCANA 1 has been developed from well-known examples of the neuropsychological testing tradition. The *Wisconsin Card Sorting Test* (WCST), in particular, has been taken as a reference. The choice to create a *hybrid* (a program with both the formal characteristics of a standardized test and those of a more open-ended situation) has been made for a number of reasons.

First, it will allow cognitive psychologists not to break with a consolidated approach of assessment. Second, it will serve as an entry-level program to IVR, to probe both patient and therapist attitudes toward this new technology. Third, although it will benefit from a solid theoretical and experimental background, it will also allow for more empirical and behaviorally oriented approaches.

Given its origins, ARCANA 1 is more suited for diagnostic purposes. Nonetheless, since it has been fully *parameterized* (can be configured in a number of ways and its cognitive demands can be graded), it may be suitable also for retraining purposes.

The artificial environment of ARCANA 1 is a virtual building (a series of rooms of variable shape with entrance and exit doors). The rooms are connected with corridors of variable length. Rooms and corridors may be empty or may contain a number of fixed or animated objects. In its basic version, however, the environment is very simple, as shown in Figures 23.8 and 23.9.[21]

The interaction is also kept as simple as possible. The user can freely navigate the environment by simply holding a pointing device (a jokerstick) in the direction of the intended movement. The doors open when touched on the knob with a virtual key.

The basic goal is to exit the castle in the shortest possible time. This implies the selection of an efficient strategy to move from one room to the next. A room can be left only by selecting the correct door. The cue for selecting the exit door is obtained by looking at the entrance door, which is marked by a yellow wall. Only one cue operates at any time and should be selected to identify the exit door, which shares with the entrance door the same cue. To be identified as a cue, a given characteristic must be categorized. For example, valid cues are the color or the shape of a door. Any combination of cues is treated as a wrong criterion. One cannot be certain that the selection is correct until the exit door is reached.

The opening of the exit door is an implicit confirmation of correctness. If the door stays shut, the strategy should be reconsidered and corrected. In the basic configuration, a shift in the criterion occurs every seven consecutive right selections. That a shift has occurred is to be inferred by an unseen lack of confirmation of a previously correct solution. Once a new solution is found by trial and error, the criterion should be maintained until the next shift.

The Cognitive Demands and the Interpretive Model

As in the standard paper-and-pencil test, motivational processes are required to carry out the task, as are a number of other special-purpose cognitive processes of the type that standard neuropsychological tests measure. For example, sustained attention, visual scanning, recognition of objects and object characteristics, spatial memory, retrospective verbal memory, categorization, concept formation, abstract reasoning, inference, utilization of nonverbal feedbacks, criterion maintenance and shifting, inhibition of impulsive behavior, and adherence to rules are all component abilities that are called into action. In addition, since IVR configures a spatially more-complex situation and the action is carried out on a broader time scale, there are a number of so-called bridge processes that enable the previously described basic cognitive abilities to be used efficiently to satisfy motivational requirements. These processes allow the creation and maintenance of goals and their realization at appropriate times.

As already mentioned, in real as well as in simulated situations, when routine actions will not achieve a goal satisfactorily, the problem-solving process required (the supervisory attentional system involves at least four stages, which can be called into action in a recursive way. An achievable goal must be specified, a plan must be formulated, a solution is attempted, and the result is assessed. Bridge processes link the schematic plan to the potential to realize it at some adequate future time.

A marker is a message relevant to a certain behavior that can be called at any point in time during a future event. Thus, a task rule would be realized through a marker becoming activated when the instructions are understood that something has to be done when a marked event occurs. In summary, the proposed function of the system is to control goal articulation, provisional plan formulation, marker allocation, and marker triggering by an appropriate event. An evaluation process can take place at any time; if the solution is not satisfactory, this would lead to a plan modification.

When applied to CyberFunk's simulation and prior information is limited to a minimum, this schema would give the following results:

- **Situation:** Being inside a building.
- **Goal articulation:** To exit as soon as possible.

- **General plan formulation or evaluation:** To proceed by trial and error until an effective strategy is identified.
- **Local plan formulation or evaluation:** Selecting a cue from the entrance door.
- **Marker creation:** Upon entering a room looking back at the entrance door to get the cue.
- **Behavior:** When entering a new room, the marker triggers the preselected behavior.
- **Solution:** Provisional solution attempted.
- **Reevaluation:** Local (or general) plan reevaluation if solution is not adequate.[22]

Evaluation of the Cognitive Performance

Cognitive performance on an IVR test such as ARCANA 1 can then be analyzed in at least two complementary ways: first, according to a quantitative scoring system that counts errors and sorts them according to a taxonomy of specific mental processes involved, as is done in standard neuropsychological tests; and second, according to the component processes model in a practical problem-solving situation as suggested. It is acknowledged, however, that in more open-ended situations, such as those that will be modeled in future system applications of the ARCANA series, a cognitive process model approach will be applied more effectively to the evaluation of performance. The latter will be also based on:

- A normative task analysis to yield a taxonomy of elementary behaviors for performing the task, their sequence, duration, frequency, relevance, and flexibility
- An analysis of the perceptual steps involved (mostly basic visual routines, such as detection, orientation, localization, and recognition
- a learning curve[23]

Automatic Scoring of Events

As in any computerized technology, IVR should also give the experimenter the opportunity to obtain objective measurements from a behaving subject. The tracking system is able to monitor a subject's head and arm movements and his body position in space. This information can be used to interpret a subject's intentions while he or she is interacting with the artificial environment.

Every move and every event in the virtual world is detected, and the time of occurrence can be stored in a report file. The latter is then analyzed to give summary reports and graphical displays of the most significant events that occurred and of their parameters in space and time. This data adds significant information for both statistical and assessment purposes. For example, the visual scanning strategy of a subject in the virtual environment of ARCANA 1 can be easily detected in this way and the data related to specific steps of the process model such as marker creation and triggering, as shown in Figure 23.8.[24]

An audiovisual monitoring device is also integrated in the IVR system of ARCANA 1. This device sample frames of the subjective vision display and synchronizes them with an outside view of the behaving subject taken by a VHS camera, as shown in Figure 23.9. A couple of combined images is then stored every 250 msec on a standard VHS tape ready to be replayed back for offline analysis.

Biomedical Data Acquisition and Analysis

It is frequently stated that quantitative measurement of psychophysiological activity during purposeful tasks allows us to quantitatively characterize individual cognitive styles. The IVR system can be connected and synchronized with other external systems devoted to biomedical data acquisition and analysis. This is obtained by triggering the external devices with input signals generated at selected time points by the IVR system. For example, CyberFunk is using this facility to recover auditory and visual event-related potentials from polygraph recordings of behaving subjects during their IVR experience. Signals from the body surface can be fed directly to an acquisition system (a commercial computerized EEG system) or, more conveniently, to a portable lightweight and battery-operated recording device that does not

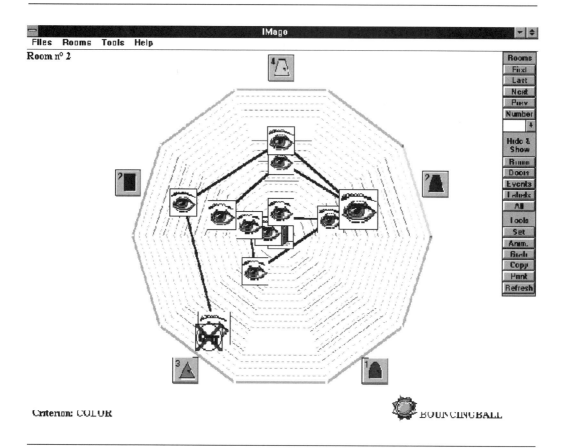

Figure 23.8 ARCANA virtual building.

encumber the subject with additional wires that connect to an external device.

The aim of recording biological signals during the IVR immersion is complex. First, it can be useful to address research questions. One that is interesting to CyberFunk is whether it can obtain a direct index of the mental resources a subject is devoting to the task. It has approached this problem, using auditory *Event-Related Potentials* (ERPs). For each subject it can generate a function that describes the relationship between sound intensity and ERP parameters (amplitude) in baseline conditions.

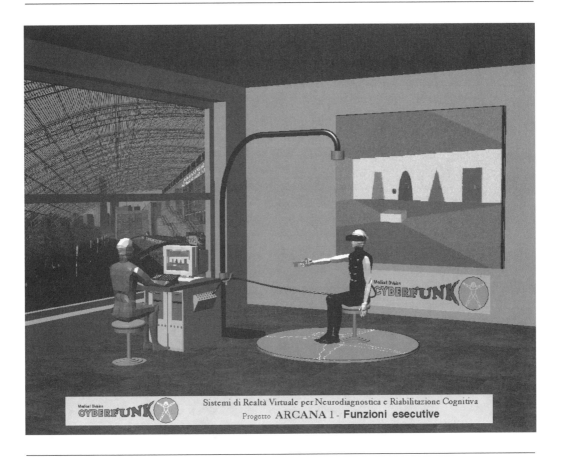

Figure 23.9 ARCANA environment.

By analogy, CyberFunk can then use this function to measure with the same units the variations of ERP parameters that it observes during IVR when the subject is supposed to be actively engaged in the primary task and only a fraction of his or her processing abilities is devoted to an auditory input, as shown in Figure 23.10.[25] The recording of body signals can serve two other important functions in IVR applications monitoring psychophysiological reactions and implementing biocybernetic paradigms. As far as the first is concerned, CyberFunk has already found it useful to record and analyze heart rate during performance in IVR systems to document the degree of cardiovascular stress imposed to the subject by the paradigm simulated and its setup.

In contrast to a VR driving simulation that CyberFunk has used in the past, the ARCANA 1 paradigm does not seem to induce as large an increase in cardiac activity of volunteers. This is important to document when developing VR applications for the disabled, since stressful paradigms may inadvertently affect a subject's performance and learning. On the other hand, mild degrees of stress may facilitate performance in apathetic individuals. Further, meaningful correlations with performance measures can be drawn to assist the interpretation, as shown in Figure 23.11.[26]

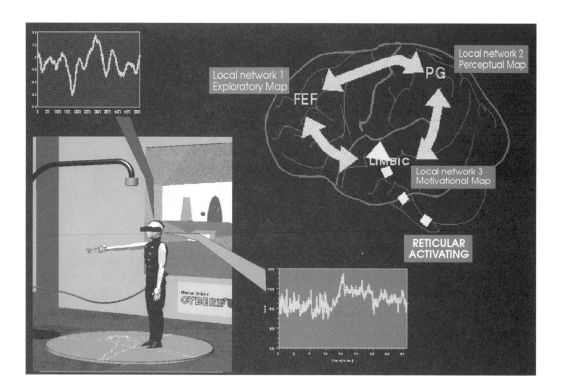

Figure 23.10 Marker creation triggering.

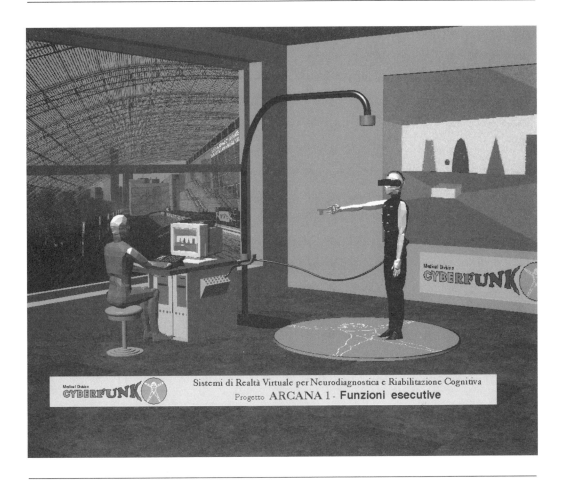

Figure 23.11 Auditory input.

The recording of eye movements during visualization of virtual environments can further improve the analysis of the scanning behavior of patients with associated impairments of oculomotor function. CyberFunk has used it to show that the commonly held belief that using HMDs with a limited total FoV greatly reduces the frequency and amplitude of saccadic EM is basically incorrect, as shown in Figure 23.12.[27]

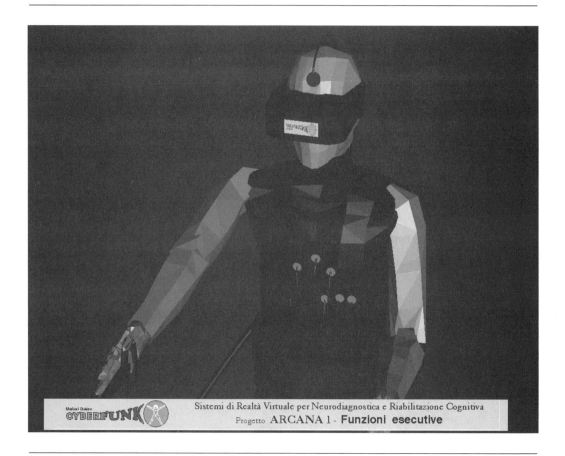

Figure 23.12 Performance measures.

Hardware and Software

Stated, there is no doubt that an affordable IVR system can be assembled from off-the-shelf technology. However, this is true only if its overall performance on the field as a real-time simulator must not be pushed to a level of absolute realism and especially if it is conceived not as an enabling device but rather as a cognitive trainer.

This consideration is, in CyberFunk's view, of paramount importance for the assessment of cost/effectiveness issues of many IVR systems proposed for training applications. As an example, it reports general specifications for such an IVR system devoted to the cognitive retraining of patients who may also happen to have a moderate limb sensory motor impairment, as shown in Figure 23.13.

In such a system no expensive engineering is requested to customize the interfaces for retraining of sensory motor skills, because the emphasis is put on the cognitive and perceptual domains. Drawing from the experience of CyberFunk Italy's Medical

Figure 23.13 Saccadic EM.

Division, which has developed the hardware and software for ARCANA 1 to meet certain specifications, the major R&D efforts had to be directed to the development of software modules required by the system.

It must be noted that the system software is not directed just to generate a virtual environment but rather to generate a virtual paradigm in which several technical aspects must be integrated:

♦ Parametric setting of the IVR in all its components: graphics and sound, dimensioning and shaping of the objects, lows of motion, strategies for the tasks, triggering and synchronization of the biomedical data.
♦ Biomedical data acquisition to be correlated to salient moments to facilitate subsequent performance analysis with the concurring need to operate on the database easily accessible.
♦ Design of operator-friendly interfaces to offer both the researcher and the therapist the possibility to have at their disposal an easy and useful instrument that would not encapsulate in a rigid context but rather offer the possibility to tailor the virtual paradigm as well as the assessment and the therapeutical plans according to their experience and the patient steps of improvement in the retraining process.[28]

CyberFunk feels that it is fundamental that there be close cooperation between the doctors and the hardware and software design engineers in order to have reciprocal exposure to the clinical needs, technological possibilities, and constraints. Only from a mutual understanding of sometimes conflicting needs can the opportunity come to develop concrete projects.

Limitations and Constraints of Present-Time VR Technology

Technological limits and constraints of IVR, however, do exist; many of them are still unavoidable and must be carefully understood and considered in relation to clinical applications. Limitations are broadly classifiable into the following categories: encumbering factors, factors introducing perceptual errors and time delays, and factors affecting novelty.

Encumbering factors limit a user's motility in various ways and are typical of HMDA (Head-Mounted Displays), datagloves, and any other device that is worn by the user and needs to be connected to the VR server. Needless to say, the encumbering should be avoided as much as possible. Patients should be informed adequately and made acquainted with the devices and their use before experiencing IVR.

Factors introducing perceptual errors and time delays typically originate from graphic computing and rendering and tracking devices. Delays of more than 100 msec are said to cause both discomfort and to affect the experience of a smooth, continuous visual environment and of motion (zooming effect).

In many IVR systems of low performance and cost significant, time delays can be introduced only when the subject stares at quite complex visual scenes. The rate at which frames can be generated then drops dramatically, say, to below 10/sec to revert to an acceptable value a few seconds later once the subject has moved his or her sight to another point in space.

The discontinuity can be so prominent to generate surprise and an orienting reaction that interrupts the ongoing cognitive processing. Encumbering factors, time delays, and the absence of sensory feedbacks typical of natural motion are also involved in the generation of so-called cybersickness.

This topic has been repeatedly covered by recent papers and will not be examined in any detail here. The introduction of faster image processors and of lightweight high-resolution HMDA, however, has considerably limited the incidence of cybersickness, thus proving that sensorial conflict is only one possible factor.

Once a specific task is identified, the sense of realism (or of novelty) can be affected by the trade-off among the amount of graphic complexity required, the level of interaction needed, and the speed of rendering. The debate between those in favor of an absolute realism and those who do not consider this requisite as a fundamental one for clinical VR applications is still unsettled.

A fundamental issue is the amount of prior knowledge of what can be used to build an internal representation of the specific environment. If this cognitive process is not greatly impaired, a sketchy version of the real world can be used without confusing the patient. Moreover, human factors that may also pose limits to applicability should be examined in greater detail.

In principle, patients with cognitive deficits are inherently at risk for showing maladaptive responses and behaviors and hence to have problems accepting an unusual experience, such as IVR, and to experience difficulties understanding the scope of its wired devices, such as HMD, data gloves, and the like.

Although psychological reactions to IVR have to be studied in greater detail, CyberFunk's still-growing experience with a variety of mentally disabled subjects exposed to IVR for relatively brief periods is completely in contrast with this expectation. Although some of them may not understand enough of the rationale and frequently take it merely as a game, most of them liked it and would experience it again. Hence, VR technology per se does not appear to be a limiting factor.

Comment

It seems that a new class of clinical tools is about to emerge from the attempt to apply IVR technology to the cognitive rehabilitation of acquired cognitive impairments. Problems of transfer to real-life situations, generalization of results, prediction, and assessment of outcome for specific behavioral-cognitive treatments may be approached from a novel stance.

CyberFunk has briefly discussed the rationale and the most relevant methodological aspects for the design of an IVR system devoted to this aim. The latter is part of an extended project, which has already been completed.

CyberFunk has also provided a few examples drawn from the ongoing preliminary clinical experience with this tool. A large number of approaches and models are amenable to be implemented by means of VR, those dealing with higher cognitive functions have attracted interest because they are the least represented in the variety of technological aids for cognitive assessment and rehabilitation.

More basic functions, such as attention, memory, and language are already successfully retrained by means of more traditional computerized procedures. There are hints, however, that IVR could be superior to the latter, thanks to its greater ability to mobilize mental resources and to be closer to the ideal rehabilitative cognitive aid—one that can easily and realistically simulate any situation and any paradigm, giving a full sense of immersion to the patient and that of full control to the therapist.

In the never-ending process of research and discovery, IVR may be the technique to bring about a new revolution in the methodologies in assessing cognitive abilities and to compensate for their impairments. Prospects are exciting, but extensive research and development will have to be carried out in order to approximate this end.

Problems of transfer of diagnostic information to real-life situations via the Internet, generalization of trained skills, and prediction of outcome for specific behavioral-cognitive treatments may be approached from a novel stance. Within a large collaborative project for the development of a cognitive retraining system based on IVR technology called ARCANA, CyberFunk has developed a system in which IVR is used to assist in the assessment of those control components of cognitive activity (so-called executive functions) that enable more basic abilities to be used efficiently.

The system is described as an example of what CyberFunk believes should be implemented to make IVR a useful clinical tool. Wearing a stereoscopic lightweight color HMD, the patient must find his or her way out of a building. Visual cues will help the patient select the correct exit doors that connect one room to the next.

A general plan will have to be drawn up, and several local strategies will have to be identified and possibly changed by the patient in order to complete the journey inside the building. Nonverbal (visual and auditory) feedback will be released by the system at every correct or incorrect move. Both the visual representation of the artificial environment and the modality of interaction are kept as simple as possible. However, the overall complexity can be increased, and every detail can be easily changed by simply typing in the modifications needed. The model can then be reconfigured according to, for example, an incremental training program or the necessity to disassemble the task into simpler subtasks.

The system stores behavioral data into exportable files and real-time images of both subjective and external views and sends synchronizing signals to other devices enabling the monitoring of biomedical data. Behavioral data analysis can be carried out according to standardized criteria, as in traditional neuropsychological tests, or to a model that classifies errors according to control cognitive processes. The recording of psychophysiological parameters enables meaningful correlations to be drawn with behavioral data. Ongoing research with this instrument is focused on its clinical validation and the assessment of all potential hazards, physical and psychological effects of IVR simulations for clinical purposes to be eventually imported to the Internet. For more information on CyberFunk, see the companion CD-ROM.

Amusement: Authoring Virtual Entertainment Worlds

Authoring Virtual Worlds is hard work. That's been primarily due to the tremendous complexity of the real world we sometimes try to simulate. In fact, some companies have developed general-purpose authoring tools to create real-time interactive 3-D worlds—supporting many special VR-specific I/O devices like trackers and head-mounted displays. These authoring tools have been successfully used by VR companies to create worlds and games. But, aside from optimization and software complexity (and obviously costs) considerations, these tools have often been a kind of all-in-a-box solution. They have forced the user to master them into building everything from 3-D graphics to sounds to GUI. And, they have also forced the user to learn new and sometimes proprietary languages to describe behaviors.

The Games Division of CyberFunk Italy Srl, Signoressa, Italy (a subsidiary of CyberFunk, Inc., of Tucson, Arizona, that is also involved in VR game development, http://www.icona.it/ CyberFunk), having developed an immersive vehicle to explore cyberspace called the CyberBuggy (which is midway between a big round surfboard and a joystick), is also developing an authoring tool called The ORB (*Other Realities Builder*). This tool is used to create interactive user worlds. Thus, the interesting thing about the ORB, is that instead of creating a very complex product covering (sometimes poorly) all aspects of the Virtual Environments creation, CyberFunk has focused upon the big problem of VR development itself, which is to turn 3-D graphics into *Actors* and give them coordination and behaviors as shown in Figure 23.14.[29]

In fact, CyberFunk did choose one professional 3-D package (Caligari TrueSpace, for the curious) to model scenes and animations. They also wrote a 3-D-scene loader and a real-time graphic engine. This was based on Microsoft's Direct 3-D (gaining access to tremendous 3-D acceleration using state-of-the-art, low-cost graphic boards and standard PCs), which merged all of the code to control the CyberBuggy. In addition, the sensors and the HMD were all focused on the behavior problem.

Now, when all of the scene from TrueSpace is loaded (including textures, lights and animations), you can load more than one scene and switch them off and on; thus enabling multilevel and multiscenario games. You can then explore the scene and select the

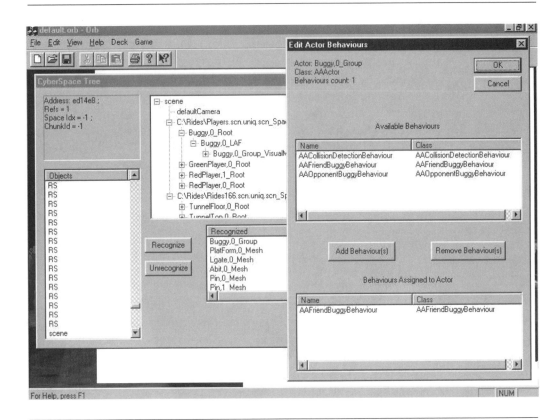

Figure 23.14 The ORB.

graphics which must have some behavior. By using a totally visual environment (the ORB was written in Visual C++, so it has a very intuitive GUI), you can turn elements of the scene into Actors and assign them different behaviors as shown in Figure 23.14. These behaviors are written in C++ and linked in, so there is no need to learn new languages. Also, adding new behaviors to the ORB enables you to create new games and experiences.

For the OOP (*Object Oriented Programming*) geeks out there, all you have to do is implement a new behavior-class-derived object, and write the body of the virtual function Simulate(). Coordination between Actors is achieved by using a message-passing architecture. For example, if you want to turn lights off and hear a scream when you collide with an ugly monster, you would assign the monster a Collision Detection behavior, as shown in Figure 23.14. The behavior would then be instructed to send an *Off* message to actor Light1 and a *Play* message to actor ScreamSound when the monster graphics collides with actor CyberBuggy.

Because the ugly monster has been animated using TrueSpace, it sometimes goes around in circles, jumping and snapping its claws. The ORB would then automatically be assigned an Animation Behavior.

Want to start a song from the CD? Just click on *Add Message* and send a *Play* message to that CD Player's special actor. Obviously, CyberFunk could have used VRML and Java instead of a third-party 3-D format and C++, but at the time, VRML was in its early infancy and didn't have animation as it does now. Furthermore, Java is still too slow for a low-cost PC-based arcade-like 3-D environment. Additionally, even if ORB is still an internal tool built around CyberBuggy and game creation, CyberFunk plans to turn it into a somewhat general-purpose tool and release it to third-party developers. For more information on CyberFunk, see the companion CD-ROM.

From Here

This chapter presented other VR research that is taking place for eventual deliverance to the Internet. The next chapter concludes by taking a peek at the next generation of VRML application development through the use of high-performance computing.

How far will high-performance VRML go? In what direction will development take place? How quickly will it evolve?

Endnotes

1 Live Picture, Inc., "The RealSpace Imaging Solution," 5617 Scotts Valley Drive, Suite 180, Scotts Valley, CA 95066, April, 1997.

2 Ibid.

3 Ibid.

4 Ibid.

5 Ibid.

6 Ibid.

7 Ibid.

8 Ibid.

9 John R. Vacca, *Dismounted Infantry Virtual Environment (DIVE) Technology*, "Virtual Reality Special Report," Vol. 2, No. 5, November-December, 1995, pp. 49.

10 Ibid., p. 50.

11 Ibid., p. 50.

12 Ibid., p. 50.

13 Ibid., p. 51.

14 Ibid., p. 52.

15 Integrated Media Systems Center (IMSC), National Science Foundation Engineering Research Center, University of Southern California, 3740 McClintock Avenue, EEB Suite 131, Los Angeles, CA 90089-2561, 1997.

16 Ibid.

17 Ibid.

18 Ibid.

19 Ibid.

20 Ibid.

21 Tullio Bortoletto, *ARCANA Project*, Cyberfunk Italy Sr1, Medical Division, Via Livenza, 5, Signoressa, Italy, 1995.

22 Ibid.

23 Ibid.

24 Ibid.

25 Ibid.

26 Ibid.

27 Ibid.

28 Ibid.

29 Aaron Brancotti, "The ORB Project," CyberFunk Italy Sr1, Games Division, Via Livenza, 5, Signoressa, Italy, 1997.

24

Summary, Conclusions, and Recommendations

It is as difficult to conceptualize *environment* on the Web as it was to imagine the graphical interface of the first Macintosh OS. As a result, people have simply imagined a futuristic cyberspace without completely understanding the present condition of the technology. These misunderstandings have established themselves as myths surrounding VRML's (*Virtual Reality Modeling Language*) presence on the Web. This book has sought to address many of these myths and promote a deeper understanding of the far reaching implications of VRML.

The development of VRML has been unique—a technology created specifically for the Internet. By definition, VRML is a file format for describing 3-D multimedia and shared virtual worlds. This technology enables the creation of viable business environments for the next generation of online games, entertainment, product demos, product support, collaborative applications, and data visualization, and provides a limitless potential to build upon the World Wide Web.

Summary

VRML implies 3-D, and 3-D is certainly one of VRML's key capabilities. However, VRML goes beyond 3-D as one the most efficient and effective technologies on the Web. VRML has the capacity to encapsulate and organize many media types including image, animation, and 3-D audio to create a cinematic experience. These media types can be embedded in VRML environments so, for example, one may navigate through a world written in VRML and experience dynamic graphical displays of moving information with sound and visual effects. VRML transforms the Web from a static, passive offering of information into a series of *worlds* with space, sound, and motion.

VRML is the next step beyond HTML. As HTML is to 2-D, VRML is to 3-D. But VRML is also object oriented and can provide all the associated benefits of object orientation including maintainability, extensibility, performance, and optimization of programming effort. VRML can also embed other programming languages, such as Java, so that worlds can become interactive and dynamic. With embedded Java, objects can be assigned behaviors and can react to the user or other objects within the world.

People have made the incorrect assumption that VRML requires a high-end graphics machine, like an SGI workstation, to view or interact with the graphics. In actuality, VRML was designed specifically for the Web and PCs. Currently, a 100-Megahertz Pentium is the minimum CPU recommended to view 3-D Web worlds, and a 3-D accelerator board will make the rendering smoother.[1] Currently, every major graphics company, without exception, is adding 3-D chips into their consumer video accelerator cards. This

3-D acceleration does not only enhance the performance of VRML worlds, but also allows increased richness, heightening detail and increasing animation capabilities. Additionally, because all 3-D objects are made up of polygons, developers have created 3-D worlds with a low polygon count for maximum performance speed. But, as more PCs make built-in 3-D acceleration the standard, the graphical information displayed on the Internet will become even more sophisticated with higher polygon counts and more sophisticated texture maps.

Because VRML enables large amounts of information to be displayed with a 3-D graphical interface, people incorrectly conclude that VRML must be a bandwidth hog. This myth often stems from the fact that in some of the worlds on the Web the content has been converted from some other 3-D format to VRML inefficiently.

Native VRML is considerably more efficient than other media types such as QuickTime movies and even static images. For example, a 20-second animation in VRML might be only about 50k, while that same animation might weigh several megabytes were it created as a GIF or MPEG file.[2] This is because VRML worlds are rendered locally. VRML is text at download time, not images as in a QuickTime movie or a bitmap file. With this smaller content footprint, VRML enables quicker download time. In addition, VRML97 contains many built-in optimization functions that help cut down excessive polygon content, making the files quicker to download and faster to navigate. One example of this is Gzip, a compression algorithm that can reduce a VRML file by a factor of 10.

VRML is not a just a technology for rapid application developers. Many artists and Webmasters have embraced VRML because of its capabilities. Currently, a basic understanding of the Internet and a familiarity with 3-D modeling and animation is required. While knowing VRML is definitely useful, many 3-D modeling packages now have VRML exporters (such as the exporter for Extreme 3-D, designed by Intervista). However, VRML exporters are very much in their infancy. Currently, exporters can convert a 3-D model into VRML, but they do not have the ability to optimize the files to make them easily downloadable. As a result, world creators often need to examine the code themselves in order to optimize the VRML file.

Given the fact that VRML is a relatively new technology, the authoring tools for VRML worlds are still evolving. But like HTML editors three years ago, new product announcements are made weekly, and soon developers will be able to move beyond the code and focus on creating powerful environments with VRML.

People who are navigating the Web today can find many entertaining VRML worlds filled with vibrant simulated spaces and cyberspace crawling with avatars. While that's a proof of the technology, it's not a proof of its usefulness. VRML is still in its infancy, but it has incredible potential. VRML will change the way we interact with our everyday information. The technology adds value to all types of information displayed in a networked community. Its implications are as far reaching and diverse as the business that is conducted every day; product demonstration, genetic manipulation, and stock chart display are just a few examples of business situations that can change drastically due to VRML. VRML can change a static, incomplete, difficult-to-learn interface into an intuitive emporium of dynamic information. For example, Visual Decisions, Inc., has created dynamic financial simulations in VRML (http://www.vdi.com). They are displaying information in ways that were previously inconceivable because of the limitations of 2-D. As more financial and scientific visualization applications become available, VRML will prove itself to be an invaluable medium. Once VRML's usefulness is fully discovered and exploited, it will undoubtedly pave the way for entirely new applications of the Internet.

Conclusions

How far can high-performance VRML go? In what direction will it develop? How quickly will it evolve? These questions can be answered by examining the various pieces of the puzzle and looking at application trends and future possibilities.

We now have lots of little pieces of the future floating around, but how they intersect or bond to one another will depend largely on the marketability of their potential outcomes. We have certainly excelled on the hardware side of high-performance VRML machines. Virtual reality software has also rapidly evolved, especially in the cinematic and advertising realms. Virtual reality, still a fledgling science, is appealing to both the would-be reality escapee and the consumer-product marketeer. Artificial intelligence, another fledgling science, still remains largely stuck in the halls of academia.

Meanwhile, the market for VR-based products is hot in three major areas: fantasy adventure games, training simulators, and sex-oriented media. These markets have experienced the type of growth that most entrepreneurs have only dreamed about during restless nights.

These market successes, as with many others, are prompting regulators and our unduly elected officials in Washington to produce some political hay. The moral concerns of the imaginary heartland and the First Amendment rights are once again clashing like titans. It is not that the governmental transients in Washington have much going for them in the way of morals, but they do like to get themselves on TV and hustle votes and campaign contributions. It is likely that political interest will attempt to choke certain aspects of the market, especially the sexually oriented graphics market. But while the politicians blow hot air, momentum in high-performance VRML development is growing.

We have been provided with a fantasy of what high-performance computer VR could do for us by our science fiction writers. They have woven a vision of reality in their millions of words of pulp-style prophecy about our future, our explorations, our quest, and indeed our destiny, and how they would all be constructed with computers at our beck and call. These dreams come to life in the concept of the Star Trek holodeck, that place where anything can happen any time we want it to, without risk to life, limb, or physical being.

One of the futures for high-performance graphics, I contend, is the development of Star Trek holodeck-like applications. These applications will serve as escape mechanisms, recreational alternatives, and training environments. It will be like Jurassic Park, with the dinosaurs replaced by anything that meets the fancy of the individuals who are willing to pay the bill. The religious could meet their god, the sex-starved could indulge in their own self-styled orgies, and those with killer instincts could slaughter and conquer. This may all be closer than we think.

Performance and Price

We have been taking large leaps in price/performance as increased power and capacity trickle down to smaller and less-expensive machines, including raw speed, memory capacity, and storage capacity. Consumer-oriented desktop units are changing very rapidly, with a price/performance improvement rate of about 100 percent per year.[3]

The more expensive systems, such as high-end Unix-based workstations, are experiencing about 100-percent price/performance improvements every 18 months. The largest systems are experiencing the same rate of price/performance improvement about every 24 months.

We also occasionally experience what I call megaleaps in commonly available price/performance improvements, which will start to come much more quickly than they have in the past. We are on the edge of our next megaleap as we migrate to 64-bit systems. This evolution will be followed with the emergence of 128-bit machines by the year 2000.

The first step, to 64-bit platforms, has been a little slow but should pick up speed during the next two years. Again, it is not the existence of the machines themselves but the commonplace availability that is key to developers being able to exploit the technology for the consumer market.

The emergence and common utilization of object-oriented development techniques will ease the move from the 64-bit platforms to the 128-bit platforms. Likewise, this opens the door for an even faster acceptance and market for 256-bit machines by the year 2005. Again, common acceptability, availability, and accessibility are the key elements to a successful market for software developers.

Software and Hardware

During the last two generations of business computers, we have seen software trailing the availability of machines by 18 to 36[4] months. However, as *de facto* standards, or market domination, solidifies in the hands of the few (like Microsoft products for PCs), mainstream business software developers are shortening the time lag between hardware availability and software availability. This lag time could potentially be reduced to just a few months as long as the haggling between dominant players and smaller applications developers doesn't heighten their licensing conflicts and developers continue the steady evolution into object-oriented design methodologies for their products.

VR and multimedia software developers, now about to reach puberty, have experienced similar lags between common hardware availability and delivery of their products. This lag will decrease rapidly. In fact, I contend, as the VR market grows consumer-oriented hardware, packagers may have difficulty keeping up with VR software products.

The leaders in the use of VR, now mostly in the entertainment industry, will always continue to push the threshold of demand for more-capable, less-expensive development platforms. This in turn will provide funding for hardware companies and will result in the development of higher-performance technology that can be more quickly trickled down to commonly available consumer machines.

We will also experience a more rapid trickling down, more like a waterfall, as hardware developers scurry to recoup their R&D investments so they can fund additional R&D. This dynamic will fuel the faster migration of VR software to 64-bit and 128-bit machines, which in turn will increase demand for these platforms and result in faster common availability.

Overall, these dynamics, although they will result in pain for those companies that cannot keep up with the rapid pace of change, will be beneficial to high-performance VRML applications developers. The primary benefit is a more open and viable market.

The secondary benefit will be obtained by those developers willing to risk the funds necessary to initiate development of VR applications or entertainment packages for future platforms. The more rapid the introduction of higher-performance consumer computers or the waterfall of price/performance, the less the risk that developers will face when preparing products for platforms that will not be commonly available for two, three, or even four years.

Although this may seem to be a long time for venture capitalists to wait for a return on their investment, it is still a shorter time between megaleaps in price/performance than we experienced during the 1980s.[5] It also lessens the pain of investment in early versions of computing platforms, because the lag between early and more-expensive versions of an architecture and the common availability of that architecture will decrease.

Artificial Intelligence and Virtual Reality

So far, consumer-oriented, graphic-based products such as Myst and a wide variety of sex games have been built on a series of pre-determined outcomes, or scripts, that are invoked by specific actions of their human players. Although these games make for great puzzles, they will rapidly fade into the Dark Ages as *artificial intelligence* (AI) and high-performance graphics merge into a new generation of AIgraphic applications.

Instead of predetermined outcomes or even simple randomly invoked outcomes available from a library, the fantasy game of the future will be more capable of emulating real life, or shall I say, real adventure. This could occur in two ways. First, and probably sooner on the evolutionary path, players will be able to intentionally create their own libraries of scripts, making them as complex as they like. This is similar to some of the virtual reality applications now on the market.

Second, and further into the future, script creation will be based on a psychological analysis of individual players. The psych battery will be built into the game or training package and will automatically develop a profile of each individual as he or she uses the software. These psycho-based scripts could potentially evolve on their own, growing more complex as player skills improve.

VR applications also extend beyond entertainment. Our military has been a leader in computer-based simulation training. These applications, to date, have been built like many of the $79 fantasy games you can buy at a local store.[6] That is, scripts and outcomes are predetermined, based on training goals.

By adding an AI feature, scripts or outcomes in these training simulators could evolve in a more natural way, based on the ability and the experience of individual trainees. The knowledge base for each trainee would be stored and reinvoked by entering an identification number and pressing the Start button.

The development of AIgraphic applications will require all-around high-performance platforms with a minimum of 64-bit massive parallel architectures, terabytes of memory and storage, and fiber-optic light speed data channels, with dynamic and logical allocation of system resources. Development platforms will likely remain in the supercomputer class, but the VR applications could be accessed via high-performance workstation servers. Other requirements for product delivery are high-resolution, floor-to-ceiling monitors to display the AIgraphic images, a high-quality sound system, and a voice-recognition interface for players to issue commands.

Market Drivers

The U.S. military and the sex industry have been leading the way in the use of computer graphics, each in its own unique fashion. For more than a decade, the military has been using graphics-based simulators for technology and battle training. This experience, combined with the potential costs savings for using simulators and the financial ability to support development, gives the military a healthy lead in the field.

If the government loosens up and moves the military technology into the private sector through a defense conversion program, VR development for commercial purposes will likely accelerate. It would make good business sense to do this, so we can probably not count on its happening.

The sex industry, in its own way, has also been a leader in developing and marketing VR-based applications. These applications range from digitized images on the low end up to pseudointeractive games on the high end. The games are becoming more and more popular and will continue to be a thriving market.

The main obstacle to growth in the sex sector is government's attempts at censorship. Although the Communications Decency Act did not pass constitutional muster, politicians can always be counted on to pander to the general public's fear and lack of knowledge. Look for another, similarly restrictive law in a house of Congress near you soon. There is a good chance the politicians will eventually win this one, and go on a smut-eradication campaign that could stifle growth in the sex sector.[7] This is bad news. Regardless of whether people agree with the intent and method of the Communications Decency Act, its passage may very well have a negative impact on the cash flow of the sex industry.

First Amendment and free-commerce issues held constant, a decrease in cash flow for developers of existing VR-based sex products will impact their ability to fund development of more-sophisticated VR AIgraphic-type products in the future. This is not good for a free-market economy.

Recommendations

This book has discussed the various facets of VRML. This final part of the book and chapter makes some valuable recommendations or tips with regard to 3-D modeling, animation, and VRML world creation. It contains the top 10 tips for the beginning VRML designer. Hopefully, your own experiences with VRML have helped save time, money, and headaches, and have resulted in sites with superior performance.

The first tip or recommendation is that you need to find a 3-D package that has robust polygon capabilities and, if at all possible, robust VRML export capabilities.[8] You need to have good polygon capabilities because you constantly need to have access to exactly how many polygons are in your scene. You also need to be able to manipulate the way each polygon faces and, if possible, the color of each polygon in a particular object. You need to be able to move individual vertices and polygons in groups as well as individually, and delete them if need be.

Another really key feature is that of polygon decimation, meaning you could take an object like a face, that has 30,000 polygons, hit the optimization feature and have it dial down some of the detail until you wind up with a 2000-polygon face. These are all things that a lot of the better 3-D packages have built into them.

3D Studio Max is probably one of the best 3-D packages for VRML right now.[9] It has a great VRML export, with the capability to export most of the features in the VRML97 spec. It also has excellent polygon-editing features as well as the optimization mentioned earlier. Other packages that have all these capabilities are Extreme 3D (with the VRML97 converter built by Intervista), SoftImage, and Alias, but Alias and SoftImage are made to do high-end stuff like Jurassic Park and other movie stuff.

The second thing you'll need is a good text editor, one that has line numbers to tell you where your errors are.[10] There are a couple like SitePad that actually color-codes the various VRML nodes to help you organize your VRML scene graph. For hacking, a text editor is always valuable.

Still other tools you'll need are an FTP tool, such as WSFTP to put your files on the Web. A Telnet tool is always valuable. Other tools are Fractal Design Painter and Photoshop for texture map manipulation, editing and creation, and a GIF for an animation utility that takes sequential GIFs and turns them into animated GIFs for animated texture maps.

The third thing to think about when creating objects for VRML is polygon-level editing.[11] This is probably one of the key effects of performance in a VRML model. A common VRML subject lately is that of VRML art galleries, VRML museums, VRML rooms, VRML offices, things like that. Everybody always wants to make a big room with VRML, giving it walls, and a carpet, pictures for texture maps and stuff like that. This is almost everybody's first VRML model. But really, there's no need to mimic physical architecture in a virtual space. In fact, this is something that doesn't even perform very well, because when you have walls in space and you get close enough to fill the screen with walls, this starts to have a hit on the video card's *blitting* capabilities.

Blitting is the video card's capability to fill the screen with a color. So even if you just have two polygons that make up a wall, the refresh rate of your browser can slow down significantly. This is because those two polygons might fill up the whole screen, and it takes the video card a long time to draw those two polygons, even though it didn't take any time for the computer to compute that. Furthermore, from a design standpoint, there really is no need for walls in VRML. There's no need for physical boundaries, and walls are only needed to delineate a separate space. So there are many reasons to just go without walls and floors at this point, and organize boundaries in other, more creative, ways.

The fourth way to help your implementation process is to use storyboarding for all the interactivity in a site.[12] Make schematic pictures of what the user will be doing each step of the way. Use just paper or whatever is comfortable for you. The point is to show exactly what users will be doing as they enter a space, including: the activities they can do, the scenes you want them to see, how do you want to compose the shots, how you want to sequence the actions, how you want to branch the interactivity, and so forth. It's a good idea to do this before you start building models as opposed to building your room and adding to it later. It helps to have a cinematic plan in mind, even if it's not linear, even if it's something that branches a lot.

Currently, one of the limitations in VRML is the lack of real-time lighting and shadows. While there is lighting, it's not quality lighting for realistic rendering. This is a necessity of real-time rendering. Basically, you just can't calculate light and shadows on-the-fly and still have the scene render 30 times a second. One way to make your scenes look good without real-time lighting is to use texture maps (the fifth recommendation) that have lighting previously calculated into them.[13] So, let's say you have a light in a room, a candelabra. You make a texture map of the floor of the room that has a glow in it from the candelabra, and is dark at the edges, so the lighting is actually in the texture map itself. That way, you don't have to worry about the real-time engine calculating shading, and your scenes will look a lot more realistic.

One tool that's available to help with this process is called LightScape (from Lightscape Technologies). It calculates the radiosity in a 3-D scene, meaning it calculates the light strength at each point on the surface of a model. LightScape takes a 3-D model, and if a light is casting a shadow or casting reflections, then it takes and subdivides the polygon, coloring each polygon with a lighting value. Then it subdivides until there's enough polygons to resolve the detail of the shadow. This is absolutely useless in VRML right now because you end up with rooms that have 50,000 polygons just for a one-walled room. But they have a capability in LightScape that allows you to calculate the radiosity solution, and gives you really nice soft glows and reflections of objects onto walls and things like that. But then it'll take that calculation and turn it into a texture map, which can then be used in VRML. This has the potential to make much more realistic VRML that still performs nicely.

But if you don't have $1000 or $2000 to pony up for LightScape, you can light your scene in your 3-D package, create a rendering of the object, using a flat nonperspective camera, and use that rendering as a texture-map for your object. So there are other ways to create lit textures in your 3-D modeling package if you're creative about it.

A good place to start with VRML now is knowing cinematography (the sixth recommendation).[14] Not necessarily knowing how to light scenes perfectly cinemagraphically, but to understand camera angles and pacing of events and things like that. Users can have interaction to browse the scene, but you can also create some compelling content by shunting the user off to some predefined viewpoint of a scene. So you can actually compose how the scene is presented to the viewer the same way a cinematographer composes a scene. This is true of pacing as well. You can make one viewpoint animate to another, pacing action that way, much the same way a movie director does. While it would be silly to constrain ourselves to cinemagraphic techniques—there's a lot more to VRML content creation—it's a good place to start.

A lot of richness can be provided in your worlds at cheap cost (without a lot of hits to performance) by using animated texture maps (the seventh recommendation).[15] If you combine this with transparent animated texture maps, you can actually have characters walking around in scenes that are just a couple of polygons wide. Now, these maps can be a lot to load. There are many frames of an animation, but you can compress them, and you can work in limited palettes and things like that. So you can make this a pretty viable way to have a lot of animation in your scenes, creating not only characters, but flames and torches for your Dungeons and Dragons junk.

Currently, it's a good idea to make animations slower than the realistic motion would be (the eighth recommendation).[16] For example, if you have a character walking, make the character walk slower with more frames in the motion. Researchers at Intervista have found that if you have too many characters in the scene, even if you don't have that many polygons, frames will start skipping, and the motion becomes choppy. If you add more frames to your animation—not necessarily more key frames, which would make your code fatter—but add more frames between the key frames, your animation will be smoother. The motion will be a little slower than normal, but it will play smoother in the browser.

The ninth performance issue (recommendation) revolves around the fact that most VRML exporters create code with a lot of whitespace embedded in it.[17] Many indentations are created for the sake of making it readable, but you may want to take out this white-space. You can do this either with something like the *DataFat Munger*, which is a Perl script; or, some other exporters that actually have settings to export without indents. This'll knock a significant amount off larger files. The other thing, of course, is Gzip, which is a compression utility that shrinks your file sizes.

There's a lot of talk currently about bandwidth problems with VRML. In one sense, it's a real red herring, because if you've got something that's so big that bandwidth becomes an issue, the computer's not going to be able to render it anyway. So if you keep your files within the limits of a garden-variety PC, bandwidth for downloading is not going to be a problem as long as you Gzip these sorts of things. Even the biggest files after Gzipping should be no more than around 30K. It takes just a few seconds to download. Almost all VRML browsers will unGzip on-the-fly. So you can put Gzipped VRML files on the Web and they'll play like a normal VRML file.

Finally, the tenth recommendation has to do with the subject of animation and key frames; while it's wise to make your animations have plenty of frames between the key frames, having more key frames is going to bloat your file.[18] But the more key frames, the more expressive the animation. You really want to learn how to animate fairly efficiently, which means compromising the number of key frames, somewhat.

Here at the infancy of VRML, with less code, you end up with quicker downloads. Have fun!

Endnotes

1 Intervista Software, Inc., "VRML Myths," 181 Fremont, Suite 200, San Francisco, CA 94105, 1997.

2 Ibid.

3 Michael Erbschloe, Consultant, educator, and writer who specializes in the strategic use of computer technology at Oklahoma State University, erbschloe@hpcwire.tge.com.

4   Ibid.

5   Ibid.

6   Ibid.

7   Ibid.

8   Intervista Software, Inc., "VRML Creation Primer," 181 Fremont, Suite 200, San Francisco, CA 94105, 1997.

9   Ibid.

10   Ibid.

11   Ibid.

12   Ibid.

13   Ibid.

14   Ibid.

15   Ibid.

16   Ibid.

17   Ibid.

18   Ibid.

Glossary

- **2-D.** Shorthand for "two-dimensional." Refers to graphics that are flat. They have width and height (represented by the x and y axes) but no depth (represented by the z axis).

- **3-D.** Shorthand for "three-dimensional." The term "3-D" can refer to a 2-D image that has the appearance of depth (it seems to be coming off the page) or it can pertain to graphics that actually have x, y, and z axes.

- **6DOF.** Six degrees of freedom: yaw, pitch, roll, up-down, left-right, front-back (or pan, zoom, swivel).

- **A-Buffering.** A variation of z-buffering that keeps track of pixels in z-planes for blending and antialiasing.

- **Accelerator.** Specialized hardware to increase speed of graphics manipulation.

- **Accommodation.** Change in the focal length of the eye's lens.

- **Action.** An operation on a scene. In Open Inventor, actions are derived from the SoAction abstract base class. Actions include the GLRenderAction, RayPickAction, WriteAction, SearchAction, GetMatrixAction, HandleEventAction, and GetBoundingBox-Action.

- **Actors.** CAD representations of players performing actions for them, as in the Mandala system. *See* **Agent**, **Character**.

- **Address Space.** The set of objects or memory locations accessible through a single namespace. In other words, it is a data region that one or more processes may share through pointers.

- **Advanced Distributed Simulation (ADS).** *See also* **SIMNET**.

- **Aesthetics.** The philosophy dealing with the human sense of pleasure and artistic merit.

- **Affine.** Any transformation composed from rotations, translations, dilatations (expansions and contractions), and shears.

- **Agent.** A software program that can carry out fairly sophisticated tasks in unknown networked environments without human intervention; in other words, a smart bot.

- **Agents.** CAD representations of human forms capable of guiding (Guides) navigators through a VR. *See* **Actor**, **Character**.

- **Algorithms.** A programmed set of mathematical formulas developed for a computer environment to perform a specific function.

- **Aliasing.** An undesirable jagged edge on many 3-D renderings on bitmapped displays. Creates jaggies along the sides of objects and flickering of objects smaller than a pixel. *See* **Antialiasing**.

- **Allocentric.** Other than egocentric, such as a bird's eye view, or adopting another person's viewpoint.

- **Altered States.** The psychology of changes in perception and other states of consciousness from changes in external and internal stimulation.

- **Alternate World Disorder.** Range of discomfort from mild headaches and disorientation to nausea from VR ("barfogenic zone"). *See also* **Simulator Sickness**.

- **Ambient Light.** General, nondirectional illumination.

- **Anchor.** Also called a link, hyperlink, or a hot link. This is the basis of hypermedia, which enables creating connections between items in a document or documents so that a user can go from one to the other in a nonlinear fashion.

- **ANSI.** American National Standards Institute. A standards body founded in 1918, as a private, not-for-profit organization that coordinates the United States national consensus standards system and approves American National Standards.

- **Antialiasing.** Removes jagged edges on bitmapped displays by interpolating neutral colors or intermediate intensities.

- **ARPAnet.** A forerunner of the Internet. The Advanced Research Projects Agency network went into service in 1969.

- **Articulation.** Objects composed of several parts that are separately moveable.

- **Artificial Intelligence.** The attempt to mimic and automate human cognitive skills through rules and knowledge representation techniques (understanding visual images, recognizing speech and written text, solving problems, making medical diagnoses, heuristic knowledge, etc.).

- **Artificial Life.** Digital agents that evolve, reproduce, grow, and change in similar ways to biological life forms.

- **Artificial Reality.** Introduced by arts and computer visualization scholar Myron Krueger in the mid-1970s to describe his computer-generated responsive environments. Krueger has emphasized the nonintrusive (Second-Person VR) systems that track people with pattern recognition techniques and display them and the surround on projection systems (*see* CAVE). As realized in his VIDEOPLACE and the Vivid Group's Mandala system, it is a computer display system that perceives and captures "a participant's action in terms of the body's relationship to a graphic world and generates responses (usually imagery) that maintain the illusion that his actions are taking place within that world." *See* **Virtual Reality, Cyberspace**.

- **Aspect Ratio.** Ratio of width to height of the field of view.

- **Augmented Reality.** This is the use of transparent displays worn as glasses on which data can be projected. This allows someone to repair a radar, for example, and have the needed data displayed on the glasses while walking around the radar.

- **Avatar.** In a virtual environment, a three-dimensional image (which may also include live video) that serves as a stand-in for the person who controls it. Its motions, gestures, and speech may be derived from the user's voice, keyboard, or other input device. More generally, an avatar is a representation of any object functioning in a virtual world, and so its meaning may cover graphical representations of bots and agents.

- **Back Clipping Plane.** A distance beyond which objects are not shown.

- **Backface Removal.** The elimination of those polygons that are facing away from the viewer.

- **Backward Raytracing.** From the eye to the object (currently how most raytracing is done).

- **Binaural.** Stereo sound incorporating information about the shadows at human ears and heads.

- **Biosensors.** Special glasses or bracelets containing electrodes to monitor muscle electrical activity. One interesting VR use is for tracking eye movements by measuring muscle movements.

- **BITFIELD.** A 32-bit mask used mainly in GL rendering commands. The range of valid masks depends on the particular command in which it is used. Refer to the OpenGL Spec for each command. Unless otherwise stated, a BITFIELD that is invalid under the GL API does not generate a protocol error.

- **Bits.** A binary digit, either a 0 or 1. The smallest element of a computer program.

- **Black Sun, The.** In *Snowcrash* by Neal Stephenson, the worldwide computer network known as the Metaverse is represented as a virtual city. The coolest place to go in all the Metaverse is the Black Sun.

- **Bodysuit.** A complete human covering supporting VR sensors and effectors (promised but never really produced by VPL). *See* **Datasuit**.

- **BOOL32.** A 32-bit integer Boolean: 1 represents True and 0 represents False.

- **BOOM.** Binocular omni-orientational monitor. A 3-D display device suspended from a weighted boom that can swivel freely about so the viewer doesn't have to wear an HMD; instead, it steps up to the viewer like a pair of binoculars. The boom's position communicates the user's point of view to the computer.

- **Bot.** A word derived from "robot," signifying a software program designed to independently carry out tasks in unknown networked environments; a more limited agent.

- **Bounding Box.** An axis-aligned box that is guaranteed to contain some part of the scene. Open Inventor uses bounding boxes to optimize certain operations.

- **BPS.** BPS is an acronym for "bits per second." It specifies how fast a modem can transfer information. Most consumer-level modems function at rates between 14,400 bps and 28,800 bps, or 14.4 Kbps and 28.8 Kbps (kilobits per second).

- **Browsers.** Software programs that will retrieve, display, and print information and HTML documents. Different browsers support different versions of the HTML standard, sometimes causing illegible information to be displayed. Most browsers also support other network protocols including FTP, GOPHER, UseNET, newsgroups, etc.

- **Camera.** Defines the eyepoint from which the scene is viewed. The Inventor SoCamera class is an abstract base class that encapsulates functionality for the two types of cameras Inventor supports: SoOrthographicCamera and SoPerspectiveCamera.

- **CAVE.** A VR using projection devices on the walls and ceiling to give the illusion of immersion.

- **Character.** A being with a virtual body in virtual reality. *See* **Agent**, **Actor**.

- **Client.** An X client. An application communicates to a server by a path. The application program is referred to *m*, a client of the window system server. To the server, the client is the communication path itself. A program with multiple connections is viewed as multiple clients to the server. The resource lifetimes are controlled by the connection lifetimes, not the application program lifetimes.

- **Client.** Part of a client/server network such as the Internet. A computer or a piece of software running on a computer that makes a request (for a Web page) is called a *client*. The computer that answers the request is called a *server*. Netscape's Navigator and Black Sun's CyberGate are both clients. Black Sun's Community Server is a server.

- **Client/Server Network.** In a client/server network, all nodes are on an equal level with one another and they can all see each other. Any node that makes a request is a *client* and any node that answers requests is a *server*. The Internet is a client/server-based network.

- **CNIDR.** Clearinghouse for Networked Information Discovery and Retrieval, the organization that continues to develop and distribute public domain versions of WAIS.

- **CommerceNet.** CommerceNet was formed to facilitate the use of an Internet-based infrastructure for electronic commerce to allow efficient interaction among customers, suppliers, and development partners to speed time to market and reduce the costs of doing business.

- **Computer-Generated Force (CGF).** A computer system that generates agents in a military simulation; it can be used with trainees in simulators fighting virtual battles, or can be run autonomously for planning of tactics.

- **Concept Map.** A browser or terms, definitions, or icons arranged in semantic proximity.

- **Connection.** A bidirectional byte-stream that carries the X (and GLX) protocol between the client and the server. A client typically has only one connection to a server.

- **Consensual Reality.** The world, or a simulation of a world, as viewed and comprehended by a society.

- **Context (Rendering).** An OpenGL rendering context. This is a virtual OpenGL machine. All OpenGL rendering is done with respect to a context. The state maintained by one rendering context is not affected by another except in the case of shared display lists.

- **Convergence.** The angle between the two eyes at a fixation point. This changes for objects at varying depths in the real world and on 3-D displays.

- **Convolvotron.** A system for controlling binaural sound production in a VR.

- **Coordinate System (xy/xyz).** A mapping system using perpendicular axes for defining and drawing graphics and geometry. If two axes are used (x and y) then the system is two-dimensional (2-D); if three axes (x, y, and z), then the system is three-dimensional (3-D).

- **Culling.** Removing invisible pieces of geometry and only sending potentially visible geometry to the graphics subsystem. Simple culling involves rejecting objects not in the view frustum. More complex systems take into account occlusion of some objects by others, e.g., a building hiding trees behind it.

- **Cyberia.** A pun on Siberia; an Autodesk project and the first VR project by a CAD company. *See* **Cyberspace**.

- **Cybernaut.** A voyager in VR.

- **Cybernetic Simulation.** Dynamic model of a world filled with objects that exhibit lesser or greater degrees of intelligence.

- **Cyberpunk.** A dystopian vision of the future, replete with technological dazzle, anomie, and jacked in cybernauts. A modern literary style.

- **Cyberscope.** A viewer that can be attached to a monitor to enable stereoscopic viewing of software-controlled images.

- **Cyberspace.** A place filled with virtual "stuff" populated by people with virtual bodies. A special kind of virtual space that promotes experiences involving the whole body. A term coined by William Gibson in his book *Neuromancer* (1984—a coincidental date!) to describe a shared virtual universe or "matrix" operating within the sum total of all the world's computer networks. *See* **Artificial Reality**, **Virtual Reality**.

- **Cyberspace Playhouse.** Social center or place where people go to play roles in simulations.

- **DataGlove.** A glove wired with sensors and connected to a computer system for gesture recognition. It is used for tactile feedback and it often enables navigation through a virtual environment and interaction with 3-D objects within it.

- **DataSpace.** A visualized representation of complex information.

- **DataSuit.** Same as a DataGlove, but designed for the entire body. Only one DataSuit has yet been built, with limited capabilities.

- **De-Rez.** Techniques to make pixels less visible in a display.

- **Deck.** A physical space containing an array of instruments that enable a player to act within, and feel a part of, a virtual space.

- **Depth Cueing.** Using shading, texture, color, interposition (or many other visual characteristics) to provide a cue for the z-coordinates or distance of an object.

- **Diffuse Reflection.** Light that is reflected in all directions from a surface.

- **Direct Manipulation.** A term coined by Schneiderman to reflect the use of computer icons or text as if they were real objects.

- **DirectionalLight.** Defines light shining in a given direction.

- **Disorientation.** Confusion about distances and directions for navigation.

- **Distributed Interactive Simulation (DIS).** A protocol for distributed virtual environments developed by the U.S. military so that computer-generated forces and manned simulators might interact on a large scale; now an IEEE standard.

- **Distributed Virtual Environment (DVE).** A virtual environment in which several users may interact and whose elements exist on two or more platforms.

- **DLL.** Dynamic Link Library. A set of routines used by Windows software packages as standard functions available for use by other software packages.

- **DNS.** Domain Name System. This is the database that links domain names to their respective IP addresses for the Internet. The computers on the Internet know each other according to their IP addresses (which are a series of numbers), not their domain names (which are a series of words). This system came about to provide a more human-centric method of managing networks.

- **Domain Name.** A domain name is assigned to a computer on a network as a way for it to be more easily identifiable to people using that network. The DNS is the database for the Internet that matches domain names to IP addresses. The domain name is used as part of a URL. When you enter the URL of a site you want to visit in your browser, the browser first makes a request to the DNS to get the proper IP address so it can find the computer you are looking for.

- **Dreaming.** A state of mind during sleep where vivid colored imagery becomes realistic and immersive. A natural counterpart to VR.

- **Droid.** Puppet that embodies a human intellect (as in *android*).

- **DSI.** Defense Simulation Internet: A component of the Internet that supports DIS and SIMNET and permits scheduled guaranteed bandwidth.

- **Dynamic Lighting.** Changes in lighting effects on objects as they and the observer move.

- **Dynamics.** The way that objects interact and move. The rules that govern all actions and behaviors within the environment.

- **EC/EDI System.** Business system built around standard EDI formats and reengineered processes to achieve all-electronic capabilities.

- **Effectors.** The output techniques that communicate a user's movements or commands to the computer and to the VR.

- **Egocenter.** The sense of self and personal viewpoint that determines one's location in a VR. *See* **Projection Point**.

- **ElapsedTime.** An engine that outputs how much time has elapsed since a given time (by default, how much time has elapsed since it was created).

- **Electromagnetic Forces.** Effects of EMF on human tissues are poorly understood and may constitute an important hazard from tracking and display devices.

- **Electronic Café International.** CAFE is an acronym for Communications Access For Everyone. The concept was born when the Los Angeles Museum of Contemporary Art commissioned Sherrie and Kit to create a project for the 1984 Olympic Festival. A telecom link between five diverse ethnic Los Angeles communities and the museum was maintained for the seven weeks of the festival, allowing users to trade video and still images, collaborate in writing and drawing on a common virtual canvas, transmit musical pieces, retrieve information, and communicate in dynamic yet nonaggressive ways. With more advanced equipment and alliances the ECI is now able to provide a virtual collaborative and real space for anyone to interact with the global village.

- **Electronic Commerce (EC).** Business environment integrating electronic transfer and automated business systems (end-user computing and computer-to-computer capabilities).

- **Electronic Data Interchange (EDI).** Computer-to-computer exchange of structured transactional information between autonomous computers.

- **E-Mail.** Electronic mail, often sent over the Internet or a commercial carrier.

- **Endoscopic.** Part of a family of new surgical procedures that avoid cutting open major portions of the patient in favor of making small holes through which tools and sensors are inserted and the surgery performed. In a VR or telepresence application, the surgeon manipulates the tools by observing the surgery site on a monitor via optical fibers and a tiny video camera.

- **Engine.** An object that reads one or more values, performs an operation on those values, and then writes the results into part of a scene. Engines can be used to program animation or to create "smart" 3-D objects with behavior.

- **ENUM.** A 32-bit enumerated value used mainly in GL rendering commands. The range of valid enumerants depends on the particular command in which it is used. Refer to the OpenGL spec for each command. Unless otherwise stated, an ENUM that is invalid under the GL API does not generate a protocol error.

- **Environment.** This a computer-generated model that can be experienced from the "inside" as if it were a place.

- **Epistemology.** The philosophical study of learning and the acquisition of knowledge.

- **ExaminerViewer.** A component with a user interface for interacting with a 3-D scene. The ExaminerViewer uses a "hold-an-object-in-your-hand-and-rotate-it" paradigm for examining a 3-D scene. It maps mouse gestures to 3-D rotations of the camera, to rotate around an object to look at it from all sides.

- **Exoskeletal Devices.** In order to provide force feedback, designers have added rigid external supports to gloves and arm motion systems.

- **Eye Tracking.** Devices that measure direction of gaze. Most HMDs do not currently support eye tracking directly.

- **Eyeball in the Hand.** A metaphor for visualized tracking where the tracker is held in the hand and is connected to motion of the projection point of the display.

- **EyeGen.** An HMD made by Virtual Research that combines visual and auditory displays.

- **Eyephone.** An HMD made by VPL that combines visual and auditory displays.

- **Face/Facet.** This term refers to a planar surface that makes up part of an object's shape in 3-D graphics. In 3-D graphics, objects are made up of polygons, and the visible part of the polygon is its *face*.

- **FAQ (Frequently Asked Questions).** A FAQ is a document that provides answers to questions that new users commonly have regarding a particular topic.

- **Field.** One or more pieces of data stored in a node or an engine.

- **Field of View.** The angle in degrees of the visual field. Most HMDs offer 60 to 90 degrees FOV. Since our two eyes have overlapping 140 degree FOV, binocular or total FOV is roughly 180 degrees horizontal by 120 degrees vertical in most people. A feeling of immersion seems to arise with FOV greater than 60 degrees. *See also* **Geometric FOV**.

- **File.** A collection of data that a computer can use for any particular purpose. Examples of file types are text and images.

- **Finite Element Modeling.** Decomposition of complex structures into small, simple elements so that engineering computations are manageable.

- **Finite-State Machine (FSM).** A mathematical description of a process as a set of states, the allowable transitions between states, and the events causing the transitions.

- **Fish Tank VR.** With stereographic display systems attached to a monitor and the scene's virtual image behind the screen, the egocentric projection is called a fish tank.

- **Flat Shading.** A shading technique in which the lighting is calculated once per facet and a single shade of color is used for the whole facet. You can turn flat shading on in your browser.

- **FLOAT32.** A 32-bit floating-point value in IEEE Single Format.

- **FLOAT64.** A 64-bit floating-point value in IEEE Double Format.

- **Force Feedback.** The computer guides a machine to offer just the degree of resistance to motion or pressure a situation would offer in real life. Representations of the inertia or resistance objects have when they are moved or touched.

- **Forms.** The capability in many browser/navigator software packages to accept input in text entry fields displayed on the user's screen. Customized forms can be easily developed to request information for company data, including time cards, expense reports, personnel records, and other such corporate data.

- **Fractal.** Any function that contains elements of self-similarity (after the work of Benoit Mandelbrot). Often used for fast texture modeling for mountains, trees, clouds, etc.

- **freeWAIS-sf.** Available from the University of Dortmund, the sf stands for structured fields. The product supports complex Boolean searches and introduces text, date, and numeric field structures within a document. FreeWAIS-sf is available at: http://ls6-www.informatik.uni-dortmund.de/freeWAIS-sf/.

- **Frustum of Vision.** 3-D field of view in which all modeled objects are visible.

- **FTP.** File Transfer Protocol. A high-level protocol that enables copying files between different systems.

- **Gateway.** Also known as an IP router. A computer that is attached to multiple TCP/IP networks for the purpose of moving packets of information between them.

- **Geometric Field of View (FOVg).** The angle in degrees of the computed visual scene. Most HMDs offer 60 to 90 degrees FOV but the scene can be computed to fit into anything from 0 to 360 degrees field of view for any particular projection point. If FOVg is larger than the FOV, then objects will appear pincushioned and distorted; if FOVg is smaller than the FOV, then objects will appear barreled and distorted.

- **Gesture.** Hand motion that can be interpreted as a sign or signal or symbol.

- **GLXContext.** A 32-bit identifier that refers to a GLX rendering context.

- **GLX_CONTEXT.** An X ID. A client refers to an OpenGL rendering context by using this uniquely assigned value. This ID, as with all X IDs, is shareable between clients.

- **GLX_CONTEXT_TAG.** A 32-bit integer used to identify the current context of a calling thread.

- **GLX_DRAWABLE.** The union of (WINDOW, GLX_PIXMAP).

- **GLX Drawables.** A GLX drawable is the GLX equivalent of an X drawable. Instead of being the union of X windows and X pixmaps, it is the union of X windows and GLX pixmaps.

- **GLX_PIXMAP.** A 32-bit identifier that refers to a GLX pixmap.

- **GLX Pixmaps.** A GLX pixmap is the GLX equivalent of an X pixmap. The difference is that a GLX pixmap has the extended visual properties described previously.

- **GLX_RENDER_COMMAND.** An OpenGL rendering command and its associated data.

- **Goggles.** Often used to refer to HMD or other displays.

- **Gopher.** An Internet protocol that directly preceded the World Wide Web, created by the University of Minnesota. It is a more basic system than HTTP.

- **Gouraud.** Shading polygons smoothly with bilinear interpolation.

- **Gouraud Shading.** Invented by Henri Gouraud in 1971, it is a shading process that interpolates colors between vertices of a facet. That is to say, lighting is calculated once per vertex and the resulting colors are blended smoothly between adjacent vertices. Also known as *smooth shading*. You can view your VRML scenes in Gouraud (smooth) shading if you like.

- **Group.** A node that contains other nodes as children.

- **Haptic Interfaces.** Interfaces that use all the physical sensors that provide us with a sense of touch at the skin level and force feedback information from our muscles and joints.

- **Head-Coupled.** Displays or robotic actions that are activated by head motion through a head-tracking device.

- **Head-Related Transfer Function (HRTF).** A mathematical description of the relationship between sound at its source and at one ear of a listener in free space. The function depends upon distance and direction, usually measured in spherical coordinates.

- **Head Tracking.** Monitoring the position of the head through various devices.

- **Heads Up Display (HUD).** A display device that lets users see graphics superimposed on their view of the world. (Created for aviators to see symbols and dials while looking out the window.)

- **Helper Application.** A program that is launched by a browser to view a particular type of data.

- **Hidden Children.** Children of a nodekit that are operated on, but you don't have direct access to them.

- **Hidden Surface.** Parts of a graphics object occluded by intervening objects.

- **Hit (Web Site).** Web jargon for a successful access to a file on a Web page. Often used to attempt to compare popularity in the context of getting so many "hits" during a given period of time. A newbie mistake is equating hits with visits. A single visit usually is recorded as several hits because each file accessed is recorded as a hit.

- **Hit (Search).** Slang for a successful match against a database. Used primarily in the context of getting so many "hits" against a database during a search, most often a keyword search.

- **HMD (Head Mounted Display).** A set of goggles or a helmet with tiny monitors in front of each eye that generate images, seen by the wearer as being 3-D. VPL Research refers to the HMDs they sell as *Eyephones*.

- **Holodeck.** Virtual reality simulation system and place used primarily for entertainment by the crew of the Enterprise in *Star Trek: The Next Generation* television series.

- **HOOD.** Swinging wraparound display. Used instead of HMD; hung from pulleys.

- **Host ID.** The portion of an IP address that identifies the host in a particular network. Used in conjunction with network IDs to form a complete IP address.

- **HotJava.** A new generation of browser technology being developed by Sun Microsystems.

- **HTML.** HyperText Markup Language. A system used to format documents for viewing by World Wide Web clients.

- **HTTP.** HyperText Transfer Protocol. Internet computer communication encoding standard for exchange of multimedia documents on the World Wide Web.

- **HTTP Linked Object.** A clickable object (text, picture, or both) that provides a path between documents, directing the browser to a new URL.

- **HTTPD.** HyperText Transfer Protocol Daemon. The server that handles Internet and World Wide Web protocols.

- **Hyperlink.** The path between two documents that allows the user to point and click on specific words on the screen and thereby move to the requested location, wherever it is.

- **Hypermedia.** When a medium is referred to as "hyper," its information is accessible through a nonlinear cross-linking process. Hyper documents contain anchors, or links, which lead to other related documents or bits of information.

- **HyperSpace.** The space of hypertext or hypermedia documents.

- **IES Photometric Data.** An (Illuminating Engineers Society) industry standard file format used to describe the shape and intensity of light energy distribution from a luminaire.

- **Image Map.** A clickable picture that directs the browser to different links depending on what part of the image is clicked.

- **Immersion.** The cognitive conviction or feeling of presence, of "being there," surrounded by space and capable of interacting with all available objects that is the hallmark of good VR.

- **Impressionists.** A 19th-century group of artists whose paintings were directed at capturing color and mood, rather than exact perspective outlines.

- **Interactive Fiction.** Dramatic creations that encourage user and viewer participation through computer technology, hypertext, group feedback, or VR.

- **Interaural Amplitude.** Differences between a person's two ears in the intensity of sound.

- **Interaural Time.** Differences between a person's two ears in the phase of sound.

- **Interface.** A set of devices, software, and techniques that connect computers with people to make it easier to perform useful activities.

- **Internet (inet).** A global network of networks growing from a Department of Defense (DARPA) funded research project.

- **InterNIC.** A collaborative project of three organizations that work together to offer the Internet community a full scope of network information services. These services include providing information about accessing and using the Internet, assistance in locating resources on the network, and registering network components for Internet connectivity. The overall goal of the InterNIC is to make networking and networked information more easily accessible to researchers, educators, and the general public. The InterNIC name signifies the cooperation between Network Information Centers, or NICS.

- **Inverse Kinematics.** A specification of the motion of dynamic systems from properties of their joints and extensions.

- **IP (TCP/IP).** Internet Protocol. Along with TCP, it is one of the foundations of TCP/IP networking. IP is responsible for the addressing and sending of data across the network.

- **IP Address.** Represented by four numbers separated by dots—a.b.c.d—where a, b, c, and d are numbers between 0 and 255. This allows for more than 4.2 billion distinct addresses.

- **Jack.** To connect to the matrix of virtual space.

- **Java.** A new, object-oriented, next programming language developed by Sun Microsystems.

- **Joysticks.** Graphic interface devices (invented by rude aviators).

- **Kinaesthetic Dissonance.** Mismatch between feedback or its absence from touch or motion during VR experiences.

- **Lag.** Delay between an action and its visual, acoustic, or other sensory feedback, often because of inherent delays in the tracking devices, or in the computation of the scene.

- **Laparoscopy.** Less invasive forms of surgery that operate through small optics and instruments; lending themselves to robotic manipulation and VR training.

- **LBE (Location Based Entertainment).** A VR game that involves a scenario based on another time and place; filling a studio or space with VR games.

- **LCD (Liquid Crystal Display).** Display devices that use bipolar films sandwiched between thin panes of glass. They are lightweight and transmissive or reflective, and ideal for HMD.

- **Light.** An object in the scene that casts light into all or part of the scene. The Inventor SoLight class is an abstract base class; Inventor supports Directional, Point, and Spot lights.

- **Link.** Another name for an anchor. Links are used to connect informational items together in hypermedia.

- **LOD (Level of Detail).** A model of a particular resolution among a series of models of the same object. Multiple LODs are used to increase graphics performance by drawing simpler geometry when the object occupies fewer pixels on the screen. LOD selection can also be driven by graphics load, area-of-interest, gaze direction.

- **Luminaire.** A complete lighting unit, including the light fixture and lamp(s).

- **Lycos.** A World Wide Web search engine developed by Carnegie Mellon University. It allows you to search on document titles and content. Lycos is a system composed of a robot that scours the Web in search of new information, which it then catalogs, indexes, and stores. The index searches document titles, headings, links, and keywords it locates in these documents.

- **Magic Wand.** A 3-D interface device used for pointing and interaction; an elongated 3-D mouse.

- **Manipulator.** An object that is part of the scene that responds to input device events and does something. For example, the TrackballManip maps mouse events into 3-D rotations.

- **Material.** An object that specifies how a shape's surface will respond to light. The lighting model used by Open Inventor for materials is fairly simple and includes diffuse color, ambient color, specular color, specular exponent, emissive color, and transparency.

- **Metaball.** A kind of "equipotential surface" around a point. You specify a point, a radius, and an "intensity" for each ball; when balls come close, their shapes blend to form a smooth equipotential surface. They seem to be very useful for modeling shapes like animals and humans. They can be rendered by most ray-tracing packages (also "blobs" or "soft spheres" or "fuzzy spheres").

- **Metaphysics.** The philosophical study of basic concepts of existence like epistemology, ontology, aesthetics, and the meaning and purpose of life.

- **Microsurgery.** A form of surgery that lends itself to robotics and VR. *See also* **Laparoscopy**.

- **MIDI.** A digital sound standard for music.

- **Mirror Worlds.** Bird's eye views of a VR in which the viewer also exists and can be seen.

- **MOO.** A MUD, object-oriented. *See also* **MUD**.

- **MOOD.** Monoscopic omni-orientational display. *See* **HOOD, HMD, Goggles, HUD, LCD**.

- **Monitor.** Display, HMD, Goggles, HUD, LCD.

- **Motion Parallax.** Objects at different distance and fixation points move different amounts when the viewpoint is dollied along the x axis (left-right).

- **Motion Platform.** A controlled system that provides real motion to simulate the displayed motion in a VR.

- **Motivation.** A psychological need, drive, or feeling that raises the intensity of an action.

- **MPEG.** Motion Picture Experts Group. A proposed International Standards organization (ISO) standard for digital video and audio compression for moving images. MPEG- 1 was defined with CD-ROM as the primary application.

- **MPEG-2.** The MPEG-2 concept is similar to MPEG-1, but includes extensions to cover a wider range of applications. The primary application targeted during the MPEG-2 definition process was the all-digital transmission of broadcast TV quality video.

- **MRI.** Magnetic Resonance Imaging. A way of making internal organs and structures visible by analyzing radio frequency emissions of atoms in a strong magnetic field. Can be made 3-D with rendering of large amounts of data.

- **MUD.** A multiuser dungeon; a place on the Internet where people can meet and browse (also a MOO).

- **Multiperson Space.** Multiplayer space involving two or more human players. A type of interactive simulation that gives every user a sense that he or she personally has a body in a virtual space.

- **Multiplayer Space.** Cyberspace that emerges from simulation that is generated simultaneously by two or more decks. Players can be made up of one human and the rest AI.

- **Multiuser.** Any protocol that supports more than one user interacting with another. These can be as simple as a text-based chat like Internet Relay Chat (IRC), or a Multi-User Domain (MUD), or as complicated as a 3-D virtual reality scene in which the people present are represented by their avatars.

- **Multiuser Dungeon (MUD).** A type of computer-controlled environment, used originally for fantasy games, in which the surroundings, two or more players, and actions are described in text displayed on a computer screen. (Use of "dungeon" to describe the space is taken from a 1973 board game called "Dungeons and Dragons.")

- **Multiuser Dungeon, Object-Oriented (MOO).** A MUD whose software obeys the rules of object-oriented programming so that the environment can be easily expanded by one or more people adding software modules.

- **Nanomanipulation.** Ability to visualize and affect objects in the nanometer range.

- **Navigation.** Refers to the computer interface that allows users to move through a virtual reality scene. Typically, the user has several options that allow for different kinds of movement. The two main types of movement involve the viewer moving around the object (called *walk*) or the object moving around the viewer (called *spin*).

- **Neural Interface.** A version of the ultimate interface that connects a VR directly to a human brain or nervous system.

- **NISO.** National Information Standards Organization (NISO), an ANSI-accredited standards development organization that serves the library, information, and publishing communities. NISO developed and maintains the Z39.50 search and retrieval standard.

- **Node.** The generic name for any object that is part of the scene, such as lights, cameras, and shapes.

- **Nodekit.** Convenient mechanism to make Open Inventor node groupings.

- **Nodekit Catalogs.** Describes how selected nodes in a subgraph are arranged and lists the available parts.

- **Nodes.** Basic item to create three-dimensional scene databases. Each holds one piece of information (description of shape, light, etc.).

- **NSFnet.** National Science Foundation network. A network backbone financed by NSF. Previously, it served as the backbone for the Internet.

- **Objects.** Graphical entities that can be dynamically created or loaded from model files. Many functions act upon them. *Tasks*: each object performs a task per frame. *Hierarchies*: objects can be "linked" together. *Sensors*: objects can be connected to sensors. *Modify*: color, texture, scale, etc. *Collision Detection*: Between objects and polygons. *Vertices*: These can be dynamically created along with the definition of a vector normal for Gouraud-shading.

- **Occipital Cortex.** The back of the brain receiving retinotopic projections of visual displays.

- **Occlusion.** Hiding objects from sight by interposition of other objects.

- **Ontology.** The metaphysics of existence.

- **Palette.** A table of color values that converts 8-bit, pseudo-color values into RGB values that can be displayed on a monitor. Also called a *color lookup table*.

- **Pan.** The angular displacement of a view along any axis or direction in a 3-D world; or a move through translation in a 2-D world.

- **Parietal Cortex.** An area of the brain adjacent and above the occipital cortex, thought to process spatial location and direction.

- **Path.** A series of nodes, each of which is a parent of the next node in the series. Paths are returned as the result of pick and search actions.

- **Paths.** Objects or viewpoints can follow predefined paths that can be dynamically created and interpolated.

- **Perceptual Acoustic Model.** A mathematical description of a physical environment's acoustical properties based on its early response to a sound impulse.

- **Perspective.** The rules that determine the relative size of objects on a flat page to give the impression of 3-D distance.

- **Phong Shading.** An algorithm published by Phong Bui-Toung in 1975. It interpolates the surface normal over the surface and recalculates the lighting on a per-pixel basis.

- **Photorealism.** An attempt to create realistic appearing images with much detail and texture.

- **Picking.** The process of determining which objects intersect a line shooting through the scene. Typically, this line is the projection of the 2-D mouse cursor into the 3-D scene.

- **Pitch.** The angular displacement of a view along the lateral axis (front/back).

- **Pixel.** An abbreviation for picture element, a picture cell; a single dot on the computer display screen.

- **Plenoptic and Plenoptic Images.** The "plenoptic function" of Adelson and Bergen is a parameterized function for describing everything that is visible from a given point in space. McMillan and Bishop plenoptic.html provide a concise problem statement for image-based rendering paradigms, such as morphing and view interpolation.

- **Plug-In.** A software module that extends the capabilities of another program. Many paint programs use plug-in filters for achieving certain effects. Browsers for the World Wide Web make use of plug-ins to extend their capabilities into audio, video, telephony, virtual reality, and many other applications. Currently there are over 50 plug-ins available for Netscape Navigator.

- **Point Cloud.** A collection of almost-invisible points in the x, y, z coordinate system that define the vertices of a 3-D world. These vertices are connected into polygons to fully define the world's structure.

- **Polygon.** A series of vertices that, when connected, define the boundary of a planar surface. The last vertex is assumed to be connected to the first. Polygons form the basis of the shapes in 3-D graphics systems.

- **POP (Points of Presence).** A term used by Internet Access Providers to indicate the number and/or geographical locations of their access to the Internet.

- **Portals.** Polygons that once passed through, automatically load a new world, or execute a user-defined function.

- **Position Trigger.** A hotspot, or sensitive spot, or button, that begins a computation when touched in some way.

- **PPP.** Point to Point Protocol. An industry-standard protocol for data transfer across serial links. Along with SLIP, PPP is commonly used for dial-up access to the Internet.

- **Presence.** A defining characteristic of a good VR system, a feeling of being there, immersed in the environment, able to interact with other objects there.

- **Production Rules.** Statements formulated in two-part, IF-THEN form.

- **Projected Reality.** A VR system that uses projection screens rather than HMDs or personal display monitors. *See* **Real Projection**.

- **Property.** A node that affects other nodes in the scene.

- **Protocol.** A set of rules used to govern the transmission and reception of data.

- **Puppet.** An avatar or other VR object that can be manipulated.

- **QTVR (QuickTime Virtual Reality).** A new multimedia standard developed at Apple Computer that "stitches" together pictures to give a 360-degree advantage point.

- **Radiosity.** A method for calculating the distribution of light energy among all the surfaces of a 3-D model.

- **Ray Tracing.** A rendering algorithm that calculates the color of pixels in the image by tracing rays of light from the user's eye through the pixel until it intersects with a surface.

- **Real Projection.** A VR projection system (a pun on rear projection).

- **Real-Time.** Appearing to be without lag or flicker (60-cps displays; highly interactive computation).

- **Renaissance.** A period of art dominated by the exploration of perspective.

- **Render.** Convert a graphics object into pixels.

- **Rendering.** A computer-generated picture of a 3-D scene.

- **Resolution.** Usually the number of lines or pixels in a display, a VGA display has 640 by 480 pixels.

- **RGB.** Red Green Blue. A color space in which colors are described in values of red, green, and blue.

- **Roll.** The angular displacement of a view along the longitudinal axis (left-right).

- **Rotation.** A three-dimensional orientation. Rotations are generally specified as an axis to rotation about and an angle of rotation about that axis.

- **Route.** The path that network traffic takes from its source to its destination.

- **Router.** A computer responsible for deciding the routes network traffic will follow and then for sending that traffic from one network to another.

- **Scan Conversion.** The change of video signals from one form (RGB) to another (NTSC, PAL).

- **Scene; Scene Graph.** A set of nodes grouped together that represent a virtual environment or 3-D world.

- **Scene Graph.** Collection of nodes, which is stored in a database managed by Open Inventor.

- **Scintillation.** The "sparkling" of textures or small objects. Usually undesirable and caused by aliasing.

- **Second Person VR.** The use of computational medium to portray a representation of you that is not necessarily realistic but still identifiable (puppet, avatar, vactor). In the Mandala system, a video camera allows you to see yourself as another object over which you have control by your own bodily movement.

- **Sensor Lagtime.** Delays in the feedback or representation of your actions caused by computation in the tracker or sensor.

- **Sensors.** Mechanisms or functions that act to change objects in response to multiple devices connected to lights, objects, viewpoints, etc., in the real world.

- **Sensory Substitution.** The conversion of sensory information from one sense to another; the use of auditory echoes and cues to "see" the shape of your surroundings.

- **Sequence (Keyframe Animation).** Interpolate images between stored frames (tweening).

- **Server.** Part of a client/server network. A computer or a piece of software running on a computer that fulfills a request (for a Web page) is called a *server*. The request comes from a client. Black Sun's server is called *Community Server*.

- **Shading.** A part of the rendering process that deals with the conversion of color information into displayable color values. The most common techniques are flat, Gouraud (smooth), and Phong.

- **Shape.** A node that represents a visible object, such as a cube, sphere, or set of polygons.

- **Shared Worlds.** Virtual environments that are shared by multiple participants at the same location or across long distance networks.

- **Shutter Glasses.** LCD screens or physically rotating shutters used to see stereoscopically when linked to the frame rate of a monitor.

- **Similar.** A potential correspondence among GLXDrawables and rendering contexts. Windows and GLXPixmaps are similar to a rendering context if, and only if, they have been created with respect to the same VisualID and root window.

- **SIMNET.** SIMNET for SIMulator NETworking, the advanced technology development of large-scale, fully interactive, widely distributed simulations created by ARPA with significant Army participation and executed by scientists and engineers from BBN and Perceptronics. Begun in 1983, the first networked simulators were operational in the summer of 1986 and the test bed network grew to 250 simulators, multiple simulations, and real platforms (a warship) linked together from 11 sites, 4 in Europe. This program proved the feasibility of real-time, shared, synthetic environments (demonstrations conducted with 1000 separately accountable entities) and has resulted in numerous follow-on programs (ADST, CCTT, etc.) in the Department of Defense as well as in the commercial/entertainment sector (Virtual World). Using networked graphics and displays built into physical mock-ups, it has been called a vehicle-based VR or synthetic environment. *See also* **DIS, ADS, DSI.**

- **Simulation.** In military contexts, depending on the degree of human interaction, described in three ways: live, involving computer-generated sensory input and real equipment; virtual, involving computer-generated sensory input and simulated equipment; or constructive, involving little or no human intervention.

- **Simulator Sickness.** The disturbances produced by simulators, ranging in degree from a feeling of unpleasantness, disorientation, and headaches to nausea and vomiting. Many factors may be involved, including sensory distortions such as abnormal movement of arms and heads because of the weight of equipment; long delays or lags in feedback, and missing visual cues from convergence and accommodation. Simulator sickness rarely occurs with displays less than 60-degrees visual angle.

- **SLIP (Serial Line Internet Protocol).** A simple protocol used to transmit data across a serial line. Like PPP, it is used commonly for Internet dial-up access.

- **Smooth Shading.** Another name for Gouraud shading, it is a type of 3-D rendering.

- **Social Computing.** The use of DVEs for social interaction.

- **SoMaterial.** A node used in Open Inventor to specify how the object looks under various lighting conditions. A SoMaterial node includes information about the way an object emits, reflects, and absorbs light, along with how shiny and transparent the object is.

- **Sound.** Accurate localization of sounds without individualized head transfer functions remains a problem.

- **Spatial Navigation.** Accurate self-localization and orientation in virtual spaces is not as easy as real-world navigation. Techniques for embedding navigational assists in complex dataspaces remain important research goals.

- **Spatial Representation System.** The cortical and other neural structures and functions that maintain spatial orientation and recognition (spatialized knowledge).

- **Spatial Superposition.** In augmented reality displays, accurate spatial registration of real and virtual images remains difficult.

- **Spreadsheets.** Early spreadsheets made the computer a valuable tool for accounting, and helped spread computers throughout industry. What is the "spreadsheet" or commercial application that will make VR a success?

- **Star Trek.** The series, based on fantasy and science fiction, offers a widely known example of a VR in its "Holodeck." Plans are also underway to use VR in a Star Trek LBE (location-based entertainment).

- **Stereopsis.** Binocular vision of images with horizontal disparities. The importance of stereopsis for immersion is not established.

- **Striate Cortex.** Visual cortex. *See* **Occipital, Parietal**.

- **Supercockpit.** An Air Force project led by Tom Furness that advanced the engineering and human factors of HMDs and VR. It used digital displays of instruments and terrain.

- **Synthetic Environments.** VR displays used for simulation.

- **Sword of Damocles.** Nickname for the first helmet-mounted display at the University of Utah.

- **Tactile Displays.** Devices like force feedback gloves, buzzers, and exoskeletons that provide tactile, kinaesthetic, and joint sensations.

- **Tactile Stimulation.** Devices like force feedback gloves, buzzers, and exoskeletons that provide tactile, kinaesthetic, and joint sensations.

- **TCP (TCP/IP).** Transmission Control Protocol. Part of TCP/IP and one of the foundations of the Internet, TCP is a connection-based protocol that provides reliable, full-duplex data transmission between a pair of applications.

- **Tele-Existence.** Remote VR.

- **Telemanipulation.** Robotic control of distant objects.

- **Teleoperation.** *See* **Telemanipulation**.

- **Telepresence.** VR with displays of real, remote scenes.

- **Telerobotic.** Robotic control of distant objects. *See* **Telemanipulation**, **Teleoperation**.

- **Telesurgery.** Surgery using Teleoperation.

- **Telnet.** Remote terminal protocol that allows a terminal attached to one host to log into other hosts.

- **Terrain.** Geographical information and models that can be either randomly generated or based on actual data. Dynamic terrain is an important goal for current SIMNET applications.

- **Texture Coordinates.** Two-dimensional numbers assigned to vertices of a polygon. These coordinates are responsible for telling the graphics engine what part of the texture appears on the polygon.

- **Texture Map.** A two-dimensional bitmap containing an image to be mapped onto the polygons representing an object. Texture mapping an image of bricks onto a rectangular surface can give the appearance of a brick wall.

- **Texture Mapping.** The technique of rendering a surface with an image to give it the appearance of texture or a painted surface. Instead of shading (or in addition to it), a color value is selected from the texture map on a per-pixel basis. This can create a visual richness while maintaining simple geometry.

- **Texture Swimming.** Unnatural motion of static textures on the surfaces of objects as they are rotated. Caused by quick and dirty texture interpolation in screen coordinates. Correctable by subdividing polygons sufficiently or by doing perspective correction.

- **Theater.** VR opens new metaphors to explore with interactive theater.

- **Thread.** One of a group of processes all sharing the same address space. Typically, each thread will have its own program counter and stack pointer, but the text and data spaces are visible to each of the threads. A thread that is the only member of its group is equivalent to a process.

- **Threads.** The GLX protocol allows multiple threads of execution to share an X connection, with each thread possibly having its own current context and drawable. In this book, the calling thread of a request is the thread that issued that request.

- **Tracker.** A device that emits numeric coordinates for its changing position in space. (Enactive tracking: Voluntarily creating the kinaesthetic cues that correlate with scene motion, without a tracker.)

- **Translation.** A three-dimensional position, specified by three numbers (*X*, *Y*, and *Z*).

- **Transparency.** How invisible and unobtrusive a VR system is.

- **Transterritorial.** Beyond physical space, as in Cyberspace.

- **Traversal.** The process of allowing each node in the scene to perform an action (for example, to draw itself).

- **Trompe l'oeil.** Perspective paintings that deceive viewers into believing they are real (a painting of the sky and clouds on the inside of a dome).

- **Type.** The class of an object; what kind of thing an object is. For example, all cubes are of type Cube. They are also of type Shape and Node.

- **Universe.** This is the "container" of all entities in a VR. Entities can be temporarily added or removed from consideration by the simulation manager. The sequence of events in the simulation loop can be user-defined.

- **URL.** Uniform Resource Locator (some people say Universal instead of Uniform). The URL provides information on the protocol, the system, and the filename so that the user's system can find a particular document.

- **VACTORS.** Virtual actors, either autonomous or telerobotic, in a VR theater.

- **Vertex.** A point at the corner of a face or a line endpoint. The vertices of a VRML world are known collectively as a point cloud.

- **View Independence.** The ability of a 3-D model or scene to be seen from any viewpoint without requiring recalculation of the light energy distribution.

- **Viewpoint.** Also referred to as a *camera position*. In VRML, the position of the viewer is the current viewpoint. There can also be preprogrammed positions in the scene that the viewer can jump to. There are a couple of different ways for users to access the viewpoints in a scene.

- **Virtual Cadaver.** A current NIH project to slice and digitize a complete human body.

- **Virtual Environment (VE).** A computer-generated, three-dimensional representation of a setting, which unlike virtual reality, need only suggest a real or imagined space, and does not have photorealism and a sense of total immersion as a primary goal.

- **Virtual Patient.** Telerobotic or digitized animation of humans with accurate disease models.

- **Virtual Prototyping.** The use of VR for design and evaluation of new artifacts.

- **Virtual Reality (VR).** A combination of technologies whose interfaces with the human user can so dominate his or her senses that he or she intuitively interacts with the immersive and dynamic computer-generated environment.

- **Virtual Reality Modeling Language (VRML).** A standard programming language, originating from a proprietary language from Silicon Graphics Inc., and designed to simplify the representation of three-dimensional objects on the Internet.

- **Virtual World.** A loose way of describing any distributed virtual environment, whether separately or in combination.

- **VISUAL_PROPERTY.** A 32-bit enumerated value indicating the property type followed by a 32-bit property value. The data type for the property value depends on the property type.

- **Visualization.** Use of computer graphics to make visible numeric or other quantifiable relationships.

- **Visuals.** In GLXm the definition of a visual has been extended to include attributes describing double-buffering capability, OpenGL rendering support, and the types, quantities, and sizes of the ancillary buffers (depth, accumulation, auxiliary, and stencil). The ancillary buffers have no meaning in the core X environment. A GLX implementation need not support OpenGL rendering for all visuals. In this book, a valid visual means a visual that has rendering support.

- **Voxel.** A cubic volume pixel for quantizing 3-D space.

- **VRML.** Virtual Reality Modeling Language (VRML). A three-dimensional interactive Web standard, pronounced "vermul."

- **VRASP.** Virtual Reality Alliance of Students and Professionals. A group founded by Karin August and her cookies, to promote the ethical and socially exciting uses of VR.

- **WAIS.** Wide Area Information Servers. A search capability that locates requested information on the Internet using a keyword or combination of keywords.

- **Waldo.** A remotely controlled mechanical puppet.

- **WebCrawler Searching.** A search engine that searches the World Wide Web by document title and content. It is part of the WebCrawler project at the University of Washington.

- **Web Site.** The virtual location for an organization's presence on the World Wide Web, usually made up of several Web pages and a single homepage designated by a unique Uniform Resource Locator (URL).

- **Windows.** On some hardware platforms, you can have multiple windows and viewpoints into the same virtual world.

- **Wireframe.** A rendering technique in which surface facets are drawn as outlines. Because no lighting or shading is done, it is extremely fast. It is the "skeleton view" of the world and is an optional rendering technique for the viewers

- **Wire Frame Outlines.** Displays of the outlines of polygons, not filled in.

- **World.** Whole environment or universe.

- **World in the Hand.** A metaphor for visualized tracking where the tracker is held in the hand and is connected to motion of the object located at that position in the display.

- **World Wide Web.** The Internet mechanism developed by Tim Berners-Lee for CERN physicists to be able to share documents. WWW allows computer users to access information across systems around the world using URLs (Uniform Resource Locators) to identify files and systems and hypertext links to move between files on the same or different systems.

- **WWW.** Generally accepted shorthand for World Wide Web. Also can be signified by W3.

- **xt.** The X toolkit. Open Inventor is separated into two libraries; libInventor is the core library containing all of the window-system-independent code. On Unix machines running the X window system, libInventorXt contains window system–specific components such as the XtRenderArea or the XtMaterialEditor. Open Inventor is being ported to Windows NT, which will have similar (but not identical) components as libInventorXt.

- **Yahoo.** Yet Another Hierarchical Officious Oracle. An extremely popular Web site that maintains a list of hypertext-linked Web sites categorized by topics and subtopics and sub-subtopics. Also available is a point-and-click, user-definable search engine.

- **Yaw.** The angular displacement of a view around the vertical, y axis (up-down).

- **Z-Buffering.** Keeping track of the Z-depth of pixels to cull them before rendering.

Index